lonely planet



# Venezuela

Kevin Raub

Brian Kluepfel, Tom Masters

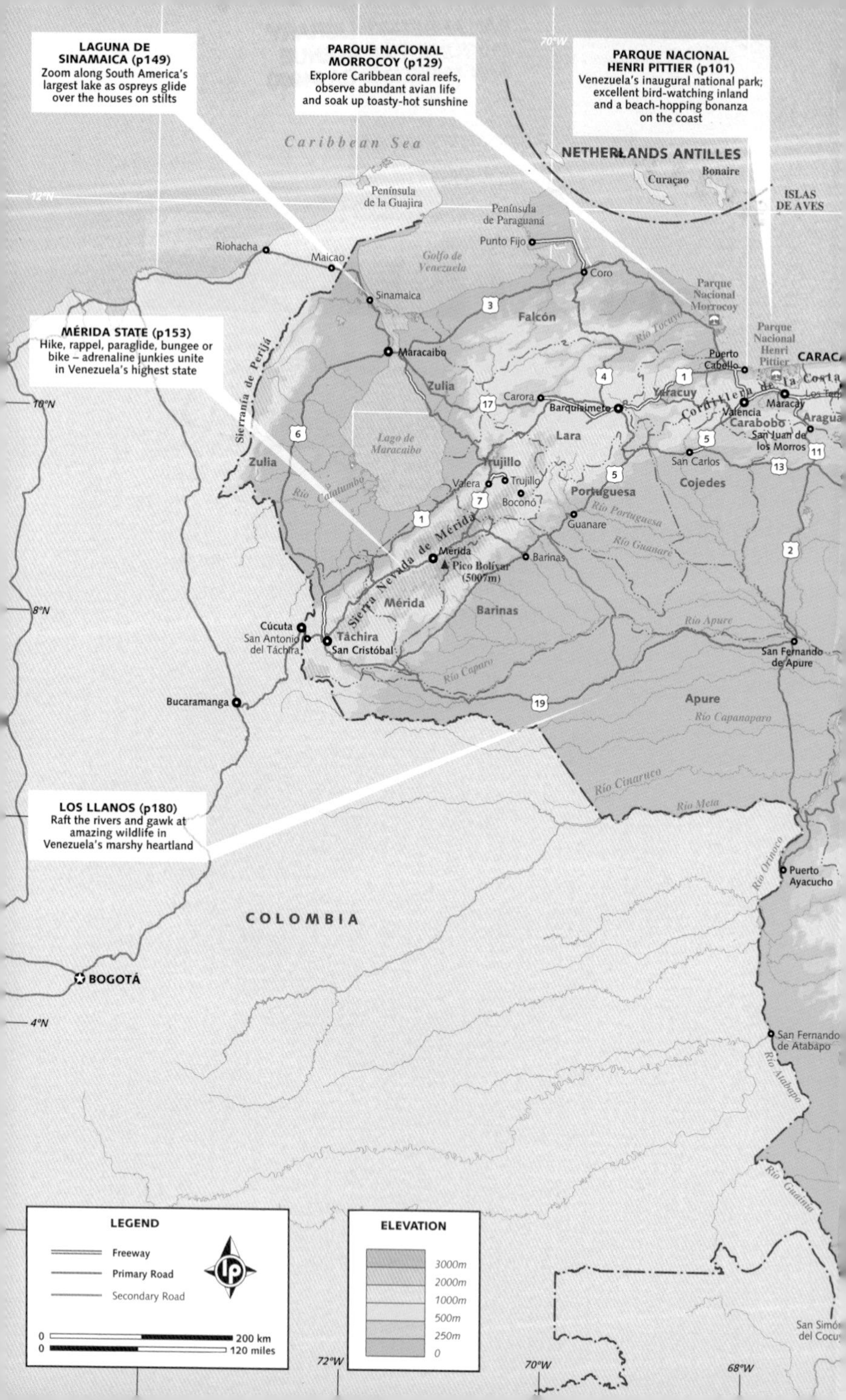
LAGUNA DE SINAMAICA (p149)
Zoom along South America's largest lake as ospreys glide over the houses on stilts
PARQUE NACIONAL MORROCOY (p129)
Explore Caribbean coral reefs, observe abundant avian life and soak up toasty-hot sunshine
PARQUE NACIONAL HENRI PITTIER (p101)
Venezuela's inaugural national park; excellent bird-watching inland and a beach-hopping bonanza on the coast
MÉRIDA STATE (p153)
Hike, rappel, paraglide, bungee or bike – adrenaline junkies unite in Venezuela's highest state
LOS LLANOS (p180)
Raft the rivers and gawk at amazing wildlife in Venezuela's marshy heartland
Caribbean Sea
NETHERLANDS ANTILLES
Curaçao
Bonaire
ISLAS DE AVES
Península de la Guajira
Península de Paraguaná
Punto Fijo
Coro
Riohacha
Maicao
Golfo de Venezuela
Sinamaica
Falcón
Parque Nacional Morrocoy
Parque Nacional Henri Pittier
Río Tocuyo
Maracaibo
Zulia
Sierranía de Perijá
Lago de Maracaibo
Río Catatumbo
Carora
Barquisimeto
Yaracuy
Puerto Cabello
CARACAS
Cordillera de la Costa
Valencia
Maracay
Carabobo
Aragua
San Juan de los Morros
Lara
San Carlos
Cojedes
Trujillo
Valera
Boconó
Portuguesa
Río Portuguesa
Guanare
Río Guanare
Sierra Nevada de Mérida
Mérida
Pico Bolívar (5007m)
Barinas
Cúcuta
San Antonio del Táchira
Táchira
San Cristóbal
Río Caparo
Río Apure
San Fernando de Apure
Apure
Río Capanoparo
Río Cinaruco
Río Meta
Bucaramanga
Río Orinoco
Puerto Ayacucho
COLOMBIA
BOGOTÁ
San Fernando de Atabapo
Río Atabapo
Río Guainía
San Simón del Cocuy
70°W
12°N
10°N
8°N
4°N
72°W
68°W
1
2
3
4
5
6
7
11
13
17
19
LEGEND
Freeway
Primary Road
Secondary Road
0
200 km
0
120 miles
ELEVATION
3000m
2000m
1000m
500m
250m
0

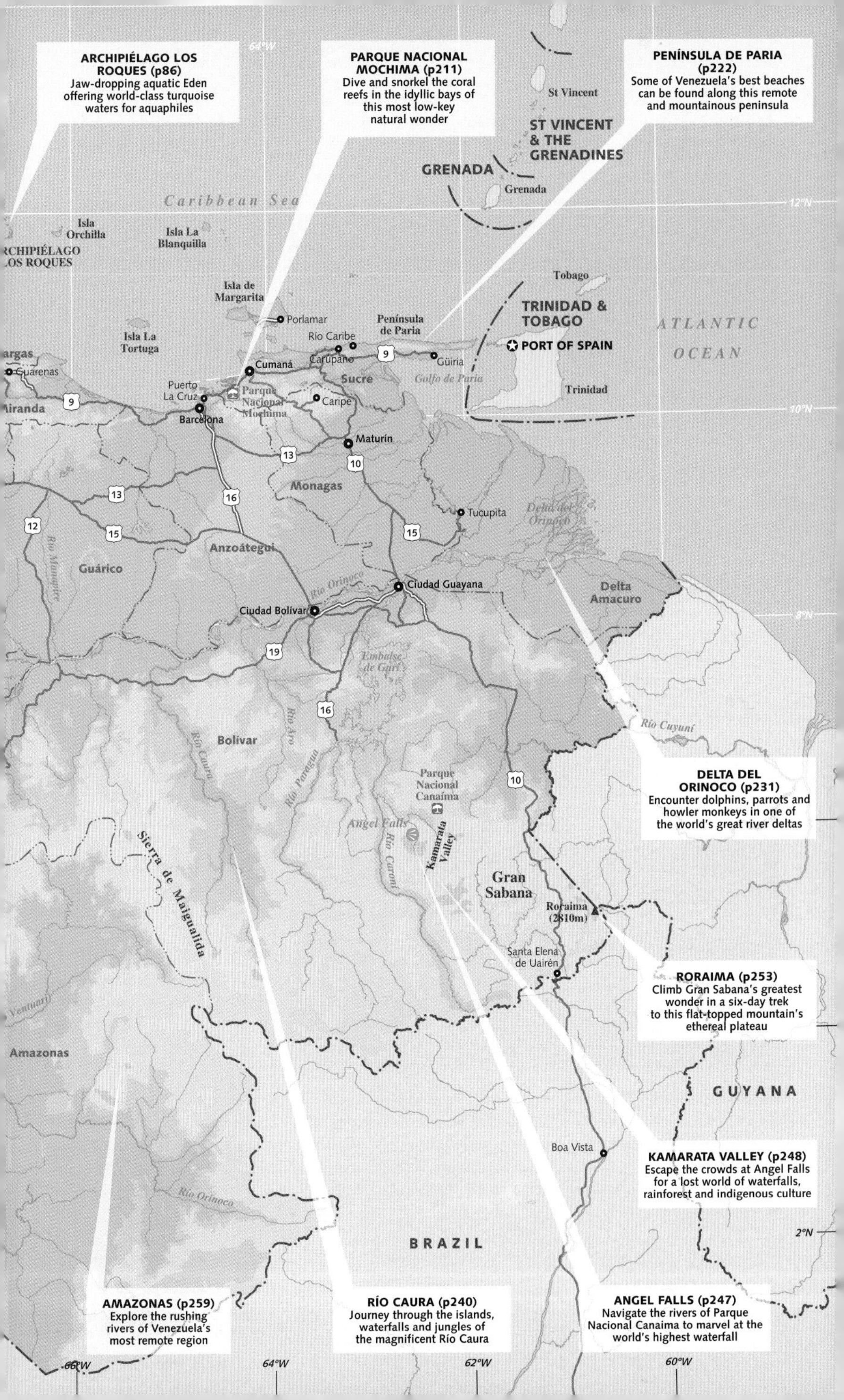

ARCHIPIÉLAGO LOS ROQUES (p86)
Jaw-dropping aquatic Eden offering world-class turquoise waters for aquaphiles
PARQUE NACIONAL MOCHIMA (p211)
Dive and snorkel the coral reefs in the idyllic bays of this most low-key natural wonder
PENÍNSULA DE PARIA (p222)
Some of Venezuela's best beaches can be found along this remote and mountainous peninsula
64°W
St Vincent
ST VINCENT & THE GRENADINES
GRENADA
Grenada
Caribbean Sea
12°N
Isla Orchilla
Isla La Blanquilla
RCHIPIÉLAGO
LOS ROQUES
Tobago
Isla de Margarita
TRINIDAD & TOBAGO
Porlamar
Península de Paria
ATLANTIC OCEAN
Isla La Tortuga
Río Caribe
PORT OF SPAIN
argas
Carúpano
9
Güiria
Guarenas
Cumaná
Golfo de Paria
Sucre
Puerto La Cruz
Parque Nacional Mochima
Trinidad
Miranda
9
Caripe
Barcelona
10°N
Maturín
13
10
Monagas
13
16
Tucupita
Delta del Orinoco
12
15
15
Río Manapire
Anzoátegui
Guárico
Río Orinoco
Ciudad Guayana
Delta Amacuro
Ciudad Bolívar
8°N
19
Embalse de Guri
16
Río Cuyuní
Río Aro
Río Caura
Bolívar
Río Paragua
Parque Nacional Canaima
10
DELTA DEL ORINOCO (p231)
Encounter dolphins, parrots and howler monkeys in one of the world's great river deltas
Angel Falls
Río Caroní
Kamarata Valley
Sierra de Maigualida
Gran Sabana
Roraima (2810m)
Santa Elena de Uairén
RORAIMA (p253)
Climb Gran Sabana's greatest wonder in a six-day trek to this flat-topped mountain's ethereal plateau
Ventuari
Amazonas
GUYANA
Boa Vista
KAMARATA VALLEY (p248)
Escape the crowds at Angel Falls for a lost world of waterfalls, rainforest and indigenous culture
Río Orinoco
BRAZIL
2°N
AMAZONAS (p259)
Explore the rushing rivers of Venezuela's most remote region
RÍO CAURA (p240)
Journey through the islands, waterfalls and jungles of the magnificent Río Caura
ANGEL FALLS (p247)
Navigate the rivers of Parque Nacional Canaima to marvel at the world's highest waterfall
66°W
64°W
62°W
60°W

# On the Road

**KEVIN RAUB Coordinating Author**
This skinny sandbar in the Archipiélago Los Roques is called Cayo de Agua (p88). I arrived early, so I had it to myself, this pristine strip of sand bound by shockingly turquoise waters. You cannot photoshop this sort of paradise! Only Mother Nature could have pulled off something this spectacular.

**BRIAN KLUEPFEL** Never smile at a crocodile? I wasn't after a 12-footer actually roared at me. My nervous smile betrays my lack of confidence in the croc's ability to read. One really appreciates how tough the *llaneros* (inhabitants of Los Llanos) are, scratching a living out of this land while living in a place where the wild beasts (p186) still kind of run the show.

**TOM MASTERS** After torrential rain all night we awoke to find the river had risen by about 5m, making crossing it and climbing up to the Mirador Laime a slippery and challenging experience! We were thoroughly soaked by the time we got there, but Angel Falls (Salto Ángel; p247) looked absolutely spectacular at full power.

*For full author biographies see p301.*

# Venezuela Highlights

Close your eyes. Don't peek. Are you ready for a surprise? The República Bolivariana de Venezuela, wrapped in petrol-politics, socialist agendas and shocking inflation, has a far less notorious side. Beyond the hyperbole is one of South America's most diverse and postcard-perfect lands, where turquoise seas rub against the continent's longest stretch of Caribbean coastline to the north and flat-topped mountains hide towering waterfalls and otherworldly landscapes in the south. In between, Venezuela is both an unparalleled adventure sports kingdom and a naturalist's paradise, boasting exotic wildlife, river deltas and more ways to get your blood pumping than a pacemaker. We're pulling back Venezuela's veil.

KRZYSZTOF DYDYNSKI

## 1 OVER THE TEPUIS AND THROUGH THE WOODS TO ANGEL FALLS

Beginning with the magnificent flight from Puerto Ordaz to Parque Nacional Canaima, a seriously spectacular aerial escapade among the tepuis (flat-topped mountains), and continuing with the dramatic boat ride along the Ríos Carrao and Churún, the journey to Angel Falls (Salto Ángel; p247) is an adventure for the ages. Upon arrival, it's all shock and awe – the mother of all waterfalls spits its life force seemingly right out from the clouds.

**Kevin Raub, Lonely Planet Author**

KRZYSZTOF DYDYNSKI

## HIKING THE HIGHLANDS ABOVE MERÍDA

Hiking the Pico Pan de Azucar (p166) was a fantastic and, compared with the glaciers, an easy way of seeing the scenic landscape around Mérida. For the descent we slid and ran down the dunelike sandy side of the mountain; that was pure fun!

**Gunther Marx, Traveler, Austria**

## 2 CONQUERING THE RORAIMA OTHERWORLD

The landscape of Roraima (p253) is like nothing you'll have ever seen, unless you've been to the moon! Strange black rocks with very peculiar shapes, alienlike frogs, carnivorous plants and extraordinary rock formations – it's an overwhelming place and well worth the five-day return trek.

**Said Fezazi, Traveler, Venezuela**

3

KRZYSZTOF DYD

RICHARD BROADWELL / A

## 4 CAY-HOPPING IN THE ARCHIPÉLAGO LOS ROQUES

I was stunned when I first landed in the Archipélago Los Roques (p86) – words can't do the color of the water justice. Each sun-scorched day and each turquoise-glistening cay outdid those of the day before, never ceasing to amaze both in their dreamscape setting and lack of crowds. The most unbelievable thing of all is that most people have never even heard of Los Roques. Except, of course, the Italians!

**Kevin Raub, Lonely Planet Author**

## CRUISING THE DELTA DEL ORINOCO

An unforgettable day in Venezuela for me was traveling around the vast channels of the Delta del Orinoco (p231), seeing Amazon River dolphins swimming beside the boat, passing Warao villages and spending the night deep in the rainforest at a rustic *campamento* (countryside lodging facility) under the stars to the tune of the jungle chorus.

**Tom Masters, Lonely Planet Author**

5

KRZYSZTOF DYDYNSKI

## CARACAS' SPA IN THE SKY

Parque Nacional El Ávila (p81) is like those amazing courtyards hidden behind the massive walls of colonial houses – a totally unexpected world opens up. On Sundays the crystal-clear waterfalls, lush vegetation and friendly hikers go a long way to help you recharge energy and face the hectic Caracas week ahead. If you take the *teleférico* (cable car), the unbelievable silence (while you soar above the hills) immediately clears your mind from all the clutter. It's better than going to a spa!

**Maria Claudia Renjifo, Traveler, Colombia**

6

STOCK CONNECTION BLUE / ALAMY

GREG JOHNSTON

7

## OFF-SEASON SUN-SOAKING IN ISLA DE MARGARITA

Visiting Isla de Margarita (p195) in low season was fantastic – the white sand beaches were empty, the water temperature was still perfect, the scenery was fantastic. To top it all off, the interior of the island is a beautiful place with dramatic mountains that remain tantalizingly inaccessible.

**Ricardo Rudas Alvarado, Traveler, Colombia**

KRZYSZTOF DYDYNSKI

## 8 DUNE-HOPPING IN CORO

The dunes outside of Coro (p118) are impressive, huge and infinite. It felt like playing in a massive sandbox. People were rolling, running or even jumping down the dunes…and always landing safely! It was interaction with nature, a cool dose of adrenaline, great exercise, and believe me, a bunch of funny pictures!

**Adrijana Mandl, Traveler, Slovenia**

## 9 FLOATING THROUGH PARQUE NACIONAL MORROCOY

As soon as the *lancha* (motorboat) pulls away from the dock in Parque Nacional Morrocoy (p129), you sort of automatically relax and your blood pressure drops 10 points. After the hustle and bustle of Caracas, and baking in Chichiriviche the day before, dropping into the Caribbean – as warm as it is – was unbelievably relaxing. I wanted to float all the way to the Dutch Antilles!

**Brian Kluepfel, Lonely Planet Author**

KRZYSZTOF DYD

KRZYSZTOF DYD

## 10 FEEL THE PRIDE OF ZULIANAS IN MARACAIBO

*Gaita* (p147) gives us the deepest sense of feeling Zuliana. It's the way we express our inextinguishable faith, and the way we get a sense of peace, love and justice – but with flavor and joy! *Gaita* shows all our tradition, how we are people brimming with life – both happy and open to other people. *Gaita* and our faith in La Chinita (p143) are the greatest way to show we are Zulianas (inhabitants of Zulia)!

**Liliana M de Viloria, Native Maracucho, Venezuela**

# Destination Venezuela

Venezuela is an intriguing beast indeed, depending on whom you ask – a *ménage à trois* of viewpoints that might be a brash, woefully troubled petrostate run by a leftist bully to a Chacao intellectual; to an oil baron, an exotic Andean-Caribbean playground for the wealthy and privileged, with crystalline coastline and mountainous majesty rivaling all of its neighboring nations; or a socialist wonderland of the future to a Chavista (supporter of President Hugo Chávez). What makes Venezuela a good time is that it's in some respects all three – a tsunami of discord and bounty of splendor that battle it out in a living, breathing, sensationalizing war of contradiction.

While other South American countries are romanticized for the tango, Machu Picchu or Carnaval, Venezuela's international reputation swirls around oil, the aggressive political style of Chávez and the next international beauty pageant winner. But through the rhetorical looking glass lies a little-known secret: Venezuela can be shockingly gorgeous and, though criminally undervisited, offers more to travelers than even the most intrepid explorers are aware. Yes, *La Tierra de Gracia* (Land of Grace), as Christopher Columbus put it in 1498, is nothing if not strangely beautiful and beautifully strange.

The sixth largest country in South America boasts Andean peaks; the longest stretch of Caribbean coastline to be found in any single nation; tranquil offshore islands set amid turquoise seas; wetlands teeming with caimans, capybaras, piranhas and anacondas; the steamy Amazon; and rolling savanna punctuated by flat-topped mountains called tepuis. The world's highest waterfall, Angel Falls (Salto Ángel), plummets 979m from the top of a tepui in Parque Nacional Canaima. Those seeking adventure will find hiking, snorkeling, scuba diving, kitesurfing, windsurfing, paragliding and more. Even better, Venezuela is relatively compact – no thrill is discouragingly too far from the next.

But Venezuela can just as well be more guns than roses. Best described as a rich nation with poor citizens, the economy is kept afloat by huge amounts of public spending, while private investors are driven away by strict currency and price controls. Oil, the battle against corruption, alarming street crime (the murder rate has increased 125% since 1998), Chávez's continued nationalization of major industries, his assistance to other Latin American Leftist governments and an acrid relationship with the US are serious issues that dominate the headlines in Venezuela. As a result, much of the bourgeoisie has jumped ship for Europe or the US, content to live abroad until the country's political and economic woes shake themselves out. As one local put it, 'Eighty percent of Venezuela is poor; the other 20% left.'

For those that stayed behind, the current state of affairs is no Hollywood honeymoon: inflation expected to reach 40% by 2011 is crippling the economy and, to add insult to injury, an energy and water crisis is leaving the country all too often in the dark and out to dry. Total power consumption has risen about 25% since 2004 while electricity rates have been frozen, leaving little incentive to save energy. Chávez has even gone so far as to temporarily ban imports of household appliances for personal use. Mandatory water rationing and controlled blackouts were commonplace at the time of writing and a state of emergency was declared. Chávez blames El Niño and global warming for the woefully depleted water

**FAST FACTS**

Population (est 2010): 28.6 million

Population growth rate: 1.5%

Adult literacy: 93%

Area: 912,050 sq km

Inflation (2010): 32%

GDP growth rate (2010): -4.8%

Unemployment (2009): 8.4%

Number of Miss World, Miss Universe and Miss Earth pageants won by Venezuelans: 12

reservoirs, but his critics aren't buying it. They say the blame is squarely on aging infrastructure and mismanagement. At the time of writing, the Guri Dam, which supplies more than two-thirds of Venezuela's power, was only 46% full – down from 60% just two months earlier – and on the verge of complete collapse.

On the brighter side, Venezuela is enamored of baseball, beauty queens, *telenovelas*, music, whisky, dance and ice-cold beers (sold in miniature bottles so consumption beats out convection every time). Its festivals are devilish delights of kaleidoscopic percussion; its natural grandeur is second to none (one dip into the stunning waters of Archipélago of Los Roques or a flyby over towering tepuis in Parque Nacional Canaima reiterates that point).

Like an undiscovered ruin, Venezuela might sit buried in discarded neglect and political hyperbole, but beneath the rhetoric is an unseen adventureland, one of the continent's last. While its politics and economics wage war, the rest of the country hides in the shadows, a diamond in the rough.

# Getting Started

Venezuela is a destination at odds with itself: after a decade of socialist government initiatives and deteriorating economic conditions, street violence and alleged authoritarian corruption have reached levels that scare many travelers away. Perhaps surprisingly, tourism is on the rise, and the travelers that do venture into the country often find Venezuela's astonishing natural wonders, pristine beaches and adventurous terrains nearly to themselves. The main things to check before your departure are the vaccination requirements (p285), weather conditions in the part of the country that you wish to visit, and the latest exchange rates and safety situations, both of which can be volatile.

## WHEN TO GO

The tourist season in Venezuela runs year-round, but consider the climate and Venezuelan holidays before finalizing your travel plans.

Venezuela has one dry season (roughly November/December to April/May) and one wet season (the rest of the year). The dry season is certainly more pleasant for traveling, particularly for hiking or other outdoor activities, though sightseeing in cities or towns won't be greatly disturbed by rain. Some sights, such as waterfalls, are actually more impressive in the wet season. Angel Falls (Salto Ángel), for example, is absolutely spectacular after heavy rains in the wet months, but in the dry season, flow can be reduced to a dribble and it's a royal pain to reach when the rivers are low. See Climate Charts (p268) for more information.

Venezuelans are mad about traveling over the Christmas season (running up till mid-January), Carnaval (several days prior to Ash Wednesday) and Holy Week (the week before Easter Sunday). During these three peak times, air and bus transportation are busy and hotels fill up quickly, so you'll have to book ahead. On the other hand, these periods are colorful and lively, with a host of festivities. Schools also break for annual vacations in August, but this doesn't significantly affect public transportation or accommodations.

## COSTS & MONEY

At first glance, Venezuela – especially Caracas – is absurdly expensive, the latter taking the honor of the most expensive Latin American city for expats in 2009. At the former official exchange rate, a Big Mac combo at McDonald's would have set you back a whopping US$16 – nearly three times the London price!

### DON'T LEAVE HOME WITHOUT...

- Recommended vaccinations (p285)
- Comprehensive insurance policy (p284)
- Photocopies of your essential documents
- Electrical adapter (p265)
- Flashlight/Torch – useful for most off-the-beaten-track excursions
- Insect repellent – essential for a Roraima trek, Los Roques and in many other areas
- Sunscreen
- Small Spanish-English dictionary and/or Lonely Planet *Latin American Spanish* phrasebook
- Flip-flops or thongs – to protect feet against fungal infections in hotel bathrooms

After the devaluation (see the boxed text, below), the price dropped to around $8, which isn't exactly a bargain, either, and it was likely to have risen significantly by the time you read this due to inflationary reaction. Banks, official *casa de cambios* (money-exchange office) and ATM machines always work with the new official rate; elsewhere, cold hard cash dollars are exchanged using the parallel exchange rate, or *dólar paralelo*, for rates that can push BsF7 for crafty financial transactions (legally known as the 'swap market') and BsF5 to BsF6 on the street, depending on the demand for non-official currency exchange. The dilemma, of course, is bringing in large amounts of cash into a country with less-than-stellar security. See below for more information.

Many of the more far-flung destinations in Guayana, Los Llanos and Amazonas, as well as many outdoor, ecotourism and adventure trips, are best visited in groups organized by travel agencies in urban centers. Even travelers who are fervently independent find themselves visiting such places as Roraima, Angel Falls and Los Llanos with groups as it's neither cost effective nor practical to make solo trips.

Budget travelers prepared for basic conditions can get by on BsF125 to BsF150 per day (considerably more in Caracas, which has little budget infrastructure). This would cover accommodations in bare-bones posadas, food in budget to midrange restaurants and travel by bus, and should still leave a small amount for some drinks and taxis. You shouldn't have to spend more than BsF50 to BsF175 per night (on average) for accommodations, and the cost will be lower if you travel with someone else, especially if you're sharing a bed (see *matrimoniales*, p265). For budget dining, the set lunch or dinner will cost BsF25 to BsF45 each. This budget wouldn't account for tours or internal flights.

**PRICE WARNING!**

Due to the Venezuelan government's strict currency controls and a high inflation rate, prices of goods and services are extremely volatile and rise frequently. Prices in this book are given in BsF, but a 25% to 32% year-on-year inflationary expectation means by the time you read this, prices will have significantly changed. Adding insult to injury, Venezuela announced 17% and 50% devaluations, respectively, of its currency post-research, which on the surface seems like a good deal for tourists, with the official exchange rate jumping from BsF2.15 to BsF4.30 to the US dollar on most tourist-related goods and services. However, this is expected to cause a significant inflationary reaction (economists predict 30% to 60% inflation in 2010), causing prices to rise considerably moving forward, erasing whatever gains the preferable exchange rate might have afforded.

An additional complication is the black market. Currency controls have pegged the bolívar fuerte to the US dollar at an artificially high rate since 2005, resulting in a two-tier market for changing money within Venezuela. Officially speaking, exchange rates in Venezuela are now fixed in a dual system: BsF2.60 per dollar for priority imports like food, health, machinery and equipment, science and technology, books and education items; and BsF4.30 for everything else (alcohol, cars, tobacco, chemicals, energy etc – a move designed to combat the black market). When changing traveler's checks, using credit cards or ATMs, or exchanging money at a bank or *casa de cambio* (money exchange bureau), you will always receive the latter rate.

An active black market (called the *dólar paralelo*) buys and sells the more stable dollars and euros, with rates boomeranging between BsF5 to BsF7 per dollar. Exchanging cash dollars this way is illegal (though exchanging titles and bonds is not). Many established posadas and tour operators will clandestinely accept payment or arrange BsF cash for you at the black market rate through online money transfers to international bank accounts. The devaluation lessened the impact of this somewhat (per design), but it can still add up if you're paying US$23 instead of US$15 per night to stay at a BsF100 budget posada, so some tourists opt to bring well-hidden cash to change or else make arrangements with an established posada or tour operator to wire money before their arrival.

Travelers who want more comfort, including midrange hotels and restaurants, will find that BsF250 to BsF400 per day should easily cover their expenses, and possibly allow an occasional flight. Midrange travelers can expect to spend between BsF200 and BsF300 per day on accommodations, less if traveling in a party or as a couple. A fine à la carte dinner will start at BsF40 to BsF60 for an average main course without drinks.

Top-end accommodations range from around BsF400 and up per night in smaller destinations to BsF600 to BsF800 in places like Los Roques, Caracas and Isla de Margarita. Top-end dining is not available in some smaller cities but can rival North American and Western European prices in Caracas and major tourist spots.

Bus is the main means of transportation, and it's reasonably priced, about BsF7 to BsF9 per hour of a journey. City buses are very cheap. Taxis aren't expensive either, particularly if you are willing to split fares with fellow travelers.

Churches and cathedrals don't have an admission charge. Most museums don't have an admission charge either, and those that do usually keep the fee low. Cultural events (cinema, theater, music etc) are all fairly inexpensive. On the other hand, a drinking session in a nightclub can deplete your funds quickly – especially if you drink at the same rate as Venezuelans.

The main cost in most travelers' budgets are organized tours. They cost roughly between BsF300 and BsF600 per day and are rarely single-day trips (though they usually include room and board).

**HOW MUCH?**

*Arepa* BsF18

Local 3-minute phone call BsF2.25

Short taxi ride BsF20 (in Caracas BsF30)

Double room in midrange hotel BsF250

One-way Caracas–Ciudad Bolívar airfare BsF290

## TRAVEL LITERATURE

Venezuela's unique table mountains have captivated writers for over a century. One of the most unusual accounts is by Sir Arthur Conan Doyle who, inspired by fabulous stories of explorers of Roraima, gave play to his imagination in the rollicking 1912 tale *The Lost World,* in which dinosaurs roam the top of the plateau.

Plenty of travelers were in turn inspired by Conan Doyle's story, including actor and author Brian Blessed, who tells how he fulfilled his childhood dream of visiting the 'Lost World' in his beautifully entertaining *Quest for the Lost World.*

*Churún Merú, the Tallest Angel,* by Ruth Robertson, is a report of the expedition to Auyantepui, during which the height of Angel Falls was measured for the first time, confirming its status as the world's highest waterfall.

The famous German geographer and botanist Alexander von Humboldt explored and studied various regions of Venezuela and describes it in his three-volume *Personal Narrative of Travels to the Equinoctial Regions of America During the Years 1799–1801.* Volume 2 covers the Venezuelan section of his journey. It may sound like a dry, scientific study, but it's fascinating reading, full of amazing details.

Of the useful local publications, *Guide to Camps, Posadas and Cabins in Venezuela,* by Elizabeth Kline, is a bilingual edition detailing 1200 accommodation options, and the bilingual *Guia Extrema,* by Arianna Arteaga Quintero, is the adventure sports bible. Both are updated yearly.

There are a number of books on Chávez and his 'Bolivarian Revolution,' though most sources take either a fervent pro- or anti-Chávez stance. Some of the more recent and widely sold titles are *Hugo Chávez: Oil, Politics, and the Challenge to the U.S.,* by Nikolas Kozloff; *Hugo!: The Hugo Chávez Story from Mud Hut to Perpetual Revolution,* by Bart Jones; *Chávez: Venezuela and the New Latin America,* by Hugo Chávez, David Deutschmann and Javier Salado; and *Hugo Chávez and the Bolivarian Revolution,* by Richard Gott.

# TOP 10

## TOP TEN HIDDEN JEWELS

Beyond Angel Falls, Roraima and Delta del Orinoco, there are plenty of lesser-known natural marvels that are just as fascinating.

1. Parque Nacional Ciénagas del Catatumbo (p150) – famous for its unique lightning without thunder
2. Salto Aponguao (p250) – Gran Sabana's most spectacular waterfall
3. Reserva Biológica de Montecano (p126) – small forest on arid Península de Paraguaná
4. Sierra de San Luis (p127) – attractive, lush mountains near Coro
5. Península de Paria (p225) – marvelous peninsula graced with coves and beaches
6. Salto Pará (p240) – lovely waterfall on the Río Caura
7. Quebrada de Jaspe (p255) – small waterfall rolling over amazing red jasper rock
8. Parque Nacional Médanos de Coro (p120) – striking mini-Sahara Desert near Coro
9. Cerro Autana (p264) – gigantic tree trunk–shaped tepui (flat-topped mountain) in Amazonas
10. Brazo Casiquiare (p259) – unusual water channel linking the Ríos Orinoco and Negro

## FESTIVALS

Dancing devils and a handful of Carnaval celebrations highlight Venezuela's festive offerings.

1. Rumba with street devils in San Francisco de Yare at the Festival de los Diablos Danzantes (p93)
2. Imbibe in Venezuela's largest Carnaval in Carúpano (p214)
3. Gorge on *sapoara* fish at Ciudad Bolívar's river extravaganza, the Feria del Orinoco (p239)
4. Shimmy and shake to Calypso rhythms at El Callao's Trinidad-influenced Carnaval (p214)
5. Party in the Andes during Mérida's Feria del Sol (p158)
6. Overdose on chocolate, beaches and dancing devils during Chuao's Festival de los Diablos Danzantes (p94)
7. Watch the locals play judge, jury and Jesus in the Good Friday Passion Play re-enactment of Tostós (p173)
8. Groove to the *gaita* at Maracaibo's Feria de la Chinta (p147)
9. Gawk at life-size burning puppets stuffed with fireworks around Mérida during Despidida del Año Viejo (p158)
10. Samba the night away during Santa Elena's Brazilian-infused Carnaval (p214)

## TUNES

From salsa to dance-funk, load up your iPod with the following Venezuelan classics and you'll own the *rumba* – and anything else the DJ spins your way.

1. *The New Sound of the Venezuelan Gozadera* (Amigos Invisibles, 1998)
2. *Songs of Venezuela* (Soledad Bravo, 1995)
3. *Donde Esta el Futuro* (Desorden Publico, 1999)
4. *40 Años 40 Exitos* (Aldemaro Romero, 2007)
5. *Al Pueblo lo que es de César* (Ali Primera, 1968)
6. *Carreño – Piano Works* (2000)
7. *Venezuela y su Folklore: A Taste of Venezuela*
8. *El Diablo Suelto: Guitar Music of Venezuela*
9. *Cómo se Llega a Belén* (Voz Veis, 2006)
10. *Oro* (Oscar D'León, 2004)

## INTERNET RESOURCES

**Lonely Planet** (www.lonelyplanet.com) Summaries on Venezuela travel; the Thorn Tree forum; travel news and links to useful travel resources.

**onlinenewspapers.com** (www.onlinenewspapers.com/venezuel.htm) Links to at least 30 Venezuelan online newspapers.

**University of Texas** (www1.lanic.utexas.edu/la/venezuela/) Comprehensive directory of Venezuelan websites provided by the Latin American Network Information Center of the University of Texas.

**Venezuela Analysis** (www.venezuelanalysis.com) Website containing articles analyzing the current political and economic issues.

**Venezuelan Embassy in the USA** (www.embavenez-us.org) Government information, including updates on visa regulations, plus plenty of links to everything from Venezuelan cuisine to beauty queens.

**Venezuela Tuya** (www.venezuelatuya.com) A comprehensive tourism portal for Venezuelan tourism.

**Zmag** (www.zmag.org/znet/places/Venezuela) Website containing articles analyzing the current political and economic issues from a pro-government perspective.

# Itineraries

## CLASSIC ROUTES

### VENEZUELA 101

**Four to Six Weeks / Caracas to Caracas**

Folks believe that since Venezuela has oil, it has never chosen to develop tourism. Whether true or not, the result is two-fold: the country's outstanding offerings remain under-visited; and those that touch down here won't have to share them with legions of fellow travelers.

Begin by spending a day or two in **Caracas** (p51), partaking in fabulous food, wild nightlife and interesting museums. From there, travel by air or an all-night bus ride to the Andean hot spot of **Mérida** (p153), an adventure sports region offering all manner of high-adrenaline activity – rafting, paragliding, trekking and mountain biking.

Next stop is **Ciudad Bolívar** (p235), where your priority is a three-day tour to the famous **Angel Falls** (Salto Ángel; p247). Back in town, take a four-day tour to the **Gran Sabana** (p250), an amazing rolling savanna dotted with table mountains and waterfalls. While there, consider the three-day summit of **Roraima** (p253), one of South America's epic treks.

Wind things down on Venezuela's Caribbean Eden, **Archipiélago Los Roques** (p86), where the swimming-pool-quality waters rival anywhere – you'll need be torn from its sandy clutches to make your flight back to Caracas and home.

**This best-of route will take four to six weeks, but can easily stretch beyond that if you are an outdoor adventure junkie, in which case plan extra days in Mérida, or an avid diver/snorkeler – Los Roques will demand more of your time.**

## CARIBBEAN COASTLINE

**One Month / Caracas to Isla de Margarita**

With the longest stretch of Caribbean coastline in any single country, Venezuela will inundate you with its wealth of beautiful beaches, islands and other natural attractions. The exquisite coral **Archipiélago Los Roques** (p86) is many people's first or last destination, easily accessible from **Caracas** (p51). Once back on the mainland, it's a West-to-East aquatic odyssey. Start in the islands, islets and cays of **Parque Nacional Morrocoy** (p129), the single prettiest stretch of Venezuelan coastline after Los Roques. A little further east, you can take the scenic, nail-biting road up and over the coastal mountains, through the wildlife-rich cloud forests of **Parque Nacional Henri Pittier** (p101) and into the coastal village of **Puerto Colombia** (p103), surrounded by secluded beaches reached only by boat or a long hike.

Taking the long haul back past Caracas, **Puerto La Cruz** (p208) is the jumping-off point to explore the stunning beaches and islands of **Parque Nacional Mochima** (p211). You can hop on a ferry to Isla de Margarita here, or continue first to the historic city of **Cumaná** (p215). You may also want to take a detour southeast to the impressive **Cueva del Guácharo** (p227), or east to **Río Caribe** (p221) and the remote, undeveloped beaches nearby, including idyllic **Playa Medina** (p222). You can then take a boat from Chacopata or Cumaná to the soft, white shores of the tourist mecca that is **Isla de Margarita** (p195).

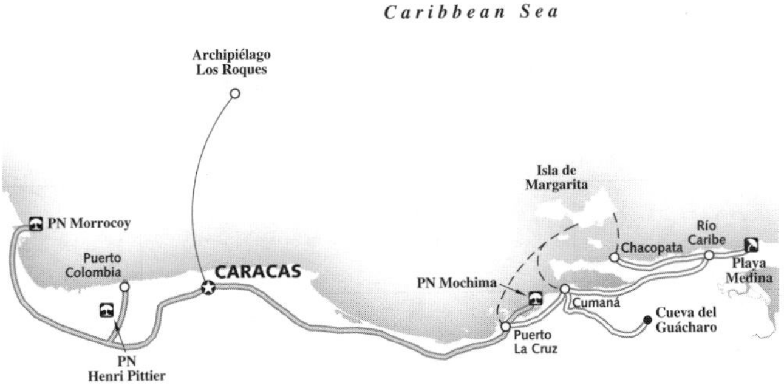


**It's possible to cover this 2244km route in three weeks at a squeeze, but if you're after rest and relaxation don't try to fit in too much. Pick and choose your destinations carefully so you can spend more time chilling out on a beach rather than sitting on a bus.**

# ROADS LESS TRAVELED

## MOUNTAINS HIGH, RIVERS LOW

**Four to Six Weeks / Ciudad Bolívar to Puerto Ayacucho**

Venezuela's natural wonders are its biggest asset, none more so than those of the famed region of Guayana, one of the country's most traveled areas. Its endless savannas, breathtaking table mountains, soaring waterfalls and broad rivers have fascinated travelers for centuries, but many are well off-the-beaten-track and best visited on an organized tour.

Guayana's major traveler base is the colonial river port of **Ciudad Bolívar** (p235), easily accessible from Caracas by daily flights or a comfortable nine-hour bus ride. Stay a few days to stroll about the colorful and charming streets before taking a tour to **Canaima** (p244) and the famous **Angel Falls** (Salto Ángel; p247). Your next adventure might involve the vast, enchanting highlands of **Gran Sabana** (p250) and the massive table mountain of **Roraima** (p253). Tours to both can be bought in Ciudad Bolívar, or you can go by bus along a spectacular road to **Santa Elena de Uairén** (p255) and buy both tours more cheaply here.

Ciudad Bolívar is also a springboard for the **Río Caura** (p240), a lovely river 200km southwest, accessible only by tour. Guayana's other big attraction is the **Delta del Orinoco** (p231), and this trip can also be organized from Ciudad Bolívar, or you can go to **Tucupita** (p231) and shop around for a tour.

Some travelers bus to **Puerto Ayacucho** (p259) to see the upper Orinoco and Amazon basins – another off-the-beaten-track adventure and another tour.

**Visiting all the listed attractions will take four to six weeks, and a large slice of your budget. Many travelers cross Guayana on their way to Brazil and just visit the main sights en route (Gran Sabana and Roraima, plus the spectacular Angel Falls). Put aside two weeks for these three sights.**

# TAILORED TRIPS

## EXTREME VENEZUELA

Need a wake-up call? In Caracas, start your day on a thrilling sunrise tandem paragliding flight from the 1800m Picacho de Galipán over **Parque Nacional El Ávila** (p81) to the beach at Camuri Chico.

Not far away from Caracas is the pretty German colonial town of **Colonia Tovar** (p100) – ain't it cute? Now, rappel down some waterfalls! Fourteen to be exact, ranging from 5m to 70m in height, on a canyoning excursion through Quebrada Tamaira to Puerto Cruz.

Most folks see **Angel Falls** (p247) from the air or from a small viewpoint several meters from its bottom. But why sit at the viewpoint staring up at Angel Falls when you can BASE jump from the top? Those with experience can take a leap of faith and hurl themselves from the summit in an exhilarating 900m BASE jump. Otherwise, rappelling down is another heart-stopping option. If that's not high enough for you, tackle the 4981m **Pico Bolívar** (p165), the highest mountain in Venezuela, a six-day trek just outside Venezuela's high-octane capital, **Mérida** (p153).

**Santa Elena de Uairén** (p255) is the jumping-off point for a 12-day kayak blockbuster on the River Karuai, where you'll navigate Class I and II rapids and encounter isolated Pemón tribes through one of the most remote and pristine areas of **Parque Nacional Canaima** (p244). All of these activities are bookable via one of the agencies listed in the Transportation chapter.

## WHERE THE WILD THINGS ARE

From the seasonally flooded plains of Los Llanos to the verdant cloud forests around Caracas, Venezuela is rich with wildlife – especially birds, over 1300 species of which have been recorded, with many existing nowhere else.

A four-day wildlife safari to **Los Llanos** (p180), organized from Mérida, is far and away the best chance to see the widest range of wildlife, including capybaras, caimans, anacondas, ocelots, anteaters and ever-elusive jaguars. The region is also one of the planet's most important bird-breeding reserves. **Parque Nacional Henri Pittier** (p101), just two hours west of Caracas by bus, is held as legendary among neotropical birders – the 1078-sq-km park is home to over 500 recorded species.

For water's-edge viewing, a trip along the **Río Orinoco** (p231), organized from **Ciudad Bolívar** (p238) or **Tucupita** (p233), is a tough act to follow: Howler and spider monkeys, Orinoco crocodiles – the largest in the Americas – giant river otters, river dolphins and manatees all inhabit the diverse Orinoco Delta.

And let us not forget the longest continuous stretch of Caribbean coastline in the Americas – you'll find world-class diving in **Archipiélago Los Roques** (p86), a plethora of waterbirds in **Parque Nacional Morrocoy** (p129) and frequent pods of dolphins in **Parque Nacional Mochima** (p211).

# History

## THE FIRST FEW MILLENNIA

It is generally believed that the first inhabitants of the Americas came from Siberia across the Bering Strait, spread over the North American continent, then moved down to Central and South America in several waves of migration.

For a concise and to-the-point introduction to the country's historic, economic, societal and contemporary issues, read *In Focus: Venezuela – A Guide to the People, Politics and Culture,* by James Ferguson.

Formerly nomadic groups began to develop into larger cultures belonging to three main linguistic families: Carib, Arawak and Chibcha. By the time of the Spanish conquest at the end of the 15th century, some 300,000 to 400,000 indigenous people inhabited the region that is now Venezuela.

The warlike Carib tribes occupied the central and eastern coast, living off fishing and shifting agriculture. Various Arawak groups were scattered over the western plains and north up to the coast. They lived off hunting and food-gathering, and occasionally practiced farming.

The Timote-Cuica tribes, of the Chibcha linguistic family, were the most advanced of Venezuela's pre-Hispanic societies. They lived in the Andes and developed advanced agricultural techniques, including irrigation and terracing. They were also skilled craftspeople, as we can judge by the artifacts they left behind – examples of their fine pottery are shown in museums across the country. No major architectural works have survived, though some smaller sites in the Andean region have recently been unearthed and will be opening for tourism in the next few years.

## THE SPANISH ARE COMING!

In 1498, on his third trip to the New World, Christopher Columbus anchored at Venezuela's northeastern tip. He originally believed that he was on another island, but the voluminous mouth of the Río Orinoco hinted that he had stumbled into something slightly larger.

John Hemming's *The Search for El Dorado* is a fascinating insight into the Spanish conquest of Venezuela and Colombia. It reads like a thriller, yet is admirably factual.

A year later, explorer Alonso de Ojeda, accompanied by the Italian Amerigo Vespucci, sailed up to the Península de la Guajira, at the western end of present-day Venezuela. On entering Lago de Maracaibo, the Spaniards saw the local indigenous people living in *palafitos* (thatched huts on stilts above the water). They called the land Venezuela (literally 'Little Venice') – perhaps as a sarcastic sailor joke, as these rustic reed dwellings didn't exactly match the opulent palaces of the Italian city they knew. The name of Venezuela appeared for the first time on a map in 1500 and has remained to this day. Laguna de Sinamaica (p149) is reputedly the place where the first Spanish sailors saw the *palafitos,* and you can see similar huts there today.

Alonso de Ojeda sailed further west along the coast and briefly explored parts of what is now Colombia. He saw local aborigines wearing gold adornments and was astonished by their wealth. Their stories about fabulous

## TIMELINE

**13,000 BC**

There is evidence of human habitation in northwest Venezuela going back more than 15,000 years. Steady agriculture is established around the 1st millennium, leading to the first year-round settlements.

**AD 1498**

Christopher Columbus lands in northeastern Venezuela. He anchors at the Península de Paria, just opposite Trinidad, becoming the first European to see the South American continent.

**1527**

Coro is made the first capital of colonial Venezuela by the Spanish. Though today a Unesco World Heritage site, it has been on the *List of World Heritage in Danger* since 2005 due to continued water damage from torrential rains.

treasures inland gave birth to the myth of El Dorado (The Golden One), a mysterious land abundant in gold. Attracted by these supposed riches, the shores of Venezuela and Colombia became the target of Spanish expeditions, an obsession with El Dorado driving them into the interior. Their search resulted in the rapid colonization of the land, though El Dorado was never found.

Venezuela is the only South American mainland country where Columbus landed.

The Spanish established their first settlement on Venezuelan soil around 1500, at Nueva Cádiz, on the small island of Cubagua, just south of Isla de Margarita. Pearl harvesting provided a livelihood for the settlers, and the town developed into a busy port until an earthquake and tidal wave destroyed it in 1541.

Officially, most of Venezuela was ruled by Spain from Santo Domingo (present-day capital of the Dominican Republic) until 1717, when it fell under the administration of the newly created viceroyalty of Nueva Granada, with its capital in Bogotá.

The colony's population of indigenous communities and Spanish invaders diversified with the arrival of African slaves, brought from Africa to serve as the workforce. Most of them were set to work on plantations on the Caribbean coast. By the 18th century, Africans surpassed the indigenous population in number.

The earliest Venezuelan town still in existence, Cumaná (p215), on the northeast coast, dates from 1521 and is an enjoyable place to visit, even though earthquakes ruined much of the early Spanish colonial architecture.

## OUT FROM UNDER THE YOKE

With few exploited gold mines, Venezuela lurked in the shadows of the Spanish Empire for its first three centuries. The country took a more prominent role at the beginning of the 19th century, when Venezuela gave Latin America one of its greatest heroes, Simón Bolívar (see the boxed text, p24).

Francisco de Miranda lit the initial revolutionary flame in 1806. However, his efforts to set up an independent administration in Caracas ended when fellow conspirators handed him over to the Spanish. He was shipped to Spain and died in jail. Bolívar then assumed leadership of the revolution. After unsuccessful initial attempts to defeat the Spaniards at home, he withdrew to Colombia, then to Jamaica, until the opportune moment came in 1817.

The Napoleonic Wars had just ended, and Bolívar's agent in London was able to raise money and arms, and recruit a small number of British Legion veterans of the Peninsular War. With this force and an army of horsemen from Los Llanos, Bolívar marched over the Andes and defeated the Spanish at the Battle of Boyacá, bringing independence to Colombia in August 1819. Though the least important of Gran Colombia's (Great Colombia) three provinces, Venezuela bore the brunt of the fighting. Venezuelan patriots fought not only on their own territory, but also in the armies that Bolívar led into Colombia and down the Pacific coast. It's estimated that a quarter of the Venezuelan population died in the independence wars.

**1577**

Caracas, founded in 1567 by Captain Diego de Losada, becomes the capital of the Province of Venezuela. A mere 60 families populate its original 25 blocks.

**1725**

Venezuela's first university, the Universidad Real y Pontificia de Caracas, is founded, and continues today at the Unesco World Heritage site of the Universidad Central de Venezuela.

**1783**

National hero Simón Bolívar is born in Caracas on July 24 into a wealthy Creole family that had emigrated some 200 years previously.

### THE SUCCESSES & FAILURES OF SIMÓN BOLÍVAR

'There have been three great fools in history: Jesus, Don Quixote and I.' This is how Simón Bolívar summed up his life shortly before he died. The man who brought independence from Spanish rule to the entire northwest of South America – today's Venezuela, Colombia, Panama, Ecuador, Peru and Bolivia – died abandoned, rejected and poor.

Simón Bolívar was born in Caracas on July 24, 1783 into a wealthy Creole family, which had come to Venezuela from Spain 200 years earlier. He was just three years old when his father died and nine years old when his mother died. The boy was brought up by his uncle and was given an open-minded tutor and mentor, Simón Rodríguez.

At the age of 16, Bolívar was sent to Spain and France to continue his education. The works of Voltaire and Rousseau introduced him to new, progressive ideas of liberalism, yet he didn't think about a political career at that stage. He married a Spaniard, María Teresa, and the young couple sailed to Caracas to start a new life at the old family hacienda in San Mateo. Unfortunately, María Teresa died of yellow fever just eight months later. Bolívar never married again, though he had many lovers. The most devoted of these was Manuela Sáenz, whom he met in Quito in 1822 and who stayed with him almost until his final days.

The death of María Teresa marked a drastic shift in Bolívar's destiny. He returned to France, where he met with the leaders of the French Revolution, then traveled to the USA to take a close look at the new order after the American Revolutionary War. By the time he returned to Caracas in 1807, he was full of revolutionary theories and experiences taken from these two successful examples. It didn't take him long to join clandestine pro-independence circles.

Bolívar's military career began under Francisco de Miranda, but after Miranda was captured by the Spaniards in 1812, Bolívar took command. Over the following decade, he hardly had a moment's rest, as battle followed battle with astonishing frequency. He personally commanded the independence forces in 35 victorious battles, including the key Battle of Carabobo, which brought freedom to Venezuela.

Bolívar's long-awaited dream of a unified republic comprising Colombia, Venezuela and Ecuador became reality, but Gran Colombia (Great Colombia) soon began to disintegrate. As separatist tendencies escalated, Bolívar assumed dictatorship in 1828, yet this step brought more harm than good and his popularity waned. A short time later, he miraculously escaped an assassination attempt in Bogotá. Disillusioned and in bad health, he resigned from the presidency in early 1830 and decided to leave for Europe.

When he reached Santa Marta, Colombia, to board a ship bound for France, he was already very ill and depressed. He died in Santa Marta, abandoned, rejected and penniless, on December 17, 1830, at the age of 47.

## GREAT COLOMBIA & GREATER PROBLEMS

Bolívar's dream of a unified republic fell apart even before he died in 1830. On his deathbed, he proclaimed: 'America is ungovernable. The man who serves a revolution plows the sea. This nation will fall inevitably into the hands of the unruly mob and then will pass into the hands of almost in-

**1811**

A congress of Venezuelan provinces declares Venezuela's independence, referred to by historians today as the First Republic of Venezuela (but actually independence wouldn't come for another 10 years).

**1819**

Four months after the Battle of Boyacá, the Angostura Congress proclaims Gran Colombia (Great Colombia), a new state unifying Colombia, Venezuela and Ecuador (though the last two are still under Spanish rule).

**1821**

Bolívar's troops defeat the Spanish royalist army on June 24 at the Battle of Carabobo, liberating Venezuela and sealing its independence. Ecuador, Peru and Bolivia soon follow.

distinguishable petty tyrants.' Unfortunately, he wasn't far off the mark. Gran Colombia began to collapse from the moment of its birth; the central regime was incapable of governing the immense country with its racial and regional differences. The new state existed for only a decade before splitting into three separate countries.

Following Venezuela's separation from Gran Colombia, the Venezuelan congress approved a new constitution and – incredibly – banned Bolívar from his homeland. It took the Venezuelan nation 12 years to acknowledge its debt to the man to whom it owed its freedom. In 1842, Bolívar's remains were brought from Santa Marta, Colombia, where he died, to Caracas and entombed in the cathedral. In 1876 they were solemnly transferred to the Panteón Nacional (p61) in Caracas, where they now rest in a bronze sarcophagus.

The Venezuelan flag was designed by Francisco de Miranda, who hoisted a yellow, blue and red striped flag on his ship in 1806 as he headed to Venezuela on his second attempt to initiate independence.

The post-independence period in Venezuela was marred by serious governmental problems that continued for more than a century. These were times of despotism and anarchy, with the country being ruled by a series of military dictators known as *caudillos*.

The first of the *caudillos,* General José Antonio Páez, controlled the country for 18 years (1830–48). It was a tough rule, but it established a certain political stability and put the weak economy on its feet. The period that followed was an almost uninterrupted chain of civil wars that was only stopped by another long-lived dictator, General Antonio Guzmán Blanco (1870–88). He launched a broad program of reform, including a new constitution, and assured some temporary stability, but his despotic rule triggered wide, popular opposition, and when he stepped down the country plunged again into civil war.

In the 1840s, Venezuela raised the question of its eastern border with British Guiana (present-day Guyana), claiming as much as two-thirds of Guiana, up to the Río Esequibo. The issue was a subject of lengthy diplomatic negotiations and was eventually settled in 1899 by an arbitration tribunal, which gave rights over the questioned territory to Great Britain. Despite the ruling, Venezuela maintains its claim to this day. All maps produced in Venezuela have this chunk of Guyana within Venezuela's boundaries, labeled 'Zona en Reclamación.'

Gabriel García Márquez' historical novel *The General in his Labyrinth* recounts the tragic final months of Simón Bolívar's life. It's a powerful and beautifully written work from one of Latin America's most celebrated literary figures.

## THE NATIONAL SOAP OPERA

The first half of the 20th century was dominated by five successive military rulers from the Andean state of Táchira. The longest lasting and most tyrannical was General Juan Vicente Gómez, who seized power in 1908 and didn't relinquish it until his death in 1935. Gómez phased out the parliament, squelched the opposition and monopolized power.

The discovery of oil in 1914 helped the Gómez regime to put the national economy on its feet. By the late 1920s, Venezuela was the world's largest exporter of oil, which not only contributed to economic recovery but also enabled the government to pay off the country's entire foreign debt. As in

**1842**

The remains of Simón Bolívar are brought from Santa Marta, where he died in 1830, to Caracas for interment in the cathedral.

**1849**

Rich lodes of gold are found in Guayana, generating one of the world's greatest gold rushes.

**1908–35**

Venezuela experiences a period of tyrannical dictatorial rule under General Juan Vicente Gómez, who is elected president three times and rules with an iron military fist.

most petrostates, almost none of the oil wealth made its way to the common citizen. The vast majority of Venezuelans continued to live in poverty with little or no educational or health facilities, let alone reasonable housing. Fast oil money also led to the neglect of agriculture and to the development of other types of production. It was easier to just import everything from abroad, which worked for a while, but proved unsustainable.

Tensions rose dangerously during the following dictatorships, exploding in 1945 when Rómulo Betancourt, leader of the left-wing Acción Democrática (AD) party, took control of the government. A new constitution was adopted in 1947, installing short-lived democracy. Just eight months after its inaugural democratic elections, the inevitable coup took place. Colonel Marcos Pérez Jiménez emerged as the leader. Once in control, he smashed the opposition, plowed oil money into public works and built up Caracas. He superficially modernized the country but the mushrooming development did not heal the country's economic and social disparities, nor the bitter resentment that lingered from the coup.

## THE BOOM/BUST CYCLE

Austerity measures introduced in 1989 by President Pérez Jiménez triggered a wave of protests, culminating in the loss of more than 300 lives in three days of bloody riots known as 'El Caracazo.'

Pérez Jiménez was overthrown in 1958 by a coalition of civilians and navy and air-force officers. The country returned to democratic rule and Rómulo Betancourt was elected president. He enjoyed popular support and actually completed the constitutional five-year term of office – the first democratically elected Venezuelan president to do so. Since then, all changes of president have been by constitutional means, although the Chávez era has seen a few hiccups.

During the term of President Rafael Caldera (1969–74), a steady stream of oil money flowed into the country's coffers, keeping the economy buoyant. President Carlos Andrés Pérez (1974–79) benefited from the oil bonanza – not only did production of oil rise but, more importantly, the price quadrupled following the Arab-Israeli war in 1973. In 1975 Pérez nationalized the iron-ore and oil industries and went on a spending spree; imported luxury goods crammed shops and the nation got the impression that El Dorado had finally materialized.

In the late 1970s, the growing international recession and oil glut began to shake Venezuela's economy. Oil revenues declined, pushing up unemployment and inflation, and once more forcing the country into foreign debt. The 1988 drop in world oil prices cut the country's revenue in half, casting doubt on Venezuela's ability to pay off its debt. Further austerity measures sparked protests that often escalated into riots, and, to make matters worse, there were two attempted coups d'état in 1992.

Corruption, bank failures and loan defaults plagued the government through the mid-1990s. In 1995, Venezuela was forced to devalue the currency by more than 70%. By the end of 1998, two-thirds of Venezuela's 23 million inhabitants were living below the poverty line. Drug trafficking and

**1914**

Caribbean Petroleum taps Lago de Maracaibo's Mene Grande oilfield. In a crude-spewing instant, Venezuela becomes one of the world's most powerful petrostates, changing the country forever.

**1947**

Venezuela holds its first-ever democratic election, in which popular novelist Rómulo Gallegos becomes president, a little over a decade after publishing his most acclaimed novels, *Cantaclaro* and *Canaima*.

**1960**

Venezuela's Energy and Mines minister initiates an oil conference in Baghdad that would eventually give birth to modern-day OPEC, the world's most powerful oil exporting organization.

crime had increased and Colombian guerrillas had dramatically expanded their operations into Venezuela's frontier areas.

## HUGO CHÁVEZ & THE BOLIVARIAN REVOLUTION

There is nothing better in political theater than a dramatic comeback. The 1998 election put Hugo Chávez, the leader of the first 1992 failed coup, into the presidency. After being pardoned in 1994, Chávez embarked on an aggressive populist campaign: comparing himself to Bolívar, promising help (and handouts) to the poorest masses and positioning himself in opposition to the US-influenced free-market economy. He vowed to produce a great, if vague, 'peaceful and democratic social revolution,' known streetside as the 'Revolución Bolivariana'.

The gripping film *Amaneció de Golpe* (1999), directed by Carlos Azpúrua, portrays Venezuelan political unrest in the early 1990s. It tells how military man Hugo Chávez led an unsuccessful coup against then-president Carlos Andrés Pérez.

Since then, however, Chávez' 'social revolution' has been rocky. Shortly after taking office, 'El Comandanté' set about rewriting the constitution, granting himself sweeping new powers. The introduction of a package of new decree laws in 2001 was met with angry protests, and was followed by a massive and violent strike in April 2002. It culminated in a coup run by military leaders sponsored by a business lobby, in which Chávez was forced to resign. He regained power two days later, but this only intensified the conflict.

While the popular tensions rose, in December 2002 the opposition called a general strike in an attempt to oust the president. The nationwide strike paralyzed the country, including its vital oil industry and a good part of the private sector. After 63 days, the opposition finally called off the strike, which had cost the country 7.6% of its GDP and further devastated the oil-based economy. Chávez again survived and claimed victory.

National politics continued to be shaky until Chávez won a 2004 referendum and consolidated his power. Emboldened by greater political support and with his pockets swollen by high oil prices, Chávez quickly moved to expand his influence beyond the borders of Venezuela, reaching out to other Leftist leaders in Bolivia, Argentina, Cuba, Uruguay, Chile and Brazil. He has openly allied himself with Cuba's Fidel Castro (quite literally, as his bodyguards are Cuban) and supported the successful Leftist candidacy of Bolivia's Evo Morales, as well as Leftist candidates in Peru and Mexico who did not win office.

In 2005, shortly after Caracas hosted the 6th World Social Forum, Chávez started a highly publicized and dubiously intentioned program to provide reduce-priced heating oil for impoverished people in the US. The program was expanded in 2006 to include four of New York City's five boroughs, providing 25 million gallons of fuel for low-income New Yorkers at 40% off the wholesale price. While the program obviously aided hundreds of thousands of poor New Yorkers, it was used as a political jab to Chávez' then enemy, former US President George W Bush.

The end of 2006 was enveloped in the lead-up to the December 3 presidential election. Chávez' closest challenger, Manuel Rosales, accused the

**1976**

Venezuela nationalizes its oil industry, creating Petróleos de Venezuela (PDVSA), the state-owned oil company. Today, gas prices in Venezuela remain the world's lowest.

**1992**

Paratrooper Colonel Hugo Chávez leads the first of two failed coups, causing shooting throughout Caracas. A second attempt, led by junior air-force officers, sees an air battle over Caracas and costs more than 100 lives.

**1998**

After vowing on national TV that he had failed 'for now,' and serving two years in prison for his involvement in the 1992 attempted coup, Hugo Chávez is elected president in a landslide victory.

North American film director Oliver Stone takes on the rise of progressive, leftist governments in Latin America in 2009's *South of the Border,* in which he attempts to 'humanize' Hugo Chávez, the documentary's focal point.

president of providing impractical political favors and aid to other countries while poverty and crime increased at home, and also challenged Chávez' government-approved land takeovers (for redistribution to the landless) and the military build-up for a hypothetical US invasion. Chávez wrote Rosales off as a lackey for the US and refused to debate him on TV. Chávez won again, with the Organization of American States and the Carter Center certifying the results.

## CHÁVEZ' SECOND TERM

Chávez has come out of the socialist closet during his second term, further increasing public works and social programs to benefit the poor (bringing basic healthcare to the *barrios,* for example) and nationalizing the country's largest telecommunication, cement and steel companies, the majority of its electricity industry and many hotels, and recreational and transport facilities. He has also managed to instill the idea of inclusion in politics among the general population, whereas previous governments blatantly excluded all but the highest echelons of society.

However, despite Venezuela's deep oil pockets and improved life for the poor, Chávez's popularity appears to be waning. Infrastructure upgrades

### HUGO CHÁVEZ: A MILITARY MIND

At age 17, Hugo Chávez Frías enrolled at the Venezuelan Academy of Military Sciences. After graduating in 1975 as a sub-lieutenant with a degree in Military Arts and Science, Chávez entered military service for several months before pursuing graduate studies in political science at Simón Bolívar University in Caracas, though he never graduated.

Over the course of his college years, Chávez and his fellow students developed a fervently left-nationalist doctrine that they termed Bolivarianism, inspired by the Pan-Americanist philosophies of 19th-century Venezuelan revolutionary Simón Bolívar and the teachings of various socialist and communist leaders.

Upon completing his studies, Chávez entered active-duty military service as a member of a counter insurgency battalion stationed in Barinas. Chávez' military career lasted 17 years, and he eventually rose to the rank of lieutenant colonel. He also held a series of teaching and staffing positions at the Military Academy of Venezuela, where he was first acknowledged by his peers for his oratorical style and spirited critique of Venezuelan government and society. At this time, Chávez established the Revolutionary Bolivarian Movement-200 (MBR-200). Afterwards, he rose to fill a number of sensitive high-level positions in Caracas and was decorated several times.

After an extended period of popular dissatisfaction and economic decline under the administration of President Carlos Andrés Pérez, Chávez staged an unsuccessful coup d'état on February 4, 1992. After prison time and a subsequent pardon. Chávez founded the left-wing, socialist Fifth Republic Movement (later dissolved into United Socialist Party of Venezuela) and launched a political career that looks to endure for one or two decades or more.

**1999**

The 1999 constitution changed the country's name from República de Venezuela to República Bolivariana de Venezuela, requiring replacement of everything bearing the name, from coins and banknotes to passports and the coat of arms.

**1999**

Violent mudslides devastate the country's central coast, claiming up to 50,000 lives and significantly altering some 60km of coastline in the state of Vargas. The towns of Cerro Grande and Carmen de Uria disappear completely.

**2006**

Chávez wins re-election with 63% of the vote and vows a more radical turn toward socialism. He is poised to hold power through to at least 2012.

like improved roads and bridges, shiny new subways and *barrio teleféricos* (cable cars) keep up appearances, but the decade ended with Venezuela struggling to combat a very serious energy and water shortage, a crisis that has struck the heart of the middle and upper classes. Widespread blackouts are commonplace throughout the country, and Chávez called on all Venezuelans to limit their showers to three minutes only (a 'Communist shower,' he said). As 2010 was ushered in, so was water rationing, with Caracas temporarily taking the brunt of the blow – up to 48 hours per week without water. Chávez supporters balked at the idea, however, and rations were suspended in Caracas, amplifying the problem elsewhere and sparking protests in Mérida. Electricity Minister Ángel Rodríguez was removed from office over the debacle, but the cabinet shakeup didn't stop there: in January alone, the Vice-President and Defense Minister, Ramón Carrizalez, his wife, Environment Minister Yubirí Ortega, and the Minister for Public Banking, Eugenio Vásquez Orellana, all resigned. Rumors blamed the electricity crisis and a disagreement with government policy, though all three politicians denied this. A month later, the energy crisis deteriorated to the point that Chávez issued a state of emergency.

Oil is Venezuela's principal natural resource. Discovered here in 1914, it soon turned Venezuela from a poor debtor nation into one of South America's richest countries. In 2008, Venezuela was the world's eighth largest oil exporter.

Chávez has instilled many controversial policies to combat the country's wild inflation and debilitating economy, too, including price controls on basic foodstuffs – a move that, on one hand, allows families to purchase the same amount of basic food with the same amount of money despite inflation, but sparks occasional food shortages of basics like milk and sugar on the other. In January 2010, Chávez announced a sharp devaluation of the *bolívar fuerte* (see p14) – the first since 2005 – creating a two-tier official exchange rate in Venezuela, a move designed to boost revenue from oil exports and limit unnecessary imports. But *Venezolanos,* fearing widespread price increases and astronomical inflation, mobbed imported electronics stores. Chávez condemned stores that raised their prices and acted: the Venezuelan Institute for the Defense of People in Their Access to Goods and Service shut down dozens of stores for price-gouging. Elsewhere, strict currency controls mean Venezuelans who travel abroad are only allowed a rationing of $2,500 in credit card and $500 cash per year to spend outside the country, leaving some feeling trapped within their own borders; and car showrooms are virtually empty.

Though Brazil's contentious approval of Venezuela's entry into Mercosur (Southern Common Market) was a major victory for Chávez and bilateral trade (final acceptance lies in the hands of Paraguay in 2010), Chávez's foreign relationships aren't faring much better than his domestic economy. Relations with Colombia remain extremely fragile over the neighboring country's accusations that Venezuela was supplying arms to FARC rebels, and its decision to allow US troops to operate out of seven of its military bases. Chávez banned Colombian car imports and was building up troops at the

**2006**

Chávez calls US President George W Bush 'the devil', in a speech to the UN. He adds that the podium area, where Bush had spoken the day before, 'smelled of sulfur' to reiterate his point.

**2007**

In a made-for-YouTube moment, King Juan Carlos I of Spain scoffs at Hugo Chávez, 'Why don't you shut up!' during the 17th Ibero-American Summit, after Chávez disrespected former Spanish Prime Minister José María Aznar.

**2008**

Chávez negotiates the release of six hostages from Colombian rebel group FARC and calls on Latin American governments to stop branding the guerrillas as 'global terrorists'.

Shot by two Irish documentary filmmakers who were inside the presidential palace during the coup d'état of April 2002, *The Revolution Will Not Be Televised* contains compelling firsthand footage of the events.

border at the time of writing, after several suspicious, cross-border deaths on both sides. Things got personal over these binational issues during a private meeting of heads of state at the Group of Rio summit in Cancun in February 2010, when Colombian President Álvaro Uribe scoffed at Chávez 'Be a man! …You're brave speaking at a distance, but a coward when it comes to talking face to face.' Chávez nearly stormed out. The Israeli ambassador was also booted out of the country in protest of Israeli's controversial three-week military campaign in the Gaza Strip in 2008–09. And, last but not least, in 2008–09 both the US and Venezuela kicked out each other's top diplomats over a political spat between the US and Bolivia, though diplomatic ties were eventually restored.

At the time of writing, popularity surveys by Datanálisis showed Chávez' approval rating fall to 46% – the first drop below 50% since 2004. Though still remarkably high for Latin America, it's a possible sign that Chávez could be running out of gas.

**2009**

Chávez scores a major victory when voters pass a constitutional amendment to eliminate presidential term limits, essentially sealing his power indefinitely – providing Venezuelans continue voting in his favor.

**2010**

Chávez' devaluation of the *bolívar fuerte*, continued water and electricity rationing, and media clampdown spark violent protests nationwide – in a National Assembly election year.

**2012**

Chávez will run for his third consecutive term in Venezuela's next presidential elections, 'unless God has planned something else, unless the people have planned something else.' A win would seal his power until 2019.

# The Culture

## THE NATIONAL PSYCHE

Venezuela is proud of its national history. The War of Independence and Simón Bolívar are championed throughout the country. However, unlike some neighboring South American nations, there are few obvious defining factors of contemporary Venezuelan culture. Many attribute this to the fact that as a petrostate, Venezuela has spent much of its existence consuming goods from abroad (food, music, clothes, movies, furniture, cars, you name it) and not needing or bothering to produce much at home.

But just like the oil pumped out of the country, Venezuela does produce raw materials and raw talent. Two things that are produced quite well in Venezuela are beauty queens and *béisbol* (baseball) players. Venezuelan women have won more international beauty competitions than those of any other country, including five Miss Worlds, six Miss Universes and countless other titles.

Historically, only the Dominican Republic has produced more foreign athletes in North America's Major League Baseball than Venezuela. Baseball is played throughout the country, too, and it's common to see casual games in construction sites or along the side of highways.

The national sport goes hand in hand with the national drinks of rum and ice-cold beer. Men in Caracas tend to opt for whisky (Johnnie Walker Black Label is the brand of choice) instead to show off their big-city sophistication.

Even in the face of deep-seated national ills, social tensions, political divisions and concerns about rising levels of crime and economic instability, Venezuelans are full of life and humor. Children are given creative, arcane or sometimes downright strange names that draw on English, Arabic and indigenous languages, and even a mix of names of landmarks like Canaima and Roraima. People are open, willing to talk and not shy about striking up conversations with strangers – particularly in the western and Andean, which that are known to be more extroverted and friendly. Wherever you are, there'll always be a *rumba* (party) brewing somewhere!

Stefanía Fernández's 2009 Miss Universe title marked the first time in the pageant's 56-year history that the same country won the crown in consecutive years.

## LIFESTYLE

As with other aspects of the country, Venezuelan lifestyle has a striking amount of variety. Venezuela holds an intriguing, if sometimes precarious, marriage of modern and traditional. This is a phenomenon found in many petrostates and certain members of the country have become ridiculously wealthy, while many have watched from the sideline. During earlier oil booms, massive amounts of consumer goods – from food and furniture to automobiles – were imported from abroad, giving certain sectors of the society a modern, if not cosmopolitan, feel. Outside of the urban centers life continued on much as usual. Tourism and the new oil boom have started to develop some of the countryside but it's still possible to see a horse and buggy roll alongside a Mercedes in traffic.

On the fringes of the country, there still exist nomadic indigenous groups who avoid contact with outsiders, including even other indigenous groups. The lives of the Ye'Kwana indigenous community near the Brazilian border have about as much in common with Caracas fashionistas, Maracaibo oil businessmen or Mérida mountain bikers as someone from the interior of Senegal has with a Parisian banker.

Such variety makes generalities difficult, but it is fair to say that most Venezuelans are family-oriented and that their lives are remarkably open and public. Family life is of central importance, and at the center of this is

### VENEZUELAN TIME & SPACE

Like many Latin Americans, Venezuelans have their own notion of time. And time-related terminology here is not necessarily predictable. For example, *mañana* (literally 'tomorrow') can mean anytime in the indefinite future. Similarly, the word *ahora* (literally 'now' or 'in a moment'), often used in charming, diminutive forms such as *ahorita* or *ahoritica,* also has a flexible meaning. If you're waiting for a bus and ask bystanders when it should arrive, take it easy when they reply *ahorita viene* (it's coming) because this can just as easily mean 'in a few hours' as 'in a minute's time'.

Venezuelans invited to lunch also regard it as normal to arrive late. So be prepared: take a newspaper! Many offices have a similarly flexible grasp of working hours. Don't expect to arrange anything if you arrive less than half an hour before it's statutory lunch break or official closing time.

Some Venezuelans, particularly rural dwellers, also have a different notion of space. If they say that something you're looking for is *allí mismito* (just around here) or *cerquitica* (very close), it may still be an hour's walk to get there. The best bet is to keep an open mind and don't be in a rush, or you'll find yourself at odds with the pace of local life.

the mother figure. Children almost always live with their families until they are married and will care for their aging parents, though this is changing as many younger people are now trying to move and work abroad.

While many books have been written on the Yanomami culture, *Into the Heart* (Kenneth Good & David Chanoff, 1991) is one of the most engaging. It describes Good's life and marriage in the Amazonian tribe.

The climate and the restricted space of the majority of Venezuelan homes create a more open, public life. Consequently, many activities take place outside the home: in front of the house, in the street, in a bar or at the market. Don't be surprised to see people dancing to the tune of the car stereo in the streets or drinking a leisurely beer together on the sidewalk curb. And Venezuelans don't hold back in these public places either. Personal affairs are discussed loudly and without embarrassment, irrespective of who may be listening. Office employees happily gossip about private love affairs and personal problems, completely oblivious to the glares of their waiting customers.

Personal space is similarly disregarded in much of Venezuela: people waiting to use public phones will squash themselves up against the person calling, and streets and parks are filled with couples kissing passionately, blind to everyone passing around them. The exception to this rule is for gays and lesbians. Sexuality is highly stereotyped in Venezuela's macho male culture, and in this environment homosexuality tends to be swept under the carpet, except in more cosmopolitan areas like Caracas and parts of Mérida.

Noise is also a constant companion in Venezuela. Locals go undisturbed by blaring music, vehicles as noisy as tanks and horns that are used constantly, even in traffic jams. Street vendors screech at potential customers, and people converse at a volume that to outsiders can suggest a heated argument.

Carlos the Jackal (aka Ilich Ramírez Sánchez), notorious assassin and a member of the Popular Front for Liberation of Palestine, was born in Caracas in 1949. He's currently serving a life prison sentence in Paris.

However, while Venezuelans are open and laid-back in their public habits, security is a high priority in the home. An estimated 37.9% of the population live below the poverty line. As such, it's all too common for haphazardly built *barrios* (shantytowns) to sit directly alongside opulent hillside mansions. In the resulting scramble for security, city apartment blocks have come to resemble enormous birdcages with their abundance of iron-barred windows and security fences.

## ECONOMY

The Venezuelan economy is a doozy. Though rich with oil revenues, little trickle-down effect means the country's income inequality index is disappointing: the richest 10% of the country earns nearly 50% of the income. Strict government currency controls, wild inflation, a rapidly growing energy and water crisis and a healthy dose of mismanagement and alleged corruption are all working against it as well.

## POPULATION

Venezuela's population density is a low 26 people per square kilometer. However, the population is unevenly distributed. Ninety-three percent of Venezuelans live in towns and cities. Over one-fifth of the country's population lives in Caracas alone, while Los Llanos and Guayana are relatively empty.

A recent study in 2005 on Venezuela's racial groups showed that 60% of the population is Mestizo (mixed race between white, African and Indian), 29% white (mostly Spaniards, Italians, Germans and Portuguese), 8% African, 1% Amercan Indian and 2% Asian (China, Japan, Vietnam, Korea, and the Middle East). There are even Venezuelans whose ancestors came from the United States: 10,000 expatriates arrived after the American Civil War (1865).

Of that 2% that are indigenous, there are about 28 highly diverse groups, comprising an estimated 800,000 people scattered throughout the country. The main indigenous communities include the Wayuú (Guajiro), north of Maracaibo; the Piaroa, Guajibo, Ye'Kwana (Yekuana) and Yanomami, all in the Amazon; the Warao in the Delta del Orinoco; and the Pemón in southeastern Guayana. Only the Warao, Pemón, Añu and the Wayuú have populations in excess of 10,000 people; the Wayuú, who live along the border with Colombia's Guajira Peninsula, are the most assimilated.

Venezuela's rate of population growth stands at 1.5%, third highest on the continent behind Paraguay and Bolivia. It has also been the destination for significant post-WWII immigration from Europe (estimated at about one million), mostly from Spain, Italy and Portugal, but it nearly stopped in the 1960s. From the 1950s on, there has been a stream of immigrants from other South American countries, particularly Colombia. Venezuela also has some Middle Eastern communities, notably from Lebanon; most have settled in Caracas.

## MULTICULTURALISM

Given that the vast majority of Venezuelans are of mixed race, it's not surprising that they profess to be a multicultural nation that doesn't judge a person by their skin color. However, under the surface there remains prejudice against the darker-skinned descendants of African slaves. The pervading ideal of beauty values light skin, blond hair and light-colored eyes – a rather sad state of affairs given that only 29% of the population are classified as 'white.' There are rarely explicit displays of racial discrimination in businesses or other public locales, but skin color is often tied to one's place in the social/economic hierarchy and people can be discriminated against on account of it.

The more openly expressed social distinction in Venezuela is of wealth and power. As in many countries, the city folk, such as the *caraqueños* (Caracas locals), frequently ridicule the lower social classes as *monos* (monkeys) and deride the 'unsophisticated' ways of the *campesinos* (country folk). Recent political turmoil has further polarized this rich-poor mentality.

In 2005, Ozzie Guillen (a native of Ocumare del Tuy in Miranda state), managed the Chicago White Sox to their first World Series championship in 88 years.

## SPORTS

Soccer? What soccer? In Venezuela, baseball rules supreme. The professional baseball league is composed of eight teams: Caracas, La Guaira, Maracaibo, Valencia, Barquisimeto, Maracay, Porlamar and Puerto La Cruz. Many Venezuelans have gone on to fame and fortune in North America's Major League Baseball, including former player and World Series–winning manager Ozzie Guillen and pitcher Anibal Sanchez, who threw a no-hitter in his rookie season for the Arizona Diamondbacks.

The biggest rivalry is between Leones del Caracas and Navegantes del Magallanes (Valencia), though in recent years Tigres de Aragua (Maracay) have dominated the championships, making it a 'three-peat' from 2006 to 2009.

**DOS & DON'TS**

- Be careful when discussing politics. Showing excessive support or disdain for the Chávez government can provoke ire in the wrong company.
- Litter is a fact of life in Venezuela. Making obvious comments about the problem will only offend people. On the other hand, don't litter just because you see locals doing it.
- Never show any disrespect for Bolívar – he is a saint to Venezuelans. Even sitting with your feet up on a bench in Plaza Bolívar may provoke piqued strangers to hassle you.
- If you ask for information or directions, don't bank on a correct answer. Polite *campesinos* (country folk) may often tell you anything just to appear helpful. Ask several people to be sure and avoid questions that can be answered by just 'yes' or 'no'; instead of 'Is this the way to…?' ask 'Which is the way to…?'

The next most popular sport is *baloncesto* (basketball), followed by *fútbol* (soccer), with a professional league playing from August to May. In the past the national side has been prone to embarrassing defeats against fellow Latin Americans, but a first-ever triumph over Brazil in 2006 has raised *fútbol* in the popularity stakes.

The Spanish *corrida* (bullfight) also found fertile soil in Venezuela, and most cities have their own *plaza de toros* (bullring). The bullfighting season peaks during Carnaval, when top-ranking matadors are invited from Spain and around Latin America.

Also thrilling – but bloodless – is the *coleo,* a rodeo popular in Los Llanos, in which four riders compete to bring down a bull after grabbing it by the tail from a galloping horse.

Less risky to participate in is *bolas criollas,* the Venezuelan variety of lawn bowling, wherein each team aims wooden balls at the smaller *mingo*. Similarly, street games of chess and dominoes have plenty of addicts throughout the country, and visitors are welcome to join in.

## MEDIA

Freedom of the press is becoming an increasingly sensitive and alarming subject in Venezuela. President Chávez' hands-on relationship with the media has had a mixed reception, invoking some mutterings of dictatorship and muzzling of free expression, and has been condemned by many international media watch groups, including International Federation of Journalists and Reporters Without Borders.

Venezuela's national soccer (football) team, *La Vinotinto* (Burgundy), is the only CONMEBOL team never to qualify for a World Cup.

Opposition media has seen broadcasting licenses pulled or other moves to shut it down or limit antigovernment editorializing. In 2009, 32 radio stations and two TV stations were taken off the air for 'failing to hand in their registration papers on time,' sparking violence in Caracas. A year later, six more TV stations, including the most popular, RCTV (already relegated to cable and satellite-only by Chávez in 2007), temporarily lost their licenses, this time for refusing to broadcast state announcements according to the Law on Social Responsibility in Radio and TV. Violent protests broke out countrywide, which resulted in at least two deaths. At time of writing four stations had been reinstated (but not RCTV).

In Jan 2010, Chávez' government revoked the broadcasting license of RCTV, a longstanding and massively popular TV station critical of his policies, for refusing to broadcast his presidential addresses.

The opposition has accused Chávez' of attempting to 'silence his critics' while a tough new media law that would allow imprisonment of journalists found guilty of 'media crimes' was being mulled over. On the other hand, the president has won the hearts of many through his use of the government-run media. He will frequently talk informally to the nation via TV appearances that can last for hours, and he hosts a regular radio program called *Aló*

*Presidente,* in which he speaks directly to the people about current issues, encouraging a feeling of inclusion and openness in his government.

## RELIGION

About 96% of Venezuelans are Roman Catholics. Many indigenous groups adopted Catholicism and only a few isolated tribes still practice their ancient beliefs. Various Protestant churches in Venezuela have also gained importance, and there are small populations of Jews and Muslims.

## ARTS

### Music

Music is omnipresent in Venezuela, though the country doesn't produce a lot of music of its own (and produces even less music for export). The most common types of popular music are salsa, merengue and *reggaetón* from the Caribbean, and *vallenato* (popular folk music from the Colombia's Caribbean region). The king of Venezuelan salsa is Oscar D'León (b 1943) who has recorded a staggering 60 albums.

North American and European popular music – everything from rock to hip-hop to house – is influential among urban youth (who account for the majority of the population). *Reggaetón* is the biggest phenomenon among youth culture; the music, much of which comes from Puerto Rico, fuses hip-hop with a hybrid of reggae, dancehall (a contemporary offshoot of reggae with faster, digital beats and an MC) and traditional Latin-music beats. It has a decidedly sexual content, with a gangsta pose and rather risqué dancing. Chávez has tried to curb the influence of foreign music, mandating that 50% of all radio airplay must be Venezuelan music and, of that, 50% must be 'traditional.' As is to be expected, few teenagers like to be told what to listen to by a politician in his 50s, but on the bright side, this '*Ley Resorte*' has been a catalyst for Venezuelans to rediscover the music within their own borders. Artists such as Adolescent's Orquesta (salsa), Chino & Nacho (*reggaetón*), Hany Kauam (pop) and Caramelos de Cianuro (rock/pop) have all benefited from the law.

*Joropo* can be divided into three regional subgenres: *llanero* (played with the nylon-stringed harp, the *cuatro,* and the maracas), *central* (played with a metal-stringed harp, maracas, voice, and *cuatro*) and *oriental* (played with additional instruments such as guitar, mandolin and accordion).

The country's most popular folk rhythm is the *joropo,* also called *música llanera,* which developed in Los Llanos (see p188). The *joropo* is usually sung and accompanied by the harp, *cuatro* (a small, four-stringed guitar) and maracas. The *joropo* song 'Alma Llanera' has become an unofficial national anthem.

*Joropo* apart, regional beats are plentiful. In the eastern part of the country you'll hear, depending on where you are, the *estribillo, polo margariteño, malagueñas, fulías* and *jotas*. In the west, the *gaita* is typical of the Maracaibo region, while the *bambuco* is a popular Andean rhythm. The central coast echoes with Afro-influenced drumbeats, a mark of the sizable population of African descent.

American actor Danny Glover secured $18 million from Venezuela's government to produce *Toussaint,* about Toussaint L'Ouverture, the leader of Haiti's slave revolt and a well-documented hero of Chávez. *Toussaint* was expected to arrive in 2010.

European classical music emerged in Venezuela only in the 19th century. The first composers of note include José Angel Lamas (1775–1814) and Cayetano Carreño Rodríguez (1774–1836), both of whom wrote religious music. The most prominent figure in Venezuela's classical music is Teresa Carreño (1853–1917), a pianist and composer.

Caracas is an exciting center of Latin pop and the 'rock *en español*' movement, which harnesses the rhythm and energy of Latin beats and combines them with international and alternative rock trends. The most famous product of this scene is the Grammy-winning Los Amigos Invisibles. The '00s has also seen the emergence of a variety of underground music styles, led by groups like KP-9000 (trip-hop), Las Americas (shoegaze), Cardopusher (breakbeat) and, perhaps most surprisingly, Los Javelin (surf rock/rockabilly).

## Dance

Given the importance of music in Venezuela, it's not surprising that dance also plays a vital role. Indeed it's all too common to hear mothers threatening their sons to learn how 'or you'll never find a girlfriend!' Dancing here is more than a pastime, it's an essential social skill. Popular dances include salsa and *cumbia*.

Dances were also an integral part of ritual in Venezuela's early civilizations. These early forms merged with colonial and immigrant influences, creating diverse and colorful folk dances. Such traditions are at their more energetic among black communities on Venezuela's central coast, where everybody rushes to dance when homegrown drummers spontaneously take to their instruments in the streets. The most dramatic time to see African-influenced dancing in Venezuela is during the Festival de los Diablos Danzantes in May/June (p270).

Barquisimeto-born conductor and violinist Gustavo Dudamel is Venezuela's latest musical phenomenon – he took over as Conductor and Music Director for the Los Angeles Philharmonic in 2009.

You can often see amateur folk-dance ensembles in action during annual feasts. Folk dance has sown seeds for the creation of professional groups that now promote their musical folklore to the public and abroad, such as Danzas Venezuela, founded by internationally famous folk dancer Yolanda Moreno.

Among the neoclassical dance groups, the best known is the Ballet Nuevo Mundo de Caracas, led by Venezuela's most famous ballerina, Zhandra Rodríguez. The Ballet Teresa Carreño and the Ballet Contemporáneo de Caracas (www.caracasballet.com) also perform in the neoclassical style. Contemporary dance is probably best represented by the groups Danzahoy (www.danzahoy.org), the Dramo (www.dramovenezuela.com) and Aktion Kolectiva (formerly Acción Colectiva; www.juliebarnsley.com/accion.htm), which is led by internationally-known dancer/choreographer Julie Barnsley.

## Cinema

Historically, Venezuela's film industry has been about as productive as its soccer team, but Chávez aimed to fix that with the creation of Vila de Cine (www.villadelcine.gob.ve) in 2006, a state-of-the-art production house that is changing the face of Venezuelan cinema. A well-funded, state-run vehicle created to derail 'the dictatorship of Hollywood,' as Chávez put it, Vila de Cine released *Miranda Returns*, a dramatic, swashbuckling epic of the life of independence hero Francisco de Miranda, as one of its flagship efforts in 2007. Though it hasn't been as prolific as expected, Vila de Cine has gained the respect of big Hollywood names like Sean Penn, Kevin Spacey and Danny Glover.

The biggest smash in new Venezuelan cinema remains 2005's *Secuestro Express* (Express Kidnapping) by Jonathan Jakubowicz. The film, which was criticized by the government for its harsh portrayal of Caracas, takes a cold look at crime, poverty, violence, drugs and class relations in the capital. *Secuestro Express* broke all box-office records for a national production and was the first Venezuelan film to be distributed by a major Hollywood studio.

Those interested in learning more about Venezuelan film should track down *Huelepega* (Glue Sniffer; Elia Schneider, 1999), which pulls no punches in its portrayal of the lives of Caracas street children, using genuine street youth, not actors, to lend the film an authenticity to its nonstop, sometimes schizophrenic, action; *Amaneció de Golpe* (A Coup at Daybreak; Carlos Azpúrua, 1999), which tells the story of how Chávez burst onto the political scene; *Manuela Saenz* (Diego Risquez, 2000), which portrays the War of Independence through the eyes of Bolívar's mistress; and *The Revolution Will Not Be Televised* (Kim Bartley & Donnacha O'Briain, 2003), a documentary

**TO PLAY AND TO FIGHT**

One of Venezuela's most important social programs is the **State Foundation for the National System of Youth and Children's Orchestras of Venezuela** (FESNOJIV; www.fesnojiv.gob.ve), commonly referred to as El Sistema ('The System'). Founded by Unesco-appointed maestro José Antonio Abreu in 1975, El Sistema promotes the collective practice of music through symphony orchestras and choruses as a means of social organization and communitarian development. Over 250,000 Venezuelan youngsters are entwined in a musical web of choruses and orchestras across the country, making El Sistema one of Venezuela's most successful government initiatives. The model has been adopted in over 25 countries throughout the world and Abreu was awarded with the Trustees Award at the Latin Grammy Awards in 2009. The spirit of the program was captured by an excellent documentary in 2005 – *Tocar y Luchar* (*To Play and To Fight*) by Venezuelan filmmaker Alberto Arvelo, himself a participant in the program.

Performances are held throughout Venezuela. The orchestra is world-renowned, has recorded several albums, been the subject of a BBC documentary and has performed worldwide. Needless to say, it's quite spectacular and heartwarming to see an orchestra full of 8-year-olds! In Caracas, the Simón Bolívar Youth Orchestra of Venezuela holds weekly performances at the Teresa Carreño Theatre (p77).

shot by Irish filmmakers who were inside the presidential palace during the coup d'état of 2002, which contains firsthand footage of the events and provides a deeply compelling – though unabashedly pro-Chávez – portrait of the man himself.

In 2009, controversial US filmmaker Oliver Stone's *South of the Border*, his attempt to humanize Hugo Chávez, debuted at the 66th Venice International Film Festival. Stone received unprecedented access to Venezuela's leader during filming and, in a somewhat shocking and out-of-character whimsical moment for Chávez, the two walked the red carpet together at the film's premiere.

Venezuelan film director Fina Torres broke into international popularity with such films as *Woman on Top* (2000), starring Penelope Cruz.

## Literature

A rich world of pre-Hispanic indigenous tales, legends and stories preserved and passed from generation to generation provided invaluable information on the pre-Columbian culture for the first Spanish chroniclers. For a taste of the first chronicles narrating the early history of Venezuela, try to hunt down *Brevísima Relación de la Destrucción de las Indias Occidentales* (1552), by Fray Bartolomé de las Casas, or *Elegías de Varones Ilustres de Indias* (Elegies of Illustrious Gentlemen of the Indes; 1589), by Juan de Castellanos. More analytical and comprehensive is one of the later chronicles, *Historia de la Conquista y Población de la Provincia de Venezuela* (The History of the Conquest and Population of the Province of Venezuela; 1723), by José de Oviedo y Baños.

The dawn of the 19th century saw the birth and crystallization of revolutionary trends. The first 30 years of that century were more or less dominated by political literature. Among the pivotal historical works was the autobiography of Francisco de Miranda (1750–1816). Simón Bolívar (1783–1830) himself also left an extensive literary heritage that included letters, proclamations, dissertations and also literary achievements such as *Delirio sobre El Chimborazo* (My Delirium on Chimborazo), which presents an expression of ideals for a nation fighting for its independence. Bolívar was influenced by his close friend Andrés Bello (1781–1865), the first important Venezuelan poet, who was also a noted philologist, historian and jurist.

Francisco Suniaga's *La Otra Isla* is a highly acclaimed novel that takes place on Isla de Margarita. It is a crime story that looks at the island's development through the eyes of native islanders and German settlers.

With independence achieved, political writing gave way to other literary forms. In the 1920s, Andrés Eloy Blanco (1896–1955) appeared on the scene

Teresa de la Parra's controversial 1924 novel *Iphigenia* so challenged the aristocracy and dictatorship of Juan Vicente Gómez that she had to go to Paris to get it published.

to become one of the best poets Venezuela has ever produced. *Angelitos Negros* (Little Black Angels) is the most popular of his numerous poems.

At the same time, several notable novelists emerged, among whom Rómulo Gallegos (1884–1969) is the most outstanding; he remains the country's internationally best-known writer. *Doña Bárbara,* his most popular novel, was first published in Spain in 1929 and has since been translated into a dozen languages. Miguel Otero Silva (1908–85) is another remarkable novelist of the period, best remembered for *Casas Muertas* (Dead Houses), a bestseller published in 1957.

Arturo Uslar Pietri (1906–2001) stands out as a novelist, historian, literary critic, journalist and even a politician, having been a minister and a presidential candidate. He was not only the most versatile writer in modern Venezuela, but also the most inexhaustible; since his first novel, *Lanzas Coloradas* (The Red Lances), published in the 1930s, he wrote tirelessly right up until his death in 2001.

The 1960s saw the start of many fresh, experimental trends in contemporary Venezuelan literature. Many writers took up magical realism, while others became more and more introspective. The increasing freedom of speech and the example of the Cuban Revolution also encouraged writers to explore the vast divides within their own oil-rich society. A groundbreaking experimental novel from the middle of the century is *El Falso Cuaderno de Narciso Espejo* (The False Notebook of Narciso Espejo), by Guillermo Meneses (1911–78); a slightly later seminal work by Adriano Gonzalez Leon (1931–2008) is the powerful magical-realism novel *Pais Portatil* (Portable Country), which contrasts rural Venezuela with a monstrous vision of Caracas.

Ednodio Quintero is another contemporary writer to look out for. His work *La Danza del Jaguar* (The Dance of the Jaguar; 1991) is one of several translated into other languages. Other contemporary writers worth tracking down include Carlos Noguera, Luis Brito García, Eduardo Liendo and Orlando Chirinos.

## Theater

Caracas has developed a strong theatrical tradition since it saw the founding of Venezuela's first venue, Teatro del Conde, in 1784. Several more theaters opened at the end of the 19th century in Caracas, Maracaibo, Valencia, Barquisimeto and Barcelona, all presenting a steady diet of European fare. The national theater was born only a few decades ago, with its major center in Caracas. Today, there are several dozen theatrical groups, most in Caracas. Rajatabla is Venezuela's best-known theater on the international scene. Other Caracas-based groups of note include La Compañía Nacional de Teatro and the Teatro Profesional de Venezuela.

Venezuela most famous and prolific contemporary playwright is Gustavo Ott (b 1963), whose plays have won numerous international awards and have been translated into at least 14 languages.

## Visual Arts

The history of Venezuelan art goes back well before the Spaniards. Surviving pre-Columbian works include a scattering of cave paintings in Bolívar and Amazonas states and enigmatic rock carvings, which have been found at about 200 locations throughout the country. Some of the best collections of petroglyphs can be seen on Piedra Pintada (p264), a 50m-high cliff near Puerto Ayacucho.

By contrast the painting and sculpture of the colonial period had an almost exclusively religious character. Although executed mostly by local artists, the style was influenced by the Spanish art of the day. But when independence loomed, painting departed from strictly religious themes and began to immortalize historical events. The first artist to do so was Juan Lovera (1778–1841), whose most famous paintings can be seen in the Capilla de Santa Rosa de Lima (p60), in Caracas.

When General Guzmán Blanco took power in the late 19th century, Venezuelan painting blossomed. The most outstanding painter of this period – and Venezuelan history as a whole – is Martín Tovar y Tovar (1827–1902), particularly remembered for his monumental works in Caracas' Asemblea Nacional (formerly known as Capitolio Nacional; p60). Another important 19th-century artist, Arturo Michelena (1863–98), received international recognition despite his short life. He spent much of his life in Paris, then the world's art capital. Another Venezuelan living in France, Emilio Boggio (1857–1920) acquired an international reputation for impressionist works influenced by Van Gogh.

The epic historical tradition of Tovar y Tovar was continued by Tito Salas (1888–1974), who dedicated himself to commemorating Bolívar's life and achievements in huge murals (see Casa Natal de Bolívar, p61, and the Panteón Nacional, p61).

Many claim that modern Venezuelan painting began with the unique expressionist Armando Reverón (1889–1954) and the transitional painter Carlos Otero (1886–1977). Francisco Narváez (1905–82) is commonly acclaimed as one of Venezuela's most groundbreaking modern sculptors. Porlamar's Museo de Arte Contemporáneo Francisco Narváez (p199), on Narváez' native Isla de Margarita, has the largest collection of his diverse and experimental works.

Recent Venezuelan art has been characterized by a proliferation of different schools, trends and techniques. One of the most remarkable examples of these movements was the painter Héctor Poleo (1918–89), who expressed himself in a variety of styles, switching easily from realism to surrealism with some metaphysical exploration in between. Equally captivating is the expressionist painting of Jacobo Borges (1931–91), who by deforming human figures turns them into caricatures.

Jesús Soto (1923–2005) is Venezuela's most internationally renowned contemporary artist. He was a leading representative of kinetic art (art, particularly sculpture, that contains moving parts). His large distinctive works adorn numerous public buildings and plazas in Venezuela and beyond (including Paris, Toronto and New York); the largest collection of his work is in the museum dedicated to him in Ciudad Bolívar (p238).

There's a lot of activity among the current generation. Watch out for the works of Carlos Zerpa (painting), the quirky ideas of José Antonio Hernández Díez (photography, video, installations) and the emblematic paintings, collages and sculptures of Miguel von Dangel. And you'll see plenty more in the Museo de Arte Contemporáneo de Caracas (p62).

The campus of Universidad Central de Venezuela in Caracas (p62 is regarded as architect Carlos Raúl 's most outstanding work and has been included on Unesco's Cultural Heritage list.

## Architecture

There isn't a lot left to see of pre-Hispanic dwellings in Venezuela, as many were made from perishable materials such as adobe, wood and vegetable fibers. However, the homes of remote indigenous communities in the Amazon still give a glimpse of the design of early indigenous structures.

The arrival of the Spanish brought the introduction of solid building materials such as brick and tile to Venezuelan architecture. The newly founded towns were direct reflections of the Spanish style, laid out on a square grid with the main plaza, cathedral and government house forming the center. But colonial architecture in Venezuela never reached the grandeur found

Internationally renowned novelist Rómulo Gallegos (1884–1969) was also Venezuela's first democratically elected president.

in neighbors such as Colombia, Ecuador and Peru. Only in the last half-century of the colonial era did a wealthier merchant class emerged to build grand residences that reflected their stature. A handful of notable examples survive in Coro (see p119).

Independence initially had little impact on Venezuelan architecture, but in the 1870s Guzmán Blanco launched a dramatic overhaul of the capital city. He commissioned many monumental public buildings in a hodgepodge of styles, from neo-Gothic to neoclassical, depending largely on the whim of the architect in charge.

A real rush toward modernity came with oil money culminating in the 1970s. This period was characterized by indiscriminate demolition of the historic urban fabric and its replacement by modern architecture. Many dilapidated colonial buildings fell prey to greedy urban planners. Accordingly, Venezuela's colonial legacy can be disappointing when compared to that of other Andean countries. On the other hand, Venezuela has some truly remarkable modern architecture. Carlos Raúl Villanueva, who began work in the 1930s, is considered the most outstanding Venezuelan architect.

# Food & Drink

Venezuelans love to eat well. From home-cooked corn turnovers and authentic Spanish paella to downright indulgent desserts, there is plenty for your taste buds to discover. The national cuisine is characterized by a rich fusion of indigenous and European roots. Caracas itself is an internationally renowned culinary melting pot, while the regions of Venezuela have their own peculiarities and specialties. The *costeños'* (coastal peoples') plates overflow with fish and exquisite seafood, while the Amazonian peoples have plenty of imaginative uses for the humble yucca (anedible root). Wheat and trout dishes dominate in the Andes, and those bursting for a BBQ platter will adore the obscenely juicy steaks in Los Llanos.

## STAPLES & SPECIALTIES

The Venezuelans have a saying: *Lo que no mata engorda* (What doesn't kill you makes you fat) – and it's true that many of their tasty common dishes appear decidedly on the fattening side, from steaks as thick as bricks to deep-fried cheese.

www.venezuelatuya.com/cocina is in Spanish (or Italian), but can at least show you some photos of typical Venezuelan dishes.

Many staples rely on the use of corn, especially *arepas* and empanadas, which are as common as hotdogs and hamburgers in the US. The *arepa* is a hamburger-sized corn pancake, split and stuffed so full of juicy fillings that it takes a special talent to avoid getting it all over your face. *Areperas* (*arepa* restaurants) offer 101 fillings to choose from, but a favorite is the tasty *reina pepiada* (chicken, mayo and avocado). They're a surprisingly heavy-going, filling snack, so don't be surprised if your jaw cramps up on the third bite.

Deep-fried empanadas (corn turnovers) filled with meat, chicken or cheeses are also a common snack. And the sweet and greasy *cachapa* pancake is another corn-based favorite, usually with slabs of cheese and ham slapped on top.

But let's not get fixated on corn alone. Other Venezuelan cuisine, collectively referred to as *comida criolla,* uses plenty of rice, yam, plantain, beans and carefully prepared meat, chicken or dozens of fresh seafood varieties. The *salsas* (sauces) make generous use of *ají dulce* (small sweet peppers) and cilantro (coriander) leaves used as a garnish. There's a vast array of tropical fruits, including papaya the size of US footballs and more types of banana than you can shake a monkey at. Venezuela is also famous for its cheap and abundant grill houses, serving steaks supplied in truckloads from the ranches of Los Llanos.

The annually updated, bilingual *Guia Gastronomica de Caracas* (Caracas Gastronomic Guide), published by Miro Popic, covers more than 600 restaurants in the capital and is a great help in discovering the local food scene. See www.miropopic.com for the latest recommendations.

Spanish, Italian, Chinese and Middle Eastern restaurants are all well represented too, thanks to sizable immigrant populations.

## DRINKS

Strong espresso coffee is excellent in Venezuela and there are some dozen ways to order it. Ask for *café negro* if you want it black, for *café marrón* if you want milk, *marrón fuerte* for less milk or for *café con leche* if you like it very milky. When it has more milk than coffee, it's given the tongue-in-cheek title of *tetero* (baby's bottle). For an extra kick, *café bautizado* (literally, 'baptized') contains a shot of rum. It's almost always served lawsuit-hot.

Given the mind-boggling variety of fruit in the country, you'll also be spoiled for choice of juices, which come as *batidos* (pure or watered down) or as *merengadas* (milk shakes). Also good for the sweet-toothed are the local

**WE DARE YOU!**

If you can track them down, these unusual Venezuelan dishes should give you plenty to chew on.

- *Hormigas culonas* – deep-fried Amazonian ants with big, juicy rear ends (hence the ungraceful name, meaning literally 'big-bottomed'). Sometimes coated in chocolate!
- *Katara* – along the same theme, the Ye'Kwana peoples' spicy sauce is made with the heads and thorax of leaf-cutter ants and is reputedly an aphrodisiac.
- *Paticas de grillo* – don't be scared off by the name (cricket legs); this tasty dish from Lara state is actually finely shredded beef.
- *Consomé de chipi chipi* – coastal clam broth; another rumored aphrodisiac.

drinks *chicha,* a thick milky liquid made with rice and sugar, and *papelón con limón,* sugarcane juice mixed with lemon.

Despite producing world-class Caribbean rum, Venezuelans prefer whisky – it boasts the highest per capita consumption of 18-year-old whisky in the world.

Tap water is generally fine to use for brushing your teeth, but is not recommended for consumption in any part of the country. Only drink bottled water or water that has been boiled for a number of minutes.

The number-one alcoholic drink is, of course, beer, sold at icy temperatures for only BsF8 a bottle (about 0.22L) in the cheapest bars and eateries. If you ever wonder why Venezuelans don't like larger bottles, the answer is simple: the beer could get warm before you finish it. Polar brand beer is the most popular.

Among Venezuelan spirits, rum heads the list; the smooth, dark Ron Añejo Aniversario Pampero is one of the best. Another specialty is the throat-stripping *miche,* an anise-flavored spirit made from sugarcane, similar to the Colombian *aguardiente,* and so called in some areas. The local production of wine is small, except for some good Altagracia wines (see p142).

Whole bottles of spirits are commonly poured over coffins (and the coffin-bearers) at Venezuelan funerals.

It's imported whisky, however, that wins the prize as the chic drink of choice, and upper-crust restaurants stock enough to rival any whisky bar. Indeed, Venezuelans manage to get through about five million cases per year.

Colorful *cocteles* (cocktails) also abound, from the hugely popular *guarapita,* a fruity combination of sugarcane spirit and fresh juices that is all too easy to gulp down, to Andean *calentados,* hot toddies to warm the cockles of your heart on cold mountain nights.

## WHERE & WHEN TO EAT & DRINK

For a filling *desayuno* (breakfast), do what many locals do and grab something from the local *panadería* (bakery). Venezuelans take their *almuerzo* (lunch) more seriously, however. In fact, it's taken for granted that a 'lunch hour' is more likely a 'lunch two hours,' and will tend to be a drawn-out social affair. For a good-value lunch, look at the *menú del día* or *menu ejecutivo,* a set meal consisting of soup and a main course. It usually costs around BsF30 to BsF45.

For a quick bite, grab some spit-roasted chicken from a *pollo en brasas* or a stuffed *arepa* from an *arepera;* markets also always offer fresh local fare. Street vending is also common, though hygiene can be iffy. Particularly popular are *churro* machines, which churn out long, thin pastry sticks sprinkled with sugar.

To linger over a more sedate evening meal, visit one of the many traditional Spanish tascas (Spanish-style bar/restaurants) found throughout the country. Here you can choose to chow down on tapas with the local barflies or sit down for a filling meal of succulent seafood or meats with the family.

**COMIDA VENEZOLANA:** *¿COMO SE DICE?*

If you are fluent in Spanish or have traveled extensively in South America, you might need a Spanish-Venezuelan dictionary to decipher the country's unique words for certain foodstuffs:

| Traditional Spanish | Venezuelan |
|---|---|
| Papaya | Lechosa (papaya) |
| Plátano | Cambur (banana) |
| Puerro | Ajoporro (leeks) |
| Apio | Celery (velery) |
| Maiz | Jojoto (vorn) |
| Maracuyá | Parchita (passion fruit) |
| Alverjas | Petipuás (peas) |
| Toronja | Greifrú (grapefruit) |
| Fríjoles Negros | Caraotas (black beans) |
| Habichuelas | Vainitas (green beans) |

In cities, upmarket restaurants come to life from 7pm to 8pm. However, in small towns, everything may be shut by 9pm.

## VEGETARIANS & VEGANS

A popular fridge magnet in Venezuela reads *Soy vegetariano, vivo de vainitas* (I'm vegetarian, I live on green beans). Sure enough, vegetarianism isn't a concept well grasped in a country where rump steak is king.

That said, it's relatively easy to get by in Venezuela if you don't mind a little monotony. The country has plenty of cheeses, eaten with ubiquitous staples such as *arepas* and *cachapas*. *Perico* is another filling made with scrambled eggs, tomato and onion. A popular appetizer is *tostónes* (hard plantain cakes), which generally come with vegan-friendly sauces. You can also consume a wide selection of beans, salads and fruit juices. When ordering salads, though, it's not enough to ask if it has any *carne* (meat) because chicken and fish are in a separate linguistic class and aren't necessarily considered meat – see the Eating Out section (p294) for ordering tips.

In tourist haunts, there are always vegetarian pizzas, pasta and omelets available, and there are even a few dedicated vegetarian restaurants in larger cities such as Caracas, though none garner rave reviews from the city's vegetarians. Self-catering is the safest option for vegans; markets have a great selection of fruit and vegetables.

Venezuela's national dish is *Pabellon Criollo*, the meal by which all grandmothers slug it out in the kitchen. It hails from Caracas and consists of *carne mechada* (shredded beef) served alongside black beans, rice and plantains.

## HABITS & CUSTOMS

At all levels of society, food preparation is done with care and eating is to be savored, not hurried. Food is a central means of showing hospitality, so expect huge portions and constant refills if you're invited to somebody's house. Festivals, especially Christmas, call for displays of generosity by filling stomachs that are already fit to burst.

If somebody invites you out to eat, you can expect him or her to pay. Of course, the flipside is that when you invite somebody out, the bill falls to you. Before tucking in, it's polite to wish your fellow diners *buen provecho* (bon appetit), and when drinking to say *salud* (good health).

The ubiquitous Venezuelan finger snack is *tequeños*, fried dough sticks stuffed with *queso blanco* (white cheese), a favorite at parties, bars, restaurants and festivals.

## EAT YOUR WORDS

Want to know what ordering a cup of *leche de burra* (donkey's milk) or a *teta* (breast) will really bring to your table? Discover the secrets of the local cuisine by getting to know the language. For pronunciation guidelines see p292.

## Menu Decoder

### FOOD

| | | |
|---|---|---|
| *aguacate* | a·gwa·*ka*·te | avocado |
| *ají* | a·*khee* | chili pepper |
| *ajo* | *a*·kho | garlic |
| *aliño* | a·*lee*·nyo | combination of spices |
| *arepa* | a·*re*·pa | small, grilled corn pancake stuffed with cheese, beef, sausage, shrimp, eggs, salad etc; Andean *arepa de trigo* is made from wheat |
| *atún* | a·*toon* | tuna |
| *batata* | ba·*ta*·ta | sweet potato |
| *berenjena* | be·ren·*khe*·na | eggplant |
| *cachito* | ka·*chee*·to | croissant filled with chopped ham; served hot |
| *camarón* | ka·ma·*ron* | small shrimp |
| *cangrejo* | kan·*gre*·kho | crab |
| *carabina* | ka·ra·*bee*·na | Mérida version of *hallaca* |
| *caraota* | ka·ra·*o*·ta | black bean |
| *carne de res* | *kar*·ne de res | beef |
| *cebolla* | se·*bo*·ya | onion |
| *chayote* | cha·*yo*·te | choko; green pear-shaped fruit |
| *chicharrones* | chee·cha·*ro*·nes | pork cracklings |
| *chivo* | *chee*·vo | goat |
| *chorizo* | cho·*ree*·so | seasoned sausage |
| *chuleta* | choo·*le*·ta | chop, rib steak |
| *churrasco a la llanera* | choo·*ras*·ko a la ya·*ne*·ra | grilled steak |
| *cochino* | ko·*chee*·no | pork |
| *cordero* | kor·*de*·ro | lamb |
| *empanada* | em·pa·*na*·da | crescent-shaped, deep-fried cornmeal turnover stuffed with meat or cheese |
| *fresa* | *fre*·sa | strawberry |
| *frijoles* | free·*kho*·les | red beans |
| *guanábana* | gwa·*na*·ba·na | soursop |
| *guasacaca* | gwa·sa·*ka*·ka | piquant sauce made of peppers, onions and seasoning |
| *guayaba* | gwa·*ya*·ba | guava |
| *hervido* | er·*vee*·do | hearty soup made of beef or chicken with root vegetables |
| *jamón* | kha·*mon* | ham |
| *langosta* | lan·*gos*·ta | lobster |
| *lau lau* | low low | catfish |
| *lechón* | le·*chon* | baked pig stuffed with its own meat, rice and dried peas |
| *lechosa* | le·*cho*·sa | papaya |
| *lechuga* | le·*choo*·ga | lettuce |
| *limón* | lee·*mon* | lemon |
| *mamón* | ma·*mon* | small, green fruit with reddish flesh |
| *mariscos* | ma·*rees*·kos | shellfish, seafood |
| *mejillones* | me·khee·*yo*·nes | mussels |
| *mondongo* | mon·*don*·go | seasoned tripe cooked in bouillon with corn, potatoes and vegetables |
| *mora* | *mo*·ra | blackberry |
| *muchacho* | moo·*cha*·cho | hearty roasted beef dish |
| *ñame* | *nya*·me | a type of yam |
| *naranja* | na·*ran*·kha | orange |
| *negro en camisa* | *ne*·gro en ka·*mee*·sa | a chocolate dessert |
| *papa* | *pa*·pa | potato |
| *papelón* | pa·pe·*lon* | crude brown sugar; flavoring for drinks |
| *parrilla (parrillada)* | pa·*ree*·ya (pa·ree·*ya*·da) | mixed grill, including steak, pork, chicken and sausages |

| | | |
|---|---|---|
| *pastel de chucho* | pa·*stel* de *choo*·cho | shredded ray with plantain and cheese |
| *patilla* | pa·*tee*·ya | watermelon |
| *pernil* | per·*neel* | leg of pork |
| *plátano* | *pla*·ta·no | plantain |
| *pollo* | *po*·yo | chicken |
| *quesillo* | ke·*see*·yo | caramel custard |
| *salchicha* | sal·*chee*·cha | sausage |
| *sancocho* | san·*ko*·cho | vegetable stew with fish, meat or chicken |
| *tocineta* | to·see·*ne*·ta | bacon |
| *tortilla* | tor·*tee*·ya | omelet |
| *tostón* | tos·*ton* | fried unripe plantain |
| *trucha* | *troo*·cha | trout |
| *yuca* | *yoo*·ka | yucca (edible root) |
| *zanahoria* | sa·na·*o*·rya | carrot |

**DRINKS**

| | | |
|---|---|---|
| *agua* | *a*·gwa | water |
| *calentado* | ka·len·*ta*·do | hot Andean drink with anise-flavored spirit, milk, herbs and brown sugar |
| *cocuy* | ko·*kooy* | sugarcane liqueur |
| *guayoyo* | gwa·*yo*·yo | weak black coffee |
| *jugo* | *khoo*·go | juice |
| *leche* | *le*·che | milk |
| *leche de burra* | *le*·che de *boo*·ra | Andean beverage made of *miche*, egg and (cow's) milk |
| *miche* | *mee*·che | anise-flavored sugarcane-based spirit; also called *aguardiente* |
| *refresco* | re·*fres*·ko | soft drink |
| *ron* | ron | rum |
| *té* | te | tea |
| *vino blanco/tinto* | *vee*·no *blan*·ko/*teen*·to | white/red wine |

## Food Glossary

| | | |
|---|---|---|
| *arroz* | a·*ros* | rice |
| *azúcar* | a·*soo*·kar | sugar |
| *bebida* | be·*bee*·da | drink |
| *carne* | *kar*·ne | meat |
| *comida* | ko·*mee*·da | food |
| *ensalada* | en·sa·*la*·da | salad |
| *frutas* | *froo*·tas | fruit |
| *helado* | e·*la*·do | ice cream |
| *hielo* | *ye*·lo | ice |
| *legumbres* | le·*goom*·bres | vegetables |
| *maíz* | ma·*ees* | corn/maize |
| *mantequilla* | man·te·*kee*·ya | butter |
| *pan* | pan | bread |
| *papas fritas* | *pa*·pas *free*·tas | fries |
| *pastel* | pas·*tel* | pastry |
| *pescado* | pes·*ka*·do | fish |
| *pimienta* | pee·*myen*·ta | pepper |
| *postre* | *pos*·tre | dessert |
| *queso* | *ke*·so | cheese |
| *sal* | sal | salt |
| *sopa* | *so*·pa | soup |
| *torta* | *tor*·ta | cake |
| *trigo* | *tree*·go | wheat |

# Environment

Tobias Mendelovici and Kevin Raub

## THE LAND

Venezuela is one of the 10 most biodiverse countries on earth. Approximately twice the size of California, and the sixth largest country on the South American continent, it claims a multiplicity of landscapes, including all four primary South American landscapes – the Amazon, the Andes, savannas and beaches – all in a single country.

The country has two mountain ranges. The lower Cordillera de la Costa reaches an altitude of 2725m at Pico Naiguatá, the tallest peak of the Cordillera El Ávila, which separates the valley of Caracas from the Caribbean. This mostly green and warm-to-temperate region is the most developed and populated of the country. The other, taller mountain range is the northernmost section of the great Andes mountain range. The tallest Andean point in Venezuela rises to 5000m at the Sierra Nevada de Mérida. These slopes give birth to rivers that roll down the treeless hills of the *páramos* (open highlands above about 3300m) to the downstream temperate forests before finally reaching Los Llanos (the Plains) and the lowlands around Lago de Maracaibo.

*Parques Nacionales de Venezuela,* edited by Oscar Todtman, is a review of Venezuela's 43 national parks. It showcases some wonderful photography.

Lago de Maracaibo is the largest lake in South America and is linked to the Caribbean Sea. The region around the lake is the traditional oil-producing region of the country. While the Maracaibo basin still produces slightly less than half of the country's oil, drilling in other areas, such as the Orinoco river delta, is displacing its significance.

The Río Orinoco watershed embraces the sparsely populated low-lying region of Los Llanos, which is characterized by prairies with a variety of savanna and forests. Los Llanos makes up nearly a third of the country. The Río Orinoco itself runs for 2150km down to the delta's wetlands and is South America's third largest river.

South of the Orinoco lies another sparsely populated area, the Guayana region. This area, which makes up nearly half the country, includes the Río Caura watershed, the largely impenetrable Amazon rainforest, and the famous plateaus of the Guayana highlands where hundreds of tabletop mountains called tepuis (flat-topped sandstone mountains with vertical flanks) tower over the forest. Geologically the Guayana highlands, are considered one of the oldest places on earth. The area also holds the world's highest waterfall – the famous Angel Falls (Salto Ángel) – which plummets nearly 1km from one of the tepuis found here.

The Río Orinoco's watershed is one of the largest and most complex fresh-water ecosystems on earth. It's home to more than 1000 fish species – more than Europe and North America combined.

Finally, let's not forget the country's 2813km-long stretch of Caribbean coast, featuring a 900,000 sq km Caribbean marine zone with numerous islands and cays. The largest and most popular of these is Isla de Margarita, followed closely by the less-developed Archipiélago Los Roques.

## WILDLIFE

Along with the variety of Venezuelan landscapes you will encounter is the amazing diversity of wildlife. One of the best places on earth to see this biodiversity is in the Guayana region, where dramatic contrasts in geology and altitude have produced a huge range of habitats for a diverse selection of plants and animals. The finest example is the 'lost worlds' atop the tepuis, where flora and fauna, isolated from the forest below and from the other tepuis, have developed independently from their surroundings. Some of the tabletop habitats have been isolated for millions of years and many of the species found on the tops of tepuis exist only on their particular summit. For example, half of the plant species found on Roraima do not exist anywhere else in the world.

## Animals

Again, diversity is the key word when it comes to describing Venezuela's fauna. There are 341 species of reptiles, 284 species of amphibians, 1791 species of fishes, 351 species of mammals and many butterflies and other invertebrates. More than 1360 species of birds – approximately 20% of the world's known species – reside in the country, and 46 of these species are endemic. The country's geographical setting on a main migratory route makes it a bird-watcher's heaven.

*The Birds of Venezuela 2003,* by Stephen L Hilty, is a must for bird-watchers. Similarly, *A Guide to the Birds of Venezuela,* by William H Phelps and Rodolphe Meyer de Schauensee, published in the 1970s, was the first of its kind and remains a classic.

The evergreen forests of the Cordillera de la Costa are a good place to look for sloths, monkeys and marsupials, and are a definite must for bird-watchers, who will delight in such rare species as Venezuela's endemic parakeets, screamers (*Anhimidae* family), trogons, rare thrushes and many species of toucan and toucanet. Parque Nacional El Ávila (p81), north of Caracas, provides an excellent starting point to search for hummingbirds, parakeets and fruit-eaters among the more than 300 species identified there. West of Caracas, Parque Nacional Henri Pittier (p101) is another birder's paradise with some 582 bird species. Further west, in the Golfete de Cuare fauna refuge (p129), you can spot one of the country's largest flamingo colonies. If you visit the Cueva del Guácharo (p227), 12km east of Caripe, you can't miss the unique *guácharo* (oilbird). This bird is about half a meter long, has reddish-brown feathers and a curved beak and lives in caves. The Andes are home to the endangered South American bear or spectacled bear, plus many birds, including curassows, quetzals, owls, hawks and a small population of the recently reintroduced Andean condor.

Along the Caribbean coastline and on its islands you will spot many waterbirds, including the colorful scarlet ibis. On some of the islands you may also see endangered parrots, such as the *cotorra cabeciamarilla* (yellow-shouldered parrot) – look for its green feathers and yellow face. Although this bird has become nearly extinct in the Caribbean, Isla de Margarita (p195) is home to one of the largest remaining populations. Dolphins are abundant along Venezuela's coastline, and around Archipiélago Los Roques (p86) you will be surprised by the health and vitality of the reefs and the abundant marine life that rivals any of the better-known diving destinations in the Caribbean. Endangered green sea turtles nest on the archipelago and in the Parque Nacional Península de Paria (p225) on the eastern mainland coast.

Updated annually, *Ecotourism Guide to Venezuela,* by Miro Popic, is a bilingual Spanish/English guidebook focusing on ecological tourism.

The seasonally flooded plains of Los Llanos (p180) are among Venezuela's best places to spot wildlife. You have a good chance of seeing capybaras (locally known as *chiguire*), spectacled caimans, monkeys, giant anteaters, armadillos, anacondas, piranhas, ocelots and even the elusive jaguar. Birds flock here by the millions: it's one of the planet's most important bird-breeding reserves, with well over 350 species, including waterfowl species such as ibises, herons, jacanas and egrets. Seed-eating birds, macaws, raptors and the strange *hoatzin* – a prehistoric-looking bird with punky yellow feathers on its head – all make their home here. South of Lago de Maracaibo, within the Parque Nacional Ciénagas del Catatumbo, you can find howler monkeys, spectacled caimans, endemic river dolphins and many birds, including ospreys, kingfishers, herons, masked ducks and ibises. Manatees and otters are also found here, but are notoriously hard to spot. In the Delta del Orinoco (p231) you can expect some of the species found in the Llanos.

Interest has all but fizzled in Venezuela's proposed *Gasoducto del Sur,* an 8000 to 15,000km natural gas pipeline that would have connected Venezuela, Argentina and Brazil – at the expense of countless hectares of Amazonian rainforest.

The Guayana region contains many rare, unique and endangered species, including the endemic birds of the tepuis (such as the amazing Cock of the Rock, with its brilliant orange crest), jaguars, pumas, otters, harpy eagles and tapirs (the largest mammal in the country). It's also home to the native, endangered Orinoco crocodile, which grows up to 8m long and is the largest crocodile in the Americas.

### Plants

Venezuela boasts 650 types of vegetation and thousands of plant species in several major habitats. Tropical lowland rainforests still cover a very large part of the country. Cloud forests are confined to the mountain slopes between 1000m and 2800m above sea level, and are a primary feature of Parque Nacional Henri Pittier (p101) and the Parque Nacional Sierra Nevada (p164). Dry forests are found mainly on the larger Caribbean islands and in the hills between Coro and Barquisimeto. The coasts and islands feature mangrove forests. Grasslands and savannas are mainly on the plains and in Parque Nacional Canaima. Finally, you can see the Mérida *páramos,* highland meadows that are found just above the cloud forests.

Otto Huber's *Ecological Guide to the Gran Sabana* provides excellent information on the environmental features of Parque Nacional Canaima, including lists of animals and plants.

The national flower, the Flor de Mayo (May Flower; *Cattleya mossiae*), is just one of the more than 25,000 species of orchid found in Venezuela's forests; its sensuous pink flower blossoms in May. Another Venezuelan specialty is the *frailejón (Espeletia),* a typical plant of the *páramos;* it has pale green leaves coated in white velvety fur, which are arranged in a rosette pattern around a thick trunk. The *frailejón* can grow to more than 3m tall and its yellow flowers bloom from September to December.

If you drive along the Caracas–Valencia highway between December and April, you are likely to see the splendid yellow blossoming of Venezuela's national tree, the *araguaney* (trumpet tree). Endemic to Roraima is the little carnivorous *Drosera roraima,* which is found in the humid areas atop of the tepui and has intense red leaves with sticky tentacles that catch insects. When visiting the Gran Sabana, look along the main road for the *morichales* (palm groves), which are groups of *moriches* (oily palms) that grow along waterways or in flood-prone areas. These are very common in the eastern plains of the Llanos as well. The adult plant features a 15m-tall trunk dotted with fan-shaped leaves, which are used by indigenous people for construction.

## NATIONAL PARKS

Venezuela's national parks offer a diverse landscape of evergreen mountains, beaches, tropical islands, coral reefs, high plateaus and rainforests. The national parks are the number-one destination for tourism within the country; Canaima, Los Roques, Mochima, Henri Pittier, El Ávila and Morrocoy are the most popular. While some parks, especially those in coastal and marine zones, are easily accessible and tend to be overcrowded by locals during holiday periods and weekends, others remain unvisited. A few of the parks offer tourism facilities, but these are generally not very extensive. For some parks, such as Morrocoy, you'll need to get a permit and pay a small fee for camping. Always ask about safety when going camping.

Some 50% of the country is protected under national law as Areas Under Special Administration (ABRAEs). Most of these protected territories are considered national parks and natural monuments, though some are designated under categories such as wildlife refuges, forests and biosphere reserves.

**Inparques** (Instituto Nacional de Parques Nacionales; www.inparques.gov.ve), an autonomous institute attached to the Ministry of Environment, was created to manage the national parks and natural monuments. Unfortunately the park authorities lack the funding, equipment, personnel and enforcement capacity to fully manage this huge territory. As a result, at least one NGO, **Bioparques** (www.bioparques.org), was created in 2002 to help pick up the slack. Some parks do require permits, and there is usually an Inparques office in most main towns,

**NOTABLE NATIONAL PARKS**

| Protected Area | Features & Activities | Best Time to Visit | Page |
|---|---|---|---|
| Parque Nacional Archipiélago Los Roques | mangrove coastline embraced by the Caribbean's turquoise waters; secluded cays with white-sand beaches & coral reefs; abundant marine life; birds (over90 species);extraordinary diving & snorkeling; fishing; sailing, windsurfing & kitesurfing; marine biological station; green turtle nesting area | year-round | p86 |
| Parque Nacional Canaima | arguably 'the jewel in the crown' with Angel Falls; hikingthe tepuis & Roraima;wildlife-watching: jaguars, anteaters, Cock of the Rock, harpy eagles, tapirs | year-round | p244 |
| Parque Nacional Guatopo | rainforest & mountains embrace a freshwaterreservoir; camping; walking trails; park ranger at La Macanilla; Hacienda La Elvira; wildlife: 50 species of bats, eight species of marsupials, howlers &capuchins, monkeys, armadillos, jaguars, harpy eagles | year-round | p93 |
| Parque Nacional Henri Pittier | steep, forested mountains rolling into Caribbean beaches; wildlife-watching: de San Juan (500 species, 22 endemic),birds, monkeys, sloths, snakes | Late June for Fiesta | p101 |
| Parque Nacional Mochima | hills with dry tropical forest penetrating deep-water beaches on the east coast;rainforest inland; diving & snorkeling; rafting; camping; wildlife: dolphins, abundant marine life, marine birds, iguanas | year-round | p211 |
| Parque Nacional Morrocoy | palm-fringed cays with sandy beaches protected by mangroves & coral reefs on the western coast; diving & snorkeling; camping; Golfete de Cuare fauna refuge; wildlife: abundant marine life, birds, alligators, large scarlet ibis colonies | September | p129 |
| Parque Nacional Sierra Nevada | snowy mountains of the Andes descend intotemperate & tropical forest; hiking & biking; Venezuela's tallest mountain Pico Bolivar (5001m); wildlife: spectacled bears & Andean condors (both endangered), deers, ocelots, *frailejón* endemic plants | year-round | p164 |

or posts at the national parks themselves, which can provide information. Other types of protected lands are managed by other organizations designated by the Ministry of Environment.

While the Venezuelan populace looks to the park system to protect the nation's biodiversity and provide a recreational amenity, local indigenous and subsistence-farming communities have lived in the parks since before they were designated as such by the government. This creates a conflict between each park's conservation needs and the local population's use of natural resources. The greatest hope in combining conservation with economic sustainability for locals lies in a planned and responsible development of ecotourism within the protected areas.

President Chávez has addressed some green issues head-on: in 2005, he announced the elimination of lead-based gasoline; a year later, he founded *Misión Arbol* (Mission Tree) to combat deforestation; and in 2007, he instituted tough new emission laws.

## ENVIRONMENTAL ISSUES

At its heart, Venezuela's biggest environmental challenge is general lack of environmental consciousness to begin with. Beyond that, nearly all of the country's environmental issues surround water and waste management (or lack thereof). Nearly 80% of Venezuela's population lives on the coast, which is widely polluted (in 2005 less than 25% of Venezuela's used water was treated before re-entering the ecosystem). There is no recycling policy, and dumping of garbage in cities, along roads and natural areas is common practice. Both Lago de Valencia and Lago de Maracaibo are heavily polluted, the former with sewage, the latter with oil. There continues to be a general lack of clear environmental policy and little to no culture of environmental stewardship outside the park areas. Much of the waste and pollution issues are a direct result of overpopulation in urban areas and a lack of civil planning and funds to cope with the rampant development. Additional worries include the continued expansion of electricity lines toward the Brazilian border and a general lack of concern for water conservation. The latter is shockingly demonstrated in the country's automatic sensor bathroom faucets through the country – one swipe of your hand and the water seemingly runs for minutes on end. Hugo Chávez addressed this specific issue in late 2009, calling for all citizens to take 'Communist showers' of no more than three minutes. Within a few months, a state of emergency was declared: Venezuela's water supplies – and subsequently its electrical power – had reached serious crisis levels.

Another major environmental issue is the illegal poaching of timber, precious metals, rare plants and tropical animals that takes place in many parts of the country, including protected areas. Pet tropical birds, for example, fetch a handsome price in the US, Asia and Europe. Amazonian hardwoods are cut from the jungle and wildcat miners pan for gold in the rivers and dump their used mercury into the water. In a proactive move in 2008, Venezuela banned gold mining in the Imataca Forest Reserve and announced the discontinuance of new open-pit mining permits anywhere in the country.

A final major ecological concern is pollution from oil refineries, oil drilling and the general destruction wrought by industry and mining: Lago de Maracaibo has witnessed many oil spills, and much of the petroleum infrastructure is old and in need of repair. Huge strip mines create moonscapes in the once fertile lands of Guyana.

Tierraviva (www.tierraviva.org), closely associated with British NGO Living Earth, is one of Venezuela's largest and most important environmental NGOs, focusing on environmental education.

This said, there is a sector of the population – including community organizations, cooperatives, nongovernmental organizations (NGOs), universities and governmental agencies – that is working to reduce environmental degradation. Following is a list of major organizations working for the Venezuelan environment:

**Conservation International** (www.conservation.org) Works on conservation issues in several Latin American countries, including Venezuela.

**Fundación Empresas Polar** (www.fundacionempresaspolar.org) Leading NGO working on biodiversity, sustainable agriculture and water-management issues.

**Ocean Futures Society** (www.oceanfutures.org) Works on environmental issues related to coastal areas.

**Planeta.com** (www.planeta.com) The 'global journal of practical ecotourism' is insightful, balanced and carries a significant amount of Venezuela-specific information.

**Venezuela EcoPortal** (www.internet.ve/wildlife) Site focusing on ecotourism and adventure trips, but with plenty of links to general information.

# Caracas

It's not often that a pretty picture is painted of Caracas. If you've seen the film *Sequestro Express* or paid much attention to the news, you'll know that violence, kidnappings and political unrest are often the attention-grabbing headlines. But there are two sides to this vibrant South American giant, once one of Latin America's most sophisticated and intellectual epicenters – a title to which small pockets desperately cling after a decade of political polarization. Your introduction to Venezuela may be an intense assault on all your senses, both thrilling and unpleasant, like opposing forces constantly colliding in a metropolyptic buzz of culture and crime.

Spreading along a high plateau that's partitioned from the sea by towering green mountains, Caracas is a dense urban fabric – for every modern skyscraper sticking out of a mass of low-rise buildings, there's a *barrio* (shantytown) carpeting the hillsides like a pandemic brick-and-mortar virus. But beneath the city's dirty fingernails (that headline-grabbing rampant violence and frightening degree of kidnappings, as well as stifling traffic and a woefully wide disparity between rich and poor), there's an impressive array of cultural activity, wonderful museums, eclectic cuisine and sunrise-be-damned nightlife. Art aficionados will appreciate the enclave of world-class museums around Parque Central, including the world's most extensive exhibition of Picasso engravings. Foodies will genuflect at the wealth of haute cuisine on offer in suburbs like Altamira and Los Palos Grandes. Night owls will overdose on the eternal pounding pulse of nightlife in Las Mercedes. Nature addicts will thrive amid the steep, wooded slopes of Parque Nacional El Ávila, where miles of walking trails wind through scented forests – all hovering just over the city like an eco-guardian angel.

## HIGHLIGHTS

- Take flight over the city in the soaring **teleférico** (cable car; p82) ride to the summit of El Ávila
- Ride the *rumba* (party) through the night at the clubs and bars of **Las Mercedes** (p76)
- Lunch in colonial style as you tasca-hop through **La Candelaria** district (p69)
- Admire art treasures at the **Museo de Arte Contemporáneo de Caracas** (p62), **Museo de Bellas Artes** (p62) and the **Galería de Arte Nacional** (p62) in the Parque Central complex
- Get lost in Venezuelan *béisbol* (baseball) madness at a Leones de Caracas game at **Estadio Universitario** (p76)

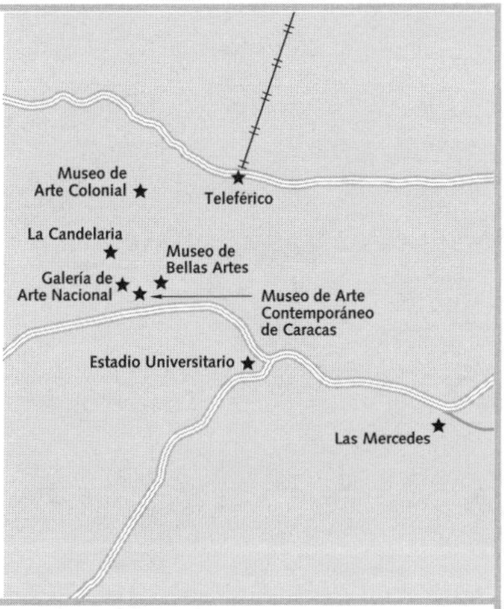


- TELEPHONE CODE: 1212
- POPULATION: 6 MILLION

## HISTORY

Caracas had a precarious beginning in 1560 when Francisco Fajardo of Isla de Margarita discovered the emerald valley – then inhabited by the Toromaima people. He founded a settlement named San Francisco, but was soon driven out by the indigenous inhabitants. A year later the town was resurrected, but years of bitter struggle against Toromaima attacks followed.

In 1567, a decisive conquest of the valley was ordered and 136 men led by Diego de Losada overcame a brave indigenous resistance before re-establishing the settlement once and for all on July 25. The new township was named Santiago de León de Caracas, 'Caracas' being the name of a decidedly less troublesome indigenous group that inhabited the coastal cordillera (mountain range).

A decade later, provincial governor, Juan de Pimentel, chose the young town to be the capital of Venezuela. But from the beginning, Caracas was besieged by vicious pirate raids, plagues and natural disasters, including a devastating earthquake in 1641. More calamity awaited the early 1700s, when a Basque trading company called the Real Compañía Guipuzcoana was based in La Guaira and given a monopoly over trade with Spain. The company's flagrantly corrupt methods aroused widespread anger among the colonists, and the ensuing riots sowed the seeds of the independence movement.

On March 28, 1750, Caracas became the birthplace of Francisco de Miranda, and on July 24, 1783, that of Simón Bolívar. The former was to pave the way to independence; the latter was to realize that aim. On April 19, 1810, a group of councilors and notable *caraqueños* denounced the Spanish governor and formed a Supreme Junta to replace the government. The political struggle raged until July 5, 1811, when congress declared the country's independence.

The following year, on Maundy Thursday, an earthquake wrecked the town, killing some 10,000 people. The conservative clergy swiftly declared that it was a punishment from heaven for the rebellion, but the independence movement was not to be stopped. It eventually reached its aim nine years later, sealed by Bolívar's victory at the Battle of Carabobo on

### CARACAS

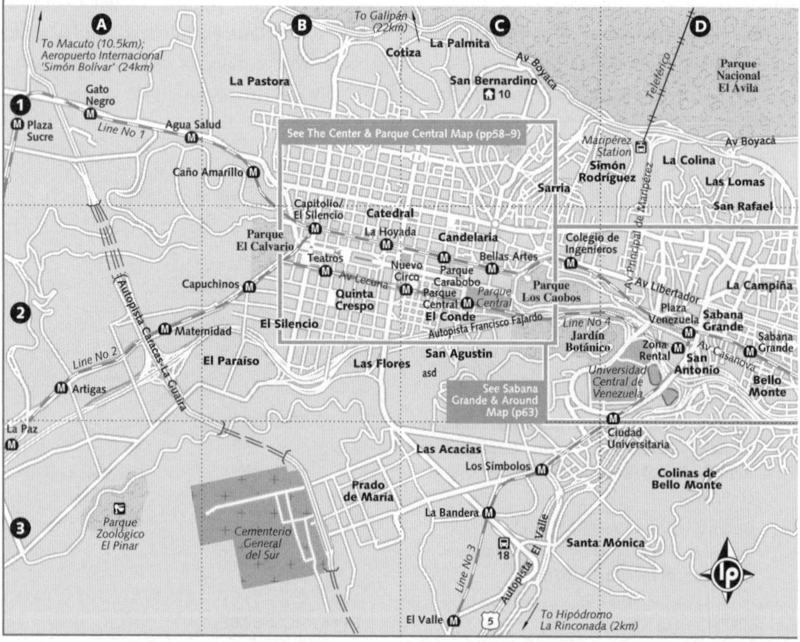

June 24, 1821. Despite this, Spain stubbornly refused to recognize Venezuela's sovereignty until 1845.

Caracas grew at a modest pace until the early 1900s, when black gold was discovered near Maracaibo and the oil boom began: changes came at breakneck speed. Oil money was pumped into modernization, transforming the bucolic colonial town into a vast concrete sprawl. Colonial buildings were demolished and their place taken by modern commercial centers and steel-and-glass towers.

Spurred on by the illusory dream of wealth, thousands of rural dwellers rushed into Caracas, but the majority never saw their share of the city's prosperity, leading a hand-to-mouth existence in *ranchos* (ramshackle huts) that covered the hills around the central districts. Over the last 50 years, the city's metropolitan population has shot up from around 400,000 to over six million.

In Hugo Chávez's political ascendance – most recently in his overwhelming re-election in December 2006 – Caracas' dispossessed see the dawning of a new era when they are finally emerging from the shadowy existence of poverty and being recognized as citizens worthy of basic rights such as health care and education. Meanwhile, the much smaller segment of the population that is comfortable laments a continuation of reduced services, legal impunity and soaring crime. The contrast in perceptions will probably continue to place a wedge in serious political dialogue as the city continues to become more polarized.

## ORIENTATION

Nestled in a long, narrow valley, the city spreads at least 20km from west to east. To the north looms the steep, verdant wall of Parque Nacional El Ávila, refreshingly free of human dwellings. To the south, by contrast, the city is devouring the hillsides, with modern *urbanizaciones* (suburbs) and derelict *barrios* invading every reasonably flat piece of land.

Extending eastward from El Silencio to Chacao, the central downtown area is packed with commercial centers, offices and hotels. The metro's main line (No 1) goes right along this axis. At the west end is the historic quarter (called the 'Center' in this chapter), recognizable

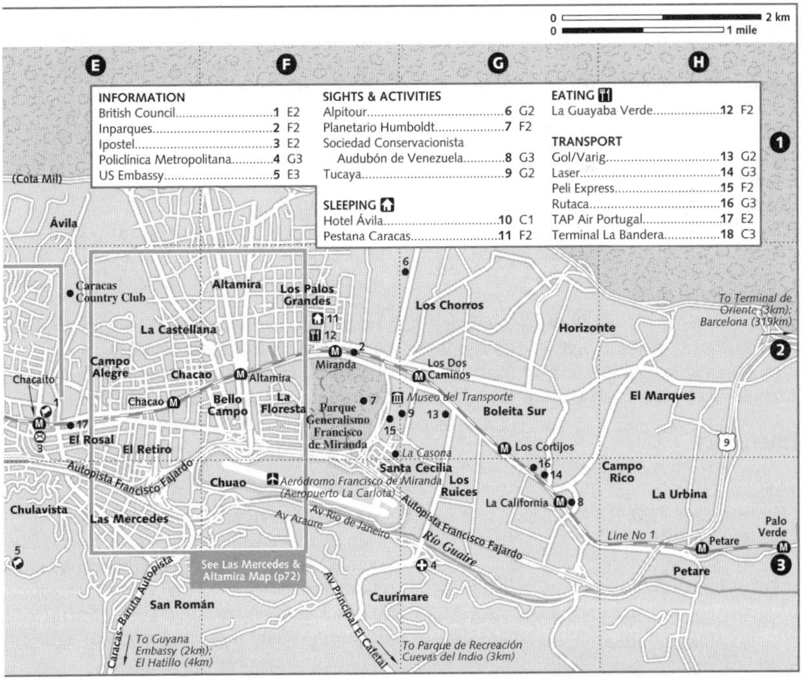

on the map by the colonial chessboard layout of the streets. About 1.5km to the east of Plaza Bolívar is Parque Central, noted for its museums and theaters. Another 2km east is Sabana Grande, centered on a busy pedestrian mall that has grown ever dangerous over the years. Continuing east, you come to Chacao, a commercial district good for upmarket shopping, and then to hip Altamira, which boasts scores of sophisticated restaurants and nightspots. El Rosal and Las Mercedes, south of Chacao, also cater to gourmands and night-trippers.

### Maps

Fold-out maps of Caracas are sold at many book and stationery stores. One useful tool is the *Guía de Calles, Avenidas, Esquinas y Metro de Caracas,* a pocket atlas with bus and metro routes, available at Tecni-Ciencia Libros (below). Also helpful are the city maps posted near metro station ticket booths.

To find topographical maps for the rest of Venezuela, ranging from 1:1000 to 1:250,000, visit the **Instituto Geográfico de Venezuela Simón Bolívar** (IGVSB; Map pp58-9; ☎ 546-1206; www.igvsb.gob.ve; Office 215, Edificio Camejo, Av Este 6; 🕘 8:30am-noon & 1:30-4pm Mon-Fri).

## INFORMATION

### Bookstores

**American Book Shop** (Map p72; ☎ 285-8779; Jardín level, Centro Comercial Centro Plaza, Los Palos Grandes; Ⓜ Altamira) Fair selection of Lonely Planet guidebooks, plus magazines in English.

**El Buscón** (Map p72; ☎ 993-8242; Centro Trasnocho Cultural, Centro Comercial Paseo Las Mercedes, Las Mercedes; 🕘 4-10pm Mon, 2-10pm Tue-Sun) Browse-worthy store with strong selection of Venezuelan literature (in Spanish), plus some English novels.

**Tecni-Ciencia Libros** Centro Comercial Sambil (Map p72; ☎ 264-1765; Nivel Acuario, Av Libertador, Chacao; Ⓜ Chacao) Centro Lido (Map p72; ☎ 952-2339; Nivel Miranda, Av Francisco de Miranda, El Rosal; Ⓜ Chacao) One of Venezuela's best bookstores, with 12 branches around town.

### Emergency

If your Spanish is not up to scratch, try to get a local to call on your behalf.

**Emergency Center** (☎ 171) Ambulance, fire and police

**Red Cross** (☎ 541-4713)

### Internet Access

It's generally easy and inexpensive to get online in Caracas. Most shopping malls have a couple of cybercafes, and many hotels provide free access for guests. Online rates are from BsF3 to BsF5 per hour. In addition to the places listed below, most CANTV Net and Telefónica communications centers (opposite) also offer internet, as well as nearly all shopping malls.

**Al Giorno** (Map p72; Blandín level, Centro San Ignacio, Av Blandín, La Castellana; per hr BsF5; 🕘 8am-8pm Mon-Fri, 10am-8pm Sat, noon-6pm Sun)

**Comunicaciones Yujemana** (Map pp58-9; Av Lecuna, Edificio San Martín, Nivel Lecuna, Parque Central; 🕘 8:30am-9pm Mon-Fri, 10am-8pm Sun)

**Cyber Office** (Map p63; Edificio San Germán, Calle Pascual Navarro at Av Francisco Solano, Sabana Grande; Ⓜ Plaza Venezuela)

**Infocentro** (www.infocentro.gob.ve; 🕘 9am-4pm or 5pm Tue-Sat) Biblioteca Metropolitana Simón Rodriguez (Map pp58-9; Esq El Conde; Ⓜ Capitolio/El Silencio) Palacio de las Academias (Map pp58-9; Av Universidad, cnr La Bolsa; Ⓜ Capitolio/El Silencio) A government project to provide internet services to all, with 30 minutes of free access available at dozens of libraries, schools and other sites. Full location list on website.

**Intermanía** (Map p72; 1a Transversal btwn Avs 2a & 3a; 🕘 9am-10:30pm Mon-Fri, 11am-10:30pm Sat & Sun; Ⓜ Miranda)

### Internet Resources

**Caracas Virtual** (www.caracasvirtual.com) Grab bag of useful info, from lists of taxi services to the history of *chicha* (sweet, milky rice beverage), plus extensive events coverage.

**Guía Gastronómica de Caracas** (www.miropopic.com/gastronomica) Reviews all the city's restaurants.

**Rumba Caracas** (www.rumbacaracas.com) Essential source for Caracas' endlessly varied nightlife.

### Laundry

A load up to 10kg, dried and folded, will cost around BsF30. Typical opening hours are from 8am to 6pm Monday to Saturday. Recommended *lavanderías:*

**Lavandería Autolanka** (Map pp58-9; Centro Comercial Doral, Av Urdaneta; Ⓜ Parque Carabobo)

**Lavandería Automática Maxi Clean** Altamira (Map p72; 2a Transversal; Ⓜ Altamira) Sabana Grande (Map p63; cnr Av Casanova & 2a Av de Bello Monte; Ⓜ Sabana Grande)

**Lavandería Chapultepek** (Map p63; Calle Bolivia; Ⓜ Plaza Venezuela) Also open Sunday morning.

### Medical Services

Caracas has a wide array of *farmacias* (pharmacies), and one in every neighborhood takes its turn to stay open all night, easily recognizable by a neon sign reading 'Turno.' Farmatodo is the nicest and most well-stocked chain and outlets are usually open 24 hours.

**Farmatodo** Chacao (Map p72; ☎ 266-6431; Av Francisco de Miranda; Ⓜ Chacao) Parque Central (Map pp58-9; ☎ 574-8719; Edificio Mohedano, Nivel Lecuna, Zona 1, Parque Central; Ⓜ Parque Central) Los Palos Grandes (Map p72; ☎ 285-7496; cnr Av Andres Bello & 3a Transversal; Ⓜ Altamira) Sabana Grande (Map p63; ☎ 761-4812; Blvd de Sabana Grande; Ⓜ Plaza Venezuela)

The following are reputable medical facilities:

**Clínica El Ávila** (Map p72; ☎ 276-1111; www.clinicaelavila.com; Av San Juan Bosco at 6a Transversal)
**Clínica Instituto Médico La Floresta** (Map p72; ☎ 209-6222; www.clinicalafloresta.com; Av Principal de la Floresta at Calle Santa Ana; Ⓜ Altamira)
**Hospital de Clínicas Caracas** (Map pp58-9; ☎ 508-6111; www.clinicaracas.com; Av Panteón at Av Alameda)
**Policlínica Metropolitana** (Map pp52-3; ☎ 908-0100; www.pcm.com.ve; Calle A-1, Urbanización Caurimare)

## Money

Many banks have ATMs on the Cirrus and Plus networks, although keep in mind extracting cash will net you the official rate.

**Banco de Venezuela** Center (Map pp58-9; Av Universidad, cnr Sociedad); La Castellana (Map p72; Av San Juan Bosco); Sabana Grande (Map p63; Centro Comercial El Recreo, Av Casanova)
**Banesco** Altamira (Map p72; Av Altamira Sur); Center (Map pp58-9; Av Universidad, cnr El Chorro); Las Mercedes (Map p72; Calle Monterrey); Sabana Grande (Map p63; Centro Comercial El Recreo, Av Casanova)
**BBVA** Chacaíto (Map p63; Plaza Chacaíto)
**Citibank** El Rosal (Map p72; Av Francisco de Miranda) Sabana Grande (Map p63; Centro Comercial El Recreo, Av Casanova)

The usual places to change foreign cash (at the official rate) are *casas de cambio* (money-exchange offices). Few do this however, so try the following outlets.

**Amex** (☎ 800-100-3555) Offers local refund assistance for traveler's checks.
**Italcambio** (☎ 565-0219; www.italcambio.com; 🕒 8:30am-5pm Mon-Fri, 9am-1pm Sat) Altamira (Map p72; Av Ávila); Maiquetía airport (International & national terminals) Sabana Grande (Map p63; Centro Comercial El Recreo, Av Casanova)

Put some serious thought into the amount you exchange or withdraw – you cannot change BsF back into dollars.

## Post

**Ipostel** (www.ipostel.gob.ve) Altamira (Map p72; Av Francisco de Miranda, Edificio PGC); Chacaíto (Map pp52-3; Centro Comercial Arta, Plaza Chacaíto) Offers poste-restante service. Address letters as follows: recipient's last name capitalized and underlined, first name, Lista de Correos, Ipostel, Carmelitas, Caracas 1010.

These international courier companies operate in Caracas:

**DHL** (☎ 205-6000; www.dhl.com.ve)
**FedEx** (☎ 205-3333; www. fedex.com/ve)
**UPS** (☎ 957-4000; www.ups.com)

## Telephone & Fax

Card-operated public phones abound. Cards (BsF2 or BsF5) are widely available in kiosks, pharmacies and shops. Metro stations have lots of functional phones and offer the additional advantage of being less disrupted by traffic noise. Both **CANTV** and **Telefónica** have many telecommunication outlets around town called 'Centros de Comunicaciones,' which offer international and domestic calls. Most of these offer reasonably priced internet access as well.

## Tourist Information

**Inatur** (www.inatur.gob.ve) Maiquetía airport domestic terminal (☎ 355-2152; 🕒 7am-8pm); Maiquetía airport international terminal (☎ 355-1442; 🕒 7am-midnight) All tourist offices are at the airport.
**Information kiosk Chacao** Altamira (Map p72; www.culturachacao.org; Plaza de Francia; 🕒 9am-5pm;

### BETWEEN THE CORNERS

A curiosity of Caracas is the center's street address system. It's not the streets that bear names here, but the *esquinas* (street corners); therefore, addresses are given 'corner to corner.' So if an address is 'Piñango a Conde,' the place is between these two street corners. If a place is situated on a corner, just the corner will be named (eg Esq Conde). However, note that a few major thoroughfares, such as Avs México and Universidad, supersede this rule.

Authorities have given numbers and cardinal-point designations to the streets (Este, Oeste, Norte and Sur), but locals continue to stick with the *esquinas*. Outside the colonial center, things don't fare much better. Street numbers are rare and most addresses are given relative to the cross-street.

## CARACAS IN...

### Two Days

On your first morning take a trip round the historical heart of the city, starting with Bolívar's birthplace and finishing at his tomb at the **Panteón Nacional** (p61). Along the way, pop in for one of the city's best coffees at **Café Casa Veroes** (p70). Sufficiently recaffeinated, head east and treat yourself to a long lunch at a traditional tasca (Spanish-style bar-restaurant) in **La Candelaria** (p69). In the afternoon, take your pick of the museums in Bellas Artes and don't miss the **Museo de Arte Contemporáneo de Caracas** (p62). Alternatively, it's worth the trip north to the **Museo de Arte Colonial** (p61). Finish off your day with a meal and perhaps a pub crawl through the bars and clubs in **Las Mercedes** (p70).

On your second day, escape the urban jungle and take a trip up El Ávila mountain on the **teleférico** (cable car; p81). Once you're back on terra firma, catch a bus out to the charming colonial suburb of **El Hatillo** (p73) for some serious souvenir shopping after a meal in one of its numerous excellent restaurants. Finally, after depositing any bulky buys back at the hotel, those who have still got a spring in their step can enjoy a meal in upmarket **Altamira** (p71) followed by a night out in the chic clubs and bars of **Centro San Ignacio** (p74).

### Four Days

If you're sticking around longer, follow the two-day itinerary, but leave El Hatillo and Altamira until your third day, spending the entire second day roaming further along the tranquil woodland paths of **Parque Nacional El Ávila** (p81). Then on your fourth day, wind down by taking a walk through the sprawling **Parque Generalismo Francisco de Miranda** (p64), followed by a blowout meal at Caracas' most exciting dining destination, **Alto** (p73), in Los Palos Grandes. Toast the town later that evening over innovative cocktails and stupendous views at the **360° Roofbar** (p75).

Ⓜ Altamira) Las Castellana (Map p72; Av Blandin, Centro San Ignacio; 🕑 9am-5pm; Ⓜ Chacao) Small tourist info booths in the southwest corner of Plaza de Francia, Centro San Ignacio and Centro Lido offering non-English-speaking staff and an essential map and cultural brochure.

**Inparques** (Instituto Nacional de Parques Nacionales; Map pp52-3; ☎ 273-2860; www.inparques.gob.ve; Av Rómulo Gallegos & Av 2a de Santa Eduvigis; 🕑 8:30am-12:30pm & 1:30-5pm Mon-Fri; Ⓜ Miranda) The national parks office has a specialized library that's accessible to tourists, though information is limited.

### Travel Agencies

**IVI Venezuela** (Map p72; ☎ 993-6082; www.iviven ezuela.com; Residencia La Hacienda, Av Principal de las Mercedes; 🕑 8am-6pm Mon-Fri) Airfares for students, teachers and people under 26 years of age; issues ISIC, ITIC cards and Hostelling International cards.

## DANGERS & ANNOYANCES

Caracas is dangerous. Since the late 1980s, crime levels have increased along with the city's rapidly growing population. Except for Chacao and to some extent Parque Central, the rest of the city is considered a *zona roja*, a high-crime area where assaults are commonplace and police protection is minimal. In particular, locals warn you to avoid the *centro* (center), Sabana Grande, Petare and La Candelaria after 6pm, when the streets in these zones tend to clear out, creating the sense of a de facto curfew.

Such warnings should not be ignored, though also tend to reinforce the paranoiac atmosphere of the place. Like any large, chaotic city, Caracas has its hazards, but that should not deter you from exploring.

Taking certain precautions will greatly reduce any risks. Try not to look like a tourist, for example, by wearing jeans instead of shorts. After dark, stick with groups of people and take walking off your to-do list unless you are in Chacao. The best approach is to stay alert and be aware of your surroundings. Never take a taxi with white plates – only yellow, which are official.

The mentality that the police are more of a threat than common criminals dominates the mindset of locals, and not without reason. With the exception of those within the municipality of Chacao (easily identified by their khaki uniforms and safari-like hats), police should be avoided. However, in Sabana Grande, the Metropolitan Police (dark blue uniforms) will find you. On the lighter side, they've been known to harass foreigners about not carrying a passport, as a means of extracting a bribe, so take a copy of it (along with your entrance stamp) when you go out (this is legal in Venezuela, no matter what they try to tell you); the harsher reality is that they are all too often accused of abusing authority by simply robbing tourists – and locals – outright.

Traffic in Caracas is a persistent danger as well, especially for those on foot. Many intersections are impossible to cross safely. Never assume you have the right of way in any crossing situation. Drivers cannot be trusted to stop at red lights – it is always safer to look for a break in traffic before crossing, preferably with other pedestrians. Motorcycle taxis zip along sidewalks or against the flow of traffic to circumnavigate jams; you never know where they're coming from. Asphyxiating fumes and incessant horn honking by gridlocked vehicles are additional annoyances.

## SIGHTS

### The Center & Around

The historic center, where the city was born, still retains glimpses of its colonial identity. Although many original houses were replaced with new buildings in the rush toward modernization, ranging from nondescript concrete edifices to futuristic tinted-glass towers, ongoing restorations continue to unearth colonial treasures. Architectural grab bag that it is, the *centro* remains a lively and colorful area and boasts some important Bolivarian sights. Most of the places mentioned below are within reasonable walking distance of metro Capitolio, unless otherwise noted.

#### PLAZA BOLÍVAR

This leafy **square** (Map pp58–9) is the nucleus of the old town. It's always alive with huddled groups of *caraqueños* engaged in conversation and children feeding freshly popped corn to the black squirrels in the trees, while vendors hawk lemonade and *cepilladas* (shaved ices) on the sidelines, the whole scene shaded by African tulip trees and jacarandas. In the center is the obligatory monument to Bolívar – the equestrian statue was cast in Munich, shipped in pieces, and eventually unveiled in 1874 after the ship carrying it foundered on the Archipiélago de los Roques.

The plaza is a favorite stage for political visionaries and religious messiahs, who deliver their passionate speeches to a casual audience. In recent years it's been a focus for supporters of President Chávez, with stalls selling videos, paintings and photos of the red-bereted leader alongside saints and musical legends.

#### CATEDRAL

Set on the eastern side of Plaza Bolívar, the **catedral** (Map pp58-9; ☎ 862-4963; 🕑 8-11:30am & 4-6pm Mon-Fri, 9am-noon & 4:30-6pm Sat & Sun) started its life in the mid-16th century as a mere mud-walled chapel. A church later replaced it, only to be flattened by the 1641 earthquake. Built from 1665 to 1713, the new cathedral was packed with dazzling gilded altars and elaborate side chapels. The wide, five-nave interior, supported on 32 columns, was largely remodeled in the late 19th century. The **Bolívar family chapel** is in the middle of the right-hand aisle and can be easily recognized by a modern sculpture of El Libertador (The Liberator) mourning his parents and Spanish bride (for more on Bolívar see the boxed text, p24). Bolívar was baptized here, but the baptismal font now stands in the Casa Natal de Bolívar (p61). Also take a look at the fine colonial altarpiece at the back of the chapel.

#### MUSEO SACRO DE CARACAS

Accommodated in a meticulously restored colonial building that stands upon the site of the old cathedral cemetery, this **museum** (Map pp58-9; ☎ 861-6562; Plaza Bolívar; admission free; 🕑 9am-4pm Tue-Sat) displays a modest but carefully selected collection of religious art. Duck through the low doorway into the dark, old ecclesiastical prison, where remains of early church leaders still lie in sealed niches. The Museo Sacro also stages concerts and recitals and has a delightful **cafe** (mains BsF58-79) inside a former chapel of the adjacent cathedral.

#### CONCEJO MUNICIPAL

Occupying half of Plaza Bolívar's southern side, the **city hall** (Map pp58-9; ☎ 409-8236; admission free; 🕑 9am-12:30pm & 2-4:30pm Mon-Fri, 10am-4pm Sat) was erected by the Caracas bishops from 1641 to 1696 to house the Colegio Seminario de Santa Rosa de Lima. In 1725, the Real y Pontificia Universidad de Caracas, the province's first university, was established here. Bolívar renamed it the Universidad Central de Venezuela, the moniker it keeps to this day, though it has moved to a vast campus outside the historic center. Today the building is the seat of the Municipal Council, but part of it is open to the public.

## THE CENTER & PARQUE CENTRAL

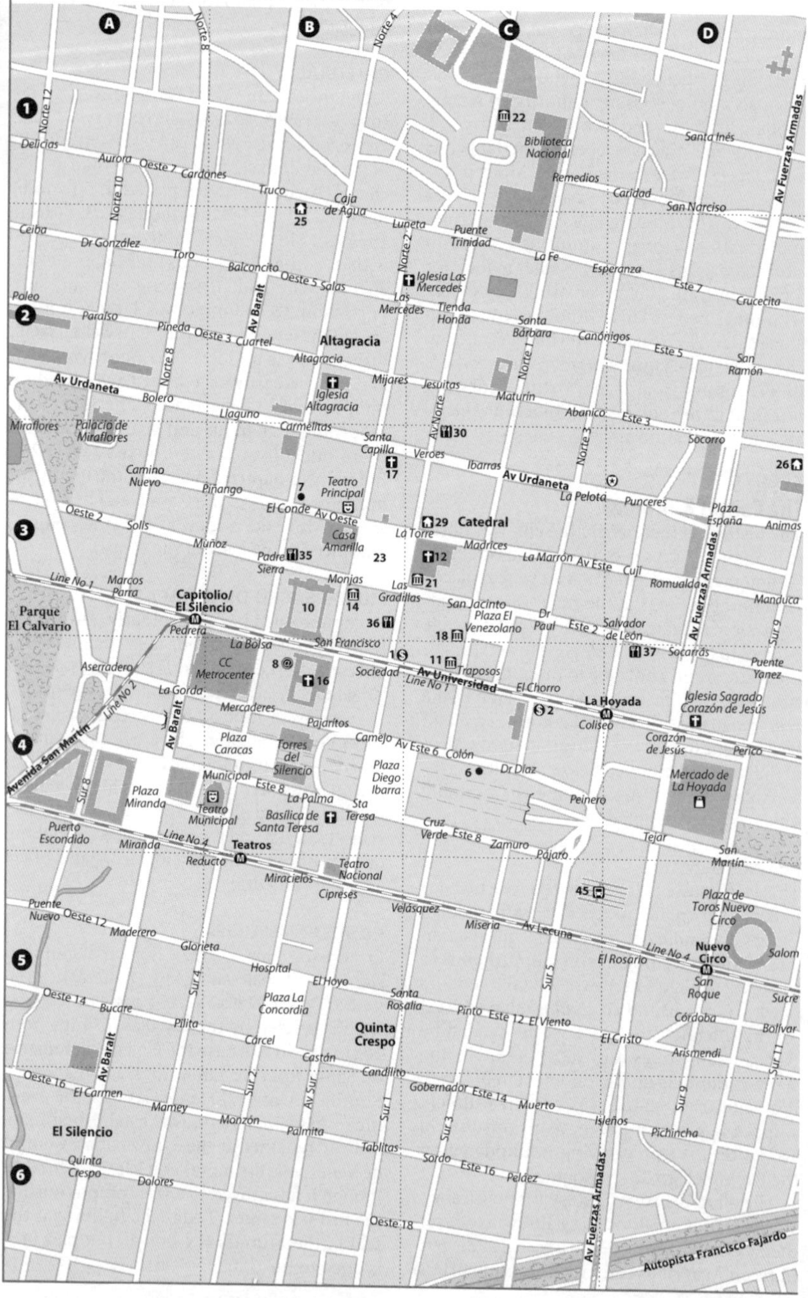

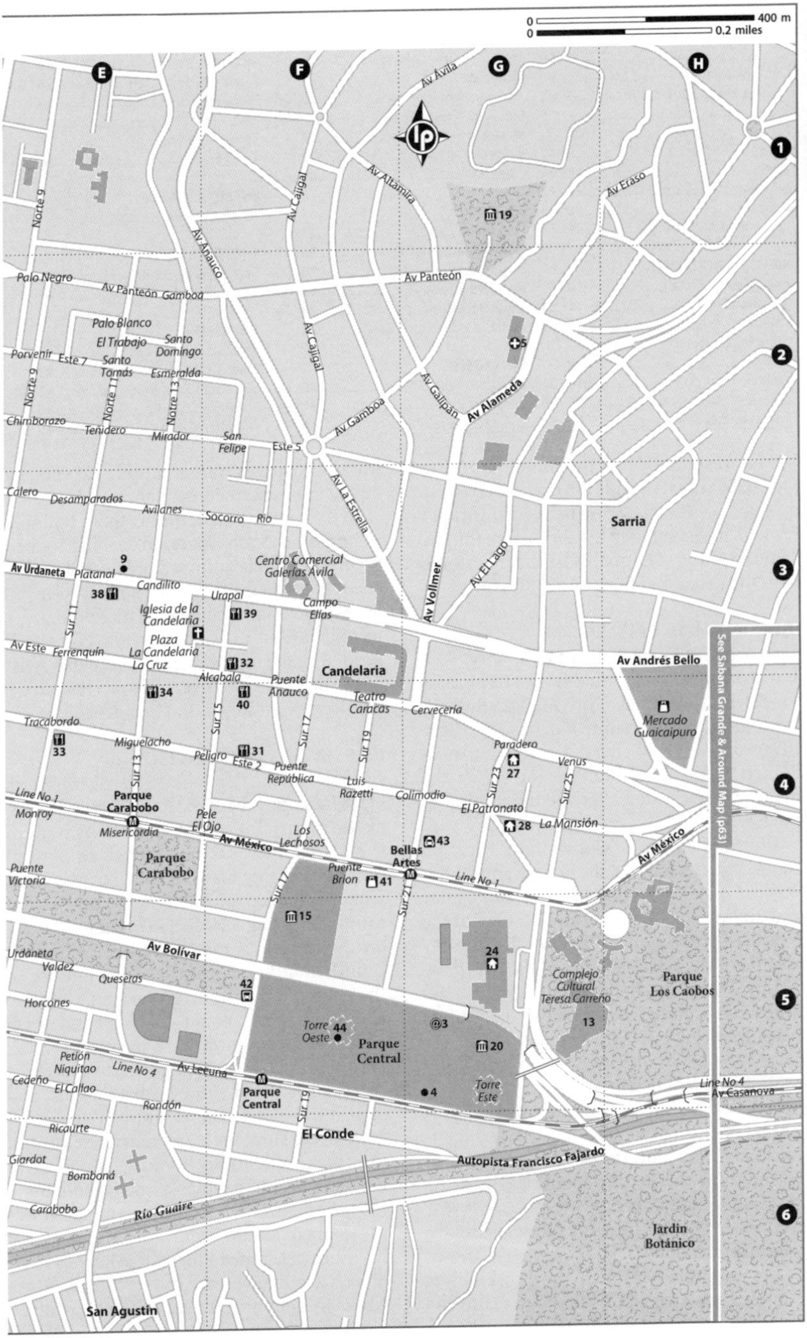
0
400 m
0
0.2 miles
E
F
G
H
1
2
3
4
5
6
Av Ávila
Av Altamira
Av Eraso
Av Cajigal
19
Norte 9
Av Anauco
Palo Negro
Av Panteón
Gamboa
Av Panteón
Palo Blanco
El Trabajo
Santo Domingo
Porvenir
Este 7
Santo Tomás
Esmeralda
Norte 9
Norte 11
Notre 13
5
Av Galipán
Av Alameda
Av Gamboa
Chimborazo
Teñidero
Mirador
San Felipe
Este 5
Calero
Desamparados
Avilanes
Socorro
Río
Av La Estrella
Sarria
Av El Lago
Centro Comercial Galerías Ávila
9
Av Urdaneta
Platanal
Candilito
38
Urapal
Campo Elías
Av Vollmer
Iglesia de la Candelaria
39
Sur 11
Plaza La Candelaria
Av Este
Ferrenquín
La Cruz
32
Candelaria
Av Andrés Bello
Alcabala
Puente Anauco
34
40
Teatro Caracas
Cervecería
Mercado Guaicaipuro
Tracabordo
Sur 15
Sur 17
Sur 19
33
Miguelacho
31
Peligro
Este 2
Puente República
Paradero
27
Venus
Sur 23
Sur 25
Luis Razetti
Colimodio
Line No 1
Monroy
Parque Carabobo
Misericordia
Sur 13
Pele El Ojo
El Patronato
28
La Mansión
Av México
Los Lechosos
43
Bellas Artes
Av México
Parque Carabobo
Puente Victoria
Puente Brion
41
Line No 1
Sur 17
Sur 21
15
See Sabana Grande & Around Map (p63)
Urdaneta
Valdez
Av Bolívar
24
Complejo Cultural Teresa Carreño
Parque Los Caobos
Queseras
42
Horcones
Torre Oeste
44
@3
Parque Central
20
13
Petión
Niquitao
Line No 4
Av Lecuna
Cedeño
El Callao
Parque Central
4
Torre Este
Line No 4
Av Casanova
Rondón
Sur 19
Ricaurte
El Conde
Giardot
Autopista Francisco Fajardo
Bomboná
Carabobo
Río Guaire
Jardín Botánico
San Agustín

**INFORMATION**

| | | |
|---|---|---|
| Banco de Venezuela | 1 | B4 |
| Banesco | 2 | C4 |
| Comunicaciones Yujemana | 3 | G5 |
| Farmatodo | 4 | G5 |
| Hospital de Clínicas Caracas | 5 | G2 |
| IGVSB | 6 | C4 |
| Infocentro | 7 | B3 |
| Infocentro | 8 | B4 |
| Lavandería Autolanka | 9 | E3 |

**SIGHTS & ACTIVITIES**

| | | |
|---|---|---|
| Asemblea Nacional | 10 | B3 |
| Casa Natal de Bolívar | 11 | C4 |
| Catedral | 12 | C3 |
| Complejo Cultural Teresa Carreño | 13 | G5 |
| Concejo Municipal | 14 | B3 |
| Galería de Arte Nacional | 15 | F5 |
| Iglesia de San Francisco | 16 | B4 |
| Iglesia Santa Capilla | 17 | B3 |
| Museo Bolivariano | 18 | C3 |
| Museo de Arte Colonial | 19 | G1 |
| Museo de Arte Contemporáneo | 20 | G5 |
| Museo de Bellas Artes | (see 15) | |
| Museo Sacro de Caracas | 21 | C3 |
| Panteón Nacional | 22 | C1 |
| Plaza Bolívar | 23 | B3 |

**SLEEPING**

| | | |
|---|---|---|
| Hotel Alba Caracas | 24 | G5 |
| Hotel Grand Galaxie | 25 | B2 |
| Hotel Inter | 26 | D3 |
| Hotel New Jersey | 27 | G4 |
| Hotel Renovación | 28 | G4 |
| Plaza Catedral Hotel | 29 | C3 |

**EATING**

| | | |
|---|---|---|
| Café Casa Veroes | 30 | C3 |
| Casa Farruco | 31 | F4 |
| La Cita | 32 | F3 |
| La Cocina de Francy | 33 | E4 |
| Lunchería Doña Agapita | 34 | E4 |
| Mi Linda Llanura | 35 | B3 |
| Pasteleria Noyer Deli | 36 | B3 |
| Restaurant Beirut | 37 | D4 |
| Restaurant El Coyuco | 38 | E3 |
| Tasca La Carabela | 39 | F3 |
| Tasca Mallorca | 40 | F4 |

**ENTERTAINMENT**

| | | |
|---|---|---|
| Teatro Teresa Carreño | (see 13) | |

**SHOPPING**

| | | |
|---|---|---|
| Gran Feria de Economiás Popular de Bellas Artes | 41 | F4 |

**TRANSPORT**

| | | |
|---|---|---|
| Aserca | (see 44) | |
| Buses to Maiquetía Airport | 42 | F5 |
| Carritos to Teleférico | 43 | G4 |
| Conviasa | 44 | F5 |
| Terminal Nuevo Circo | 45 | C5 |

The western side of the building houses the **Capilla de Santa Rosa de Lima**, where congress declared Venezuela's independence in 1811 (though it was another 10 years before this became a reality). The chapel has been restored with the decor and furniture of the time.

### IGLESIA SANTA CAPILLA

This neo-Gothic **church** (Map pp58-9; ☎ 860-8894; Av Urdaneta, cnr Sta Capilla; 7am-6pm Mon-Fri, 2-6pm Sat, 9am-6pm Sun), one block north of Plaza Bolívar, is modeled on the Sainte Chapelle of Paris. It was ordered by General Antonio Guzmán Blanco in 1883 and built on the site of the first mass celebrated after the foundation of the town.

Illuminated by a warm light through stained-glass windows, the marble and whitewashed interior has an elaborate stone altar and an unusual open-work vault. One of the treasured possessions of the church is the sizable painting *Multiplication of the Bread*, by Arturo Michelena, hanging in the right-hand aisle and shrouded in plastic for unspecified reasons during our visit.

### ASEMBLEA NACIONAL

As part of his mad dash toward modernization in the 1870s, Guzmán Blanco commissioned an ambitious, neoclassical seat of congress, the **National Assembly** (Map pp58-9; ☎ 483-8240; admission free; 9am-noon & 2-5pm Mon, Wed & Fri), to occupy the entire block just southwest of Plaza Bolívar. It was formerly known as the Capitolio Nacional. The two-building complex was erected on the site of a convent, whose occupants were promptly expelled by the dictator and their convent razed.

In the central part of the northern building is the famous **Salón Elíptico**, an oval hall topped by an extraordinary domed ceiling with an all-encompassing mural, which almost seems to move as you walk beneath it. The painting, depicting the Battle of Carabobo, was completed in 1888 by the most notable Venezuelan artist of the day, Martín Tovar y Tovar. It's put on public view on July 5, Independence Day.

### IGLESIA DE SAN FRANCISCO

Just south of the Capitolio Nacional, the **Church of San Francisco** (Map pp58-9; ☎ 484-5707; Av Universidad, cnr San Francisco; 6am-noon & 3-6pm) was built in the 1570s, but was remodeled on several occasions during the 17th and 18th centuries. Guzmán Blanco, unable to resist his passion for modernizing, placed a neoclassical facade on the church to match the just-completed capitol building. Fortunately, the interior of the church didn't undergo such an extensive alteration, so its colonial character and much of its old decoration have been preserved. Have a look at the richly gilded baroque altarpieces distributed along both sidewalls, and stop at the statue of San Onofre, in the right-hand aisle. He is the most venerated saint in the church due to his miraculous powers of bringing health, happiness and a good job.

It was in this church in 1813 that Bolívar was proclaimed 'El Libertador,' and also here that his much celebrated funeral was held in 1842, after his remains were brought from Santa Marta in Colombia, 12 years after his death.

### CASA NATAL DE BOLÍVAR

Bolívar's funeral took place just two blocks from the house where, on July 24, 1783, he was born. The interior of **Bolívar's birthplace** (Map pp58-9; ☎ 541-2563; btwn cnrs San Jacinto & Traposos; admission free; 🕑 9am-4:30pm Tue-Fri, 10am-4:30pm Sat & Sun) has been enthusiastically reconstructed. The walls are splashed with a score of huge paintings by Tito Salas depicting Bolívar's heroic battles and scenes from his life. All *caraqueños* take cheesy photos – notebooks in hand – under the backyard tree under which Simon Rodriguez was said to have taught Bolívar to read and write.

### MUSEO BOLIVARIANO

Just a few paces north of the Casa Natal de Bolívar, this **museum** (Map pp58-9; ☎ 545-3396; btwn cnrs San Jacinto & Traposos; admission free; 🕑 9am-4:30pm Tue-Fri, 10am-4pm Sat & Sun) has more successfully preserved its colonial style and displays a variety of independence memorabilia, from muskets to medals and shaving sets to swords. It also has some fascinating documents and letters written by the man himself, and numerous portraits. More on the morbid side are the coffin in which the remains of Bolívar were brought from Santa Marta in Colombia and the *arca cineraria* (funeral ark) that conveyed his ashes to the Panteón Nacional.

### PANTEÓN NACIONAL

The entire central nave of the imposing **National Pantheon** (Map pp58-9; ☎ 861-7131; Av Norte; admission free; 🕑 9am-4:30pm Tue-Fri, 10am-4pm Sat & Sun) is dedicated to national hero Simón Bolívar, underlining the almost saint-like reverence with which he is held in Venezuela. His bronze sarcophagus is placed in the chancel, and the path to reach his tomb is covered by a ceiling filled with paintings of Bolívar's life, all done by Tito Salas in the 1930s.

No less than 140 white-stone tombs of other eminent Venezuelans are crammed into the aisles. One tomb is empty and open, symbolically awaiting the remains of Francisco de Miranda, who died in a Spanish jail in 1816 and was buried in a mass grave. There are two more empty tombs, but they are sealed. One is dedicated to Antonio José de Sucre, who was assassinated in Colombia and whose remains are in the Quito cathedral; he is considered by Ecuadorians as the liberator of their country. The other tomb commemorates Andrés Bello, a Caracas-born poet, writer and friend of Bolívar's who later went to live (and die) in Chile. In 2001, Chávez added the tomb of Guacaipuro, who organized Venezuela's first indigenous army by stealing swords from the Spanish (little did he know the Spaniards had guns, so his newly formed army didn't last long in battle). He is the only non-Caucasian to be honored here.

The pantheon is at the opposite, northern edge of the old town, five blocks due north of Plaza Bolívar. A church once stood on the site, but it was destroyed in the 1812 earthquake. After reconstruction, it continued as a place of worship until 1874, when Guzmán Blanco decided that it would make a suitable resting place for revered Venezuelans. The progressive president himself, who died in Paris in 1899, rests here.

Take note of the surrounding plaza, which is peppered with Masonic symbols. Many of Venezuelans founding fathers were Freemasons.

### MUSEO DE ARTE COLONIAL

The **Museum of Colonial Art** (Map pp58-9; ☎ 551-4256; www.quintadeanauco.org.ve; Av Panteón; admission incl 45-min tour adult/student BsF10/5; 🕑 9-11:30am & 2-4:30pm Mon-Fri, 10am-4pm Sat & Sun) is considered one of the finest museums of its kind in Latin America. Housed in an elegant country mansion known as **Quinta de Anauco**, it's laid out around a charming patio and enclosed by lush, shady gardens. A ball was staged here in honor of Simón Bolívar's very last night in Caracas: he was never to return alive.

When built in 1797, the mansion was well outside the historic town. Today it's just a green oasis in the inner suburb of San Bernardino, a 10-minute walk northeast of La Candelaria. (Alternatively, catch Metrobús 421 from metro Bellas Artes.)

## Parque Central & Around

Parque Central is not, as you might expect, a green area, but rather a concrete complex of five high-rise residential slabs of somewhat apocalyptic appearance, crowned by two 54-story octagonal towers, the tallest in the country (Tower Oeste was devastated in a fire in 2004 and remains closed).

The Parque Central area is Caracas' art and culture hub, boasting half-a-dozen museums and the major performing arts center. The park is 1.5km southeast of Plaza Bolívar, next to the Bellas Artes metro station.

#### MUSEO DE ARTE CONTEMPORÁNEO DE CARACAS

Occupying the eastern end of the Parque Central complex, the **Museum of Contemporary Art** (Map pp58-9; ☎ 573-8289; www.fmn.gob.ve; Parque Central; admission free; ⏰ 9am-5pm) is by far the best in the country, if not on the continent. In a dozen halls on five levels, you'll find big, bold and sometimes shocking works by many prominent Venezuelan artists, including Jesús Soto, famous for his kinetic pieces.

There are also some remarkable paintings by such international giants as Chagall, Matisse, Monet, Leger and Miró. The pride of the museum is a collection of 100 or so engravings by Picasso, created from 1931 to 1934. Part of the exhibition space is for changing displays that showcase both locally and internationally renowned artists. There's also a pleasant cafe in the adjacent sculpture garden.

#### MUSEO DE BELLAS ARTES

The **Museum of Fine Arts** (Map pp58-9; ☎ 578-0275; Parque Central; www.fmn.gob.ve; admission free; ⏰ 9am-5pm Mon-Fri, 10am-5pm Sat & Sun; Ⓜ Bellas Artes) is a beautiful museum with lots of breathing room housed in two buildings, a functional modern six-story building and a graceful building radiating from a neoclassical-style courtyard with a pond and weeping willow – both were designed by Venezuelan architect Carlos Raúl Villanueva. The museum features permanent exhibitions from Egypt and China and on Cubism, as well as mostly temporary exhibitions in 18 galleries. It includes a little shop selling contemporary art and crafts and a cafe.

#### COMPLEJO CULTURAL TERESA CARREÑO

Rising like a gigantic concrete bunker across the street from Parque Central (and linked to it by a footbridge), the **Complejo Cultural Teresa Carreño** (Teresa Carreño Cultural Complex; Map pp58-9; ☎ 574-9333; www.teatroteresacarreno.gob.ve; tours BsF0.60; ⏰ tours 9am-5pm Tue-Sat) is a modern performing arts center. Opened in 1983, it has an enormous main auditorium, theater and side hall that regularly host concerts, ballets, plays and recitals by local and visiting performers.

Guided tours around the complex are conducted throughout the day; call in advance if you need an English-speaking guide. At the back of the building is a small museum dedicated to Teresa Carreño (1853–1917), Venezuela's most renowned pianist (see p35).

#### GALERÍA DE ARTE NACIONAL

The new, nearly completed **National Art Gallery** (Map pp58-9; www.fmn.gob.ve; Av Mexico; admission free; ⏰ 9am-5pm Mon-Fri, 10am-5pm Sat & Sun; Ⓜ Bellas Artes) was inaugurated by Hugo Chávez in 2009 and now stands as Venezuela's physically largest museum. Construction on its nearly 31,000 sq meters originally began in 1989 but was abandoned in the mid-'90s. Architect Carlos Gómez persevered and construction resumed in 2006. Its exhibition galleries are complete and house a selection from the 7000-piece collection that embraces five centuries of Venezuelan artistic expression. Anything from pre-Hispanic art to mind-boggling modern kinetic pieces may be showcased here in temporary exhibitions. Venezuela's four most important artists – Arturo Michelena, Armando Reverón, Carlos Cruz Diez and Jesús Soto – are well represented, including in the museum's most important work, Michelena's somber portrayal of Francisco Miranda in a Spanish jail, *Miranda en La Carraca* (1896).

A permanent cafe, museum shop and car park have yet to be built – and appeared stalled yet again during time of research.

### Sabana Grande & Around

Though it's still an important nucleus that is packed with hotels, restaurants and shops, Sabana Grande has sadly lost luster. Its once pleasant pedestrian promenade, the Blvd de Sabana Grande – which extends from Plaza Venezuela to Plaza Chacaíto – is rampant with crime and corruption. The only attraction worth seeing is the University Central de Venezuela. It's generally OK during the day when it's loaded with people; at night, it's a no-go area without trusted locals in tow.

#### UNIVERSIDAD CENTRAL DE VENEZUELA

With its 85,000 students, the **UCV** (Map p63; ☎ 605-4050; www.ucv.ve; Ⓜ Ciudad Universitaria) is Caracas' (and Venezuela's) largest university and is a hub of cultural activity.

The vast campus was designed and built all in one go in the early 1950s by Carlos Raúl Villanueva. Dotted with abstract sculptures and murals throughout its grounds by international artists like Fernán Leger, Jean Arp and Wilfredo Lam, the entire complex was declared a World Heritage Site by Unesco in 2000 for its innovative blending of art and architecture.

# SABANA GRANDE & AROUND

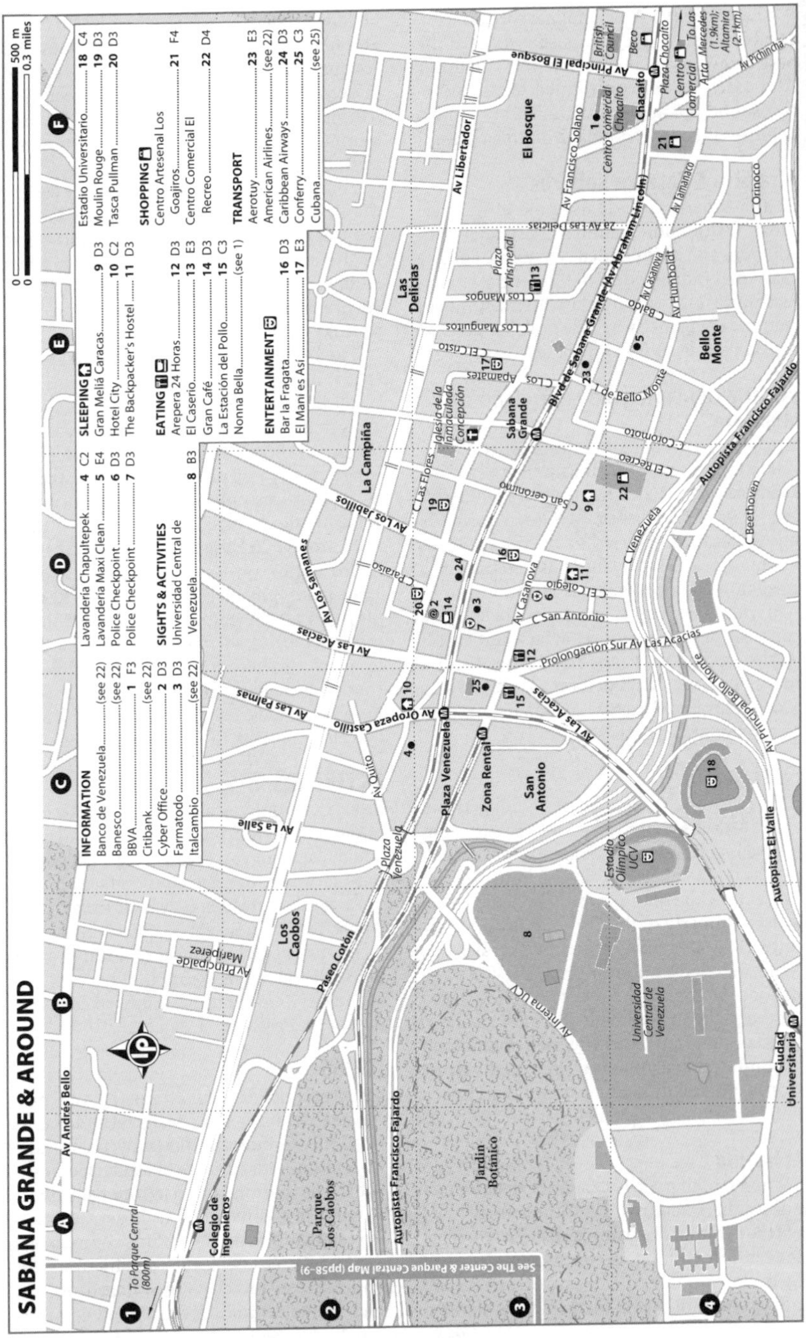

The excellent Aula Magna concert hall, capable of seating 2700, is said to have the best acoustics in the country. US sculptor Alexander Calder contributed to this superior sound quality by hanging a set of *nubes acústicos* (acoustic clouds) from the ceiling.

## Altamira & Eastern Suburbs

East of Sabana Grande lie some of Caracas' most fashionable suburbs, especially in Altamira and its immediate environs. Further east, you gradually descend the social ladder, reaching a low point at Petare, an independent colonial town once worth a stroll, but deemed too dangerous at the time of research.

### PARQUE GENERALISMO FRANCISCO DE MIRANDA

Situated on a portion of a former coffee plantation, the 82-hectare **Parque Generalismo Francisco de Miranda** (Map pp52-3; Av Francisco de Miranda; admission free; 5am-4:30pm Tue-Sun; Ⓜ Miranda), formerly known and still referred to by *caraqueños* as Parque del Este, is the largest in Caracas, and a stroll through its expanses is a botanical odyssey, with many plants and trees labeled. You can visit the snake house, aviary and cactus garden, and on weekends enjoy astral displays in the **Planetario Humboldt** (Map pp52-3; ☎ 234-9188; www.planetariohumboldt.com; adult/child BsF5/2; shows hourly 1-4pm Sat & noon-4pm Sun).

### LA ESTANCIA

This renovated fragment of a 220-year-old coffee **hacienda** (Map p72; ☎ 208-6463; www.pdvsa.com; Av Francisco de Miranda; admission free; 9am-5pm Mon-Fri, 8:30am-7pm Sat & Sun; Ⓜ Altamira) houses a fine museum with rotating works by Venezuelan artists. Property of the Simón Bolívar family until 1895, it is now owned by Petróleos de Venezuela Sociedad Anónima (PDVSA), the national oil company. Free concerts are staged on the patio on weekends (Saturday at 4pm, Sunday at 11am) and the well-manicured grounds offer a much-appreciated respite from Caracas' diesel and dust, as well as a great location for a picnic.

## El Hatillo

Set in the rolling hills of Caracas' heterogeneous southern suburbs, the 16th-century town of **El Hatillo** (www.elhatillo.com.ve) lived its own life for centuries until it was eventually absorbed by the burgeoning city. Its narrow streets and pretty plaza still retain many of their colonial buildings, now painted in sugary, bright colors and filled with art galleries, craft shops and restaurants (see p73). It remains a lovely and convenient nearby getaway for *caraqueños*, worlds away from the chaotic city. The only bummer is there are no accommodation options in the small *pueblo* (town).

Located 15km southeast of the city center, the little village overflows with visitors on the weekend. There's a magical atmosphere in the afternoon and early evening, when children can still be found skipping in the square and *sapitos* (tiny frogs) begin their squeaky chorus.

The biggest and best craft shop is Hannsi (p77), half a block north of the plaza, but you'll find countless other boutiques tucked away in the narrow streets. Also take a look at the parish church on Plaza Bolívar, which has a particularly well preserved exterior, though its interior was radically (and rather controversially) modernized.

Metrobús 202 leaves from near Altamira metro station on weekdays from 5:30am to 10am and 4pm to 10pm (BsF0.70, 30 minutes). To return, grab the Metrobús from the same stop back; alternatively, take a local bus to metro Chacaíto from Paseo El Hatillo, the shopping mall at the corner of Calle Santa Rosalia and Calle Belle Vista. A taxi rank is also here; the trip back to Altamira costs BsF50.

# ACTIVITIES

**Hiking** in Parque Nacional El Ávila (p82) is one of the more rewarding outdoor endeavors. If you'd like to join an organized group, contact one of the *centros excursionistas* (see p283).

**Parque de Recreación Cuevas del Indio** (☎ 273-2882; Av Principal de la Guairita; 8:30am-4pm Tue-Sun) is a favorite rock-climbing spot; local climbers flock here on the weekend. It's 9km southeast of the city center on the southern continuation of Av Principal el Cafetal.

# TOURS

For an overview of this complex city, you might consider taking a tour. Major hotels like the Hotel Alba Caracas and Hotel Ávila can arrange full-day tours that include El Hatillo for around BsF131 per person, for up to four people.

For a less conventional view of Caracas, **Leo Lameda** (☎ 0412-998-1998; leosupersoul@hotmail.com; full-day tour BsF380) leads walking tours, hitting some of the city's less-visited pockets, such as the central university and cemetery,

### FUNDACIÓN BIGOTT: HANGING ON TO HERITAGE

If you'd like to dig a little deeper into traditional Venezuelan culture – perhaps learn to play *joropo* music with the *bandola llanera* (a string instrument) in the style of Anselmo López, or how to create your very own Festival de los Diablos Danzantes masks (p94) – you'll want to pay a visit to **Fundación Bigott** (off Map p72; ☎ 205-7111; www.fundacionbigott.com; Calle El Vigía, Petare; 8am-8pm Mon-Fri, 9am-2pm Sat; M Petare). In a restored colonial home sitting prominently on richly preserved Plaza Sucre in the independent colonial town of Petare, Fundación Bigott offers extensive workshops in traditional Venezuelan culture, including traditional celebrations, music, gastronomy, popular arts and artesian crafts. Workshops generally last three months and cost a measly BsF15, but one-day classes are sometimes offered. There is also an extensive research library open to the public (2pm to 6pm Monday to Friday) and a small store where you can pick up CDs, books and other *fundación*-sponsored cultural items.

Petare is a dodgy area and is best reached by taxi, a BsF40 ride from Altamira.

while offering plenty of illuminating historical insights along the way.

For Caracas-based tour providers of other parts of Venezuela, see p282.

## FESTIVALS & EVENTS

The biggest religious feast in Caracas is the **Semana Santa** (Holy Week) celebration in Chacao, which begins with the Bajada de Palmeras (literally, 'taking down of the palms') on the Friday before Palm Sunday, when hundreds of young men ascend Mt Ávila to collect royal palm fronds for the procession, a tradition that dates back over two centuries. Holy Week culminates with solemn processions on Maundy Thursday and Good Friday, concluding with the Quema de Judas (Burning of Judas) on Easter Sunday.

The week around July 25 witnesses an increase in concerts, exhibitions and theater performances, organized to celebrate the anniversary of Caracas' foundation on July 25, 1567. The **Temporada de Danza** runs for several weeks in July and August, bringing together some of the leading national dance groups, plus international guests. In late October and early November, the **El Hatillo Jazz Festival** highlights major figures from across the Latin jazz spectrum.

## SLEEPING

Accommodation in Caracas is more expensive than elsewhere in the country and rooms are scarcer than most cities of its size. The following price breakdowns reflect that reality and you should always book as far in advance as possible. All hotels listed in this chapter have rooms with private bathrooms, and most include air-conditioning and TVs.

On the whole, Caracas' budget accommodations are poor, lacking charm and located in unimpressive, almost always unsafe areas. Most budget haunts double as love hotels (renting by the hour) and some as brothels. Caracas also has plentiful four- and five-star hotels charging hefty rates, though some top-end hotels offer temptingly low rates on weekends; ask in advance.

You will be incalculably happier and safer if you sleep in the eastern suburbs and visit the attractions in the city center by metro during the day.

### The Center & Parque Central

Other than the options listed below, decent, reasonably priced accommodations are scarce in the old core of town. And though the zone bustles during the day, by 8pm or 9pm everything shuts down and there's not a soul about, so you won't want to linger long outside the confines of your lodging.

#### BUDGET

**Plaza Catedral Hotel** (Map pp58-9; ☎ 564-2111; plazacatedral@cantv.net; Plaza Bolívar; s/d/tr incl breakfast BsF130/170/240; M Capitolio/El Silencio; ) Some travelers have been less than pleased, but it's still hard to fault this cheapie option smack dab on the corner of the plaza: the best rooms have big balconies facing it. Light sleepers may want an interior room, however, as the cathedral's bells clang every 15 minutes.

**Hotel Grand Galaxie** (Map pp58-9; ☎ 864-9011; www.hotelgrandgalaxie.com; cnr Caja de Agua; s/d/ste BsF140/170/190; ) This modern, eight-story tower is an oddity in the otherwise rough-and-tumble Altagracia area, four blocks north of Plaza Bolívar. It's often packed with visiting employees of the nearby Education Ministry, whom you may run into at the adjacent tasca, which glows an atmospheric violet.

**Hotel Inter** (Map pp58-9; ☎ 564-6448; btwn Animas & Calero; s/d/q BsF150/180/230; Ⓜ Parque Carabobo; Ⓟ ❄) Don't expect a warm welcome, but this crotchety old guesthouse conveniently placed near the tasca zone of La Candelaria. It has good budget rates and super-funky bathrooms.

### MIDRANGE & TOP END

**Hotel New Jersey** (Map pp58-9; ☎ 571-4624; Av Este, cnr Paradero; s/d BsF200/250; Ⓜ Bellas Artes; ❄) This basic and clean low-rise in the somewhat easier-going section of the center near Parque Central makes a shady budget choice. Rooms are relatively large and well maintained, with a cheery palette of colors and assorted decorative elements from over the decades – though it must be said, from a security standpoint, that this was the only hotel in Caracas that let us see a room unaccompanied. The atmospheric attached tasca is usually packed with businesspeople.

**Hotel Renovación** (Map pp58-9; ☎ 571-0133; www.hotelrenovacion.com; Av Este 2 No 154, cnr El Patronato; s/d/ste BsF200/250/260; Ⓜ Bellas Artes; ❄) This exceedingly narrow, orange-brick building is on the eastern edge of the central grid, a relatively safe zone near the museums. The hotel has some of the city's friendlier staff, and the rooms, though basic, are zealously looked after and painted in bright primary colors.

**Hotel Ávila** (Map pp52-3; ☎ 555-3000; www.hotelavila.com.ve; Av Jorge Washington; s/d incl breakfast BsF350/420; ❄ 📶 🏊) Built by Nelson Rockefeller in the 1940s, the Ávila is a throwback to a less traffic-choked age. Enjoying a secluded position at the base of the Ávila range, the grand old hotel has two ivory wings offering commanding balcony views. There's no air-con but at these cool heights the ceiling fans are more than adequate, and you'll be lulled to sleep by the chorus of tree frogs. A huge buffet breakfast is served out on the rear deck near an oval aquamarine pool. Its steadfast refusal to update its well-worn elevator insures it remains a relic of a bygone era. From the metro Belles Artes, take Metrobús 421, a 15-minute ride.

**Hotel Alba Caracas** (Map pp58-9; ☎ 503-4203; www.hotel-albacaracas.com.ve; Av Sur 25 at Av México, Parque Central; s/d BsF537/600; Ⓜ Bellas Artes; ❄ 📶 🏊) The government took over this former Hilton in 2007, but it remains a five-star option in an unbeatable location – facing Parque Central and connected by a footbridge to the Teresa Carreño cultural complex. Its trump cards are a convenient location for museum hopping, lofty views of the concrete jungle from the top floors, tennis courts, a couple of pools and a state-of-the-art gym. Ironically enough, however, is it the socialist hotel that is one of the few in the city to charge for wi-fi, a whopping BsF17 per hour.

## Sabana Grande & Around

The dodgy neighborhood of Sabana Grande previously was the go-to spot for budget accommodations for shoestring travelers – albeit in love motels, not hostels – but the area has declined to such a state that sleeping here is nearly a guarantee of assault, robbery or endless harassment. Day or night, prostitution, petty theft and violent street crime thrive – and it's not a place to wander aimlessly or appear foreign (within our first two hours there, we were stopped twice by police and creatively robbed by a group if teenagers). It does, however, still house the city's only (sort of) hostel and some relatively safe options on the higher end (if you are entering or exiting with a driver or private taxi), and a few lively nightclubs. Never walk here at night without a local, never withdraw money from any ATM outside a shopping mall and never close the eyes in the back of your head.

There are two **police checkpoints** in the area – one that some say is sitting specifically to hassle backpackers around the corner from The Backpacker's Hostel. Both should be avoided if possible.

### BUDGET

**The Backpacker's Hostel** (Map p63; ☎ 761-5431; Calle El Colegio; s/d/tr/q BsF80/120/140/170) Occupying the second floor of the Nuestro love motel, this is Caracas' only shoestring-oriented option amid a hostel atmosphere. It's run by a doting Portuguese couple and offers up-to-date travel information, free luggage storage and a 2nd-floor terrace where travelers gather under a mango tree, firing back *cervezas* (beers) and ogling the gritty streets below. It's ultra-basic, but fills a niche. Sadly, you need a teleporter to get in and out safely given its location in Sabana Grande.

### MIDRANGE & TOP END

**Hotel City** (Map p63; ☎ 793-5785; Av Bolivia; s/d BsF230/260; Ⓜ Plaza Venezuela; Ⓟ ❄) Not only is the Hotel City a well-maintained, comfortable nest with quirky design nuances (Asian tearoom shower doors alongside European country-house tiling) set amid this zone's mean streets, it also allows a quick getaway: the metro station is practically on the doorstep. It's not luxurious, but boasts extra comfort in this price range; a friendly, service-oriented staff; and a landmark location, recognized citywide, in the shadow of the Previsora building.

**Gran Meliá Caracas** (Map p63; ☎ 762-8111; www.granmeliacaracas.solmelia.com; Av Casanova cnr Calle El Recreo; r incl breakfast from BsF722; Ⓜ Sabana Grande; ) One of Caracas' grand dames, the 436-room Gran Meliá is its largest luxury hotel. It's set back from Sabana Grande's tough streets by a gala driveway, leading to an urban oasis featuring a startling sunset-toned lobby, wildly popular pool with cascading fountain, and a restaurant that makes its Sunday brunch look like a work of art. It's cheaper than Altamira and Las Mercedes' luxury options, but you won't come out ahead due to the compulsory need to use taxis for any movement whatsoever.

## Las Mercedes & Around

For easy access to the city's chief restaurant and nightlife zone, stay in Las Mercedes or El Rosal, though anything outside the luxury category is likely to rent rooms by the hour.

**The Hotel** (Map p72; ☎ 951-9268; www.thehotel.com.ve; Calle Mohedano; r BsF605, ste from BsF925; Ⓜ Chacaíto; ) This sleek, boutique business hotel offers a collision of Bali and Milan inside an L-shaped white sentinel building in modish Las Mercedes. Everything is designed for the hip young exec, from the lobby brimming with flat-screen TVs to the globally decorated DVD-equipped rooms. Shower-shy folks should avoid if not traveling solo: these all-glass numbers next to the bed leave little to the imagination (echoing local sentiment that it's merely a boutique love motel!).

**Hotel Paseo Las Mercedes** (Map p72; ☎ 993-1244; www.hotelpaseolasmercedes.com; Centro Comercial Paseo Las Mercedes; r from BsF616; ) Since so much of Caracas life revolves around shopping complexes, it figures that a hotel should be part of one. The prevalence of white wicker furniture gives an oddly Club Med feel to the rooms at this upscale offering in the chic mall of the same name, but with lower prices than other top-end hotels in the city (rates drop another BsF120 on weekends) and a prime location for restaurants and nightlife, it's hard walk away based on inept decor.

## Altamira & Around

The upmarket district of Altamira has some good midrange accommodations that are well worth considering. Travelers who'd prefer not to brave the rougher climes of Sabana Grande and the center will find this a safe, attractive area, based around a large bustling plaza and dotted with excellent restaurants and nightspots – all just 15 minutes from the center by metro.

### MIDRANGE

**Hotel Gioly** (Map p72; ☎ 286-7767; cnr Av San Ignacio de Loyola & Calle Páez; d/tr BsF220/250; Ⓜ Chacao; ) There's no tourism-oriented hospitality at this 45-room, is-it-or-isn't-it love motel (they shy from reservations), but it's hard to beat for price and location, set on a bustling, working-class but safe commercial street in Chacao, just two blocks south of Centro San Ignacio. Recently renovated rooms are surprisingly nice, with LCD televisions and some with extra room for small tables. You can walk to everything in Altamira, La Castellena, El Rosal and Los Palos Grandes from here, day or night.

**Hotel La Floresta** (Map p72; ☎ 263-1955; www.hotellafloresta.com; Av Ávila; s/d/tr incl breakfast from BsF255/310/330; Ⓜ Altamira; ) La Floresta is a 10-story block of smallish rooms with attached balconies; those on the north side get a good glimpse of the mango-dotted La Estancia estate. Ongoing renovations have boosted the comfort level on floors seven to nine. A continental breakfast in the downstairs lounge is on the house, though you'd be better off at the cafe next door.

**Hotel Altamira** (Map p72; ☎ 267-4284; Av José Félix Sosa, cnr Av Altamira Sur; r BsF280; Ⓜ Altamira; ) Positioned away from the plaza on a quiet street, the climate-cooled Altamira is a good, clean and basic choice for thrifty travelers who want relative safety. Front-facing rooms have a small balcony, which may not have picture-perfect views but which do give an interesting angle on the city, looking over a small, haphazardly built *barrio* to the skyscrapers and mountain beyond.

**Hotel Campo Alegre** (Map p72; ☎ 265-3946; 2a Calle de Campo Alegre; s/d/tr BsF280/320/360; Ⓜ Altamira; ) Tucked away in a quieter location than some midrange options in the area, this secure, somewhat friendly option is clean and fuss-free. It's walking distance from both Chacao and Altamira Metro stations, supermarkets and Centro San Ignacio and there's a generous 2pm check-out time.

**Hotel Residencia Montserrat** (Map p72; ☎ 263-3533; Av Ávila; r/tr BsF325/BsF446; Ⓜ Altamira; ❄) This seven-story box with a checkerboard facade holds an excellent position just down from Plaza de Francia and the metro. Accommodations are far more basic than the lobby suggests, with faux mid-century-modern furniture and an aged air, but the soccer field–size suites with kitchens and ample balconies (the checker squares) give oblique views of the plaza.

**our pick** **Hotel Residencial El Cid** (Map p72; ☎ 263-2611; cumarucidhotel@hotmail.com; Av San Felipe btwn 1a & 2a Transversal; s/d/tr BsF381/484/618; Ⓜ Altamira; ❄ 💻) Setting itself apart from the rest in a nondescript zone west of the plaza, this safely enclosed hotel sports a suitably faded Spanish aristocrat theme. Noble carved hardwoods abound in the old-school lobby and computer room, while apartments pack in a salon with DirectTV, kitchenettes and heavy, colonial wood furniture. It offers the most character of the midrangers here as well as a cute and feisty front desk staff.

### TOP END

**our pick** **Pestana Caracas** (Map pp52-3; ☎ 208-1900; www.pestana.com; 1a Av, Santa Eduvigis; s/d incl breakfast BsF923/969; Ⓜ Miranda; ❄ 📶 🏊) If you're missing LA, this Portuguese-owned luxury chain is Caracas' newest and hippest hotel, a perfect homesickness treatment. Opened in 2008, it's truly the city's only fully equipped modern design hotel and packs in plenty of coolness within its walls. The rooftop infinity pool and adjacent hotspot lounge – featuring a kaleidoscopic array of clean-lined acrylic bar stools – are Caracas' latest see-and-be-seen abode. The 195 rooms lean a tad too minimalist, but such is how it goes when you're paying more for cool than comfort.

**Hotel Centro Lido** (Map p72; ☎ 957-7777; www.lidotelhotelboutique.com; Av Francisco de Miranda; s/d/tr incl breakfast BsF934/985; Ⓜ Chacao; ❄ 📶 🏊) Though the Caracas Palace is amidst more pleasant surroundings, this upscale business hotel in the heart of Francisco de Miranda in El Rosal offers way more heart and jazz. Rates include use of the spa and the gymnasium-sized fitness center, and they often throw in a bottle of wine as well. Rooms are sizable, with extra-large marble bathrooms. If your Caracas business trip has you and yours apprehensive, it's located in Centro Lido mall, so you could conceivably not leave your hotel if you so chose.

**Hotel Caracas Palace** (Map p72; ☎ 771-1000; www.caracaspalace.com; Av Luis Roche, cnr Av Francisco de Miranda; s/d incl breakfast from BsF1074/1204; Ⓜ Altamira; ❄ 📶 🏊) This former Four Seasons lost much of its soul when the luxe Canadian chain pulled out of Caracas a few years ago – it's now a massive piece of modernist architecture that feels somewhat Soviet in its eerie quietness. Located right across from the pleasant Plaza de Francia, its saving grace is a wonderful cascading split-level pool on an elevated deck.

**Hotel Altamira Suites** (Map p72; ☎ 285-2555; www.hotelaltamirasuites.com; cnr 1a Av & 1a Transversal; ste from BsF1213; Ⓜ Altamira; ❄ 📶 🏊) Sitting on lush grounds a few blocks north of Plaza de Francia, this extremely secure corporate hotel is designed for longer stays. Suites come in two classes but the layout is the same, with a kitchen, living room and narrow balconies. Ongoing renovations have thrown in a masculine touch to the kitchens, and brighter hallways on floors 2 to 4 and 10 to 13. The hip 360° Roofbar (p75) offers a panoramic cocktail for the city's bold and beautiful.

## EATING

You could eat out three times a day for several years without ever visiting the same restaurant twice in Caracas. For more ideas, the indispensable **Guía Gastronómica de Caracas** (Caracas Gastronomic Guide; www.miropopic.com/gastronomica) is a must-have resource for discovering the local cuisine scene.

If you're on a budget, keep an eye out for the *menú del día* or *menú ejecutivo* (set menu with two or three courses) for BsF40 to BsF60. Inexpensive rotisseried chicken restaurants and *areperas* (restaurants selling *arepas* – small, thick corn pancakes) also abound. For breakfast, go to any of the ubiquitous *panaderías* (bakeries). During lunch, countless tascas come alive, particularly in La Candelaria (opposite) – though tread very carefully in this area at night.

Trendy suburbs such as Las Mercedes, Altamira and La Castellana boast dozens of upmarket restaurants serving a worldwide range of delicacies. Depending on the exchange rate secured, some of the city's finest dining experiences can be had for less than you might expect. For example, a BsF100 main course is around $23 at the official rate, but as low as $15 at the parallel rate.

With everyone devoting so much time to shopping, malls can also provide substantial options, with food courts offering far more than the usual bland franchises. You'll find a particularly worthy selection at El Recreo, Tolón, Sambil and Paseo Las Mercedes shopping malls (p77).

## Restaurants

### THE CENTER & PARQUE CENTRAL

While it doesn't abound in chic restaurants, the center has plenty of low-priced eateries, many of which serve local fare known as *comida criolla.* La Candelaria, the area east of Av Fuerzas Armadas, is swamped with top-end tascas.

#### Budget

**Restaurant Beirut** (Map pp58-9; Salvador de León a Socarrás; Mains BsF17-29; lunch Mon-Sat; M La Hoyada) Don't let the facade deter you – this atmospheric lunch place serves up northern Lebanese cuisine in a far more welcoming atmosphere than first impressions call for.

**Lunchería Doña Agapita** (Map pp58-9; ☎ 573-4398; Av Sur 13 btwn La Cruz & Miguelacho; cachapas BsF23-29; 8:30am-7:30pm; M Parque Carabobo) Excellent *cachapas* (corn pancakes that end up looking like a ménage-a-trois of a pancake, omelet and taco) stuffed with ham and/or cheese are griddled to oblivion at this no-nonsense spot.

**Restaurant El Coyuco** (Map pp58-9; ☎ 572-6246; Av Urdaneta, btwn Candilito & Platanal; half chicken with sides BsF27; lunch & dinner; M Parque Carabobo) Mouthwatering grilled chicken is what's served up in this vast, smoky dining hall on the main drag. Order your bird *con todo* for sides of yucca, salad and a *hallaquita* (mini tamale) – then fight the masses for a table.

#### Midrange & Top End

**La Cocina de Francy** (Map pp58-9; ☎ 576-9849; Av Este 2, cnr Tracabordo; mains BsF45-75; breakfast & lunch Mon-Sat; M Parque Carabobo; ) Instead of Spanish fare, this tasca-style restaurant specializes in delicious Venezuelan cuisine rooted in ancestral recipes. Check out the *pelao guayanés,* a soulful chicken stew laced with herbs and olive oil, or the *pabellón criollo,* Venezuela's national dish of rice, black beans, fried plantains and shredded beef. The burlap tablecloths and funky art are a nice touch.

**Mi Linda Llanura** (Map pp58-9; ☎ 863-2799; Edificio Capitolio, Piso 2, cnr Padre Sierra, Centro; mains BsF48-60; Thu-Sun; M Capitolio/El Silencio) For a taste of Los Llanos in the capital, this rooftop party terrace has breezy views over the Asemblea Nacional and serious *llanero* cuisine, such as *carne en vara* (beef on a stick), all set to a

### TASCAS – THE SPANISH CONNECTION

The legacy of an early-20th-century wave of immigration from Spain and the Canary Islands, tascas (Spanish-style bar-restaurants) are dotted around town, but are most heavily concentrated in the Candelaria neighborhood at the east end of the center – there are 20 within a four-block stretch around the zone's central plaza, making tasca-hopping an entirely feasible activity. The following places retain an extraordinary degree of Iberian character, down to the tile murals, cured hams hanging from the rafters and tie-clad waiters who cultivate that peculiarly Spanish brand of brusqueness. Unfortunately, crime has forced most of the once-thriving nightly camaraderie here out of the center after dark – it's much safer to make it a nice, long lunch. Entrees generally feed two.

**Tasca Mallorca** (Map pp58-9; ☎ 572-5974; Av Este btwn Alcabala & Puente Anauco; mains BsF28-130; M Parque Carabobo; ) This small, cozy place has just a few tables alongside the bar.

**Tasca La Carabela** (Map pp58-9; ☎ 578-3029; Av Urdaneta, cnr Urupal; mains BsF38-130; lunch Mon-Sat; M Parque Carabobo; ) Time stands still in this animated spot by the plaza, where an entire wall is dominated by a wooden ship relief.

**Casa Farruco** (Map pp58-9; ☎ 572-9343; Av Este 2 btwn Peligro & Puente República; mains BsF49-159; M Parque Carabobo; ) Decorated with beautiful tile work and ship models, this atmospheric locale offers tranquil dining upstairs and a boisterous bar downstairs.

**La Cita** (Map pp58-9; ☎ 572-8180; cnr Alcabala; mains BsF58-117; lunch & dinner; M Parque Carabobo; ) This corner classic is one of the liveliest in the zone, with ham hocks hanging from the bar and a roaring lunch crowd. Go for the *caldeirada mero con mariscos*, a fish and seafood stew.

country-fried soundtrack of *joropo*. The top floor dining room is rowdier than the other one floor below.

**our pick** **Café Casa Veroes** (Map pp58-9; ☎ 564-7457; Casa de Estudio de la Historia de Venezuela Lorenzo Mendoza Quintero, Veroes a Jesuitas; mains BsF65-85; lunch Mon-Fri; M Capitolio/El Silencio; ) On your walk up to Pantéon Nacional, search out this hidden, open-air cafe tucked away in the leafy backyard of a home-turned-museum donated by the Polar beer family – it's a true local's secret. There's a daily rotating chalkboard menu of modern Venezuelan creations and some of the city's best coffee. You might not make it to the Pantéon.

### SABANA GRANDE & AROUND

Av Francisco Solano is Sabana Grande's major culinary artery. Here budget restaurants, cafes and snack bars abound, though considering safety before cost-cutting isn't a bad idea in this area. Lunch is generally fine, but after dark you're better off heading to Altamira or Las Mercedes, where the food is far more interesting.

#### Budget

**Arepera 24 Horas** (Map p63; Av Casanova, cnr Prolongación Sur Acacias; arepas BsF18-22; 24hr; M Plaza Venezuela) Open round-the-clock as the name suggests, this big, busy, open-air joint is always good for a well-stuffed *arepa* – choose from classic *caraqueños* fillings in the display case, such as *carne mechado*, a shredded beef.

#### Midrange

**El Caserio** (Map p63; ☎ 762-0614; cnr Av Francisco Solano & Av Los Mangos; mains BsF38-78; lunch & dinner; M Sabana Grande) This charming, Spanish-owned tasca features low, wood-beamed ceilings extending out from an atmospheric central bar, the whole surroundings of which are packed on weekends and for important soccer matches. The seafood and steaks are both excellent, as are the waiters decked out in traditional *bufanda* bandanas around their necks. There's a guard out front, so safety is a priority.

**La Estación del Pollo** (Map p63; ☎ 793-3366; cnr Av Casanova & Av Acacia; half-chicken with sides BsF44; noon-11pm; M Plaza Venezuela) This popular dining hall has racks upon racks of chickens roasting over coals and attentive waiters rushing them to your table, along with the obligatory side of yucca laced with *guasacaca* sauce.

### LAS MERCEDES & AROUND

Eating out is a passion for *caraqueños*, and nowhere is that more obvious than in the fashionable dining district of Las Mercedes. Competition here is fierce, with 100 restaurants closely packed into a 30-block area. Unfortunately it's not a great place to walk around: SUVs and other status vehicles jam the streets and sidewalks function more as car parks than pedestrian thoroughfares. From Chacaíto metro station, take the 'CC Expreso' exit to catch Metrobús 222 to Las Mercedes.

#### Budget

**Restaurant Real Past** (Map p72; ☎ 993-6702; Av Río de Janeiro btwn Calle Monterrey & Av Jalisco; pastas BsF18-24; lunch & dinner) Catering to students and other cash-strapped types, Real Past prides itself on house-made pasta and excellent pizza at dirt-cheap prices.

**La Casa del Llano** (Map p72; ☎ 991-7342; Av Río de Janeiro; mains BsF19-27; 24hr) A veritable *arepa* factory, this huge no-nonsense diner sticks to traditional plain fare. Hungry locals flock here not just for the *arepas* but for charcoal-grilled steaks and hearty soups.

#### Midrange & Top End

**Café Olé** (Map p72; ☎ 993-9059; cnr Calle California & Calle Jalisco; mains BsF43-82; breakfast, lunch & dinner) This chain has caught on like a California wildfire in Caracas, but here lies its beginnings. Sophisticated wraps, burgers, sandwiches and salads are served in an artistic cafe atmosphere and on a lovely candlelit patio. There's enough hotness here to sink a Cold War battleship. Additional locations include Centro San Ignacio.

**our pick** **Mokambo** (Map p72; ☎ 991-2577; Calle Madrid, cnr Monterrey; mains BsF49-91; lunch & dinner daily, plus breakfast Sat & Sun) Expertly fusing Mediterranean and Caribbean elements in a upscale, jungly setting, Mokambo offer scrumptious and surprising dishes, such as duck risotto in orange-sesame reduction; or the local cheese plate, made in the suburbs by an ex-Argentine guerrilla, current *Opositión* cheesemonger.

**El Maute Grill** (Map p72; ☎ 991-0892; Av Rio de Janeiro; steak BsF82-104; lunch & dinner) Don't let the ramshackle exterior alter your course: this steakhouse – wildly popular with *chavistas* – serves some of the best beef around, in an open-air courtyard surrounded by brick walls full of Venezuelan-empowering pop culture.

### ALTAMIRA & AROUND

Altamira is an area dotted with upmarket restaurants, hip cafes, discos and bars, as are its neighboring suburbs of La Castellana and Los Palos Grandes.

#### Budget

**Automercados Campitos** (Map p72; ☎ 263-0098; Av Blandin, cnr Calle San Marino; 7am-9pm Mon-Sat, 8am-7pm Sun; M Chacao) For self-caterers.

**Pastissima** (Map p72; ☎ 264-0101; Av San Marino, cnr Calle Guaicaipuro; pizza BsF5.50-7.50, pasta BsF37-55; lunch Mon, lunch & dinner Tue-Sun; M Chacao) This smart pasta deli offers a wealth of homemade ravioli, tortellini and gnocchi, which you marry with fresh sauces of your choice, and individual gourmet pizzas, all handily available for takeaway. Tough to beat for the price.

**Gran Horizonte** (Map p72; Av Blandin; arepas BsF13-23, mains BsF25-69; 24hr; M Chacao) This wildly popular all-hours *arepera* near the Centro San Ignacio is a perfect spot for your first *arepa* – try the *mixto con pernil* and douse each bite in its house salsas (go easy on the red one). Sandwiches, soups and salads are also served.

**El Budaré de la Castellana** (Map p72; ☎ 263-5475; Av Eugenio Mendoza; arepas BsF17-25, mains BsF26-68; 24hr; M Altamira) This bustling, two-level restaurant offers good *cachapas, arepas* and other Venezuelan standards. Mention it to a local and you'll consistently hear one thing: 'classic.'

**Helados 4D** (Map p72; ☎ 121-7313; Av 4a btwn 3a & 4a Transversal, Altamira; ice cream BsF21-66; lunch & dinner; M Altamira) The only thing Venezuelans love more than cheap gas is this Italian-style ice cream. Get in line. Enjoy!

**Miga's** (Map p72; cnr 1a Transversal & Av Luis Roche; sandwiches BsF29-36; breakfast, lunch & dinner) A slightly spiffier indoor/outdoor bakery-cafe with army of servers pimping super-fast breakfasts (BsF14 to BsF28), hefty sandwiches, sweet pastries and a handful of rarer fare like shrimp and calamari wraps and Thai salads.

**Chef Woo** (Map p72; ☎ 285-1723; 1a Av, Los Palos Grandes; mains BsF29-72; lunch & dinner; M Altamira) This lively, neighborhood Chinese restaurant is popular for its tasty Szechuan fare and even more so in the evening for its cheap beer.

**El Mundo del Pollo** (Map p72; ☎ 267-2011; cnr Av Blandin & Calle Mohedano; chicken combos BsF37-50; lunch & dinner; M Chacao) Puts other South American *pollerías* to shame: the rotisserie chicken served here, in a clean, well-to-do carnivore's temple, is transcendent!

#### Midrange & Top End

**Café Il Botticello** (Map p72; ☎ 266-1618; 2a Transversal; pizzas BsF32-54; lunch & dinner Mon-Sat; M Altamira) Small enough to fill up fast, this unpretentious Italian bistro produces some decent pizza.

**Nobu** (Map p72; ☎ 285-9009; Centro Comercial Las Cúpulas, 2a Av, cnr 5a Transversal; sushi rolls BsF35-68, mains BsF41-69; lunch & dinner; M Miranda) It's not everyday that sushi this good comes this cheap, nor is it usually paired with Thai food, but you'll cure the Asian cravin' here, at any rate. Nobu is one of a string of modish restaurants with terrace seating at a 'gastronomic shopping mall' in a quiet corner of the Los Palos Grandes district. There is no affiliation with world-renowned Japanese chef Nobu Matsuhisa – in fact, he should probably sue.

**Evio's Pizzeria** (Map p72; ☎ 283-6608; 4a Av btwn 2a & 3a Transversal; pizzas BsF37-130; lunch & dinner; M Miranda) There's pizza and then there's the city's best. When famous Venezuelan composer Evio de Marzo isn't performing, he makes gourmet pizza – six styles to be exact. Locals pack this joint for their favorite – goat cheese and sundried tomato – as well as pasta, empanadas and ice-cold Polar.

**La Guayaba Verde** (Map pp52-3; ☎ 285-9245; www.guayabaverde.com; Av Rómulo Gallegos, Edificio Pascal, Santa Eduvigis; set menu BsF45, mains BsF58-62; lunch Mon, lunch & dinner Tue-Sat; M Miranda) This wonderful *comida venezolana* hotspot got an upgrade both in space and location, moving from the edgier center to the safe confines of Santa Eduvigis. Here you'll find Chef Eduardo Castañeda's healthy-ish takes on his country's dynamic cuisine, from a Trinidad- and Tobago-influenced curried shrimp wrapped in roti to upscale *tequeños*, a local staple of bread dough stuffed with white cheese.

our pick **Catar** (Map p72; ☎ 285-0649; Cuadra Gastronómica, 6a Transversal; mains BsF45-76; lunch & dinner Tue-Sat, lunch Sun; M Miranda) One of several restaurants in the culinary mall known as the Cuadra Gastronómica, Catar has aggressively eclectic food, with a funky, mismatched decor to match. The emphasis is on fresh, natural ingredients, which show up in artistically presented sandwiches, carpaccios and lovely artisanal pizzas. Don't miss it.

**Chirú** (Map p72; ☎ 285-1960; Centro Comercial Las Cúpulas, 2a Av, cnr 5a Transversal; mains BsF59-83; lunch & dinner Tue-Sun; M Miranda) Next door to Nobu, this popular spot with terrace seating does eclectic Chinese-Peruvian, or Chirú cuisine, and a damn fine job at that. The *degustación*

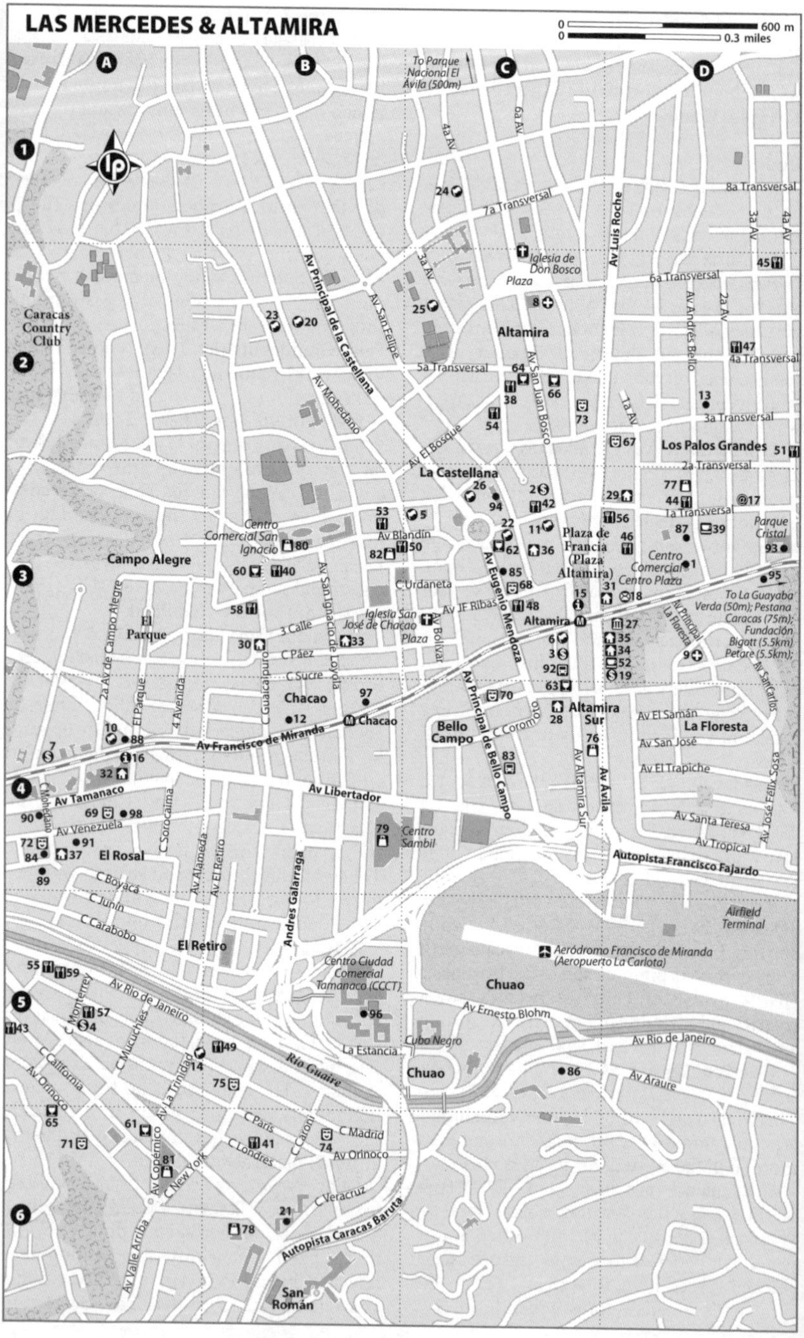
LAS MERCEDES & ALTAMIRA
0
600 m
0
0.3 miles
A
B
C
D
1
2
3
4
5
6
To Parque Nacional El Ávila (500m)
8a Transversal
7a Transversal
6a Transversal
5a Transversal
4a Transversal
3a Transversal
2a Transversal
1a Transversal
4a Av
3a Av
6a Av
2a Av
1a Av
Av Luis Roche
Av Andrés Bello
Iglesia de Don Bosco
Plaza
Altamira
Av San Juan Bosco
Av Principal de la Castellana
Av San Felipe
Av Mohedano
Av El Bosque
La Castellana
Los Palos Grandes
Caracas Country Club
Centro Comercial San Ignacio
Av Blandín
C Urdaneta
Av JF Ribas
Iglesia San José de Chacao
Plaza
Av Bolívar
Av Eugenio Mendoza
Plaza de Francia (Plaza Altamira)
Centro Comercial Centro Plaza
Parque Cristal
To La Guayaba Verda (50m); Pestana Caracas (75m); Fundación Bigott (5.5km); Petare (5.5km);
Av Principal La Floresta
Av San Carlos
Campo Alegre
El Parque
2a Av de Campo Alegre
El Parque
4 Avenida
3 Calle
Av San Ignacio de Loyola
C Páez
C Sucre
C Guaicaipuro
Chacao
Av Francisco de Miranda
Chacao
Av Principal de Bello Campo
Bello Campo
C Coromoto
Altamira Sur
Av Altamira Sur
Av Ávila
Av El Samán
La Floresta
Av San José
Av El Trapiche
Av José Félix Sosa
Av Santa Teresa
Av Tropical
Autopista Francisco Fajardo
Av Tamanaco
C Mohedano
Av Venezuela
El Rosal
C Sorocaima
Av Libertador
Centro Sambil
Av Alameda
Av El Retiro
Andres Galarraga
C Boyacá
C Junín
C Carabobo
El Retiro
Airfield Terminal
Aeródromo Francisco de Miranda (Aeropuerto La Carlota)
Chuao
Centro Ciudad Comercial Tamanaco (CCCT)
Av Ernesto Blohm
Av Rio de Janeiro
Cubo Negro
La Estancia
Chuao
Río Guaire
Av Araure
C Monterrey
C Mucuchíes
Av La Trinidad
C California
Av Orinoco
C París
C Caroní
C Madrid
C Londres
Av Orinoco
Av Copérnico
C New York
C Veracruz
Autopista Caracas Baruta
Av Valle Arriba
San Román

*de ceviche* (raw fish or seafood marinated in lime juice and spices) is outstanding, as is the *chupe de camerones*, an Incan-style shrimp chowder.

**Aprile** (Map p72; ☎ 264-5775; 4a Av & 5ta Transversal; mains BsF62-80; lunch & dinner Tue-Sun; Ⓜ Altamira) Much of Caracas' high society has left the country or disappeared under the radar during the Chávez era – this is one of the spots you'll find them. The marble bar attracts a beautiful, mature drinking crowd, while the limited Italian menu serves up excellent *ceviches* (try the salmon martini!), carpaccios and risottos.

**Alto** (Map p72; ☎ 284-3655; 1a Av at 3a Transversal de Los Palos Grandes; mains BsF78-145, menu BsF320; lunch & dinner Mon-Fri, dinner Sat) *Caraqueños* bowed down yo Chef Carlos Garcia's bold cuisine and decor from the moment the doors opened in 2007: Alto became an instant culinary icon. Local ingredients built around a vanguard Euro-Catalonian framework make dishes like *cordero al café* (rack of lamb in coffee sauce) worth shelling out the big bolívares. Reservations essential.

### EL HATILLO

Well known for its numerous eating outlets, the outlying colonial village of El Hatillo boasts an extraordinary variety of cuisines for adventurous palates.

**INFORMATION**

| | | |
|---|---|---|
| Al Giorno | (see 80) | |
| American Book Shop | 1 | D3 |
| Banco de Venezuela | 2 | C3 |
| Banesco | 3 | C3 |
| Banesco | 4 | A5 |
| Brazilian Embassy | 5 | C3 |
| Canadian Embassy | 6 | C3 |
| Citibank | 7 | A4 |
| Clínica El Ávila | 8 | C2 |
| Clínica Instituto Médico La Floresta | 9 | D3 |
| Colombian Embassy | 10 | A4 |
| Dutch Consulate | 11 | C3 |
| El Buscón | (see 78) | |
| Farmatodo | 12 | B4 |
| Farmatodo | 13 | D2 |
| French Embassy | 14 | A5 |
| German Consulate | (see 26) | |
| Information Kiosk Chacao | (see 80) | |
| Information Kiosk Chacao | 15 | C3 |
| Information Kiosk Chacao | 16 | A4 |
| Intermanía | 17 | D3 |
| Ipostel | 18 | D3 |
| Italcambio | 19 | D3 |
| Italian Consulate | 20 | B2 |
| IVI Venezuela | 21 | B6 |
| Japanese Consulate | 22 | C3 |
| Lavandería Automatica Maxi Clean | (see 42) | |
| Spanish Embassy | 23 | B2 |
| Suriname Embassy | 24 | C1 |
| Tecni-Ciencia Libros | (see 32) | |
| Tecni-Ciencia Libros | (see 79) | |
| Trinidad & Tobago Embassy | 25 | C2 |
| UK Embassy | 26 | C3 |

**SIGHTS & ACTIVITIES**

| | | |
|---|---|---|
| La Estancia | 27 | D3 |

**SLEEPING**

| | | |
|---|---|---|
| Hotel Altamira | 28 | C4 |
| Hotel Altamira Suites | 29 | D3 |
| Hotel Campo Alegre | 30 | B3 |
| Hotel Caracas Palace | 31 | D3 |
| Hotel Centro Lido | 32 | A4 |
| Hotel Gioly | 33 | B3 |
| Hotel La Floresta | 34 | D3 |
| Hotel Paseo Las Mercedes | (see 78) | |
| Hotel Residencia Montserrat | 35 | D3 |
| Hotel Residencial El Cid | 36 | C3 |
| The Hotel | 37 | A4 |

**EATING**

| | | |
|---|---|---|
| Alto | (see 67) | |
| Aprile | 38 | C2 |
| Arábica Coffee Bar | 39 | D3 |
| Automercados Campitos | 40 | B3 |
| Auyama Café | 41 | B6 |
| Café Il Botticello | 42 | C3 |
| Cafe Olé | 43 | A5 |
| Cafe Olé | (see 80) | |
| Café St Honoré | 44 | D3 |
| Catar | 45 | D2 |
| Chef Woo | 46 | D3 |
| Chirú | 47 | D2 |
| El Budaré de la Castellana | 48 | C3 |
| El Maute Grill | 49 | B5 |
| El Mundo del Pollo | 50 | B3 |
| Evio's Pizzeria | 51 | D2 |
| Flor de Castilla | 52 | D3 |
| Gran Horizonte | 53 | B3 |
| Helados 4D | 54 | C2 |
| La Casa del Llano | 55 | A5 |
| Miga's | 56 | D3 |
| Mokambo | 57 | A5 |
| Nobu | (see 47) | |
| Pastissima | 58 | B3 |
| Restaurant Real Past | 59 | A5 |

**DRINKING**

| | | |
|---|---|---|
| 360° Roofbar | (see 29) | |
| Barra Bar | 60 | B3 |
| Birras Pub & Café | 61 | A6 |
| Gran Pizzería El León | 62 | C3 |
| Greenwich Pub | 63 | C4 |
| Lola | 64 | C2 |
| Malabar | 65 | A6 |
| Suka | (see 80) | |
| Uvas | 66 | C2 |

**ENTERTAINMENT**

| | | |
|---|---|---|
| Celarg | 67 | D2 |
| Cool Café & Pub | 68 | C3 |
| Copa's Dancing Bar | (see 89) | |
| Discovery Bar | 69 | A4 |
| El Sarao | 70 | C4 |
| El Teatro | 71 | A6 |
| Juan Sebastián Bar | 72 | A4 |
| Little Rock Café | 73 | C2 |
| Rosalinda | 74 | B6 |
| Rumbar | 75 | B5 |
| Teatro Trasnocho Cultural | (see 78) | |

**SHOPPING**

| | | |
|---|---|---|
| Artesanía Altamira | 76 | C4 |
| Casa Curuba | 77 | D3 |
| Centro Comercial Paseo Las Mercedes | 78 | B6 |
| Centro Commercial Sambil | 79 | B4 |
| Centro San Ignacio | 80 | B3 |
| Fashion Mall Tolón | 81 | A6 |
| Mercado Chacao | 82 | B3 |

**TRANSPORT**

| | | |
|---|---|---|
| Aeroexpresos Ejecutivos | 83 | C4 |
| Aerolíneas Argentinas | 84 | A4 |
| Aeropostal | 85 | C3 |
| Air Canada | 86 | C5 |
| Air France | (see 93) | |
| Air France/KLM | (see 93) | |
| Alitalia | 87 | D3 |
| American Airlines | 88 | A4 |
| Aserca | 89 | A4 |
| Avianca | 90 | A4 |
| Avior | 91 | A4 |
| Buses To El Hatillo | 92 | C3 |
| Continental Airlines/Copa Airlines | (see 32) | |
| Cubana | (see 87) | |
| Delta Airlines | (see 32) | |
| Iberia | 93 | D3 |
| KLM | (see 93) | |
| LAN | (see 80) | |
| Lufthansa | 94 | C3 |
| Mexicana | 95 | D3 |
| Santa Bárbara | (see 32) | |
| TACA/LACSA | 96 | B5 |
| TACA/LACSA | 97 | B4 |
| Tam | 98 | A4 |
| Venezolana | (see 1) | |

**Hannsi Café** (☎ 963-5577; Calle Bolivar 12; snacks BsF5-15; lunch & dinner) This lovely cafe/gourmet food shop attached to the Hannsi crafts store is a gem, full of quick eats, fresh juices, excellent coffee and artisanal honey, hot sauce, coffee and cigars from all over Venezuela.

**Dulces Criollos** (☎ 961-3198; Calle La Paz; sweets BsF6-13; 8am-11pm) The sweet-toothed will have a field day in this traditional candy store on the plaza, which sells gooey cakes, jellied fruits and other local confections.

**La Gorda** (☎ 963-7476; Calle Santa Rosalia 9; mains BsF34-69; lunch & dinner) 'The fat lady' has been serving traditional Venezuelan dishes for decades. This is where some five-star hotels send guests who want to eat 'local.'

**Espetería** (☎ 961-5823; Calle Bolívar 9-1; kebabs BsF39-56; lunch & dinner Wed-Mon) Madeira-style kebabs are grilled – and served – on swords at this stone-walled eatery opposite the Hannsi crafts store.

our pick **Hajillo's** (☎ 961-4289; Calle Miranda; mains BsF45-72; lunch & dinner Tue-Sun) A block west and half a block north of the plaza, this small chef-managed restaurant offers some adventurous culinary hybrids of Venezuelan and Asian fare, with assuredly aphrodisiacal ingredients. Try the mango rice for a true experience: curried chicken and rice comes along with a cornucopia of flavor enhancers to mix in. Perfection!

### Cafes

A profusion of southern European-style cafe-bakeries offers a good selection of pastries and cookies in their display cases. These *pastelerías* (pastry shops) invariably have Italian espresso machines and prepare excellent, strong, hotter-than-Hades coffees of all ilk.

**Pasteleria Noyer Deli** (Map pp58-9; ☎ 541-1102; Av Norte, btwn Las Gradillas & Sociedad; snacks BsF4.50-8.50; 7am-7pm Mon-Sat; M Capitolio/El Silencio) This particularly appealing cafe-bakery near the Plaza Bolívar has fantastic apple strudel and other decadent treats.

**Flor de Castilla** (Map p72; ☎ 261-1955; Av Ávila; snacks BsF7-11, breakfast BsF19-37; breakfast, lunch & dinner; M Altamira) Equipped with a fresh juice bar and front terrace seating, this makes a perfect morning coffee stop for those lodged at nearby hotels. The cannolis, éclairs and other pastries are of an especially high standard.

**Café St Honoré** (Map p72; ☎ 286-7982; Av Andrés Bello, cnr 1a Transversal; pastries BsF8-18, sandwiches BsF43-63; breakfast, lunch & dinner; M Altamira) The greenery-enclosed deck at this modish bakery is perhaps the area's trendiest meeting place. Aside from amazing pastries, there are well-stuffed baguettes, quiche and breakfast specials.

**Gran Café** (Map p63; ☎ 763-6792; cnr Blvd de Sabana Grande & Pascual Navarro; sandwiches BsF15-42, mains BsF25-67; 7am-midnight; M Plaza Venezuela) 'It's not what it used to be,' you'll hear repeatedly in reference to the sad decay of the surrounding zone, but the Gran Café's boulevard terrace still makes a fine place to relax over coffee and croissants and people-watch for a while, hysterical warnings notwithstanding.

**Arábica Coffee Bar** (Map p72; ☎ 286-3636; Av Andrés Bello btwn 1a Transversal & Av Francisco de Miranda; breakfast BsF28-55; breakfast, lunch & dinner; M Altamira) Caffeine junkies unite here over the house-roasted beans whose waft is discernable up and down the block. Espresso, lattes and macchiatos on tap.

## DRINKING

The youthful bar scene centers around the districts Las Mercedes and La Castellana – the safest areas for nocturnal festivities. To that end, many shopping malls have become bastions of perceived security, especially for the well-to-do, and offer an authentically Venezuelan nightlife culture that feeds off the fear at street level. It doesn't require a high level of security awareness to realize that all those charming outdoor patios surrounded by lush vegetation are less about ambience and more about creating a barrier between the harsh realties of Caracas at street level and the inner sanctum of the city's middle and upper classes. To that end, the Blandin level of Centro San Ignacio in La Castellena and the fifth floor of Fashion Mall Tolón in Las Mercedes are both full of upscale watering holes and worth a wander.

### LAS MERCEDES & AROUND

Las Mercedes is the true pub-crawl area, full of rowdy bars fueled by *reggaetón* alongside more refined hotspots for a conversation and a cabernet.

**Birras Pub & Café** (Map p72; ☎ 992-4813; Av Principal de las Mercedes at Av Copérnico; from 5pm) Almost deviant in its lack of security, Birras is a rough-around-the-edges pavement bar at street level, totally exposed to the realities of sundown Caracas – no foliage fences or palm walls to hide behind here. Like Gran Pizzería El León, revelers flood its haphazardly-strewn plastic tables, where the Polars and Soleras pile up into the wee hours, but here without fuss over class or status.

**Maroma Roots** (Map p72; ☎ 993-0513; Calle París btwn Calles Mucuchíes & Monterrey; from 9pm Tue-Sun) The

Rasta bar. The upstairs lounge is where the real skanking goes on – a dim, smoky environment where a DJ works from the front section of an old bus, pumping out a righteous blend of dub, dancehall and more commercial reggae.

**Auyama Café** (Map p72; ☎ 991-4489; Calle Londres btwn Calles New York & Caroni; noon-late Mon-Sat) The *rumba* never stops at this boisterous, open-air lounge with a broad front terrace and various brightly lit salons. It's for a slightly more mature set, who may want to engage in more animated conversation than sweat-soaked shamelessness on the dance floor, but it doesn't stop the karaoke singing or salsa dancing.

**Malabar** (Map p72; ☎ 991-3131; Av Orinoco; 5pm-late Mon-Sat) Nouveau-vintage Malabar is one of the most sophisticated choices in Las Mercedes. Down a long hallway that heads behind the seemingly closed daytime-only restaurant of the same name, you'll find the jet set sipping classy cocktails and nibbling on Ital-Asian fusion on a gorgeous terraced seating arrangement split down the middle by a cascading, Zen-like stream.

### ALTAMIRA & AROUND

**Gran Pizzería El León** (Map p72; ☎ 263-6014; Plaza La Castellana; M Altamira) In Caracas nightlife terms, this famous beer-guzzling spot is known as a *predespacho* (pre-party), the first stop on a bender that can go until sunrise. It's an open-air affair on a vast terrace below towering buildings. At the weekend, you'll find masses of college-age drinkers and beyond jovially debating over row upon row of beer bottles, but it swells on most any night.

**Greenwich Pub** (Map p72; ☎ 267-1760; cnr Av Altamira Sur & Av José Félix Sosa; M Altamira) This supposedly English pub (No lager? No English speakers? No shepherd's pie?) is small, dark and dungeony, with a rock-and-roll attitude. The crowd gets progressively younger and the music more up-to-date as the weekend draws near.

**our pick** **360° Roofbar** (Map p72; ☎ 284-1874; Hotel Altamira Suites, cnr 1a Av & 1a Transversal; 5pm-late; M Altamira) This innovative open-air lounge atop the Altamira Suites attracts hip scene-makers, who come to chill out on hammocks and sofas in the 19th floor restaurant and sip innovative cocktails over startling panoramic views of the city on the circular rooftop terrace. Access is through the hotel's rear entrance on 1a Av – and subject to a coolness size up.

**Barra Bar** (Map p72; ☎ 264-5019; Centro Comercial Mata de Coco, Av San Marino; M Chacao) Tucked in a pedestrian alley next to the SENIAT building, this intimate lounge has futuristic decor, a few couches for making out, and electronica, jazz and salsa at conversation-friendly levels.

**Suka** (Map p72; ☎ 263-5249; Blandín level, Centro San Ignacio, Av Blandín; 7pm-late Mon-Sat; M Chacao) Sexy Moroccan souk meets Karma Sutra chic at this dark and sultry bar full of patrons sipping creative cocktails like melon mojitos, *orgasmartinis* and *tangerinhas*. DJs spin nightly.

**Lola** (Map p72; ☎ 265-8703; 5a Transversal & Av San Juan Bosco; M Altamira) There is Japanese fusion at this trendy, bi-level restaurant, but it's all about rubbing elbows with the cornucopia of hotness that permeates the bar at this Altamira hotspot, full of Caracas movers, shakers, and those that look so good, it hardly matters if they just stand still – there's no room to move, anyway.

**Uvas** (Map p72; ☎ 266-9927; Centro Comericial L'Orangerie, 6a Av & 5a Transversal; from 5pm Mon-Sat) This cozy wine bar feels as if you're drinking *in* a wine crate. The vino is concentrated on Europe and South America, with oddly little by the glass; accompaniments range from Spanish tapas to heartier fare such as coq au vin to an ample cheese menu. Lots of space for single travelers to mingle but service is irritating.

## ENTERTAINMENT

Your best bet to find out what's going on is the daily *Guía de la Ciudad* (City Guide) in the newspaper *El Universal* (www.eluniversal.com) which has brief descriptions (in Spanish) of the day's music, theater, cinema and art events. Also look out for the monthly brochure put out by the municipality of Chacao, available at various hotels and cultural venues around town. It has useful listings of events in Altamira, La Castellana and El Rosal.

For many, the nightlife is the best reason to come to Caracas. On the weekend, beautiful young things clad in designer labels swarm to Las Mercedes, El Rosal, Altamira and La Castellana. Check out the excellent website www.rumbacaracas.com for up-to-the-minute trends.

Many venues, especially gay ones, will require your *cédula* (ID) for entrance. A copy of your passport or local driver's license should suffice.

### Live Music

In addition to the venues listed here, check the places under Drinking and Nightclubs, many of which also host live acts, especially toward the weekend.

### ROCK & JAZZ

**Juan Sebastián Bar** (Map p72; ☎ 951-0595; Av Venezuela at Calle Mohedano; 5pm-2:30am Mon-Sat; Ⓜ Chacaíto) A longtime bastion of jazz in Caracas, the refined club remains one of the most attractive environments anywhere for hearing jazz. If you wish, you can grab a seat right at the bandstand – there's a counter to place your drink along the front of it.

**Little Rock Café** (Map p72; ☎ 267-8337; 6a Av btwn 3a & 5a Transversal; noon-midnight Sun-Wed, to 5am Thu-Sat; Ⓜ Altamira) In other words, something like the Hard Rock Cafe but smaller. Wackily decorated with images of musical icons and related paraphernalia, the club hosts rock and metal bands on the weekend, along with a pool table, burgers and Tex-Mex food.

**Discovery Bar** (Map p72; Av Tamamaco, Torre Impres, Planta Baja; 9pm-late Tue-Sat; cover BsF20-40; Ⓜ Chacaito) A down-to-earth, genuine alt-rock dive, catering to a hyper-aware crowd who come for the alternative rock, reggae and ska that permeates the shotgun-style room all opening nights besides Wednesday, when they wax intellectual with Latin jazz fusion.

## Nightclubs

The hedonistic dance clubs of Caracas bear testament to Venezuelans' religious devotion to having a good time. Most clubs open from Tuesday to Saturday, but the real action cranks from Thursday to Saturday after midnight. *Caraqueños* are famed for their inexhaustible energy, and you can expect the *rumba* to roll till daybreak. Most clubs adhere to strict door policies – forget about sneakers or a T-shirt, and dress to impress.

### LATIN DANCE

**El Maní es Así** (Map p63; ☎ 763-6671; Calle El Cristo at Av Francisco Solano; 2pm-late Tue-Sun; Ⓜ Sabana Grande) This is one of Caracas' longest-standing and hottest salsa spots, where everything revolves around the dance floor and the live combos. The intense rhythmic ensembles that perform here regularly will inspire rump shaking in the staunchest lead-footers. Take a taxi in and out.

**Rumbar** (Map p72; Calle New York, cnr Calle Madrid; 9pm-late Tue-Sat) Bodies are pressed together here on the small dance floor like a Mumbai passenger train at rush hour. Salsa, merengue and *reggaetón* fuel the sweat-soaked atmosphere, only relieved by a mild-by-comparison outdoor patio seating.

**El Sarao** (Map p72; ☎ 267-1660; Centro Comercial Bello Campo, Av Principal de Bello Campo; admission Wed-Sat BsF70; from 6pm; Ⓜ Altamira) A longstanding destination for middle-class *rumberos*, this massive, subterranean space provides a continuous flow of rum, copious plasma TVs, great live music and enough wicker furniture to fashion an apocalyptic ark. The BsF70 is recoupable in drinks and is often waived for tourists. Access is through the parking garage.

**Rosalinda** (Map p72; ☎ 993-9893; Calle Madrid btwn Veracruz y Caroni; 6pm-3am Tue-Wed, to 6am Thu-Sat) Backpackers will be shooed away, but hipsters, icons of fashion, the rich, famous and an odd mix of out-of-place misfits clamor for face time inside this Las Mercedes club, the hottest spot in town at the time of research. The shotgun-style space is backdropped by backlit stenciled mirrored walls that beam the merengue, *reggaetón* and Latin pop right back at ya.

### ROCK/ELECTRONICA

**El Teatro** (Map p72; ☎ 993-0023; Edificio D&D, Calle Orinoco; 8pm-5am) This eclectic newcomer on the rise offers two dueling rooms, one usually devoted to rock, the other electronica, drum and bass or hip-hop. It skews towards wealthy, alterna-twentysomethings, who appreciate the more casual door (only rule: no shorts) and expands its artistic edge to stage plays and stand-up comedy on Mondays.

**Moulin Rouge** (Map p63; ☎ 761-1990; www.moulinrouge.com.ve; Av Francisco López; admission BsF10-100; 10pm-6am Tue-Sat; Ⓜ Sabana Grande) Behind the flamboyant windmill facade is Caracas' leading venue for live alternative rock, with two environments: the performance hall and an adjacent lounge for drum and bass, trance and techno sessions by resident DJs – and, of course, a mock stripper pole just for fun. The crowd is under 30, pleasantly mixed and all too willing to rock until the metro conveniently resumes operation at 5:30am.

## Sports

**Estadio Universitario** (University Stadium; Map p63; ☎ 0500-226-7366; tickets BsF25-120; Ⓜ Ciudad Universitaria) *Béisbol* (baseball) is the local sporting obsession. Professional-league games are played from October to February at this 18,500-seat stadium, home to the Leones de Caracas (Caracas Lions; www.leones.com),

**GAY & LESBIAN CARACAS**

Caracas has by far the most open gay community in what is still a relatively conservative country. When looking for gay-oriented venues, the code phrase to watch for is *'en ambiente.'* For additional options, check www.rumbacaracas.com and look for *Orbiguia*, a pocket GLBT nightlife guide and directory of gay spots throughout Venezuela.

**Bar La Fragata** (Map p63; ☎ 762-1684; Calle Villaflor; from 6pm; Ⓜ Sabana Grande) Thumping beats and cheap booze guarantee a packed house most nights at this mostly male establishment.

**Cool Café & Pub** (Map p72; ☎ 265-5784; Edificio Lara, Av Eugenio Mendoza; closed Sun; Ⓜ Altamira) There's usually some performance event going on at this relaxed lounge for a mixed crowd, though the transexual cabaret acts are the biggest draw.

**Copa's Dancing Bar** (Map p72; ☎ 951-3947; Edificio Taeca, Calle Guaicaipuro; 10:30pm-6:30am Wed-Sat; cover BsF40-50; Ⓜ Chacaíto) A classic spot for men and women, with a well-stocked bar, an eclectic musical mix, a tight dance floor and irritating door security.

**Tasca Pullman** (Map p63; ☎ 761-1112; Edificio Ovidio, Av Francisco Solano; from 6:30pm; Ⓜ Plaza Venezuela) One of the most frequented *en ambiente* bars in Sabana Grande, the cozy Pullman has an egalitarian vibe. Though primarily a place to meet and chat, spontaneous dancing is not uncommon.

on the grounds of the Universidad Central de Venezuela. Tickets may be purchased up until game time, usually 7:30pm Tuesday to Friday nights, 6pm Saturday and 4:30pm Sunday; or in advance between 10am and 5pm Monday to Friday at Galerias El Recreo in Sabana Grande (right).

### Theater

If you'd like to catch a show – and if your Spanish is up to it – there are a dozen regular theaters in the city. Performances are generally from Thursday to Sunday, with ticket prices anywhere from BsF40 to BsF70 (some theaters offer discount admission on Thursday).

Following are some of the city's more reliable stages. Another good source for information on plays is the 'Eventos' page of www.caracasvirtual.com.

**Celarg** (Map p72; ☎ 285-2721; www.celarg.org.ve; Centro de Estudios Latinoamericanos Rómulo Gallegos, Av Luis Roche, cnr 3a Transversal; Ⓜ Altamira)

**Teatro Teresa Carreño** (Map pp58-9; ☎ 574-9333; www.teatroteresacarreno.gob.ve; Complejo Cultural Teresa Carreño; Ⓜ Bellas Artes) See p62.

**Teatro Trasnocho Cultural** (Map p72; ☎ 993-1910; www.trasnochocultural.com; Centro Comercial Paseo Las Mercedes) Dedicated to pushing the boundaries of conventional theater.

## SHOPPING

*Caraqueños* adore shopping, and the streets of La Candelaria, Sabana Grande, Chacaíto, Chacao and the historic center are all tightly packed with stores and malls to satisfy that need.

### Shopping Malls

To fully appreciate the national love affair with shopping, you need only visit one of Caracas' huge shopping malls. Even if you don't normally enjoy hanging around malls, it's instructive to see how they've become a sort of alternate reality to the often harsh landscape of the streets. As safety has deteriorated over the 2000s, everything has moved indoors – *caraqueños* now shop, eat, drink, celebrate and even sleep there, effectively creating an idealized microcosm of normal life in these temples of consumerism.

**Centro Comercial El Recreo** (Map p63; ☎ 761-2740; www.elrecreo.com.ve; Av Casanova; 10am-9pm Mon-Sat, noon-8pm Sun; Ⓜ Sabana Grande) Escape Sabana Grande's mean streets!

**Centro Comercial Paseo Las Mercedes** (Map p72; Av Principal de las Mercedes) Includes an excellent hotel (p67) and a cutting-edge arts center. From the metro Chacaíto, take Metrobús 221.

**Centro Comercial Sambil** (Map p72; ☎ 267-2101; www.sambilmall.com; Av Libertador; 10am-9pm Mon-Sat, noon-8pm Sun; Ⓜ Chacao) Touted as South America's largest shopping mall.

**Centro San Ignacio** (Map p72; ☎ 263-3953; www.centrosanignacio.com; Av Blandín; 10am-8pm Mon-Sat, 1-8pm Sun; Ⓜ Chacao) A major nightlife destination, boasting dozens of bars and clubs along the lower level, and the best mall within striking distance of a metro station.

**Fashion Mall Tolón** (Map p72; www.cctolon.com; Av Principal de Las Mercedes; 9am-9pm) A winner for its high-end dining and nightlife.

### Souvenirs

To pick up the obligatory hammocks, papier-mâché devil masks or stuffed piranhas, check out the biggest craft shop of them all at **Hannsi** (☎ 963-7184; www.hannsi.com.ve; Calle Bolívar 12; ⏲ 10am-7pm Mon-Thu, to 8pm Fri-Sun), in El Hatillo (p64), one of the best souvenirs shops you'll see. The massive store is divided by region and 20% of its inventory represents neighboring countries. The narrow, winding streets around Hannsi also house numerous high-quality craft stores, so take your time to dip into them all.

**Artesanía Altamira** (Map p72; ☎ 265-2007; Av Ávila, Altamira Sur; ⏲ 7:30am-6:30pm Mon-Sat; Ⓜ Altamira) A veritable profusion of basket work is to be found here, along with other assorted knick-knacks – the kind we all buy and ask ourselves 'Why?' later.

**Casa Curuba** (Map p72; ☎ 203-9368; Av Andrés Bello) Stunning wares here, all fashioned from exotic hardwoods. The high-quality stock includes beautiful picture frames, boxes and bowls, especially from the state of Lara. *The* spot for a discerning gift or souvenir.

**Centro Artesanal Los Goajiros** (Map p63; btwn Blvd Sabana Grande & Av Casanova; ⏲ 7am-8pm Mon-Fri, to 6pm Sun; Ⓜ Chacaíto) A below-street-level corridor of stalls just west of Plaza Chacaíto offers a mixed-bag of Orinoco crafts (woven hammocks and bags, carved blowguns, musical instruments) and hippie gear (Rasta caps, Guatemalan wallets).

Next door to the new Galería de Arte Nacional (p62) is the **Gran Feria de Economiás Popular de Bellas Artes**, where you'll find *Chavista* memorabilia. Check row *Rosa Mistica*, Stall 46.

## GETTING THERE & AWAY

### Air

The **Aeropuerto Internacional 'Simón Bolívar'** (www.aeropuerto-maiquetia.com.ve), 26km from central Caracas, has two terminals, one for international and the other for domestic flights, 400m apart. There's a free, though infrequent, shuttle service between the terminals.

The **international terminal** (☎ 355-3110) has a good range of facilities, including an Inatur tourist office branch (p55), car-rental desks, *casas de cambio*, banks, ATMs, post and telephone offices, restaurants, cafes and a slew of travel agencies. The **domestic terminal** (☎ 355-2660) provides all of the same facilities.

Do not change money with touts at the airport (what good is BsF6 to the dollar if they end up counterfeit?). Allow four hours before departing international flights, – between Caracas traffic, lengthy airport lines and the Guardia Nacional's antidrug wing, who randomly select travelers postimmigration to subject them to further searches, x-rays and fingerprinting.

For a list of international flight connections, see p277. For domestic connections and airline offices in Caracas, see p279. Fares vary widely by airline – here are a few domestic one-way examples from Caracas, but do shop around: Gran Roques (BsF520), Ciudad Bolívar (BsF290), Las Piedras (BsF275), Porlamar (BsF197), Maracaibo (BsF268), Mérida/El Vigía (BsF378), Puerto Ayacucho (BsF376) and Puerto Ordaz (BsF219).

At the time of writing, the international/domestic airport tax was a hefty BsF162.50/32.50, plus a BsF110 departure tax (the latter is usually built into the ticket). The international tax is payable with cash (BsF or USD) or domestic credit/debit card. To check for any further increases, see the airport website – they change often, and if you buy your ticket before a price change and fly after, you will be forced to pay the difference.

You can change your money (dollars only) upon arrival, but see the explanation of official/black market exchange rates first (p14). Note that airport *casas de cambio* do not change *bolívares fuertes* back into foreign currencies; if you get stuck with any, consider using them to buy liquor or cosmetics at the duty-free shops.

To phone from the terminal, buy a phone card at a newsstand. Maiquetía has the same area code as Caracas, so just dial the local Caracas number.

### Boat

Passenger boats from Caracas to Isla Margarita have been discontinued, but you can you book tickets for departures in Puerto La Cruz (p210) at **Conferry** (Map p63; ☎ 0501-2663-3779; www.conferry.com; Torre Banhorient, cnr Av Casanova & Av Las Acacias; ⏲ 8am-5:30pm Mon-Fri; Ⓜ Plaza Venezuela). Fares run from BsF73 to BsF93 for the four-hour *convencional* boat and BsF151 to BsF261 for the two-hour *expreso* boat.

There's no passenger service to Los Roques.

### Bus

Caracas has three public bus terminals – two intercity stations and a central one for shorter journeys. In addition, several smaller, less chaotic private terminals cover the same destinations.

See the bus table (p80) for standard fares and trip duration. Fares range from conventional to *'bus-cama'* service with seats that recline to serve as beds.

### TERMINAL LA BANDERA

The **Terminal La Bandera** (Map pp52-3; ☎ 693-6607; Av Nueva Granada; Ⓜ La Bandera), 3km south of the center, handles long-distance buses to anywhere in the country's west and southwest. The terminal has a **left-luggage office** (1st hr BsF2, per hr thereafter BsF1; 6am-8pm Mon-Sat, 7am-7pm Sun) on the right side of the top level and a friendly, Spanish-only information desk near the ticket offices.

The terminal's layout can be confusing. To get to the ticket offices, go up the ramp to the top level. Ignore the numerous touts attempting to shoo you over to their bus companies. A chart inside the entrance shows where the 40 or so bus companies go and the locations of their ticket offices, all of which are on the left side. Below is a list of the most reliable lines serving the most destinations, along with their window location numbers.

**Expresos Flamingo** (☎ 693-7572; 40)
**Expresos Los Llanos** (☎ 0414-730-1303; 41)
**Expresos Mérida** (☎ 693-5559; 44)
**Expresos Occidente** (☎ 693-6489; 1)

All buses depart from the level directly below the ticket offices, with the exception of buses to Maracay and Valencia. To reach those, you must go to the other end of the terminal, then down one level. From the same location, por puestos (collective taxis/minibuses) travel to San Felipe (BsF52, 3½ hours), La Victoria (BsF10, 1½ hours), Puerto Cabello (BsF50, 2½ hours), Barquisimeto (BsF80, four hours) and Maracay (BsF35, 1½ hours), departing as they fill.

The terminal is inconveniently not linked to La Bandera metro station, 350m away through a chaotic, unsafe neighborhood. From the metro, take the Granada/Zuloaga exit, cross the avenue and turn left. Leaving the terminal, go down the ramp to the left and proceed 350m, past two gas stations, and cross at the stoplight to the metro. Alternatively, you'll find secure taxis inside the station, departing from opposite the por puesto stand.

### TERMINAL DE ORIENTE

The newly renovated and far less chaotic **Terminal de Oriente** (☎ 243-2603; Autopista Caracas-Guarenas) handles all traffic to the east and southeast of the country, with the exception of the state-run **SITSSA** (☎ 241-0323; www.sitssa.gob.ve), which services the entire country. These brand-new, government-subsidized buses are the cheapest way to get around the country, though departures aren't as frequent and space fills up faster. Sample fares include Coro (BsF40), Valencia (BsF10), San Fernando de Apurre (BsF35), Maracay (BsF10), Tucupita (BsF30) and Puerto Ayacucho (BsF60). All buses are new Marco Polo coaches with air-conditioning and televisions, and security in the terminal is nearly airport-level.

From Oriente, you'll also find international buses to Colombia. **Expresos Amerlujo** (☎ 241-2578) operates the most direct routes to Cartagena (BsF450) and Santa Marta (BsF340). The terminal is on the eastern outskirts of Caracas, on the highway to Barcelona, 5km beyond Petare (about 18km from Caracas' city center). It's accessible by local buses (BsF2, 20 minutes) from metro Petare: take the 'Av Francisco de Miranda' exit, go left to the avenue and left again to find the bus stop. Take extra care here – this area is shady. A taxi from Altamira will cost about BsF45; straight to the airport, around BsF160. The terminal features ATMs, a helpful information desk and a left-luggage office (per hour BsF1 to BsF2).

### TERMINAL NUEVO CIRCO

Buses servicing regional destinations (La Guaira, Los Teques, Santa Teresa, Ocumare del Tuy etc) still depart from the old central **Nuevo Circo regional bus terminal** (Map pp58-9; Av Lecuna; Ⓜ Nuevo Circo), though it's absolute chaos. Be prepared to wait in long lines and – when your bus finally arrives – to scramble on.

### PRIVATE TERMINALS

Modern, comfortable buses from these smaller stations are pricier than those out of the major terminals but make up for it in convenience and straightforward access. All of the terminals listed have ATMs and snack bars. In order of comfort and reputation:

**Aeroexpresos Ejecutivos** (Map p72; ☎ 266-2321; www.aeroexpresos.com.ve; Av Principal de Bello Campo; Ⓜ Altamira) Services Maracay, Valencia, Barquisimeto, Maracaibo, Maturín, Ciudad Bolívar, Puerto La Cruz, Puerto Ordaz, El Tigre and San Félix.

**Peli Express** (Map pp52-3; ☎ 286-0144; Av Intercomunal; Ⓜ Los Dos Caminos) Has a terminal on the east side of Parque del Este, just south of the Museo del Transporte, with several lines servicing Puerto La Cruz, San Cristóbal,

Mérida, Maracaibo, Barinas, Carúpano, Coro, Valencia, Cumaná and Ciudad Bolívar, among other places.

**BUSES FROM CARACAS TO MAJOR DESTINATIONS**

| Destination | Duration | Fare (BsF) |
|---|---|---|
| Barcelona | 5hr | 44-50 |
| Barinas | 9hr | 22-25 |
| Barquisimeto | 5½hr | 54-64 |
| Carúpano | 9hr | 69-75 |
| Ciudad Bolívar | 9hr | 67-80 |
| Coro | 9hr | 65-103 |
| Cumaná | 7hr | 69-75 |
| Guanare | 5hr | 34-63 |
| Güiria | 15hr | 80-85 |
| Maracaibo | 12hr | 83-114 |
| Maracay | 2hr | 20 |
| Maturín | 8hr | 63-73 |
| Mérida | 13hr | 95-120 |
| Puerto Ayacucho | 17hr | 75-80 |
| Puerto La Cruz | 5hr | 57-67 |
| San Antonio | 12hr | 59-97 |
| San Cristóbal | 10hr | 95-120 |
| San Fernando | 8hr | 29-54 |
| Tucupita | 12hr | 78 |
| Valencia | 3hr | 25 |
| Valera | 11hr | 40-73 |

## GETTING AROUND

### To/From the Airport

Caracas' main airport is at Maiquetía, near the port of La Guaira on the Caribbean coast, 26km northwest of the city center. If you only have an overnight stop in Maiquetía, you may prefer to skip the journey into Caracas and stay the night on the coast (see p83).

The private **airport bus service** (UCAMC; Map pp58-9; ☎ 576-9851; www.ucamc.com; Av Sur 17 btwn Mexico & Av Lecuna; BsF18) is the fastest bus option between central Caracas and Maiquetía airport, with departures from its private terminal near Parque Central from 5:30am to 7pm (buses leave when full). At the airport, the airport bus picks up and drops off passengers by the domestic terminal only, departing between 7am and 9:30pm. An infrequent shuttle service connects the two terminals, but it's quicker to hike it. The bus ride normally takes 30 to 50 minutes. A cheaper **airport bus service** (SITSSA; ☎ 892-1922; www.sitssa.gob.ve; BsF8) is run by the government from the Hotel Alba Caracas (Map pp58–9), but it leaves only hourly from 6:30am to 5:30pm. Buy your tickets at least 20 minutes beforehand from the office in the hotel's shopping promenade, then board outside by the fountain. At the airport, it departs from the domestic terminal from 7:30am to 7pm. Buy tickets at the office next door to Inatur.

If you travel into the city during rush hour, it's faster to get off at the Gato Negro metro station and continue by metro, although the area is considered unsafe.

Kiosks in both terminals as well as international baggage claim sell prepaid tickets at posted prices for the **official airport taxis** (☎ 355-2211) – to Las Mercedes/Altamira costs BsF165, Sabana Grande BsF155, Catia la Mar BsF55 and Macuto BsF80; credit cards are accepted. Taxis are black Ford Explorers with yellow placards on the side. Unregistered taxis are not recommended because of reports of robberies and kidnappings. Do not wander outside of the main airport terminals at night.

Check the correct fare with the tourist office before boarding a taxi to avoid overcharging. The fares from the city back to the airport are generally 20% to 30% lower.

### Bus

Two kinds of buses operate on Caracas streets: city-run Metrobúses (BsF0.70), and privately run carritos, which are slightly more expensive. The latter are generally in worse shape, with blaring radios and beat-up seats, but go to many destinations inaccessible by metro. They can also be useful for a quick hop along the main east–west thoroughfares when you don't feel like going underground. Route destinations are posted on the windshield. Metrobuses run to the same schedule as the metro while carrito lines generally stop running after 9pm.

### Metro

The French-built **metro** (www.metrodecaracas.com.ve; 🕓 5:30am-11pm) is fast, easy to use, cheap, air-conditioned and provides access to most major city attractions.

The metro has four lines and almost 50 stations with a total length of more than 70km. The longest line, No 1, goes east–west along the city axis. To determine which side of the tracks to use, look for the sign showing the train's final destination. On line 1, westbound platforms are marked 'Dirección Propatria;' eastbound, 'Dirección Palo Verde.'

The system also includes a number of 'Metrobús' routes, buses that link some suburbs to metro stations. This means you can easily get to San Bernardino, Prados del Este, El Hatillo and other suburbs that are

**CARACAS TRAFFIC**

Venezuela has the planet's cheapest gas – at a whopping US$1.13 (at the official rate) to fill a 50L tank, there really is no incentive to park the car, is there? For perspective, 50L costs around BsF5, cocktails at 360° Roofbar start at BsF31! The result is some of the planet's most horrendous traffic to go along with it. From dawn to dusk and later, the city becomes a congested nightmare. Some two million cars jam the streets of the capital daily, with vehicles crawling at an average rate of 15km per hour. It can take an hour to get from Sabana Grande to Altamira at midday, a journey that takes under 10 minutes on the metro. The notorious gridlock leaves large sections of the city paralyzed for much of the day, and incessant horn-honking and asphyxiating fumes are facts of life. The toll on the environment – not to mention people's lungs and nerves – is disregarded.

not reached directly by metro. The Metrobús routes are described in the appropriate sections of this chapter. All of the metro lines and Metrobús routes are marked on the Caracas maps posted in every metro station.

Yellow single-ride tickets cost BsF0.50 for a ride of any distance; *boletos de ida y vuelta* (roundtrip tickets) cost BsF0.90. Consider buying the **multiabono** (BsF4.50), an orange multiple-ride ticket valid for 10 metro rides; not only do you save money, but you also avoid the seemingly interminable queues at the ticket booth every time you need to use the metro. *Multiabono* tickets can only be purchased from ticket booths, while single and roundtrip tickets are also available from vending machines. Single roundtrip 'Metrobús' fares cost BsF1.40.

### Taxi

Identifiable by the 'Taxi' or 'Libre' sign, taxis are unmetered, so always fix the fare before boarding. Official daytime rates from Plaza Bolívar to Sabana Grande or Parque Central to Las Mercedes are BsF40 and BsF35, respectively. Sabana Grande to Altamira is BsF40 as well. Rates increase around 30% after dark.

Use only white cars with yellow plates and preferably those from taxi ranks, of which there are plenty, especially outside shopping malls. Alternatively, request one by calling any of the numerous companies that provide dispatch service. Several companies, including **Móvil-Enlace** (☎ 577-3344; www.taximovilenlace.com), service the entire Caracas area around the clock. Other reliable services include **Teletaxi** (☎ 753-4155) and **TaxiTaxco** (☎ 576-8322). Hotels will usually have taxi companies on standby.

**Veronica Crepinsek** (☎ 0416-096-0682; amthaad@hotmail.com; per hr BsF110, airport transfer BsF190-218) is a likable English/German-speaking driver with ample experience transporting foreign travelers. Her service includes check-in assistance.

# AROUND CARACAS

This section includes only what lies between the city and the coast. For other one-day destinations out of Caracas see the Central North chapter (p84).

## PARQUE NACIONAL EL ÁVILA

The steep, verdant mountain range that dominates Caracas to the north provides an easily accessible refuge from the chaos of the city. The **national park** (🕑 6am-5pm) stretches along about 90km of Cordillera El Ávila, which forms a natural east–west wall between the city and the sea.

A remarkable diversity of wildlife inhabits the park's varied ecosystems, which range from dry-season forest to subtundra. Birdwatchers will find hundreds of species to ogle and will likely spot flocks of green parakeets or hear the song of the great kiskadee, which Venezuelans say sounds like its local name, *cristofué* ('Christ was'). It may take more patience, though, to get a glimpse of a gorgeous collared trogon or groove-billed toucanet. Reptiles and snakes, both poisonous and benign, also populate the slopes, along with numerous small mammals such as armadillos, porcupines and squirrels. Early-morning visitors can eavesdrop on howler monkeys conversing from the treetops. There are even a few jaguars and mountain lions roaming about the more densely vegetated patches of the northern slopes.

The southern slope, overlooking Caracas, is virtually uninhabited but is crisscrossed with dozens of walking trails. The northern face, running down to the sea, is dotted with hamlets and haciendas, yet few tourist trails are on this side. The park is crossed north–south by a few 4WD tracks and the *teleférico* (cable car).

### Teleférico Warairarepano

Rising high above the city to the peak of El Ávila (2175m), the **Teleférico Warairarepano** (Warairarepano cable car; ☎ 792-7050; adult/child BsF25/10; 🕒 10am-8pm Tue, to 10pm Wed-Thu, 10am-midnight Fri & Sat, to 8pm Sun, closed Mon Jul 22-Sep 15, noon-8pm Tue, 10am-10pm Wed-Thu, 10am-midnight Fri & Sat, to 8pm Sun Sep 16-Jul 21) was reopened with fanfare in 2002 after a 25-year hiatus. Built by a German company in 1956, the old *teleférico* line consisted of two routes: the now inoperable 7.5km run from El Ávila down to Macuto on the coast, and the reconstructed 4km run from Maripérez station, next to Av Boyacá in Caracas, to Pico El Ávila (2250m). The *teleférico* is now owned and operated by the government.

The summit offers breathtaking views of Caracas and the Valle del Tuy beyond; towards the north is a stunning panorama of the coastline and the Caribbean Sea stretching away to the horizon. The area around the *teleférico* station has been developed as a sort of fun park with a playground, 3D cinema and an ice-skating rink, as well as several restaurants and numerous stands along the main path selling coffee, hot chocolate and snacks.

The path from the *teleférico* station leads to the circular 14-story **Hotel Humboldt**. Built in 1956, the hotel is an extraordinary landmark visible from almost every point in the city. It was closed when the cable car stopped running, but is in the middle of restoration with a planned opening for April 2010 (but don't count on it). If you're curious and want to have a snoop inside, there are **tours** (adult/child BsF5/2.50; 🕒 noon-3:30pm) of the installations; or stop by the piano bar, open from 4pm nightly until one hour prior to the cable car closing.

Views are usually best before the mid- to late-afternoon clouds start snaking across the mountaintop, enveloping the complex in an eerie fog that hides objects within even a few meters. At these times it can get surprisingly chilly so be sure to pack a sweater. But when the views vanish and the cold sets in, there's always the Swiss fondue restaurant to warm you up.

Regular pickup trucks (to the left as you exit the *teleférico*) carry visitors to the northern-slope hamlet of **Galipán** (BsF4, five minutes), where you'll find a string of good, inexpensive restaurants – folks come here for *pernil* (pork leg – sandwiches and strawberries and cream), horseback rides and a couple of posadas with cabins. Nicer restaurants, with stupendous views and outstanding service (by Caracas standards) are tucked down narrow roads further inside the mountain (try Il Picaccio Trattoria). Galipán is also linked by covered pickup to Macuto on the coast (BsF15, one hour, on weekends only), an unforgettable journey down a winding cobblestone road through a series of cloud-forest villages, further down revealing astounding views of the Caribbean coast.

Carritos to Maripérez station, labeled 'Sarria – Teleférico,' run from just north of Bellas Artes metro station (BsF1.50, 15 minutes).

### Hiking

Of all Venezuela's national parks, El Ávila provides the best infrastructure for walkers. There are 200km of walking trails, most of them well signposted. Half a dozen camping grounds distributed around the park are equipped with sanitary facilities, and there are many other more basic places designated for camping. Potable water is available at points along the trails.

A dozen entrances lead into the park from Caracas; all originate from Av Boyacá, commonly known as 'Cota Mil' because it runs at an altitude of 1000m (closed to traffic on Sunday between 6am and 1pm, it's a popular place for riding bikes and jogging). The *guardaparques* (park rangers) may provide information and suggestions about routes, and you should tell them where you intend to hike. Before you come, however, pick up the useful brochure on Parque Nacional El Ávila published by ECOgraph Proyectos y Diseños, which includes a 1:25,000 map of the park. It can be found at Tecni-Ciencia Libros (p54) and other local bookstores. Keep in mind, however, that some tracks may be difficult to find and there are few distance markers.

There are plenty of options for a half- or full-day hike. One recommended way is to catch a bus from the east side of Plaza de Francia in Altamira (by the Hotel Caracas Palace) to the Sabas Nieves entrance, from which it's a 300m hike up to the ranger post. From there, you can pick up an easy-to-handle nature trail along the southern slope that passes a series of streams, waterfalls and caves. Another trail from Sabas Nieves climbs the mountain, one of four main ascents to the park's highest points, Pico Oriental (2640m) and Pico Naiguatá (2765m). One of the most scenic routes is along the Fila Maestra, following the crest of the Ávila range from Pico de Ávila to Pico Naiguatá and rewarding hikers with splendid views toward both the valley of Caracas and the Caribbean Sea.

Start early, as it can get extremely hot by midmorning. The dry season is from December to April, but be prepared for a few showers in the upper reaches all the same. Take rain gear and warm clothes.

## LITORAL CENTRAL

The northern face of El Ávila park slopes steeply down to the sea, leaving only a narrow, flat strip of land between the foothills and the shore, referred to as the 'Litoral Central.' This strip has developed into a chain of coastal towns, including, from west to east, Catia La Mar, Maiquetía, La Guaira, Macuto, Caraballeda and Naiguatá.

Sadly, most of the area was devastated by mudslides caused by torrential rains in December 1999, with up to 50,000 people buried under the mud. Once popular seaside resorts for *caraqueños*, Caraballeda and Naiguatá were destroyed, along with much of the colonial town of La Guaira, though Macuto was mostly spared. Restoration efforts have proceeded slowly and haphazardly – just check that new, strangely designed promenade in Macuto – and it will take decades before the urban fabric is fully rebuilt, if ever.

For travelers, the zone's chief function is as an overnight alternative to Caracas near the airport, but is only an option if you are afraid of or have no interest in Caracas, or if you are arriving late and have an early domestic departure the following morning. Catia La Mar, just west of the airport, has the closest and finest lodging but little else to recommend it. A 20-minute ride in the opposite direction is Macuto, a somewhat safer, less disheveled spot with some crumbling colonial architecture, a string of more budget-oriented hotels and a few beaches. Macuto has the additional advantage of being located at the start of a wonderful backdoor route to Caracas via the *teleférico*.

### Sleeping & Eating
#### CATIA DEL MAR & MACUTO

**Hotel Plazamar** ( ☎ 339-5242; plazamarhotel@hotmail. com; Plaza de las Palomas, Calle Macuto, Macuto; d/tr/q from BsF 100/130/160; ✗ ) Though basic, this family-run hotel packs a lot of punch for the price, including friendly service, travel advice, air-con and wi-fi. It's right on the central Plaza de las Palomas (Pigeon Plaza, a name adopted for obvious reasons) and is as hospitable as can be (English and Italian are spoken if Mom is around).

**Il Prezzano** ( ☎ 351-2626; reserva@ilprezzano.com.ve; Av Principal de Playa Grande; s/d/tr/q BsF180/202/221/245; ✗ 🛜 ) Towards Playa Grande, you'll find this hospitable lodging on a lively corner with an attached tasca specializing in pasta. Rooms are amply sized, the tiles are spic-and-span and you're a stone's throw from a Laundromat, pharmacy and additional cheap eats. For added comfort, you can also try the Buenavista or Marriot Playa Grande, both nearby.

**Posada del Hidalgo** ( ☎ 355-5144; Av La Playa, Urbanización Alamo, Macuto; s/d/tr from BsF200/220/230; ✗ ) This motel-like structure full of Andalusian character offers straightforward, if smallish and humid, units. There's a very popular tasca in front serving great seafood, which might make up for the hard-headed front desk staff. Airport transfer from BsF70.

**Hotel Eurobuilding Express** ( ☎ 700-0700; www. hoteleuroexpress.com; Av La Armada, Catia del Mar; d/ste from BsF648/672; ✗ 🛜 🏊 ) A flashy alternative amidst an otherwise blighted zone, the Eurobuilding is situated directly on the road departing from the terminal. Rates include shuttle to or from the airport and an ample breakfast at the hotel's Mr Grill restaurant. Half-day rates are available, too, so you can while away long hours between flights at the gym, pool and tennis courts.

**Brisas del Mar** ( ☎ 615-6470; Av La Playa, Macuto; mains BsF27-130). The go-to spot in Macuto, this lively restaurant does a little bit of everything, including pizza and pasta.

### Getting There & Away

Shuttle buses travel regularly between Parque Central in Caracas and the airport (p80), from which taxis charge around BsF50 to BsF55 to Catia La Mar and BsF70 to BsF80 for Macuto. Some hotels include airport transfer in the rate. From the airport, take official taxis only if your hotel has not arranged a transfer. Metrobús 603 from Metro La Paz also combs this part of the coast.

Another option is to go straight over the Ávila range to Caracas. Pickup trucks ply the cobblestone road to Galipán (BsF15, one hour), a village on the mountain's northern slope, affording amazing views of the coast along the way. These depart from the west end of Macuto, near the Hotel Macuto. From Galipán it's another 10 minutes by pickup to the *teleférico* station down to the city. (Note: one-way fares offered only on the way down.)

# The Central North

Though Venezuela's Central North dangles no iconic traveler's mecca (like Angel Falls) and no transcendent nomadic rites of passage (like Roraima), this dense area – all within an earshot of Caracas – is rife with both aquatic and earthly delights and boasts one of the continent's most stunning and unforgettable landscapes: the magical Archipiélago Los Roques.

Located about 175km off the coast, this otherworldly collection of islands and cays, a national marine park, offers some of the most glorious beaches and underwater wildlife you'll ever see anywhere, a dazzling don't-miss for anyone in the country. Though honeymooners, sport fishers, divers and sun-and-sand addicts flock to its shores year-round, it remains advantageously off the radar, helping to maintain its rustic appeal.

Back on land, six national parks carpet the landscape in all directions from Caracas. Most notably is Parque Nacional Henri Pittier, where the endearing towns of Choroní and Puerto Colombia still retain their colonial feel, while the enticing beaches and coves along the park's coast (some accessible only by boat) attract heaps of *venezolanos* and backpackers. Here too are some of the country's best festivals, heavily influenced by Afro-Venezuelan culture – the occasional spontaneous party and drum session might pop up when you least expect it. Amid the mainland's comely hills and valleys are several hidden gems, easily reached on day trips from Caracas. The pretty 19th-century German town of Colonia Tovar, which lies scattered along the upper reaches of a mountainside, is an Alpine oasis, seemingly straight out of the Black Forest. The world's second-hottest thermal waters are toward the west at Las Trincheras, a rustic mini-resort that can make for a blistering good time. And don't forget the important battlefield of Carabobo – Venezuelans certainly never will – where national hero Simón Bolívar clinched Venezuelan independence, helping birth the modern-day countries of Venezuela, Colombia, Ecuador, Panama, Peru and Bolivia.

### HIGHLIGHTS

- Immerse yourself in Venezuela's aquatic Eden, the stunningly beautiful **Archipiélago Los Roques** (p86)
- Walk off the hearty sausages in the German-themed town of **Colonia Tovar** (p100)
- Take in a fat dose of Venezuelan patriotism at **Campo Carabobo** (p111)
- Beach-hop the days away in idyllic **Parque Nacional Henri Pittier** (p101)
- Scorch off a skin layer in the piping-hot springs of **Las Trincheras** (p112)

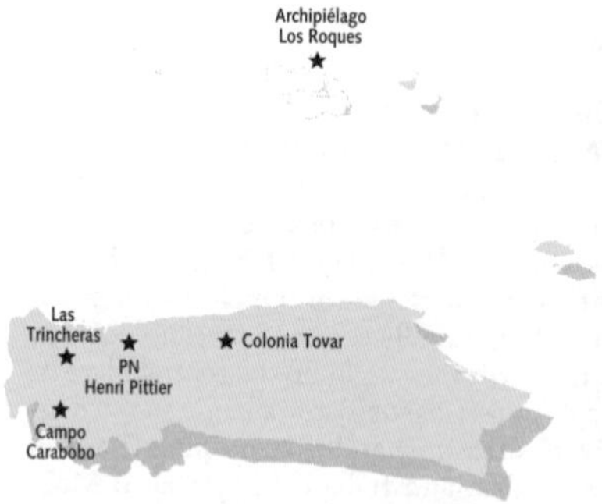

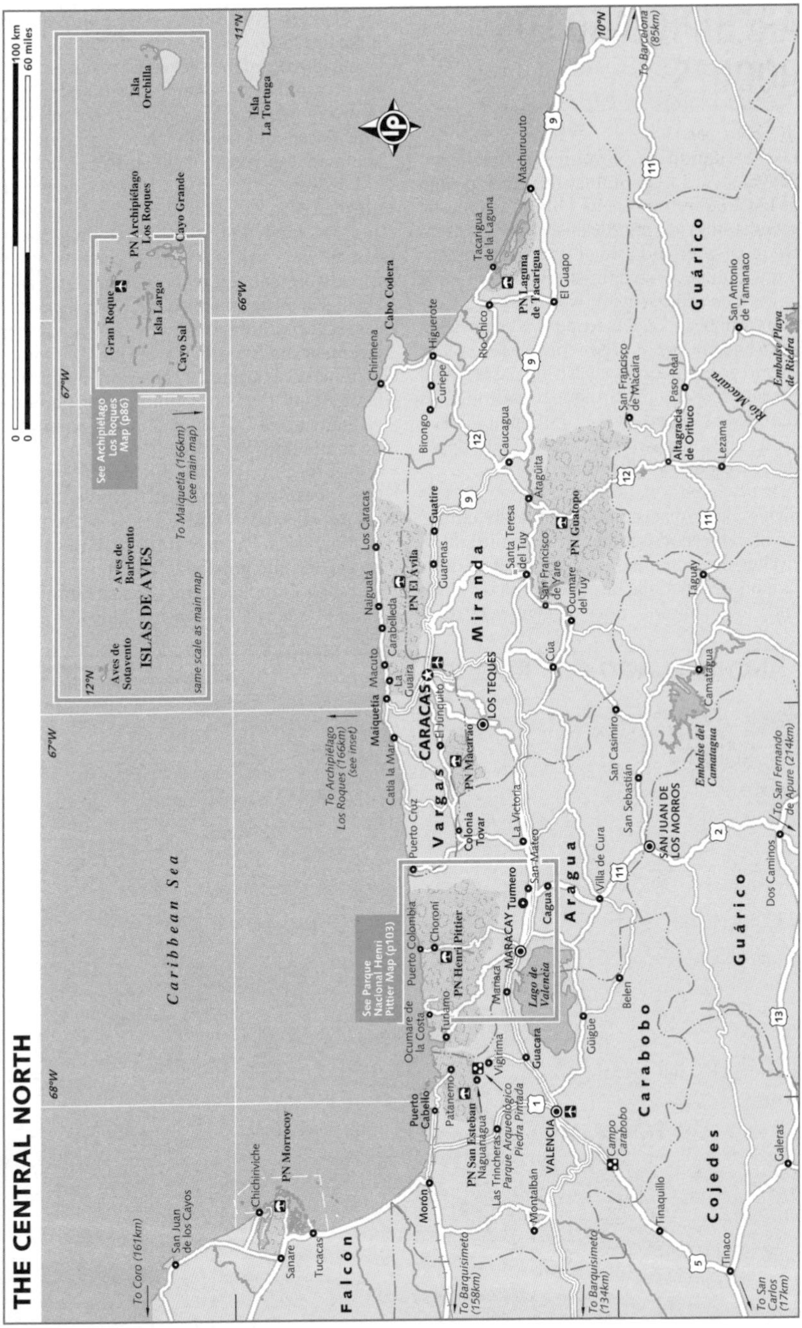
THE CENTRAL NORTH
0 100 km
0 60 miles
Caribbean Sea
Isla La Tortuga
Isla Orchilla
ISLAS DE AVES
Aves de Sotavento
Aves de Barlovento
same scale as main map
To Maiquetía (166km) (see main map)
See Archipiélago Los Roques Map (p86)
Gran Roque
PN Archipiélago Los Roques
Isla Larga
Cayo Sal
Cayo Grande
12°N
11°N
10°N
68°W
67°W
66°W
To Archipiélago Los Roques (166km) (see inset)
Falcón
Carabobo
Cojedes
Aragua
Vargas
Miranda
Guárico
To Coro (161km)
San Juan de los Cayos
Chichiriviche
PN Morrocoy
Sanare
Tucacas
Morón
Puerto Cabello
Patanemo
PN San Esteban
Naguanagua
Las Trincheras
Parque Arqueológico Piedra Pintada
Vigirima
Montalbán
VALENCIA
Campo Carabobo
Tinaquillo
Tinaco
Galeras
To Barquisimeto (158km)
To Barquisimeto (134km)
To San Carlos (17km)
Guacara
Güigüe
Belen
Ocumare de la Costa
Turiamo
See Parque Nacional Henri Pittier Map (p103)
Puerto Colombia
Choroní
PN Henri Pittier
Mariara
MARACAY
Lago de Valencia
Turmero
Cagua
San Mateo
La Victoria
Colonia Tovar
Villa de Cura
Puerto Cruz
Catia la Mar
Maiquetía
Macuto
La Guaira
CARACAS
El Junquito
PN Macarao
LOS TEQUES
Caraballeda
Naiguatá
Los Caracas
PN El Ávila
Guarenas
Guatire
Chirimena
Cabo Codera
Higuerote
Birongo
Curiepe
Caucagua
Río Chico
PN Laguna de Tacarigua
Tacarigua de la Laguna
Machurucuto
El Guapo
Santa Teresa del Tuy
San Francisco de Yare
Ocumare del Tuy
Cúa
Araguïta
PN Guatopo
San Casimiro
San Sebastián
SAN JUAN DE LOS MORROS
Camatagua
Embalse del Camatagua
Taguay
Altagracia de Orituco
Lezama
San Francisco de Macaira
Paso Real
Río Macaira
Embalse Playa de Piedra
San Antonio de Tamanaco
Dos Caminos
To San Fernando de Apure (214km)
To Barcelona (85km)
1
2
5
9
11
12
13

# ARCHIPIÉLAGO LOS ROQUES

**☎ 0237 / pop 1300**

Like Fernando de Noronha in Brazil and Providencia in Colombia, the Archipelago of Los Roques represents ultimate domestic getaway bliss to Venezuelans, many of whom are in wonder and awe of its tropical splendor without ever stepping foot on its pristine sands. You will be equally wowed as well. This fine Caribbean kaleidoscope is a Venezuelan Eden and one of South America's island gems. Rustic constructions awash in pastel-hued charm serve as a picturesque backdrop to its centerpiece, a perfect collision of sun-baked sands and cerulean-jade waters that pepper the seascape in all directions.

Proclaimed a national park in 1972, this idyllic collection of small coral islands harbors rich coral reefs and comes virtually unspoiled, rivaling the swimming-pool-clarity of far more famous destinations like Bora Bora or Turks and Caicos, but with none of their overcrowding or expense. The archipelago's only village is the tiny Gran Roque, while most islands are uninhabited and the silence is broken only by the occasional buzz of motorboats and splash of diving pelicans. It's a much more relaxed, slow-paced and friendly place – a complete alternate reality from mainland Venezuela.

Los Roques lies about 160km due north off the central coast under a scorching sun and dazzlingly blue skies. Stretching 36km east to west, the archipelago consists of 42 islands big enough to bother naming, and about 250 other unnamed islets, sandbars and cays scattered around a crystal-clear, glittering lagoon brimming with marine life. The whole archipelago is around 2211 sq km in size, but Gran Roque is the focal point, being home to virtually all of its population, accommodations and transportation.

In order to preserve the habitat, protective zones have been created where tourists are not allowed or where access is limited to daytime visits. The only area with unrestricted access and the possibility of camping is the so-called Zona Recreativa, which comprises Gran Roque and the nearby islands.

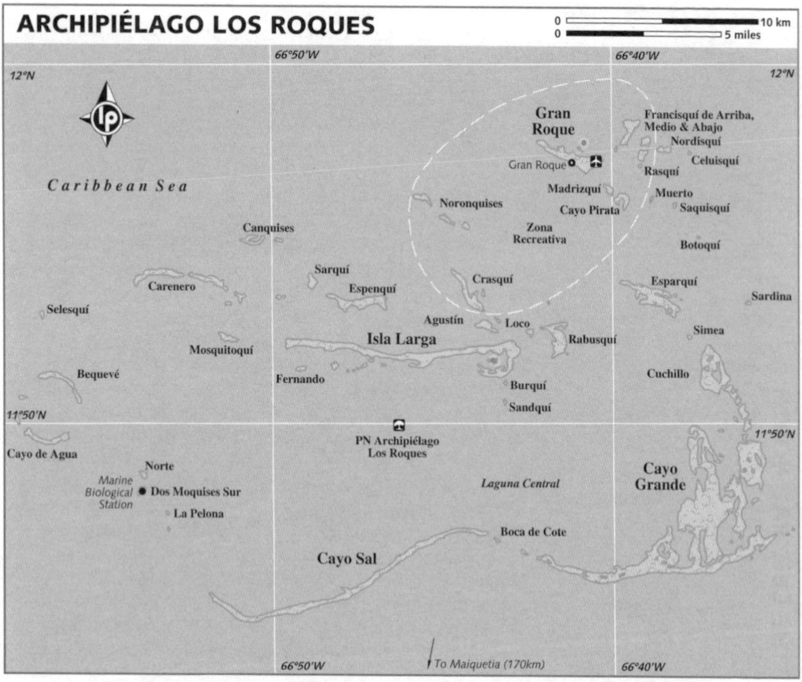

### THE VENEZUELAN BERMUDA TRIANGLE?

Paradise may be but a mere 160km from Aeropuerto Internacional 'Simón Bolívar' in Caracas, but recent history has left many folks wishing they could navigate Venezuela's Caribbean coastal waters to Archipiélago Los Roques on a Jet Ski, in a paddleboat or even with little more than a really nice pair of fins – anything but a plane! Since 1997, at least 15 planes – mostly Cessnas and Beechcrafts – have crashed, declared emergencies or otherwise disappeared along the route, earning comparisons to the mysterious Bermuda Triangle. The worse accident was in 2008, when a commercial Transaven flight to Los Roques disappeared into the water, killing all 14 aboard. Luckily, Aerotuy flies Dash 7s!

All foreign visitors to Los Roques pay the BsF55 national park entry fee upon arrival (BsF35 for Venezuelans).

## When to Go

Tourist peaks include late December and early January, Carnaval (late February to early March), Semana Santa (Holy Week, culminating in Easter) and August. Prices are at their highest during these times, and reservations are a must. The slowest periods are May to July and September to November, when beaches are less crowded and bargaining might be possible.

The average temperature is about 82°F, with highs around 91°F in July and lows around 75°F in January. Rainfall is practically nonexistent, except for rare showers between September and January.

## History

The archipelago has long been a stopping-off point for sailors, pirates and explorers. It was used as much as a thousand years ago by indigenous peoples; who temporarily inhabited the islands to catch fish, turtles and queen conch. Dos Mosquises was one of their prime staging areas.

In colonial times the islands saw a steady trail of foreigners, mostly from the Netherlands Antilles and England. In the 1920s fishermen from Isla de Margarita were attracted by the abundance of fish and gradually settled the archipelago's main island, Gran Roque, pushing out the Dutch by the 1950s. Known as *roqueños,* the fishermen's descendants now make up the majority of the local population.

Another recent influx of inhabitants is Italians, drawn here almost 20 years ago by restaurateur Vincenzo Conticello. He wrote home about the archipelago's wonders, and the rest is history. Today there are so many Italians here (most running posadas) that speaking Italian is as useful as speaking Spanish.

## Wildlife

The birds are a constant source of entertainment on the archipelago – from the continual rising and splashing falling of pelicans to mesmerizing frigates soaring effortlessly high overhead. Around 92 species of birds have been recorded on the islands, including 50 that migrate from North America. The only native mammal is the fishing bat, and there are also some reptiles, including four species of turtle and plenty of lizards, salamanders and iguanas. In terms of flora, the islands are sprinkled with grasses, thorny cacti, low bushes and mangroves.

But the islands' most attractive wildlife is actually underwater. The waters teem with riotously colorful fish, rays, barracudas, sea stars, mollusks, crabs, octopuses and lobsters, to name just a few. Any quick trip snorkeling around the archipelago's reefs will be rewarded by glimpses of everything from exquisite angelfish to the lumpish sea cucumbers. And of course the corals themselves are extraordinary, with names as exotic as their appearance, from the grooved brain coral to the orange elephant-ear sponge and the devil's sea whip.

Los Roques is particularly famous for its delicious lobsters, though they have been overfished in recent years. There's now a ban on fishing lobster from May to October, but Los Roques still accounts for over 90% of national production.

## Activities

Los Roques is a well-established sport fishing destination for Americans, though the principal activity remains relaxing, whether dozing in a hammock, cooling off in crystal-clear waters or soaking up the sun on pristine beaches (you'll find mostly Italians and Brazilians doing that). Crasquí claims one of the archipelago's longest ribbons of sand, but boat operators will most commonly drop passengers off at the islands of Francisquí and Madrizquí – these tend to be the most crowded. There are many other beautiful beach destinations, however, each one outshining the previous, all culminating at Cayo de Agua, a dreamy heavenscape on the sea and Los Roques' most postcard-perfect location (Inparques only allows 60 people per day to visit).

One word of warning: beaches on Los Roques are shadeless and the sun is relentless, made all the more powerful by reflection off the immaculately white sand. Umbrellas often come with package deals, but you'll still need sun block, along with a hat and sunglasses. Insect repellent wards off late-afternoon *puri-puri*, the region's tiny and very irritating biting flies (see p90).

#### SNORKELING & SCUBA DIVING

Los Roques is one of Venezuela's top destinations for snorkeling. Among the best places are Boca de Cote, Crasquí and Noronquises (here you can swim with the sea turtles), but there are other excellent sites closer to Gran Roque. The most popular spot is the so-called *piscina* (literally 'swimming pool') on Francisquí de Arriba. You can rent snorkeling equipment in Gran Roque for about BsF35 a day.

Scuba diving is also fabulous here, and there is a wealth of good places to explore. Diving is organized by several companies, including **Aquatics Dive Center** (SSI; ☎ 0414-777-0196; www.scubavenezuela.com), **Ecobuzos** (PADI; ☎ 0414-793-1471; www.ecobuzos.com) and **Arrecife Divers** (SSI & DAN; ☎ 0414-249-5119; www.divevenezuela.com) Two-tank dives with all the equipment range from BsF385 to BsF570.

#### WIND SPORTS

Los Roques is also a top-notch spot for windsurfing of all levels. It's organized by Elias at **Vela Windsurf Center** (www.velawindsurf.com) on the island of Francisquí de Abajo, which rents equipment (per hour/half-day/day BsF150/250/350) and can provide lessons for beginners (two hours including equipment BsF250). Get more information from Arhuna (Elias' brother) at Restaurant El Canto de la Ballena (p92) on Gran Roque. He can also give you advice on the local surfing action.

Vela Windsurf Center also rents kayaks (BsF250 per day) and is beginning to delve into paddleboarding. For general information, enquire at **Oscar Shop** (☎ 291-9160; oscarshop@hotmail.com; 6am-6:30pm) by the Gran Roque airport.

#### OTHER ACTIVITIES

Los Roques is also renowned as one of the world's finest areas for **game fishing**, particularly for bonefish. These trips are expensive and require permits, so it's often best to arrange one in advance through a specialized company; for example, Alpitour (p282) in Caracas. In Gran Roque, **Posada Mediterráneo** (☎ 0414-215-2219; www.posadamediterraneo.com) organizes game-fishing tours that go for BsF2100 per day (not including a rather forcefully 'suggested' tip of BsF420). Inparques (see opposite) can also give you some fishing information.

You can go **sailing** (per person per day BsF1250) around Los Roques on one of several sailing yachts that anchor off Gran Roque. They have cabins equipped with berths and provide meals on board, and can take you for several days around the islands. Ask at Oscar Shop for more information.

### Tours

If you don't have much time or just want a quick taste of Los Roques, taking a one- or two-day tour is an easy way out, but nobody ends up wanting to leave so quickly. A day tour is good value, as it's not much more expensive than the airfare. Two-day tours give a better insight but are much more expensive as the tour companies often use upmarket accommodations.

An all-inclusive one-day tour from Maiquetía costs weekday/weekend BsF1072/1400, including the roundtrip flight, a boat excursion from Gran Roque to one or two of the nearby islands, lunch, soft drinks, one hour of snorkeling (equipment provided) and free time on the beach. Different operators may go to different islands and often have their own preferred snorkeling areas.

The two-day package adds an overnight stay in Gran Roque plus all meals, and it costs weekday/weekend BsF3224/4580 (depending on the season and posada standard). Many tours are run by the small airlines that fly to Los Roques (see p283), though plenty of travel agencies in Venezuela offer tours also. Note that tour prices don't include the BsF55 entry fee to the national park.

If you plan on staying two or more days, it's often better value to go it alone. Just buy a roundtrip ticket and arrange all the rest in Gran Roque. **Oscar Shop** (☎ 291-9160; oscarshop@hotmail.com) provides boat transportation to the islands, organizes full-day boat tours, and rents out snorkeling equipment and beach chairs. It also provides general tourist information.

Try to avoid tourist peaks, when flights and accommodations are in short supply and prices are at their highest.

## Getting There & Away

### AIR

Flights to Los Roques are messy. Once there were at least five airlines covering the route, but at time of research, there were only a few left after various crashes, bankruptcies and business divorces, and flights were being cancelled or delayed with annoying regularity. The Maiquetía–Los Roques one-way fare is generally around BsF520 but can be double or half that. The flight takes 40 minutes. You can also fly between Los Roques and Porlamar, on Isla de Margarita (one way BsF720, 1½ hours). It is not a good idea to book an international connection on the same day as a Los Roques flight. Normally only 10kg of free luggage is permitted on flights to Los Roques; every additional kilogram costs BsF5.

**Aereotuy** (LTA; ☎ 0237-221-1306; www.tuy.com)
The *most* reliable at the time of research but that's no compliment.

**Rainbow Air** (☎ 0424-146-1424; makorotours@gmail.com)

**Sundance Air** (☎ 0414-016-5577; jomicoltours@gmail.com)

### BOAT

There are no passenger boats to Los Roques.

## GRAN ROQUE

Lying on the northern edge of the archipelago, Gran Roque is the main island and has a distinct Caribbean feel. It's small – you can walk from one end of the island's four-street fishing village to the other in less than 10 minutes. It's also a friendly place and accounts for the archipelago's biggest population, a mere 1280 souls in all.

Gran Roque's sandy streets, where locals walk barefoot, are lined with one-story, brightly painted concrete houses. There's also one bank, a handful of supermarkets, a school and no less than 60 posadas. The only land vehicles you'll see are a water and garbage truck, plus maybe a golf cart or two. In contrast, the waterfront is packed with fishing boats, tour vessels and visiting yachts – all covered by a vast army of pelicans. The island also has an airstrip by the village, which handles all tourist flights. You practically land on the sand.

Unlike the other islands, which are sandy and flat, Gran Roque has several massive rocky humps along its northwestern coast – the tallest is 110m – and cliffs that plunge vertically into the sea. Climb the hill crowned with an old lighthouse, known as the Faro Holandés, for sweeping views over the village, islands, coral reefs and the crystal-clear turquoise sea. The lighthouse was built in the 1870s and used until the early 1950s.

### Information

The island's only bank, **Banesco** (☎ 221-1265; Plaza Bolívar; 🕑 8am-noon & 2-5pm Mon-Fri, 8am-2pm Sat), arranges cash advances on Visa and MasterCard with a maximum of BsF800 per day (the ATM limit is also BsF800 per day). However, it's wise to bring cash (dollars or euro) in case your cards don't work. Though credit card acceptance is on the rise, most posadas still don't accept them (some nicer restaurants do).

**Inparques** (National Institute of National Parks; ☎ 0416-614-2297; 🕑 8am-noon & 2-5pm Mon-Fri, 8am-noon Sat & Sun), at the far end of village, oversees the running of the national park and can give advice on places to camp and snorkel. **Oscar Shop** (☎ 0414-291-9160; oscarshop@hotmail.com; 🕑 6am-6:30pm), right by the airport, is a combination of shop, tour agency, boat operator and tourist office, all run by the knowledgeable Oscar. Upon arrival at Gran Roque, you will pass his kiosk on your way into the village. It's essential stopping.

For internet access there's **Enzosoft** (🕑 8am-10pm; per hr BsF20), or try the free state-sponsored Infocentro near the school. Enzosoft also has local and international telephone services. For minor ailments limp to the **medic** (☎ emergencies 0425-712-1120; 🕑 9am-noon & 4-7pm Mon-Fri) near the school – just a bed in a doctor's home, really.

### Sleeping

The small island village of Gran Roque has exploded with posadas over the last decade. There are now over 60 on the island, about half of them Italian-run. Most posadas will have a luggage tout meet you at the airport to escort you and your luggage (via hand cart) included in the price. Note that there are no addresses in Los Roques.

Unless you're camping, accommodations will be pricy – even in low season there are few options under BsF400 for two people. Breakfast, dinner or both are often included in the price – lunch (usually sandwiches for the beach) can be available on request. In high season most posadas offer full pension rates only. Single travelers get whacked with a 30% or more single supplement fee in any season.

Food is also expensive, because everything except fish has to be shipped in from the mainland. You can save money by staying at a posada that offers bed only (just the cheaper ones do this in low season), while patronizing the island's few inexpensive eateries and supermarkets.

The island has an electricity and desalination plant, though there are frequent blackouts (bring a flashlight and consider high-end options with generators). Water should be used sparingly.

Prices listed here are for high season, per person per night with breakfast only unless otherwise noted. These peak dates include late December to early January, Carnaval (late February to early March), Semana Santa (Easter) and all of August. Reservations are an absolute must during these times and many posadas have five to seven-day minimum stays, full board only (which often includes a daily excursion). Other times, prices can drop 20% to 50% depending on the posada (top end ones offer the biggest discounts), bargaining is a possibility, and you can always choose between B&B, half-board or full board.

Additionally, most posadas require a wire transfer deposit to secure a room, but it's not a bad option to pay your entire bill in full, alleviating the worry over the infrequent credit card acceptance and iffy ATM machine.

### I VAANT TO CHUPAR YOUR BLOOD!

*Puri-puri* are very annoying sand flies that love to feast on travelers' exotic blood. They're tiny little things that are barely visible, and you won't feel much after the first chomp – but after a while the bite will start to itch...and itch...and itch...for days on end! It's important not to scratch too much (though, frankly, this will be impossible) because it's relatively easy to pick up an infection in the tropics. If you do get seriously bitten and can't resist scratching, try going to a Venezuelan pharmacy and getting some anti-itch pills or cream. And consider covering up with clothing or repellent next time you're lined up on the beach buffet.

### BUDGET

**Doña Magali** (☎ 0414-120-4096; r per person incl breakfast BsF150; ❄) This roquena-owned guesthouse isn't rolling out any red carpets, but offers bare-bones basic shelter – save those chilly air-conditioners, a nice budget bonus. It's right on the plaza.

**Posada Gremary** (☎ 0414-260-1993; www.posadagremary.com; r per person incl breakfast BsF180; ❄ 📶) Staff is a bit unpolished and the whole place could use a fresh slap of paint, but for the price, amenities like wi-fi and air-con, and location right on the northwest corner of Plaza Bolívar, it's a good shoestring option – just don't expect homespun hospitality.

**Doña Carmen** (☎ 0414-318-4926; richardlosroques@hotmail.com; Plaza Bolívar; r per person incl breakfast BsF200; ❄) Nine decent and clean rooms, set along a colorful outdoor hallway, greet you at this long-running posada on Plaza Bolívar. All have air-con except the two fronting the beach (which come with ocean breezes instead). Your towels are folded into bird shapes.

The cheapest option in Los Roques is to camp. Camping is allowed on all the islands within the Zona Recreativa, including Gran Roque, and is free. After arrival go to the far end of the village to the Inparques office for a free camping permit. The staff will tell you which islands are open for camping and can give you other practical tips. On Gran Roque the camping area is next to the Inparques office and set near the beach in a shady grove. Toilet and shower facilities are available at nearby posadas (Inparques has a list) for a small fee. Oscar Shop rents basic tents. However, there have been reports of thefts, so you might think twice if you have to spend all of your time guarding your stuff rather than enjoying the beaches.

Also be on the lookout for Posada Eva, a longtime backpacker haunt that had lost its concession at the time of research but was scheduled to reopen in a new location near the lagoon in 2010.

### MIDRANGE

**Ranchito Power** (☎ 0414-141-3568; www.ranchitopower.com; r per person incl breakfast BsF240) Tiny and simple, this is a great six-room, Italian-run budget option offering clean rooms with crotchety fans, along with a nice rooftop area in which to hang out. Guests can use the kitchen.

**Roquelusa** (☎ 0414-369-6401; r per person incl breakfast BsF250; ❄) Located at the far end of the village near the Inparques office is this basic cheapie with a few rough edges, but a big plus is that all eight rooms offer chilly air-con. This part of the neighborhood is a little noisy.

**El Botuto** (☎ 0414-238-1589; www.posadaelbotuto.com; r per person incl breakfast BsF263) The stiff staff certainly isn't charming any travelers during their stay, but this six-room posada close to the Inparques office offers smallish but pleasant rooms, most with mosquito nets and tiny outdoor patio showers. There's a relaxing front area with shade and water views.

**Guaripete** (☎ 0212-286-4932; www.posadaguaripete.com; r per person incl breakfast BsF385; ) Seven pleasant rooms with fan and mosquito nets are available at this pretty, Italian-run posada, and a shady upstairs terrace comes strewn with relaxing hammocks.

### TOP END

**La Lagunita** (☎ 0414-291-9151; www.posadalagunita.com; Calle La Laguna; r per person incl breakfast BsF450; ) This friendly, Italian-run posada offers up seven excellent rooms with TV and safe box (room five is especially nice) and a pleasant rooftop terrace with an established traveler's scene. But the big bonus here is an included nightly aperitif for all, and free cocktails across the board – even for your days on the beaches – for full pensioners.

**La Cigala** (☎ 236-5731; www.lacigala.com; r per person incl breakfast BsF540; ) This refined, eight-room boutique posada is extra-friendly and well run, by a tri-lingual couple and a lovely staff. Whitewashed in understated Med-Italian accents, minimalist rooms are a tad tiny but staff offers extra-personalized attention to make up for it. It sits on privileged real estate mere steps from the runway.

**El Paraiso Azul II** (☎ 0237-221-1218; www.posadaelparaisoazul.com; r per person incl breakfast BsF600; ) Here's another Italian-run posada sporting eight clean, comfortable rooms with clean wood accents. You'll find sinks in the sleeping area in the smaller rooms. It also has a sunny rooftop patio and airy bar area.

**Natura Viva** (☎ 0212-952-8722; www.naturavivalosroques.com; r per person incl breakfast BsF850; ) The 14 rooms at this vaguely maritime-themed posada are steeped in unexpected touches such as Victorian doorknobs. They surround a pastel-hued courtyard above which sits a beautiful rooftop terrace with sea views and boat-shaped bar.

**Piano y Papaya** (☎ 0414-281-0104; www.pianoypapaya.com; d incl breakfast BsF900; ) Behind the church, this bright, fresh posada has just five spacious, vanilla-scented rooms with mosquito nets and paintings by the artistic owner, along with a wonderful lounging area in front. It's a good deal (prices are per room, not per person). French and Italian are all spoken.

**our pick Acuarela** (☎ 0212-953-4235; www.posadaacuarela.com; r per person incl meals BsF1250; ) Almost everyone's favorite top end, this artistic posada comes with 12 gorgeous and creative rooms. It also boasts open-topped patios and a breezy rooftop terrace with hammocks. Italian Chef Cossimo Muscoguiri, who hails from Puglia via a New York City restaurant, is an absolute culinary Da Vinci – this is one posada where you don't want to skimp on the meal plan. Outside guests are also welcome at the restaurant with reservations (three-course meal BsF150 to BsF200). Prices here are for high season, when full board is mandatory, as is a seven-day minimum. English, French and Italian are spoken.

**Mediterráneo** (☎ 0414-215-2219; www.posadamediterraneo.com; r per person incl meals & daily excursion BsF1800; ) True to its name, this spotless whitewashed posada comes with airy Mediterranean feel and caters to mainly to sport fishers, especially from January to May (hence the questionable design choice of planting their triumphant fishing photos in each room). There's a great rooftop terrace, common spaces are beautifully decorated and all rooms have a flat-screen with DirecTV. Prices here reflect the high season option of full board only.

## Eating & Drinking

Since almost all posadas serve meals for their guests, there's only a handful of independent restaurants in Gran Roque. A few folks sell cheap empanadas out of their homes or from kiosks.

**Brisas de Los Roques** (breakfast BsF10-30; breakfast, lunch & dinner) Early risers and caffeine junkies will appreciate the 6am opening time. Everyone else comes for down-to-earth *arepas*, empanadas, grilled meats and pasta. The bar stays open late.

**Mama Julia** (arepas BsF20; breakfast & lunch) Perfect hangover-curing *arepas* are the star at this wooden kiosk by the lagoon, served from 6am.

**La Chuchera** (☎ 221-1417; Plaza Bolívar; pizza BsF26-100, mains BsF28-85; lunch & dinner Tue-Sun) The Venezuelan owner of this restaurant, located on Plaza Bolívar and offering cool music, spent time in the US, so he knows a thing or two about service. On the menu are hamburgers, pasta, simple but well-done daily catches, and, oddly, good pizza (served after 4pm) *not* made by an Italian. In fact, no Italians here have a pizzeria, which is just weird.

**Aquarena Cafe** (☎ 0414-131-1282; mains BsF35-70; ⏰ lunch & dinner) There's Cuban-style *ceviche* (marinated raw fish or seafood), sushi, burgers, fresh fish and salads (all set to reggae muzak) at this beachside cafe on the sand. Before 1pm, there's only juices and espresso. It's near Macanao Lodge.

**Bora la Mar** (☎ 325-7814; 1-/3-course menu BsF80/150; ⏰ dinner) The chosen spot for sundown drinks and world-famous the island over for its piña coladas, Bora la Mar is a simple place run by a sweet Spanish woman. The kitchen needs to ease up on the salt a bit, but the food – just one choice per night, served on pleasant tables in the sand – is better than expected.

**El Canto de la Ballena** (☎ 0237-221-1160; breakfast BsF100, 5-course menu BsF170; ⏰ breakfast, lunch & dinner) Though we were greeted by several empty tables and a closed kitchen (on a Saturday night at 8:20pm – reservations are mandatory for dinner, we learned), the gourmet wares served family-style on this restaurant's breezy wood deck make for a pleasant tropical evening (count yourself lucky if you get the tuna sashimi). Space is limited and there is only nightly seating – obviously, call ahead.

**La Gotera Art Café** (☎ 221-1369) Bean-bag chairs, romantic lights, a mellow vibe and tasty drinks make this swanky beachside spot a great place to hang out, inside or out under the shady grove.

## OTHER ISLANDS

The nearest island to Gran Roque is **Madrizquí**, about 1km to the southeast. It was the favorite island among affluent *caraqueños* (people from Caracas), who built summer beach houses here before the archipelago was made a national park. Connected to Madrizquí by sandbar is **Cayo Pirata**, which harbors fishing shelters known as *rancherías* and a restaurant to eat fresh lobster in season. **Francisquí**, also close to Gran Roque, is actually composed of three islands, and the most popular one – Francisquí de Arriba – has a casual but excellent restaurant. Beautiful and serene **Crasquí** has good snorkeling and some *rancherías,* while **Rasquí** is the only island (other than Gran Roque) with a posada.

### Sleeping & Eating

Wherever you stay you'll never be far from a beach, but for that ultimate castaway feeling you can stay outside Gran Roque.

Camping is free: all you need is a permit from Inparques. Permits are available for the nearby islands of Madrizquí, Cayo Pirata and Francisquí. Further away, you can also camp on Noronquises and Crasquí. You must be self-sufficient and bring all camping gear, food and water to all but Crasquí. Also don't forget your snorkeling gear, insect repellent for small biting flies, a hat and strong sun block.

**Restaurant Don Luis** (☎ 0414-019-0466) The simple beach restaurant on Crasquí offers fried fish plates for BsF50 and camping is allowed on the property – right in front of the crystalline sea. Miss Deysi will cook for you and allow you to use her facilities if you eat at her restaurant. For added comfort, there are two small rooms as well (full room and board goes for BsF300 per person). She also rents four-person tents for BsF80 per day.

**Rancho de la Langosta** (lobster per kg BsF150) During lobster season from November to May, this bucolic seaside shack on Cayo Pirata allows you to pick your lobster of choice from the sea, then fires it up for you then and there – a real treat for lobster connoisseurs.

**Rasquí Island Chalet** (☎ in Gran Roque 0412-310-1962; www.rasqui.net; per person BsF1235) The only posada outside Gran Roque is this rustic chalet on idyllic sands in tiny Rasquí. The three cabins are comfortable (though a dodgy staircase leads to the two second-floor rooms) and there's a communal kitchen and barbecue. Rates include roundtrip boat transportation, all meals and wine and beer with meals. In low season rates drop by 30% to Bs950 per person. For more information go to Posada Acquamarina in Gran Roque.

There are a couple of fried-fish restaurants run by fishermen on Crasquí. Otherwise your only formal eating option outside Gran Roque is the pleasant and casual **Restaurant Casamarina** (mains BsF40-100; ⏰ lunch), located on Francisquí de Arriba. It has a great shady wood deck and the seafood spaghetti is a star. Snorkeling equipment and umbrella rentals are available.

### Getting There & Away

Oscar Shop or other boat operators in Gran Roque will take you to the island of your choice and pick you up at a prearranged time and date. Most boats leave by 9:30am, especially for destinations further away. Roundtrip fares per person include Madrizquí (BsF25, seven minutes), the Francisquises (BsF30, 10 minutes), Crasquí or Noronquises (BsF60, 25 minutes) and Cayo de Agua (BsF120, 1½ hours). Full day tours to Cayo de Agua, Dos Mosquises and Espenquí or Boca de Coté and Crasquí cost BsF120. A private boat and captain for a day costs BsF1200.

# MIRANDA STATE

## SAN FRANCISCO DE YARE

☎ 0239 / pop 22,000

Strolling around the colonial streets of this small, sleepy town, it's difficult to imagine the mayhem that reigns here annually during the Festival de los Diablos Danzantes (Dancing Devils). This colorful festival sees visitors arrive in their thousands as the village is transformed into a huge mass of frenzied, costumed revelers in devil masks dancing to the hypnotic rhythm of drums and maracas.

San Francisco de Yare lies 70km by road southeast of Caracas. The town was founded in 1714 and boasts a fine mid-18th-century church, the Iglesia de San Francisco, and some well-preserved colonial architecture.

### Sights

The **Casa de los Diablos Danzantes** (Calle Rivas; admission free; 8am-7pm), one block down from the plaza, shelters a small museum with a collection of papier-mâché devil masks and photos from previous festivals. The family living in the house to the left of the museum as you face it can open the museum if it's closed when you arrive.

You can stop by workshops manufacturing devil masks to see the production process and buy masks at good rates. One of the best is **Artesanía El Mocho** (☎ 222-9191; Calle Ribas), led by Manuel Sanoja. It's two blocks down from the museum, above the small Bodega San Antonio. **Artesanía Morgado** (☎ 222-9345; Calle Ribas 19), one block down from the museum, is run by noted local artisan Juan Morgado – a 'living Unesco site,' as he calls himself – and a mask maker since 1963. Knock on the entrance door around the corner on Calle Santa Eduviges if it appears closed.

### Sleeping & Eating

There are no regular hotels in San Francisco de Yare proper. There is a upscale love motel, Hotel El Rufugio, on the outskirts of town that may relent on their maximum eight-hour requirement during the festival. Otherwise, there's **Hotel Tahay** (☎ 231-7116; Calle Miranda; d/tr BsF100/120), in nearby Santa Teresa del Tuy (a love motel as well) or try additional options in Ocumare del Tuy. There are several basic places to eat in San Francisco de Yare, especially around the cute-ish plaza.

### Getting There & Away

There's no direct transportation from Caracas to San Francisco de Yare, but you can get there easily with one connection from the Nuevo Circo regional bus terminal. Take one of the frequent buses to Ocumare del Tuy (BsF5, 1½ hours) or Santa Teresa del Tuy (BsF5, 1½ hours) and change at your destination. Frequent buses shuttle between San Francisco de Yare and Santa Teresa (BsF1.70).



## PARQUE NACIONAL GUATOPO

This national park is an important biological enclave covered by lush rainforest in the otherwise heavily developed and populated hinterland of Caracas. Thanks to the wide range of elevations and copious rainfall, the park's vegetation is varied and exuberant, and includes palms, ferns, orchids and huge trees up to 40m high.

The rich mammal world includes jaguars, pumas, tapirs, armadillos and sloths, to name just a few. Guatopo is also good for birdwatching: macaws, parakeets, woodpeckers, hummingbirds, honeycreepers and dozens of other bird species are easily spotted in the forest canopy. But keep an eye on the ground as well – there are also some poisonous snakes, including the coral snake and the (more common and dangerous) macagua.

Established in 1958, Guatopo is about 100km by road (60km as the crow flies) southeast of Caracas. The park encompasses 1225 sq km of the rugged Serranía del Interior, a mountain range that splits off the Cordillera de la Costa and winds inland. The altitude in the park ranges between 200m and 1430m above sea level. The park is also a major water source for the region, since several dams have been built around the park, creating *embalses* (reservoirs).

The climate here is wet and warm. The rainiest months are October to December, while the driest ones are March and April, but rain gear is recommended at any time of the year. Insects are also plentiful, so bring

**DANCING WITH DEVILS**

The Festival de los Diablos Danzantes (Dancing Devils) is a kaleidoscopic spectacle. Up to a thousand devil dancers clad in red costumes and wearing monstrous masks strut around in everything from marching movements in double file to spasmodic squirms accompanied by the stirring clamor of drums. The devil dancers take to the streets on the Wednesday, one day before Corpus Christi (held in honor of the Eucharist), and on the holy day itself. So why do the devils come out on this holiest of days?

The ceremony manifests the struggle between evil and good, and the eventual triumph of the latter. No matter how profane the devil dances look, the devils come to the church to submit themselves to the Eucharist before returning to their whirling dances. Locals believe that the dance ritual will ensure abundant crops, welfare, prosperity and protection against misfortune and natural disasters. For the devils, the dance is their religion.

The festival blends Spanish and African traditions: its origins lie in Spain, where devils' images and masks featured in Corpus Christi feasts in medieval Andalusia. But when the festival was brought to the New World in colonial times, it found a fertile soil among the black slaves, who introduced the traditional African-style masks and the rhythm of drumbeats so characteristic of their homeland. Some saw this as an act of protest against the white god, a symbol of Spanish oppression and cruelty. But the profane and the divine gradually merged, producing a striking cross-cultural ritual.

While the ceremony's African roots are palpable, the dances are not performed exclusively by blacks. Devil dances have been preserved only in areas with the heaviest import of African slaves, including the towns of Naiguatá (Vargas); Cata, Chuao, Cuyagua, Ocumare de la Costa and Turiamo (Aragua); Canoabo, Guacara, Los Caneyes, Patanemo and Tocuyito (Carabobo); Tinaquillo (Cojedes); and San Francisco de Yare (Miranda). The celebrations in Chuao and San Francisco de Yare are best known.

Dances and costumes have their own characteristics in each community, especially the papier-mâché masks, which differ notably from town to town. San Francisco de Yare churns out large, elaborate masks depicting horned demons, monsters and fantastic animals painted in every color of the rainbow. Meanwhile, the masks from Chuao are smaller and painted with just three colors (white, black and red).

repellent. The temperature ranges between 77°F and 86°F, but drops to about 59°F on the highest peaks.

## Orientation

The paved but pothole-ridden road between Santa Teresa del Tuy and Altagracia de Orituco winds through the middle of the park, passing all the recreational areas and starting points for walks. Public transportation from Caracas does travel along this road sporadically, but it's infrequent and dies in the afternoon. Given that the last bus back to Caracas leaves around 4pm, a one-day trip leaves you limited time in the park. If you decide to do this, leave very early and go directly to Agua Blanca – the best starting point for walks. Altagracia de Orituco, just beyond the park, has several hotels but is otherwise dull as daisies. Having your own transportation gives you more flexibility.

There are some basic lodging and camping facilities in the park. The following section details the major stopovers on the route, from north to south, with their tourist facilities.

Bring all food and water with you. There is a small restaurant at Los Tepes and limited snacks available at Agua Blanca, but only on weekends.

## Sights & Activities

### LA MACANILLA

There's a *guardaparque* (park ranger) based here who can give you information about the park (7:30am to 3pm Monday to Friday, 7am to 4:30pm Saturday and Sunday), but no other services are available. And, incidentally, it was closed on our visit, so don't count on it.

### AGUA BLANCA

Thirteen kilometers on, Agua Blanca is the park's major recreational area and has a *guardaparque* and the safest camping. There's an intriguing reconstructed **trapiche** (traditional sugarcane mill; 7:30am-3pm Mon-Fri, 7am-4pm Sat & Sun), complete with its huge cauldrons and ladles, and you can also take a bath in nearby *pozos* (ponds).

From here a 3km walking trail heads to Santa Crucita; allow up to 1½ hours to walk it at a leisurely pace. There's also another, shorter (1.5km) trail between Agua Blanca and Santa Crucita that takes just 45 minutes, running on the opposite (eastern) side of the road – so you can take a roundtrip without returning the same way.

Agua Blanca attracts day-trippers on weekends, but is usually quiet on weekdays. It has a picnic area, toilets, a guarded car park, a snack kiosk (open on weekends) and some accommodation options. There are also five two-person **cabañas** (BsF10), which are very rustic timber structures on stilts, scattered around the forest. They have no beds, so bring mats and sleeping bags. To stay at them simply check with the nearest park rangers. There's also a **camping ground** (per person BsF5). Bring your own food and water.

### SANTA CRUCITA
The next stop, Santa Crucita, is 1.5km from Agua Blanca. There is a small lagoon here, and you can pitch your tent in the unguarded grassy camping site. As well as the two trails coming here from Agua Blanca, there are two short local walking loops, one skirting around the lagoon (700m) and another one going through the nearby forest (800m).

### EL LUCERO & QUEBRADA DE GUATOPO
The park's **administrative center** ( ⌚ 7:30am-3pm Mon-Fri, 9am-4:30pm Sat & Sun) is El Lucero, 5.5km down the road from Santa Crucita. There are *guardaparques* here to provide information. Quebrada de Guatopo, 2km beyond El Lucero, has a picnic area, a creek with small waterfalls and swimming holes, and yet another (unguarded) camping ground. Again, bring your own food and water.

## ALTAGRACIA DE ORITUCO
☎ 0238 / pop 53,000
Lying outside the national park's boundaries and a 30-minute bus ride from Agua Blanca is Altagracia de Orituco. It's a distinctly ordinary town, but big enough to have a collection of hotels and restaurants.

The **Hotel Tasca Galicia** ( ☎ 334-3354, s/d/tr BsF80/120/140; ☒ ) is near buses to Caracas and offers decent (if noisy) rooms. Four blocks down Av Pellón y Palacio is the best choice,

the **Hotel Amazor** ( ☎ 334-1174; francidelamw@hotmail.com; Calle Pellón y Palacio 16; s/d/tr BsF95/125/140; ☒ ☎ ). Rooms smell a little greasy, but there's cable TV and a restaurant.

### Getting There & Away
There are hourly buses from the Nuevo Circo regional terminal in Caracas to Altagracia de Orituco (BsF20, four hours), but they go via San Casimiro and don't pass through the park. There are also faster *camionetas* (minibuses) that run to Altagracia from about 8am to 5pm and depart when full. They go via Santa Teresa and the park, and can let you off at any point along the road. In Altagracia, buses to the park and private carritos to Caracas (BsF400) depart one block from Hotel Galacia at Redoma Chala in front of Inversiones Don Jose. Buses to Caracas depart from the intersection of Avs Ilustres Próceres and Hurtado Arcano. The last transportation back to Caracas leaves Altagracia around 4pm. After that, you're stuck with the carrito option only.

# ARAGUA STATE

## MARACAY
☎ 0243 / pop 443,000
Maracay, the 300-year-old capital of Aragua state, isn't necessarily luring travelers in with a warm welcome and a wealth of don't-miss attractions, but as a popular stopover en route to and from Parque Nacional Henri Pittier, it packs in enough colonial relic and museums to hold your attention for a day. You can wander some of the city's parks and leafy plazas, including the country's largest Plaza Bolívar, as well as Venezuela's only aeronautical museum.

At an altitude of about 450m, the city has a hot climate (warmer than Caracas, but more pleasant than Maracaibo), with an average temperature of 77°F and most rain falling between April and October.

If you made the mistake of not entering the country with plenty of cash, it's a good idea to stock up on cash here if you're heading to the coast, as there is only one bank in Puerto Colombia, but it isn't friendly to foreign cards.

### History
Founded in the mid-16th century, Maracay has long taken advantage of the valley's fertile soil, growing dozens of crops from cacao

to sugarcane. It was a slow-growing town, however, and by 1900 the population had reached a mere 7000. Indeed, the city would have probably continued at this unhurried rate if it hadn't been for Juan Vicente Gómez, probably the most ruthless of all Venezuelan *caudillos* (dictators). He first came here in 1899, and after seizing power in 1908, he settled in Maracay and ruled both state and country from here until his death in 1935. He set about turning the town into a city worthy of being capital, building a grandiose bullring, opera house, zoo, splendid hotels and an air-force school that became the cradle of Venezuelan aviation.

After his reign, a second wave of city development came with the freeway linking Caracas with Maracay in the 1950s. Around this time, Venezuela also developed the most powerful air force in Latin America, much of it based in Maracay. The city is still an important military base, and the unsuccessful coup of 1992 began with the rebels' planes flying to Caracas from here.

## Information

Internet cafes in Maracay are common.

**Banco de Venezuela** (Calle Mariño)
**Banesco** (Av Páez)
**Farmatodo** (☎ 232-2049; cnr Avs Las Delicias & Urb La Soledad; 🕑 24hr) A large, well-stocked pharmacy north of the center.
**Instituto Autónomo de Turismo de Aragua** (Iatur; ☎ 242-1967; www.intur.gov.ve; Hotel de Golf Maracay, Av Las Delicias; 🕑 9am-2pm Mon-Fri) Dreadfully located 2km north of the center, but full of national park info.
**Ipostel** (Av 19 de Abril)

## Sights

### PLAZA GIRARDOT

The historic heart of Maracay, Plaza Girardot (for once, not Plaza Bolívar) is crowned by a large obelisk topped with a bronze eagle, erected in 1897. It commemorates the North American volunteers who joined the independence war forces led by Francisco Miranda, but were captured and hanged in 1806 by the Spaniards.

The only colonial building left by the square is the handsome **catedral** on its eastern side. The cathedral was completed in 1743 and not much has changed since. The white-washed exterior is particularly attractive when the late-afternoon sunlight strikes the facade.

### CASA DE DOLORES AMELIA

Set on the northern side of Parque Bicentenario, this fine **mansion** (☎ 245-1618; 🕑 7am-7pm Mon-Fri) was built in 1927 by Gómez for his favorite mistress, Dolores Amelia Núñez de Cáceres. Designed in the neo-Sevillan style, the building has been nicely restored, but today is a medical facility. Tourists can take a look around the inner patio, which is clad with glorious *azulejos* (ornamental tiles), reminiscent of the Alhambra in Granada.

### SANTUARIO DE MADRE MARÍA DE SAN JOSÉ

This saintly **sanctuary** (admission free; 🕑 8:30am-noon & 2:30-5pm Tue-Sun), one block east of Plaza Girardot, is the most revered city site. Choroní-born Madre María (1875–1967) was beatified by papal decree in 1995. Her remains were exhumed and, to everybody's shock, the corpse was allegedly intact. You can see her diminutive body in a crystal sarcophagus in the Santuario (though the face and hands are covered with masks).

### PLAZA DE TOROS MAESTRANZA

This large Spanish-Moorish construction, possibly the most stylish and beautiful bullring in the country, was modeled on the one in Seville and built in 1933. It was originally called 'Calicanto,' but was then renamed in memory of César Girón, Venezuela's most famous matador, who died in 1971. A monument of him fighting a bull stands in front of the ring. If you want to have a snoop inside, try getting in through the back door on the eastern side.

### MUSEO AERONÁUTICO

This is the only **aeronautical museum** (Av Santos Michelena; admission free; 🕑 9:30am-5pm Sat & Sun) in the country and well worth a look. There are about 40 aircraft on display, including four helicopters. Many are warplanes from the 1920s to the 1950s that once served in the Venezuelan air force. The collection's gem has to be a beautifully restored French Caudron G3 from the 1910s, reputedly still in perfect working order.

In the middle of the exhibition grounds is a statue of Juan Vicente Gómez: the first and only monument to the *caudillo*, unveiled amid great controversy in 1995.

The museum is open only on weekends. If you arrive on a weekday, enquire at the

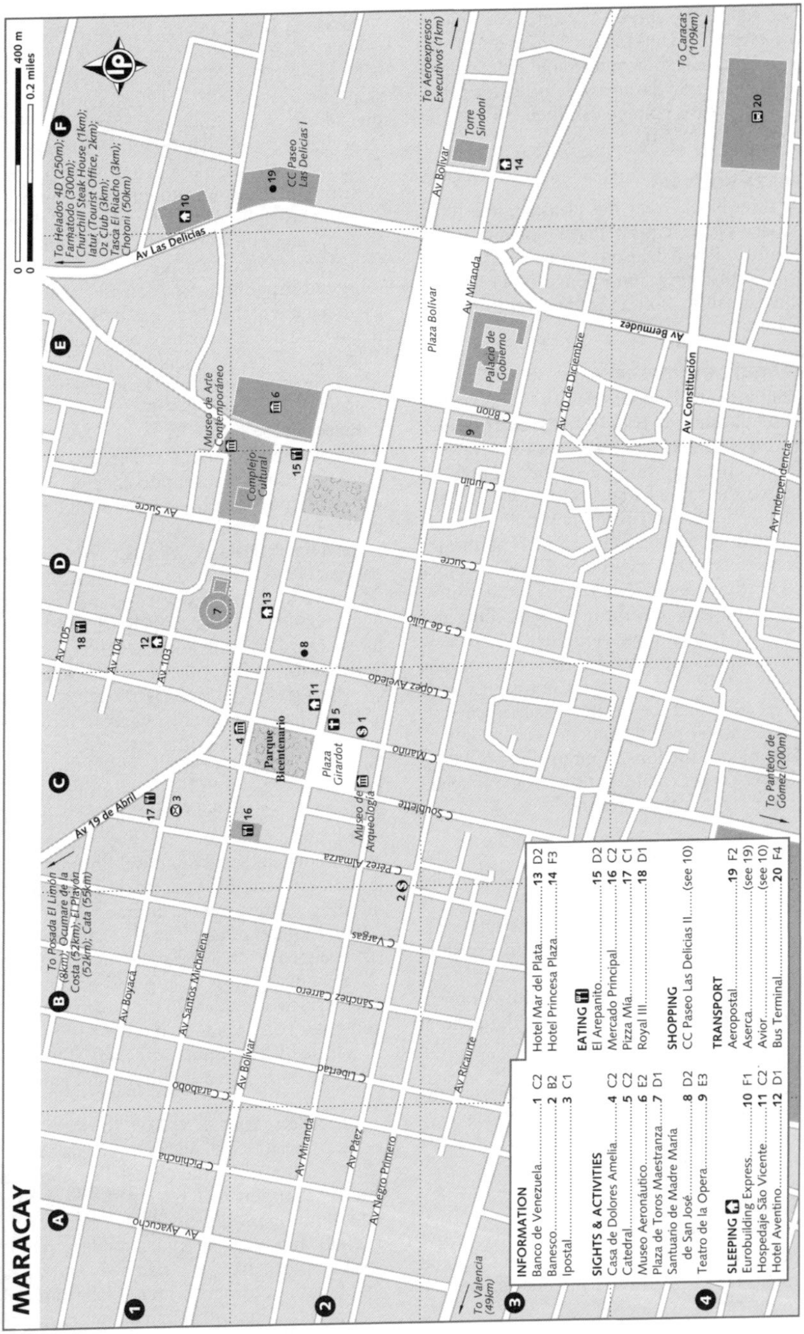
MARACAY
0 400 m
0 0.2 miles
To Posada El Limón (8km); Ocumare de la Costa (52km); El Playón (52km); Cata (55km)
To Helados 4D (250m); Farmatodo (300m); Churchill Steak House (1km); Iatur (Tourist Office, 2km); Oz Club (3km); Tasca El Riacho (3km); Choroní (50km)
To Aeroexpresos Ejecutivos (1km)
To Caracas (109km)
To Valencia (49km)
To Panteón de Gómez (200m)
Av Las Delicias
Av 19 de Abril
Av Bolívar
Av Miranda
Av Bermúdez
Av Constitución
Av Independencia
Av 10 de Diciembre
Av Sucre
Av 105
Av 104
Av 103
Av Boyacá
Av Santos Michelena
Av Páez
Av Negro Primero
Av Ricaurte
Av Ayacucho
C Pichincha
C Carabobo
C Libertad
C Sánchez Carrero
C Vargas
C Pérez Almarza
C Soublette
C Mariño
C López Aveledo
C 5 de Julio
C Sucre
C Junín
C Brion
Plaza Bolívar
Palacio de Gobierno
Torre Sindoni
CC Paseo Las Delicias I
Museo de Arte Contemporáneo
Complejo Cultural
Parque Bicentenario
Plaza Girardot
Museo de Arqueología
INFORMATION
Banco de Venezuela 1 C2
Banesco 2 B2
Ipostal 3 C1
SIGHTS & ACTIVITIES
Casa de Dolores Amelia 4 C2
Catedral 5 C2
Museo Aeronáutico 6 E2
Plaza de Toros Maestranza 7 D1
Santuario de Madre María de San José 8 D2
Teatro de la Opera 9 E3
SLEEPING
Eurobuilding Express 10 F1
Hospedaje São Vicente 11 C2
Hotel Aventino 12 D1
Hotel Mar del Plata 13 D2
Hotel Princesa Plaza 14 F3
EATING
El Arepanito 15 D2
Mercado Principal 16 C2
Pizza Mía 17 C1
Royal III 18 D1
SHOPPING
CC Paseo Las Delicias II (see 10)
TRANSPORT
Aeropostal 19 F2
Aserca (see 19)
Avior (see 10)
Bus Terminal 20 F4

side gate at the end of Av Santos Michelena (best from 8am to 11am or 2pm to 3pm) and somebody may show you around. The soldiers at the gate may be unaware of this service, in which case politely ask them to call the supervisor (NCO).



#### PLAZA BOLÍVAR

At three blocks long, this pleasant, tree-filled square is the largest Plaza Bolívar in the country. It was laid out by architect Carlos Raúl Villanueva and opened in 1930. The monument to Bolívar is identical to that in Caracas.

#### TEATRO DE LA OPERA

Commissioned by Gómez in 1934, this Soviet-esque **theater** (☎ 233-6043; Av Miranda at Calle Brión; ⏰ box office 8:30am-noon & 2:30-6pm Mon-Fri) was intended to be the best in the country, to match the capital status of the city. An immense budget of two million bolívares was allotted for the structure alone. The theater was constructed swiftly, and by December 1935 (the month Gómez died) it was almost ready, missing only the imported ceiling and interior furnishings. Nonetheless, the new government halted work, and its decorations were moved to theaters in Caracas. It wasn't until 1973 that the theater finally opened. It can seat 860 people and stages a variety of visiting productions, from opera to folkloric dance. There is a tiny but smart cafe attached to the right of the entrance.

#### PANTEÓN DE GÓMEZ

In typical dictator style, once Gómez had taken a firm grip of Venezuela, he set about building himself a grandiose **mausoleum** (admission free; ⏰ 8am-3pm Mon-Fri, to noon Sat). Finished in 1919, this rather pretentious pantheon structure is topped by a white Moorish dome and houses the tomb of the general and members of his family. Curiously, the interior walls are covered with the kind of thanksgiving plaques normally reserved for saints, each reading 'Thanks for the favors,' and signed with initials. A taxi to here costs BsF20.

### Sleeping

Maracay's cheapest accommodations are love hotels that rent rooms by the hour. Late at night, take care around the bus station and in the center.

**Posada El Limón** (☎ 283-4925; www.posadaellimon.com; Calle El Piñal 64, El Limón; hammock BsF40, dm BsF80, d/tr BsF220/275; ❄ 📶 🏊) If you'd like to skip Maracay entirely, this lush complex in the suburb of El Limón is run by a Dutch-Venezuelan couple. Their secure complex is filled with colorful mosaics and leafy patios with mountain views. Rooms are comfortable and tastefully arranged, and backpackers will appreciate the dorm or hammock option. Other pluses include a peaceful pool, wi-fi, tours and airport transfers; downsides include legging it out of the residential neighborhood if you want to eat something other than pizza delivery, and a general sense of abandonment when the owners are away. From the bus station, a taxi here costs BsF25.

**Hospedaje São Vicente** (☎ 247-0321; Av Bolívar Este 3; s/d BsF80/120; ❄) About as friendly as fire, these tiny rooms set around a concrete courtyard with too many caged birds should serve penny-pinchers only.

**Hotel Mar del Plata** (☎ 246-4313; mardelplatahotel@gmail.com; Av Santos Michelena Este 23; s/d/tr BsF100/120/140; ❄) Maracay's most pleasant deal and a central budget option is this peaceful hotel, which features neat rooms with hot water and cable TV.

**Hotel Aventino** (☎ 245-7087; www.hotelaventino.com; Calle López Aveledo 15; s/d from BsF195/200; ❄ 📶) This great choice looks a bit like an exotic birdcage as you enter through the extensive security bars draped with plants. The well-groomed rooms have several button controls for the cable TV, air-con, lights and cheesy ambient music, and a nationalist newspaper arrives on your doorstep. Secure and well-located, this is the best bang for your buck if you don't minding shelling out for midrange.

**Hotel Princesa Plaza** (☎ 223-1008; www.hotelprincesaplaza.com; Av Miranda Este; s/d BsF239/299; ❄ 📶) Edging close to top-end quality, the large Princesa lies next to the 30-story brick-and-glass Torre Sindoni. It offers good-value (if a little bland) rooms with cable TV, plus little comforts like a hairdryer and laundry service.

**Eurobuilding Express** (☎ 200-1111; www.eurobuilding.com.ve; Centro Comercial Las Delicias II; s/d from BsF600/648; ❄ 📶) This upmarket hotel lies above a swanky shopping mall filled with restaurants and boutiques. It's bend-over-backwards friendly and offers spacious, modern rooms with comforts like king-size beds and wi-fi, and boasts a business center, a solarium and two Jacuzzis. Enter through elevators via the lowest floor in the mall. It's a straight shot down Av Las Delicias for equally swanky bars and restaurants.

## Eating & Drinking

There are plenty of reasonably priced places to eat scattered throughout the city center. Some of the cheapest typical meals are in the Mercado Principal (try Felipe's cheap soups), open 7am to 3pm only. The city's upmarket restaurants lie along Av Las Delicias north of the city center (taxis around BsF20).

**Royal III** (☎ 247-1813; cnr Calle López Aveledo & 3a Transversal; sandwiches BsF17-45; ⏰ breakfast, lunch & dinner) This massive, well-heeled *panaderia/pastelaria* (bakery/pastry shop) does it all: 59 sandwiches, loads of stuffed croissants, pizza and a wealth of sweets and treats. Sit at the long counter or in a cluster of tables under stained glass.

**El Arepanito** (☎ 237-8621; Av 19 de Abril at Junín; arepas BsF18-20; ⏰ 24hr Sat, breakfast, lunch & dinner Sun-Fri) This very popular *arepera* has a pleasant, plant-filled front patio along with an air-conditioned dining room. It also serves good pizza and cheap grilled meats, and is open 24 hours on Saturday.

**Helados 4D** (☎ 232-0976; Av Las Delicias, Torre Maracay; ice cream BsF20-63; ⏰ breakfast, lunch & dinner) Venezuelan's best ice cream chain is a good spot to cool your jets with yummy, creamy Italian gelato. Go for a small – they pile it on.

**Pizza Mia** (☎ 245-6010; Av 19 de Abril; pizzas BsF28-96; ⏰ lunch & dinner) This popular pizza chain has nine locations in Maracay. The pizza is reminiscent of a home attempt with canned vegetables, assuming your home is not in Italy. But it's a cheap option that gets the job done and *maracayeros* seem to love it.

**Tasca El Riacho** (☎ 242-4050; Av Las Delicias; mains BsF31-98; ⏰ lunch & dinner) This tasca (Spanish-style bar-restaurant) has a huge curvaceous bar, large seating areas and a sophisticated atmosphere that comes alive in the evening. The live music's not so good (bad Juanes covers) but it cooks up paella, *noquis* (potato dumplings), rabbit and trout dishes and Portuguese specialties.

**our pick Churchill Steak House** (☎ 241-1020; Av Las Delicias, Centro Comercial La Floresta; steaks BsF75-95; ⏰ lunch & dinner) Embracing its old-schoolness with ferocity, this 30-year-old, London-themed French steakhouse boasting stained-glass windows, extra low ceilings and salmon furnishings will knock you out. If the *churrasco salomo* isn't one of the best steaks you've had anywhere, you just like being argumentative. Finish things off with the decadent *tres leches* cake. The lounge is a trip as well.

**Oz Club** (☎ 451-3320; Av Las Delicias; ⏰ 9pm-5am Wed-Sat) Ever wonder what it's like to attend P Diddy's White Party? In the same complex as El Riacho, this all-white club (collared shirt or some sort of jacket required) is where the *rumba's* (party) at, in a Johnnie Walker-on-the-Nile theme. Don't wear white or nobody will see you.

## Getting There & Away

### AIR

The nearest non-military airport is in Valencia, 50km to the west. **Avior** (☎ 232-8861; www.aviorairlines.com; Centro Comercial Paseo Las Delicias II, Local 2-MZ-30) is in a shopping mall just above the Eurobuilding Hotel. **Aeropostal** (☎ 232-3789; Centro Comercial Paseo Las Delicias I, Local AV-57) and **Aserca** (☎ 232-5960; Centro Comercial Paseo Las Delicias I, Local M-64) are next door.

### BUS

It's about a 20-walk from Maracay's confusing and hectic bus terminal to Plaza Bolívar, but there are frequent city buses (BsF1.50) that head into the center. Look for buses marked 'Terminal' along Av Las Delicias to head back to the terminal. For transportation to Puerto Colombia, see p103.

Destinations from the central terminal include Valencia (BsF7, one hour, frequent), Caracas (BsF17, 1½ hours, frequent), Barquisimeto (BsF35, three hours), Puerto La Cruz (BsF60, seven hours), San Fernando de Apure (BsF55, seven hours, frequent), Maracaibo (BsF70, 8½ hours) and Ciudad Bolívar (BsF75, nine hours).

From the Terminal Extraurbano, next door on the southern end of the terminal complex, destinations include Coro (BsF14, seven hours), Mérida (BsF21, 11 hours) and San Cristóbal (BsF19, 12 hours).

The government-owned **SITSSA** (☎ 246-0887; www.sitssa.gob.ve) services San Fernando de Apure (BsF30), Puerto Ayacucho (BsF50) and Coro (BsF30), among others, from the Terminal Extraurbano.

### Private Terminals

**Aeroexpresos Ejecutivos** (☎ 232-2977; www.aeroexpresos.com.ve; Av Bolivar Este, Frente Ingeniería Militar) Services Valencia (BsF15), Caracas (BsF20), Maracaibo (BsF75), Puerto La Cruz (BsF75), Puerto Ordaz (BsF81) and Maturín (BsF60).

## COLONIA TOVAR

☎ 0244 / pop 9000

Every post-colonial country seems to have a ubiquitous European architectural playground that offers a tranquil piece of the motherland tucked away in a completely unexpected location. Unfortunately, the whole thing usually ends up feeling more like a pounding Oktoberfest hangover than anything remotely approaching European authenticity. Colonia Tovar represents Venezuela's Eurovision, in the form of a German village lost in Araguan cloud forest in the Cordillera de la Costa, about 60km west of Caracas. Though every bit as contrived as similar settlements around the world, Colonia Tovar is a refreshing change of pace for Venezuela, a tidy and scenic town of red-tile-roof cabins and Fachwerk architecture tumbling down mountainsides in all directions, far away from the coarser reality found at lower altitudes.

But what really sets this German *stadt* apart from other faux European enclaves is its almost cultish history. It was founded in 1843 by a group of 376 German settlers from the Schwarzwald (Black Forest), recruited by Italian Agustín Codazzi (see the boxed text, opposite). Isolated from the outside world by a lack of roads and rules prohibiting marriage outside the colony, the village followed the mother culture, language and architecture for a century. It wasn't until the 1940s that Spanish was introduced as the official language and the ban on marrying outside the community was abandoned.

In 1963 a paved road from Caracas reached Colonia Tovar, marking a turning point in the history of the tiny town. Today, only the older generations understand German and the town's Germanness is all but gone save the impressive Fachwerk architecture, hearty cuisine (though strong German mustard and good sauerkraut are suspiciously absent) and the odd blonde-haired, blue-eyed *niño* here and there. Though Venezuelans roaring through the town's otherwise serene streets are endlessly irritating, Colonia Tovar still makes for a relaxing and interesting stopover on the route west.

### Information

The village has a few banks (with ATMs), though exchanging money at the weekend can be difficult. Tour agencies will sometimes change money and give information about the area. For internet access and telephones head to CANTV, just below the church.

The **Instituto Autónomo de Turismo de Aragua** (Iatur; ☎ 661-5123; Calle Bolivar, Sector La Plaza; 🕑 8:30am-5pm) sits besides the church, just in front of Hotel Selva Negra, and offers local tourist info, though not in English (or German).

### Sights & Activities

Stroll about the steep, winding streets to soak up the quaint atmosphere and see some fine examples of traditional German architecture. Visit the fun and creaky **Museo de Historia y Artesanía** (☎ 251-5403; admission BsF2; 🕑 9am-6pm Sat & Sun) to learn about the region's history, from grinding stones to antiquated swords to fossilized crocodile vertebrae.

Don't miss the quirky black-and-white **church**, a pretty L-shaped building with stained-glass windows and a high altar joining two perpendicular naves. The patron saint of the town, San Martín de Tours, looks down from the altar.

There are various walking options around the town, including a hike up to **Pico Codazzi** (2425m), the highest peak in the area. You'll first need to reach the pass, which is 5km out of Colonia Tovar on the road toward La Victoria (walk or take a taxi). Here a path branches off to the right and leads up to the top, about a half-hour's walk. Hiring a guide is recommended, since it's easy to get lost.

### Festivals & Events

Colonia Tovar hosts the annual chamber music event **Festival Internacional de Música de Cámara** (www.festivalcoloniatovar.com.ve) at the end of November.

### Sleeping & Eating

Colonia Tovar is an easy day trip from Caracas, but for overnight stays there are plenty of hotels and cabañas, most with their own restaurants. Private bathrooms and hot water are the norm, and some also have heated rooms (air-con is unnecessary). The accommodations are good but not cheap. Reserve ahead for weekend stays.

**Cabañas Leo** (☎ 355-1623; Calle Hessen; d/t from BsF160/210) One of Colonia Tovar's best deals is this small family posada with only five rooms, all with cable TV and supposed hot water (rooms with a kitchen cost extra). There's a cute grassy garden in front and a concrete patio in back with views and a mumbling parrot. It's next to Cabañas Silberbrunnen.

**Cabañas Silberbrunnen** (☎ 355-1490; matildedebreidenbach@hotmail.com; Calle Hessen; d/tr from BsF210/240;

### A LIFE LESS ORDINARY

Swashbuckler, explorer, soldier, pirate, merchant and cartographer – it was the multi-talented Italian Agustín Codazzi (1793–1858) who founded Colonia Tovar in 1843. Codazzi led an extraordinary life: at 17 he was fighting in the Napoleonic army, then took to international commerce and later managed a casino in Constantinople (now Istanbul).

When Codazzi heard that Bolívar was recruiting foreigners for a new Venezuelan army, he was the first to enroll. However, on his way south he met the French corsair Louis Aury, and together they landed on Providencia, a Colombian island. From there they ransacked Spanish galleons, reaped huge rewards, and – as a bonus – contributed to the defeat of the Spaniards.

After the war Codazzi was commissioned to draft maps of Venezuela. But after a while the Venezuelan government began to look for European migrants eager to settle and work in Venezuela to help revive the devastated economy. Codazzi set about selecting a place with acceptable climatic conditions, then returned to Europe and collected a group of several hundred German peasants (the nationality he thought most adaptable), bringing them to Venezuela and founding Colonia Tovar. By then the Venezuelan authorities had lost enthusiasm for the program, and Codazzi dedicated himself to mapping. His excellent maps are now the pride of national archives in Venezuela and Colombia.



) Twenty-two clean, neat rooms on flowery grounds are available at this friendly complex set into the hillside. Get them with or without a kitchen. Located in a *calle ciega* (blind alley) just below the church.

**Hotel Restaurant Kaiserstuhl** ( ☎ 355-1859; Calle Bolivar, Sector La Plaza; d/tr/q BsF280/320/380; ) In the heart of town, Kaiserstuhl's rooms are the least cheesy in town, with nice stone archways and tolerable bedspreads. The airy German restaurant, staffed by waitresses in traditional dress, is one of the town's best.

**Hotel Selva Negra** ( ☎ 355-1415; www.hotelselvanegra.com; d from BsF350; ) Located to the right of the church through some big iron gates, Selva Negra is the oldest and the biggest lodge in town. It's like a little village in itself, with 46 homey, picturesque cabañas scattered along the grassy hillside, each sleeping two to five guests and boasting old-style furniture. There's a good antique-style restaurant, spa services and even an outdoor playground for the kids.

**Café Muhstall** ( ☎ 265-1452; Calle Bolivar; mains BsF29-96; breakfast, lunch & dinner) This lively cafe inside a 170-year-old Fachwerk construction on the plaza churns out hearty German fare that is quite good – go for the Plato Alemán, a nicely-sized sampler plate, and wash it all down with local Tovar pilsner (now produced in La Victoria).

**Das Bäcker Café** ( ☎ 355-1536; Calle Bolivar; pizzas BsF40-68) If your arteries give way just thinking about any more German sausages, head to this friendly cafe for surprisingly tasty, well-presented pizza. Typical fare is also on offer, *natürlich.*

## Getting There & Away

The trip from Caracas requires a change at El Junquito. In Caracas, carritos leave from the metro stop Yaguara (BsF3, 45 minutes to 1½ hours, weekends) – watch your back in this area. From El Junquito, por puesto vans take you the remainder of the journey (BsF5, one hour).

If you don't want to go back the same way to Caracas (or want to continue further west), you can take an exciting ride south down to La Victoria. Over a distance of only 30km, the road descends about 1300m. Buses depart regularly from Colonia Tovar (BsF8, one hour) on Calle Codazzi in front of Panaderia Herr Peter; grab a seat on the left side for better views. From La Victoria you can catch a bus to Caracas (BsF10, 1½ hours), Maracay (BsF4.50, one hour) and Valencia (BsF10, two hours).

# PARQUE NACIONAL HENRI PITTIER

☎ 0243

Venezuela's oldest national park, created in 1937, Henri Pittier offers a gorgeous coastline for beach lovers, a huge variety of species for bird-watchers, a few trails for hikers, colonial towns for architecture buffs and rolling African drumbeats for *rumba* ravers.

Named for its founder, Swiss botanist Henri Pittier, the park covers 1078 sq km of the Cordillera de la Costa, the coastal mountain range (considered the northern continuation of the great Andean system). The cordillera exceeds 2000m in some areas, then plunges down to the Caribbean coast in the north.

This mountainous region has a staircase of different zones: from Maracay, you ascend steeply through semi-dry deciduous woods to evergreen rainforest and, further up, to dense cloud forest – all over a remarkably short distance. Over the crest and descending for another hour northward to the sea, you get the same sequence in reverse, plus arid coastal scrub followed by beaches, mangroves and coconut groves at the base.

The park is famous for its birds. Almost 600 species have been identified in the park – this represents 43% of the bird species found in Venezuela and 7% of all the birds known in the world. Hardly any other park of this size in the world claims this diversity. An added bonus is that Paso Portachuelo (1128m) is on a bird and insect migratory route. The animal world here is also rich and includes tapirs, deer, pumas, agoutis, peccaries, ocelots, opossums, armadillos, monkeys, snakes, frogs and bats.

Let's not forget the beaches – many splendid and secluded crescents of sand glisten along the national park's coastline. The bays are small and the beaches short but wide, some of them shaded from the relentless tropical sun by swaying coconut palms. A few beaches are accessible by road, but other more solitary coves can only be reached by boat – offering all the beauty of an easily accessible paradise, but without the crowds.

The national park is also home to various towns and villages. One of the biggest and most visited is Puerto Colombia, at the end of the eastern road. It's the park's main tourist destination and offers the widest choice of services. El Playón, toward the end of the western road, is a bit rougher and less popular with foreign tourists.

### ORIENTATION

The park's highest point is Pico El Cenizo (2436m). From its east–west ridge, the cordillera rolls dramatically down north to the coast, and south to Maracay. Two roads, both paved, cross the park from north to south. Both originate in Maracay and go as far as the coast. The western road leads from Maracay to El Playón and then ends at the town of Cuyagua.

The eastern road heads from Maracay to Choroní, then 2km further on ends at Puerto Colombia. It's narrower, poorer and more twisting, but it climbs up to 1830m and is more spectacular. Both roads are about 55km long and are occasionally blocked by landslides in the rainy season. There's no road connection between the coastal ends of these roads; an expensive boat ride is the only way to get from one to the other.

The coast has rocky cliffs interspersed with golden sandy bays filled with coconut groves – some almost totally virgin and undeveloped.

### ACTIVITIES

#### Walking & Hiking

The area along the coast, where most of the towns and villages are located, offers the simplest and best options for walkers. Carrying water and shade protection is crucial, however, as these coastal paths are often unshaded.

It's possible to walk from Puerto Colombia a few hours west to Aroa or east to Chuao. Another trail begins 6km south on the road from Choroní, at the place known as 'El Mamón'; the walk from here to Chuao will take five to seven hours. The route is confusing in parts because of various side paths, so consider taking a local guide (see below).

Further up the mountains, the trails are few and far between. The terrain is covered by thick forest, and rainfall is high. The cordillera's northern slopes receive more rain than the southern ones, and the upper parts are pretty wet most of the year. The driest months are January to March.

### TOURS

Many posadas in the Puerto Colombia area offer tours. For something more personal ask around for guides who can take you on hikes in the area and give you more information and attention.

**Casa Luna** (☎ 951-5318, 0412-176-8114; www.jungletrip.de) The personable owners of the posada in Puerto Colombia (p104), Claudia Beckmann and Emilio Espinoza, also act as guides. They do one- and two-day tours of the national park (BsF140 to BsF350), along with day trips to area beaches for groups (BsF300 to BsF900). They can also organize airport transfers to/from Caracas (BsF140 per person for groups of three or more). English and German are spoken.

**Virgilio Espinal** (☎ 991-1106, 0416-747-3833; www.cocuy.org.ve; senttovivi@hotmail.com) 'Vivi' is a good English-speaking guide for walks and specializes in serious bird-watching. Knowledgeable about the park, Vivi operates a rustic mountain refuge known as 'El Cocuy,' near

## PARQUE NACIONAL HENRI PITTIER

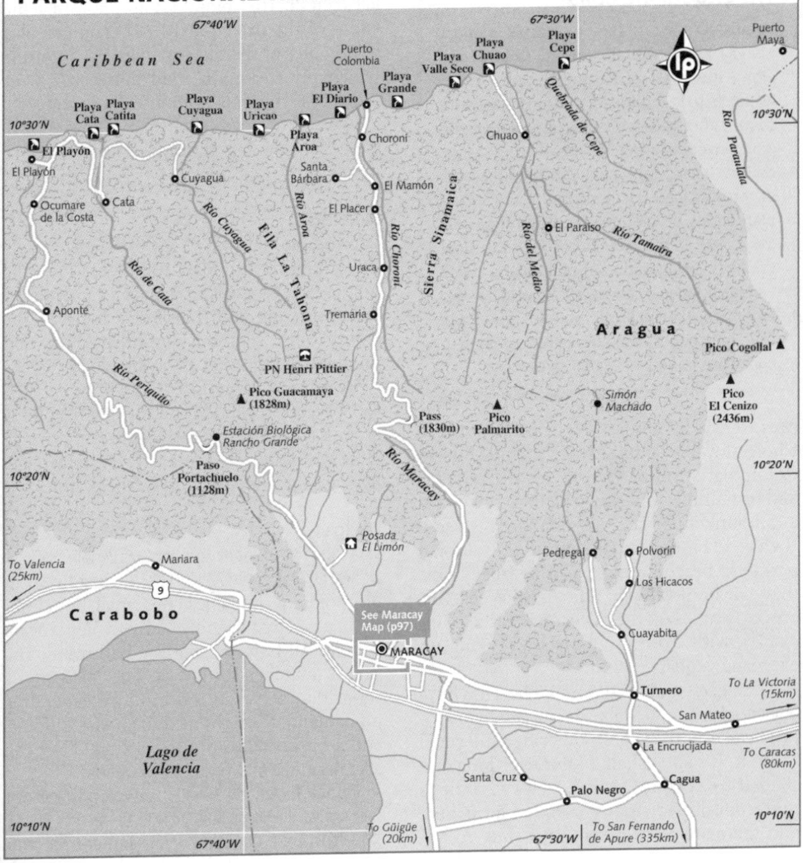


the village of Uraca (40 minutes from Puerto Colombia), which serves as a base for tours ranging from two hours to several days. Day rates range from BsF90 to BsF360.

### GETTING THERE & AWAY

Most travelers get to the park via Maracay's bus terminal. Both the eastern and western roads are very curvy, so if you're very prone to motion sickness consider downing the proper pill. Also consider taking a bus rather than a por puesto; buses take longer but are slower on the curves.

Buses to Puerto Colombia and Choroní leave regularly from Anden 5 (platform 5) and run from 6:30am to 7pm (BsF15, two hours). Por puesto offices to these destinations are just outside the southern gate of the terminal in the car park of the gas station (BsF30 per person, 1½ hours). They depart from here as early as 4am and as late as 11pm.

Boats in Puerto Colombia can take you to any beach you wish. The charge is by boat, so the fare depends on the number of passengers (usually up to 10). Prices are negotiable and possibly inflated, so always try to bargain.

Note that transportation prices for buses, por puestos and boats may rise on weekends, when demand is high.

## Puerto Colombia

This attractive and well-visited coastal town was once the area's local port. It has developed into one of Venezuela's most popular travelers' destinations, and attracts backpackers like

### THE CHOCOLATE COAST

Venezuela's world-famous cocoa is most heavily concentrated around **Chuao** and along the coast of Parque Nacional Henri Pittier (p101), home to the most rare and sought after variety, Criollo. Chocolatiers the world over seek out its virtually bitter-free, delicate taste, and you'll find broad swaths of red-scorched cocoa drying in the sun at plantations in the area. Representing only 5% to 10% of the world's cocoa production, Criollo is considered a delicacy among cocoa varieties, and you can seek it out on a day trip to Chuao, where locals peddle everything from hot chocolate to chocolate ice cream to chocolate liqueurs – a real sweet treat.

bees to honey. Unlike sleepy and nostalgic Choroní a few steps further inland, Puerto Colombia is full of young crowds, posadas and restaurants and can get a little rowdy (in a rambunctious way, not a dangerous way). It's a great base for excursions to the national park and beaches, and has a laid-back vibe that can be positively addictive. Weekends are party times on the malecón (coastal boulevard), with drumming circles revving up everyone's spirits.

The closest and most popular beach is **Playa Grande**, a 10-minute walk by road east of town – just head over the pedestrian bridge and you'll reach it. It's about half a kilometer long and shaded by coconut palms. Playa Grande is quite developed; many people camp here and there are a few restaurants (but no hotels). It also gets very busy (and littered) on weekends.

For a good view and photo opportunity, climb to **Cristo Mirador**, east of town and up the hill about 20 minutes. You can go further for higher panoramas, too. Before you set off, though, ask locals if it's safe: there's always some danger of robbery in isolated places.

### INFORMATION

**BNC** (Calle Morillo) is the only bank in the Puerto Colombia/Choroní area but its ATMs rarely, if ever, work with foreign cards, and they do not exchange money, so arrive sufficiently loaded down with cash. There are a couple of internet places in town; **Coffe Mey** (10am-8pm Mon-Sat, noon-6pm Sun; per hr BsF10), next to Posada Túcan, has a good (and chilly) connection.

A green open bus called 'El Tren' shuttles between Puerto Colombia and Choroní at the whim of the driver (BsF1.50). You can also hop in any of the old cars marked 'Interno,' which ply the main road between towns. Otherwise the walk is about 20 minutes.

Buses to Maracay (BsF15, two hours) leave from the new bus terminal at the entrance to town.

### SLEEPING

Puerto Colombia has plenty of places to stay – everything from budget to luxury – and the number keeps growing. You can camp on the beach or sling your hammock between the palms (both free), but don't leave your tent unattended. Showers are available for BsF3.

Be warned: prices rise by a whopping 30% to 100% on weekends and for major holiday periods (Christmas to early January, Carnaval, Holy Week and all of August). The rates listed here are for midweek and off-peak times.

#### Budget

**Casa Luna** (☎ 951-5318; www.jungletrip.de; Calle Morillo 35; dm from BsF30, d/tr/q BsF70/100/120; ) Just five simple rooms are available at this small, hostel-like posada run by a friendly German-Venezuelan couple. All but one shares a bathroom, and there's a kitchen for guests. They also offer a room that serves as a dormitory depending on demand. It's right next to Hostal Colonial and a bit noisy, so bring earplugs. They can also organize all of your tour needs.

**Posada Tucán** (☎ 264-4961; www.posadatucan.com; Calle Morillo; d with fan BsF80, d with air-con from BsF115; ) Run by a German-Peruvian couple, this casual place has eight colorful, comfortable rooms with posturepedic German mattresses, though the walls need touching up. Area tours and airport transfers are available and there's a wonderful kitchen area.

**Casa Nova** (☎ 615-1375; www.jungletrip.de; Parcellamiento San Antonio 7a; d/tr from BsF100/160; ) Tucked away off the main drag, this new, Casa Luna-affiliated midrange offers an upgrade in creature comforts in its seven rooms – all with private bathrooms and hammocks – and all the same English support as its predecessor, in a more tranquil location. There's a spacious communal kitchen as well.

**Posada Riqui Riqui** (☎ 991-1061; casa.riqui.riqui@gmail.com; Calle Morillo 56; d/tr/q/apt BsF160/180/240/290; ) This exceptional posada is set on lovely planted grounds with a bit of a hacienda feel. There are 10 rooms in all, with three tasteful new second-floor options offering the most character and style, though at the sacrifice of space. Hammocks and a small pool offer relaxation and there's a wonderful barbecue area. The personable German owner will include breakfast with reservations.

#### Midrange

**La Posada de Choroní** (☎ 991-1191; www.laposadadechoroni.3a2.com; Calle Morillo 17; s/d/tr 250/290/330; ) A good peaceful choice, boasting a lovely courtyard with potted plants and lined with attractive hallways. Rooms are small but tidy and well done. Small continental breakfast included.

**Posada Tom Carel** (☎ 991-1220; www.posadatomcarel.com; Calle Trino Rangel 11; d/tr/q BsF260/306/408; ) A wonderfully friendly, family-run option named after the doting owners, Tom and Carel. The vibrant rooms are found through a path strewn with plants and intricate tile-and-pebble mosaic floors. Inside, you'll find them cramped, but the hammocks slung across the tops of the beds and the choice of fans or air-con elevate this midrange above others in town proper.

**Posada Semeruco** (☎ 991-1264; www.posadasemeruco.com; Calle Morillo 65; d with/without air-con from BsF280/235, tr BsF340; ) This elegant posada, situated near the Guardia Nacional post, is housed in a colonial-style building set around a sunny courtyard with hammock chairs, wrought-iron tables and a small fountain. The 11 rooms have handsome, old-style furniture and come with comforts like a fridge and a coffeemaker. Its annex (same contact details) is not quite as large or nice, but is 25% cheaper and closer to the beach.

**Posada Pittier** (☎ 991-1028; www.posadapittier.com; Calle Morillo; d/tr/q BsF300/350/400; P ) This cute posada packs more character than most, with tasteful abstract art and nine rooms filing around a grassy area with hammocks lining the open hallways. The well-landscaped backyard pool area, flanked by *palapa* (open thatched hut) seating, is an oasis of calm. It's on the main road at the very entrance to town; look for the coral-colored outside wall.

#### Top End

**Posada La Casa de las García** (☎ 235-6894; www.posadalasgarcia.com; Calle El Cementerio; d/tr/q incl breakfast BsF430/570/650; ) This centuries-old family hacienda is well worth the walk out of town. Its grounds have pretty gardens, while the 15 charming, old-style rooms boast antique furniture along with modern touches like hairdryers and rain-style showers. Hammock chairs hang in the open hallways. A newer extension at the back of the house has stylish, bright rooms with garden baths and at least one TV/DVD.

**Hostal Casagrande** (☎ 991-1251; www.hostalcasagrande.net; Calle Morillo 33; d/tr/q BsF530/680/720; ) The 19 large, beautiful rooms in this stunning colonial-style hotel come with lovely artwork and rustic furniture. Even the halls are nice, and there's a jungly courtyard with hammocks and a shallow, birdbath-like pool for cooling off. There are spa services and an annex with more rooms. It's opposite the church.

### EATING & DRINKING

Restaurants are numerous and fried fish is the local staple. Budget eating is provided by a cluster of shack eateries on the way to Playa Grande (beware a lack of hygiene, however). There are midrange choices near the boat docks and at the beach itself.

Several posadas have their own restaurants. If you're vegetarian and willing to walk 20 minutes inland to Choroní, try the tiny restaurant in the Posada Colonial El Picure (p106), which has a few veggie dishes.

**Restaurante Brigettli** (Calle Morillo 37; breakfast BsF10-25; breakfast) Hostal Colonial itself is about as friendly as a tornado to a trailer park, but this independent breakfast-only cafe in the back does do excellent foreigner-friendly breakfasts here for non-guests. Options include American and continental styles, pancakes or one of several *criollo* choices. Open from 7:30am.

**Brisas del Mar** (☎ 991-1268; Calle Los Cocos; mains BsF25-45; breakfast, lunch & dinner) You'll be surprised that this food comes out of this kitchen. Brisas del Mar is noisy and a bit rough-around-the-edges, sitting on a rambunctious corner near the harbor, but it turns out down-to-earth seafood, pastas and meat dishes that are surprisingly well presented.

**Bar Restaurant Araguaneyes** (Calle Los Cocos 8; mains BsF28-78, pizza BsF42-78; breakfast, lunch & dinner) This lively restaurant offers good international and *criollo* food, pizzas in the evening, and is also open for breakfast. There's a fair list of cocktails that are best enjoyed from the airy roof terrace. Skip the greasy *dorado* (a river fish).

our pick **Bokú** (☎ 215-5404; Calle Morillo; dinner menu BsF55-68; dinner) In a candlelit backyard enclosed by a bamboo fence, this gourmet surprise is a travel memory in culinary form.

 



Never mind the confusing ordering system, you choose between one or two courses and two drinks are included, all made with Santa Teresa rum. There are only a few options on the nightly changing menu. Our *caprese* salad and grilled albacore left our palate shocked and awed.

our pick **Jalío Surf Bar** (☎ 991-1269; Calle Concepcion; from 9:30pm) This imaginative bar, run by an snazzy *Italiana,* is way too hip for Henri: Moroccan-esque day beds, hippie-tinged decor, edgy music and an artsy crowd converge over exotic cocktails such as white chocolate daiquiris and strawberry mojitos – a funky step forward from Polars on the malecón.

## Around Puerto Colombia

Beaches in the area are normally visited by boat, though some of them can also be reached on foot after a long, hard, sweaty hike. Negotiate with boat operators at the river's mouth in Puerto Colombia.

**Playa Aroa** (BsF20 per person one way, 15 minutes one way) is a lovely place with no services, though nearby **Playa Uricao** (BsF25 per person one way, 20 minutes) might have a weekend snack shack. There's good snorkeling but no shade at **Playa Valle Seco** (BsF20 per person one way, 15 minutes) while **Playa Cepe** (BsF25 per person one way, 25 minutes) is on a bay and has some services, including a restaurant and midrange posada. Determine a pick-up time with the boat operator, and pay him when he picks you up. The trip may be quite rough if the waves are high, so be prepared to get wet.

**Chuao**, about 8km east of Choroní as the crow flies, is a small, friendly village known for its cacao plantations (see the boxed text, p104) and Diablos Danzantes celebrations (see p94). Villagers live in almost complete isolation here: there is only one road in and out. A visit here means you'll quickly find yourself OD'ing on chocolate liqueurs, ice cream and hot chocolate. La Luzonera is a good posada on the plaza. Chuao also has a so-so beach, which you can reach by boat from Puerto Colombia (BsF20 per person one way, 20 minutes).

### A LITTLE HISTORY...

The park's coastline has been inhabited for centuries. Interestingly, all the old towns are set well back from the waterfront; Ocumare de la Costa, Cuyagua, Cata, Choroní and Chuao were all founded several kilometers inland from the sea to protect themselves against the pirates who roamed the coast. Puerto Colombia and El Playón are relatively recent settlements.

There was also a big African population in these older towns, and their legacy has been preserved in the sensual culture and music. Drums have long been an integral part of life, and today their pulsating beat immediately sparks dancing on weekend nights and holidays – particularly during the Fiesta de San Juan on June 23 and 24.

## Choroní

An oasis of peace, charming Choroní is the place to escape the crowds of Puerto Colombia, which is about a 20-minute walk away. There's not much to do in this 385-year-old village other than greet the villagers as you wander the interesting, narrow colonial streets, which are lined with fine pastel houses. The deeply shaded Plaza Bolívar has a lovely parish church, **Iglesia de Santa Clara**, with a finely decorated ceiling. The wall over the high altar has been painted to look like a carved retable (altar ledge).

Madre María de San José was born in Choroní in 1875 and dedicated her life to service for the poor. The house where she lived and worked is on the plaza. She later continued her work with the poor in Maracay, where she founded a religious congregation. She died at the respectable age of 92 and was beatified in 1995.

The **feast of Santa Clara**, the patron saint of the town, is celebrated in August.

### SLEEPING & EATING

The town has two pleasant colonial hotels on the main street (one with a restaurant), but eateries and services are few and far between.

**Posada Colonial El Picure** (☎ 991-1296; posadapicure@hotmail.com; Calle Miranda 34; d/tr/q BsF160/200/250; ) Just four simple but clean rooms come with high ceilings at this pleasantly serene colonial building. They're set around a concrete courtyard with talking parrots and a tiny restaurant serving excellent home-cooked food, including vegetarian dishes (mains BsF20 to BsF70). There's an eight-room annex with air-con nearby.

**Hostería Río Mar** (☎ 991-1038; Calle Miranda; s/d/tr BsF180/220/250; ) This attractive mustard-

**DETOUR**

Located at the end of the national park's western road, **El Playón** is the main town in this area and offers more than a dozen places to stay. It's much larger and rougher than Puerto Colombia but has none of its colonial charm, which makes it less attractive and less popular, though it is swarming with nice beaches. Highlights in the area include **Playa Maya**, a beautiful and isolated bay beach with no services, 1½km to the west; and, just beyond, **La Cienaga**, which has good snorkeling, diving and kayaking, (the last two organized through **Posada de la Costa Eco-Lodge** (☎ 993-1986; www.ecovenezuela.com; Calle California 23; s/d incl breakfast BsF384; ). Five kilometers eastward is the area's most famous beach, **Playa Cata**. The beach is a postcard-perfect crescent of sand bordering Bahía de Cata, and marred only by two ugly apartment towers looming over the beach.



yellow house hides a good little hostel behind its heavy wooden door and wood-barred windows. It has nine small and simple but neat rooms with high ceilings, most with bathtubs. There's no common area, but a couple of hammocks hang in the dark hallway. It's just a few doors down (and across the street) from Posada Colonial El Picure.

# CARABOBO STATE

## VALENCIA

☎ 0241 / pop 1,408,000

Founded in 1555, five years before Caracas, Valencia is the country's third-largest metropolis and one of the first Spanish settlements in Venezuela. Though not a huge tourist draw, it does boast a few museums and surrounding attractions, wonderful food and nightlife, and is an important air and land transportation hub. Set at an altitude of around 500m, Valencia has an average temperature of about 77°F, with hot days ameliorated by the evening breeze that rolls down from the mountains.

### History

Valencia has had a violent and tumultuous history. It had not yet reached its seventh birthday when Lope de Aguirre, the infamous adventurer obsessed with finding El Dorado, sacked the town and burned it to the ground. Twenty years later, the town, not yet fully recovered, was razed by Carib people. Then in 1667 the town was seized and destroyed again, this time by French pirates. The town's proximity to Lago de Valencia didn't help, either. The disease-breeding marshes brought about smallpox epidemics that decimated the population and scared away many survivors. Then in 1812 a devastating earthquake shook the Andean shell, leaving Valencia in ruins yet again.

And as if all that wasn't enough – the war for independence came to Valencia. Just two years after the earthquake, the town was besieged by royalist troops under the command of José Tomás Boves (fittingly known as 'the Butcher'). The ensuing slaughter left 500 people dead. Over the next seven years no fewer than two dozen battles were fought around the town, ceasing only on June 24, 1821, when Bolívar's decisive victory at Carabobo secured Venezuela's independence.

The year 1826 saw Valencia become the first town to oppose Bolívar's sacred union, Gran Colombia. Its inhabitants called for Venezuelan sovereignty and, four years later, this demand became a reality. Congress decreed formal secession here and made Valencia the newborn country's capital, before switching it to Caracas a year later.

The town caught new economic wind in its sails after WWII, and today Valencia is Venezuela's most industrialized city.

### Information

#### INTERNET ACCESS

CANTV/Movilnet and Movistar outlets are prevalent through the city.

#### LAUNDRY

**Mr Wash** (☎ 858-2904; Av Cedeño, Centro Comercial Angela; 8am-noon & 2-6pm Mon-Fri, 8am-1pm Sat; Ⓜ Cedeño) *Servicio completo* (full service) costs BsF14.

#### MEDICAL SERVICES

**Farmatodo** (24hr) Located 2.5km north of center.

#### MONEY

**Banco de Venezuela** (Av 101 Díaz Moreno at Calle 101 Libertad)

**Banesco** (Av 101 Díaz Moreno)

### POST

**Ipostel** (Calle 100 Colombia; 8am-5pm Mon-Fri)

### TOURIST INFORMATION

**Dirección de Turismo de Carabobo** ( 858-9506; www.carabobo.gov.ve; 3rd fl, Edificio Valenap, Av Bolívar Norte & Penalver; 8am-noon & 1-5pm Mon-Fri) Located above BOD bank, the tourist office is about 750m north of Plaza Bolívar.

## Dangers & Annoyances

Valencia is a dicey city that all but clears out in the city center at night. Taxis here will not stop for passengers in the street after dark – they must be called – so keep a number handy or always ask whatever establishment you are visiting to call one for you. Some are resistant, so politely insist or ask for a manager. Beware of the gringo surcharge as well.

## Sights

### PLAZA BOLÍVAR

The heart of the historic town, this plaza boasts the inevitable monument to Bolívar, though this one claims a certain novelty. The bronze figure, pointing toward Campo Carabobo, stands on a 10m-high white Italian marble column cut from a single block of stone. The monument was unveiled in 1889.

### CATEDRAL

The colonial **cathedral** (Av 99 Urdaneta) is about 420 years old, but it's been altered by so many generations that today it's a hodgepodge of historical styles. The latest restoration was in the early 1950s, which saw the ceiling plastered with an intricate design resembling cake frosting.

The cathedral's most revered treasure, the figure of Nuestra Señora del Socorro, is kept in the chapel in the left transept on an elaborate red-and-gold stage. Carved in the late 16th century, the sorrowful Virgin in black has an expression of perpetual shock and sadness. She was the first statue in Venezuela to be crowned (in 1910) by Rome, and her original gold crown is encrusted with so many precious stones it has to be stored in a safe.

#### CASA PÁEZ

This beautifully preserved **historic mansion** (☎ 857-1272; Av 98 Boyacá at Calle 99 Páez; admission free; 9am-noon & 3-5.30pm Tue-Fri, 9am-2pm Sat & Sun) is the former home of Venezuela's first president, General José Antonio Páez. He distinguished himself by forging a formidable army of *llaneros* (plainsmen) who fought under Bolívar, contributing greatly to the achievement of independence. In 1830, on the day Venezuela split from Gran Colombia, Páez took power as the first acting president and established his residence in the new capital.

Restored and furnished with period fittings, the house is today a museum. The walls of the cloister lining the lovely central patio are graced with fascinating murals depicting the nine battles the general fought. The work was done by Pedro Castillo and supposedly directed by Páez himself. Ask the attendant to show you the tiny prison and torture room at the back of the house. Wall paintings by unfortunate prisoners can still be seen here, though they have been altered by schoolchildren, making the original scrawlings hard to decipher from the 5th-grade graffiti.

#### CASA DE LA ESTRELLA

The sovereign state of Venezuela was born in this **historic house** (☎ 825-7005; Calle 100 Colombia at Av Soublette; admission free; 9am-5pm Tue-Fri, 10am-5pm Sat & Sun; M Lara) on May 6, 1830, when Congress convened here and decreed secession from Gran Colombia. Erected as a hospital around 1710 (thus being the city's oldest existing house), after independence the building was remodeled as a college, which later became the Universidad de Valencia. Extensively restored over recent years, it's now a museum. The few exhibits on display include a brief history of Valencia's past posted on boards and a 12-minute video on the history of the house.

#### MUSEO DE BÉISBOL

This **museum** (☎ 841-1313; Centro Comercial Sambil, Mañongo; adult/child BsF8/5; noon-9pm Mon-Sat, to 8pm Sun) in the popular Centro Comercial Sambil, 5km north of the city, is totally devoted to baseball fanaticism. It even has a pitching machine under the distinctive half-dome baseball roof of the shopping mall. Buses to Sambil run from the town center (BsF1.50); taxis here are BsF30.

### Festivals & Events

The two major local events are **Semana de Valencia**, in late March, and the **Fiestas Patronales de Nuestra Señora del Socorro**, in mid-November. The former features cultural events, an agricultural fair, parades, bullfights etc. The latter is a religious feast in honor of the city's patron saint, in which the crowned Virgin is taken out of the church and paraded in a procession.

Every two years in October, the prestigious Salón Arturo Michelena opens in the **Ateneo de Valencia** (☎ 858-0046; www.ateneodevalencia.com; Av Bolívar) and goes on for five months until March. This is Venezuela's oldest visual arts show, held every year since 1943. It presents a variety of styles and forms, including painting, photography, sculpture, performance, video and installations. The rest of the year it hosts a variety of rotating exhibitions.

### Sleeping

The cheapest accommodations are concentrated a few blocks around Plaza Bolívar, but these hotels are very basic and the center is not safe after sundown. They also tend to be dingy love hotels, with a check-in of 6pm or later (for overnight stays, that is).

#### BUDGET

The following budget choices are all part-time love hotels, which doesn't make them unsafe *inside* – just a bit seedy at times.

**Hotel Continental** (☎ 857-1004; Av 98 Boyacá No 101-70; s/d with fan BsF38/75, with air-con BsF70/95; ) This colonial-style hotel in a striking green-and-yellow building is the cheapest budget option in the center. It's declining, but offers good security and service, along with decent rooms. You can flag down a bus to CC Sambil right in front.

THE CENTRAL NORTH

**Hotel Carabobo** (☎ 858-8860; Calle 101 Libertad No 100-37; d/tr BsF90/105; ❄) Ideally located just off Plaza Bolívar, this hotel still has one foot in the 1970s with some lurid vinyl furniture remaining in the dark lobby and poor maintenance in places. However, things brighten up with better lighting and occasional art as you ascend to spacious, clean rooms, some with excellent views of the hotel generators.

**Hotel Caribe** (☎ 857-1157; Calle 100 Colombia No 96-68; d with/without air-con BsF100/70; ❄) The basic doubles at this hotel are set around a surprisingly sunny courtyard in back, which comes with potted palms. Rooms are tiny and dark with no hot water, however.

### MIDRANGE & TOP END

**Hotel El Diamante** (☎ 858-1595; Av 103 Carabobo; d with/without Jacuzzi BsF265/220; M Lara; ❄ wi-fi) With the exception of the smoky front desk, there's a professional atmosphere in this modern, secure hotel, the best value in the center. The well-kept rooms are clean, spacious and comfortable; they also come with cable TV and wi-fi. The only complaint is that the water is sporadically hot, lukewarm otherwise. There's an intimate tasca (Spanish-style bar-restaurant) on the 2nd floor that does room service.

**Hotel Emperador** (☎ 858-2433; Av Miranda; d/tr BsF370/410; ❄ wi-fi) Stranded away just north of the center, but in a safer area, this modern 81-room tower has touches of art deco throughout, with large rooms that feature minibars, small tables, work desks and cable TV. There's also a restaurant. When the station opens, it will be steps from the metro.

**Hotel Dinastía** (☎ 858-8139; www.dinastiahotel.com; Av 99 Urdaneta at Av Cadeño; s/d/q BsF370/375/490; M Cedeño; ❄ wi-fi) A wonderfully friendly and clean choice in the center, offering 100 or so rooms with minibars, roomy desks, hairdryers and large bathrooms. There's a smart bistro/bar as well. Think a step above a nice chain hotel.

**Lidotel** (☎ 841-1999; www.lidotelhotelboutique.com; Av 4, Jardines de Mañongo; s/d BsF839/950; ❄ wi-fi pool) Opened in 2008, this modern boutique hotel sits just behind Centro Comercial Sambil. Sizable rooms are stylishly appointed in a burnt-orange-and-chocolate motif. All the amenities and services a discerning traveler expects are here, including a hip, minimalist restaurant/bar, pool, business center and gym. It's a slicker choice than the InterContinental, the other top dog.

## Eating

The center has plenty of cheap eateries in the backstreets, where set meals can be found for just a few bucks. However, the area is not renowned for quality dining or safety. Restaurants here tend to close by 8pm except for the tascas, which by that time turn into drinking venues.

The city's upmarket restaurants are north along Av Bolívar and especially in El Viñedo, which is about 2.5km north of the center. This trendy area lies on Av Monseñor Adams, which is just west off of Av Bolívar. A taxi here costs between BsF20 and BsF40 depending on who's driving but be warned: getting a taxi back can be a challenge. By end of 2011, it should all be accessible by metro.

**Aramarjomi** (☎ 858-5062; Av Montes de Oca; shawarma BsF12-18, menu BsF20; ⏰ lunch Mon-Sat; M Lara) This Syrian-bent Arab spot on pleasant Plaza Sucre does cheap and tasty shawarma, kebabs, falafel and other Middle Eastern delights. A real treat when you are sick of *arepas* (which, of course, you are).

**Calabacín y Nueces** (☎ 858-6550; Calle 102 Independencia at Av Urdaneta; menu BsF23; ⏰ lunch Mon-Sat; M Cedeño; V) For vegetarians and non-vegetarians alike, the best budget option in the center is this healthy spot. It serves up hearty meat-free set meals, delicious cakes, fresh juices and salads.

**Bambu** (☎ 824-1177; Av Monseñor Adams 105; meals BsF35-65; ⏰ dinner Mon-Sat) Located by the Plaza las Esculturas in El Viñedo is this sleek and contemporary restaurant-bar-disco. Kick back on beanbag chairs on the terraced wood decks in front, sipping *mojitos* that go down like Shirley Temples. The food is great – try the signature *chupe de mariscos* (seafood stew, served in a bread bowl). It turns into a hip nightclub after 10pm from Thursday to Saturday (it's dead Monday to Wednesday); the crowd is cougar out one eye, young hipster out the other, all chillaxin' to loungy vibes at the beginning of the evening that are progressively stirred into a frenetic pace by the night's end.

**Kaffas Coffee Shop** (☎ 825-7555; cnr Av 101 & Transversal D, Centro Commercial MC Tower; mains BsF49-84; ⏰ lunch & dinner) The name doesn't do this trendy cafe justice. There *are* 40 types of coffee, but this beautiful patio fills up with pretty people for good wine and an extensive menu of gourmet fusion (try the rich risotto *succhini*, which feeds two). Cheaper fare includes sandwiches and crepes. It's the cornerstone of a very hip block in El Viñedo.

**Casa Valencia** (☎ 823-4923; Av Bolívar Norte; mains BsF61-128; lunch & dinner) Oozing classic Venezuelan ambience – aqua chairs, lime tablecloths, a bamboo roof and a honker of a central grill flanked by dangling lanterns – this elegant restaurant in old-hacienda style is worth a splash-out meal for its excellent grills and seafood. The *punta trasera* steak is carnivorous rapture: cooked to perfection and sized just short of overindulgence. There are scattered veggie options as well.

## Drinking

Valencia has a very trendy side and its hippest venues are all north of the center, mostly in or near El Viñedo. Look out for the free *Cover* guide (www.cover.com.ve), which outlines all the hotspots with a handy map as well.

**Bar 21** (☎ 825-5330; Centro Comercial CC La Viña Siglo XXI, Av Salvador Feo la Cruz; 6pm-3am Wed-Sat) It's mostly standing room-only at this box-shaped bar teeming with youngish wannabe players, their *chicas* and an oddly eclectic mix otherwise fighting for legroom due to some serious space issues.

## Getting There & Away

### AIR

The **airport** (☎ 513-9889; www.iaaec.gob.ve) is about 7km southeast of the city center (taxis BsF60). Domestic destinations include Caracas and Porlamar.

**Dutch Antilles Express** (www.flydae.com) and **Avior** (☎ 826-3118; Av San José de Tarbas at Av Paseo Caribe, Torre BOD) have direct flights to Curaçao. **Copa** (☎ 0800-826-7200; Av Mañongo at Av Palma Real, Centro Comercial Via Veneto, Planta Florencia) has a direct flight to Panama City.

**Aeropostal** (☎ 832-9761; Aeroporto Arturo Michelena) flies direct to Porlamar once daily. **Aserca** (☎ 820-8200; Av Andres Eloy Blanco at Calle 137C) and **Santa Barbara** (☎ 832-0874; Aeroporto Arturo Michelena) operate flights to Caracas.

### BUS

The bus terminal, in the Big Low Center about 4km northeast of the city center, is easily accessible by frequent local buses or taxi (BsF30). The terminal is large and has many facilities, including restaurants and telephone and internet services. Some shops will store luggage; look for 'Guarda Equipaje' signs.

Frequent destinations include Maracay (BsF7, one hour), Puerto Cabello (BsF7, one hour), Barquisimeto (BsF30, 2½ hours), Caracas (BsF20 to BsF40, 2½ hours) and Coro (BsF40 to BsF65, five hours).

Evening buses to faraway destinations include Maracaibo (BsF65 to BsF75, nine hours), San Cristóbal (BsF80, 10 hours), Mérida (BsF70 to BsF80, 10 hours) and San Antonio del Táchira (BsF70, 12 hours).

Several of the nicer companies, like **Expresos Merida** (☎ 737-1073, www.expremeca.com), **Expresos Los Llanos** (☎ 871-7791) and, the most luxurious, **Aeroexpresos Ejecutivos** (☎ 871-5767; www.aeroexpresos.com.ve), offer small, air-conditioned subterminals within the terminal or just outside. The latter offers services to Maracay (BsF15), Caracas (BsF24), Barquisimeto (BsF30), Maracaibo (BsF65), Puerto La Cruz (BsF75), Maturín (BsF82) and Puerto Ordaz (BsF81).

There are half a dozen buses a day to San Fernando de Apure (BsF50, eight hours), where you can change for the bus to Puerto Ayacucho.

## Getting Around

### METRO

Valencia's dazzling new **metro** (www.metrovalencia.gob.ve; 6am-8:30pm Mon-Fri, to 7:30pm Sat & Sun), opened in 2007, is thus far operating with seven immaculate stations along Line 1 in a north–south direction. Metro stations Cedeño and Lara are of the most interest to tourists, though the early closing time won't help get you off the streets at night. Line 2, currently in construction and due to open by 2011, will connect the center to El Viñedo (Metro Josefa Camejo). A single ride costs BsF0.50.

### TAXI

For security reasons, taxis won't stop here at night for passengers in the street. **Taxi Movil Cars** (☎ 858-9330) provides reliable service.

# CAMPO CARABOBO

For a taste of unadulterated Venezuelan patriotism, visit the **Carabobo Battlefield** (admission free; 6am-6pm Tue-Sun), 32km southwest of Valencia. This is the site of the great battle fought on June 24, 1821, in which Bolívar's troops decisively defeated the Spanish royalist army with help from the lancers of General Páez and British legionnaires. A milestone in Latin American history, the victory effectively sealed

Venezuela's independence. To commemorate the event, a complex of monuments has been erected on the battle ground.

Toward the end of the 1km entrance into the complex is a building on the right; inside is a diorama cubicle which screens historical films on the site. The end of the entrance road turns into the **Paseo de los Héroes**, a formal promenade lined with bronze busts of the battle's heroes. Beyond is the large **Arco de Triunfo** (Triumphal Arch) and the **Tumba del Soldado Desconocido** (Tomb of the Unknown Soldier). Two unflinching, deadpan soldiers guard the tomb and its flaming torch; their shockingly red gala period uniforms seem more suitable for a Siberian winter than for the baking sun of Carabobo. Fortunately for them, the changing of the guard takes place every two hours (starting at 8am).

Just behind the arch is the impressive **Altar de la Patria**, a massive monument – the largest in Venezuela. Designed by Spanish sculptor Antonio Rodríguez del Villar and unveiled in 1930, the monument depicts the main heroes and allegorical figures, all fashioned in stone and bronze. On the top is an equestrian statue of Bolívar.

About 1km to the west is the **mirador**, a viewpoint from which Bolívar commanded the battle. It has a large model of the battlefield and a panoramic view over the whole site.

You can wander the site at will or find a guide hanging around the area; they give free tours (in Spanish) starting at about 8am or 9am. The park has plenty of grassy expanses for picnicking, and a few drinks and snacks are sold in a building near the Paseo de los Héroes – make an afternoon of it.

There was an unstaffed information booth at the time of research.

### Getting There & Away

Frequent suburban buses (marked 'Campo Carabobo') leave from Valencia's Av Lara to the battlefield (BsF1.50, 45 minutes). They'll drop you off at the beginning of the entrance road. Take a hat and water, as it's a hot 15-minute walk up this long entrance road to the monuments. To avoid a long walk back, just head behind and to the left of the monuments to a side gate, carefully cross the highway to a bus stop and flag the local bus back to Valencia. A taxi from Valencia costs BsF60.

## LAS TRINCHERAS

☎ 0241

Located 18km north of Valencia, the thermal springs of Las Trincheras – with temperatures of up to 198°F recorded – are the world's second hottest (after some in Japan). The rustic site has been known for centuries and attracted explorers and naturalists throughout history, including Alexander von Humboldt, who used the waters to boil eggs in four minutes. In 1889 thermal baths and a hotel were built. In 1980 the old hotel was restored, a new one constructed beside it, and the murky-looking pools were remodeled. There are now three pools with temperatures ranging from 97°F to 118°F, as well as fountains, a sauna and a sociable mud bath where everybody slaps warm gloopy *lodo* on each other and lets it cake in the sun (mind the monkeys here).

The springs are renowned for their therapeutic properties and recommended for the treatment of a variety of ailments, including rheumatic, digestive, respiratory and allergic problems. They also freshen and smooth the skin, and help with general relaxation.

You can either choose a **day pass** (adult/child BsF15/10; 7am-9pm Tue-Sun, to 4pm Mon, mud bath until 5pm) or stay in the on-site hotel, using the baths and other facilities at no extra cost. The hotel also has a pool exclusively for guests, plus a bewilderingly long list of health treatments and massages (lower your expectations).

### Sleeping & Eating

**Centro Termal Las Trincheras** (☎ 317-9969, in Caracas 0212-661-3724; www.trincheras.com.ve; d/tr/q BsF125/150/200; ) The on-site hotel, steeped in aged colonial appeal, offers around 100 light, comfortable rooms with hot water and cable TV. The price includes use of the baths, sauna and other facilities. There are three food options and the main restaurant offers all-day service for hotel guests and day visitors. It's usually easy to get a room during the week, but on weekends the hotel is full to bursting and reservations are a must. There is also a Corp Banca ATM in the lobby.

For half the price and none of the quality, you can hole up across from the bath complex at **Posada El Bosque** (☎ 317-9969; d/tr with fan BsF70/90), where you'll find eight basic rooms and a small restaurant serving fried fish and the like for BsF20 to BsF30. A far more inviting option is the pleasant **Restaurant El Ñaññа** (mains BsF20-52; ⌚ lunch & dinner) just down the road.

For simple family rooms look around town for signs that read 'Se Alquilan Habitaciones.'

### Getting There & Away

From Valencia, take one of the frequent Puerto Cabello buses, which can drop you at the freeway bridge in Las Trincheras. From here it's a 10-minute walk to the baths. Taxis from Valencia cost BsF60. A warning to day-trippers: buses heading back to Valencia will not pick you up at the bridge after sunset.

## PUERTO CABELLO

☎ 0242 / pop 178,500

You'd have to go out of your way to end up in the once vital port city of Puerto Cabello, 58km north of Valencia, but those who do might find just enough crumbling colonial architecture to fascinate themselves for a day or two. The scenic, restored colonial town center is once again heading toward decay, but still holds on loosely to its kaleidoscopic facades and overhung balconies, which dominate the picturesque landscape of the old town center.

Puerto Cabello began life in the mid-16th century as a simple wharf built on the bank of a coastal lagoon. During the 17th century the Dutch-run port grew fat on its contraband trade with Curaçao. It wasn't until 1730 that the Spanish took over the port, after the Real Compañía Guipuzcoana moved in. This company built an array of forts, and by the 1770s Puerto Cabello was the most heavily fortified town on Venezuela's coast. Thus, during the War of Independence, it became an important royalist stronghold, and was the last place in Venezuela to be freed from Spanish rule.

Today, Puerto Cabello boasts two old forts, a lively malecón and a new government hell-bent on modernizing the tourism infrastructure (plans call for a revamped marina, an over-water mall, a new airport and a *teleférico* (cable car) to Fortín Solano). The town is also a jumping-off point for several pretty beaches on the road toward Patanemo as well as Isla Larga, a favorite diving and snorkeling spot inside Parque Nacional Esteban, which also boasts several hikes that eventually join up with those located in Parque Nacional Henri Pittier (p101).

### Information

**Cybercafe** (Calle Miranda; ⌚ 9am-9pm Mon-Sat, to 6pm Sun) Near the Hotel Fortín.

**Ipostel** (⌚ 8am-4:30pm Mon-Fri) Near the end of the malecón.

**Tourist Office** (Calle Bolivar, Paseo El Malecón; danmendes@hotmail.com) At the time of writing, tourism director Daniel Mendes was operating out of the marina office across from Teatro Municipal, with plans to relocate to a permanent location. Email for more details.

Local banks include **Banco de Venezuela** (Calle Colón), at the end of the malecón, and **Banco Mercantil** (Plaza Bolívar).



### Sights

#### SPANISH FORTS

North of the old town, and separated from it by the entrance channel to the harbor, is colonial Fortín San Felipe, later renamed **Castillo Libertador** (admission free; ⌚ dawn-dusk). It's a fine-looking fort, though in a state of disrepair. It was constructed in the 1730s to protect the port and warehouses. During the War of Independence, the fort was for a time in the patriots' hands, but it was lost to the royalists in 1812. Francisco de Miranda was jailed here before the Spanish sent him to prison in Spain. The fort was recovered in 1823, and later served General Gómez as a jail, mostly for political prisoners. Upon Gómez' death in 1935, the prison closed down and no less than 14 tons of chains and leg irons were thrown into the sea. The fort is within the naval base, and tourists need authorization to visit – only groups of 20 or more are permitted.

On the 100m-high hill to the south of the city sits another fort, **Fortín Solano** (admission free; ⌚ dawn-dusk), built in the 1760s to secure commercial operations. Reputedly the last colonial fort built in Venezuela, it commands excellent views of the city and the harbor. The road to the fort branches off from the road to San Esteban on the outskirts of Puerto Cabello. Thus, you can combine a visit to the fort with the trip to San Esteban. Even if you want to visit only the fort, take a San Esteban carrito to the turnoff to avoid walking through a shabby *barrio* (shantytown).

#### OLD TOWN

The part of the old town to the west of Calle Comercio was restored in recent years and some of the facades painted in bright colors. Though in decline again, it remains a pleasant area to explore or watch the world go by from the open-air restaurants on the tree-shaded waterfront boulevard, Paseo Malecón.

Don't miss the two historic streets Calle de los Lanceros and Calle Bolívar; they're both next to each other and off the plaza. Note the overhanging balconies and massive doorways, including the fair-sized **Museo de Historia** (Calle Bolívar 43; admission free; 8am-noon & 1-5pm). Built in 1790 as a residence, this decaying building has graceful facades over both streets. There isn't much in the way of artifacts, though there are some interesting paintings, especially that of the slaves overhanging the staircase. Be careful on the second floor – the floor is ready to give way at any moment. At the northern end of Calle de los Lanceros is the **Iglesia del Rosario**, a handsome yellow church built in 1780. The bell tower is made of wood – unique in Venezuela.

**Plaza Bolívar**, at the southern edge of the colonial sector, boasts yet another fine equestrian statue of Bolívar. The massive, somewhat ugly edifice built from coral rock and occupying the eastern side of the plaza is the **Catedral de San José**. It was begun in the mid-19th century and completed only some 100 years later.

The colorful **Teatro Municipal** (361-9411; Calle Bolívar; 8am-5pm Mon-Fri depending on events) dates from 1880 and is a replica of one in Havana, Cuba. It's a beautiful theater with 617 seats, two balconies and a huge 640kg chandelier. Ballerina Ana Pavlova, tango songbird Carlos Gardel and violinist Augusto Brandt have all performed here. Free tours (in Spanish) are given.

### SUBURBAN BEACHES

To reach the beaches outside of town, catch a carrito from the bus terminal toward Patanemo (BsF3, 30 minutes). Along the way, you can hop off at **Balneario Quizandal**, about 7km by road from the city. This beach is quite developed, with a car park, showers and restaurants, though it's mainly of interest as a jumping-off point for boats to the gem of the area, **Isla Larga**, one of five islands that make up the aquatic side of Parque Nacional Esteban (BsF17 per person one way). Here you'll find a beautiful, sandy island popular with day-trippers. There are two wrecks near the island, a bonus attraction for snorkelers and divers. *Jaco*, an Italian cattle boat, is easily seen while snorkeling; the German ship *Sesostris*, on the other hand, sits at 18m and is better viewed on a dive. **La Tienda de Buceo** (0414-143-0223 in Valencia; www.venezueladiving.com; Av Bolivar Norte, Centro Comercial HS Center, Valencia), is a good English-speaking dive operator in the area.

Also try **Playa Patanemo**, the best mainland beach in the area, with wide sands and shaded by coconut palms, about 16km east of Puerto Cabello.

## Sleeping & Eating

Budget accommodations in town tend to double as shady love hotels (this is a port, after all). There is a fairly atmospheric string of simple bars/restaurants on Playa Blanca, on the southern end of the malecón, but imbibing here means mingling with possible trouble. Tread within your comfort zone, especially at night. Be on the look out for La Casa de Chocolate, a small dessert kiosk on the malecón at the beginning of Calle de los Lanceros, serving a cornucopia of homemade deserts from somebody's kitchen.

**Hotel Bahía Azul** (361-4033; Av Santa Bárbara 11-93; s/d/tr BsF150/180/280; P ) The secure Bahía Azul has 15 large, good-value, spotless rooms with cable TV, thin mattresses and small vanities. No hot water.

**Hotel El Fortín** (361-4356; Calle Miranda; d/tr BsF160/200; ) The clean and comfortable El Fortín is one of the better budget options in town. The uniform, spacious rooms have cable TV, hot water and telephone. Both of the above options are in rowdier streets several blocks from the charming old town.

our pick **Posada Santa Margarita** (361-7113; www.posadasantamargarita.com.ve; Calle Bolívar No 4-36; d with fan/air-con BsF290/380; ) Boasting more character than nearly every hotel in this region, this 275-year-old house, rescued from ruin, right on historic Calle Bolívar comes with a wonderfully charming old-time atmosphere. The brightly painted rooms have high ceilings, creaky wood floors and comfortable furnishings. There are relaxed sitting areas, steep staircases, a tiny pool and heaven-sent showers, and the cost includes a fab breakfast. The towels are a piece of art – folded into elephants!

**Pizzería da Franco** (361-6161; Paseo Malecón; pizza BsF35-55; lunch & dinner) This seafront spot boasts opera on the radio and a Italian owner frantically switching between *La Liga* and *Serie A* on the DirecTV. It ain't Napoli, but the pizzas are decent, made by a 15-year-old *venezolano* during our visit. There's terrace seating outside facing the malecón.

**Restaurant Los Lanceros** (☎ 361-8471; Paseo Malecón; mains BsF40-80; lunch & dinner) In an old colonial building with a sea view, this upmarket Spanish restaurant has terrace seating along with a small, pleasant, air-con bar area. On the menu are paella, seafood and meat dishes. Go for the catch of the day *al ajillo* (sautéed with garlic).

## Getting There & Away

### AIR

The airfield is 7km west of Puerto Cabello, next to the freeway. There are no scheduled tourist flights, though there is talk of a new airport in the near future.

### BOAT

At the time of writing, the new **ferry building** (Calle Puerto Cabello) sits unused due to a government change and takeover. Plans remain to rev up passenger services from Puerto Cabello to Bonaire, Curaçao and Isla de Margarita, but don't hold your breath.

### BUS

The bus terminal is on Calle Urdaneta, about 800m west of Av Bolívar. Frequent carritos run between the terminal and the center, but you can walk it in 10 minutes.

Buses depart every 15 minutes to Valencia (BsF7, one hour), which has frequent connections to Caracas. Other destinations include Tucacas (BsF10, 1¼ hours) and Chichiriviche (BsF14.50, 1¾ hours), departure points for Parque Nacional Morrocoy, as well as San Felipe (BsF13.50, 1¾ hours) and Barquisimeto (BsF29, three hours).

Carritos to San Esteban depart regularly from outside the bus terminal in front of Loterias El Emperador in Puerto Cabello (BsF2, 25 minutes), from where hiking trails begin into Parque Nacional San Esteban.

# The Northwest

If Venezuela was a restaurant, the northwest would be the chef's *menu de dégustation* – a chance to savor all the delicious morsels that make up the country. There's something for every taste – rainforests and deserts, coral islands and beaches, caves and waterfalls, and South America's largest lake.

Colorful Coro is one of the oldest settlements in the New World, and a popular traveler's chill-out spot. Nearby are two strikingly different environs – the desert wildness of the Peninsula de Paraguaná, and the misty green forests of the Sierra de San Luis. The favorable winds off Adícora, on Paraguaná's east coast, have made it the top spot for budget kitesurfers in Venezuela.

The white-sand cays of Parque Nacional Morrocoy beckon beach-lovers with warm Caribbean waves and colorful reefs. Or escape the heat, if you prefer, and head for the hills – relax in the small colonial towns around Barquisimeto, sample Venezuela's finest wines in Carora or indulge in an all-night, cigar-smoking séance with the faithful at the shrines of María Lionza.

## HIGHLIGHTS

- Let the afternoon breeze gently rock your hammock, or fly down a dune on a sandboard in colorful, oh-so-groovy **Coro** (p118)
- Test your mettle against wind and wave going kitesurfing in **Adícora** (p126)
- Work on your tan lines on the white-sand beaches of the **Parque Nacional Morrocoy** (p129)
- Discover *gaita*, the music of **Maracaibo** (p147), during the Feria de la Chinita in November
- Marvel at the unique lightning phenomenon of **Catatumbo** (p150)

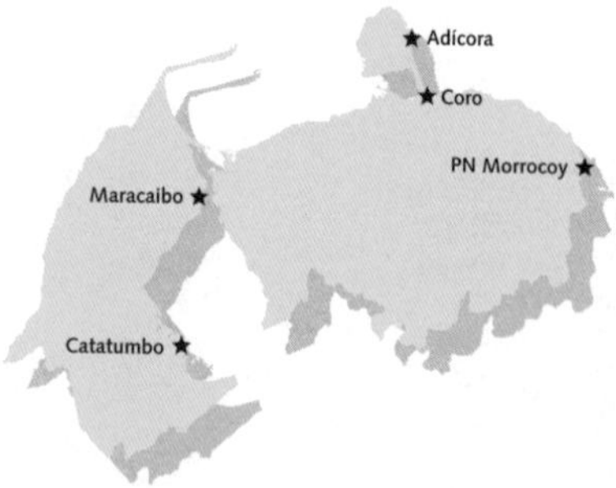

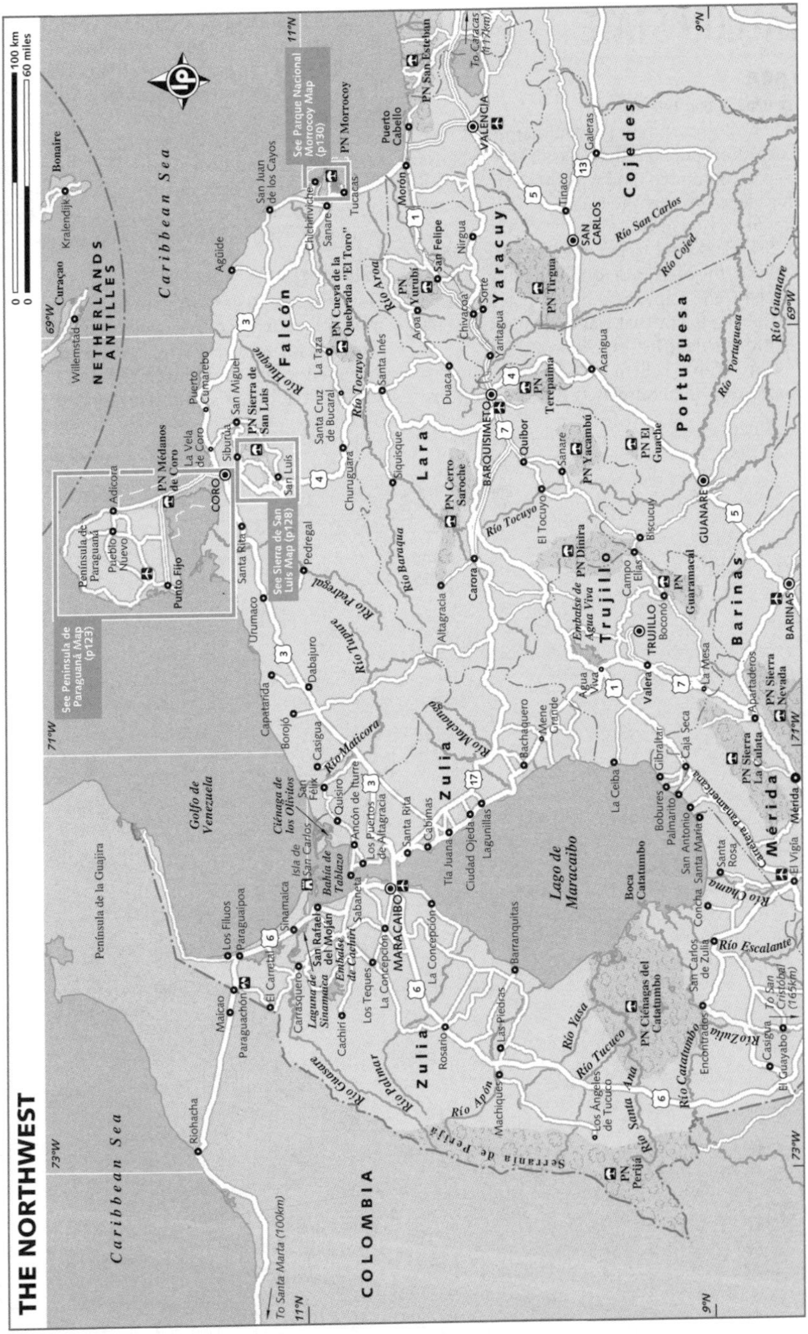


THE NORTHWEST

 



# FALCÓN STATE

## CORO

☎ 0268 / pop 198,700

When you're swinging in your hammock on a Coro afternoon and that coastal breeze blows in, you can understand why the natives called this place *curiana*, the Caquetío word meaning 'place of winds.'

Travelers tend to get stuck here, enjoying the heat, the breeze, or strolling along cobblestoned Calle Zamora, a bright patchwork of Caribbean flavor that was added to Unesco's World Heritage list in 1993.

Coro is an excellent base for exploring two interesting and completely different regions: the arid Península de Paraguaná (p122) and the lush, mountainous Sierra de San Luis (p127). They can each be toured in a day (see Tours, p120), or you can linger for a while and explore them on your own.

Coro is one of the oldest settlements in the New World, and became the first capital of Venezuela in 1528. It's also the capital of Falcón state, and boasts several universities, bringing a young and cultured air to the proceedings.

### Orientation

Coro's center, where you are likely to spend most of your time, is small, compact and pleasant for leisurely strolls. Conveniently, all but one of the important sights and a lion's share of the hotels and restaurants are here.

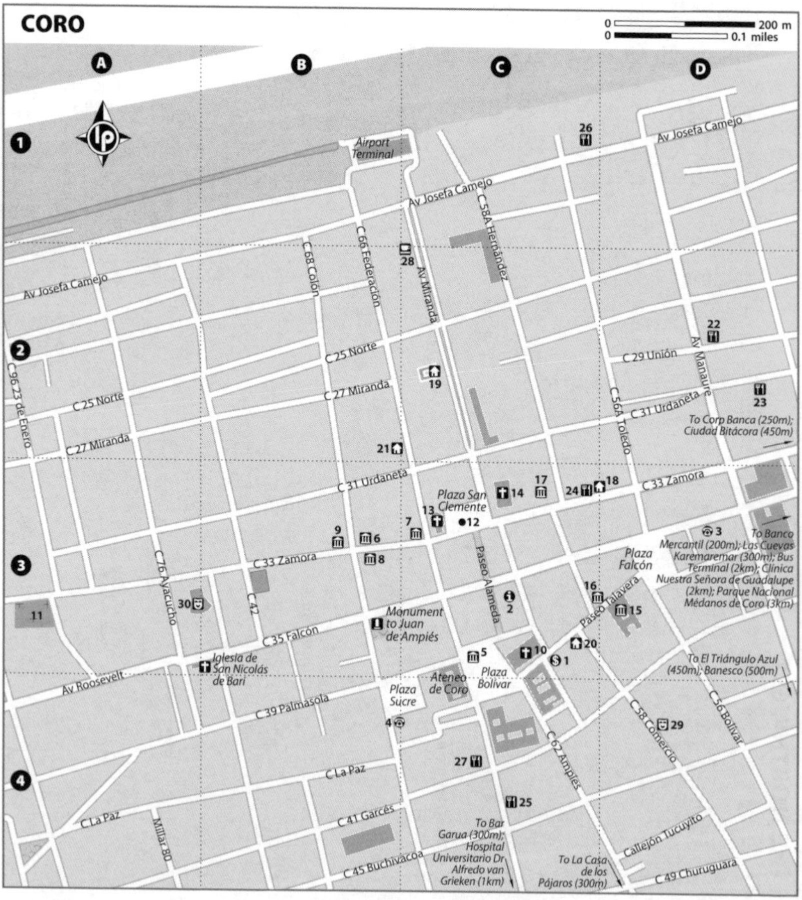

Probably your only trip away from the center (and a recommended one) will be a visit to Parque Nacional Médanos de Coro.

## Information

### EMERGENCY

**Ambulance** (☎ 171)
**Fire** (☎ 171)
**Police** (☎ 171)

### MEDICAL SERVICES

**Clínica Nuestra Señora de Guadalupe** (☎ 252-6011; Av Los Médanos)
**Hospital Universitario Dr Alfredo van Grieken** (☎ 252-5700; Av El Tenis)

### MONEY

**Banco de Venezuela** (Paseo Talavera)
**Banco Mercantil** (Calle 35 Falcón) Two blocks east of Av Manaure.
**Banesco** (Av Manaure) Eight blocks south of Calle Falcón.
**Corp Banca** (Calle 33 Zamora) Three blocks east of Av Manaure.

### TELEPHONE

**Movistar** (Calle 35 Falcón)
**CANTV** (Av Los Medanos) Across from the bus terminal; also has internet.

### TOURIST INFORMATION

**CorFalTur** (Corporación Falconiana de Turismo; ☎ 252-4198, 253-0260; www.visitfalcon.com; Paseo Alameda; 🕑 8am-noon & 2-6pm Mon-Thu, 8am-4pm Fri) The office is on the central pedestrian mall just north of Plaza Bolívar. It publishes a variety of guides in different languages.

## Sights

### HISTORIC MANSIONS & MUSEUMS

All of the city's interesting museums are in restored colonial buildings. The **Museo de Arte de Coro** (☎ 808-3603, 251-5658; Paseo Talavera; admission free; 🕑 9am-12:30pm & 3-7:30pm Tue-Sat, 9am-4pm Sun), in a beautiful 18th-century mansion, is a branch of the Caracas Museo de Arte Contemporáneo and, like its parent, features thought-provoking and well-presented temporary exhibitions.

Diagonally opposite, in another great historic mansion, the **Museo de Arte Alberto Henríquez** (☎ 252-5299; Paseo Talavera; admission free; 🕑 8am-noon & 2-6pm Tue-Fri, 9am-noon Sat & Sun) also has modern art – shows change regularly but are always worth a visit. At the back of the mansion is the first synagogue in Venezuela, (founded 1853) though the present furnishings are all replicas.

For an insight into the colonial past, go two blocks north to the **Museo Diocesano Lucas Guillermo Castillo** (☎ 251-1298; Calle 33 Zamora; admission BsF5; 🕑 9am-noon & 3-6pm Tue-Sat, 9am-2pm Sun), named after a local bishop. Accommodated in 15 rooms of a 17th-century Franciscan convent, the museum boasts an extensive collection of religious and secular art from the region and beyond, including Venezuela's oldest tempera painting and some extraordinary statues of the Madonna carved in wood. It's one of the best collections of its kind in the country. All visits are guided (in Spanish only), and the tour takes about 45 minutes.

A short walk west is the **Casa de los Arcaya** (☎ 251-0023; Calle 33 Zamora) with its attractive, tile-roofed balconies.

The **Casa de las Ventanas de Hierro** (Calle 33 Zamora; admission BsF5; 🕑 8am-6pm Mon-Sat) is noted for a splendid 8m-high plaster doorway and the wrought-iron grilles (brought from Seville, Spain, in 1764) across the windows. It now shelters a private collection of historic objects collected by the family over generations. Nearby, the **Casa del Tesoro** (Calle 33 Zamora) houses an art gallery, while the **Casa de los Soto** (Calle 33



**INFORMATION**
Banco de Venezuela ........ 1 C3
Cor Fal Tur ........ 2 C3
Movistar ........ 3 D3
Post Office ........ (see 5)
Public Telephones ........ 4 B4

**SIGHTS & ACTIVITIES**
Araguato Expeditions ........ (see 21)
Casa de las Cien Ventanas ........ 5 C3
Casa de las Ventanas de Hierro ........ 6 B3
Casa de los Arcaya ........ 7 C3
Casa de los Soto ........ 8 B3
Casa del Tesoro ........ 9 B3
Catedral ........ 10 C3
Cementerio Judío ........ 11 A3
Cruz de San Clemente ........ 12 C3
Iglesia de San Clemente ........ 13 C3
Iglesia de San Francisco ........ 14 C3
Museo de Arte Alberto Henríquez ........ 15 D3
Museo de Arte de Coro ........ 16 C3
Museo Diocesano Lucas Guillermo Castillo ........ 17 C3

**SLEEPING**
Casa Tun Tun ........ 18 D3
Estancia Da Domenico ........ 19 C2
Posada Turística Don Antonio ........ 20 C3
Posada Turística El Gallo ........ 21 B2

**EATING**
Pizzería La Barra del Jacal ........ 22 D2
Restaurant El Conquistador ........ 23 D2
Restaurant El Tinajero ........ 24 C3
Restaurant Punto Criollo ........ 25 C4
Restaurante Shangri La ........ 26 C1
Viva Mejor ........ 27 C4

**DRINKING**
El Café de Andrés ........ 28 C2

**ENTERTAINMENT**
La Casa de la Poesía ........ 29 D4
Teatro Armonía ........ 30 A3

 

Zamora) is a private residence and cannot be visited but is worth looking at from the outside. The home of today's post office on the corner of Plaza Bolívar (corner of Ampíes/Paseo Talavera) is an orange-red structure commonly known as the **Casa de las Cien Ventanas** (House of One Hundred Windows), a unique example of colonial architecture. (We'll take their word for it – we didn't actually count the windows.)

#### COLONIAL CHURCHES

The massive, fortress-like **catedral** (Plaza Bolívar) was begun in the 1580s and finished half a century later, making it the oldest surviving church in Venezuela. There are no remainders of its early history inside, but the 1790 baroque main retable is a good example of late colonial art.

Two blocks north is the 18th-century **Iglesia de San Francisco** (Calle 33 Zamora). The cupola of the 1760s Capilla del Santísimo Sacramento, at the top of the right aisle, is a very fine piece of Mudejar art, showing the strong influence of Moorish style in medieval Spain.

Just a stone's throw to the west of San Francisco is another 18th-century church, the **Iglesia de San Clemente** (Calle 33 Zamora). Note the anchor hanging from the middle of the ceiling, which commemorates St Clement's martyrdom (he was drowned after being weighed down with an anchor).

In the barred pavilion on the plaza between the two churches is the **Cruz de San Clemente** (Plaza San Clemente). This is said to be the cross used in the first mass celebrated after the town's foundation. It's made from the wood of the *cují* tree, a slow-growing species of acacia that is found in this arid region.

#### CEMENTERIO JUDÍO

Established in the 1830s, Coro's **Cementerio Judío** (cnr Calles 33 Zamora & 23 de Enero) is the oldest Jewish cemetery still in use on the continent. It's normally locked and the keys are kept in the Museo de Arte Alberto Henríquez (p119). Enquire there for a guide to show you around.

Jews came to Coro from Curaçao in the early 19th century, a period of intensive trade with the Dutch islands. The cemetery was founded by Joseph Curiel, whose tomb is one of the most elaborate; sadly the grave of his 10-year-old daughter, dated 1832, is the oldest.

#### PARQUE NACIONAL MÉDANOS DE CORO

Just northeast of the city is a spectacular desert landscape, dominated by sand dunes up to 30m high, giving an impression of being in the middle of the Sahara. The **Parque Nacional Médanos de Coro** (www.losmedanos.com, in Spanish; admission free; 9am-6pm) was created in 1974 to protect this unique environment on the isthmus of the Península de Paraguaná.

To get to the park from the city center, take the Carabobo bus from Calle Falcón and get off 300m past the large Monumento a la Federación. From here it's a 10-minute walk north along a wide avenue to another public sculpture, the Monumento a la Madre. A few paces north there is nothing but sand.

Be cautious – armed robbery of tourists in Los Médanos has been reported. Go in the late afternoon, when the security presence is strongest, and take only what you need.

### Tours

Budget full-day tours (BsF220 to BsF250 for up to four persons) to Península de Paraguaná and the Sierra de San Luis are organized by the managers of the **Posada Turística El Gallo** (☎ 252-9481; www.hosteltrail.com/posadoelgallo; Calle 66 Federación No 26) and **La Casa de los Pájaros** (☎ 252-8215; www.casadelosparajos.com.ve; Calle Monzón No 74).

**Araguato Expeditions** (☎ 251-1590, 460-7424; www.araguato.org; Calle 66 Federación No 16) Named for the ubiquitous red howler monkey, Araguato offers tours countrywide, including Los Llanos, as well as local sandboarding expeditions (see the boxed text, p121). Araguato has a cozy posada, Casa del Mono, in the same building.

### Sleeping

**La Casa de los Pájaros** (☎ 252-8215; www.casadelospajaros.com.ve; Calle Monzón No 74; dm or hammock per person BsF30, d/tr BsF140/170, ) The 'House of Birds' is owned by Venezuelan architect Roberto, who is constantly expanding and rebuilding this very unique home. There's seven deliciously cool rooms (including air-con dorm rooms), guests can use the kitchen and internet, and Roberto can also organize local tours.

**Posada Turística El Gallo** (☎ 252-9481; www.hosteltrail.com/posadoelgallo; Calle 66 Federación No 26; hammock/dm/d/tr with shared bathroom BsF30/60/80/120, d/tr with bathroom BsF120/180) What El Gallo lacks in luxury, the French owner Eric makes up for with an encyclopedic knowledge of tourism

**SURFING THE SANDS OF CORO**

The climb, calf-deep in sand, seems interminable. You reach the top of the dune, breathless. Wax the board, strap both feet in and *zoom* – you've zipped down 100m in seconds flat. Despite the difficulty – or maybe because of it – sandboarding the finger of land known as Los Médanos is both exhilarating and addictive.

Only the basics are required: a board (rentable at any of Coro's tourist agencies), some sunblock, and a little *joie de vivre*. It's hands-down the best way to see the sunset over Coro, and afterwards you can reward yourself with an icy-cold and vitamin-rich *cocada* – coconut juice, condensed milk and cinnamon over ice – from La Gran Cocada, at the park entrance.

A background in snowboarding is helpful but by no means required. Should you lose your balance, just lean back and let the bottomless *arena* (sand) cushion the blow. Weeks after you return from Venezuela, you'll still find the sands of Paraguaná in your shoes – and your memory.

in the region. The rooms are simple, with no private facilities, but clean and to the point, plus there's laundry service and a kitchen. For those wanting a little bit more comfort, it also offers an additional six rooms with bathrooms in a separate building.

**Casa Tun Tun** (☎ 404-0347; www.hosteltrail.com/casatuntun; Calle 33 Zamora btwn Calles 56A Toledo & 58A Hernández; s/d/tr with shared bathroom BsF80/100/150, wtih private bathroom BsF100/120/180) Tun Tun (Knock Knock) is a friendly posada with room for 18 people in a mixture of dorms and private rooms. Facilities include a barbecue, laundry service, free coffee and a wicked old vinyl jukebox.

**Posada Turística Don Antonio** (☎ 253-9578; Paseo Talavera No 11; d/tr BsF120/160; ❄ ☰) This acceptable posada has been rebuilt in a colonial style and you can't argue with its location – smack dab in the heart of Coro. It has nine comfy *matrimoniales* (doubles) and three triples, all equipped with bathrooms and air-conditioning.

**Estancia Da Domenico** (☎ 252-7703, 0414-687-6874; www.estanciadadomenico.net; Av Miranda btwn Calles 27 Miranda & 31 Urdaneta; s/d/tr/ste BsF120/190/210/290; ❄ ☰) This is a comfortable small hotel, with walls draped in artwork – the works are for sale – and all the usual luxuries you might want, including air-con, cable TV, wi-fi, laundry service and a yummy restaurant on the ground floor.

## Eating

**Restaurante Shangri La** (☎ 0416-967-2535; Av Josefa Camejo at Toledo; meals BsF3-10; 🕑 6am-9pm; V) Lee Tzu serves up veggie breakfasts and lunches in this new, small joint near the airport, as well as a variety of herbal teas to cure what ails you. The *Flor de Jamaica* is a guaranteed 'cleanser'!

**Restaurant Punto Criollo** (☎ 252-2043; Calle 66 Federación; breakfasts BsF8-15, lunches BsF15-30; 🕑 7am-3pm Mon-Sat) This simple eight-table place offers filling breakfasts and gets completely packed with patrons at lunchtime – and deservedly so. The *solomo criollo* is killer (not literally!).

**Viva Mejor** (Calle Federacion at Garces No 52; set lunch BsF20; 🕑 6am-9pm; V) Another yummy veggie choice, closer to the center. Try the *yoyos* – whole-wheat empanadas stuffed with plantains and cheese, as well as the scrumptious veggie Mexican tacos.

**Pizzería La Barra del Jacal** (☎ 252-7350; Calle 29 Unión; meals BsF45-55) This attractive open-air restaurant offers more than just pizzas, and is a refreshing spot to sit with a beer, especially in the evening when a gentle breeze dissipates the heat of the day.

**Restaurant El Conquistador** (☎ 252-6794; Calle 31 Urdaneta; meals BsF45-80; ❄) Satisfactory food, white-gloved waiters and a tastefully decorated interior make El Conquistador one of the best eateries in town. Go for *parrilla aire* (mixed grill), *mar y tierra* (surf and turf) or *paella valenciana*, which are among its specialties.

## Drinking

**Bar Garua** (cnr Calles Monzon & 68 Colón; 🕑 7pm-late Tue-Sat) This classic old-time bar has been here since 1943. Sit with a cold one and soak up the atmosphere, or chat to some of the friendly locals.

**El Café de Andrés** (☎ 253-0870, 0414-740-5065; Av 27 Miranda btwn Av Josefa Camejo & Calle Norte; 🕑 6:30pm-late Thu-Sat) Just across the street from the Hotel Cumberland, this funky bar-cum-restaurant is one of the hippest joints in town. Come early for the food, and linger late over drinks for the live music, which kicks in around midnight.

## Entertainment

**Cine en la Calle** (Paseo Talavera) A free open-air cinema casts Venezuelan and Latin American films against the wall on buildings between

Plaza Bolívar and Plaza Falcón every Tuesday at 7pm.

**Pacha Mama** (☎ 252-8675; Calle 58 Comercio) A French-owned open-air cafe inside the Casa de la Poesia. Local collegians flock here for the cheap beer and rock/reggae/funk flowing through the garden. Ecological furniture from recycled materials ups the PC quotient.

**Teatro Armonía** (Calle 35 Falcón) The city's main performing arts venue. Free concerts by the local philharmonic orchestra (considered to be the best in the country) are held every Thursday at 7:30pm.

## Getting There & Away

### AIR

The **Aeropuerto Internacional José Leonardo Chirinos** (Av Josefa Camejo) was closed at the time of research, with no schedule for reopening.

You may have to fly to Punto Fijo (p124) to get to the peninsula via air.

### BUS

The **Terminal de Pasajeros** (☎ 252-8070; Av Los Médanos) is about 2km east of the city center, and is accessible by frequent city transportation. SITSSA buses go to Maracay (BsF35) and Caracas (BsF40) each evening. There are por puestos to Punto Fijo (BsF25, 1¼ hours, 90km), Maracaibo (buseta BsF35, por puesto BsF60, bus BsF60 to BsF70, four hours, 259km) and Valencia (BsF49, five hours, 288km) leaving every half-hour until about 6pm. Most of the direct buses to Caracas (BsF61, seven hours, 446km) depart in the evening, but you can take one of the buses to Valencia and change.

Several direct buses go nightly to Mérida (BsF70 to BsF74, 12 hours, 782km) and to San Cristóbal (BsF83, 12 hours, 698km); all these buses depart in the evening and go via Maracaibo. If you're in a hurry, go to Barquisimeto (BsF50, seven hours, 418km) and change there.

Within the region, there are buses to Adícora (BsF9), on the eastern coast of Península de Paraguaná, as well as por puesto jeeps to Curimagua (BsF20) in the Sierra de San Luis (from the Mercado Nuevo). Buses to Valencia can drop you off in Tucacas (four hours, 203km), but for Chichiriviche (3¾ hours, 195km) you'll have to get off at the junction in Sanare (3¼ hours, 184km) and change; busetas pass frequently (BsF5, 20 minutes). You have to pay the full fare to Valencia for both destinations (BsF49).

# PENÍNSULA DE PARAGUANÁ

☎ 0269 / pop 273,000

You get the feeling Paraguaná wishes it was still an island – in geography and character, it has more in common with the nearby Dutch Antilles than the continent just a thin strip of sand away. Beautiful beaches, of course, lead the list of attractions, and a favorable onshore wind has made Adícora the leading budget spot for windsurfing and kitesurfing in the country.

Flat as a pancake and dry as a parched mouth, the peninsula is punctuated only by the singular Cerro Santa Anta (830m), which rises abruptly from the middle of the plain, and can be seen from every angle. Only 40 scant days of rain per year water this arid landscape, which is covered in *cardón,* a columnar cactus tree, whose wood is used to make striking furniture.

Paraguaná offers a striking contrast of desert and beach, wind and waves, colonial towns and nature reserves, pink flamingos and colorful salt mines. There's enough to keep you here for a while.

### HISTORY

The original inhabitants of Paraguaná were the now extinct Amuay, Guaranao and Caquetío people, all belonging to the Arawak linguistic family. Europeans first saw Paraguaná in 1499, when Alonso de Ojeda landed at Cabo de San Román, on the northern tip of the peninsula. Some 130 years later, the Dutch settled the nearby islands of Curaçao, Aruba and Bonaire, and since then there has been a steady mix of Spanish, Dutch and indigenous cultural influences.

The earliest colonial towns emerged inland, close to Cerro Santa Ana, as it provided the only source of fresh water. Some of the towns' old urban fabric remains, including several churches.

Things began to change with the oil boom. In the 1920s a terminal was built in Punto Fijo; refineries were constructed in the 1940s, and Punto Fijo embarked on a boom that continues today. The rest of the peninsula, however, hasn't rushed into modernity. It's still dotted with small old towns and their tiny colonial churches.

### ORIENTATION

There's an array of paved but rather pockmarked roads on the peninsula, except in the almost uninhabited northwest. Having an independent means of transportation is an advantage here, but buses and por puestos are common and service most of the larger localities, including Punto Fijo, Santa Ana, Moruy, Pueblo Nuevo and Adícora.

The usual springboard for the peninsula is Coro, from where buses go to Adícora and Punto Fijo. Los Taques, close to Las Piedras airport, has a growing reputation for its seaside posadas. Punto Fijo is much better serviced by public transportation, but otherwise it's an unremarkable place. It's better to go to the more pleasant Adícora and use it as a base for further excursions, such as viewing flamingos at Laguna de Tiraya or hiking up Cerro Santa Ana. Day tours around the

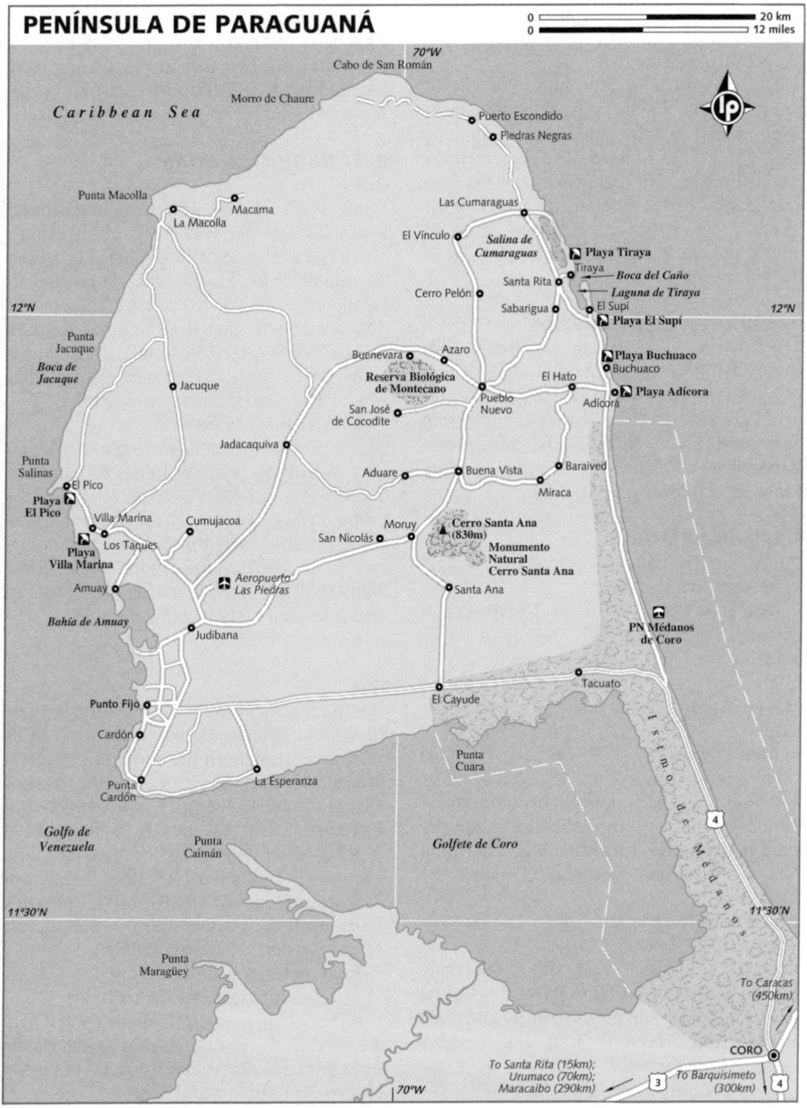

peninsula organized from Coro (p120) are worth considering if you want just a quick taste of Paraguaná.

## Punto Fijo

Punto Fijo is the only city on the peninsula, and first appeared on maps in 1925, when an oil terminal was built serving Lago de Maracaibo. Its two refineries, in Amuay and Punta Cardón, are among the largest in the world, but don't expect a tour – even journalists get turned away.

Today Punto Fijo is an industrial city of about 140,000 inhabitants, and the center of commerce on the peninsula. As such, it has a good range of hotels and restaurants – establishments that are scarce elsewhere on Paraguaná – but is otherwise of marginal interest. You're better off venturing 30 to 60 minutes to reach the comfortable posadas in the hills or on the beaches of Taques.



### ORIENTATION & INFORMATION

The downtown is based on two north–south streets, Av Bolívar and Av Colombia, along which many stores, hotels, restaurants and banks are located. Useful banks include **Banco de Venezuela** (cnr Av 21 Bolivia & Calle 78 Comercio), **Banco Mercantil** (cnr Av 17 Bolívar & Calle 86 Girardot) and **Corp Banca** (cnr Av 21 Bolivia & Calle 81 Falcón).

### SLEEPING & EATING

Punto Fijo has a few places to stay and most have their own restaurants.

**Hotel El Cid** (☎ 245-5743; cnr Av 17 Bolívar & Calle 78 Comercio; s/d/tr/ste BsF120/140/215/300; ❄ 💻) This amazing one-stop shop has everything you might need – a glitzy internet cafe, telephone *cabinas*, a groovy bar and restaurant, and even a disco.

**Hotel Presidente** (☎ 245-8964, 245-5156; cnr Av 14 Perú & Calle 79 Arismendi; d BsF130-150, tr BsF180, ste BsF200-240; ❄) The rooms in this modern establishment are unimpeachable, as are the even better suites, furnished with charming Nixon-era hardwood desks. Conspire the night away.

**Casa de las Tres Ventanas** (☎ 277-0627; lastresventanas@cantv.net; Calle Principal, Los Taques; d/tr BsF285/350; ❄) This upmarket posada offers B&B-style service, sunset views from its garden courtyard, Mediterranean meals to order and tourist excursions around Paraguaná. It's just five minutes from the beach, and 15 minutes to the airport or Punto Fijo.

**Hotel La Península** (☎ 245-9734, 245-9776; hotelpeninsula@cantv.net; Calle Calatayud; d BsF290-370, tr/ste BsF440/640; ❄ 🏊) On Punto Fijo's southeastern outskirts, La Península is one of the city's top offerings, with well-maintained rooms, two restaurants, swimming pool and shaded bar, across from a casino. A planned parking garage should add convenience for drivers.

**Fuente de Soda Tasca-Restaurant Imperial** (☎ 246-5987; cnr Av 17 Bolívar & Calle 78 Comercio; meals BsF20-60) This oasis of air-con and beer may be your salvation if you get stuck in Punto Fijo. Good solid food, especially the *chivo* (goat), and a big-screen TV and bar to while away the hours.

### GETTING THERE & AWAY

#### Air

Punto Fijo's airport, **Aeropuerto Internacional Josefa Camejo** (☎ 246-0278), is about 10km northeast of the city and is labeled in all the air schedules as 'Las Piedras.' There are no public buses to the airport; a taxi from the city center will cost BsF40. Santa Barbara and Conviasa each have three daily flights to Caracas (BsF164 to BsF235) and Conviasa has one to Maracaibo (BsF116 to BsF155).

FBO is a freight/charter company that takes passengers to Curaçao – the price rises if you stay overnight. Insel also goes to Curaçao; Tiara has a daily flight to Aruba. Airlines come and go frequently on this particular route – particularly the smaller charter carriers – so check around before buying. **Santa Bárbara** (☎ 0212-204-4000) has flights to Curaçao and Aruba, but only from Valencia, Maracaibo or Caracas.

#### Bus

Punto Fijo has not yet built a central bus terminal; bus companies have their own offices scattered throughout the city center. **Expresos Occidente** (cnr Calle 78 Comercio & Av 21 Bolivia), **Expresos Alianza** (cnr Calle 85 Altagracia & Av 18 Colombia) and **Expresos San Cristóbal** (cnr Calle 90 Artigas & Av 18 Colombia) service long-distance routes, including Caracas (BsF63 to BsF73, 8½ hours, 536km), Maracaibo (BsF81, 5½ hours, 349km), Barquisimeto (BsF55), Barinas (BsF68) and Mérida (BsF81, 15 hours, 872km).

Regional buses depart from the market square. Buses to Coro (BsF9, 1¼ hours, 90km) run every half-hour until about 6pm. There are also hourly buses to Pueblo Nuevo via the freeway and Santa Ana, and busetas to Pueblo Nuevo via Judibana and Moruy.

### Santa Ana

Originally a Caquetío settlement, Santa Ana was founded in the 1540s. Once Paraguaná's major urban center, it's now a quiet little town, renowned mostly for its colonial church – one of the prettiest country churches in Venezuela. It's also a convenient starting point for a hike to the top of the dramatic Cerro Santa Ana.

The church on Plaza Bolívar was built in the 16th century – the first church on the peninsula – and was remodeled at the end of the 17th century. The unusual bell tower was built around 1750. The church is often open during the day, but if you find it locked, go to the Casa Parroquial, on the northern side of Plaza Bolívar, and somebody may open it up for you.

Santa Ana has several basic places to eat, and a nice posada, Posada e Diego, on the plaza opposite the church; the Inparques office is one block north. Buses between Pueblo Nuevo and Punto Fijo pass on the main road every hour or so.

### Moruy

Moruy is most famous for its *silletas paraguaneras,* chairs made from the wood of the *cardón* cactus, which thickly covers most of the peninsula. You can buy them on the roadside stalls here, and also in the neighboring hamlet of San Nicolás.

A short 6km northwest of Santa Ana, Moruy's lovely colonial church also attracts visitors. Completed in 1683, it's modest in internal furnishing and decoration, but is beautifully proportioned and has a charming facade.

Moruy is a popular starting point for hikes up Cerro Santa Ana. There's nowhere to stay overnight in the village and only a couple of places for a meal. Busetas and buses run regularly to Punto Fijo, Pueblo Nuevo and Santa Ana.

### Cerro Santa Ana

This unexpected mountain rises 830m from the plains, in sudden and striking defiance of the parched flatness below. Its three peaks are visible from nearly every point on the peninsula. The mountain, along with its environs (19 sq km altogether), has been decreed a natural monument and is under the control of Inparques.

Climbing the mountain, you pass through three totally different ecosystems – the xerophytic desert species at the base, through cloud forest at 500m and, at the very summit, the plants of the semi-*páramo* (open highland), including orchids and bromeliads.

Two ways lead to the top. The main route begins at Moruy and heads eastward for 1500m along an unpaved road to the Inparques post and a bivouac area. From here, a proper trail heads to the highest peak. It's about a three-hour walk up to the summit (two hours back down).

Another starting point is the town of Santa Ana, from where a rough road from the Inparques office heads north to another bivouac site (a 30-minute walk). The trail that begins here leads to the lowest, eastern peak, and continues westward along the crest to the main peak. This route is not clear at some points, so be careful not to get lost.

Because of the extreme midday heat, Inparques only permits hikers to start uphill from 7am to 9am. You should register before departure at the respective post, but there's no charge. Hikers need to return by 3pm and mark their return on the list.

The peak is always windy and frequently shrouded in cloud. Occasionally it rains in the upper reaches, especially during the wet months (September to January). Take along a sweater, waterproof gear and proper shoes – the path near the top can be muddy.



### Pueblo Nuevo

**pop 8000**

Pueblo Nuevo is the largest town in the inland portion of Paraguaná. It became the capital of Paraguaná in 1829 but the oil boom eventually stripped it of the title in favor of Punto Fijo.

Although it continues to maintain importance as an agricultural center, its economy now depends primarily on the arts and crafts industry – especially pottery, for which it is well known – making it a good place to go shopping. It still contains some fine colonial houses and a church dating from 1758, although the latter was remodeled in the 20th century.

#### SLEEPING & EATING

**Posada de Luis** (☎ 988-1072, 0414-696-3019; Calle Falcón; d/tr BsF150/180) This likeable, neat, 10-room posada, 300m west of Plaza Bolívar, is the main place to stay in the center of Pueblo Nuevo.

our pick **Casa de los Vientos** (☎ 808-5000, 0416-564-4027; per person BsF220) Near the hamlet of Sacuragua, between Pueblo Nuevo and Buena Vista, sits this beautiful Gaudí-inspired minicastle, a world apart from the torrid peninsula. Stay in a room in the house or one of the tree-shaded, self-contained cabins the owner built himself. Price includes air-con, TV, dinner and breakfast; Mr Pages can also organize transportation around the peninsula.

**Restaurant Popular y El Caney de Taca** (☎ 808-5005; Calle Falcón; meals BsF12-25) It's indeed popular, serving straightforward, tasty meals at low prices.

#### GETTING THERE & AWAY

There are frequent buses, busetas and por puestos to Punto Fijo (via Moruy) and Adícora, and two busetas a day direct to Coro.

### Reserva Biológica de Montecano

This small wooded area, only 16 sq km, is the only remaining lowland forest on the peninsula. Amazingly, it provides a habitat for 62% of the plant species of Falcón state and attracts a great variety of birds. The **Montecano biological reserve** (admission free; 8:30am-8pm) is about 7km west of Pueblo Nuevo. It is run by Infalcosta, a Coro-based institute established in 1995 for the development and conservation of Falcón's arid coastal areas.

The visitors center is on a narrow road leading to the village of San José de Cocodite, 2km south of Pueblo Nuevo. There are frequent por puestos from the Pueblo Nuevo terminal that will leave you at the gate (BsF3). A 2km looped path with nine stations winds through the reserve – an easy walk through an unusual habitat full of amazing plants and birds. You'll even find a small lagoon on the way. The best times to see the birds are early in the morning and late afternoon – and you avoid the burning heat of midday. You can also arrange a guided tour if desired.

### Adícora

The small town of Adícora, on Paraguaná's eastern coast, is set at the tip of a narrow, eastern-pointing strip of land and has beaches on both sides, a scant five minutes' walk apart. It's most famous for its windsurfing and kitesurfing, but also boasts fine, colorful Caribbean streets and a reasonable choice of accommodations and restaurants.

Reputedly founded in the middle of the 16th century, it was once one of the most important ports in western Venezuela. Prosperity came in the 18th century when the Compañía Guipuzcoana built a trading base here. Strolling around the streets, you'll still find brightly colored Dutch-Caribbean houses characterized by barred windows on pedestals, topped with decorated caps.

#### ACTIVITIES

Adícora has gained international fame as a **kitesurfing** and **windsurfing** center, with some of the best wave and wind conditions on Venezuela's coast. The winds are strongest and most consistent from January to May, and the calmest from September to November, and the breeze is always onshore, ensuring you don't make an unplanned visit to the Dutch Antilles. It's a choice spot, virtually untouched by tourism, beautifully relaxed and informal, and not too expensive.

Joachim Wicher (aka Archie) and Pachi, German and Venezuelan respectively, can be found on the Playa Sur (South Beach), and offer similar windsurfing and kitesurfing courses, equipment rental and simple accommodations.

You'll pay around BsF800 for a two-day kitesurfing class. You generally have to take the class before you're permitted to rent gear (around BsF400 per day) and go solo. Windsurfing is a bit cheaper, around BsF150 per day for equipment rental and beginner's instruction for another BsF150. Both offer instruction in a variety of languages.

**Archie's Kite & Windsurfing** (☎ 988-8285, 511-8894; www.kitesurfing-venezuela.com) Archie offers instruction in multiple languages and rents simple rooms, including some that have air-con. Long-term visitors in a dorm bed pay BsF60, furnished apartments go for BsF120, and bungalows for four to six people BsF200. He sometimes leads kitesurfing and barbecue excursions to more remote, 4WD-only accessible beaches.

**Windsurf Adícora** (☎ 0416-769-6196; www.windsurfadicora.com) The biggest and most reliable facility, run by Pachi. It offers windsurfing and kitesurfing, plus good accommodations. The four rooms go for BsF60 per person with air-con, wi-fi and TV, and there's a common kitchen.

#### SLEEPING & EATING

Adícora has a better choice of places to stay than most other towns on the peninsula. Prices are higher on weekends, when tourists arrive. Some locals rent out rooms in their homes, which can make for some of the cheapest and safest forms of lodging – ask around. But don't rent unattended cabañas or beach houses; these places are easy prey for robbers. There are restaurants in the buildings along the beach, though most of them are only open on weekends.

**Posada Casa Rosada** (☎ 988-8004; Calle Malecón; d/tr BsF180/300; ) This beautifully restored colonial building surrounds a garden courtyard and serves up German-influenced food in the peaceful front restaurant. One of the family-sized rooms comes self-contained with a kitchen and fridge.

**Hacienda La Pancha** (☎ 511-1269, 0414-969-2649; r per person BsF260; P ) This luxurious uber-posada is just five minutes west of Adícora in the hills. Brightly decorated and well run, La Pancha offers six comfortable rooms, an excellent restaurant and a lush garden with hammocks. Price includes dinner, breakfast and friendly dogs.

**Posada Guadalupana** (☎ 988-8178; Calle Comercio; www.turismodeplaya.com; self-contained apt/detached house BsF280/400; ) Self-contained apartments are the name of the game in this old colonial building. Each apartment has a well-furnished kitchen with stove and fridge, and there's also a separate detached beach house for up to 20 persons available.

#### GETTING THERE & AWAY

Adícora is linked to Coro (BsF8, one hour, 50km) by half a dozen buses a day, the last departing at around 5pm. There are also por puestos to Pueblo Nuevo and busetas to Punto Fijo. Transportation varies heavily with the season – during peak tourist times, more buses and por puestos ply this route.

### Lagunas & Salinas

Flamingos feed at **Laguna de Tiraya,** about 6km north of Adícora. Peak season is November to January, but you can be pretty sure of finding some birds almost year-round. The flamingos generally come to the western shore in the afternoon after doing their morning fishing on the eastern side. The lagoon is accessible by the paved road to Santa Rita (which skirts the western shore of the lagoon), but there is no public transportation. You can walk or try to hitch (the traffic is mainly on weekends), or take a taxi from Adícora.

Further north, between Santa Rita and Las Cumaraguas, is the **Salina de Cumaraguas**, where salt is mined using rudimentary methods. The lagoon is noted for its beautiful colors, ranging from milky pink to deep purple.

If you have your own transportation, you can explore the region further north as far as **Cabo de San Román**, which is the northernmost point in Venezuela, and from where, on a clear day, you can see as far as Aruba. If you're without a car, there are irregular por puestos (BsF6) on a paved road from Las Cumaraguas to Pueblo Nuevo via El Vínculo. Be prepared for the heat: take water, sunscreen, sunglasses and a hat.

### Beaches

The beaches on Paraguaná don't match those of Morrocoy or Henri Pittier and the lack of coconut palms means that they usually lack shade. Like all beaches in Venezuela, Paraguaná's beaches are quiet on weekdays and swamped on the weekends.

The beaches on the eastern coast stretch almost all the way from Adícora to Piedras Negras. **Adícora** is the most popular and well-kept beach resort; the beaches at **El Supí** and **Buchuaco** are often covered with litter. **Tiraya** is less popular with holidaymakers because it's harder to reach. On the western coast, the popular beaches include **Villa Marina** and **El Pico**, both serviced by local transportation from Punto Fijo.

## SIERRA DE SAN LUIS

☎ 0268

For those seeking relief from the coastal heat, or a chance to do some hiking, the Sierra de San Luis offers green mountains chock-a-block with tiny colonial towns, waterfalls, caves and a dozen *simas* – deep vertical holes in the earth. There's a good choice of walking paths and excellent bird-watching, and an array of hotels and restaurants to cater to most tastes.

The sierra is a vital source of water for the whole coastal area, including the Península de Paraguaná. About 200 sq km of this rugged terrain was made into a national park in 1987. Elevations within the park range from 200m to 1501m on Cerro Galicia, the park's highest point. Average temperatures range between 60°F and 75°F, according to altitude. Annual rainfall is moderate, not exceeding 1500mm, and the wettest months are October to December.

### Orientation

Curimagau, San Luis, and Cabure are the major towns of the Sierra, all accessible by public transportation from Coro. Curimagua

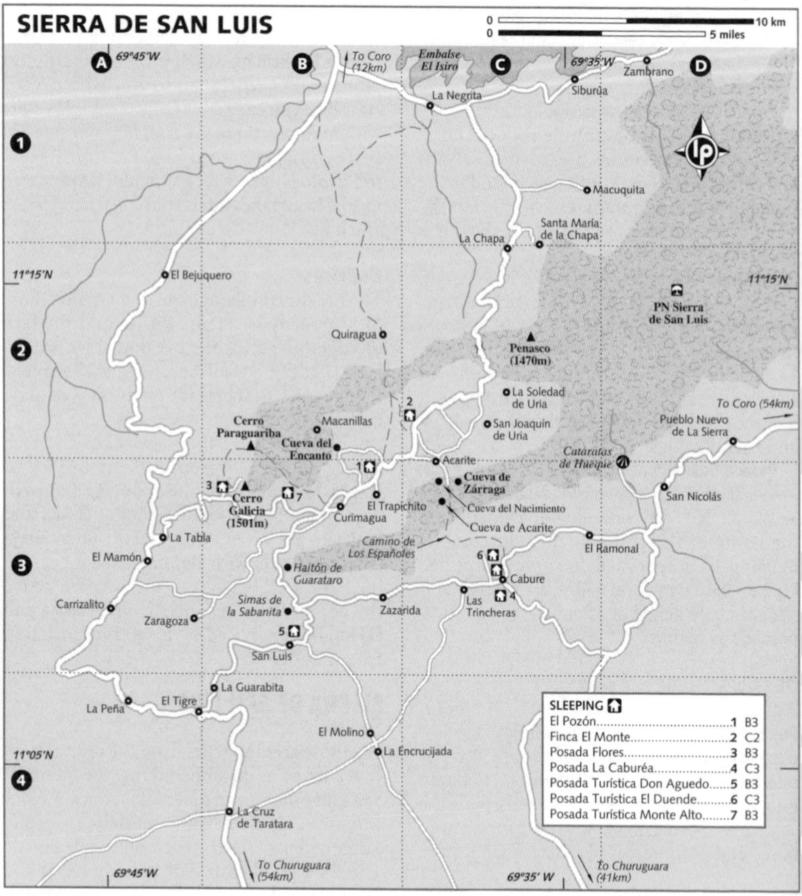


is the closest to Coro (45km) and is the only one regularly serviced. Curimagua and its environs also have the best choice of accommodations and provide the most popular and convenient base for visiting the region. You can go there on your own and stay in a posada, from where you can explore the sierra. Some posada owners will offer excursions, or at least provide information on what to see and how to get there. The Swiss owner of **Finca El Monte** (☎ 404-0564; fincaelmonte@yahoo.com) is one of the few in the mountains who speaks English, and offers walking tours throughout the Sierra de San Luis.

You can also take a day tour to the sierra from Coro (see Tours p120), which covers most of the sights listed here.

## Sights

The most popular attraction in the mountains is the **Camino de los Españoles**, an old Spanish trail between Cabure and La Negrita; its best-preserved part is near Acarite, where there is a brick Spanish bridge dating from around 1790. You have to walk the trail to see the **Cueva de Zárraga** and the **Cueva del Nacimiento**, both spectacular local caves. It's about a three-hour walk to cover the whole trail. Be sure to wear stout shoes and bring water and insect repellent.

Midway between Curimagua and San Luis is the **Haitón de Guarataro**, an impressive local *sima*. It's 305m deep, but the mouth is only about 12m in diameter. Northeast of Cabure is the **Cataratas de Hueque**, the largest and the most spectacular of the region's waterfalls.

You may see the amazing *heliconia* (false bird of paradise) flower on your way down.

Of the three main towns, **San Luis** is possibly the most picturesque. Founded in 1590, it's the oldest Spanish settlement in the area and has preserved some of its colonial architecture, including a fine church.

You can also walk a loop up **Cerro Galicia**, to **Cerro Paraguariba**, and then back to Curimagua. The trail is hard to follow, so be sure to take a local guide – it's both easy and dangerous to get lost.

## Sleeping & Eating

Accommodations in the Sierra range from small, family-run posadas to larger hotels, some with their own nightclubs. Many places come alive only on the weekend, when city holidaymakers can fill hotels to capacity. Unless otherwise noted, all places listed here are open during the week, have rooms with bathrooms and provide meals.

### CURIMAGUA & AROUND

**Posada Flores** (☎ 426-566-1516; www.posadafloresdesalome.com; per person BsF60; ) This relatively new posada provides a great observation point for birds from its back garden filled with fruit trees, and has a lovely weekend package of two nights with excursions (BsF480).

**our pick Finca El Monte** (☎ 404-0564; fincaelmonte@yahoo.com; s/d/tr BsF60/100/126; V) Friendly Swiss couple Ernesto and Ursula run this cozy family posada. They serve delicious meals (vegetarian on request), organize walking tours in the area, and also roast, grind and serve homegrown organic coffee. Just 5km northeast of Curimagua, on the road to Coro, this is hands down the best traveler's option in the sierras.

**Posada Turística Monte Alto** (☎ 416-5243; d BsF120, cabañas BsF250-350; P) About 2km west of Curimagua, this agreeable posada, stuck to a steep hillside, offers five *matrimoniales*, two cabañas (for four to five guests) providing great views and a no-nonsense restaurant.

**El Pozón** (☎ 0426-769-2607; d BsF130) Just down the road from Finca El Monte is this quiet family home, which offers comfortable rooms and a restaurant that serves up home-style creole cooking. They grow their own fruit and coffee and have a special interest in traditional and herbal remedies, including – wait for it – whole, pickled snake, curled up in a jar of rum.

### SAN LUIS

**Posada Turística Don Aguedo** (☎ 666-3073; Calle Principal; d BsF280; P) This charming place at the foot of the mountain has seven perfectly acceptable rooms with bathrooms and fans, and a rustic restaurant serving filling meals. It's an oasis of tranquility and air-con with breakfast included.

### CABURE

**Posada Turística El Duende** (☎ 809-9066, 661-1079; d BsF120) At the end of the Camino de los Espanoles, and 1.5km up a steep, recently paved road from town, this oasis of tranquility has five cute, pink rooms and a flowering garden set around a 300-year-old ceiba tree. There's a rustic restaurant and bar, too. The Duende's son has a nice six-room posada across the road, and a bit more modern at that.

**Posada La Cabureña** (☎ 661-1093; Calle Bolívar; d/tr BsF185/216; ) Next to the church, this six-room place provides neat, homey rooms with air-con, bathrooms and hot water. The sheer number of pictures on the walls makes you feel as if you are in a provincial museum – if a bit claustrophobic.

## Getting There & Away

The usual point of departure for the Sierra is Coro. Por puesto jeeps to Curimagua (via La Chapa) depart from the Mercado Nuevo from 5am until midafternoon (BsF20, 1½ hours, 45km). There are also infrequent por puestos to Cabure (via Pueblo Nuevo de la Sierra), some of which continue up to San Luis. Be sure to specify precisely where you want to go.

# PARQUE NACIONAL MORROCOY

One of the most spectacular coastal environments in Venezuela, Parque Nacional Morrocoy comprises a strip of mainland and an offshore area dotted with islands, islets and cays. Some islands are skirted by white-sand beaches and surrounded by coral reefs. At the eastern edge of Falcón state, Morrocoy is one of the most popular parks among those looking for beaches and diving.

The park is also well known for its variety of waterbirds, including ibis, heron, cormorant, duck, pelican and flamingo. They permanently or seasonally inhabit some of the islands and coastal mangroves, especially the **Golfete de Cuare**, which is one of Venezuela's richest bird-breeding grounds and has been declared a wildlife refuge.

Venezuelan beachgoers come en masse on holidays and weekends and leave the islands littered. The fragile environment has suffered, though you can still enjoy somewhat deserted beaches on weekdays. More significantly, some of the coral has died, especially closest to the surface, purportedly the result of a chemical leak in the 1990s. Biologists claimed that up to half of the hard coral was dead. It has begun to rebound, but it's likely to take decades for the full recovery. Cayo Sombrero was the least touched by this tragedy and the best coral diving and snorkeling is to be found there.

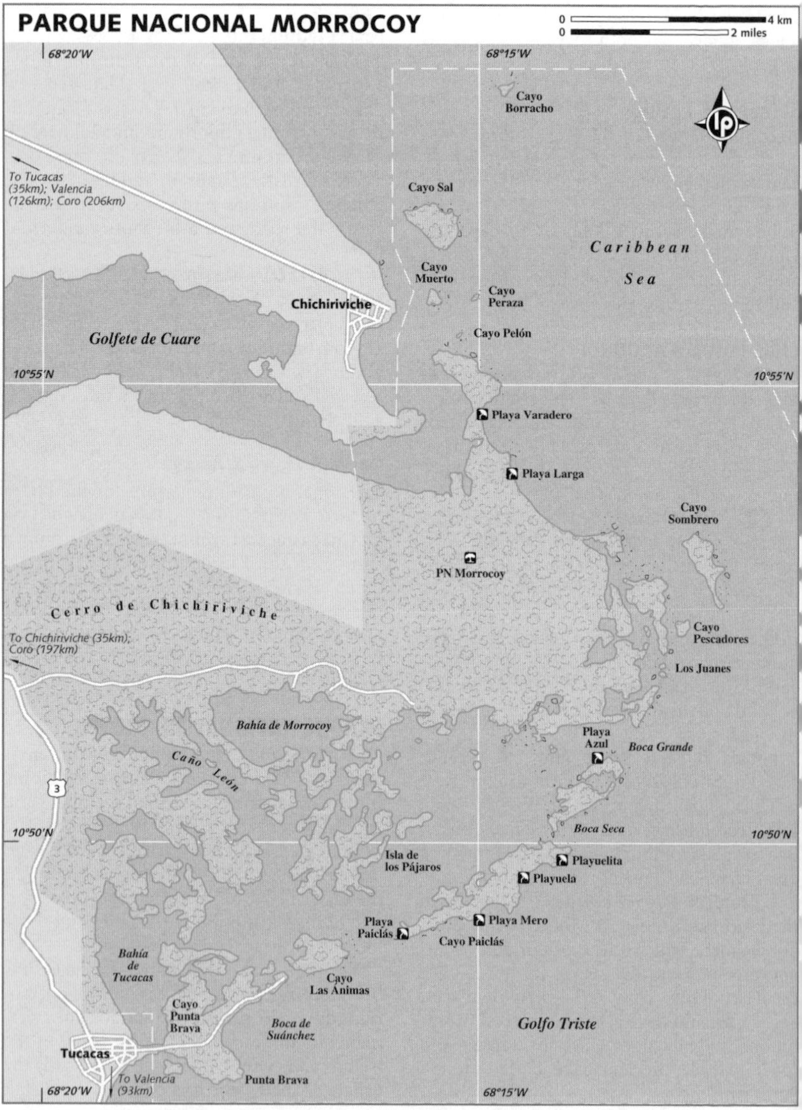

### Orientation

The park lies between the towns of Tucacas and Chichiriviche, which are its main gateways. Both have well-organized boat services to the islands, as well as an array of places to stay and eat. If you have a tent or a hammock you can stay on the islands themselves, but don't plan on it – access has been severely restricted due to past human-made pollution.

The most popular island is Cayo Sombrero, which has fine coral reefs and some of the best beaches. It's more exposed to the open sea than most other islands, and the breeze means that it has fewer insects. Other places good for snorkeling include Playuela and Boca Seca.

### Sleeping & Eating

Camping is permitted on four islands: Cayo Sal, Cayo Muerto, Cayo Sombrero and Cayo Paiclás; it is officially allowed during the month of August, the week after Christmas, and the week of Carnaval. In practice, however, the right to camp has been suspended for the past two years due to pollution.

If you plan on staying in a hammock, make absolutely sure you take along a good mosquito net. All four of the islands have beach restaurants and/or food kiosks, but some may be closed on weekdays in the low season.

Before you go camping, you need to contact the Inparques office in Tucacas (see p132) and shell out a camping fee of BsF10 per person per night, payable at the Banesco in Tucacas or in cash at the Inparques office.

When camping on the islands, take sufficient water, some food to save on predictably overpriced beach eateries, snorkeling gear, good sun protection and a reliable insect repellent. The small biting gnats *(puri-puri)* are particularly nasty early in the morning and late in the afternoon. You can use gas camping stoves, but no open fires are permitted.

### Getting There & Away

Boats to the islands normally take up to seven or eight people and charge a flat rate per trip. Prices to all islands and beaches are posted next to the ticket office close to the loading dock in Tucacas. The fares are roundtrip per boat, not per person. The fare to the farthest islands, such as Cayo Sombrero or Cayo Pescadores, is around BsF300. Closer destinations include Cayo Sal (BsF120), Cayo Peraza (BsF140), Cayo Pelón (BsF140) and Cayo/Playa Veradura (BsF170). The boat will pick you up from the island when you want to return. On off-season weekdays you can usually bargain. Some hotels arrange excursions, too.

Chichiviriche has two piers: the Embarcadero Playa Norte, near the eastern end of Av Zamora, and the Embarcadero Playa Sur, about 1km southwest. Boat fares are the same at both piers. As in Tucacas, the boat takes a maximum of seven to eight passengers, and the fare given is per boat. Popular shorter trips include Cayo Muerto (BsF100), Cayo Sal (BsF120) and Cayo Pelón (BsF140), whereas Cayo Sombrero (BsF300) is the leading further destination. As in Tucacas, the return time and fare haggling are up to you.

## CHICHIRIVICHE

☎ 0259 / pop 12,000

Chichiriviche is the northern gateway to Parque Nacional Morrocoy, providing access to half a dozen neighboring cays. Accommodations, food and boats are in good supply, and it's a big step up from Tucacas.

Access to the town is from the west, by the 12km road that runs along a causeway through mangrove swamps. This area is a favorite feeding ground for flamingos, which gather here mostly between August and January; however, a small community can remain up to March or even April. November is usually the peak month, when up to 5000 birds are in the area.

### Orientation

Upon entering the town proper, the access road divides. Its main branch, Av Zamora (also called Av Principal), continues straight ahead to the bus terminus and the town center, ending at the waterfront next to the northern pier. This area boasts a number of hotels, restaurants and other businesses.

### Information

In the absence of a tourist office you can ask hotel managers for local information. The **Banco Industrial de Venezuela** (Av Zamora) gives advances on Visa cards, but that's about all it can do for you; it doesn't accept MasterCard. Chichiriviche has no diving schools.

### Sleeping

**Morena's Place** (☎ 815-0936, 0424-453-3450; posadamorenas@hotmail.com; Sector Playa Norte; r per person BsF65) This three-room posada offers the only dorm beds in town. It's in a fine old house near the waterfront, a 400m up the beach on the left

THE NORTHWEST

from the pier. It's run by friendly, English-speaking Carlos, who also offers a laundry service, budget meals and tours.

**Villa Gregoria** (☎ 818-6359; aagustinm@yahoo.es; Calle Mariño; d with air-con BsF100-150; ) This Spanish-run and Spanish-looking posada, near the bus terminus, has good rooms with bathrooms. The rooms on the upper floor are brighter and more attractive – and you can relax in a hammock or an armchair on the great terrace. The owner organizes transfers to Coro and Puerto Cabello.

**Hotel Capri** (☎ 818-6026; hotel_capri@cantv.net; Av Zamora; d BsF140-160, self-contained apt BsF350; ) The Capri offers self-contained apartments with kitchen, fridge, microwave and all the goodies you might need, just steps from the waterfront.

**Posada La Negra** (☎ 815-0476; Calle Mariño No 32; d/tr BsF180/250; ) This colorful old Carib building's owner will welcome you into her large family home and look after you personally. All rooms have air-con and TV, and you can even use her kitchen and fridge.

**Caribana Hotel** (☎ 815-1491; Paseo Bolívar; d/tr BsF185/195; ) The refurbished Caribana offers neat rooms with fine tile work and comfortable beds, and tours can be organized.

**Hotel Mario** (☎ 818-6811; www.hotelmariomorrocoy.it; Calle Zamora; s/d/tr BsF265/290/380; ) The largest hotel (with the most complete facilities) in Chichiriviche, the Mario specializes in weekend package deals that include transportation from Caracas, plus breakfast, dinner and boat excursions.

**Hotel Gabón** (☎ 815-0055, 815-1023; www.hotelgabon.com; Calle Marina; d BsF364-375, ste BsF610-672) This hotel sits rights on the waterfront, with impeccable rooms (pay extra for the sea view!), airy rooftop bar and a pool. You can't miss this one – check the waterfront skyline for the big blue-and-red dome.

## Eating

**Restaurant La Esquina de Arturo** (Av Zamora; breakfasts BsF10-15, set lunches BsF15-25; closed dinner) Budget travelers are likely to appreciate the straightforward tasty meals in this tiny, rustic place.

**Rica y Dely** (☎ 815-0813; Av Zamora; pizzas BsF15-25, fish BsF25-40) Yes, *Baywatch* (a David Hasselhoff look-alike) has moved one door down, but he still serves a mean pizza, and he'll still show you his tattoo!

**El Sazón Tropical** (☎ 0416-433-8258; Av Zamora 23; breakfasts BsF21, meals BsF30-50) For good ol' down-home creole cookin', look no further than this affordable restaurant. There's even a respectable paella to share, if you have the patience to wait for it.

**Restaurant Txalupa** (☎ 818-6425; El Malecón; meals BsF50-80; noon-10pm) This respectable Basque-run establishment does good fish and seafood at reasonable prices, with nice views of the fishing boats on the shore and the islands on the horizon. Try *crema de mero,* the local fish soup.

## Getting There & Away

Chichiriviche is about 22km off the main Morón–Coro highway and is serviced by half-hourly buses from Valencia (BsF20, 2½ hours, 126km).

There are no direct buses to Chichiriviche from Caracas or Coro. To get there from Caracas, take any of the frequent buses to Valencia (2½ hours, 158km) and change there for a Chichiriviche bus. From Coro, take any bus to Valencia, get off in Sanare (BsF30, 3¼ hours, 184km) at the turnoff for Chichiriviche and catch one of the many busetas that pass by. To go to Barquisimeto, go to Morón (BsF12, two hours) and switch for Barquisimeto service (BsF30).

# TUCACAS

**☎ 0259 / pop 25,000**

This ordinary, hot town on the Valencia–Coro road has nothing to keep you for long. It's worth a day trip to go to the island or for scuba diving, but staying in 'ChiChi' is a much better and safer option because of Tucacas' proximity to the national highway.

## Orientation

Buses stop at the intersection of the town's lifeline, Av Libertador, and the Morón–Coro road. A bridge 1km to the east leads to Cayo Punta Brava, part of the national park. A 15-minute walk from the bridge along the paved road will bring you to the beach, which is shaded with coconut palms; more beaches lie further east on the same island, accessible by road.

To visit other islands in the park, go to the *embarcadero* (landing dock) close to the bridge, which is packed with pleasure boats waiting for tourists.

## Information

Tucacas has no reliable tourist office – try the scuba-diving operators. The office of **Inparques** (☎ 812-2176; Av Libertador; 8am-12:30pm & 2-5pm).

THE NORTHWEST

which you need to contact if you want to camp on the islands, is close to the bridge. Pay your camping fee at **Banesco** (Av Libertador), which also gives cash advances on Visa and MasterCard (from the cashier, not the ATM). **Banco Provincial** (Carretera Coro-Morón) has a useful ATM, but it's 2km south of the center. The diving schools will all be happy to accept your cash dollars as well.

### Activities

There are two scuba-diving operators in town. Both offer diving courses and guided tours run by licensed instructors, and have shops selling diving and snorkeling gear, some of which can be rented. Expect to pay roughly BsF1600 to BsF2000 for a four-day NAUI open-water course and BsF450 to BsF600 per day for a local diving trip.

**Submatur** (☎ 812-0082, 0414-841-7333; www.morrocoydivingsubmatur.com; Calle Ayacucho No 6) is owned and managed by Mike Osborn from Guyana. With 40-odd years' experience, it is one of the oldest diving schools in the country. Two-day and longer diving trips in a sailing boat to Bonaire and Islas Las Aves can also be organized (BsF900 per day).

**Frogman Dive Center** (☎ 812-4112, 0414-340-1824; www.frogmandive.com; CC Bolivár – Local No 3, Plaza Bolívar) is just off Plaza Bolívar, run by Valencia native Manuel Collazo.

### Getting There & Away

Tucacas sits on the Valencia–Coro road, so buses run frequently to both Valencia (BsF15, 1½ hours, 91km) and Coro (BsF30, 3¾ hours, 197km). Buses from Valencia pass through regularly on their way to Chichiriviche (BsF6, 30 minutes, 35km).

# LARA & YARACUY STATES

## BARQUISIMETO

☎ 0251 / pop 1,018,900

The Revolution marches on in Barquisimeto, if a bit slowly. The city's solar-inspired crowning glory – the Monumento al Sol Naciente, a circular sundial of massive stones on the scale of Stonehenge – is complete, and has become a favored nocturnal drinking spot for local youth. But the other civic improvements – a proposed modern trole bus line; a new, Epcot-center style intercity bus terminal; a shiny new civic center and redeveloped botanical gardens – are still in the works.

Yet Barquisimeto has good food, shopping, and is the perfect jumping-off point for the surrounding region – a beautiful land of arid hills, Venezuela's best wine and the mysteries of María Lionza (p137).

Originally founded in 1552, Barquisimeto moved three times before eventually being established at its present-day location in 1563. Its growth was slow, as the indigenous tribes in the region were fierce in defending their territory. It wasn't until the 20th century that the city really developed to become a thriving commercial and industrial center and the capital of Lara state.

### Orientation

Barquisimeto's center, spreading to the north of Plaza Bolívar, has a regular grid pattern, easier to navigate by landmarks because the street corners are irregularly marked. Its main commercial street, and nearly complete pedestrian boulevard, is Av 20, heavily packed with shopping centers and stores. A trole bus line is planned to run down it –still a pipe dream, according to many locals.

The area around Plaza Bolívar is quieter, but becomes a ghost town after dark, so don't plan on night walks there. More attractive and relaxing is the city's eastern sector, along Av Lara and Av Los Leones, about 3km east of the center. Dotted with shopping malls, well-appointed restaurants and trendy night spots, it's a destination for the city's beautiful people.

### Information

#### EMERGENCY

**Ambulance** (☎ 171)
**Fire** (☎ 171)
**Police** (☎ 171)

#### MEDICAL SERVICES

**Clínica Razetti** (☎ 232-7111, 231-9011; Calle 27 btwn Carreras 21 & 22)
**Hospital Central Universitario Dr Antonio María Pineda** (☎ 251-3846; cnr Av Las Palmas & Av Vargas)
**Policlínica de Barquisimeto** (☎ 254-0044; cnr Av Los Leones & Av Madrid) Northeast of town.

#### MONEY

**Banco de Venezuela** (cnr Av 20 & Calle 31)
**Banco Mercantil** (cnr Carrera 19 & Calle 29)
**Banco Provincial** (cnr Av 20 & Calle 31)
**Banesco** (cnr Carrera 19 & Calle 27)
**Corp Banca** (cnr Av 20 & Av Vargas)
**Italcambio** Airport (☎ 443-1910; 🕒 7am-7pm); City

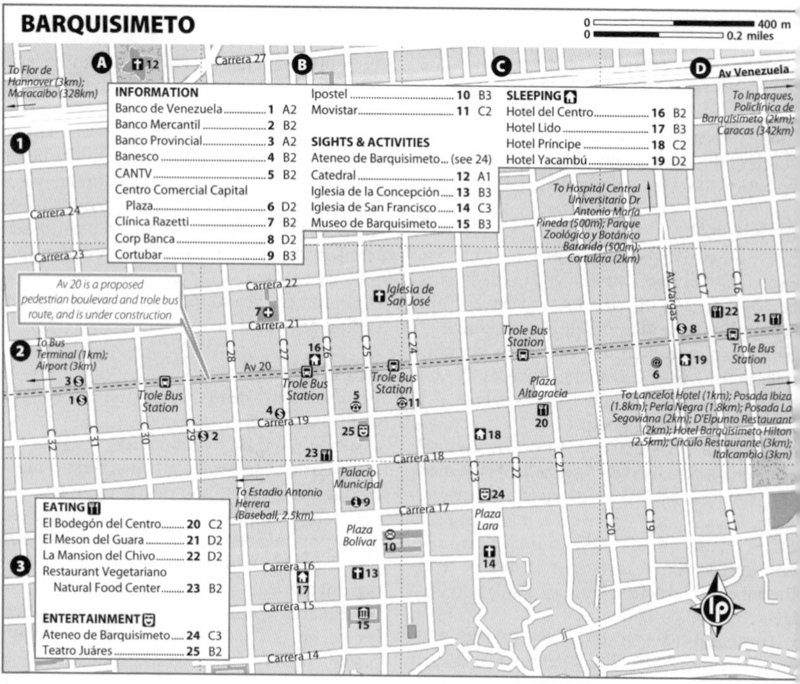


(☎ 254-9790; Centro Empresarial Barquisimeto, Av Los Leones; 8:30am-4pm)

### POST

**Ipostel** (Plaza Bolívar)

### TELEPHONE

Both of these also have internet.
**CANTV** (Carrera 19 btwn Calles 25 & 26)
**Movistar** (Carrera 19 btwn Calles 24 & 25)

### TOURIST INFORMATION

**Cortubar** (Corporación de Turismo Barquisimeto; ☎ 710-1802; Plaza Bolívar, 8am-noon & 2-6pm Mon-Fri) The city tourist office, on the plaza in a blue-and-yellow building.
**Cortulara** (Corporación de Turismo del Estado de Lara; ☎ 255-7544, 255-6613; http://cortulara.lara.gob.ve; Edificio Fundalara, Av Libertador; 8am-noon & 2-6pm Mon-Fri) It's over 2km northeast of the center, near the Complejo Ferial. To get there, take Ruta 12 bus from anywhere along Carrera 19 in the center. The office operates information desks in the bus terminal and at the airport. Its website is an excellent source of information on the region.
**Inparques** (☎ 254-2933, 254-8118; Parque del Este; Av Libertador; 9am-noon & 2-5pm Mon-Fri) The office provides information about the national parks in the region, Yacambú and Terepaima, and books accommodations in the parks.

## Sights

The lovely **Plaza Bolívar**, full of splendid tall palm trees, is the birthplace of the city. The pretty **Iglesia de la Concepción** (Plaza Bolívar), on the square's southern side, was Barquisimeto's first cathedral, but it was destroyed in the earthquake of 1812 and rebuilt 30 years later in a different style.

A few steps south of the church is the **Museo de Barquisimeto** (☎ 717-1022; Carrera 15 btwn Calles 25 & 26; admission free; 9am-5pm Tue-Fri, 10am-5pm Sat & Sun), in an imposing historical building with a rectangular courtyard centered on a chapel. It was built in the 1910s as a hospital, and later authorities decided to demolish it to make way for modern buildings. Thanks to public protests, though, it was restored and turned into a museum. Its rooms house various temporary exhibitions, usually interesting and well displayed.

The tiny **Plaza Lara**, two blocks east of Plaza Bolívar, is the city's only area with colonial character, thanks to the restored historic buildings lining the square. It's no doubt the finest historic plaza in town and is charmingly shaded with old trees. On the northern side of the plaza is the **Ateneo de Barquisimeto** (☎ 232-4655; cnr Carrera 17 & Calle 23), a busy center for cultural activities. Go in and check what's on.

The handsome **Iglesia de San Francisco** (Plaza Lara), on the southern side of the plaza, was built in 1865 and carried the distinction of being Barquisimeto's second city cathedral, until the modern **Catedral de Barquisimeto** (cnr Avs Venezuela & Simón Rodríguez) was constructed in the 1960s. It's a bold, innovative design, noted for its parabolic concrete roof and a centrally located high altar. The cathedral is open only for mass (normally at 6pm weekdays, with more services on Sunday), so plan accordingly.

At **Estadio Antonio Herrera Guitierrez** (Av Rotaria; www.cardenalesdelara.com; admission BsF10-40), the color red doesn't necessarily imply revolutionary activity – it's simply the color of the hometown Cardenales de Lara, one of the country's eight baseball teams. Venezuelan *béisbol* features dancers and fireworks between innings. The season runs from October to December. Take the Ruta 5 bus (BsF2.50, 30 minutes) from downtown to the baseball stadium entrance.

**Parque Zoológico y Botánico Bararida** (☎ 252-4774; cnr Av Los Abogados & Calle 13; admission BsF5; 9am-5pm Tue-Sun), 1.5km northeast of the center, is a large park with an artificial lake and cafes, in addition to the city's zoo and botanical gardens. Here you'll see some of Venezuela's usual plants and animals, such as the tapir, jaguar and capybara – but as with many South American zoos, it can be depressing for the animal-lover.

**Flor de Venezuela aka Flor de Hannover** (Av Venezuela, cnr Av Bracamonte) – was the nation's contribution to the World Expo in Hannover, Germany in 2000. Created by local architect Fruto Vivas, the three-story glass-and-iron structure has 10m 'petals' – when the hydraulics open the flower, it's 39m in diameter – more impressive at night when bathed in green, tropical floodlights. It houses thousands of plants inside.

## Festivals & Events

The city's biggest annual event is the **Fiestas Patronales de la Divina Pastora**. The patron saint's day is January 14, and its central feature is a solemn procession parading the image of the Virgin Mary from the shrine in Santa Rosa village into the city. The celebrations go for several days before and after the saint's day, and include agricultural fairs, concerts and sports events held in the Complejo Ferial (fairgrounds).

## Sleeping

Most visitors will want to stay in the city center for good accommodations that are close to the main sights. The eastern suburbs offer the city's best lodgings, but at a steep price. If you're in transit and looking for a place to crash for a night, there are half a dozen basic hotels in an unattractive area on the northern side of the bus terminal that differ significantly in standards and rates.

**Hotel del Centro** (☎ 808-0378; Av 20 btwn Calles 26 & 27; d BsF80-90, tr BsF100; ) Hidden among dozens of shoe shops, the Hotel del Centro is just about the cheapest acceptable option in the center. Rooms are basic but surprisingly large, and all have private bathrooms and cable TV. (Splurge on the air-con for BsF10.) Some of the rooms on the upper floors provide bird's-eye views of the busy commerce below.

**Hotel Lido** (☎ 231-5568; Carrera 16 btwn Calles 26 & 27; d/tr BsF140/190; ) The bundles of towels and room keys on the reception desk clue you in to the popularity of this central hotel. Just one block from the Plaza Bolívar, this small place is not a Sheraton, but all rooms have air-con and bathrooms, and it isn't expensive.

**Hotel Yacambú** (☎ 252-6746; fax 251-3229; hotel yacambu@gmail.com; Av Vargas btwn Av 20 & Carrera 19; d/tr/ste BsF200/220/300; ) Nestled on a busy avenue, Yacambú has already passed its years of glory, yet it still does a ample business. Grab one of the two suites: they are noticeably better than the ordinary rooms and have balconies. The hotel has an enjoyable, inexpensive restaurant.

**Posada La Segoviana** (☎ 252-8669; www.posadalase goviana.com.ve; Calle 7 btwn Carreras 2 & 3, Urbanización Nueva Segovia; d BsF230-250, tr BsF295, ste BsF365-430; ) This was Barquisimeto's first posada, set in a quiet residential eastern suburb. With just 16 rooms, it provides personalized service and cozy ambience, but it's often full, so book well in advance.

**Posada Ibiza** (☎ 267-9221; Calle 3 No 1-71; d BsF250-290, ste BsF324-353; ) This minimalist-style posada is decorated in black, white and chrome, and still shimmers with newness. Very comfortable rooms offer air-con, hot water and cable TV. There's a popular restaurant downstairs.

**Hotel Príncipe** (☎ 231-2111, 231-2544; fax 231-1731; Calle 23 btwn Carreras 18 & 19; d/tr BsF270/280; ) This big hotel has 140-plus rooms, plus an

THE NORTHWEST

outdoor pool, restaurant and bar. Some rooms are a bit musty, but if everything else is full, the 'Prince' is an acceptable, central option.

**Lancelot Hotel** ( ☎ 252-2021; www.lancelotsuite.com; cnr Av 20 & Calle 2; s/d/tr BsF300/350/400, ste BsF450-500; ✗ 🖳 🛜 ) You can see the mighty ramparts of this castle-themed hotel from afar. It's a comfortable place to lay aside the chain-mail underwear, especially in the Jacuzzi-equipped suites. The 'Lance' is conveniently situated midway between the center and the restaurants along Av Vargas.

**Hotel Jirahara** ( ☎ 710-6111; www.jiraharahotel.com.ve; Urbanización Nueva Segovia, Carrera 5 btwn Calles 5 & 6; d BsF500-680, ste BsF800-1750; ✗ 🖳 🛜 🍴 ) Named for the local indigenous tribe, this five-star former Hilton has lost none of its glory. All of the rooms have floor-to-ceiling windows and most have high-speed internet access. Facilities include a gym, an outdoor pool and a ballroom.

## Eating

The city center is packed with places to eat, particularly Av Vargas and its environs and, to a lesser extent, Av 20. The best restaurants, though, are in the eastern suburbs.

**Restaurant Vegetariano Natural Food Center** (cnr Carrera 18 & Calle 26; meals BsF18-25; 🕙 11am-4pm Mon-Fri; 🇻 ) This popular and central vegetarian spot serves straightforward set lunches and snacks.

**El Bodegón del Centro** ( ☎ 231-6556; cnr Carrera 19 & Calle 21; meals BsF25-40; 🕙 11am-11pm Mon-Sat) Cured hams hang behind the large bar in this tasca-style restaurant that does solid, stick-to-your-ribs food. Ignore the menu and ask for the special of the day instead.

**El Meson del Guaro** (Av 20 & Carrera 15; meals BsF30-60) Sip on a 'Ton Collins' or 'Fruyt Ponch' at this old-school local favorite, designed with the beef-, shrimp- and chicken-lover in mind. The black-vested waiters can be a bit overly solicitous, but try the *parrilla* (mixed grill) for two spread over your blood-red tablecloth.

**D'Elpunto Restaurant** ( ☎ 254-8367; Urbanización Nueva Segovia, cnr Carrera 1 & Calle 4; meals BsF35-70; 🕙 noon-3pm & 7-10:30pm Mon-Sat, noon-5:00pm Sun) D'Elpunto serves *comida creativa* (creative food). The waiters will be happy to explain the intricacies, including the *salomo en salsa erotica* (beef shoulder in erotic sauce). Yowsa!

**La Mansion del Chivo** ( ☎ 252-5069; Carrera 21 & Calle 17; meals BsF40-90) There's a dumbwaiter, real waiters, local wines and classic '80s videos

competing with baseball on the TV. And the food? Leave a pile of bones behind after a *chivo asado* (barbecued goat).

**Perla Negra** ( ☎ 267-9221; Calle 3 No 1-71; meals BsF40-60 🕙 7am-11pm) Perla Negra is a hip black-marbled bar-restaurant inside the Posada Ibiza. It serves up breakfast and wicked portions of steak, pasta and three different risottos, and the bar invites you to linger long after your meal.

## Entertainment

**Ateneo de Barquisimeto** ( ☎ 232-4655; cnr Carrera 17 & Calle 23) This is a busy center of cultural activities on Plaza Lara, including musical works and changing art exhibitions.

**Teatro Juáres** ( ☎ 231-6743; cnr Carrera 19 & Calle 25) The city's main theater center, Teatro Juáres hosts other cultural events as well, including music performances.

## Getting There & Away
### AIR

The **Aeropuerto Jacinto Lara** ( ☎ 441-9940; Av Vicente Landaeta) is 4km southwest of the center. The Ruta 7 city bus runs between the bus terminal and the airport, or you can take a taxi (BsF40 to BsF50). Caracas flights to and from Barquisimeto are serviced by **Aeropostal** ( ☎ 800-284-6637), with two flights on weekdays and one on the weekend.

Aserca also has three to four departures a day to Caracas (BsF224 to BsF276). To other destinations, you need to go via either Caracas or Maracaibo.

### BUS

Barquisimeto straddles an important crossroads, with roads and buses leading in all directions. The large and busy **Terminal de Pasajeros** ( ☎ 442-2189; cnr Av Rómulo Gallegos & Carrera 24), 2km northwest of the center, is linked by frequent city buses to the center and other districts. The Ruta 12 bus (often blue in color) runs from Carrera 22 in the center to the terminal and returns along Carrera 19, so is close to all hotels in the center mentioned here.

Buses depart regularly throughout the day to Valencia (BsF50 to BsF60, three hours, 183km), Maracaibo (BsF80, five hours, 328km) and Caracas (BsF80, 5½ hours, 341km). Half a dozen buses depart nightly to Mérida (BsF54 to BsF60, eight hours, 449km). Buses to Coro (BsF30, seven hours, 418km) go every two to three hours. Buses within

---

**THAT VOODOO THAT YOU DO – THE CULT OF MARÍA LIONZA**

A striking amalgam of native indigenous creeds, African voodoo and Christian practices, the cult of María Lionza involves magic, witchcraft, esoteric rites and trance rituals.

The cult is pantheistic and involves a constellation of deities, spirits and other personalities. At the top of the hierarchy is María Lionza, a female deity usually portrayed as a beautiful woman riding a tapir. One story of her origin tells of a woman from a dark-skinned tribe who gave birth to a light-skinned, green-eyed girl of surpassing beauty. The girl grew up to be venerated by her tribe and eventually by the surrounding peoples. As the years passed, her life became the stuff of legends and ever since she has been revered by her devoted followers.

Often referred to as La Reina (Queen), María Lionza is followed by countless divinities – historical and legendary personages, saints and powers of nature – usually grouped into *cortes* (courts). The most popular deities include Cacique Guaicaipuro, the Virgen de Coromoto, Negro Felipe, Dr José Gregorio Hernández and even Simón Bolívar.

the region (to Quíbor, El Tocuyo, Sanare and Chivacoa) run frequently.

## CHIVACOA

☎ 0251 / pop 54,000

Chivacoa, 58km east of Barquisimeto on the road to Valencia, is the jumping-off point for Cerro de María Lionza, the holy mountain that is home to the cult of María Lionza (see the boxed text above). Don't miss browsing through the *perfumerías* for cigars and candles – indispensable ritual accessories – and hundreds of strange essences, perfumes and lotions. Have a look at the books and brochures dealing with magic, witchcraft and foretelling, and a complete stock of plaster figures of the deities in every size and color.

### Sleeping & Eating

In Chivacoa there are a few places to stay and most have their own restaurants.

**Hotel Venezia** (☎ 883-0544; Centro Comercial Venezia, cnr Calle 12 & Av 9; d BsF100-110, tr BsF130; P ❄) Marginally better than the rest, all the rooms in this brightly colored hotel have (very small) bathrooms and air-con. The hotel surrounds a pleasant courtyard of small shops, including a yummy pizza restaurant and bar – a refreshing place to sit and relax in the evening, when a cooling breeze moderates the day's heat.

**Hotel El Gran Luso** (☎ 883-0366; cnr Calle 10 & Av 12; d BsF100-120, tr BsF160, ❄) Not the most central location, but still a cheap, acceptable option. All rooms have bathrooms and air-con, and a reasonable tasca-style restaurant lurks downstairs.

**Hotel Abruzzese** (☎ 883-0419; Av 9 btwn Calles 10 & 11; d BsF120-140, tr BsF160; ❄) A block from Plaza Bolívar, Abruzzese has neat rooms with private facilities. Ask for a room with a balcony.

### Getting There & Away

Plenty of buses run between Barquisimeto and Valencia or San Felipe, all of which call in at the Chivacoa bus terminal. There are also direct buses from Barquisimeto to Chivacoa, marked 'Chivacoa Directo' (BsF8, one hour, 58km), as well as por puestos (BsF10, 45 minutes). To get into Chivacoa from the terminal take por puesto Ruta 4 (BsF1.20) – walk through terminal to the other side.

## CERRO DE MARÍA LIONZA

The Cult of María Lionza counts an ever-growing number of devotees in Venezuela, Colombia, Puerto Rico and the Dominican Republic. Its most sacred area – and the focus for pilgrimages – is the mountain range referred to as the Cerro de María Lionza, south of Chivacoa. Devotees come here year-round, mostly on weekends, to practice their rites. The biggest celebrations are held on October 12 (Discovery of America Day) and during Semana Santa (Holy Week), when thousands of people cram themselves into this tiny place, where screaming in tongues and walking on fire and broken glass sometimes take place.

The followers have built several sanctuaries along the northern foothills of the mountains. The most important of these are Sorte and Quiballo (or Quibayo). Both have their own *altar mayor* (high altar), where the initial celebrations are performed, before the group and its medium head off to the shrine of their choice. It's at these shrines scattered over the forested rugged land where the proper rites are performed, which may last the whole night or longer and usually include a trance séance.

Cerro de María Lionza is part of a much larger mountain formation known as the Macizo de Nirgua. Covered with thick rainforest, the range is rich in endemic species. In 1960, Inparques formally reserved the 117-sq-km area as the Monumento Natural María Lionza, in an attempt to protect the region from overuse by the cult's followers. However, the religious significance of the place overshadows its natural wealth.

### Quiballo

Quiballo is really just a collection of several dozen shabby shacks that are either *perfumerías* or basic places to eat. The high altar (really, little more than a shack itself) sits on the riverbank and shelters a bizarre collection of images, including figures of Bolívar, various indigenous caciques and numerous statues of María Lionza.

Come on the weekend, or during a holiday period, if you can, when you can join the faithful as they sit in front of the altar, smoke cigars and light candles.

Quiballo is far larger than Sorte, and has both the Inparques office and a Guarda Nacionál post, and seems to be more accustomed to casual visitors. However, it's not a tourist spot by any definition. Behave sensibly and modestly, and don't openly use your camera, which may arouse hostile reactions from cult believers.



### Hiking Cerro de María Lionza

From the Quiballo altar, a path goes over the bridge to the opposite bank of the river (in which the faithful perform ritual ablutions) and then splits into a maze of paths that wind up the mountain, some climbing to the very top. All along the paths are *portales* (gates), shrines dedicated to particular deities or spirits. On the top are Las Tres Casitas (Three Little Houses) of María Lionza, Negro Felipe and Cacique Guaicaipuro. Technically, the trip to the top can be done in less than three hours. In practice, though, it may take far, far longer, for various reasons.

Followers of the cult point out that the trip is full of drawbacks and dangers. At each portal you have to ask the appropriate spirit for permission to pass. This is done by smoking cigars, lighting candles and presenting offerings. Those who continue on without permission may be punished by the spirits. Some, local stories claim, have never returned.

The Inparques staff members have a far more pragmatic standpoint. They don't recommend the trip to the top because of muddy paths, snakes and the possibility of getting lost.

An additional problem is robberies. Try not to venture too far on your own and keep your wits about you. If you're desperate to go to the top, consider taking a local guide, for both safety and orientation.

Wandering around, especially on weekends, you may come across a group of faithful practicing their rituals. Keep away unless you're invited or unless you are with a guide who will introduce you.

### Sleeping & Eating

There are no hotels in either Sorte or Quiballo, but you can camp in a tent or sling a hammock on the river bank as the pilgrims do. Never leave your tent and belongings unattended. It's much better to hang your hammock in a cabaña in Quiballo for a small fee. You won't starve at the shack restaurants (BsF17 to BsF20 for chicken or *mondongo;* seasoned tripe), but their offerings are mostly basic.

### Getting There & Away

Jeeps and vans to Quiballo (BsF2.50, 20 minutes, 8km) depart when full from Chivacoa's Plaza Bolívar. They run regularly on weekends, but there may be only a few departures on weekdays. Jeeps to Sorte (BsF2.50, 15 minutes, 6km) are even less frequent. The jeeps travel 4km south on a paved road to the María Lionza roadside altar, then turn right onto a rough road and continue through sugarcane plantations for another 4km to Quiballo. The road to Sorte branches off to the left 1km past the altar.

## QUÍBOR

☎ 0253 / pop 50,500

This swiftly growing satellite town, 35km southwest of Barquisimeto, is a thriving folk-art and craft center. It's also worth stopping here to have a look at the pre-Columbian indigenous heritage of the region, but not worth staying the night – it's a bit dusty and down at the mouth.

### Sights

The **Cementerio Indígena de Quíbor** (cnr Av 8 & Calle 12), just off the Plaza Florencio Jiménez, is a pre-Hispanic cemetery accidentally discovered in 1965. Numerous tombs and more than 26,000 pottery pieces have been excavated from what is thought to be a burial ground for tribal elders of an aboriginal community that lived here around the 3rd century AD.

Most of the finds from the graveyard are now on display in the **Museo Antropológico de Quíbor** (☎ 491-3781; cnr Calle 12 & Av 10; admission free; ⏰ 9am-4pm Tue-Sun), two blocks north of Plaza Bolívar. The collection includes indigenous tombs, funerary urns, mortuary offerings and a lot of pottery.

One of the oldest colonial relics, dating from the town's foundation in 1620, is the **Ermita de Nuestra Señora de Altagracia** (Calle 13 btwn Av 19 & Av 20), a fortress-like church on the northern edge of Quíbor. The large **Iglesia de Nuestra Señora de Altagracia** (Plaza Bolívar) is also named after the patron saint, but was only built in 1808 and was reconstructed after the earthquake of 1881.

The best place to see (and buy) crafts is the **Centro de Acopio Artesanal** (cnr Av Rotaria & Cubiro Rd; ⏰ 9am-5pm), 1km southeast of Quíbor. The center stocks crafts made in Quíbor and in the nearby towns and villages, such as Tintorero, Guadalupe, Cubiro and Sanare.

### Getting There & Away

Buses between Barquisimeto and Quíbor run frequently from 6am to 6pm (BsF5, 45 minutes, 35km). There are also por puestos (BsF7, 30 minutes). In Barquisimeto, they depart from the bus terminal; in Quíbor, they line up at the corner of Av 6 and Calle 12, one long block south of Plaza Bolívar. Buses to El Tocuyo run along Av 7, lining Plaza Bolívar.

## EL TOCUYO

☎ 0253 / pop 49,500

The glory days of El Tocuyo, 30km southwest of Quíbor, are still palpable in the ruins of colonial churches, in the museums and in the stories of old inhabitants. Referred to as the 'Mother City of Venezuela,' this was once a wealthy town and Venezuela's capital. Devastated by an earthquake in 1950, El Tocuyo is today not much more than an ordinary modern city, yet it's worth coming to see what's left of the past.

### History

Founded in 1545 in a verdant valley of the Río Tocuyo, Nuestra Señora de la Pura y Limpia Concepción del Tocuyo swiftly developed into one of Venezuela's most important towns. Around 200km from the coast, it still had sea access via a navigable river. Just two years after its foundation, the authorities moved the seat of government here from Coro, and the town became the province's capital for the next 30 years. Splendid colonial churches and mansions popped up and the city was a starting point for expeditions to explore and settle the colony. Barquisimeto and Caracas were founded from El Tocuyo.

In 1577 the capital was transferred to Caracas, but El Tocuyo continued to expand. It was here that the Spanish first introduced sugarcane to the continent, a crop that could be harvested year-round thanks to favorable climatic conditions.

Unfortunately, a serious earthquake in 1950 ruined all seven colonial churches and a good number of opulent public buildings. The job was completed by Colonel Marcos Pérez Jiménez, Venezuela's then-dictator. On his orders, most of the damaged structures were demolished and a new town was built on the site. El Tocuyo is now a modern town with just a handful of restored or reconstructed historic buildings.

### Sights

The **Iglesia de Nuestra Señora de la Concepción** (Carrera 11 btwn Calles 17 & 18) is the town's most important monument. The church was badly damaged in the 1950 earthquake and was bulldozed. It was later reconstructed and its whitewashed exterior is noted for its unusual bell tower and fine facade. The church is open only for religious services, normally held at 6pm on weekdays, with more masses on Sunday. If you can't make it to the service, go to the Casa Parroquial beside the church, and someone may to let you in.

None of the other colonial churches were restored or reconstructed, but two were left in ruins, untouched from the day of the earthquake: the **Iglesia de Santo Domingo** (cnr Carrera 10 & Calle 19) and the **Iglesia de Belén** (Carrera 12 btwn Calles 15 & 17). One of the few buildings that somehow withstood the quake is the **Convento de San Francisco** (Plaza Bolívar), though the adjacent church didn't make it. Today the building is occupied by the Casa de la Cultura – go inside to see its spacious two-story arcaded courtyard.

El Tocuyo has two small museums relating to its history. The **Museo Arqueológico JM Cruxent** (Plaza Bolívar; admission free; ⏰ 8am-4pm Mon-Fri) has a small collection of pre-Hispanic pottery, photos depicting the damage by the 1950 earthquake, and regional crafts. Note the remains of a 30m-long steam riverboat from around 1850, proving that the Río Tocuyo was navigable for large vessels.

The **Museo Lisandro Alvarado** (Calle 17 btwn Carreras 10 & 11; admission free; 9am-noon & 2-5:30pm Mon-Sat), named after the locally born politician, doctor and anthropologist, features old maps, documents, paintings and etchings and a variety of historic objects. Look for an amazing old bell from the defunct San Francisco Church.

## Sleeping & Eating

**Posada Colonial** (663-0025; Av Fraternidad btwn Calles 17 & 18; d BsF100-125, tr BsF156; ) The most enjoyable and central place to stay, a stone's throw from Plaza Bolívar, this colonial-style posada has 24 neat rooms and a pool in the garden surrounded by coconut palms. Ask for one of the rooms upstairs, which have balconies.

**Hotel Venezia** (663-1267; cnr Calle 2 & Carrera 9; per person BsF100) If the posada can't accommodate you for some reason, this is another marginally cheaper but less attractive option behind the hospital.

Tocuyo even has its own vegetarian restaurant, Restaurant Vegetariano, two blocks from the bus terminal on Carrera 9, at the corner of Calle 18.

## Getting There & Away

Buses between Barquisimeto and El Tocuyo (BsF8, 1¼ hours, 65km) run at least every half-hour until about 6pm. There are also por puestos (BsF10, one hour).

# SANARE

0253 / pop 18,000

This refreshingly cool holiday spot sits high above the heat of the plains, and its curving, twisting mountain streets, awash in greenery and dotted with flowerpots, leave little doubt as to why the town bears the nickname the 'Garden of Lara.' Founded in 1620, it's surrounded by forested hills and boasts some fine historic architecture and a handsome parish church, the three-nave Iglesia de Santa Ana. The **Instituto de Turismo de Municipio** (449-0139; Plaza Bolívar; 8:30am-3:30pm Mon-Fri) is in the *alcaldia* (town hall).

## Sleeping & Eating

Sanare has at least half a dozen places to stay and most have their own restaurants.

**Hotel Taburiente** (449-0148; hoteltaburiente@hotmail.com; Av Miranda; d/tr BsF80/120) Nestled right behind the church, this neat and very central 21-room hotel is a good deal and it, too, has its own restaurant. Ask the Suzanne Somers look-alike to cook you up something special.

**Posada Turística El Cerrito** (0414-550-4077; Calle Providencia; d/tr BsF100/130) About 500m south of Plaza Bolívar – take Calle 18 from the square up the steps and past the *bolla criolla* (bocce) court – this is a charming and stylish place. Built in a colonial style, the posada has 14 rooms (with bathrooms) lining a patio, plus a budget restaurant.

**Hotel La Fumarola** (449-0754; Sector Palo Verde; d BsF200; ) Probably the most comfortable option, La Fumarola is 3km north of Sanare on the road to Quíbor. It has 22 rooms which hold up to six persons, a restaurant and a pool.

## Getting There & Away

Minibuses run regularly between Barquisimeto and Sanare (BsF10, 1¼ hours, 57km) until mid-afternoon.

# CARORA

0252 / pop 105,400

This colorful, slumbering colonial town was founded in 1569 and has preserved much of its colonial architecture, despite several serious floods. The historic center has been restored and is a charming place, particularly Plaza Bolívar.

Carora's main claim to fame, however, is its wine – Venezuela's best – and you can visit the vineyards and wineries and see the whole production process (but only at harvest time). Though commercial production only began in 1990, the wine has already won international medals.

## Information

### MONEY

**Banco de Venezuela** (cnr Av Francisco de Miranda & Calle 20)

**Banco Provincial** (cnr Av 14 de Febrero & Carrera Lara)

**Banesco** (cnr Carrera Lara & Calle Rivas)

### TELEPHONE

**CANTV** (Av 14 de Febrero btwn Carreras Lara & Bolívar) Also has internet.

### TOURIST INFORMATION

**Centro de Información y Atención Turística** (Av Francisco de Miranda; 8am-noon & 2-5pm Mon-Fri,

THE NORTHWEST

### CARORA: LAND OF WINE & SONG

There are two good reasons to visit Carora: wine and music.

At **Bodegas Pomar** (☎ 421-2191, 421-2225; www.bodegaspomar.com.ve; Carretera Lara-Zulia), 3km south of the Carora city center, 17 varieties of wine are marketed under the Viña Altagracia label (the site of the 125-hectare vineyard).

Each harvest season (three weeks in August and September) Bodegas Pomar is open to visitors. A full-day tour includes breakfast, lunch and two tastings (BsF420). Packages include music and a more expansive wine tasting (BsF690 to BsF820). No open-toed shoes are permitted and you must wear long pants. It's recommended to book in advance through the **Caracas office** (☎ 0212-202-8907; clubpomar@empresas-polar.com).

Carora is also the home of legendary classical guitarist Alirio Diaz, who studied under Andrés Segovia. Born in neighboring La Candelaria in 1923, the maestro still comes into town many mornings for his coffee, and each autumn the *Concurso Internacional de Guitarra Alirio Diaz* (www.aliriodiaz.org) brings out the best young classical guns from around the world, competing for a $10,000 prize. Because of his advanced age, Diaz no longer performs, but the guitar competition is held in theaters around Carora and Barquisimeto, and is open to the public. (There must be something magical in the water around these parts – world-renowned conductor Gustavo Dudamel of the Los Angeles Symphony Orchestra hails from neighboring Barquisimeto.)

8am-3pm Sat & Sun) It's in a kiosk in front of the bus terminal.

## Sights

The historic quarter, centered on the postcard-like Plaza Bolívar and populated with elegant tall palm trees, is neat, well kept and colonial in style, even though not all the buildings date from that period. Have a look at the mid-17th-century **Casa Amarilla** (Plaza Bolívar), Carora's oldest surviving building, now a public library, and **El Balcón de los Álvarez** (Plaza Bolívar), a two-story 18th-century house where Simón Bolívar stayed in 1821. The **Casa de Juan Jacinto Lara** (cnr Calle San Juan & Carrera Torres) is the birthplace of the hero of the War of Independence, who gave his name to the state.

The town has some fine colonial churches. The main one, the mid-17th-century **Iglesia de San Juan Bautista** (Plaza Bolívar) shelters an amazing, richly gilded main retable dating from 1760. The church is only open in the late afternoon, but if you enquire in the Casa Parroquial, right behind the church, someone is likely to open it for you.

The **Capilla San Dionisio** (cnr Carrera Torres & Calle Comercio) dates from 1743. It's used only for special ceremonies, such as funerals, and is closed at other times. About 300m northeast of San Dionisio, in the middle of arid woodland, is the striking ruin of the **Iglesia de la Purísima Concepción**, commonly referred to as the 'Portal de la Pastora.' You'll get a good view of the ruin from the dike at the end of Calle Comercio.

The **Capilla del Calvario** (cnr Carrera El Calvario & Calle Comercio) has a beautiful facade, a fine example of local baroque. Its simple interior features an interesting main retable, plus two side retables on both walls. The chapel is often open in the morning, but if it's locked, the keys are kept in Casa Parroquial.

## Sleeping

**Hotel Irpinia** (☎ 421-6362; cnr Carrera Lara & Av 14 de Febrero; s/d/tr BsF80/120/130; ❄ 📶) Another convenient place in the center, Irpinia has 36 neat, spacious rooms with bathrooms and air-con. Take one facing the inner courtyard – they are quieter.

**El Rincón del Bogavante** (☎ 444-2941; Plaza Torres; d/tr/ste BsF100/120/130; ❄) Bean bags in all the rooms give it a retro-seventies hipness feel and push the hotel's grooviness quotient through the roof. Comfortable and very central, it also offers a solid tasca downstairs, plus there's an internet cafe on the plaza.

**Posada Madre Vieja** (☎ 421-2590, 0424-511-0856; Av Francisco de Miranda; d/tr BsF220/220; ❄ 📶) Set in spacious, garden-like grounds, Madre Vieja offers 16 rooms in a two-story building away from the noisy road and has an enjoyable restaurant in a palm-leaf thatched *churuata* (hut).

## Eating

**Parrilla Barí** (☎ 421-6745; Av 14 de Febrero at Lara; meals BsF15-40) The restaurant of Hotel Parilla Barí looks extremely basic, yet the food is OK, portions are generous and almost none of its 40-plus dishes costs more than BsF25.

### Getting There & Away

Carora is about 3km north off the Barquisimeto–Maracaibo freeway. The **Terminal de Pasajeros** (Av Francisco de Miranda) is on the southeastern outskirts of town, about 600m northwest off the freeway. The terminal is linked to the town's center by city minibuses.

Carora has half-hourly buseta connections with Barquisimeto (BsF20, 1½ hours, 103km), and there are also por puestos (BsF20, 1¼ hours). It's an interesting trip on a good autopista (freeway) across arid, hilly countryside. Ordinary buses to Maracaibo (BsF40 to BsF50, 3½ hours, 225km) come through from Barquisimeto infrequently; you may opt for a por puesto or go to the highway and wait once the morning buses have left. Buses to Caracas come through from Maracaibo but do not always stop here; it is likely to be faster to go to Barquisimeto and change there.



# ZULIA STATE

## MARACAIBO

☎ 0261 / pop 1,891,800

Founded as a trading post in 1574, Maracaibo was a backwater on the shores of the vast Lago de Maracaibo until 1914, when drillers struck oil. By the late 1920s Venezuela had become the world's largest exporter of oil, with two-thirds of the nation's output coming from beneath the lake. Today, it's the capital of Zulia, Venezuela's richest state, and an important port. The *maracuchos,* as local inhabitants are called, feel that they are producing the money that the rest of the country is spending.

Stroll about the old town, if you have a day or two, and sit in the shade of the leafy plazas, enjoying a fresh, icy *coco frio.* Wander through Las Pulgas – the flea market – getting lost in the seemingly endless variety of hawkers and merchants. At night, stick to the new town, for the myriad restaurants to be found there – it's where Maracaibo's oases of pleasure cluster, as though seeking refuge from the littered, barren streets.

Maracaibo is a sweltering stop for travelers on the way to or from Colombia's Caribbean coast. Stay a day or two to visit some of the city's icons, including the old holy basilica and the brightly painted restored houses on Calle Carabobo.

With a few more days up your sleeve, it's well worth exploring the city environs, noted for a colorful blend of tradition and modernity. In particular, be sure to make a detour to see the old *palafitos* on the shores of Laguna de Sinamaica. Five hundred years ago, Spanish sailors saw these houses on stilts and named the place 'Little Venice' – Venezuela.

### Dangers & Annoyances

Maracaibo can be a dicey place to walk around, and is also very hot. Take good care of your personal valuables while walking, and if someone advises you to take a taxi, it's probably best to heed that advice, even for a couple of blocks. In fact, let the hotel or restaurant call a reliable one for you.

### Orientation

Maracaibo is a big metropolis with vast suburbs, but the tourist focus is on the historic center to the south and the new center to the north. Getting between the two is easy and fast. The new center offers a far better choice of hotels, restaurants and other facilities, and it's moderately safer at night. The old quarter boasts more sights, but they can all be visited on one or two leisurely daytime trips.

### Information

#### EMERGENCY

**Fire** (☎ 171)
**Police** (☎ 171)

#### MEDICAL SERVICES

**Hospital Central** (Map p144; ☎ 722-6404; Av El Milagro btwn Calles 94 & 95)

#### MONEY

Major banks in Maracaibo have plenty of branches and the city also has a few *casas de cambio.*

**Banco de Venezuela** Historic Center (Map p144; cnr Av 5 & Calle 74); New Center (Map p146; cnr Av Bella Vista & Calle 71)
**Banco Mercantil** New Center (Map p146; cnr Av Bella Vista & Calle 67)
**Banco Provincial** Historic Center (Map p144; cnr Av El Milagro & Calle 97); New Center (Map p146; cnr Av Bella Vista & Calle 74)
**Banesco** New Center (Map p146; cnr Av Bella Vista & Calle 71)
**Casa de Cambio Maracaibo** New Center (Map p146; ☎ 797-2576; Av 9B btwn Calles 77 & 78); Av El Milagro

(Map p144; ☎ 792-2174; Centro Comercial Lago Mall, Av El Milagro).
**Corp Banca** Historic Center (Map p144; cnr Av Libertador & Av 14); New Center (Map p146; cnr Av Bella Vista & Calle 67)
**Italcambio** Airport (☎ 736-2513); Av 20 (off Map p146; ☎ 783-2040; Centro Comercial Montielco, cnr Av 20 & Calle 72); Av El Milagro (off Map p146; ☎ 793-2983; Centro Comercial Lago Mall, Av El Milagro)

### TELEPHONE

**CANTV** (Map p144; Local 43, Centro Comercial Plaza Lago, Av Libertador)
**Movistar** Bus Terminal (Map p144; Av 17); Centro Comercial La Redoma (Map p144; Local 52-53, Av Libertador); Paseo Ciencias (Map p144; Calle 96 No 10K-29)

### TOURIST INFORMATION

**Corpozulia** (Corporación de Desarrollo de la Región Zuliana; Map p146; ☎ 794-9424; www.corpozulia.gov.ve; Edificio Corpozulia, Av Bella Vista btwn Calles 83 & 84; 8am-4pm Mon-Fri) Located 2km north of the historic center, accessible by the Bella Vista por puestos.
**Corzutur** (Corporación Zuliana de Turismo; Map p146; ☎ 783-4928; www.zuliaturistica.com; Edificio Lieja, cnr Av 18 & Calle 78; 8am-4pm Mon-Fri) Located 2km northwest of the historic center.

## Sights

### HISTORIC CENTER

The historic center boasts most of the tourist sights, a short walk from each other. The axis of this sector is the **Paseo de las Ciencias**, a seven-block-long greenbelt laid out after the demolition of the colonial buildings that formed the core of Maracaibo's oldest quarter, El Saladillo. This controversial plan, executed in 1973, effectively cut the very heart out of the old town. The only structure not pulled down was the blue-colored neo-Gothic **Iglesia de Santa Bárbara** (Map p144; cnr Av 8 & Calle 95).

At the western end of the Paseo is the **Basílica de Chiquinquirá** (p144), which features the venerated Virgin of Chiquinquirá, affectionately referred to as La Chinita, the patron saint of Zulia. Legend has it that the image of the Virgin, painted on a small wooden board, was found in 1709 by a humble *campesina* (peasant woman) on the shore of Lago de Maracaibo. Upon being brought to her home, the image began to glow. It was then taken to the church and allegedly miracles started to happen. Pilgrims gather here year-round, but the major celebrations are held in November (p145).

The eastern end of the Paseo de las Ciencias is bordered by **Plaza Bolívar** and the 19th-century **catedral** (p144; cnr Av 4 & Calle 95). The most revered image in the cathedral is the Cristo Negro, or Cristo de Gibraltar, as it was called originally in the church of Gibraltar, a town on the southern shore of Lago de Maracaibo. The town was overrun and burned by indigenous groups in 1600, but the crucifix miraculously survived, even though the cross to which the statue was nailed was incinerated. The image is in the chapel to the left of the high altar.

The arcaded mid-19th-century **Palacio de Gobierno** (p144; Plaza Bolívar) is also called the Palacio de las Águilas (Palace of the Eagles) for the two condors placed on its roof. Next door is the late-18th-century Casa Morales, better known as **Casa de la Capitulación** (☎ 725-1194; Plaza Bolívar; admission free; 8am-noon & 1-6pm Mon-Fri), for it was here that the Spaniards who were defeated in the naval battle of Lago de Maracaibo signed the act of capitulation on August 3, 1823, sealing the independence of Gran Colombia. This is the only residential colonial building left in the city. It has been restored, fitted with period furniture and decorated with paintings of heroes of the War of Independence.

Across the street from the casa is the mighty art deco **Teatro Baralt** (p148), which you can tour.

A short walk north from the center is **Museo Urdaneta** (Map p144; Calle 91A No 7-70; admission free; 8:30am-3pm Mon-Fri), which is dedicated to Maracaibo-born General Rafael Urdaneta, the city's greatest independence hero. Built on the site of Urdaneta's birth, it features a collection of objects, documents, paintings and other memorabilia related to the general and the events of the period.

Calle 94, better known as **Calle Carabobo**, has been partly restored to its former appearance, and is notable for its brightly colored facades and grilled windows. The most spectacular part of the street is between Avs 6 and 8. Also worth visiting is the **Mercado Artesanal San Sebastián** (Map p144; cnr Av El Milagro & Calle 96), a colorful Guajiro craft market full of hammocks and other crafts.

South of the Paseo de las Ciencias lies **Las Pulgas** – the flea market. Streets are crammed with stalls selling everything from fresh fish to pirate DVDs. Here also is **Plaza Baralt**, the historic trading district from Maracaibo's earliest days, and the imposing old market building, which operated as the Mercado Principal from 1931 to 1973. It has been wholly remodeled and refurbished, and re-opened as the **Centro de Arte de Maracaibo Lía Bermúdez** (Map p144).

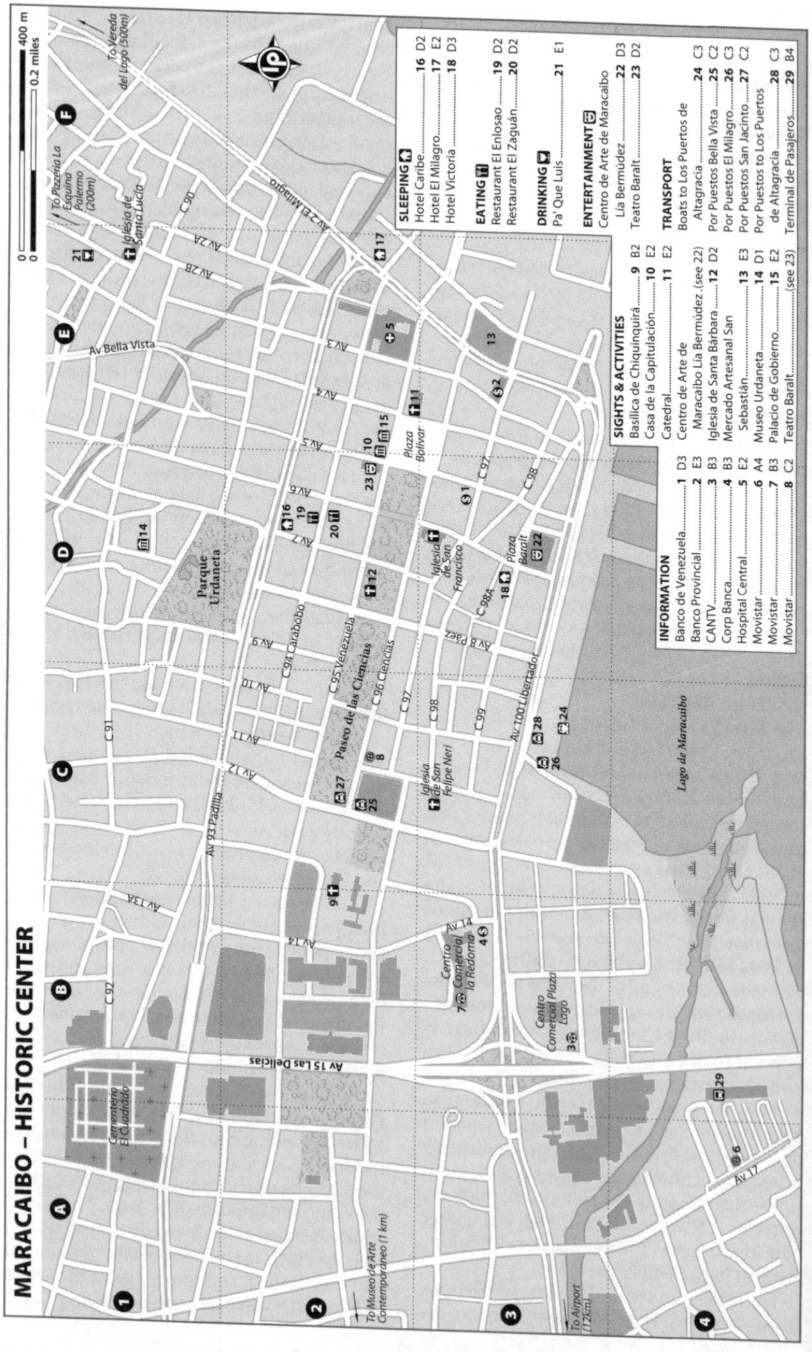
MARACAIBO – HISTORIC CENTER
0 400 m
0 0.2 miles
INFORMATION
Banco de Venezuela 1 D3
Banco Provincial 2 E3
CANTV 3 B3
Corp Banca 4 B3
Hospital Central 5 E2
Movistar 6 A4
Movistar 7 B3
Movistar 8 C2
SIGHTS & ACTIVITIES
Basílica de Chiquinquirá 9 B2
Casa de la Capitulación 10 E2
Catedral 11 E2
Centro de Arte de Maracaibo Lía Bermúdez (see 22)
Iglesia de Santa Bárbara 12 D2
Mercado Artesanal San Sebastián 13 E3
Museo Urdaneta 14 D1
Palacio de Gobierno 15 E2
Teatro Baralt (see 23)
SLEEPING
Hotel Caribe 16 D2
Hotel El Milagro 17 E2
Hotel Victoria 18 D3
EATING
Restaurant El Enlosao 19 D2
Restaurant El Zaguán 20 D2
DRINKING
Pa' Que Luis 21 E1
ENTERTAINMENT
Centro de Arte de Maracaibo Lía Bermúdez 22 D3
Teatro Baralt 23 D2
TRANSPORT
Boats to Los Puertos de Altagracia 24 C3
Por Puestos Bella Vista 25 C2
Por Puestos El Milagro 26 C3
Por Puestos San Jacinto 27 C2
Por Puestos to Los Puertos de Altagracia 28 C3
Terminal de Pasajeros 29 B4
Cementerio El Cuadrado
Av 15 Las Delicias
Av 93 Padilla
Av 100 Libertador
Av Bella Vista
Av 2 El Milagro
Parque Urdaneta
Paseo de las Ciencias
Plaza Bolívar
Plaza Baralt
Iglesia de San Francisco
Iglesia de San Felipe Neri
Iglesia de Santa Lucía
Centro Comercial la Redoma
Centro Comercial Plaza Lago
Lago de Maracaibo
To Airport (12km)
To Museo de Arte Contemporáneo (1 km)
To Vereda del Lago (500m)
To Pizzeria La Esquina Palermo (200m)

## NORTHERN SUBURBS

The lakeshore **Vereda del Lago** (Map p146; cnr Av El Milagro & Calle 81), 5km north of the center, features the Aquamania water park (BsF50), paint-ball court, and the city's best-dressed and surgically enhanced joggers.

Northwest of the city center, on the university's grounds, the strikingly modern **Museo de Arte Contemporáneo del Zulia** (off Map p144; ☎ 759-4866; Av Universidad; admission free; ☾ 9am-5pm Tue-Sun) stages temporary displays of modern art in its huge exhibition halls.

## Festivals & Events

Maracaibo's major annual event is the **Feria de la Chinita**, which springs to life around November 10 and continues until the coronation of the Virgin on November 18. Apart from religious celebrations, the week-long festival includes various cultural and popular events such as bull-fights, *toros coleados* (rodeo with bulls), street parades and, obviously, music – above all the *gaita* (see the boxed text, p147). The best time to listen to the *gaita* is on the eve of November 18, when groups gather in front of the basilica to play the *Serenata para la Virgen*.

The Feria de la Chinita marks the beginning of the Christmas celebrations, reflected in the illumination of Av Bella Vista and a general holiday atmosphere.

## Sleeping

### BUDGET

The historic center is the most convenient place to stay, but doesn't offer anything special in the way of accommodations. The northern suburbs provide better lodgings and are a bit safer after dark, but you'll be away from most of the major sights.

**Hotel Caribe** (Map p144; ☎ 722-5986; Av 7 No 93-51; s BsF60-150, d BsF100-190, tr BsF100-225; ☒ ) Just two blocks from the Plaza Bolívar, the 60-room Caribe has a slightly updated section at the back. These rooms have noiseless, efficient air-con, but there's no way to adjust the temperature.

**Nuevo Hotel Unión** (Map p146; ☎ 793-3278; Calle 84 No 4-60; d BsF80-90, tr BsF120; ☒ ) Just a few steps from the Corpozulia tourist office, this small budget spot offers six basic rooms with air-con and cable TV.

**Hotel Victoria** (Map p144; ☎ 322-6159, 721-2654; Plaza Baralt; s/d/tr BsF100/110/155; ☒ ) This white colonial building is your best budget bet in the old town, with 32 very basic rooms and

a pleasant common area to sit for a chat at the end of the day. Try to snag a room with a balcony view over the busy market plaza.

**Hotel El Milagro** (Map p144; ☎ 722-8934; Av El Milagro No 93-45; d/tr BsF170/195; ☒ ) Homely from afar, the corridors of the Miracle Hotel are clad almost entirely in eerie white tile, with spick-and-span rooms to match. The newer section has slightly nicer rooms.

### MIDRANGE

There are no mid-priced or upmarket hotels in the old city center; they've all opted for newer, more elegant districts, mainly in the northern part of the city.

**Hotel Doral** (Map p146; ☎ 797-8385; cnr Av 14A & Calle 75; s BsF190, d BsF210-230, tr BsF250; ☒ ) This small 22-room hotel isn't anything particularly memorable, yet it has quiet, acceptable air-con rooms and the room rate includes breakfast in the adjacent restaurant.

**Hotel Maracaibo Cumberland** (Map p146; ☎ 722-2944; www.hotelescumberland.com; Calle 86A No 4-150; s/d/ste BsF224/235/308; ☒ ☒ ) Roughly midway between the old and new centers, this five-floor 88-room hotel is a good compromise between quality and price, and has a breezy rooftop terrace.

**Apart Hotel Suite Golden Monky** (Map p146; ☎ 797-3285; goldenmonky@hotmail.com; Calle 78 No 10-30; s/d/tr/ste BsF245/265/330/420; ☒ ☒ ) Central and convenient, the Golden Monky offers a variety of rooms and suites and a pool; the restaurant downstairs is pretty good value, too. Don't wander at night without a taxi.

**Gran Hotel Delicias** (Map p146; ☎ 797-0983; www.hotel delicias.com; cnr Av Las Delicias & Calle 70; d/tr BsF280/360, ste BsF410-450; ☒ ☒ ☒ ) 'Deliciously different,' and the clocks in the lobby prove it. It is one of the cheapest hotels in town that has its own pool – a bonus you'll surely appreciate in this steamy climate. There's a good-value restaurant and a disco, too.

### TOP END

**Hotel Kristoff** (Map p146; ☎ 200-4000; www.hotelkristoff. com; Av 8 No 68-48; s BsF431, d BsF641-720, ste BsF1389-2977; ☒ ☒ ☒ ☒ ) The stylish four-star Kristoff, done up in dark woods and marble floors, has a wide range of facilities, including a restaurant, spa, gym and a deliciously palm-fringed pool with an outdoor bar.

**Hotel El Paseo Best Western** (off Map p146; ☎ 792-4422; www.hotelelpaseo.com.ve; cnr Av 1B & Calle 74; d/ste BsF425/510, ☒ ☒ ☒ ) This waterfront high-rise hotel's 63 unusually large rooms all have bath-

## MARACAIBO – NEW CENTER

**INFORMATION**
Banco de Venezuela 1 C3
Banco Mercantil 2 C1
Banco Provincial 3 C3
Banesco 4 C2
Casa de Cambio Maracaibo 5 C4
Colombian Consulate 6 C2
Corp Banca 7 C1
Corpozulia 8 D5

**SLEEPING**
Apart Hotel Suite Golden Monky 9 B4
Gran Hotel Delicias 10 A2
Hotel Doral 11 A4
Hotel Kristoff 12 C2
Hotel Maracaibo Cumberland 13 C6
Nuevo Hotel Unión 14 D5

**EATING**
El Budare de Juana 15 C2
La Churuata 16 C2
Restaurant Los Soles 17 D3
Ristorante Da Vinci 18 B3

**DRINKING**
Bahia Rastabar 19 D3
Bar Alvarito 20 A3

**ENTERTAINMENT**
Centro de Bellas Artes 21 D2

**TRANSPORT**
Budget 22 B4
Hertz (see 12)

## GAITA – THE MUSIC OF MARACAIBO

Is the party inside or outside? Amid the pastel-colored homes on Plaza Santa Lucia, a bottle of rum is passed from the car trunk around the circle, ice-filled cups awaiting the sugarcane elixir. The locals are swathed in button-down shirts as bright as their homes, a Caribbean rainbow of pink, yellow and blue. The pizzerias and *areperas* on the street are open late and doing a booming business.

Inside Pa' Que Luis, the percussion thumps. Empty cases of Polar Light, in rows of six by six, are quickly filled with spent bottles.

What is *gaita zuliana*? It's a highly percussive ensemble music, where songs of love, humor and protest all are infused with a shout-it-out-loud *maracucho* vocal line and the insistent strumming of the four-stringed *cuatro*, backed up by a tub-thumbing *furro*, a drum made from a leather membrane and what looks like a broom handle. Like Zulia itself, it's lively and loud.

This is *gaita* – the music of the *marachuchos* – and barrio Santa Lucia its spiritual home.

*Gaita* is Maracaibo's musical identity – what tango is to Buenos Aires. It's a lively percussion- and voice-based sound, performed by a small band, with lyrics often improvised on religious or political themes. It evolved in Maracaibo's central quarter of El Saladillo, part of which was razed for the Paseo de las Ciencias.

A classical *gaita* ensemble includes the *cuatro* (a small, four-stringed guitar), *tambora* (large wooden drum) and *furruco* (another drum-based instrument). Ricardo Aguirre (1939–69), nicknamed 'El Monumental,' is considered one of the greatest *gaita* singers. Another living favorite is Pillopo Coquivacoa, while Los Cardenales del Exito have been playing since 1962 and remain a point of pride for Zulianas.

*Gaita* is most popular from October to January, peaking during the Christmas season, when it can be heard everywhere – in bars and buses, on the street and on the beach. Plenty of restaurants and bars across town stage live *gaita* music in that period.

Back inside Pa' Que Luis, a cup of ice is passed to the *tambora* player in the backline, and the *furruco* man in the front row takes time during a song to answer his cell phone. One thing that never stops flowing is the *cerveza* (beer). Baseball caps hang from the ceiling, and the walls are lined with photos and newspaper clippings of famous clients such as shortstops Luis Aparicio and Ozzie Guillen. The *maracuchos* are out in full force!

THE NORTHWEST

rooms, hot water, silent air-con, cable TV and a fridge. Downstairs is a business center with internet access and a small pool. Be sure to ask for a room with lake views.

**Venetur Hotel del Lago Maracaibo** (off Map p144; ☎ 794-4222; fax 793-0392; www.venetur.gob.ve; Av El Milagro; s/d BsF645/680, ste BsF700-1000; ) Opened in 1953, this massive five-star hotel is Maracaibo's institution. The portraits of Chávez and Bolivar in the lobby tell you who's running the show now. It has two restaurants, a sizeable swimming pool and sauna.

## Eating

Most upmarket restaurants are nestled in the northern sector of the city, in particular in the new center around Plaza República. The historic center hosts a lot of cheap eateries, but nothing really posh or classy.

**El Budare de Juana** (Map p146; ☎ 798-3219; cnr Av 8 & Calle 70; juices BsF 6-8, arepas BsF10-15; 7am-11pm) This clean and efficient *arepera* – part of a local chain – serves 25 different kinds of delicious *arepas* (stuffed corn pancakes) and a dozen freshly made juices to wash the food down.

**Restaurant El Enlosao** (Map p144; Calle 94; meals BsF15-40) Set in a charming historic mansion, the Casa de los Artesanos, El Enlosao serves unpretentious but tasty Venezuelan food at low prices. The *parrilla* is so copious that you may struggle to finish it.

**Restaurant El Zaguán** (Map p144; ☎ 717-2398; cnr Calle 94 & Av 6; meals BsF30-40) A few paces away from El Enlosao, the white tablecloths and leather-bound menus of El Zaguán greet you with the air-con set to arctic – surely a plus in the midday heat. Try the *papelón* (sugarcane drink with lemon). In the evenings you can eat outside in the shade of two beautiful old ceiba trees.

**La Esquina de Palermo** (Map p144; Ave 2a at Calle 88, Santa Lucia Barrio; pizzas BsF33-145) Salsa music blares, balconies overhang the street, and there are 145 pizzas to choose from – great for a group outing. Sample the Maracucha pizza with fried banana, or La Orgia – need we say more?

**Restaurant Los Soles** (Map p146; ☎ 793-3966; www.lossoles.com.ve; Av 5 de Julio No 3G-09; meals BsF41-61) Run by a Mexican family, this bright, airy new spot brings some authentic Mexican flavor to town. You can have your tacos and enchiladas outside if you want, but the colorful interior offers deliciously cool air-conditioning.

**Restaurant El Girasol** (off Map p146; ☎ 792-4422; Hotel El Paseo Best Western, cnr Av 1B & Calle 74; meals BsF50–80; ⏰ noon-3pm & 7pm-midnight) This is the only revolving restaurant in the country – an entire circle takes about two hours and the floor-to-ceiling windows provide for great views – you might even see the Catatumbo lightning in the distance. You can sit at the bar or dine on international cuisine, including a fair choice of pasta and seafood.

**Ristorante Da Vinci** (Map p146; ☎ 798-8934; www.grupodavinci.com.ve; Av 11 btwn Calles 75 & 76; meals BsF75-90) With a mock Renaissance fountain in front of the restaurant, Da Vinci is, predictably, an Italian affair, is consistently popular with locals for its fine food and relaxed atmosphere.

**La Churuata** (Map p146; ☎ 798-9685; www.lachuruata.com; cnr Calle 72 & Av 8; meals BsF80-105; ⏰ noon-midnight) Far from the palm-thatched jungle hut the name suggests, this trendy steak house combines delicious food with enjoyable decor. There's also an adjacent bar.



## Drinking

**Bahia Rastabar** (Map p146; ☎ 622-2159; Av 3G at Calle 77 5 de Julio) DJs spin trendy reggae and *reggaetón* in this youthful bar, conveniently across the street from Los Soles Restaurant. Outdoor tables are more relaxed, and what's not to like about a bar that has drinks like 'Mango Funk'?

**Bar Alvarado** (Map p146; ☎ 0414-165-8892; Calle 72 at Ave 13) A young 20-something crowd dominates this massive club, which encompasses two floors on trendy Calle 72. Cheap drinks and loud music: what more might one require?

## Entertainment

Have a look in *Panorama* (www.panorama.com.ve), Maracaibo's major daily paper, for what's going on in the city.

**Centro de Arte de Maracaibo Lía Bermúdez** (Map p144; ☎ 723-1355, 723-0166; Av Libertador btwn Avs 5 & 6) The center has an auditorium where it hosts musical events, theater and art-house films. It also stages temporary exhibitions.

**Centro de Bellas Artes** (Map p146; ☎ 791-2950; Av 3F No 67-217) Bellas Artes has a multipurpose auditorium used for concerts, art-house films and theater performances. It's also home to the Orquesta Sinfónica de Maracaibo and the Danza Contemporánea de Maracaibo.

**Teatro Baralt** (Map p144; ☎ 722-3878; cnr Calle 95 & Av 5) Inaugurated in 1932, this is the main central venue for theater performances, but it also stages other events. Half-hour guided tours are run from 9am to noon weekdays, if there are no other activities in the theater. Don't forget to look in the basement!

## Getting There & Away

### TO/FROM COLOMBIA

Three bus companies – **Bus Ven** (☎ 723-9084; www.busven.com), **Expresos Amerlujo** (☎ 787-7872; www.expresosamerlujo.com) and **Expreso Brasilia** (☎ 0212-243-7100; www.expresobrasilia.com) – run air-conditioned buses to Cartagena via Maicao, Santa Marta and Barranquilla (all in Colombia). All three have early morning departures daily from Maracaibo's international bus terminal, although the Bus Ven and Expreso Brasilia service originates in Caracas. Expect to pay roughly BsF190 for Santa Marta and BsF290 for Cartegena. The buses cross the border at Paraguachón (you actually change buses there) and continue through Maicao, the first Colombian town.

Note that the international terminal in Maracaibo is not in the same location as the national one. If taking a taxi, be sure to specify which one you are going to.

It's cheaper to go by por puesto to Maicao (BsF60, 2½ hours, 123km) and change there. It's also your only option if you miss the early morning buses. Por puestos depart regularly from about 5am to 3pm and go as far as Maicao's bus terminal. From there, several Colombian bus companies operate buses to Santa Marta (BsF35, four hours, 251km) and further on; buses depart regularly until late afternoon.

All passport formalities are done in Paraguachón on the border. Venezuelan immigration charges a BsF55 *impuesto de salida* (departure tax), paid in cash by bolívares by all tourists leaving Venezuela.

You can change bolívares into Colombian pesos at the Maracaibo terminal or in Paraguachón or Maicao, but don't take them further into Colombia: they're difficult to change beyond Maicao. Wind your watch back one half-hour when crossing from Venezuela to Colombia.

Ask for 90 days, when entering Colombia.

### AIR

The **Aeropuerto Internacional La Chinita** (☎ 735-8094; Av El Aeropuerto), about 12km southwest of the city center, is not linked by city buses; take a taxi (BsF60). Maracaibo is serviced by most major airlines, including **Aeropostal** (☎ 800-284-6637), **Aserca** (☎ 735-3607), **Avior** (☎ 735-1910) Conviasa and **Venezolana** (☎ 783-5158).

There are more than a dozen flights daily to Caracas (BsF311 to BsF481), serviced by all the listed airlines. There are also daily flights to Valencia, Porlamar and Las Piedras.

Aeropostal has two direct flights to Valencia (BsF500 to BsF554), and Conviasa has three flights daily to Las Piedras (BsF116 to BsF182).

International carriers are American (Miami), Copa (Panama), Venezolana (Aruba), Avior (Curaçao) and Aires (Colombia Bogota, Baranquilla and Cartagena).

For other destinations you usually have to change planes in Caracas.

### BUS

The large and busy **Terminal de Pasajeros** (national terminal; Map p144; ☎ 722-1443; Av 15) is about 1km southwest of Maracaibo's historic center. City buses link the terminal to the center and to other districts.

Ordinary buses to Coro (BsF40, four hours, 259km) and Valera (bus BsF20, por puesto BsF30, four hours, 238km) run every half-hour. Buses to Barquisimeto (*bus-cama* BsF40, five hours, 328km) depart every hour and stop en route in Carora (BsF35, 3½ hours, 225km). There are regular departures to Caracas (BsF70 to BsF80, 10½ hours, 669km), though most buses depart in the evening. Four or five buses depart nightly for Mérida (BsF60, nine hours, 523km).

### CAR & MOTORCYCLE

Maracaibo has all the major car rental companies. All have desks at the airport, but some also maintain offices in the city.

**Budget** Airport (☎ 735-1256); City (Map p146; ☎ 798-3107; Calle 76 No 13-08)
**Hertz** Airport (☎ 735-0832); City (Map p146; ☎ 797-4656; Hotel Kristoff, Calle 68)
**Thrifty** (☎ 735-1631; airport)

### METRO

Maracaibo has a brand-spanking, new green-and-white air-conditioned Metro (www.metrodemaracaibo.gob.ve), with six stations modeled after the city's famous bridge, in operation, as of this writing with a total of 14km of track. The Libertador station is a 200m walk from the bus terminal, but connections to the city center have not been made yet. One ride costs BsF1.50.

## Getting Around

City transportation is serviced by buses and por puesto cars. You are most likely to need them to get between the historic center and the northern suburbs, which are linked to each other by three main roads: Av El Milagro, Av Bella Vista and Av Las Delicias. El Milagro por puestos depart from Av Libertador (Map p144). The Bella Vista por puestos leave from the corner of Av 12 and Calle 96 (Map p144). From the same corner, por puestos depart for San Jacinto and run north along Av Las Delicias.

It can sometimes be difficult to hail a regular cab in the street. Two radio taxi companies to try are **Unión Taxi 976** (☎ 793-9151) and **Radio la 13** (☎ 736-5273).

# AROUND MARACAIBO

## Laguna de Sinamaica

The most popular tourist sight around Maracaibo, Laguna de Sinamaica, is noted for the *palafitos* – houses built on pilings along the lakeshore. Reputedly it was here that the Spanish explorers Alonso de Ojeda and Amerigo Vespucci saw native people living in *palafitos* in 1499, and gave Venezuela its name (see p22).

Today there is even a posada on stilts, called **Posada Keitchikaru** (☎ 0416-228-3285). Three rooms (BsF100) can accommodate four persons each. Pleasure boats take tourists for trips around the lagoon and its side water channels to see the famous *palafitos*. Boats from Puerto Cuervito or San Rafael de Mojan can take you around Laguna Sinamaica – a spectacular if sometimes bone-jarring ride across the glassine and seemingly endless stretches of Lake Maracaibo. Some houses are still traditionally built of *estera*, a sort of mat made from a papyrus-like reed that grows in the shallows. If you ignore the TV antennas sticking out from the roofs, they probably don't look much different from their predecessors 500 years ago. Many houses, though, are now built from modern materials, including timber, brick and tin.

Sinamaica, with its abundant avian population, low-key locals and deep, still waters seems a world away from the madness of

### AN ELECTRIFYING JOURNEY ON THE CATATUMBO RIVER

The moon hangs low over Lago Maracaibo, illuminating the ceiba trees and water lilies, and cackles and cries that seemed innocent in the daylight hours become downright creepy now.

Crawling along the Catatumbo River delta at night, the boat's searchlights point out spectacled caiman, herons, the owl-like potoo and even tree boas dangling from the branches, ready to devour an unsuspecting bird.

Then there is the lightning, which happens most, but not all of the time. (Around 300 days a year, most say.) And when it does happen, the results can be nothing short of spectacular.

Centered on the mouth of the Río Catatumbo at Lago de Maracaibo, the phenomenon consists of frequent flashes of lightning with no accompanying thunder, which gives an eerie sensation. Even though the luminosity and frequency of the lightning have diminished over recent decades and it can stop for some days, on clear dry nights you are in for an unbelievable and shocking experience.

Various hypotheses have been put forth to explain the lightning, but the theory that stands out is based on the topography of the region. The clash of the cold winds descending from the freezing highlands with the hot, humid air evaporating from the lake is thought to produce the ionization of air particles responsible for the lightning.

Boat tours of the Río Catatumbo can be organized from Merida (p159). The night tour is a must for those who want to see the bizarre lightning, while the morning and afternoon tours are better for viewing the animals, vegetables and minerals of the basin. You may see frolicking *araguato* (red howler monkey) families and a cornucopia of birdlife, including scarlet macaws and toucans. Lucky visitors may even see the docile manatee, or sea cow.

On a typical tour, you may also visit a *trapiche*, or old-fashioned sugarcane processing station (buy the sample!); tour Hacienda La Victoria, an old coffee plantation with the original 19th-century English-built equipment; and hit La Palmita waterfalls, 18km from Catatumbo, for a refreshingly cool splash on the way back to Mérida. Many tours also stop in colonial Jají, an amazingly pristine colonial village.



Maracaibo city. Watch an osprey glide out of a treetop to snag a fish in the murky waters, or watch a boatload of schoolchildren in uniform get picked by boat from their school-on-stilts, and it's easy to forget that an hour ago you were sitting in bumper-to-bumper traffic at the bus terminal.

Laguna de Sinamaica is 60km north of Maracaibo and makes for an easy day trip from the city. Take a bus heading to Guana or Los Filuos from the Maracaibo bus terminal and get off in the town of Sinamaica (BsF8, two hours, 60km). From there, por puestos do a short run on a side road to Puerto Cuervito (BsF2, 10 minutes, 5km), on the edge of the lagoon.

## Isla de San Carlos

You can almost sense the ghosts of days gone by – from buccaneer Henry Morgan to the 1950s political prisoners wailing in their dank cells – at the **Castillo de San Carlos**, which was built in the 1670s to guard the lake entrance from pirates. Even though the mouth was largely protected by a sandbar, many marauders were eager to cross over and sack Maracaibo. The fort was in Spanish hands until the 1823 Battle of Lago de Maracaibo; after their defeat it passed to the republicans.

Finally decreed a national monument, it was extensively restored in the late 1980s to become a tourist attraction.

San Carlos Island is about 45km north of Maracaibo, and with its fine white-sand beaches and the castle, it makes a great day trip. With ambition and the right boat pilot, you can visit San Carlos and Sinamaica in the same day.

### GETTING THERE & AWAY

The fort is accessible by boats from the town of San Rafael del Moján. San Rafael, 39km north of Maracaibo, is serviced by a number of buses and por puestos (BsF5 to BsF10) from the city's bus terminal. The terminal at Moján was under construction at the time of research.

## Parque Nacional Ciénagas del Catatumbo

The (literally) striking feature of this area is the lightning (see the boxed text, above), which continues almost uninterrupted without any claps of thunder. Tours organized from Mérida (p159) are the best way to see the Catatumbo lightning close up.

# The Andes

You might imagine that Simón Bolívar himself – that guy for whom nearly every plaza in the country is named – stopped and took a deep breath himself when he marched through the Andes on the 'Admirable Campaign,' the final steps in the country's independence. Scenic Trujillo – where he decreed death to every resistor – and its surrounding villages, like Boconó and Niquitao, retain much of the colonial character of days gone by and make for some great trekking.

But save your breath and energy for Mérida, the adventure capital of the country, where two- and four-wheel vehicles, ropes, pick-axes, hang-gliders and yes – your own two feet – take you higher than you might imagine, soaring above even the condors in a parapente glider, or looking down on the rest of Venezuela from the shrouded mists of Eagle's Pass. Leap from vertigo-inducing bridges, rappel into canyons, bike down or glide off mountains: you'll be completely exhausted and exhilarated by your time in the highlands.



**HIGHLIGHTS**

- Find mountain hospitality in the remote mountain village of **Los Nevados** (p165)
- Careen down waterfalls on a **canyoning trip** (p157), or soar above the condors on a **paragliding trip** (p155), organized from Mérida
- Go mountain trekking to **Pico Bolívar** (p165) and **Pico Humboldt** (p165), Venezuela's highest peaks
- Watch the mysterious Good Friday passion play in **Tostós** (p173)
- Stare out the eye-holes of the massive 47m statue of the **Virgin Mary** (p169) in Trujillo

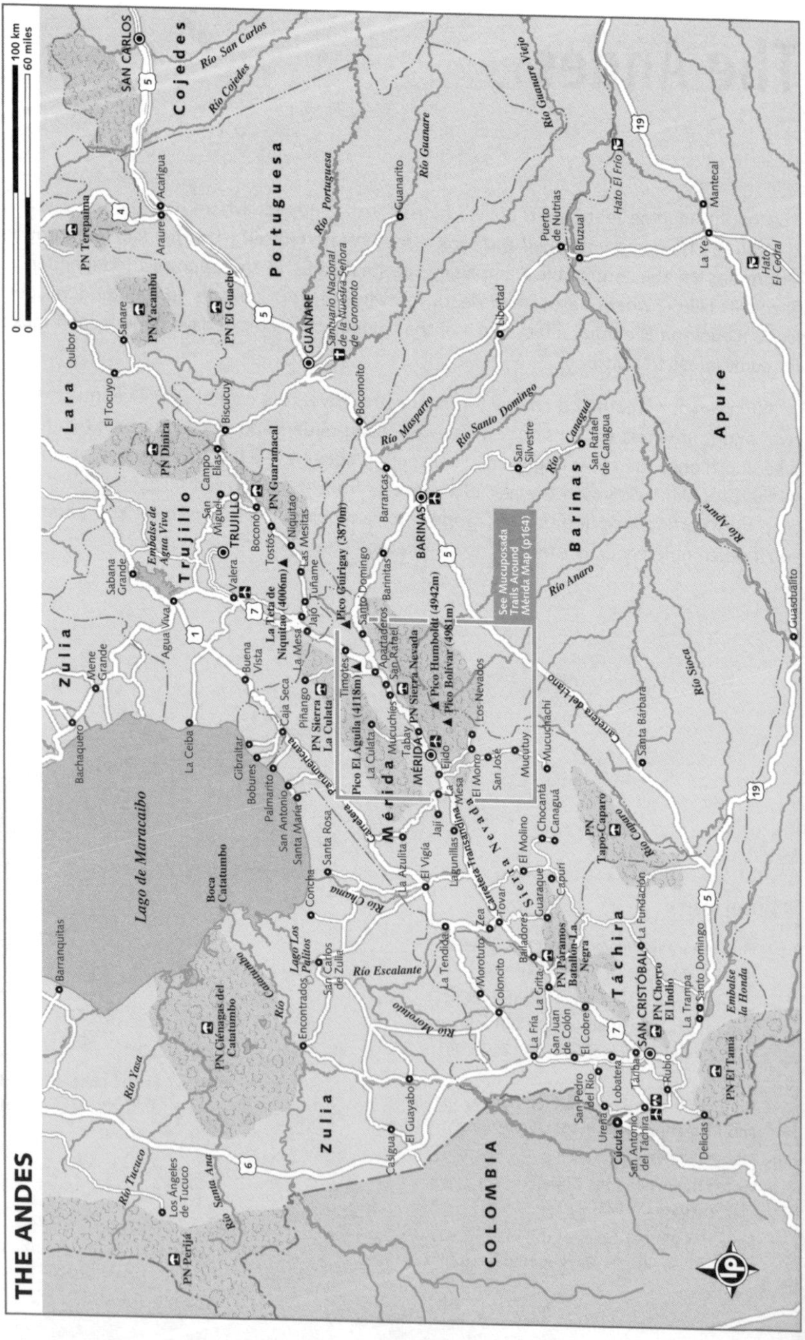
THE ANDES
0 100 km
0 60 miles
Lago de Maracaibo
Zulia
Lara
Trujillo
Portuguesa
Cojedes
Mérida
Barinas
Apure
Táchira
COLOMBIA
SAN CARLOS
GUANARE
TRUJILLO
BARINAS
MÉRIDA
SAN CRISTÓBAL
Cúcuta
Valera
Acarigua
Araure
Quíbor
Sanare
El Tocuyo
Biscucuy
Boconoito
Guanarito
Barrancas
Barinitas
Santo Domingo
Timotes
Apartaderos
San Rafael
Mucuchíes
Tabay
La Culata
Ejido
Jají
La Mesa
Tovar
Zea
Bailadores
La Grita
El Vigía
La Azulita
Lagunillas
Santa Rosa
San Antonio
Santa María
Palmarito
Bobures
Gibraltar
La Ceiba
Bachaquero
Mene Grande
Agua Viva
Sabana Grande
Buena Vista
Caja Seca
Piñango
Jajó
Tuñame
Las Mesitas
Niquitao
Tostós
Boconó
Campo Elías
San Miguel
Concha
Encontrados
San Carlos de Zulia
Barranquitas
Boca Catatumbo
El Guayabo
Casigua
Los Ángeles de Tucuco
La Fría
San Juan de Colón
El Cobre
Lobatera
Táriba
Rubio
Ureña
San Antonio del Táchira
San Pedro del Río
Delicias
La Tendida
Morotuto
Coloncito
Guaraque
Capurí
Chocantá
Canaguá
El Molino
Mucuchachí
Mucutuy
San José
El Morro
Los Nevados
Santa Bárbara
La Fundación
La Trampa
Santo Domingo
Libertad
Puerto de Nutrias
Bruzual
La Ye
Mantecal
San Silvestre
San Rafael de Canagua
Guasdualito
Hato El Frío
Hato El Cedral
Pico El Águila (4118m)
Pico Humboldt (4942m)
Pico Bolívar (4981m)
Pico Guirigay (3870m)
La Teta de Niquitao (4006m)
PN Sierra Nevada
PN Sierra La Culata
PN Guaramacal
PN Dinira
PN Yacambú
PN El Guache
PN Terepaima
PN Tapo-Caparo
PN Páramos Batallón-La Negra
PN Chorro El Indio
PN El Tamá
PN Ciénagas del Catatumbo
PN Perijá
Santuario Nacional de la Nuestra Señora de Coromoto
Embalse de Agua Viva
Embalse la Honda
Lago Los Patillos
Sierra Nevada
Carretera Panamericana
Carretera Transandina
Carretera del Llano
Río San Carlos
Río Cojedes
Río Portuguesa
Río Guanare
Río Guanare Viejo
Río Masparro
Río Santo Domingo
Río Canaguá
Río Anaro
Río Apure
Río Sioca
Río Caparo
Río Chama
Río Escalante
Río Motatán
Río Catatumbo
Río Yasa
Río Tucuco
Río Santa Ana
See Mucuposada Trails Around Mérida Map (p164)

# MÉRIDA STATE

## MÉRIDA

☎ 0274 / pop 234,200

An adventure-sports playground, Mérida is the sort of place people come to stay a couple of days and end up spending a couple of weeks. With a just-right climate, great restaurants and nightlife, and the mountains towering snowy and oh-so-near, Mérida makes a lovely short holiday, but an even better base camp for extended adventures throughout the region.

With gargantuan mountain views looming over the city in every direction, it's no surprise that mountain trips are a main attraction – Pico Bolívar (4981m) is just 12km away, and there are numerous mountaineering and hiking opportunities for every fitness level. Sadly, Mérida's famous *teleférico*, the world's highest and longest cable-car system, had been closed for more than a year at the time of research.

Adrenaline junkies will find a huge range of adventure sports to indulge in, from paragliding and white-water rafting to mountain biking, canyoning and zip-lining. You can even bungee-jump off the viaduct at the entrance to Mérida with **Factor Pendulo** (☎ 0416-8787-932). Additionally, most wildlife safaris – a highly recommended trip – to Los Llanos leave from Mérida.

Mérida is a student town – more than 50,000 students from several universities flood the city every year – giving it a young face and a bohemian, cultured air. It also means you'll find some of the best nightlife in Venezuela. Foodies will also be delighted to discover a wide selection of excellent, reasonably priced restaurants serving a variety of cuisine.

### History

Founded deep in the heart of the Andes and separated by the high mountains from both Colombia and Venezuela, nothing much happened in the tiny town of Mérida during its 250 years under Spanish dominion. In 1812 an earthquake devastated the center, further hindering its development.

After Venezuela's independence, the isolation that had retarded Mérida's progress suddenly proved to be its ally. During the federation wars in the mid-19th century, when Venezuela was plunged into full-blown civil war, the city's solitude attracted refugees fleeing the bloodshed, and the population began to grow.

It was not, however, until the 1920s that access roads were constructed, and its transition from a town into a city really took place only over the past few decades. Why, now there's even a statue of Charlie Chaplin and a monument to Beethoven here, a sure sign of urban savoir faire.

### Orientation

You can never get lost in Mérida – just remember that uphill is always north and west, and downhill, south and east. Bounded on either side by two parallel rivers, the town sits on a sloping *meseta* (alluvial terrace) and stretches 12km from the colonial center in the north toward Ejido, its working-class suburb, in the south.

The bus terminal is about 2km south-by-southwest from the center, linked to downtown by frequent city buses.

### Information

#### EMERGENCY

**Fire** (☎ 171)
**Police** (☎ 171)

#### LAUNDRY

Some posadas offer laundry service; if yours doesn't, there are many central facilities.

**Lavandería Andina** (Map p156; Av 7 Maldonado No 22-45)
**Lavandería Patty** (Map p156; cnr Av 8 & Calle 24)
**Lavandería La Especial** (Map p156; cnr Av 4 Simón Bolívar & Calle 15 Piñango)

#### MEDICAL SERVICES

**Clinica Albarregas** (Map p154; ☎ 244-8101, 244-7283; Calle Tovar 1-26)
**Clinica Mérida** (Map p154; ☎ 263-0652, 263-6395; Av Urdaneta 45-145)

#### MONEY

**Banco de Venezuela** (Map p156; Av 4 Simón Bolívar btwn Calles 23 Vargas & 24 Rangel)
**Banco Mercantil** (Map p156; cnr Av 5 Zerpa & Calle 18 Fernández Peña)
**Banesco** (Map p156; Calle 24 Rangel btwn Avs 4 Simón Bolívar & 5 Zerpa)
**BBVA** (Map p156; Av 4 Simón Bolívar at Calle 14 Ricaurte)

#### POST

**Ipostel** (Map p156; Calle 21 Lazo btwn Avs 4 Simón Bolívar & 5 Zerpa)

#### TELEPHONE

**CANTV** (Map p156; cnr Calle 26 Campo Elías & Av 3 Independencia) Also has internet.

**Movistar** (Map p156; Calle 20 Federación No 4-64) Also has internet.

### TOURIST INFORMATION

**Cormetur** (Corporación Merideña de Turismo; ☎ 0800-637-4300; cormeturpromocion@hotmail.com) Main tourist office (Map p154; ☎ 262-1603, 263-4701; cnr Av Urdaneta & Calle 45; 🕑 8am-noon & 2-6pm Mon-Fri); Airport (Map p154; ☎ 263-9330; Av Urdaneta; 🕑 7am-6pm); Bus terminal (Map p154; ☎ 263-3952; Av Las Américas; 🕑 7am-7pm); Mercado Principal (Map p154; ☎ 262-1570; Av Las Américas; 🕑 7am-7pm Mon & Wed-Sat, to 2pm Tue & Sun); Teleférico (Map p156; ☎ 252-1997; Parque Las Heroínas; 🕑 7am-6pm Wed-Sun)

**Inparques** (Map p156; ☎ 262-1356, 262-1529; http://sierranevada.andigena.org; Teleférico, Parque Las

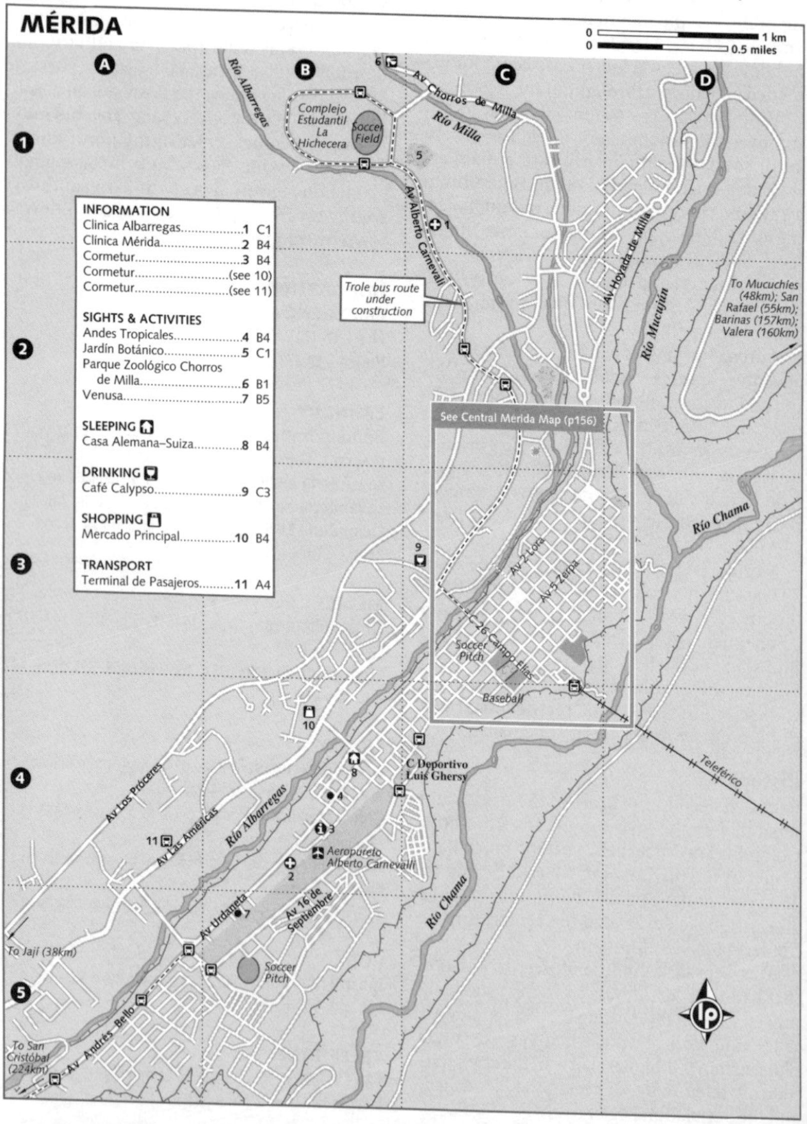

Heroínas) Offers permits for Parque Nacional Sierra Nevada and Parque Nacional Sierra La Culata.

## Sights

Mérida is a delightful place for a leisurely stroll. Marvel at the bustle in the central **Plaza Bolívar** (Map p156) near the city's business heart; or, at the north end of town, sit yourself down in a leafy spot in the redeveloped **Plaza Milla** (Map p156), a shady spot for a delicious picnic.

Check out the monumental **Catedral de Mérida** (Map p156). Begun in 1803, based on the plans of the 17th-century cathedral of Toledo in Spain, it was not completed until 1960, and probably only then because things were sped up to meet the 400th anniversary of the city's founding.

Next to the cathedral, the **Museo Arquidiocesano** (Map p156; ☎ 252-1238; Plaza Bolívar; admission BsF5; 🕑 9-11:30am & 2:30-3:30pm Mon-Fri, 10:30am-2:30pm Sat) features a fine collection of religious art. Note the Ave María bell cast in AD 909, thought to be the world's second-oldest surviving bell. It must have been brought from Spain by the missionaries and somehow ended up in the church of Jajó. By the early 20th century, though, it was unused and intended to be melted for reuse. Luckily, a priest from Valera sent it to Mérida for a closer inspection, thus saving it from destruction.

Across the plaza is the **Casa de la Cultura Juan Félix Sánchez** (Map p156; ☎ 808-3255; Plaza Bolívar; admission free; 🕑 9am-8pm Mon-Fri, to 5pm Sat). Rooms on the upper floor are used for temporary exhibitions of work by local artists and craftspeople. On the ground level there's a craft shop (see p162).

The building of the Universidad de los Andes, just off the plaza, houses the **Museo Arqueológico** (Map p156; ☎ 240-2344; cnr Av 3 Independencia & Calle 23 Vargas; admission BsF1; 🕑 8am-noon & 2-6pm Tue-Sun), which has a pottery collection dating from 25,000 BC to 50,000 BC.

The large, modern Centro Cultural Tulio Febres Cordero shelters the **Museo de Arte Moderno Juan Astorga Anta** (Map p156; ☎ 252-4380; Calle 21 Lazo btwn Avs 2 Lora & 3 Independencia; admission free; 🕑 9am-5pm Tue-Sat). It stages changing exhibitions of modern art by Venezuelan artists, and sometimes concerts.

Set in a beautiful 300-year-old mansion with a courtyard, the **Museo de Arte Colonial** (Map p156; ☎ 252-7860; cnr Av 4 Simón Bolívar & Calle 20 Federación; admission BsF1.50; 🕑 9am-4pm Tue-Sat) has a small but carefully assembled collection of sacred art, dating mostly from the 18th century.

The small Parque de las Cinco Repúblicas boasts Venezuela's oldest **Bolívar monument** (Map p156; Calle 13 Colón btwn Avs 4 Simón Bolívar & 5 Zerpa), dating from 1842. The small bust sitting atop a high, massive column looks totally out of proportion.

Visit the **Parque Zoológico Chorros de Milla** (Map p154; ☎ 244-3864; Av Chorros de Milla; admission BsF5; 🕑 8am-5pm Tue-Sun) on the northern outskirts of the city, 4km from the center. Set on a mountain slope along the Río Milla and named after the waterfalls in the park, the small, scenic zoo features a selection of local fauna, including jaguars, condors, anacondas, capybaras, tapirs and capuchin and spider monkeys. Don't miss walking uphill along the creek to see the waterfalls.

Not far from the zoo is the **Jardín Botánico** (Map p154; ☎ 416-0642; Av Alberto Carnevali; admission weekdays/weekend free/BsF5; 🕑 8am-5pm Tue-Sun). Inaugurated in 2000, the botanical garden is still young, and only a portion of the total 44 hectares is open to the public. Featuring a miniature cloud forest and more than 600 bromeliad species, it's worth visiting, particularly on Saturday or Sunday, when an unusual 'aerial path' is open for visitors (www.senderosaereos.com, in Spanish). You 'walk,' rappel and skim using ropes between platforms built atop four tall trees. The 'trip' takes between 45 minutes and 1½ hours and costs BsF40 to BsF50.

## Activities

Mérida is the adventure-sports capital of Venezuela, and offers excellent conditions for activities as diverse as canyoning, paragliding, rock-climbing, rafting, mountaineering, bird-watching and horseback riding. There's even bungee jumping *(pendulo)* from a nearby bridge. There are heaps of local tour operators – see p159 for details.

### HIKING & TREKKING

There are excellent hiking and trekking opportunities on the trails linking the many remote villages in the mountains around Mérida (see the boxed text, p166) and in the Parques Nacionales Sierra Nevada (p164) and Sierra La Culata (p166).

### PARAGLIDING

Of Mérida's wide array of adventure sports, paragliding is easily the most iconic – there's

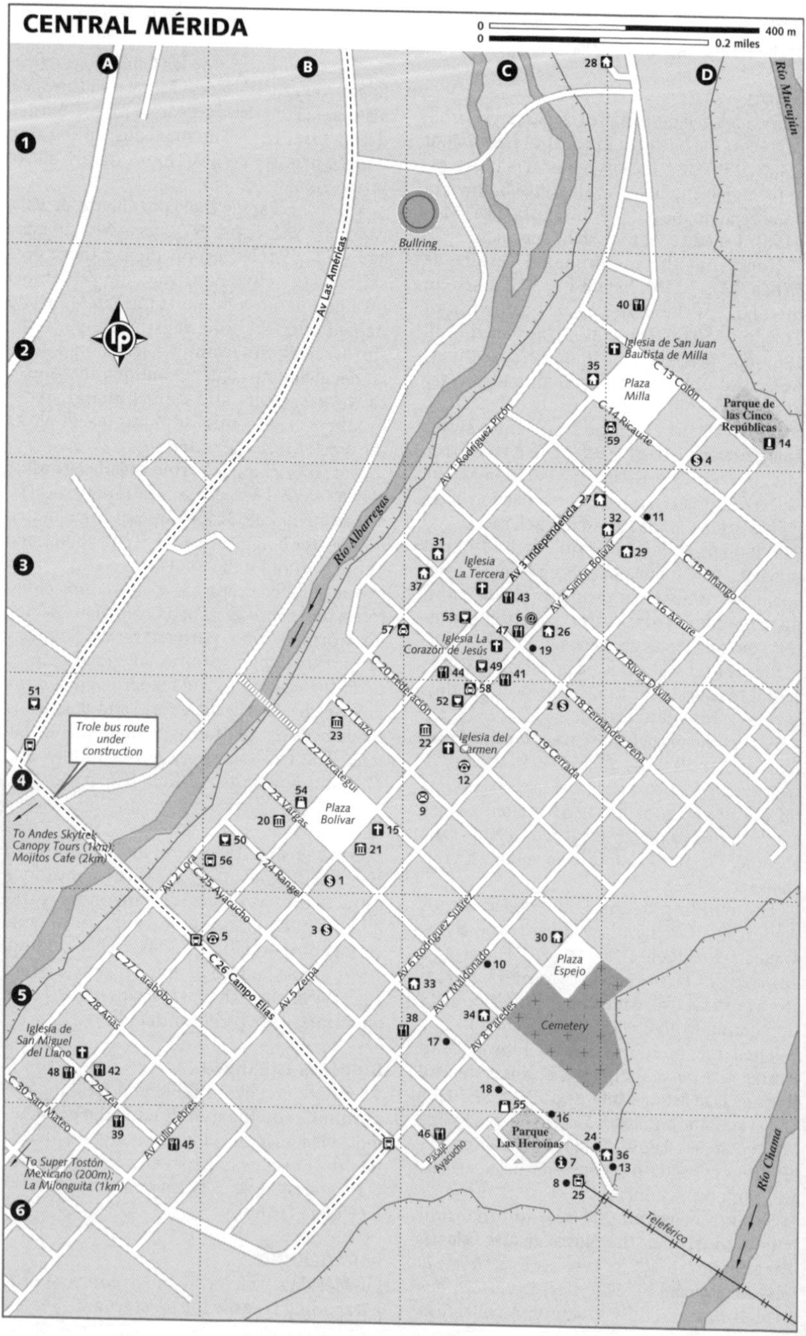
CENTRAL MÉRIDA
0
400 m
0
0.2 miles
A
B
C
D
1
2
3
4
5
6
Bullring
Río Mucujún
Av Las Américas
Río Albarregas
Av 1 Rodríguez Picón
Iglesia de San Juan Bautista de Milla
Plaza Milla
C 13 Colón
C 14 Ricaurte
Parque de las Cinco Repúblicas
Av 3 Independencia
Av 4 Simón Bolívar
Iglesia La Tercera
Iglesia La Corazón de Jesús
C 15 Piñango
C 16 Araure
C 17 Rivas Dávila
C 18 Fernández Peña
C 19 Cerrada
C 20 Federación
C 21 Lazo
C 22 Uzcátegui
C 23 Vargas
C 24 Rangel
C 25 Ayacucho
C 26 Campo Elías
C 27 Carabobo
C 28 Arias
C 29 Zea
C 30 San Mateo
Iglesia del Carmen
Plaza Bolívar
Trole bus route under construction
To Andes Skytrek Canopy Tours (1km); Mojitos Cafe (2km)
Av 2 Lora
Av 5 Zerpa
Av 6 Rodríguez Suárez
Av 7 Maldonado
Av 8 Paredes
Plaza Espejo
Cemetery
Iglesia de San Miguel del Llano
Av Tulio Febres
To Super Tostón Mexicano (200m); La Milonguita (1km)
Pasaje Ayacucho
Parque Las Heroínas
Teleférico
Río Chama
1
2
3
4
5
6
7
8
9
10
11
12
13
14
15
16
17
18
19
20
21
22
23
24
25
26
27
28
29
30
31
32
33
34
35
36
37
38
39
40
41
42
43
44
45
46
47
48
49
50
51
52
53
54
55
56
57
58
59

even pictures of paragliders on the side of the city's garbage trucks. Most visitors glide on tandem gliders with a skilled pilot, so no previous experience is necessary. The usual starting point for flights is Las González, an hour-long jeep ride from Mérida, from where you glide for 20 to 30 minutes down 850 vertical meters. The cost of the flight (BsF360) includes jeep transportation. For an extra BsF70 you may buy a CD containing a short video and photos of your flight.

You can also take a paragliding course that lasts approximately one week, covering theory (available in English) and practice (including solo flights); the cost is BsF5000 to BsF6000. The course allows you to fly solo, but you'll still have to rent a paraglider (BsF300 per flight, BsF3000 to BsF3500 per week, transportation included).

**Parapente Merida** (☎ 0414-746-0210; www.parapentemerida.com) is a group of the most seasoned pilots in town (all with more than 12 years of flying experience) who offer piloted flights as well as week-long courses.

### CANYONING & RAFTING

Canyoning is one of the more recent adventure sports to become popular in the area. Not for the faint of heart, it consists of climbing, rappelling and hiking down a river canyon, and through its waterfalls. It's been described by travelers as 'awesome, terrifying, beautiful, insane but amazing' and 'quite possibly the maddest thing you can do without getting killed.' Full-day, all-inclusive canyoning tours go for around BsF350.

White-water rafting takes place on some rivers on the Andes' southern and western slopes. It can be included in a tour to Los Llanos or done separately as a two- to four-day rafting tour (BsF250 per day). It's normally a wet-season activity, but some rivers allow for year-round rafting. Arassari Trek (p159) offers some of the most adventurous canyoning and rafting tours.

### CANOPY TOURS

Zip-lining, or canopy touring, is the latest craze to hit altitude-addicted Mérida. Two sites offer wickedly quick zips through the tree tops, high above the orange trees and banana plants below. **Andes Skytrek Canopy Tours** (☎ 0424-733-3566; Ave Los Porceros, sector Las Quebraditas) is a 2km walk from town (look for the big tire at the entrance to the road) and currently has three stations. **Trioleza** has two stations totaling 120m and a precarious wooden bridge, open daily in the high season and on weekends in the low season (BsF20 for children and BsF30 for adults). Trioleza trips are organized by Guamanchi Expeditions (p159). You can also do this activity at the city's **Jardín Botánico** (p155) on the weekends.

### MOUNTAIN BIKING

Biking has taken Venezuela by storm, and several tour companies organize trips and

**INFORMATION**

- Banco de Venezuela .......... **1** B4
- Banco Mercantil .......... **2** C4
- Banesco .......... **3** B5
- BBVA .......... **4** D2
- CANTV .......... **5** B5
- Ciber Café El Russo .......... **6** C3
- Cormetur .......... **7** C6
- Inparques .......... **8** C6
- Ipostel .......... **9** C4
- Lavandería Andina .......... **10** C5
- Lavandería La Especial .......... **11** D3
- Lavanderia Patty .......... (see 36)
- Movistar .......... **12** C4

**SIGHTS & ACTIVITIES**

- Arassari Trek .......... **13** D6
- Bolívar Monument .......... **14** D2
- Casa de la Cultura Juan Félix Sánchez .......... (see 54)
- Catedral de Mérida .......... **15** B4
- Cumbre Azul .......... **16** C6
- Gravity Tours .......... **17** C5
- Guamanchi Expeditions .......... **18** C5
- Iowa Institute .......... **19** C3
- Museo Arqueológico .......... **20** B4
- Museo Arquidiocesano .......... **21** B4
- Museo de Arte Colonial .......... **22** C4
- Museo de Arte Moderno Juan Astorga Anta .......... **23** B4
- Natoura Adventure Tours .......... **24** C6
- Teleférico .......... **25** C6

**SLEEPING**

- Hotel El Tisure .......... **26** C3
- Hotel Mistafí .......... **27** C3
- Hotel Prado Río .......... **28** C1
- La Casona de Margot .......... **29** D3
- Mérida Suites .......... **30** C5
- Posada Alemania .......... **31** C3
- Posada Casa Sol .......... **32** D3
- Posada Guamanchi .......... (see 18)
- Posada La Montaña .......... **33** C5
- Posada Los Escaladores .......... **34** C5
- Posada Luz Caraballo .......... **35** C2
- Posada Patty .......... **36** D6
- Posada Vene-Suiza .......... **37** C3

**EATING**

- Buona Pizza .......... **38** C5
- Café Mogambo .......... **39** A6
- Casa Andina .......... **40** D2
- Europe Art Cafe .......... **41** C3
- Heladería Coromoto .......... **42** A5
- La Abadía .......... **43** C3
- La Mamma & Sushi-Bar .......... **44** C3
- La Sevillana .......... **45** A6
- La Trattoria da Lino .......... **46** C6
- Restaurant Vegetariano .......... **47** C3
- TéCafé .......... **48** A5

**DRINKING**

- Alfredo's Bar .......... **49** C3
- Birosca Carioca .......... **50** B4
- El Bodegón de Pancho .......... **51** A4
- El Hoyo del Queque .......... **52** C4
- Gurten Café Poco Loco .......... **53** C3

**SHOPPING**

- Casa de la Cultura Juan Félix Sánchez .......... **54** B4
- Mercado Artesanal .......... **55** C5

**TRANSPORT**

- Buses to Bus Terminal .......... **56** B4
- Por Puestos to La Culata .......... **57** B3
- Por Puestos to Los Aleros .......... **58** C4
- Taxi .......... **59** D2

rent bikes. Shop around, as bicycle quality and rental prices may differ substantially between companies. One of the more popular bike tours is the loop around the remote mountain villages south of Mérida known as Pueblos del Sur. For a more challenging ride, try a trip up and back to El Refugio in Parque Nacional Sierra la Culata. The downhill through the high grasslands really gets the adrenaline pumping (you can do the same from the villages above the parapente site south of town). Bike rental varies from BsF100 to BsF120 a day. For information on the national biking craze, visit www.ciclismototal.net.

#### WILDLIFE-WATCHING

A recommended excursion out of Mérida is a wildlife safari to Los Llanos (p180), the immense savanna south of the Andes that offers some of Venezuela's best wildlife-watching. Most tour companies in Mérida offer this trip, usually as a four-day tour for about BsF1000.

There is excellent bird-watching in the Sierra Nevada around Mérida. The most popular destination is the Humboldt Trail, which winds its way from the Inparques office at La Mucuy to the summit of Pico Humboldt (p165). The most popular high-mountain trekking area is the Parque Nacional Sierra Nevada, east of Mérida, which has all of Venezuela's highest peaks, including Pico Bolívar, Pico Humboldt and Pico Bonpland (4883m). Climbing these peaks shouldn't be attempted without a guide unless you have climbing experience. Guided trips are offered by most of Mérida's tour operators (opposite). It's normally walked as an overnight or multiday hike, but also makes a great birding day trip, where you are likely to see scores of bird species and the occasional *oso frontino* (spectacled bear).

### Courses

Mérida is a very good place to study and practice Spanish. In the Andes, Spanish is spoken more slowly than in other parts of the country,

#### MÉRIDA – A LAND OF FIESTAS

There's always an excuse for a party, and in no place is this more so than Mérida. The biggest annual bash is unquestionably the **Feria del Sol**, held in the week before Ash Wednesday. There's music, dancing, sports events, bullfights and – of course – a beauty pageant.

The mountain towns around Mérida are also rich in festivities, most of which have religious roots and are linked to the religious calendar. You can take it for granted that every village will be holding a celebratory feast on the day of its patron saint. There are frequent local buses to all the following destinations; enquire at the tourist office for details.

**January – Paradura del Niño** Game in which villagers 'steal' the infant Jesus from his crib, then search for him and celebrate his 'finding'; it's popular throughout the region for the entire month.

**January 6 – Los Reyes Magos (Epiphany)** Particularly solemn carol-singing ceremony in the town of Santo Domingo.

**February 2 – Los Vasallos de la Candelaria** Ritual dances in La Parroquia, Mucuchíes, Bailadores and La Venta.

**Easter – Semana Santa (Holy Week, leading up to Easter)** Observed in many towns and villages, including La Parroquia, Lagunillas, Santo Domingo, Chiguará and La Azulita.

**May 15 – Fiesta de San Isidro Labrador** A type of agrarian rite in honor of the patron saint of farmers, celebrated with processions featuring domestic animals and crops; it's most elaborate in Apartaderos, Mucuchíes, Tabay, Bailadores and La Azulita.

**July 25 – Fiesta de Santo Apóstol** Held in Lagunillas, Ejido and Jají.

**September 30 – Los Negros de San Gerónimo** Celebrated in Santo Domingo.

**October 24 – Fiesta de San Rafael** Patron saint's day feast in San Rafael.

**December 8 – Fiesta de la Inmaculada Concepción** Spectacular display of some 20,000 candles, which are lit in the evening in the main plaza of Mucurubá.

**December 29 – Fiesta de San Benito** Event held in honor of Venezuela's only black saint, in which the locals take to the streets in red-and-black costumes (and sometimes black-colored faces) and spend the day dancing to the rhythm of drums and parading from door to door; observed in Timotes, La Venta, Apartaderos and Mucuchíes.

**December 31 – Despedida del Año Viejo (Farewell to the Old Year)** Midnight burning of life-sized human puppets, often stuffed with fireworks, which have been prepared weeks before and placed in front of the houses; celebrated regionally.

**NATIONAL PARK PERMITS**

Some of Mérida's tour operators can provide information about the tours discussed in this chapter, as well as other do-it-yourself tours. Don't ignore their comments about safety measures. If you are going to stay overnight in either the Parque Nacional Sierra Nevada or Parque Nacional Sierra La Culata, you need a permit from Inparques. Permits cost BsF7 per person per night and BsF12 per tent and are issued on the spot by Inparques outlets at the park's entry points, including one next to the cable-car station (see p154), one in La Mucuy and another one by Laguna Mucabají. If you are climbing Pico Humboldt or Pico Bolívar, you should go with a certified guide (travel agencies in Mérida charge about BsF350 per day). Bring your passport, as most rangers will ask to see your identification before granting a permit. Don't forget to return the permit after completing your hike – this is to make sure nobody is left wandering lost in the mountains.

so you are likely to find it easier to understand. The city has several language schools and the prices of language courses tend to be lower here than just about anywhere else in the country.

There are also plenty of students and tutors offering private lessons – enquire at popular traveler hotels and tour companies.

Institutions offering Spanish courses include the following:

**Iowa Institute** (Map p156; ☎ 252-6404; www.iowainstitute.com; cnr Av 4 Simón Bolívar & Calle 18)

**Venusa** (Map p154; ☎ 263-7631; www.venusacollege.org; Edificio Guilam, Av Urdaneta 49-49)

## Tours

Mérida is chock-a-block with tour companies, and the competition helps keep prices reasonable. Mountain trips figure prominently in most agencies' offerings; for treks to nearby Pico Bolívar and Pico Humboldt, expect to pay BsF350 to BsF400 per person per day.

Trekking to the mountain village of Los Nevados is another popular mountain trip. Most companies offer trips there, but you can easily do it on your own. It's a two- to three-day trip.

If you've got a hankering for some off-the-beaten-track hiking, check out the *mucuposadas* (see the boxed text, p166). Tours organized by **Andes Tropicales** (Map p154; ☎ 263-8633; www.andestropicales.org; cnr Av 2 Lora & Calle 41), the travel-agency wing of the not-for-profit development company, is especially recommended. (It can also organize domestic/international airline tickets, and transfers to and from the trail heads.)

Special-interest tours readily available in Mérida focus on paragliding, canyoning, wildlife-watching, mountain biking, rafting, rock climbing and horseback riding. Some companies handle rental of mountaineering equipment, camping gear and bikes; if you just need equipment, not a guide or a tour, check **Cumbre Azul** (Map p156; ☎ 251-0455; www.cumbreazul.com; Calle 24 Rangel No 8-153), which specializes in rental.

Following are the best established and most reliable local tour companies:

**Arassari Trek** (Map p156; ☎ /fax 252-5879; www.arassari.com; Calle 24 Rangel No 8-301) This Swiss-owned outfit pioneered many of the most popular tours in Mérida, including trips to Los Llanos and to Catatumbo. It offers a full range of some of the most creative rafting, canyoning, biking, trekking and mountaineering tours, and also sells domestic and international airline tickets.

**Cocolight** ( ☎ 0414-756-2575; alanconda@gmail.com, catatumbo@cocolight.com) Respected British naturalist Alan Highton has recently formed his own specialty company, Cocolight, for Catatumbo tours, with a unique camp. See www.cocolight.com for details.

**Gravity Tours** (Map p156; ☎ 252-1279; www.gravity-tours.com.ve; Calle 24 Rangel btwn Av 7 & 8) This decade-old, established company has young, experienced bilingual guides, and owner Gustavo Viloria has led many Audubon trips to Venezuela and is a keen and expert wildlife-spotter. A provider of fun and safe trips.

**Guamanchi Expeditions** (Map p156; ☎ 252-2080; www.guamanchi.com; Calle 24 Rangel No 8-86) This hands-on tour company, one of the longest-operating in Mérida, is owned and run by John Peña, a long-time mountain guide. It offers a selection of well-prepared tours up the mountains and down to Los Llanos, and also runs rafting and canyoning trips. It has bicycles for rent, and the staff is happy to provide information on do-it-yourself biking and walking trips. Check out its posada in Los Nevados.

**Natoura Adventure Tours** (Map p156; ☎ 252-4216; www.natoura.com; Calle 31 at Avenida Don Tulio) Managed by José Luis Troconis, this heavyweight travel agency specializes in custom-tailored travel and adventure tourism, and will happily organize your trip for you from overseas. It uses good gear and conducts tours in small groups, with quality guides. Only open Monday to Friday.

**Chal Tours** (☎ 0274-252 5344; www.chaltours.com.ve; Av 3 Independencia, btwn Calles 28 & 29, Mini Centro Acuario, Local 5-C Mérida, Edo Mérida) Mérida-born Roger Manrique is a Mérida-born naturalist who specializes in ornithology and biology-based tours, such as bird-watching and a 'butterfly odyssey', with his 20-year old company Chal Tours .

There are plenty of other tour operators in town, many of which nestle around Parque Las Heroínas and along Calle 24 Rangel. They may be reliable and will cost much the same or even less than those listed. Shop around, talk to other travelers and check things before deciding.

## Sleeping

Mérida has heaps of places to stay all across the center. Most of these are posadas, which are usually small, inexpensive family-run guesthouses with a friendly atmosphere. Nearly all have hot water and provide laundry facilities, and some allow guests to use the kitchen.

The line between hotel and posada, though, is increasingly blurring, as some of the newer posadas outstrip hotels in luxury and service. Should you prefer a conventional hotel, however, there are several reasonable midrange-to-high-end places to lay your head for the night.

### BUDGET

**Posada Patty** (Map p156; ☎ 251-1052; Calle 24 Rangel No 8-265; r without bathroom per person BsF30, per person in either dm or matrimonial BsF50) Friendly Colombian Patty offers some of the cheapest beds in town. They're on the spartan side, with shared bathrooms, but the price is unbeatable. You can use the kitchen and fridge, and Patty also offers some of the cheapest laundry services around (and not just for the guests).

**Posada Alemania** (Map p156; ☎ 252-4067; Av 2 Lora No 17-76; dm/s BsF40/60, d BsF100-120; wi-fi) This Venezuelan-run posada is a popular one. Rooms surround a central garden courtyard, and there's a good kitchen guests can use. The owner runs a tour agency from the posada.

**Posada Vene-Suiza** (Map p156; ☎ 252-4961; cnr Av 2 Lora & Calle 18 Fernández Peña; dm per person BsF40, s without bathroom BsF50, d with/without bathroom BsF120/80) The Vene-Suiza is a similar style as the Alemania, and is just that little bit nicer. It offers 10 rooms set around a colonial-style courtyard, and has a quiet terrace with hammocks at the back, with views of the mountains.

our pick **Posada Guamanchi** (Map p156; ☎ 252-2080; www.guamanchi.com; Calle 24 Rangel No 8-86; d with/without bathroom BsF120/90, tr with/without bathroom BsF165/135) This rambling posada with four floors, a terrace and two kitchens is the sort of place where rough-stubbled, fleece-wearing, sun-reddened mountain climbers stumble into the rooftop lounge with cries of 'dude, wicked cool!' Grab a double at the back, if you can; they have great views.

**Posada Los Escaladores** (Map p156; ☎ 252-2411; www.elescalador.com; Calle 23 Vargas No 7-70; d/tr BsF150/250) The 'Mountain Climbers' is a good place to begin or end a mountain adventure. It's just around the corner from most of the agencies, and the posada rents rain jackets, too. Good, clean value.

**Posada La Montaña** (Map p156; ☎ 252-5977; posadalamontana@intercable.net.ve; Calle 24 Rangel No 6-47; s/d/tr BsF150/195/220; wi-fi) This classic, well-run posada is a perennial favorite for its location, well-kept rooms and helpful staff. Rooms have bathrooms, safety deposit boxes, minibars and a terrace tempts with hammocks and gorgeous mountain views. The restaurant downstairs serves high-quality meals, including solid breakfasts.

**Casa Alemana-Suiza** (Map p154; ☎ 263-6503; www.casa-alemana.com; cnr Av 2 Lora & Calle 38 No 130; d/ste BsF150/250) In the south end of town, this posada has a different feel from the more touristy center. The rooms are spacious and quiet; treat yourself, if you can, to a suite with a Jacuzzi. The roof deck has great views of the mountains and Alemana-Suiza can also organize tours all over the country.

**Posada Luz Caraballo** (Map p156; ☎ 252-5441; fax 252-0177; Av 2 Lora No 13-80; s/d/tr BsF160/250/270) Facing the tree-filled Plaza Milla, the Luz offers 42 rooms spread over three floors. Popular with tour groups and serving basic meals downstairs, this well-maintained posada can't quite shake that just-a-motel feeling. Ask for a room in the new wing on the third floor: the old one is rather downtrodden.

**La Casona de Margot** (Map p156; ☎ 252-3312; www.lacasonademargot.com; Av 4 Simón Bolívar No 15-17; d/tr BsF180/220; wi-fi) The stylish rooms in this old colonial building boast such high ceilings that some rooms have been lofted – perfect for a large family. Free coffee, fluffy white towels and a small garden patio add to the allure.

### MIDRANGE & TOP END

**Hotel El Tisure** (Map p156; ☎ 252-6072; www.venaventours.com/hoteltisure; Av 4 Simón Bolívar No 17-47; s BsF200, d BsF290-320, tr BsF360, ste BsF440-480; wi-fi) Owned by a

Frenchwoman from Martinique, this delightfully cozy hotel and friendly staff will appeal to those with European tastes, and is exceptional value for the price. Good location, and a quality bar and restaurant downstairs.

**Mérida Suites** (Map p156; ☎ 251-2459; fax 251-2650; www.meridasuites.com; Av 8 Parades btwn Calles 21 Lazo & 22 Uzcategui; d/tr BsF240/280; P ) This swish hotel offers five fully self-contained apartments with kitchen, pots and pans, stove, fridge, computer with broadband and washer-dryer combos. It's set in a central yet tranquil spot, just opposite the Plaza Espejo. Discounts are available for stays longer than a week.

**Hotel Mistafí** (Map p156; ☎ 251-0729; www.hotelmistafi.com.ve; cnr Av 3 & Calle 15; d/tr BsF270/300, ste BsF455-485; ). The marble halls are classy, but frequent large groups means that noise-wise, the ostentatious Mistafí can be a bit boomy. For a touch of tranquility with your Scotch, ask for a room at the back – they have mountain views.

**Hotel Prado Río** (Map p156; ☎ 252-0633; www.hotelpradorio.com.ve; Av 1 Rodríguez Picón; s BsF280, d BsF380-400, tr BsF420-650, ste BsF810-1520; ) Set in vast, walled-in grounds, the Prado Río offers the faded glory of the Venezuelan *bourgeois*, now maintained by a small army of Bolivarian worker-bees. Besides the 13 spacious rooms in the main hotel building, there's a colony of 66 cabañas arranged in the form of a Mediterranean town with a further 84 rooms. The complex is well maintained and adorned with flowers, and has its own restaurant, a large swimming pool and outdoor bar.

our pick **Posada Casa Sol** (Map p156; ☎ 252-4164; www.posadacasasol.com; Av 4 Simón Bolívar btwn Calles 15 Piñango & 16 Araure; d/tr/ste BsF290/320/375; ) This exquisite guesthouse challenges the definition of a posada, with a sense of luxury and service normally expected from a fine hotel. Walls dripping with cast-iron sculpture, stained glass, high-thread-count sheets, multilingual staff and breakfast under an ancient avocado tree all add up to a very memorable experience. Splurge on a minisuite, if you can.

## Eating

our pick **Heladería Coromoto** (Map p156; ☎ 252-3525; Av 3 Independencia No 28-75; ice cream BsF9-20; 2:15pm-9pm Tue-Sun) The most famous ice cream parlor in South America, Coromoto holds the *Guinness Book of Records* title for most number of ice-cream flavors. Eat your heart out, Baskin-Robbins: this place has more than 900 for you to taste (about 70 varieties available per week). Try the tuna flavor, a Diet-Coca Cola cone, or even a Mexican sundae – black bean, beef, chili, onion and tomato. *¡Olé!*

**Te'Café** (Map p156; cnr Av 3 Independencia & Calle 29 Zea; meals BsF15-25; 8am-midnight; ) Choose from breakfasts, sandwiches, pizza and delicious herbal tea infusions at this hip, open-air cafe-restaurant. The cafe is blessed with wi-fi, and is a good place for a coffee by day or a beer by night. Try the New York Café – with a gob of ice cream on top, of course.

our pick **La Trattoria da Lino** (Map p156; ☎ 252-9555; Pasaje Ayacucho; meals BsF15-30) If you are after a fine Italian lunch (until 4:30pm weekdays), you won't go wrong coming to this well-appointed restaurant with a delicate Mediterranean touch. Savor the homemade gnocchi with a glass of merlot.

**Café Mogambo** (Map p156; ☎ 252-5643; cnr Calle 29 Zea & Av 4 Simón Bolívar; breakfast BsF20-25, meals BsF45-65) With its prominent 1920s-style bar, art deco plasterwork, soft lighting and antique ceiling fans, mood is the name of the game in this trendy bistro, a haven for wine buffs. Breakfast and dinner is served, and on weekend nights you'll hear live jazz drifting in from trios in the corner.

**Super Tostón Mexicano** (Map p156; ☎ 0414-374-0937; Ave 4 Simón Bolívar btwn Calle 32 & 33; meals BsF25-36) *Que?* You wanted Mexican food and Venezuelan mixed together? *No hay problema* – here, traditional Mexican dishes like chalupas and tamales all get served on top of a mini *tostón*, the traditional fried banana dish of Venezuela. Becoming a fast (literally) favorite for *meridenas*.

**Casa Andina** (Map p156; ☎ 252-4811; Av 2 Lora No 12-30; set meal BsF25, meals BsF30-35) Budget eaters, rejoice – with the best, cheapest set meals in town, this historic restaurant-cum-museum is worth the short walk to the edge of town. Tables surround a lovely garden patio, and a few front rooms house a collection of pre-Hispanic stone and pottery pieces.

**Restaurant Vegetariano** (Map p156; Av 4 Simón Bolívar No 17-84; meals BsF25-30; 8am-9pm) This salad-lover's delight is a welcome refuge from the usual Venezuelan deep-fried yumminess. Wholemeal (baked) empanadas, natural juices, good bread and desserts.

**Europa Art Cafe** (Map p156; Av 4 Simón Bolívar No 19; meals BsF25-30; 9am-9pm) Indigenous-themed photos line the wall of this German-owned establishment, chock-a-block full of simple fare including German sausage and meatballs, Hungarian goulash and Russian potato salad. Breakfasts of yogurt and granola are a bit easier on the arteries. Friendly staff, good-value set lunch.

**La Mama & Sushi Bar** (Map p156; ☎ 252-9437; Calle 29 Zea btwn Avs 4 Simón Bolívar & 5 Zerpa; meals BsF30-50) Mama moved recently from Calle 16 but still serves up a hearty pizza, has a nice wine list and a sushi bar.

**Buona Pizza** (Map p156; ☎ 252-7639; Av 7 Maldonado No 24-46; pizza BsF30-60) Convenient, central and open till late, this is a recommended budget pizza outlet: Takeaway is available.

**La Abadía** (Map p156; ☎ 251-0933; www.grupoabadia.com; Av 3 Independencia No 17-45; meals BsF30-70; noon-11pm) This meticulously reconstructed former monastery is a Mérida institution, and serves good-quality salads, meat and pasta – plus you get 30 minutes of free internet before or after your meal.

**La Sevillana** (Map p156; ☎ 252-9628; cnr Tulio Febres & Calle 29 Zea; meals BsF30-70) Wine racks line the walls of this classic Spanish seafood restaurant, where the specialty is fish, just about any which way you like it – there's even German and Chilean dishes on the menu.

## Drinking

Party nights in Mérida are, of course, Thursday, Friday and Saturday. Things don't normally get popping until 10pm or 11pm, and go until late, late, late.

**Alfredo's Bar** (Map p156; cnr Av 4 Simón Bolívar & Calle 19 Cerrada) This bar competes for the cheapest beer in Venezuela, and at prices like these (about BsF4 per bottle) plenty of people come to dance, or just watch baseball. The large outdoor area at the back pumps the *reggaetón* (fusion of music styles including hip-hop and reggae) to the stars, and a smaller front lounge swings with salsa and merengue.

**Birosca Carioca** (Map p156; ☎ 252-3804; www.biroscacarioca.com; Calle 24 Rangel No 2-04; to 3am) As its Facebook page says, 'if you're someone who hates *reggaetón*, this is your place.' It plays plenty of ska, rock and reggae, and occasionally hosts live music events. The student crowd forgoes glassware in favor of bright-blue plastic sand-castle buckets – try not to lose track of which straw is yours.

**Café Calypso** (Map p154; Centro Comercial Viaducto; 9am-late Mon-Sat) This mild-mannered shopping center cafe has a secret identity. By day, it's a tranquil coffee bar. Come back at night, though, and Mr Hyde emerges, when international DJs freak it up with the techno and the barman serves up some of the tastiest *caipirinhas* and *mojitos* in town. Open till 3am, and sometimes later, the Calypso rarely fills up before midnight.

**El Bodegón de Pancho** (Map p156; ☎ 244-9819; Centro Comercial Mamayera, Av Las Américas) Within walking distance from the center, El Bodegón is one of the oldest discos in town, and it continues to draw crowds. The timber-decked ground-level hall has the charm of an old tavern and vibrates with Latin rhythms, with bands usually playing on Friday. Upstairs is a large dance floor, which blasts out hip-hop, trance and the like.

**El Hoyo del Queque** (Map p156; ☎ 252-4306; cnr Av 4 Simón Bolívar & Calle 19 Cerrada) Some say this is the best bar in Mérida. Others disagree. No, they say, it's the best bar in Venezuela. It is definitely the hottest spot on Mérida's 'hot corner.' Whatever side you take, this rocking bar attracts a big crowd every night, often spilling into the street.

**Gurten Café Poco Loco** (Map p156; ☎ 251-2379; Av 3 Independencia btwn Calles 18 Fernández Peña & 19 Cerrada) This Swiss-owned sports bar packs them in till late with a mixture of rap, *reggaetón* and salsa. The owner loves *fútbol* and it's on every hour the bar is open.

**Mojitos Cafe** (Map p156; Centro Comercial el Terminal) Perhaps El Ché would not have appreciated this for-profit venture, but the red-juice-and-white-rum drink named in his honor is a wicked capitalist delight, as is the house specialty, the *mojito*. Get your revolution on in this two-story salute to Papa Fidel's island. It's just a 150m walk to the bus terminal, across from Parque de los Ninos and is perfect for recovery from, or preparation for, a long trip!

**La Milonguita** (Map p156; ☎ 244-5939; Ave Las Americas, Sector La Otra Banda, Centro Comercial Plaza Mayor) For pure dancing delight, La Milonguita is a dance academy/night spot where you can boogie to tango and salsa every weekend, often with live music. During the day, sip on an Argentinean *máte* in the cafe.

## Shopping

Mérida is a good place to buy local crafts.

**Casa de la Cultura Juan Félix Sánchez** (Map p156; ☎ 808-3255; Plaza Bolívar; 9am-noon & 3-6pm Mon-Sat) The large, well-stocked craft shop on the ground level offers a wide variety of authentic, locally made handicrafts.

**Mercado Artesanal** (Map p156; Parque Las Heroínas; 9am-6pm) This small, arty crafts market sits just opposite the Parque Las Heroínas, near the *teleférico,* and is home to a dozen stalls selling arts and crafts.

**Mercado Principal** (Map p154; ☎ 262-1570, 262-0437; Av Las Américas; 7am-4pm) This vast, busy and colorful main city market has dozens of stalls selling arts and crafts. Some of the city's best traditional food is also to be found on the 2nd floor. Try dishes such as *pechuga rellena a la merideña* (chicken breast stuffed with ham and cheese, breaded, deep-fried, and slathered in mushroom sauce). On the ground floor, hit the bull's-eye with a *levantón andino* (Andean 'big lifter'), a milkshake reputed to enhance virility, made of half a dozen fruits, vegetables, raw quail eggs, raisin wine and the special ingredient – two raw bulls' eyes, slit open and squeezed into the blender.

## Getting There & Away

### AIR

The **Aeropuerto Alberto Carnevalli**, 2km southwest of Plaza Bolívar, has been closed since late 2008 and now the nearest airport to Mérida is in **El Vigia**, 1¼ hours away by por puesto – many tour companies will arrange transportation. Conviasa and Santa Barbara have two flights per day to and from Caracas (BsF206 to BsF377).

### BUS

The **Terminal de Pasajeros** (Bus Terminal; Map p154; ☎ 263-3952; Av Las Américas) is 3km southwest of the city center; it's linked by frequent public buses, which depart from the corner of Calle 25 Ayacucho and Av 2 Lora.

Alianza and Expresos Merida each have three daily buses to Caracas (BsF81) and Valencia (BsF71). Alianza also runs to Punto Fijo (BsF8) and Coro (BsF75). Expresos Merida goes to Barquisimeto (BsF55, six hours, 418kms) and Ciudad Bolívar (BsF144) as well as Coro (BsF75, 12 hours, 782km). Transportes Barinas has six daily buses to Barinas, the last one at 5pm (BsF24, four hours, 157km), and four to Valera (BsF30). Por puestos run to Barinas for BsF35; busetas to El Vigia (BsF8.50, 1¼ hours), Barinas (BsF30) and San Cristobal (BsF35, six hours, 224km) run frequently. Express Coromoto goes to Maracaibo twice daily via executive service or *bus-cama* (BsF46 to BsF55, 8:30am and 1:30pm).

Regional destinations, including Apartaderos and Jají (BsF4.50), are serviced regularly throughout the day.

### CAR & MOTORCYCLE

Driving in Venezuela is a heart-stopping experience for locals, let alone tourists with little background in the country's chaotic and difficult driving conditions. That being said, a small sedan-style car rented by the local companies will cost around BsF400 to BsF450 daily, including insurance and unlimited mileage.

**Budget** (☎ 262-2728) You must be 23 years of age or older and have an international driver's license and at least US$2500 on a credit card for security deposit.

## Getting Around

The city is well serviced by small buses and minibuses, but they stop running around 8pm to 9pm, leaving taxis as the only alternative. Taxis are cheap, so you may prefer to move around by taxi anyway. They are particularly convenient for trips to and from the bus terminal, when you're carrying all your bags with you. The trip between the city center and the bus terminal will cost about BsF15 each way. A trole bus line connecting Mérida to Ejido, its densely packed working-class suburb 12km to the south, is up and running, but there is no service to the center of town yet.

**Línea Las Mercedes** (☎ 0426-702-3928, 0424-742-5872) is a reliable taxi company with radio service, located conveniently on Plaza Milla. The company organizes taxi trips around the region, including to Jají, El Águila, Mucuchíes and San Rafael.

# AROUND MÉRIDA

The region that surrounds Mérida offers plenty of attractions, both natural and cultural. Many sights are accessible by road, so you can get around by public transportation. This is particularly true of the towns and villages on the Carretera Transandina and surrounding mountain slopes and valleys. Many of them have preserved their historic architecture and old-time atmosphere.

Exploring the region is quite easy, as transportation and accommodations along the Carretera Panamericana are in good supply. Virtually every sizable village on the road has at least one posada or hotel, and there are plenty of roadside restaurants.

Just outside of Mérida and accessible by buseta are **Laguna de Urao**, good for a refreshing dip (open from 7am to 5pm; take any bus toward Lagunillas), and the **Hacienda**

**La Victoria/Museo de Café** (☎ 0275-411-1731), an old coffee plantation in the town of Santa Cruz de Moro features original 18th-century British harvesting and milling equipment and a tasty cafe. It also houses the small Museum of Immigration. Take any La Estrella or Expresos Tovar por puesto toward Santa Cruz for this tasty visit.

## Parque Nacional Sierra Nevada

The most popular high-mountain trekking area is the Parque Nacional Sierra Nevada, east of Mérida, which has all of Venezuela's highest peaks, including Pico Bolívar, Pico Humboldt and Pico Bonpland (4883m). Climbing these peaks shouldn't be attempted without a guide unless you have climbing ex-

MUCUPOSADA TRAILS AROUND MÉRIDA

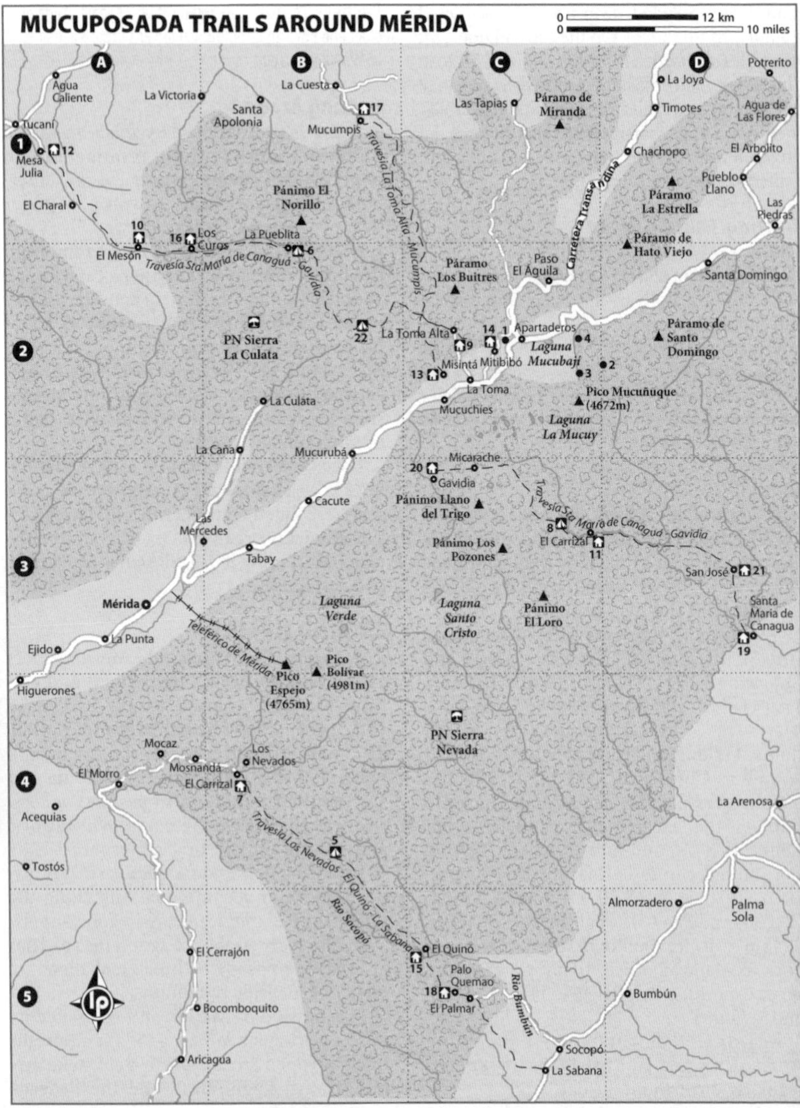

perience. Guided trips are offered by most of Mérida's tour operators (p159).

**Pico Bolívar**, Venezuela's highest peak (4981m), is one of the most popular peaks to climb (boy, were Venezuelans disappointed when its official height was lowered below 5000m based on new technology). Given the country's mania for Bolívar monuments, it's no surprise that a bust of the hero has been placed on the summit. The climb requires a rope, and ice and snow equipment in the rainy season, which will be provided by your guide. What you can do without a guide is hike along the trail leading up to Pico Bolívar. It roughly follows the cable-car line, but be careful walking from Loma Redonda to Pico Espejo – the trail is not clear and it's easy to get lost.

Venezuela's second-highest summit, **Pico Humboldt** (4942m), is also popular with high-mountain trekkers. There's not much here in the way of mountaineering, but the hike itself is marvelous. The starting point for the trek is La Mucuy, accessible by road from Mérida. A four- to six-hour walk from La Mucuy will take you up to the small **Laguna La Coromoto** (3200m), where trekkers normally camp the first night. The next day, it's a four-hour walk to reach **Laguna Verde** (4000m), one of the largest lakes in the area. Some hikers stay here the second night, or you can walk for another hour to **Laguna El Suero** (4200m), a tiny lake almost at the foot of the glacier. It gets freezing at night, so have plenty of warm clothes. Pico Humboldt is a two- to four-hour ascent, depending on the weather. You reach the snow line at about 4850m. Further up, crampons and an ice axe are recommended, and keep an eye out for crevasses. Again, this climb is best done with an experienced local guide, particularly in the rainy (snowy) season.

Back at Laguna El Suero, you can return the same way to La Mucuy or continue along the route known as **La Travesía** to the cable-car top station at Pico Espejo (4765m). After an initial 500m ascent from the lake, the trail to **Pico Espejo** (four to six hours) goes for most of the way at roughly the same altitude of nearly 4700m. You can then climb Pico Bolívar before returning to Mérida by foot. The whole loop normally takes four to six days.

A milder, less stressful hike is up to tranquil **Los Nevados**. For a two-day, one-night stay, take a jeep from Plaza Las Heroinas to Los Nevados (BsF70, five hours). Spend the afternoon trekking around Los Nevados, and spend the night in a nearby posada, of which there are several in the BsF80 to BsF150 range. The best of these is Bella Vista (thankfully with hot water!). The next day, go on horseback from Los Nevados to Valle del Indio (BsF30, four hours). Note that it is customary to tip the *arriero*, or horse wrangler, BsF30. Back in Los Nevados, have lunch in town and then take the jeep back to Mérida (BsF70). For the three-day, two-night option many hikers choose to go through a guide or tour agency from Mérida. Follow the same procedure for the first day, but on the second take a mule from Los Nevados to Estacion Loma Redonda (BsF40 each mule, plus *arriero's* tip, five hours). From Loma Redonda, trek 3.5km (about two hours) down to rustic **Posada Pedro Pena** (BsF70). Chill out there, and on the third morning trek down to La Mucunutan, and from there hop the jeep back to Mérida.

Rather than stay in Los Nevados itself, you can also walk an extra hour past the village to the 200-year-old **Hacienda el Carrizal** (☎ 263-8633; per person incl dinner & breakfast BsF83), part of the *mucuposada* network (see the boxed text, p166). It's a working farm that produces maize, wheat and potatoes, and you can either walk back to Los Nevados the next day, or use it to begin the five-day, four-night trans-Andean trek to El Quinó and La Sabana.

| SIGHTS & ACTIVITIES | | |
|---|---|---|
| Centro de Investigaciones de Astronomia (CIDA) | 1 | C2 |
| El Tisure | 2 | D2 |
| Laguna Los Patos | 3 | C2 |
| Laguna Negra | 4 | C2 |
| **SLEEPING** | | |
| Boca e' Monte | 5 | B4 |
| El Oso | 6 | B2 |
| Hacienda el Carrizal | 7 | B4 |
| Los Morritos | 8 | C3 |
| Mucuposada Agüita Azul | 9 | C2 |
| Mucuposada El Cafetal | 10 | A1 |
| Mucuposada El Carrizal | 11 | C3 |
| Mucuposada El Mirador | 12 | A1 |
| Mucuposada El Nidal del Gavilán | 13 | C2 |
| Mucuposada El Trigal | 14 | C2 |
| Mucuposada La Paragüita | 15 | C5 |
| Mucuposada Las Rositas | 16 | A1 |
| Mucuposada Los Bordones | 17 | B1 |
| Mucuposada Los Laureles | 18 | C5 |
| Mucuposada Los Samantes | 19 | D3 |
| Mucuposada Michicaba | 20 | C3 |
| Mucuposada San José | 21 | D3 |
| Pan de Azúcar Pico Pan de Azúcar | 22 | B2 |

### MUCUPOSADAS – ANCIENT TRAILS, HOT WATER

A spider's web of ancient trails links the many remote villages in the mountains around Mérida, in the Sierra Nevada and Sierra de la Culata. Until recently it has been difficult to explore this area – there was little in the way of accommodations, services or guides.

This is slowly changing, due largely to the efforts of Andes Tropicales (p159), a European Union microfinancing project whose goal is to promote rural tourism in the region. Since the mid-1990s it's been offering small, easily repaid loans to indigenous mountain villages to help them create the services necessary to attract visitors.

The result? A unique network of trails, with *mucuposadas* – '*mucu*' means 'place of' in the local dialect – each spaced a day's travel apart, permitting comfortable and relaxed four- to five-day treks, with hot showers and home-cooked food to look forward to every night. So remote, in fact, are some of these villages that a local guide or a GPS device are necessary, to prevent getting lost. You can even download the GPS data free of charge from the Andes Tropicales website.

The *mucuposada* trails follow more or less the existing ancient pathways through the mountains, and trek through cloud forest, pastureland, the glacial landscapes of the *páramo* (open highland) and even coffee and cacao plantations. In most cases the *mucuposadas* are the only places to stay in very remote, very beautiful locations.

The network has been extended in recent years to 21 posadas throughout the country, including treks around La Gran Sabana from Puerto Ordaz and a five-day trek from Mérida to Barinas.

This is sustainable, rural ecotourism at a budget price – the *mucuposadas* charge roughly BsF58 to BsF117 per night, including dinner and breakfast; tours organized by Andes Tropicales currently cost around BsF200 to BsF250 per day, local guide and mules included.

## Parque Nacional Sierra La Culata

The Parque Nacional Sierra La Culata, to the north of Mérida, also offers some amazing hiking territory, and is particularly noted for its desertlike highland landscapes. Take a por puesto to La Culata (departing from the corner of Calle 19 Cerrada and Av 2 Lora), from where it's a three- to four-hour hike uphill to a primitive shelter known as El Refugio, at about 3700m. Continue the next day for about three hours to the top of **Pico Pan de Azúcar** (4660m). Be sure to return before 4pm, the time the last por puesto tends to depart back to Mérida.

Some guided tours don't return the same way, but instead descend southeast through an arid moonscape-like terrain to a chain of mountain lakes and on down to Mucuchíes via natural hot springs. Trails are faint on this route, and it's easy to get lost if you don't know the way; don't wander too far unless you're an experienced trekker.

Another interesting area for hiking is further east, near **Pico El Águila** (4118m). Take a morning bus to Valera and get off at Venezuela's highest road pass, **Paso del Cóndor** (4007m), about 60km from Mérida. Bolívar marched this way on one of his campaigns, and a statue of a condor was built here in his honor (hence the name of the pass).

There's a roadside restaurant where you can have a hot chocolate before setting off. Take the side road up to Pico El Águila (a 20-minute walk), crowned with a communications mast to reach the panoramic beauty of the *páramo* (open highland), dotted with *frailejones* (espeletia) – hairy, spiky succulents with bright yellow flowers shooting from their centers.

Back at the pass, walk 5km south to **Laguna Mucubají** (3540m). The path leads through another splendid *páramo*, before descending to the Barinas road and the lake, one of the largest in the region. There is an Inparques post here that will provide information about the area. From here it's an hour's walk through reforested pine woods to **Laguna Negra**, a small beautiful mountain lake with amazingly dark water. A 45-minute walk further uphill will bring you to another fine lake, **Laguna Los Patos**.

A trail from Laguna Mucubají leads 7km south up to the top of **Pico Mucuñuque** (4672m), the highest peak in this range, which is known as the Serranía de Santo Domingo. The roundtrip will take the good part of a day. It's a rather difficult hike, as the trail is not clear in the upper reaches and you have to ascend over 1100m from the lagoon. Ask for detailed instructions at the Inparques post by Laguna Mucubají.

### Jají & Around

The best known of the mountain villages is Jají (*ha*-hee). It was extensively reconstructed in the late 1960s to become a manicured, typical (some say Disney-ish) *pueblo andino* (Andean town), and its delightful Plaza Bolívar is surrounded by a whitewashed church and old balconied houses that now host craft shops. Jají has a few posadas and restaurants should you like to linger longer, and you can visit an old coffee hacienda on the town's outskirts.

The town is about 38km west of Mérida, easily accessible by buses from the bus terminal (BsF4.50, 50 minutes). A bonus attraction is the spectacular access road from Mérida, which winds through lush cloud forest.

About 8km before Jají, beside the road, is the **Chorrera de las González**, a series of five waterfalls. You can stop here to bathe in the falls' ponds, or just to have a look. Instead of returning by bus straight back to Mérida, you can walk 1.5km along the road (toward Mérida) to a junction, take a right turn and walk another 7km to **La Mesa**, a fine old town. Por puestos from La Mesa will take you to the larger town of Ejido, where you change for Mérida. It's a great day trip out of Mérida.

### Mucuchíes & Around

For something a little less touristy, check out Mucuchíes, a 400-year-old *pueblo andino* which is especially proud of its beautiful parish church on Plaza Bolívar. It was here the locals gave Simon Bolívar 'Nevado', a *mucuchíes* (mastiff hybrid) puppy that accompanied him during his final battles. There's a monument to Nevado and The Liberator at the town's entrance. Stroll about the adjacent streets to see the lovely little houses; some of them are craft shops, offering attractive handmade textiles, particularly ponchos woven on archaic looms. You may need to buy a poncho if you stay for a while – it gets a bit chilly at night. The town has plenty of accommodations.

About 7km further up the road is the village of **San Rafael**, noted for its amazing, small stone chapel built by local artist Juan Félix Sánchez, who died in 1997 and is buried inside. This is his second chapel; the first, in similar style, was built two decades ago in the remote hamlet of **El Tisure**, inaccessible by road. You can walk there in five to six hours or rent a mule.

Any bus to Valera, Barinas or Apartaderos will drop you at Mucuchíes or San Rafael. Alternatively, enquire at Mérida's tour operators or tourist offices about transportation to Mucuchíes.

### CIDA Astronomical Observatory

North of San Rafael, at an altitude of about 3600m, is the **Centro de Investigaciones de Astronomía** (CIDA; ☎ 0274-245-1450; www.cida.ve, in Spanish), an astronomical observatory with four telescopes and a museum of astronomy. It's normally open to the public only on weekends, but during peak holiday seasons (Christmas, Carnaval, Easter, August) it's open daily. CIDA is off the main road, and there is no public transportation on the access road to the observatory, but visits can be organized from Mérida by any tour company. Tours (BsF120 per person) depart on Saturday at 2pm (daily in high season) from Parque Las Heroínas and return around midnight. A nice option is staying down the road at the 16-person **Mucuposada Santa Barbara** (☎ 263-6884),

THE ANDES

#### CLIMATE & WEATHER IN THE MOUNTAINS

As a general guide, the Venezuelan Andes enjoy a dry season from December to April. May and June are periods of changeable weather, with a lot of sunshine, but also frequent rain (or snow at high altitudes). It is usually followed by a short, relatively dry period from late June to late July before a long, really wet season begins. August to October are the wettest months, during which hiking can be miserable. The snowy period – June to October – may be dangerous for mountaineers.

The weather changes frequently and rapidly, even in the dry season. Rain (or snow, at upper reaches) can occur any time, and visibility can drop dramatically within an hour, leaving you trapped high up in the mountains for quite a while. Be careful and hike properly equipped, with good rain gear and warm clothing, as well as some extra food and water. Particular care should be taken on remote trails, where you may not meet anyone for days. Also keep in mind the risk of altitude sickness.

just a 4km walk to CIDA, and hiking back in the moonlight.

# TRUJILLO STATE

## VALERA

☎ 0271 / pop 137,400

Founded in 1820, Valera began to grow rapidly after the construction of the Carretera Transandina was completed in the 1920s. Today it's the largest and most important urban center in Trujillo state and the state's only real city – far larger and more populous than the state capital, Trujillo.

However, it's rather unattractive and its only real tourist value is as a transportation hub, with regular bus connections within the mountains and beyond. Your best option is to stay in Trujillo, which is only 40 minutes away.

### Getting There & Away

#### AIR

The Valera airport was closed at the time of research with no timetable for reopening.

#### BUS

The **Terminal de Pasajeros** (☎ 225-5009; Av México) is about 1.5km northeast of the center. To get there, take the northbound city bus marked 'Terminal' from Av Bolívar.

There are a dozen buses a day to Caracas (BsF68 to BsF75, 9½ hours, 584km); most depart in the evening, and all go via Barquisimeto, Valencia and Maracay. There is a SITSSA bus that goes to Caracas (BsF45) in the morning. Ordinary buses to Barquisimeto (BsF20, four hours, 243km) run every one to two hours. Expresos Valera has regular departures to Maracaibo (BsF78, four hours, 238km).

Transporte Barinas has four buses daily to Mérida (BsF40, five hours, 160km) along the spectacular Carretera Transandina. The road winds almost 3500m up to Paso del Cóndor (at 4007m the highest road pass in Venezuela), before dropping 2400m down to Mérida. There are also por puesto taxis to Mérida (BsF50, four hours). Buses to San Cristobal cost BsF50 and to Valencia from BsF46 to BsF78, depending on level of service.

Por puesto minibuses to Trujillo (BsF5, 40 minutes, 35km) depart every 10 to 20 minutes from the bus terminal, and to Boconó (BsF15, 2¼ hours, 106km) every 30 minutes.

Buses to Jajó (BsF5, 1½ hours, 48km) depart from the corner of Calle 8 and Av 4 (locally known as Punto de Mérida) every 40 minutes from 7am to 5pm.

Two or three jeeps a day to Tuñame (BsF10, two hours, 74km) depart from Av 6 between Calles 9 and 10.

## TRUJILLO

☎ 0272 / pop 14,300

Browsing Trujillo's markets, elbow-to-elbow with the locals in these crowded mountain streets, you need only look up to lift your soul and change your spirit– green vistas surround the town in every direction. A flicker of a place set high up in the Andes, where time seems to stand still, there is something here for everybody – the citydweller on a mountain getaway, the lover of native handicrafts and the bargainhunter will all find reasons to smile.

Trujillo is the capital of Trujillo state, despite the certain grumblings of much larger Valera, just 35km to the southwest. At 450 years and counting, Trujillo boasts some fine colonial architecture, and its trump card is the world's largest statue of the Virgin Mary – from her eyes at the top some say you can see as far as Lago de Maracaibo on a clear day.

Trujillo was the first town to be founded in the Venezuelan Andes (in 1557), but the continuous hostility of the local Cuica indigenous group caused it to be moved several times. It was called the 'portable city' because seven different locations were tried before the town was permanently established at its present site in 1570.

Located in a long narrow valley, El Valle de los Cedros, Trujillo has an unusual layout – it's only two blocks wide but extends more than 2km up the mountain gorge. Despite new suburbs at the foot of the historic sector, Trujillo remains a small and provincial place, in both appearance and spirit.

### Information

#### MONEY

**Banco de Venezuela** (cnr Av 3 Colón & Calle 2 Comercio)
**Banco Provincial** (Av 2 Bolívar btwn Calles 2 Comercio & 3 Miranda)
**Banesco** (Av 19 de Abril, Edif Baraju)

#### TELEPHONE

**CANTV** (cnr Av 2 Bolívar & Calle 5 Carrillo)
**Movistar** (cnr Av 1 Independencia & Calle 5 Carrillo)

THE ANDES

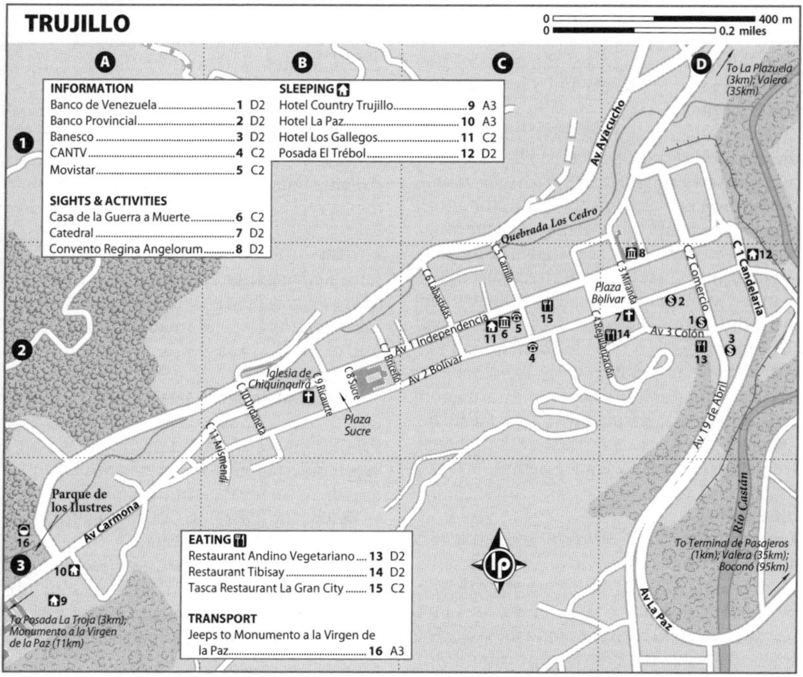


### TOURIST INFORMATION

**Cortrutur** (Corporación Trujillana de Turismo; ☎ 236-1455, 236-1277; ⏲ 8am-5pm Mon-Fri) The office is in La Plazuela, 3km north of Trujillo.

## Sights

### OLD TOWN

Trujillo's historic quarter stretches along two parallel east–west streets, Av 1 Independencia and Av 2 Bolívar. In the eastern part of the sector is the leafy **Plaza Bolívar**, the town's historical heart and still the nucleus of the city's life today. The mighty **catedral** (Plaza Bolívar), completed in 1662, has a lovely whitewashed facade and some charming old altarpieces inside.

There are some graceful historic buildings around the plaza, including the **Convento Regina Angelorum** (cnr Av 1 Independencia & Calle 3 Miranda). Built in the early 17th century as a convent, it's now the public library. Do go inside to see its splendid courtyard. You'll find more surviving colonial houses west of the plaza, on Av 1 Independencia and Av 2 Bolívar. The best approach to sightseeing is to take either of the two streets uphill and return down by the other one. They merge 10 blocks further up to become Av Carmona, but the best architecture is within a few blocks of the plaza.

At **Casa de la Guerra a Muerte** (☎ 236-6879; Av 1 Independencia No 5-29; admission free; ⏲ 8:30am-6pm Mon-Fri, to noon Sat & Sun) exhibits include old maps, armor, period furniture, pre-Columbian pottery and even a fully equipped kitchen with a historic stove. It was in this house that Bolívar signed the controversial Decreto de Guerra a Muerte (Decree of War to the Death), under which all captured royalists were to be summarily executed. The table on which the proclamation was signed and the bed in which Bolívar slept are part of the exhibition.

### MONUMENTO A LA VIRGEN DE LA PAZ

This gigantic, 47m-high monument is said to be the world's tallest **statue of the Virgin Mary** (admission BsF5; ⏲ 9am-5pm). Frankly, it bears an eerie, uncanny resemblance to Darth Vader. Inaugurated in 1983, the massive, concrete statue stands on a 1700m-high mountaintop overlooking Trujillo, 11km southwest of the town. The internal elevator and staircase smell rather bad, yet provide access to five *miradores* (lookout points), the highest of which peeks out through the Virgin's eyes. You can enjoy views over much of Trujillo state, and on a clear day you can even see the peaks of the Sierra Nevada de Mérida and a part of Lago de Maracaibo.

Jeeps to the monument leave from next to the Parque de los Ilustres in Trujillo. They depart upon collecting at least five passengers and charge BsF4 per head one way for a 20-minute trip. On weekdays the wait may be quite long, but you can pay for five seats and have the jeep to yourself. It's best to start early, as later in the day the Virgin is often shrouded by clouds, even in the dry season. If you feel like some exercise, the monument is a two- to three-hour walk uphill from town. Some hardy bicyclists also make the ride uphill. For more information on bicycling in Venezuela, which has taken the nation by storm in recent years, see the national federation's website: www.fvc.net.ve.

### Sleeping

**Posada El Trébol** (☎ 236-6078; Calle 1 Candelaria No 1-53; d/tr BsF70/80; ) A sense of luxury pervades this tasty option, with 20 bright rooms offering both tranquility and a very central location, just steps from Plaza Bolívar and the center of town. They'll bring beer to your room from the *cervezeria* – you can't beat that.

**Administradora Marisol Habitaciones Confortables** (Calle 1 Candelaria; d/tr BsF80/100; ) Two blocks downhill from Plaza Bolívar, this inviting, 15-room hotel has changed its name recently. Rooms are clean and quiet and have fridges and bathrooms with hot water, but it's a step down from Trébol at a higher price.

**Hotel Los Gallegos** (☎ 236-3193; Av 1 Independencia No 5-65; d BsF135; ) A luscious if eclectic selection of Edwardian and wicker furniture adorns this neat, well-run posada. Hot water, cable TV and friendly staff make this 32-room hotel a reasonable choice.

**Hotel La Paz** (☎ 236-4864, 236-5157; cnr Calle 15 & Av Carmona; s/d/tr BsF140/190/200; ) This seven-story edifice, a bit out of proportion for this site, offers 28 spacious suites, though they are rather on the basic side and pretty worn out.

**Posada La Troja** (☎ 236-7009; Via Monumento a La Paz; 4-person/6-person room BsF180/220; ) This rustic place is about 3km uphill from town, halfway to the Virgin statue. Wooden doors and ladders lead up to the *troja* (storage attic), and Mary and Marcos even have a pet red howler monkey and a homey restaurant. All rooms have capacity for four to six persons.

OUR PICK **Hotel Country Trujillo** (☎ 236-3942, 236-3646; Av Carmona; d BsF230-260, ste BsF280; ) The Country is definitely the best high-end place in town, offering spacious, air-conditioned rooms that have wide, comfortable beds, fridges and stylish furniture. It has a fair-sized swimming pool (nonguests BsF30), and a relaxed restaurant by the pool that serves local cuisine.

### Eating

**Tasca Restaurant La Gran City** (☎ 236-5254; Av 1 Independencia; meals BsF15-20, set meal BsF18) It's nothing special by Caracas standards, but here it's one of the best eateries in town, and it also offers a solid *menú ejecutivo*.

**Restaurant Andino Vegetariano** (Av 3 Colón btwn Calles 2 Comercio & 3 Miranda; set meal BsF20; lunch, Mon-Sat) Simple and modest, this is the only vegetarian spot in town, serving a filling *menú ejecutivo* (set meal) at lunch only.

**Restaurant Tibisay** (cnr Calle 4 Regularización & Av 3 Colón; meals BsF20-30; Mon-Sat) Mind your matches, the local firemen eat here. You can see why – it serves solid, stick-to-your-ribs food in an unpretentious cafeteria atmosphere, and with prices to match.

### Getting There & Away

The **Terminal de Pasajeros** (Av La Paz) is 1km northeast of the town's center, beyond Río Castán, and is accessible by urban minibuses. The terminal is rather quiet, and the only really frequent connection is with Valera (BsF12, 40 minutes, 35km). A few night buses go to Caracas (BsF80 to BsF85, 9½ hours, 589km). Transportation to Boconó (BsF12, two hours, 95km) is infrequent and thins out in the late morning. You may need to go to Valera, from where minibuses to Boconó depart regularly until about 5pm.

## BOCONÓ

☎ 0272 / pop 48,000

Simón Bolívar called Boconó the 'Garden of Venezuela,' and it's easy to see why. The region is famed for its lush natural vegetation, and for the cultivation of vegetables, coffee and orchids.

Boconó is a peaceful town nestled on the banks of the Río Boconó, and surrounded by the greenest of green hills. The town is 95km southeast of Trujillo, and the journey there, via a winding mountain road, is a spectacular attraction in itself. The mountain air will come as a welcome respite for lovers of cooler climes – the average temperature is just 68°F.

Boconó is an important regional craft center, known particularly for its weaving, basketry and pottery, and there are plenty of home workshops and craft shops in town. The surrounding region is dotted with pretty little towns such as Tostós and Niquitao, for which Boconó is a convenient jumping-off point.

Boconó was founded in 1560 on one of the sites chosen for Trujillo, but when the state capital made one of its several moves, some of the inhabitants decided to stay on. Isolated for centuries from the outside world, Boconó grew slowly and remained largely self-sufficient. It wasn't until the 1930s that the Trujillo–Boconó road was built, linking the town to the state capital and the rest of the country, although a sense of isolation is still palpable around the place.

## Information

### MEDICAL SERVICES

**Hospital Rafael Rangel** (☎ 652-2513; Av Rotaria)

### MONEY

**Banco de Venezuela** (Av 2 Sucre btwn Calles 5 Bolívar & 6 Jáuregui, Edif Banco de Venezuela)
**Banco Provincial** (cnr Av 4 Independencia & Calle 4 Vargas)
**Banesco** (cnr Av 4 Independencia & Calle 4 Vargas)

### POST

**Ipostel** (cnr Calle 5 Bolívar & Av 2 Sucre)

### TELEPHONE

**CANTV** (Plaza Bolívar)
**Movistar** (cnr Calle 4 Vargas & Av 4 Independencia)

## Sights

The **Museo Trapiche de los Clavo** (☎ 652-3655; www.museotrapichedelosclave.org.ve; Av Rotaria; admission free; 8am-5pm) occupies the walled-in compound of a 19th-century hacienda. The core of the museum is the original *trapiche* (sugarcane mill) and exhibits related to traditional sugar production, but there's more to see. One of the buildings features rotating exhibitions. In the southwestern corner is a pleasant open-air restaurant, and in the northern end are craft workshops – look for the textile workshop, where you can see artisans weaving blankets on rustic looms.

The **Ateneo de Boconó** (☎ 652-1131; Calle 3 Páez) is another place where you can see local weavers at work in their textile workshop on the upper floor. The Ateneo runs arts-and-crafts exhibitions from time to time. Down the road from the Ateneo is the **Paseo Artesanal Fabricio Ojeda** (cnr Calle 3 Páez & Av Cuatricentenario), a craft market featuring a collection of craft stands.

The small **Museo Campesino Tiscachic** (☎ 652-3313; Calle Tiscachic; admission free; 9am-3pm Mon-Fri) has quite an interesting exhibition of crafts – mostly woodcarving, pottery and basketry – fashioned by local artisans. It's in the Centro de Servicios Campesinos Tiscachic, 150m northeast of town past the bridge and off the road to Valera. The center hosts a lively food market on Saturday.

## Sleeping

**Posada Turística Los Andes** (☎ 652-1100; Calle 3 Páez No 1-08; s/d BsF50/80, d/tr with bathroom BsF80/100) This basic posada surrounds a pleasant courtyard with flowering red plants. Some rooms lack windows and bathrooms but there's hot water and it's cheap.

our pick **Posada Turística Jardín Boconés** (☎ 652-0171; Calle 1 Girardot No 3-05; d/tr BsF120/150) This romantic, 100-year-old house has a leafy central garden shaded by two old mango trees. It has eight cheerful, tranquil rooms, all with bathrooms and hot water. Meals are available on request or you can use the kitchen. Rooms upstairs have nice views and there's a beautiful garden and small library.

**Posada Machinipé** (☎ 652-1506; www.posadamachinipe.com.ve; Calle 5 Bolívar No 6-49; d/tr BsF120/140; ) This cozy posada feels so much like home, you might not want to leave. And what's the hurry? The Machinipé is a relaxing holiday spot, the nine rooms are all super-duper comfy, and the friendly owners will happily organize tours to regional attractions such as the Teta de Niquitao, and are excellent sources of local information.

**Posada Turística Su Punto** (☎ 652-1047; Av José María Hernández; d BsF120-130, tr BsF160; P ) This groovy posada, decorated throughout with antiques and crafts, has eight spotless rooms in four bungalows, and a good restaurant. It's good value, although a bit far from town.

**Hotel Campestre La Colina** (☎ 652-2695; www.hotel_lacolina.com.ve; Vía Las Guayabitas; d/tr BsF180/210, 5-6 person chalet BsF400-450) Set on a slope next to the river, this relaxing place with a country feel has a colony of chalets scattered over its spacious grounds, a hotel building with balconies overlooking the river, and its own restaurant.

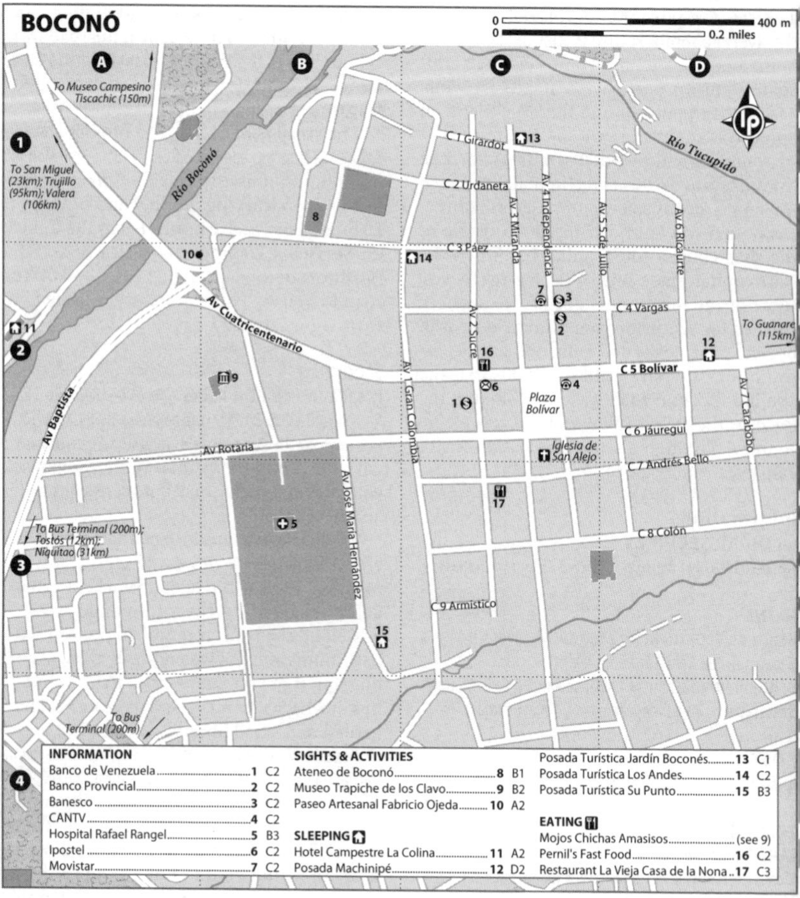


THE ANDES

## Eating

**Pernil's Fast Food** (cnr Calle 5 Bolívar & Av 2 Sucre; snacks BsF10-15) This smart, modern, convenient corner spot has already conquered local stomachs thanks to its tasty sandwiches, hamburgers, *arepas* (corn pancakes stuffed with juicy fillings) and Middle Eastern shawarmas.

**Mojos Chichas Amasisos** (Museo Trapiche de los Clavo, Av Rotaria; breakfast BsF10-15, lunch BsF15-30; 8am-3pm) This small outdoor nook is tucked away in the grounds of the Museo Trapiche, and offers creole breakfasts as well as pasta, fish, beef and chicken for lunch.

**Restaurant La Vieja Casa de la Nona** ( 0416-414-9056; Calle 7 Andrés Bello btwn Avs 2 Sucre & 3 Miranda No 4-29; meals BsF20-30) Dining on home-style creole tucker in 'Grandma's Old House,' you can't help but smile. The walls are lined with classic movie posters – and did we mention the food? It doesn't get much more down-home than this.

## Getting There & Away

All transportation options arrive and leave from the bus terminal just south of town except for Transporte Las Delicias, which has its own terminal in the center.

Minibuses heading to Valera (BsF12, 2¼ hours, 106km) depart when full until about 5pm. Minibuses to Trujillo (BsF12, two hours, 95km) cost about the same, but stop running in the late morning.

There are a few nightly buses to Caracas (BsF38 to BsF40, 10 hours, 542km), operated by two companies, Transporte Las Delicias and Expresos Los Andes. They all go via Guanare. If your aim is Guanare (BsF10, 3½ hours, 115km) and you miss the last mid-afternoon bus, catch a Caracas-bound bus. There are minibuses to San Miguel (BsF3, 40 minutes, 27km) every hour or so.

Jeeps to Niquitao (BsF4.50, 50 minutes, 31km) depart from Av Sucre about every 30 minutes until 5pm or 6pm on weekdays. On weekends, they leave when full (every one to two hours). The Niquitao jeeps don't enter Tostós, but there are direct jeeps to Tostós (BsF4.50, 20 minutes, 12km) departing from the same stop. Also from this stop are jeeps to Las Mesitas (BsF10, 1½ hours, 44km), beyond Niquitao. In theory, three jeeps run per day, at 1pm, 3pm and 5pm, but only the first two are reliable.

## TOSTÓS

During Holy Week, diminutive Tostós is the focus of nationwide attention for its celebrations of **Vía Crucis Viviente**, a stunning passion play re-enacting the last days of Christ's life. This blend of religious ceremony and popular theater, performed by locals playing the parts of Jesus, the apostles and Roman soldiers, is held on Good Friday. On that day the town fills up, and the crowd's emotions become almost hysterical when Christ is crucified. The rest of the year, Tostós is as it has been for more than 380 years: a sleepy town picturesquely tucked into the hillside.

The town is 12km southwest of Boconó and can be easily reached by regular por puesto jeeps (BsF3, 20 minutes).

## NIQUITAO

**☎ 0271 / pop 5000**

Niquitao is another pretty colonial town, spectacularly set in a long valley surrounded by mighty mountains. Founded in 1625, it still has much of its historic fabric in place, particularly around Plaza Bolívar. Niquitao is famous for its fruit wines, including blackberry and strawberry wine, and for its *sanjonero*, a strong, locally distilled bathtub gin.

The town sits at an altitude of nearly 2000m and has a typical mountain climate, with warm days and chilly nights – come prepared. It's a good base for excursions (see right).

### Sleeping & Eating

Niquitao has a few posadas to stay in and most can provide meals.

**Posada Mamá Chepy** (☎ 885-2173; Calle Páez; d/tr BsF70/70) Mama's place is a healthy walk from downtown, and would be hard to locate in the dark, but it's still a decent value for Niquitao. Set about 400m uphill from the Plaza Bolívar (look for the blue phone booth), it offers six rustic rooms, and Mamá serves home-cooked meals from her kitchen, if you ask nicely.

**Posada Don Tobias** (☎ 885-2074; Av Bolívar; d/tr BsF80/120; P) Don Tobias is half a block from the plaza, and has 18 no-frills rooms, all with nice beds and hot water. Handily, owner Laudencio (not Tobias!) has vehicles to take you to nearby tourist spots, including La Teta.

**Posada Turística Niquitao** (☎ 885-2042; www.ptn.ciberexpo.com; Plaza Bolívar; s/d/tr BsF200/200/270) Set in a meticulously restored colonial mansion, reputedly almost 400 years old, the Niquitao is the most stylish and elegant lodging option. Its 16 rooms are comfortable and spotless, and its own restaurant specializes in local cuisine.

### Getting There & Away

Jeeps (taking up to 12 passengers) service Niquitao from Boconó (BsF4.50, 50 minutes, 31km) every 30 minutes on weekdays and every one to two hours on the weekends.

From Niquitao there is a 13km road (partly paved but in bad shape) winding uphill to Las Mesitas. Jeeps service this route from Boconó. Beyond Las Mesitas, a rough road leads to the town of Tuñame (transportation is scarce on this stretch), from where a better road continues downhill to Jajó. Tuñame has a couple of basic posadas and a jeep link to Valera.

## AROUND NIQUITAO

Niquitao is a convenient base for trips to the surrounding mountains, including Trujillo state's highest peak, **La Teta de Niquitao** (4006m). You can walk there from Niquitao, but it will take two days roundtrip, so be prepared for camping. You can also go by jeep; the day trip to the top will include a two- to three-hour jeep ride uphill via Las Mesitas to the Llano de la Teta, followed by an hour's walk to the summit.

Another possibility is to climb **Pico Guirigay** (3870m). It's also a long, hard hike, or an easy day trip by jeep plus an hour's walk to the top. Jeep excursions can be arranged through hotel managers in Niquitao, who can also suggest other interesting destinations in the region. A jeep taking up to 10 people will cost BsF600 to BsF700 for a full-day trip (check tour prices offered by Posada Machinipé in Boconó or Don Tobias in Niqutao). Horseback-riding trips can also be arranged in Niquitao.

For shorter excursions around Niquitao you won't need a jeep or a guide. One good day trip is to **Viaducto Agrícola**, a spectacular old iron bridge over the lush Quebrada El Molino. You can go down to the stream of El Molino, 80m below the bridge, and take a refreshing bath. The bridge is on the Niquitao–Las Mesitas road, a 30-minute walk from Niquitao.

In the same area, a bit further up the road, is the site of the **Batalla de Niquitao**, which took place on July 2, 1813, and was one of the important battles of the War of Independence. The battlefield is a memorial site, with busts of the battle heroes. There is one empty pedestal where you can place your head among the heroes!

Another easy trip out of Niquitao is to **Las Pailas**, scenic waterfalls in the Quebrada Tiguaní. It's a nice picnicking spot and a leisurely walk uphill from the town. You can bathe here too, though the water is pretty cold.

# TÁCHIRA STATE

Most travelers who find their way to Táchira are in transit to Colombia, and don't stay for long. There are some small charms to be found on the way, however, and there are growing facilities to accommodate travelers. Proximity to the border has raised safety concerns in recent years, although some tour agencies in Mérida still offer tours.



## SAN CRISTÓBAL

☎ 0276 / pop 279,100

This bustling, commercial city feeds off trade with Colombia, and spreads its business across a green-as-green mountain slope, down steep streets, past old men playing chess in the leafy plazas and across the sidewalk. It's called 'La Ciudad de la Cordialidad' (the Friendly City), perhaps because everyone has a smile, and something they want to sell you. Flip-flop lovers, beware – wear shoes on these busy commercial streets or your toes will be trod on.

Set at a pleasant 800m, San Cristóbal is surrounded by misty green hills, scattered with the dotted beginnings of its growing suburbs. It's a good base to explore the local national parks, or stop in town for a day or two and for some museum-gawking and shopping among the manic street stalls. January is especially lively, when the city goes mad for two weeks celebrating its Feria de San Sebastián.

Founded in 1561 by Juan de Maldonado, the town was ruled from Nueva Granada (present-day Colombia) for more than 200 years, but didn't grow any bigger than an obscure hamlet. In 1777 it came under Venezuelan administration, but remained small and linked to Colombia because of the lack of roads to anywhere in Venezuela. A trip to Caracas was at least a two-week boat expedition by river down to Lago de Maracaibo and then by sea along the coast. It wasn't until 1925 that the winding Carretera Transandina reached San Cristóbal from Mérida, and it was only in the 1950s that the Carretera Panamericana was completed, providing the city with a fast, lowland link to the center of the country.

Today San Cristóbal is the capital of Táchira state and a thriving commercial center fueled by the proximity of Colombia, just 40km away. It's an important transit point on the Carretera Panamericana between Venezuela and Colombia; you'll pass through if you are traveling to or from anywhere in Colombia except the Caribbean coast.

### Orientation

San Cristóbal's historic quarter is centered on a triangle of three squares – Plaza Maldonado, Plaza Bolívar and Plaza Sucre – but the city has expanded in all directions far beyond its downtown area. The focus of the new development has moved to the east and north, with the ironically named Barrio Obrero (literally, 'Working-Class Suburb') 1.5km northeast of the center, where you'll find the cream of city's restaurants and nightclubs. The tourist office, Cotatur, is 1km further to the northeast.

### Information

#### MONEY

**Banco de Venezuela** (cnr Calle 8 & Carrera 9)
**Banco Provincial** (cnr Av 5 Francisco de Hevia & Calle 15)
**Banesco** (cnr Av 5 Francisco de Hevia & Calle 4)
**Corp Banca** (cnr Av 5 Francisco de Hevia btwn Calle 7 & Calle 8)

#### POST

**Ipostel** (Edificio Nacional, Calle 4 btwn Carreras 2 & 3)

#### TELEPHONE

**CANTV** (cnr Av 5 Francisco de Hevia & Calle 5)
**Movistar** (Av 7 Isaias Medina Angarita No 9-97)

### TOURIST INFORMATION

**Cotatur** (Corporación Tachirense de Turismo; ☎ 357-9655, 357-9578; cnr Av España & Av Carabobo; 🕑 8am-noon & 2-5:30pm Mon-Fri) The tourist office is 2.5km northeast of the city center, accessible from the bus terminal or from buses in the center; look for the Línea Intercomunal white bus with green stripes. Cotatur has desks at the airport terminals of Santo Domingo and San Antonio, open during flight times only.

**Inparques** (☎ 347-8347; Parque Metropolitano, Av 19 de Abril; 🕑 8am-12:30pm & 2-6pm Mon-Fri) Just south of town, Inparques provides information about the national parks in the region.

**Fundacion Proyecto AVE** (Archivo Visual Especializado; ☎ 276-356-8037; www.proyectoave.org; Pasaje Acueducto btwn Carreras 21 & 22) A collaborative effort of photographers, graphic designers, biologists and scientists promoting ecotourism in Venezuela. Through its image bank, audiovisual library of wildlife, eco-store and online magazine, it seeks to educate nationals and visitors about the abundant flora and fauna in Venezuela and how to best preserve it through literature and educational programs.

## Sights

San Cristóbal began its life around what is now Plaza Maldonado. The monumental, twin-towered **catedral** was completed in the early 20th century, after the previous church had been wrecked by an earthquake. It houses the venerated statue of San Sebastián, the city's patron saint. Next door to the cathedral is the fine, neocolonial **Palacio Episcopal**. On the northern side of the plaza is the massive, late-19th-century **Edificio Nacional**, the city's largest historic building, today home to public offices, courts of law and the post office.

Plaza Bolívar is not a colonial square, either. The oldest building here is the stylish **Ateneo del Táchira** (☎ 342-0536), built in 1907 as the Sociedad Salón de Lectura. Today it hosts a cultural center with its own art gallery and an auditorium staging theater performances and screening art-house movies. Stop inside to see what's on.

There are more historic buildings on and around Plaza Sucre, including the large **Palacio de Gobierno**. Also known as the Palacio de los Leones, because of the stone lions on its roof, this palace-like edifice was built in the 1910s as a government house.

Another early 20th-century mansion houses the **Museo de Artes Visuales y del Espacio** (☎ 343-3102; cnr Carrera 6 & Calle 4; admission free; 🕑 9am-noon & 1:30-6pm Mon-Sat). Its 14 rooms feature changing exhibitions of paintings and sculpture by local artists.

The **Complejo Ferial** (cnr Av España & Av Universidad), 4km northeast of the center, is a large fairground and sports complex, complete with exhibition halls, a stadium, a velodrome and Venezuela's second-largest bullring. About 1.5km north of the complex is the **Museo del Táchira** (☎ 353-0543; Final Av Universidad; admission free; 🕑 8am-5:30pm Tue-Fri, 10am-6pm Sat & Sun). Situated in a spacious old coffee and sugarcane hacienda, the museum features interesting exhibitions on the archaeology, history and ethnography of the region.

San Cristóbal's curiosity is the **Puente Libertador**, an old suspension bridge across the Río Torbes, constructed during the Gómez regime by the same company that built the Eiffel Tower. This intricate iron structure was brought from Europe and assembled in the 1920s, and has carried vehicular traffic ever since. The bridge is off Av Antonio José de Sucre, 5km north of the center; to get there, take any bus to Táriba, Cordero or Palmira.

## Festivals & Events

San Cristóbal's major annual bash is the **Feria de San Sebastián**, held in the second half of January. It includes agricultural and industrial fairs, bullfights, bicycle races and other sports events, a crafts fair, popular music, dances and parades, plus a lot of food and drink. Many events take place at the Complejo Ferial.

## Sleeping

For upmarket accommodations, head to the northeastern suburbs, beyond Barrio Obrero. The city center has a good choice of inexpensive lodging but nothing really upscale.

**Hotel El Andino** (☎ 343-4906; Carrera 6 btwn Calles 9 & 10; r BsF80) Just half a block from the Plaza Bolívar, this is your last choice in the center, acceptable, secure and family run, although also popular as a *por rato* (love motel). Some rooms have no bathroom.

**Hotel Grecón** (☎ 343-6017; Calle 16 btwn Av 4 & 5; s/d BsF110/120; ❄ 📶) The cheapest option you'll find for air-con and cable TV in town, the Grecón is a small hotel offering 55 spotless rooms and nice patio views of the mountains, it's a short walk south to the center.

**Hotel Central Park** (☎ 341-9077; cnr Calle 7 & Carrera 4; s/d/tr BsF130/150/160; ❄) The former Hotel Horizonte (taxis still know it by this name) is spartan but clean, and just fine for the price. All rooms have hot water and some have air-con.

**Suite Ejecutivo Dinastía** (☎ 343-9530; cnr Calle 13 & Av 7 Isaias Medina Angarita; s/d/tr BsF168/201/224; ) An offspring of the more expensive Hotel Dinastía, one block to the north, this small place provides comfortable and quiet rooms (not suites as its name would suggest). You can use the wi-fi/internet at the bigger hotel and it's a step up from the rest of the hotels in the center.

**Posada El Remanso** (☎ 342-1587; www.elremanso.com.ve; Av Principal de Pueblo Nuevo, Los Naranjos; d BsF250-310, tr BsF280-350, ste BsF360-390; ) This small, ambitious posada is a first-rate joint. It offers 14 comfortable rooms in a quiet residential suburb close to the tourist office. Room rates include breakfast, and it can provide lunch and dinner on request.

our pick **Posada Los Pirineos** (☎ 355-6528; posadapirineos@cantv.net; Ave Francisco Cardenas btwn Calle 15 & Av Carabobo; s/d/tr BsF350/370/450; ) Los Pirineos offers 15 plush rooms, each in a different color scheme and style, and named for individual *pueblos* in Táchira state. With fresh flowers and a terrace with mountain views, Dona Josefina's inn is easily San Cristóbal's best. Meals available on request.

**Castillo de la Fantasía** (☎ 353-0848, 353-0848; castillodelafantasiahotel@yahoo.es; Av España, Pueblo Nuevo; d BsF400-467, ste BsF534-667; ) The 'Fantasy Castle' is an opulent eclectic mansion, if a bit on the tacky side. Built in 1988, it will take you back in time a century or more with its 38 old-fashioned rooms (each different and individually named), stylish furniture and ancient statues. Yet it has most of the modern amenities, including noiseless air-con and Jacuzzi. Breakfast is included in the room rates.

**Hotel Valle de Santiago** (☎ 342-5090; www.hotelvalledesantiago.com.ve; Av Las Pilas, Santa Inés; s/d BsF425/480, ste BsF529-585; ) This is one of the city's best hotels, set in a stylish brick building 1.5km northeast of the center. Modern, small (27 rooms) and comfortable, it provides most facilities you'd wish for, including a well-appointed restaurant, gym and wee lobby bar. Room rates include breakfast.

## Eating

The city's main dining quarter is Barrio Obrero, which has loads of restaurants, including some of the best in town. A good place to start is Carrera 20, sarcastically nicknamed by the locals the 'Calle del Hambre' (Street of Hunger). The center also has lots of restaurants, though mostly budget ones, including numerous greasy spoons serving set lunches for BsF15 to BsF20.

**Tienda Naturista Gustico** (☎ 0416-579-0609; Calle 7 btwn Av 7 Isaias Medina Angarita & Carrera 8; juices BsF4.50, set lunch BsF10) This storefront veggie place cranks out the homemade yogurt, wholemeal bread, wholemeal empanadas and other yummy snacks well into the afternoon. It also sells vitamins and herbal remedies.

**Tostadería Grecón** (☎ 343-6017; Av 5 Francisco de Hevia btwn Calles 15 & 16; arepas BsF12-15; dinner only) Perhaps connected to the Grecón hotel via an underground labyrinth, come here for some of the best *arepas* in town with a huge choice of fillings. Open until 1am!

**Restaurant La Bologna** (☎ 343-4450; Calle 5 No 8-54; meals BsF20-30) The Italian owner still includes several pasta and ravioli dishes, on the menu since 1968. It also serves up hearty, economical Venezuelan food and is popular with locals and tourists alike. The large potted plants and tasteful decor bring a little bit of elegance to the center.

**La Guitarra Andaluza** (☎ 356-0573; Pasaje Acueducto btwn Carreras 20 & 21; meals BsF20-45; noon-4pm & 6-9pm) This classic Spanish restaurant sits in the heart of Barrio Obrero and offers a good mixture of steak, chicken and pasta dishes, as well as a good wine list. Some weekend nights there's live salsa. Next door there's a flashy, recently opened tapas joint (Sotto) under the same ownership. It caters to the young and wealthy, with a nice list of brochettes and cocktails. Open until late.

## Getting There & Away

### AIR

San Cristóbal's airport, **Aeropuerto Base Buenaventura Vivas** (☎ 234-7013), is in Santo Domingo, about 38km southeast of the city, but not much air traffic goes through there. The airport in San Antonio del Táchira (p178) is far busier and just about the same distance from San Cristóbal.

### BUS

The vast and busy **Terminal de Pasajeros** (☎ 346-1140; Av Manuel Felipe Rugeles, La Concordia) is 2km south of the city center and linked by frequent city bus services.

More than a dozen buses daily go to Caracas (BsF80 to BsF85, 13 hours, 825km). Most depart in the late afternoon or evening for an overnight trip via El Llano highway. Ordinary buses to Barinas (BsF40, five hours, 313km) run every hour or so between 5am and 6:30pm.

Busetas to Mérida (BsF35, five hours, 224km) go every 1½ hours from 5:30am to 7pm, but they may depart before their scheduled departure time if all seats are taken. The 7pm bus is unreliable if fewer than 10 passengers show up. Five buses depart nightly for Maracaibo (BsF70, eight hours, 439km); por puestos cost BsF90. You can also get to Puerto Cruz (BsF125), Barquisimeto (BsF65) Coro (BsF70) and Carora (BsF70).

Busetas to San Antonio del Táchira (BsF8, 1¼ hours, 40km), on the Colombian border, run every 10 or 15 minutes; it's a spectacular but busy road. If you're in a hurry, consider sharing a por puesto (BsF10 to BsF15), or take a taxi.

## SAN PEDRO DEL RÍO

**☎ 0277 / pop 5000**

The tiny town of San Pedro del Río is Táchira's little architectural gem. With narrow cobblestone streets lined with red-tile-roofed, single-story whitewashed houses, it looks like a typical old Spanish town straight out of a picture postcard. It has been extensively restored and is well cared for and clean. Particularly lovely is Calle Real, the town's central nerve, along which most craft shops, ice cream shops and restaurants have nestled.

San Pedro has become a popular weekend haunt for Venezuelans from the region, mostly from San Cristóbal, 40km away. On these days, food and craft stalls open and the town blossoms. During the rest of the week, by contrast, San Pedro is an oasis of peace and solitude.

### Sleeping

**Posada Turística Paseo La Chirirí** (☎ 291-0157; Calle Los Morales 1-27; d/tr BsF100/200) One block west of Plaza Bolívar, La Chirirí doesn't have the yesteryear's air of the Escuela (below), but has nine equally clean rooms, a barbecue area and a craft shop. Some rooms come with nice, big balconies – grab one if you can.

**Posada Turística Mi Vieja Escuela** (☎ 291-3720; cnr Calle Real & Carrera Calanzancio; r/tr BsF120/250; ❄) Located in an old school, Escuela will learn you a thing or two about hospitality. It's got seven neat rooms, some with air-con, and a lovely central patio to soak up the afternoon sun. It does a filling breakfast on request, and organizes walks and excursions in the local area.

### Eating

Dining spots have mushroomed since tourists began to come, but most of them open only on weekends. Local specialties include *gallina* (boiled and roasted hen) served with yucca, rice and salad, which can be found on the menu of most restaurants. The whole bird with accompaniments (BsF40) will feed four to six people. You also might try the *leche de burra* (donkey's milk) made of condensed milk and other delights.

Open more regularly than most other restaurants, **La Casona de los Abuelos** (☎ 291-4830; cnr Calle Real & Carrera General Márquez; meals BsF25-45) is a large, colonial-style mansion that serves typical local fare, including *gallina*.

Other Calle Real restaurants worth trying include Río de las Casas, El Saguan de la Estufa (both open seven days from 7am to 8pm), El Balcón and **El Refugio de San Pedro** (Plaza Bolívar).

### Getting There & Away

From San Cristóbal, take the half-hourly Línea Colón bus to San Juan de Colón and ask the driver to take you into San Pedro (BsF6.50, 1¼ hours, 40km). To return from San Pedro to San Cristóbal, go to the Línea Colón brick building office at the entrance to town – the people there will phone the next arriving bus and get you a seat.

If you are coming from the north (eg from Mérida or Maracaibo), get off at the turnoff to San Pedro, about 9km past San Juan de Colón (the driver will know where to let you off). Going to Mérida from San Pedro, it's easiest to take a bus back to San Cristóbal and change for direct service.

## SAN ANTONIO DEL TÁCHIRA

**☎ 0276 / pop 48,500**

San Antonio sits on the busy San Cristóbal–Cúcuta road and lives off trade with bordering Colombia. It's a pleasant enough place, but there's not much reason to visit, and the budget-conscious will find better and cheaper facilities across the border in Cúcuta, a much larger town. Wind your watch back half an hour when crossing from Venezuela to Colombia.

### Information

#### IMMIGRATION

**DIEX** (Carrera 9 btwn Calles 6 & 7; 24hr) This office puts exit or entry stamps in passports.

All tourists leaving Venezuela are charged a BsF55 *impuesto de salida* (departure tax). You need to buy stamps for this amount in a shop (open 24 hours) across the road from DIEX. Nationals of most Western countries don't need a visa for Colombia, but all travelers must get an entry stamp from DAS (Colombian immigration). The DAS office is just past the bridge over the Río Táchira (the actual border), on the right.

#### MONEY

While there are plenty of *casas de cambio* (money exchange offices) in the center, particularly on Av Venezuela and around the DIEX office, you will get significantly better rates for all currency transactions on the opposite side of the bridge – a five-minute walk – or in Cúcuta. None of the money exchanges will touch your traveler's checks. There are a few banks around Plaza Bolívar:

**Banco de Venezuela** (cnr Calle 3 & Carrera 9)
**Banco Sofitasa** (Carrera 8 btwn Calle 5 & 6)

#### POST

**Ipostel** (cnr Carrera 10 & Calle 2)

#### TELEPHONE

**CANTV** (cnr Calle 4 & Carrera 13)
**CANTV** (Av Venezuela btwn Calle 4 & 5) Also has internet.
**Movistar** (cnr Av Venezuela & Calle 4)

#### TOURIST INFORMATION

**Tourist information desk** (Aeropuerto Juan Vicente Gómez) Open only during flight times; 2km northeast of town.

#### TRAVEL AGENCIES

**Turismo Internacional** (☎ 771-5555; Av Venezuela 4-04)
**Turismo Turvinter** (☎ 771-0311; Av Venezuela 6-40)
**Turismo Uribante** (☎ 771-1779; Av Venezuela 5-59)

### Sleeping & Eating

San Antonio del Táchira has a number of decent places to stay and each has it its own restaurant.

**Hotel Casa Colonial** (☎ 771-2679; Carrera 11 No 2-55; s/d/tr BsF70/90/90; ❄) Chattering parakeets and two caged peacocks greet you at the Colonial, where the mattresses may well date from the colonial era. Rooms are very, very basic but have private facilities, and are easily the cheapest in town.

**Hotel Terepaima** (☎ 960-7207; Carrera 8 No 1-37; s/d/tr BsF90/90/120; ❄) This grandmotherly place has 10 rooms, but only a few with air-con. Service is a bit arthritic, but it's on a quiet, tranquil street, and the rustic restaurant below serves good set meals. Of the hotels listed here, likely your last choice.

**Hotel Don Jorge** (☎ 771-1932; hoteldongjorge@hotmail.com; cnr Calle 5 & Carrera 9; d/tr/ste BsF150/170/220; ❄) Clean, neat and to-the-point, the Don Jorge has had more than 20 years to get it right, and continues to deliver well maintained, good-value rooms. Arguably the best-value accommodations in town.

**Hotel Adriático** (☎ 771-5757; cnr Calle 6 & Carrera 6; s/d/tr BsF160/160/185; ❄) You can't go wrong with the Adriático, which offers 45 fair-sized rooms with air-con. Some rooms have balconies, if you want to watch the world go by. The hotel restaurant is reasonable and not expensive. There's laundry service, too.

### Getting There & Away

#### TO/FROM COLOMBIA

Buses, also called *colectivos* (BsF5), and por puestos (BsF10) run frequently to Cúcuta in Colombia (12km). You can catch both on Av Venezuela, or save yourself some time by walking across the bridge, getting your Colombian entry stamp from the DAS office (on your right), and looking for a shared taxi on the other side. Ask for 90 days when entering Colombia.

Buses go as far as the Cúcuta bus terminal. Most, but not all, pass through the center – be sure to ask if you're planning on stopping for a while. You can pay in bolívares or pesos.

The Cúcuta terminal is dirty, busy and unsafe – one of the poorest in Colombia – so watch your belongings closely and beware of con artists. Buy your ticket directly from the bus office.

From Cúcuta there are frequent buses to Bucaramanga (BsF96, six hours, 148km) and two dozen buses daily to Bogotá (BsF200, 16 hours, 568km).

#### AIR

The **Aeropuerto Juan Vicente Gómez** (☎ 771-2692), 2km northeast of town, can be reached by Ureña buses. They depart from Plaza Miranda, but if you don't want to go that far, you can catch them on the corner of Calle 6 and Av Venezuela.

**Rutaca** has two daily flights to Caracas (BsF300).

There are no direct flights to Colombia from San Antonio; go to Cúcuta across the border, from where you can fly to Bogotá, Medellin and other major Colombian cities (for a much better price than you'd get for a flight to those cities from Maracaibo or Caracas).

#### BUS

The bus terminal is midway to the airport. Half a dozen bus companies operate buses to Caracas (BsF80 to BsF95, 14 hours, 865km), with a total of seven buses daily. All depart between 4pm and 7pm and use the El Llano route. Most of these bus companies also have offices in the town center: **Expresos Los Llanos** (☎ 771-2690; Calle 5 No 4-26), **Expresos Mérida** (☎ 771-4053; Av Venezuela 6-17), **Expresos Occidente** (☎ 771-4730; cnr Carrera 6 & Calle 6) and **Expresos San Cristóbal** (☎ 771-4301; Av Venezuela 3-20). They all sell tickets, but then you have to go to the terminal anyway to board the bus.

No direct buses run to Mérida; go to San Cristóbal and change there. Por puestos to San Cristóbal leave frequently from the corner of Av Venezuela and Carrera 10 (BsF10 to BsF15, 1¼ hours, 40km).

# Los Llanos

Like the Wild West of yore, Los Llanos is the mythological heart of Venezuela, and birthplace of President Hugo Chávez. The tough-guy cowboys living rough and riding the plains are the fierce *llanero* warriors of song and story, praised by Simón Bolívar himself as the best soldiers he ever had.

Sandwiched between the soul-stirring sky and the endless plains is where you'll find the real star of any visit – the jaw-dropping diversity of bird and animal life. Look out into the night and you may find a bowlful of caiman eyes looking back at you from the lagoon. Chuckle at the enormous herds of capybara, the world's largest rodent, as they frolic in the marshy undergrowth. Come the dry season, a thousand scarlet ibises rise in a cloud of feathered pink from a shrinking oasis, prepared for their annual migration.

Cruise along the flattened landscape, taking in the smells of *rayado* (massive, salted catfish) and *naiboa* (cassava and brown sugar bread) along the roadside stands. Visit the home of Venezuela's patron saint, the Virgen de Coromoto: an astonishing cathedral in the middle of the plains in homage to her draws pilgrims from every corner of the country.

This is the land that inspired a national obsession – *joropo,* the hypnotically fast finger-picking of the harp-playing *llaneros*. You can hear it live in the bars of Barinas, and there's an impressive statue of legendary *arpista* Juan Vicente Torrealba on the road outside Camaguán.

### HIGHLIGHTS

- Venture out on a wildlife safari amid caimans, dolphins and birds, organized from the **hatos** (p182)
- Join the pilgrims at the astonishing **Santuario Nacional de Nuestra Señora de Coromoto** (p190)
- Learn to dance to the pulsating rhythms of **joropo music** (p188)
- Explore the spiritual capital of **Guanare** (p188)

## Geography & Climate

Sometimes called the Serengeti of South America, the Los Llanos ecosystem stretches across 300,000 sq km in Venezuela (plus another 250,000 sq km in Colombia). It's mostly covered by grass, with ribbons of gallery forest along the rivers and islands of woodland scattered around.

Rivers are numerous and, in the wet season, voluminous. The main ones are the Apure, Meta, Arauca and Capanaparo, all of which are left-bank (south) tributaries of the Orinoco.

The climate is extreme in both wet and dry seasons, resulting in either floods or droughts. The wet period lasts from May to November and brings frequent and intense rains. The rivers overflow, turning much of the land into lagoons. In the dry season, December to April, the sun beats down upon the parched soil and winds blow the dust around.

## Getting Around

You can fly into Barinas, but you'll have to rely on land transportation to take you into the heart of the savanna. San Fernando de Apure is accessible by paved roads from Maracay/Caracas in the north and Barinas/Guanare in the northwest. There's also a paved road from San Fernando southward to Puerto Páez, on the Colombian border.

# TOURING LOS LLANOS

## Budget Tours

While it is possible to visit Los Llanos independently, the enormity of the plains, the travel time involved and the scarcity of rural accommodations make tours the best option for wildlife viewing, especially for those on a budget. The majority of budget tour companies leading safaris to Los Llanos are based in Mérida, but a few are cropping up in the coastal towns. Expect to pay between BsF900 and BsF1000 for a four-day, three-night excursion; remember, as always, you tend to get what you pay for.

A typical budget tour includes off-road safaris in a jeep (sitting on the roof is recommended, but strictly optional – hang on to the bars!), a boat tour (in season), horseback riding, piranha fishing and usually bird-watching in the morning or evening. Most guides will try to catch an anaconda or river turtle for you but environmentalists strongly discourage this practice; see p184. Some may also offer whitewater rafting to break up the lengthy trip to and from Mérida. Most tours include the services of a bilingual guide.

Accommodations are in basic *campamentos*, and most tour companies have their own. Sleeping can be in beds or hammocks, with shared bathrooms and cold water. Food is simple and filling, but nothing special.

There are many tour agencies offering trips to Los Llanos and there is no shortage of quality, bilingual guides. Some of the most reputable include:

**Araguato Expeditions** (p120) Based in Coro, this outfit is a small tour company that offers expeditions Venezuela-wide, including to Los Llanos.

**Arassari Trek** (p159) Pioneered budget tours to Los Llanos, and continues to be one of the best in the business. Most of their guides are respected naturalists, including Alan Highton and Roger Manrique.

**Gravity Tours** (p159; gravityxtreme@hotmail.com) Has its own camp and a rafting guide from Venezuela's national team for one- to two-day river trips. Guides are excellent wildlife spotters.

**Guamanchi Expeditions** (p159) Offers tours to Los Llanos, led by a variety of well-prepared guides.

## Campamentos

Budget tours from Mérida stay in *campamentos* near Barinas or Mantecal. There's also a *campamento* inside the Parque Nacional Cinaruco-Capanaparo.

**Las Churuatas del Capanaparo** (☎ 0212-235-1287, 0247-511-4315; fmatas@trolk.com.ve; Margen sur del Capanaparo, La Macanilla) is a remote camp that sees few foreign tourists; situated on the southern bank of the Río Capanaparo, 110km south of San Fernando de Apure. It's just inside the Parque Nacional Cinaruco-Capanaparo, the only national park in Los Llanos. The owner, Riverito, is quite the *llanero* story-teller, and charges BsF150 per day for very basic accommodations in one of the seven *churuatas* – palm-thatched huts with beds for four people, plus hammocks, cold-water bathrooms and electricity. The price includes breakfast and dinner prepared by his wife, Rosario, but safaris are extra and go for BsF200, depending on your choice of walks, boat trips, horseback riding or fishing. There are also indigenous settlements nearby that you can visit. The camp is not far from the San Fernando–Puerto Páez highway, near the ferry crossing on the Río Capanaparo. Call in advance and they can arrange to pick you up in Puerto Páez. In the rainy season be sure to bring insect repellent.

## Hatos

The *hatos* are large cattle ranches that also offer accommodations and ecotourism safaris. Unlike in the rainforests of the Amazon, cattle production has done minimal damage to the ecosystems of these vast, grassy wetlands, and the poor level of nutrients in the soil makes it difficult to fatten livestock for market. So it comes as no surprise that many of the *hatos* have turned to ecotourism, and most have strict conservation measures in place to maintain this abundant natural resource – the plentiful wildlife.

Excursions are basically photo safaris in a jeep or boat (or even tractor or horseback). There's usually one trip in the morning and another in the afternoon – the best times to observe the wildlife and to avoid the unbearable midday heat. Boat trips are more common in the rainy period, while jeep rides prevail in the dry season. Visitors are taken deep into wilderness areas where animals, and especially birds, are plentiful and easy to see. Among the mammals and reptiles, capybaras and caimans are particularly common (see the boxed text, p186). Fishing for piranhas is also an activity offered by most of the *hatos*. Ask to eat what you catch; they are tasty.

Visits to some *hatos* are available only as an all-inclusive package, which has to be booked and paid beforehand, usually in Caracas. Packages are normally three-day, two-night visits that include full board and one or two excursions each day. Other *hatos* are more flexible,

**LOS LLANOS**

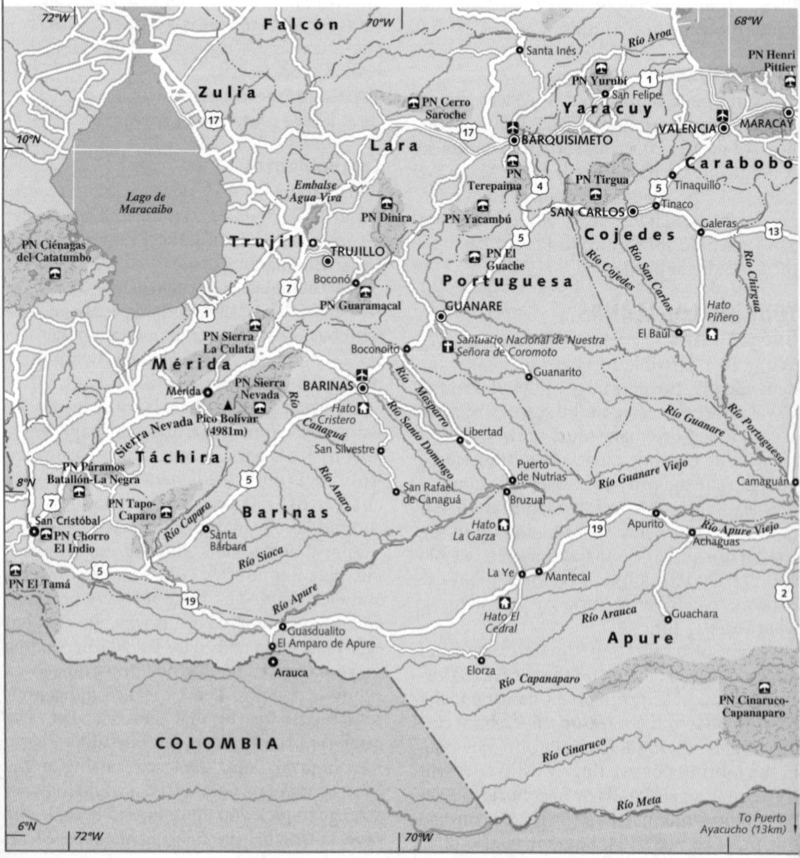

allowing visitors to come without paying beforehand, stay a day or two and pay accordingly. Expect to pay between BsF300 and BsF400 per person per day, which adds up to some BsF1000 to BsF1200 for a three-day tour.

Bilingual guides can vary from place to place and are not always on duty. Be sure to ask in advance if a guide who speaks your language will be there during your stay.

### HATO PIÑERO

The best-known ranch in the Llano Alto (Upper Plain), **Hato Piñero** (Map pp182-3; ☎ in Caracas 0212-991-1135, 0212-992-4413; www.hatopinero.com; Biotur Hato Piñero, 6th fl, Edificio General de Seguros, No 6-B, Av La Estancia, Chuao, Caracas; per day May-Nov BsF339, Dec-Apr BsF389) is in Cojedes state, close to the town of El Baúl. It's accessible by road from the central states. If you are coming from Caracas, head to Valencia; from there it's about 220km south.

Owned by the Branger family and set 22km down a rough red-clay road from the highway, Piñero has a somewhat different spectrum of wildlife from that of the ranches in the Llano Bajo (Lower Plain). Set on the northern edge of the plains, this 800-sq-km ranch also has plateau and gallery forest on the rolling hills, and is surrounded by four rivers. The wet season comes later (in late May or early June) and ends earlier (in September). Although capybaras and caimans are not ubiquitous here, there is a large variety of other animals, including ocelots, monkeys, anteaters, agoutis, foxes, tapirs and iguanas. This is largely the

effect of hunting and logging bans, which were introduced as early as the 1950s.

The family's Fundación Branger seeds the *hato's* biological station, where many significant discoveries have been made about the unique Llanos ecosystem. Their private herbarium, where the potential medicinal properties of the indigenous plant life are investigated, is one of a kind. Neighboring Hato Paraima has been seized by the government, to the detriment of Piñero's cattle that need its higher ground in the wet season. The battle over land rights continues.

The delightful colonial guesthouse, complete with an old-fashioned cattle-weighing scale, has 25 rooms with bathrooms. Packages can be booked in Caracas; they include full board and excursions. The ranch can provide transportation to and from Caracas (BsF660 roundtrip for up to four people).

### HATO EL CEDRAL

About 65km southwest of El Frío is **Hato El Cedral** (Map pp182-3; ☎ in Caracas 0212-781-8995; www.elcedral.com; 5th fl, Edificio Pancho, No 33, Av La Salle, Los Caobos, Caracas; per person per day BsF392, for Venezuelan citizens BsF336; ). If you want to experience the Revolution first-hand, come to El Cedral, which is now the property of the Bolivarian government. You'll eat with the workers, and there's a school on the grounds for their children. Most say the level of service has gone down since the government takeover, but it's still worth visiting for its unbelievable array of wildlife and quadrilingual guide, Rafael, who speaks French, German, English and Spanish.

The ranch itself covers 530 sq km and has around 15,000 head of cattle. More than 300 bird species have been recorded on the ranch, as well as 8000 capybaras (sadly diminished from 20,000 in recent years) and numerous other species. Among the marvelous avian specimens you may spy are the punk-rock-meets-prehistoric yellow-spiked *hoatzin*, and the boisterous orinoco goose.

The *campamento*, 7km west off the road, provides comfortable lodging in 25 air-conditioned double rooms, all equipped with bathrooms with hot water; there is also a tiny pool. The dining room serves typical Creole food and several different excursions are offered, by boat or specially prepared minibus, and there are sometimes optional night walks available (for a small extra fee).

El Cedral requires advance booking in Caracas. The *hato* can provide a car from Barinas (BsF400 roundtrip for up to four people) or phone **Bell-Fred Taxi** (☎ 0426-572-5899).

### HATO LA GARZA

For those seeking luxury in exclusive surroundings, look no further than **Hato La Garza**

#### DROP THAT ANACONDA!

For many years, guides have been giving tourists the thrill of snatching a live anaconda from its watery lair and holding it up for a group picture. Not only is that practice dangerous to the tourists, but often to the animal itself.

Dr Jesus Rivas, a biologist from the Universidad Central de Venezuela (see www.anacondas.org), has been studying the reptiles for many years, and raises many concerns about anaconda grabbing. 'Most times a tour guide handles a snake with little consideration for the harm it might do,' he says. 'The first thing they do is to pull it by the tail to the middle of the road…sometimes dragging its heavy body on the ground against the direction of the scales.'

The snake's head is usually shut tightly to take a photo. Because of its needle-like, non-opposing teeth, this can cause the snake to cut open its own gums, resulting in bleeding. If the animal does manage to bite its handler, it's more to the snake's detriment than the handler's, who will pull away, causing the snake to lose teeth and open wounds that may become infected.

Over-handled snakes may shy away from basking on banks, which gravid (pregnant) females need to do to warm their brood. If she does not get enough sun, she may lose her brood entirely or have many stillborns, or they may flee safe water havens in the dry season and die.

'Proper handling of an animal, one time, does not necessarily harm the snake if the person does it well. But rough handling along with high frequency is completely bad news,' says Rivas. The lure of high-season tips is tempting to guides, but results in 'harassing the animals way too much.'

'It would be best if people stay away from anacondas without handling them,' concludes Rivas. And you may be lucky enough to see one basking or crossing the road.

**WHEN TO GO ON A WILDLIFE SAFARI IN LOS LLANOS**

Wildlife is abundant in both rainy and dry seasons. The main difference is that in the dry season (considered the high season, which therefore has higher prices) most animals flock to scarce sources of water, which makes them easy to watch. In late March or early April, just before the first rains, the crowds of caimans or capybaras can be unbelievable!

In the wet season, on the other hand, when most of the land is half-flooded, animals are virtually everywhere, but are harder to spot because they are not concentrated in certain areas.

Year-round, take a hat, sunglasses and sunblock; in the wet season, bring wet-weather gear as well. Whenever you come, don't forget a flashlight, mosquito repellent, good binoculars and a camera.

(Map pp182-3; ☎ 0273-414-1176; www.hatogarza.com; per person BsF1600; ) about halfway between Bruzual and Mantecal. La Garza is a water-buffalo and cattle ranch of 65 sq km, and has been a nature reserve since the mid-1990s. Three main rivers cut across the property and a quarter of the land is gallery forest, making it a good spot for wildlife watching.

Managed by scions of the Swarovsky optical fortune, La Garza offers excursions in jeep or by boat depending on the season, and is one of the few *hatos* to offer safaris on horseback. For the hardy, there's even an excursion through the paddies on a tractor – you need strong legs and good balance – but you'll get far enough into the wetlands to maybe spot a *jabiru*: at 1.4m, it's South America's tallest flying bird.

Accommodations are in one of three large suites or two twin rooms, all with private terraces, king-size beds and hot water. The theme is rustic but relaxed – fans instead of freezing air-con, and no televisions to spoil the tranquility. Most of the food served is grown organically on site, and you may even dine on the local *bufalo*. There's also a richly decorated bar, an extensive wildlife library and a pool area with a view of both the savanna and the forest.

Booking and payment in advance are stringently required. You must transfer a 50% deposit to the *rancho's* bank account (in BsF) 15 days prior to arrival. They can organize pickup from Barinas (two hours, BsF250).

There is also a small landing strip that can accommodate light planes. There is currently no charter service available.

### HATO CRISTERO

A short 28km south of Barinas lies **Hato Cristero** (Map pp182-3; ☎ 0273-223-5060, 0414-454-4193; www.hatoelcristero.com; adult/child per day BsF550/BsF450; ). Converted into an ecotourist resort in the mid-1990s, Don Humberto's 1100-hectare ranch sits on the edge of the Upper Llanos and is one of the smaller *hatos*. It offers good wildlife viewing, in particular bird-watching, although you won't find nearly as many capybaras, caimans or anacondas as you would in the Lower Llanos.

Hato Cristero is the closest ecotourist resort to both Barinas and Mérida, and thus makes an especially good option if you are short on time.

It offers jeep and horseback safaris and there's usually an optional night-time excursion available. If you want to chill, a winding path leads through butterfly-strewn grounds to a cascading waterfall and a pond full of turtles. Lodging is in air-conditioned, cane-ceilinged cabins with large bathrooms and hot water, TV, fridge and safety-deposit box. There are 12 rooms, including triples, doubles and singles (six more are under construction), plus a swimming pool. Much of the food served here is grown or produced on the farm, including homemade cheese.

A taxi from Barinas costs about BsF70.

## BARINAS

☎ 0273 / pop 295,000

Barinas is the biggest city in Los Llanos, as well as President Chávez' birthplace and seat of power – both his father and brother have been governors of the state. Named for the Varyná indigenous tribe, it's the capital of a vast agricultural and ranching region, and the discovery of oil has given an edge of prosperity to the town. It's also an important transportation hub, and an ideal jumping-off point for adventures in Los Llanos.

The city has had a turbulent past, and recently night-time kidnappings have become a very real threat (always take a cab at night, and ask your hotel for a trustworthy company). It's a likeable place, however, and the humid, muggy climate takes the edge off the small-town hustle and bustle. The center is compact and walkable, and is surrounded by large, leafy suburbs.

### THE WILDLIFE OF LOS LLANOS

Apart from the legendary anacondas and piranhas, Los Llanos is most famous for the myriad birds that gather seasonally to breed and feed, or live permanently on the grassy plains and wetlands. About 360 bird species have been recorded in the region, which accounts for a quarter of all the bird species found in Venezuela. Waterbirds and wading birds predominate, and the list includes ibises, herons, cormorants, egrets, jaçanas, gallinules and darters. The *corocoro colorado*, or scarlet ibis *(Eudocimus ruber)*, noted for its bright red plumage, appears in large colonies in the dry season. Three-quarters of the world's *corocoro* population lives in Venezuela.

As for mammals, the most common local species (apart from the omnipresent cattle, of course) is the *chigüire*, or capybara *(Hydrochoerus hydrochaeris)*. This is the world's largest rodent, growing up to about 60kg, with a face like a guinea pig's and a coat like a bear's. It's equally at home on land and in the water, feeding mainly on aquatic plants. Other local mammals include armadillos, peccaries, opossums, anteaters, tapirs, ocelots and the occasional jaguar. Two interesting aquatic mammals are the *tonina*, or freshwater dolphin *(Inia geoffrensis)*, and the *manatí*, or manatee *(Trichechus manatus)*, which inhabit the large tributaries of the Orinoco. Both are endangered species, and numbers of the latter are dangerously low.

Also threatened with extinction is the largest American crocodile, the Caimán del Orinoco *(Crocodylus intermedius)*. These huge reptiles once lived in large numbers and grew up to 8m from head to tail, but the population was decimated by ranchers, who killed them for their skins. Far more numerous is the *baba*, or the spectacled caiman *(Caiman crocodylus)*, the smallest of the family of local caimans, growing up to 3m in length.

## History

Barinas' long and checkered history began in 1577 when it was founded by Spanish conquerors from Pamplona in Nueva Granada (now Colombia). At the beginning of the 17th century, tobacco gave the town an economic base and overseas fame, as Barinas was the only region in the colony that the Spanish Crown allowed to grow tobacco. Other crops, including sugarcane, bananas and cacao, were subsequently introduced to the region, as was raising cattle. By the end of the 18th century, Barinas was Venezuela's largest and wealthiest town after Caracas.

The civil wars that plagued Venezuela during the 19th century affected the development of the town and the state, but afterwards a steady revival began. Agriculture and the cattle industry were joined by a short-lived timber industry, which took advantage of the extensive tropical forest in the region, chopping it down rapidly and indiscriminately. Meanwhile, oil was discovered in the region south of Barinas and is today pipelined to the coast near Morón.

## Information

### MONEY

**Banco de Venezuela** (cnr Av 7 Marqués del Pumar & Calle 6 Plaza)

**Banco Mercantil** (cnr Av 7 Marqués del Pumar & Calle 11 Cruz Paredes)

**Banco Provincial** (cnr Av 7 Marqués del Pumar & Calle 9 Carvajal)

**Banesco** (cnr Av 7 Marqués del Pumar & Calle 11 Cruz Paredes)

**Corp Banca** (cnr Av 5 Libertad & Calle 10 Camejo)

### POST

**Ipostel** (Calle 9 Carvajal btwn Avs 4 Montilla & 5 Libertad)

### TELEPHONE

**Movistar** (cnr Av 7 Marqués del Pumar & Calle 4 Arzobispo Méndez)

### TOURIST INFORMATION

**Corbatur** (Corporación Barinesa de Turismo; ☎ 552-7091; www.descubrebarinas.com.ve; Calle 4 Arzobispo Mendez, Edif Vifrán; 🕑 8am-noon & 2-6pm Mon-Fri)

## Sights

The unusual, two-block-long Plaza Bolívar still boasts buildings dating from the city's fat days. The pastel-colored, graceful **catedral** was built in the 1770s, except for the bell tower, which was added in 1936.

Across the plaza is the imposing **Palacio del Marqués**, occupying one entire side of the square. Commissioned by the Marqués de las Riberas de Boconó y Masparro as his private residence and constructed in the 1780s, the palace reflected the owner's wealth and Barinas' prosperity at the time. It was partly ruined during the

Wars of Federation in the mid-19th century, but was later restored. It now houses governmental offices, including the tourist office.

Also set on the plaza is the colonial-style **Casa de la Cultura** (☎ 552-3643), built in the 1780s as the town hall and jail. José Antonio Páez, a republican hero, was imprisoned here but managed to escape, liberating 115 of his fellow prisoners in the process. The building was the town jail until 1966, but today it houses a cultural center and auditorium, staging art exhibitions and various cultural events.

Named after a local poet, the **Museo Alberto Arvelo Torrealba** (☎ 532-4984; cnr Calle 5 de Julio & Av 6 Medina Jiménez; admission free; 8am-noon & 2-5pm Mon-Sat) is set in a splendid 200-year-old mansion with a charming patio and a tree-shaded garden. It features an exhibition related to the history of the city and the region.

The **Museo de Arte Colonial y Costumbrista San Francisco de Asís** (☎ 533-4641; Av 6 Medina Jiménez btwn Calles 2 Pulido & 3 Bolívar; admission free; 8am-12pm & 2-6pm Mon-Fri) has a bizarre, 30,000-piece private collection of old objects, including kerosene lamps, hospital beds, jukeboxes, crucifixes, chamber pots, fire extinguishers, wedding dresses, surgical instruments, turtle shells – you name it. It's stunning. The friendly attendants have stories about every single exhibit. Note the first gas-street lamps from Plaza Bolívar.

In the vast grounds of the Universidad Nacional Experimental de los Llanos Ezequiel Zamora (Unellez), 3km southwest of the center, the **Jardín Botánico** (☎ 546-4555; Av Alberto Torrealba; admission free; 8am-3pm Mon-Fri) has many beautiful trees, a plant nursery and a small zoo featuring local species.

## Sleeping & Eating

There's a variety of accommodation choices in the center and along Av 23 de Enero. Avoid the cheap hotels around the bus terminal: they are both unclean and unsafe.

**Hotel Marqués** (☎ 552-6576; Calle 3 Bolívar No 2-88; d BsF90-110, tr BsF120; ) The only real budget option in the center, the Marqués offers 50 spotless, freshly painted rooms, all with air-con and cable TV. It's a block away from the Plaza Bolívar and close to everywhere you might want to go in the center.

**Hotel Internacional** (☎ 552-2343; Calle 4 Arzobispo Méndez; d BsF145-190, tr BsF220; ) The 48-room, three-star Internacional is the oldest hotel in town and great value. Built in the early 1950s (when there was still no reliable road connection with Caracas), it has large rooms, high ceilings, spacious common areas and a no-nonsense restaurant serving copious meals. Ask for a room overlooking the lovely courtyard with a fountain.

**Hotel Turístico Varyná** (☎ 533-3984; hotelvarinat@cantv.net; Av 23 de Enero; d BsF220-230, tr BsF240-260; ) This motel-style place, set on a busy thoroughfare, still manages to provide a surprising amount of tranquility in a colony of 10 single-story cabins, each of which has four rooms with a bathroom and hot water.

**Hotel Bristol** (☎ 532-1425; hotelbristol@cantv.net; Av 23 de Enero; s/d BsF460/490, ste BsF670-840; ) Popular with business travelers, the decor in the Bristol hasn't changed for a couple of decades, but it has all the amenities, plus a convention hall in the same building.

## Drinking

**El Emperador** (☎ 533-4938; Calle 3 Bolívar btwn Avs 8 Sucre & 9 Briceño Méndez) Packed on weekends, this is the biggest party in the center. It also offers a peaceful, wood-paneled side bar for a quiet drink, and *parrilla* (mixed grill) at lunchtime during the week.

**Club Folklorico La Casa de Llano** (☎ 533-4938; Avenida 23 de Enero) This is the place to get in touch with your inner cowboy! The original cowboy poets and singers of the plains sing and play live *joropo* from Thursday to Sunday evenings. There's also a nice dinner selection, heavy on beef and chicken, naturally.

## Getting There & Away

### AIR

The small **Aeropuerto Nacional de Barinas** (☎ 533-2063; Av Codazzi) is 1.5km southwest of Plaza Bolívar. **Avior** (☎ 532-1203) has a daily flight to Caracas (BsF345), **Conviasa** (☎ 247-341-3178) has two flights (BsF358) and **Rutaca** has an early morning flight (BsF384).

### BUS

The **Terminal de Pasajeros** (Av Cuatricentenaria), 2km west of Plaza Bolívar, is serviced by local buses. Barinas has regular buses southwest to Maracaibo (BsF70, five hours, 313km) and northeast to Caracas (BsF65 to BsF70, 8½ hours, 512km). Buses to Guanare (BsF10, 1¼ hours, 85km) run every half-hour from 4am to 6pm.

There are frequent departures to Mérida (157km). The smaller por puesto vans (BsF30, three hours) are faster than the full-size buses

### JOROPO – MUSICAL PULSE OF LOS LLANOS

A skinny calico cat saunters across the cement dance floor and under a table. The *plink-plink* of the harpist tuning up tickles the ears; a sizzling *asada* (roast meat) on the table tingles the nose. The bass line bounces happily around the staccato rhythm of the *cuatro* (four-string small guitar), and the maracas player shuffles his hands up and down like a man mixing fruit juices.

A thick-set *llanero* in black cowboy hat and checked short-sleeved work shirt takes the microphone and begins reciting song-stories as the band keeps pace behind him: Rosalinda, the girl who broke his heart; the legendary tale of the fisherman and the beast; odes to family and the *llanero* way of life that the audience alternately laughs, cries or shouts along with.

Later, these spoken-word epics are replaced by the tuneful melodies of a young woman from Barquisimeto with an angelic voice and painted-on jeans. The swinging ceiling fans hanging from the bamboo ceilings beat time to the music, often mimicking the triple meter of the European waltz.

You're in the **Club Folklorico La Casa de Llano** (p187) of Barinas, and this is the *joropo*, the music of the *coleo* (rodeo)-loving, hard-riding, beef-eating Venezuelan cowboy.

Also known as the *música llanera* (Llanos music), the *joropo* is believed to have its origins in the Spanish flamenco, but it has changed considerably over the centuries in its new home. It's usually sung and accompanied by a small band that normally includes the *arpa llanera* (a local harp), a *cuatro* and maracas (gourd rattles).

The harp came over from Spain during the colonial period, and in the 20th century made its way into *joropo* music. By that time, it had evolved into a smaller and less elaborate version of its European parent. Normally associated with lyrical salon music, the harp has found a totally new form of expression in *joropo*. Presumably reflecting the hard life of the *llaneros*, it sounds clear and sharp, often even wild. The harp is sometimes replaced by the *bandola*, a mandolin derivative with a pear-shaped body and four nylon strings. The *cuatro* (also of European origin) accompanies the melody played by the harp or the *bandola*.

*Joropo* can be performed with or without words, and often is accompanied by a waltz-like dance, but whichever form you get to see, whether in the bars of Barinas or inside an air-conditioned *hato*, this heartfelt expression of the Venezuelan plains is well worth a listen.

(BsF25, five hours). The road, which winds up the mountain slopes, is spectacular; sit on the right for some dramatic views.

Several companies, including Expresos Los Llanos and Expresos Zamora, operate buses southeast into Los Llanos, with half a dozen departures daily to Puerto La Cruz (BsF100, nine hours, 469km). It's a hypnotic (some would say monotonous) way to travel right across the best part of Los Llanos.

## GUANARE

☎ 0257 / pop 114,000

Since its founding nearly 400 years ago, Guanare has been famous as a spiritual center. You can hardly throw a stone in Guanare without hitting a church or other religious monument (although you probably shouldn't do that).

Guanare is famed above all for its Virgen de Coromoto (or Nuestra Señora de Coromoto), the country's patron saint. It was around here in 1652 that the Virgin miraculously appeared before an indigenous chief and left him an image of herself (see the boxed text, p190). The site became a destination for pilgrims from around the region. The canonization in 1942 of the Virgin as the patron saint of Venezuela contributed to even larger floods of the faithful; today it's Venezuela's major pilgrimage center, attracting half a million visitors a year.

The focus of pilgrimages has moved to the exact place of the Virgin's apparition, 25km south of Guanare, where a huge sanctuary has been built, yet Guanare continues to pull in pilgrims as the Virgin's traditional home and the only city in the area.

### Information

#### MONEY

**Banco de Venezuela** (cnr Carrera 6 & Calle 15)
**Banco Mercantil** (cnr Carrera 5 & Calle 6)
**Banco Provincial** (cnr Carrera 5 & Calle 20)
**Banesco** (cnr Carrera 6 & Calle 16)

#### TELEPHONE

Both of these also have internet, with costs ranging from BsF5 to BsF10:

**CANTV** (Carrera 6 btwn Calles 16 & 17)
**Movistar** (Carrera 5 btwn Calles 10 & 11)

### TOURIST INFORMATION

**Corpotur** (Corporacíon Portugueseña de Turismo; ☎ 251-0324; Pabellón de Exposiciones, Av IND; ⏲ 8am-noon & 1-4pm Mon-Fri) The office is opposite the Instituto Nacional de Deporte, 1.5km southwest of the center.

## Sights

The most important religious monument is the **Basílica Catedral de Nuestra Señora de Coromoto** (Plaza Bolívar; ⏲ 6:30am-noon & 2-8pm Mon-Fri, 6:30am-7:30pm Sat & Sun). It was constructed from 1710 to 1742, but the 1782 earthquake almost completely destroyed it. The holy image of the Virgin, which had been kept inside, was saved and returned to the reconstructed church. It resided here until 1999, when it was taken to the new *santuario* (p190).

Once inside the church, your eyes will immediately be caught by a three-tier main retable (altar ledge), an excellent piece of colonial baroque art made in 1739. It later took 16 months to gild. In front of the retable stands the elaborate 3.4m-high *sagrario* (tabernacle), made entirely of silver. A painting on the dome over the high altar depicts the legend of the Virgen de Coromoto. The colorful stained-glass windows were commissioned in Munich, Germany.

The mid-18th-century **Convento de San Francisco** (☎ 251-6483; cnr Carrera 3 & Calle 17) no longer serves its original purpose as a convent. In 1825, Venezuela's first college was opened here. Today, the building accommodates the offices of the Universidad Nacional Experimental de los Llanos. You can enter its spacious courtyard, which has retained much of its old style and charm. The adjacent church is now used for university meetings and symposiums.

Opposite the church is a splendid two-story colonial mansion, one of the few buildings remaining from the Spanish period. It's now home to the **Museo de la Ciudad de Guanare** (☎ 253-0832; cnr Carrera 3 & Calle 17; admission BsF3; ⏲ 8am-4pm Tue-Fri, to 2pm Sat), and features exhibits related to the town's history. Don't miss visiting the rooms on the upper floor, which shelter a small but fine collection of historic religious art.

Two blocks north is **Parque Los Samanes** (cnr Carrera 1 & Calle 16; admission free; ⏲ 8:30am-5pm Tue-Sun), named after the species of spreading tree that grows in the park. You'll find an impressive specimen in front of the entrance. Bolívar's troops reputedly camped here in 1813.

There are several monuments dedicated to the Virgen de Coromoto in the town center, including the 1928 statue on **Plaza Coromoto**, seven blocks east of Plaza Bolívar along Carrera 5. On the same square you'll find a charming sculptured scene depicting the miraculous appearance of the Virgin to the native Cacique and his family.

Outside the center, just 500m west of the tourist office, is the **Museo de los Llanos** (Complejo Ferial José Antonio Páez; admission free; ⏲ 8am-5pm Mon-Fri & 10am-5:30pm Sat & Sun), which has an archeological collection from the region.

## Festivals & Events

As might be expected, Guanare's annual celebrations revolve around the Virgen de Coromoto. Most pilgrims flock to the city in time for the **Fiesta de la Virgen de Coromoto** on September 8, the anniversary of the Virgin's appearance.

Guanare is also noted for its **mascarada**, a three-day-long celebration that culminates in a parade of *carrozas* (floats) and a very realistic re-enactment of Jesus Christ's crucifixion during Semana Santa.

## Sleeping

**Posada del Reo** (☎ 808-0373; cnr Calle 16 & Carrera 3; s/d/tr BsF80/85/90; ❄) This former jail (the rooms are called *celdas* or cells), now a women's cooperative, could use a coat of paint. You'll sometimes be charmed (irritated?) by the local youth orchestra rehearsing next door.

**Hotel Italia** (☎ 253-1213, 251-4277; Calle 20 btwn Carreras 4 & 5; d BsF90-120, tr BsF120; ❄) This rambling budget option sprawls over four floors and pouts with an air of glory days gone by. The 87 rooms are neat and clean and all have air-con, cable TV and hot water (although in this climate, we have to wonder – why?).

**Hotel del Este** (☎ 251-7165; Carrera 12 & Av Unda; s/d/tr BsF90/100/120) This otherwise unremarkable offering is clean, neat and not far from the bus station. More importantly, it's just across the street from a busy commercial center that's open late, making it safe to wander a short ways for a late-night bite.

**Motel La Góndola** (☎ 251-2802, 253-1480; cnr Carrera 5 & Calle 3; d BsF110-120, tr/ste BsF150/200; ❄) Around 400m west of Plaza Coromoto, the palm-shaded motel is quiet and good value. Its 42 fair-sized rooms are arranged around two spacious courtyards, while the cozy restaurant serves palatable food at economic prices.

**A VENEZUELAN MIRACLE**

According to legend, on a sunny day in 1652, as indigenous Chief Coromoto and his wife were crossing a stream near their hut, a radiant lady of incredible beauty appeared and walked over the water toward them. While they stared at the divine creature, she started talking to them in their own language. She urged the chief to go with his tribe to the white men to have holy water poured over their heads so that they could go to heaven.

Astonished and confused, the chief promised to comply. He told the story to the Spaniard who owned a nearby plantation and with his permission the whole tribe soon moved onto the settler's land and built their huts. They were put to work on the plantation and given religious instruction.

As months passed, though, the chief was increasingly unhappy with the indoctrination and wanted to return to his native pastures. One day he refused to assist in religious acts and went back to his hut. While he tried to rest and calm his anger, the beautiful lady suddenly appeared again, radiating with rays of light more dazzling than the midday sun.

This time the chief was not in a peaceful mood. He grabbed his bow and arrows, but the shining vision moved quickly around. He then tried to catch her in his hands but the dazzling creature vanished. When he opened his hand all he found was a small image of the divine lady.

Angry and irritated, he threw the image down and ran into the dark night. While he was madly running through the woods, he was bitten by a venomous snake. Only then, moments before his death, did he ask to be baptized, and he told his tribe to do likewise.

The radiant lady, named the Virgen de Coromoto after the chief, is today the patron saint of Venezuela, while the tiny image he found in his hand is the object of devotion by millions of Venezuelans.

## Eating

**Los Toldos** (☎ 0414-792-8929; Av Simón Bolívar; meals BsF20-35) It hasn't got a menu, it hasn't got air-con – heck, it doesn't even have four walls – but this massively popular spot cranks out the *asado*, fresh off the grill. It does monster, heart-clogging *arepas con queso* (corn pancakes filled with cheese), and some mighty fine juices, too.

**El Bodegón de Pedro Miguel** (☎ 251-4358; cnr Calle 15 & Carrera 8; meals BsF30-50; closed Sunday) A long-standing tasca-style restaurant, with a long menu, moderate prices and a dim interior. It serves good chicken, pasta and seafood.

## Getting There & Away

### BUS

The **Terminal de Pasajeros** (Av UNDA) is 2km southeast of the city center, and is serviced regularly by local transportation. To get there from the center, take the eastbound busetas 12 or 24 from Carrera 5.

Guanare sits on El Llanos highway, so there is a fair bit of traffic heading southwest to San Cristóbal (BsF55 to BsF65, 6½ hours, 398km) and northeast to Caracas (BsF60 to BsF70, seven hours, 427km). There are hourly buses to Barquisimeto (BsF20, 3½ hours, 173km) and several departures a day to Boconó (BsF15 to BsF20, 3½ hours, 115km). Buses to Barinas (BsF10 to BsF15, 1¼ hours, 85km) frequently until 6pm. If you are heading to Mérida, go to Barinas and change.

# SANTUARIO NACIONAL DE NUESTRA SEÑORA DE COROMOTO

☎ 0257

The **Santuario Nacional** (☎ 251-5071, 251-5427; 8am-6pm) marks the holy site where the Virgen de Coromoto (see the boxed text, above) allegedly appeared in 1652. A cross was placed here after the event, and was later replaced with a chapel, but the site was isolated and rarely visited. Instead, the pilgrims flocked to Guanare's church, which for centuries boasted the holy image and effectively acted as the Virgin's shrine.

In 1980 the construction of a huge church at the actual site of the apparition commenced and was completed for the papal visit in February 1996, when 300,000 faithful attended a mass. The holy image of the Virgin has been brought to the site from Guanare.

From the outside, this all-concrete cathedral looks something like a cross between an aging rustbelt sports stadium and a Spielberg spaceship; from the inside, it looks like – and has the acoustics of – a rock concert hall. Alone in the church, the overwhelming sound is of twittering bird song, echoed and amplified by the vast acres of concrete curvature.

Some saving grace is to be found, however, in the marvelous stained-glass windows on the wall behind the high altar, which depict the history of the apparition as portrayed by Venezuelan artist Guillermo Márquez.

The high altar is said to be at the exact location where the Virgin appeared. The holy image is in an elaborate reliquary right behind the altar. You can get close and see the tiny image through the magnifying glass: its colors are almost totally washed out and the picture is faint and indistinct.

You can go up to a 36m-high viewing platform, built between the two towers (76m and 68m) and providing vast panoramic views; it's accessible by elevator for a nominal fee. A museum in the basement of the church features religious paraphernalia related to the Virgin and a collection of votive offerings.

### Getting There & Away

The Santuario is 25km south of Guanare – 10km by the main road toward Barinas, and then a further 15km by the paved side road branching off to the south. Small buses, operated by Línea Los Cospes, depart every 15 minutes from the corner of Carrera 9 and Calle 20 in Guanare, and will deposit you right at the church's entrance (BsF6, 40 minutes).

## SAN FERNANDO DE APURE

☎ 0247 / pop 79,000

The capital of Apure state, San Fernando is an old river port hundreds of miles away from any sizable urban center. The remoteness, the river and the lazy pace of life give the city a certain charm though most visitors come to San Fernando on their way to the *hatos* (p182) in the surrounding region, which boast some of the best wildlife-watching Los Llanos has to offer, it's certainly worth an afternoon stroll among the impressive monuments on Paseo Libertador.

San Fernando started as a missionary outpost at the end of the colonial era. Sitting on the bank of the large Río Apure, in the very heart of Los Llanos, the town developed into an important trading center, growing rich on the trade in heron and egret feathers and caiman skins. By the early 20th century, it was Venezuela's second-largest river port after Ciudad Bolívar. Today, cattle raising is the major activity in the region, followed by farming. Crops and livestock are funneled through San Fernando and trucked north to Caracas and the central states of Aragua, Carabobo and Miranda.

### Information

#### MONEY

**Banco Mercantil** (Paseo Libertador btwn Carreras 8 Aramendi & 9 Colombia)
**Banco Provincial** (Plaza Páez)
**Banesco** (cnr Paseo Libertador & Av 1 de Mayo)
**Corp Banca** (cnr Av Miranda & Calle 14)

#### TELEPHONE

**CANTV** (cnr Calle 18 Piar & Carrera 4) Also has internet ranging from BsF5 to BsF10.
**Movistar** (Bus Terminal)

#### TOURIST INFORMATION

**Coratur** (Corporacion Apureña de Turismo; ☎ 342-9963; Calle Rodríguez Rincones; 🕑 8am-noon & 2-6pm Mon-Fri)

#### TRAVEL AGENCIES

**Carmen Estrada** (0416-248-9030; cbestrada_864@hotmail.com) Although she closed her Dona Barbara agency and now operates out of Caracas, Ms Estrada remains a wealth of information on the Llanos and San Fernando.

### Sights

Walk along Paseo Libertador, the city's main thoroughfare. At its northern end is a circular plaza, its large **fountain** adorned with six charmingly kitsch concrete caimans. Beside the fountain is the **Monumento a Pedro Camejo**, a bronze equestrian statue of one of the bravest lancers to have fought in Bolívar's army. Camejo, who died in the battle of Carabobo, is known as Negro Primero, as he was the first black person to distinguish himself in the War of Independence.

Just east of the fountain is the ornate, two-story **Palacio Barbarito**, built by the Italian Barbarito brothers at the turn of the 19th century. At that time the Río Apure used to pass by just a few meters from the palace pier, and boats came directly from Europe up the Orinoco and Apure. The brothers made a fortune on heron and egret feathers during the 1910s' bonanza, but later on, when the business deteriorated, they sold the palace and left. It then passed through the hands of various owners who divided and subdivided it repeatedly, so much of the original internal design has been lost.

About 600m south along Paseo Libertador is the **Monumento a Los Llaneros**, dedicated to the tough *llanero* soldiers who made up the backbone of Bolívar's army. Another 600m down the Paseo is the huge **Monumento a San Fernando**, an allegorical monument to the city presented by the city itself.

The Plaza Bolívar, six blocks west of Paseo Libertador, boasts a modern tent-like **catedral** and an old **Masonic lodge**, and is pleasantly shaded with trees.

## Sleeping

**Hotel La Torraca** (☎ 342-2777, 342-2676; Paseo Libertador; d BsF100-110, tr/ste BsF130/150; ) The reception desk doesn't look very promising, but don't worry – the 48 rooms, distributed over three floors, are airy, bright and good value. Most of them look over the back and are quiet, but if you want some action, take a front room with a balcony and watch the world go by on the busy Paseo Libertador.

**Gran Hotel Plaza** (☎ 342-1504, 342-1255; Plaza Bolívar; s/d/tr BsF140/180/220; ) This is possibly San Fernando's top place to stay, though don't expect any Sheraton-like luxuries. It has 42 fairly reasonable rooms with views over the peaceful and leafy plaza. Uber-'70s bedspreads bring to mind grim visions of the Brady Bunch.

**Nuevo Hotel Apure** (☎ 341-0119, 341-2646; Av María Nieves; s/d BsF230/230; ) This motel-style, 29-room establishment offers comfy, quiet accommodations and a good, inexpensive restaurant. There's a mixture of older rooms and newer ones, so check out a few first – the new generation has king-size beds for no extra charge. Has nice high, wood ceilings.

## Eating

**Arepas La Estación** (Av Carabobo; arepas BsF10-15; 5:30pm-3:30am) This is a food kiosk, serving great *arepas* (stuffed corn pancakes) with 20 different fillings and open till late.

**La Taberna de Don Juan** (☎ 342-6259; Av Carabobo; meals BsF30-60) Don Juan is a respectable, slightly upmarket restaurant, hosting discos and live music – *joropo* – on Thursdays. It serves up quality international fare, including *paella valenciana*, and there's a nice internet cafe with air-con right next door.

**Italian's Pizza** (Av Carabobo; pizzas BsF40-85; 4:30-10:30pm Wed-Mon) This two-level pizza parlor pumps out the best – and quite possibly only – pizzas in town. Try the *super italia* (tuna, green olives and sausage), and finish the damage with one of four ice-cream flavors (BsF10 to BsF15).

**Restaurant Casa Bermejo** (☎ 342-7613; Paseo Libertador; meals BsF50-110) Set at the foot of the giant Monumento a San Fernando, this stylish spot sports waiters in peach shirts and ties and brightly colored tablecloths. It serves up good pasta, steak and seafood, especially the *bagre* or *dorado*, a yummy river fish that is not often seen on local menus. Shorts and flip-flops not welcome.

## Getting There & Away

### AIR

The **Aeropuerto Nacional Las Flecheras** had no service at the time of research.

### BUS

The bus terminal is on the northern outskirts of the city, near the river. You can either walk there (five minutes from Plaza Bolívar) or take a taxi (BsF8).

There are several departures a day to Caracas (BsF45 to BsF50, eight hours, 398km), or you can go by any of the half-hourly buses to Maracay (BsF52, seven hours, 319km) and change there. Half a dozen buses a day travel to Barinas (BsF45 to BsF52, nine hours, 469km) on a remote road across the heart of the plains. Keep a look out for animals.

**Transporte Campesino** has three trips daily along another interesting route, south to Puerto Ayacucho (BsF50, six hours, 299km) via Puerto Páez. The road is now paved all the way and traversable year-round, but the bridges over the Capanaparo and Cinaruco are incomplete, so the trip includes *chalana* (ferry) crossings across these two rivers and, obviously, across the Orinoco between Puerto Páez and El Burro. It's a very enjoyable trip. You can also reach San Cristobal (BsF69) and Valencia (BsF46 to BsF55) from here.

# The Northeast

Home to Venezuela's biggest holiday island, Isla de Margarita, the northeastern region sees many tourists both domestic and foreign, but most limit their activities to spending time on Margarita's beaches before flying out to Angel Falls, the Delta del Orinoco or the Andes. This makes some sense if you're doing a whistle-stop tour of the country, but if you have more time there are plenty of other areas to explore in the region, including the stunning beaches of the Península de Paria, many of which are vastly superior to the overcrowded and overdeveloped sands of Margarita. Other idyllic stretches of Venezuela's coastline include the dazzling islands and beaches of Parque Nacional Mochima and the ethereal landscapes of the rugged and remote Península de Araya.

The northeast isn't just about its pretty beaches, however. Inland there are lush mountains and verdant valleys to explore. This region also boasts Venezuela's most famous cave, and is home to fascinating wildlife, obscure hiking trails and a scattering of historical forts, towns and churches where the Spanish first conquered and settled.

## HIGHLIGHTS

- Find an unknown beach on **Isla de Margarita** (p195)
- Explore the picturesque islands of **Parque Nacional Mochima** (p211)
- Enjoy the stunning hillsides and secluded beaches east of **Río Caribe** (p222)
- Truly escape from the crowds to the remote tropical beaches of **Isla La Tortuga** (p213)
- Be amazed by the nocturnal, whiskered birds of **Cueva del Guácharo** (p227)

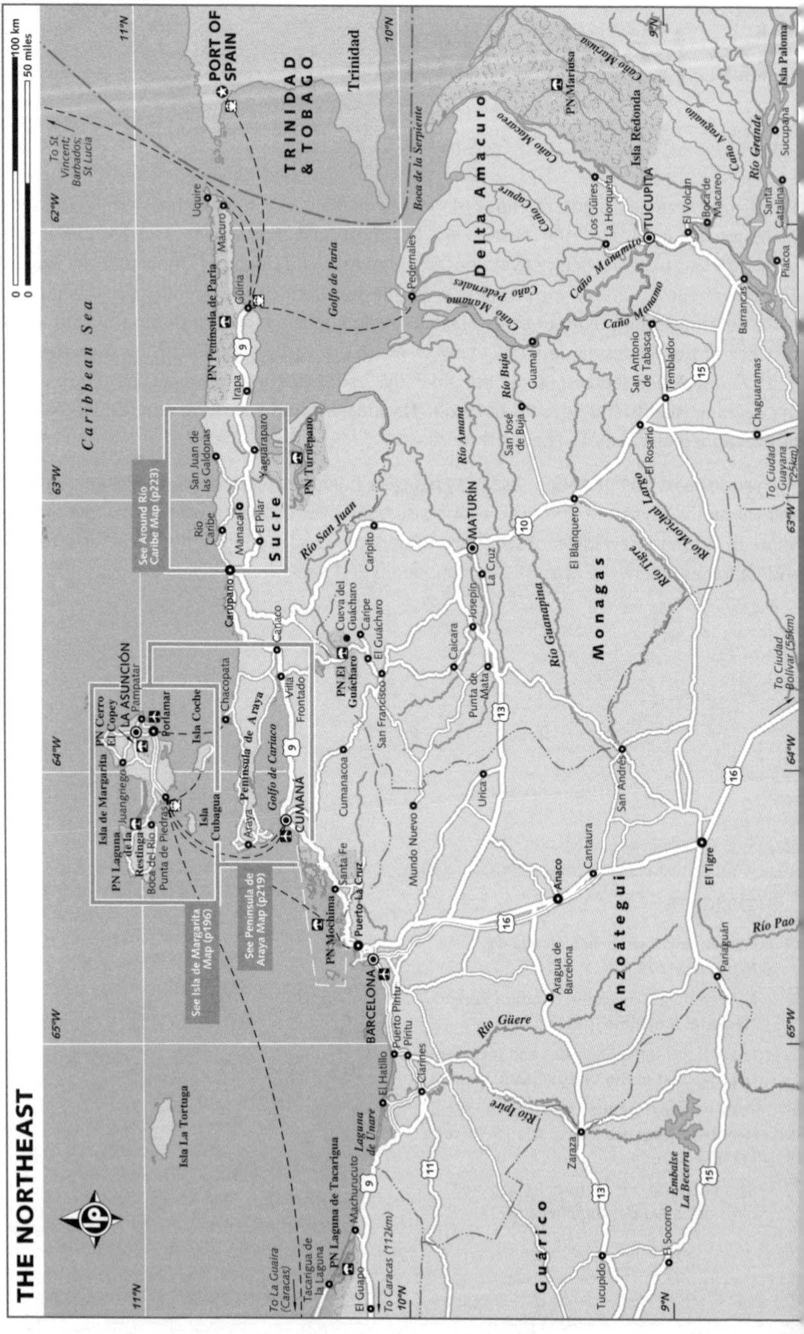
THE NORTHEAST
0 100 km
0 50 miles
Caribbean Sea
Isla La Tortuga
To La Guaira (Caracas)
To Caracas (112km)
To St Vincent; Barbados; St Lucia
PORT OF SPAIN
TRINIDAD & TOBAGO
Trinidad
Boca de la Serpiente
Golfo de Paria
Uquire
Macuro
Güiria
PN Península de Paria
Irapa
Yaguaraparo
San Juan de las Galdonas
PN Turuépano
See Around Río Caribe Map (p223)
Río Caribe
Manacal
El Pilar
Sucre
Carúpano
Río San Juan
Caripito
Cueva del Guácharo
Caripe
El Guácharo
PN El Guácharo
San Francisco
Cañaco
Villa Frontado
Chacopata
Península de Araya
Golfo de Cariaco
Araya
CUMANÁ
Cumanacoa
Isla Coche
Isla Cubagua
Isla de Margarita
PN Cerro El Copey
LA ASUNCIÓN
Pampatar
Porlamar
Juangriego
PN Laguna de la Restinga
Boca del Río
Punta de Piedras
See Isla de Margarita Map (p196)
See Península de Araya Map (p219)
PN Mochima
Santa Fe
Puerto La Cruz
BARCELONA
Puerto Píritu
Píritu
Clarines
El Hatillo
Laguna de Unare
Machurucuto
PN Laguna de Tacarigua
Tacarigua de la Laguna
El Guapo
Mundo Nuevo
Urica
Caicara
Jusepín
Punta de Mata
MATURÍN
La Cruz
Río Amana
San José de Buja
Río Buja
Guamal
Pedernales
Caño Mánamo
Caño Pedernales
Delta Amacuro
Caño Capure
Caño Macareo
PN Mariusa
Caño Mariusa
Isla Redonda
Los Güires
La Horqueta
Caño Manamito
TUCUPITA
El Volcán
Boca de Macareo
Caño Araguao
Río Grande
Sucupana
Isla Paloma
Santa Catalina
Piacoa
Barrancas
Temblador
San Antonio de Tabasca
Chaguaramas
El Rosario
El Blanquero
Río Morichal Largo
Río Tigre
Monagas
Río Guanapiña
To Ciudad Guayana (25km)
To Ciudad Bolívar (55km)
San Andrés
Cantaura
Anaco
El Tigre
Anzoátegui
Aragua de Barcelona
Río Güere
Pariaguán
Río Pao
Río Unare
Zaraza
Embalse La Becerra
Tucupido
El Socorro
Guárico
11°N
10°N
9°N
62°W
63°W
64°W
65°W

# ISLA DE MARGARITA

☎ 0295 / pop 385,000

How to be fair to Venezuela's top beach destination? While Isla de Margarita itself certainly has some of the country's best beaches and enjoys a dramatic, mountainous interior to boot, its unchecked development, traffic-clogged roads and creeping urban sprawl has made something of a joke out of its tropical paradise reputation. That said, there are lots of reasons to come here (just ask any Venezuelan where they want to go on holiday), but if you come expecting a Caribbean idyll, you'll be disappointed.

With an area of 1071 sq km, Isla de Margarita is Venezuela's largest island, 69km from east to west and 35km from north to south. Lying 40km off the mainland, it is composed of what were once two islands, now linked by a narrow, crescent-shaped sandbank, La Restinga. The island houses five major nature reserves, among them two national parks.

Margarita's urban sprawl around the island's largest town, Porlamar, now extends unbroken to the nearby towns of Los Robles and Pampatar. These areas, full of glitzy shops, huge hotels and beach bars, are the favored haunts of holidaying Venezuelans, though more discerning travelers may want to avoid this corner of the island and escape the crowds. By far the best bits of the island are to be found elsewhere – the terrific beaches of Playa El Agua and Playa El Yaque, the inland mountains, the quiet fishing villages around Juangriego and the largely untouched Península de Macanao are the real highlights of any visit here.

Margarita boasts a rich spectrum of habitats, from mangrove swamps to mountainous cloud forest and extensive semidesert. It features two fine Spanish forts, one of the oldest churches in the country and a sprinkling of little old towns, some of which are vivid centers of craftwork. The well-developed tourist infrastructure means that there are all kinds of activities on offer, from snorkeling trips to world-class windsurfing.

The island's typically Caribbean climate is glorious year-round: temperatures are between 75°F and 85°F, mitigated by evening breezes. The rainy period lasts from November to January, with rain falling mostly during the night. Peak seasons include Christmas, Easter and the August holiday period. May, June and October are the quietest months.

## Getting There & Away

### AIR

All major national airlines fly into the modern **Aeropuerto Internacional del Caribe General Santiago Mariño** (☎ 269-1027), and destinations within Venezuela include Caracas, Barcelona, Cumaná, Canaima, Valencia, Maturín and Los Roques. As well as charter flights from North America and Europe, there are international connections to Port of Spain in Trinidad and Tobago.

Except for Aserca, the following airline offices are located in Porlamar:

**Aereotuy** (LTA; Map p198; ☎ 415-5778; Av Santiago Mariño)

**Aeropostal** (Map p198; ☎ 263-1374; www.aeropostal.com; Centro Comercial Galerías, Av 4 de Mayo)

**Aserca** (OCA; ☎ 269-8990; www.asercaairlines.com; Av Bolívar, Centro Comercial Provemed, Pampatar)

**Conviasa** (VCV; Map p198; ☎ 0500-266-84272; www.conviasa.com; Centro Comercial Galerías local 27, Av 4 de Mayo)

**Laser** (LER;Map p198; ☎ 263-9195; www.laser.com.ve, in Spanish; Calle Maneiro)

**Rutaca** (RUC; ☎ 263-9236; www.rutaca.com.ve; Centro Comercial Jumbo, Av 4 de Mayo)

### BOAT

Puerto La Cruz and Cumaná are the main jumping-off points to Margarita; car ferries arrive at Punta de Piedras (29km west of Porlamar). Frequent buses (BsF3, 35 minutes) run between Punta de Piedras and Porlamar; taxis charge BsF40 to BsF50. There are also small passenger-only boats to the island from the dock of Chacopata, on the Península de Araya; these go directly to Porlamar.

#### From Puerto La Cruz

This route is served by **Conferry** (Map p198; ☎ 0501-2663-3779; www.conferry.com, in Spanish; Av Llano Adentro, Porlamar; 🕑 8am-noon & 2-5pm Mon-Fri, 8am-noon Sat), which has several departures daily. Check the website for exact times and dates.

Regular ferries cost from BsF38 to BsF50 for adults (depending on class) and cars are BsF67 to BsF78 (depending on size); the trip takes about 4½ hours. Express ferries cost BsF95 to BsF146 for adults and cars are BsF112 to BsF140; the trip takes two hours.

Additionally, the route is operated by the passenger-only hydrofoil **Gran Cacique Express**

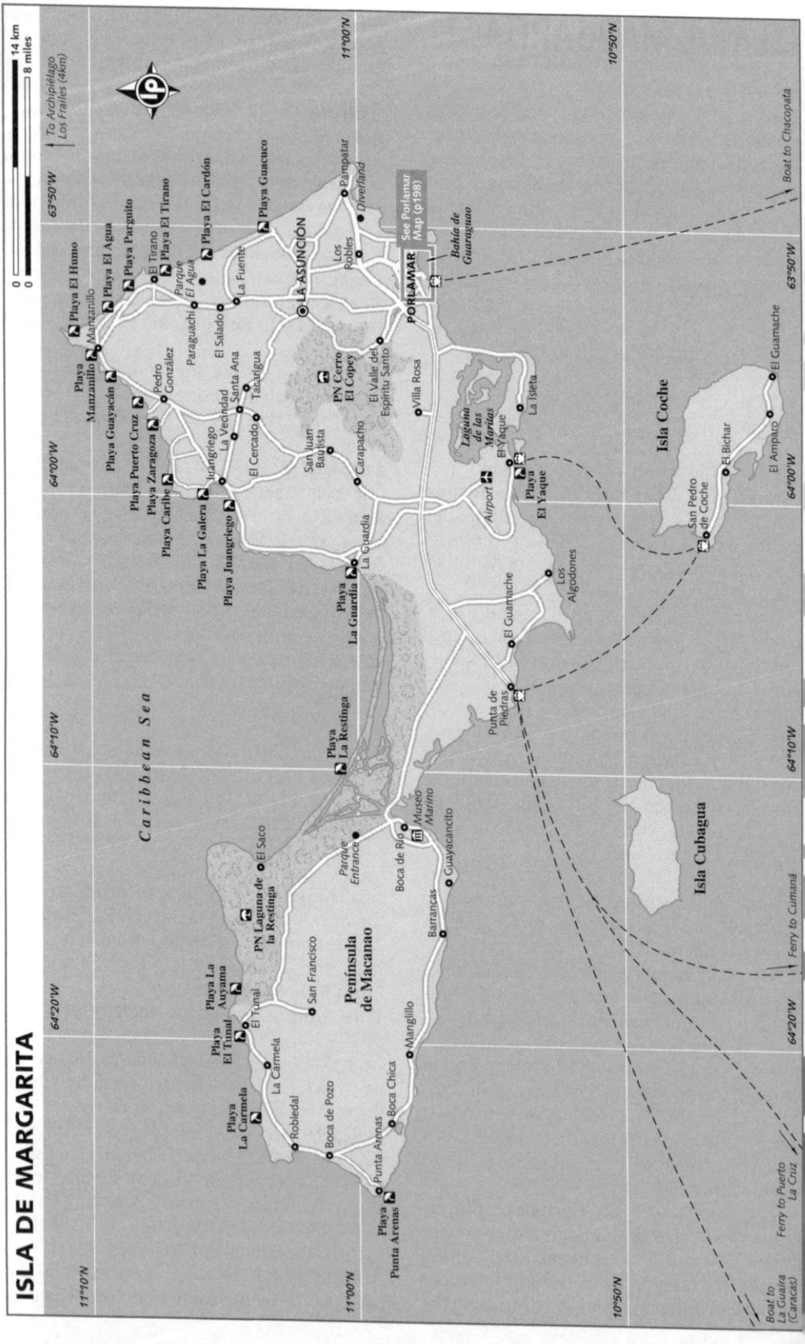
ISLA DE MARGARITA
0 14 km
0 8 miles
To Archipiélago Los Frailes (4km)
Caribbean Sea
LA ASUNCIÓN
PORLAMAR
See Porlamar Map (p198)
Bahía de Guaraguao
Pampatar
Diverland
Los Robles
La Fuente
El Salado
Paraguachí
Parque El Agua
El Tirano
Manzanillo
Playa El Humo
Playa El Agua
Playa Parguito
Playa El Tirano
Playa El Cardón
Playa Guacuco
Playa Manzanillo
Playa Guayacán
Pedro González
Playa Puerto Cruz
Playa Zaragoza
Playa Caribe
Playa La Galera
Playa Juangriego
Juangriego
La Vecindad
Santa Ana
Tacarigua
El Cercado
PN Cerro El Copey
El Valle del Espíritu Santo
Villa Rosa
San Juan Bautista
Carapacho
La Guardia
Playa La Guardia
Laguna de las Marites
El Yaque
Playa El Yaque
La Isleta
Airport
Los Algodones
El Guamache
Punta de Piedras
Playa La Restinga
Museo Marino
Boca de Río
Guayacancito
Parque Entrance
El Saco
PN Laguna de la Restinga
Península de Macanao
San Francisco
Barrancas
Playa La Auyama
El Tunal
Playa El Tunal
La Carmela
Playa La Carmela
Robledal
Boca de Pozo
Manglillo
Boca Chica
Punta Arenas
Playa Punta Arenas
Isla Coche
San Pedro de Coche
El Bichar
El Amparo
El Guamache
Isla Cubagua
Boat to Chacopata
Ferry to Cumaná
Ferry to Puerto La Cruz
Boat to La Guaira (Caracas)
11°10'N
11°00'N
10°50'N
64°20'W
64°10'W
64°00'W
63°50'W

(☎ 264-2945; www.grancacique.com.ve; Edificio Blue Sky, Av Mariño; 8am-noon & 2-6pm Mon-Fri, 8am-2pm Sat), with the choice of tourist or VIP class (BsF57/82, two hours). On all ferries, children aged two to seven and seniors over 65 pay half-price.

#### From Cumaná

From Cumaná, **Gran Cacique** (☎ 0293-431-5577; www.grancacique.com.ve), has two to three daily pedestrian-only departures (tourist/VIP BsF60/80, two hours) to Punta de Piedras. Its affiliate **Naviarca** (☎ 239-8439) has four daily car-ferry departures (adults BsF40, children BsF20, cars from BsF70, 4½ hours). In Margarita, Naviarca tickets are available only at Punta de Piedras (☎ 239-8232).

#### From Peninsula de Araya

The cheapest route to Isla de Margarita is on the passenger-only boat service that ferries people between Chacopata and Porlamar. Boats run approximately every two hours, or when full, from 8am until about 4pm Monday to Saturday and until 2pm Sunday. The schedule can be unreliable – if there are few passengers around, some departures may be canceled. Boats hold up to 70 passengers and are not for the queasy at sea. The trip takes one hour to 1½ hours (BsF25).

### Getting Around

Margarita's smart and modern airport is in the southern part of the island, 20km southwest of Porlamar. There is no public transportation that can take you from the airport to your destination; you'll have to spring for a taxi (BsF50).

Porlamar is the island's transportation hub, where frequent small buses (called *micros* or busetas) service towns and beaches around the eastern part of the island. Public transportation on the Península de Macanao is very poor.

There are about a dozen car-rental companies opposite the airport's international terminal, and many have offices in Porlamar as well. Due to the competition, this is one of the cheapest places in Venezuela to hire a car. Roads and signposting on the island are both very good by national standards.

For more laid-back sightseeing, plenty of travel agencies will happily show you around. They offer general-interest tours, specific trips (eg Laguna de la Restinga) and activities (eg horseback riding, fishing, snorkeling, scuba diving). The Archipiélago Los Frailes, northeast of Margarita, is a popular destination for snorkeling and diving.

There are fast and cheap connections to the nearby island of Coche from El Yaque (BsF50, 20 mins) leaving daily between 8am and 2pm and returning in the afternoon.

## PORLAMAR

**pop 143,000**

The unofficial capital of Margarita and the only place on the island that can be called a city, Porlamar is a scruffy and unattractive place for the most part. For many bargain-hungry Venezuelans however, it is Margarita, a duty-free port of bright and loud stores with its own decent beach and plenty of eating and drinking options. Most travelers will find Porlamar a place of little interest, though, and should take care here after dark. To the city's east Porlamar now merges with Los Robles and Pampatar to form an ugly urban scar on the bottom-right-hand corner of this once pristine island.

Porlamar has come a long way since 1536, when it was founded. Less than 40 years later, Christopher Columbus sailed past the island on his way to the mainland. You can glimpse some of the city's past in the older part of town; tree-shaded Plaza Bolívar is the historic center.

### Information

#### EMERGENCY

**Police** (☎ 264-1494; Centro Comercial Bella Vista, cnr Calle San Rafael & Av Terrenova)

#### INTERNET ACCESS

Most internet places charge BsF4 per hour.

**Cyber Café Am@zonas** (Av Raúl Leoni; 8am-10pm) Also does international calls.

**Internet Café** (Hotel Boulevard, Calle Marcano; 8am-8pm)

**La Comarca** (Calle Fermin; 9am-8pm)

#### LAUNDRY

**Lavandería Edikö's** (Calle Fermín; 8am-7pm Mon-Sat, 8:30am-1pm Sun)

**Lavandería La Burbuja** (☎ 263-2115; Calle Maneiro; 7am-7pm Mon-Sat)

#### MEDICAL SERVICES

Many clinics and pharmacies are clustered on and around Av 4 de Mayo, near the hospital.

**Clínica La Fe** (☎ 262-2711; Av Jóvito Villalba, Los Robles) A good clinic outside the center.

**Hospital Central Dr Luís Ortega** (☎ 261-1101, 261-6508; Av 4 de Mayo) The most convenient medical clinic on the island.

PORLAMAR
INFORMATION
Banco de Venezuela 1 B3
Banco Mercantil 2 B3
Banesco 3 C2
Corp Banca 4 B3
Cyber Café Am@zonas 5 D3
Hospital Central Dr Luís Ortega 6 C2
Internet Café (see 13)
Ipostel 7 B4
La Comarca 8 D1
Lavandería Edikö's 9 D3
Lavandería La Burbuja 10 B4
SIGHTS & ACTIVITIES
Museo de Arte Contemporáneo Francisco Narváez 11 C3
SLEEPING
Casa Lutecia 12 D2
Hotel Boulevard 13 B3
Hotel Central 14 B3
Hotel Colibrí 15 C2
Hotel Flamingo City 16 C1
Hotel Imperial 17 D3
Hotel Jinama 18 B4
Hotel María Luisa 19 D3
Residencias Virginia Mar 20 D1
EATING
4D 21 D2
El Pollo de Carlitos 22 A3
El Rancho de Pablo 23 D3
Jumbo Arepa 24 D1
La Casa de Rubén 25 D3
Mediterraneo Bluu Café 26 D2
Panadería 4 de Mayo 27 D1
Pollos El Cacique 28 C3
Positano 29 D2
Restaurant Punto Criollo 30 B3
Restaurant Rancho Típico Mandinga 31 D3
Vivaldi Panadería 32 D2
DRINKING
Cheers 33 C2
El Rancho de Pablo (see 23)
SHOPPING
Ciudad Comercial Jumbo 34 D1
Handicraft Stalls 35 D3
TRANSPORT
Aereotuy (LTA) 36 D3
Aeropostal (see 49)
Boats to Chacopata 37 C4
Buses to El Valle 38 B3
Buses to Juangriego 39 B3
Buses to La Asunción 40 C3
Buses to La Restinga 41 B4
Buses to Pampatar 42 C3
Buses to Playa El Agua 43 B3
Buses to Punta de Piedras 44 B4
Buses to Punta de Piedras 45 B3
Car-rental Companies 46 D3
Chacopata Tickets 47 C4
Conferry 48 B1
Conviasa 49 D1
Gran Cacique 50 C3
Laser 51 C4
Por Puestos & Taxis to Airport 52 B3
Rutaca 53 D1
0 800 m
0 0.4 miles
To Police (200m)
To Los Robles (5km); Clínica La Fe (5km); Corpotur (5km); Diverland (7km); Centro Comercial Sambil (7km); Rampatar (10km)
To Centro Comercial Costa Azul (2km); British Bulldog (2km); Señor Frog's (2km); La Samanna de Margarita (3km); Kamy Beach (6km)
To Airport (20km); Punta de Piedras (29km)
Bahía de Guaraguao
Río El Valle
Puerto de la Mar
Old Lighthouse
Hotel Bella Vista
Plaza Bolívar
Catedral
Av 4 de Mayo
Av Santiago Mariño
Av Raúl Leoni
Av Miranda
Blvd Gómez
Blvd Guevara

#### MONEY

Most stores accept cash dollars for payment using the official exchange rate, though some will give you the black-market rate (negotiate).

**Banco de Venezuela** (Blvd Guevara)
**Banco Mercantil** (Calle San Nicolás)
**Banesco** (Av 4 de Mayo)
**Corp Banca** (Calle Velázquez)

#### POST

**Ipostel** (☎ 416-3583; Calle Maneiro; 🕑 8am-noon & 1-4:30pm Mon-Fri)

#### TOURIST INFORMATION

**Corpotur** (☎ 262-2322; Centro Artesanal Gilberto Menchini, Av Jóvito Villalba, Los Robles; 🕑 8:30am-12:30pm & 1:30-4:30pm Mon-Fri) This government-run tourist office is rather unhelpfully located midway between Porlamar and Pampatar.

### Sights & Activities

Porlamar's only real tourist sight is the very enjoyable **Museo de Arte Contemporáneo Francisco Narváez** (☎ 261-8668; cnr Calles Igualdad & Díaz; 🕑 9am-5pm Mon-Fri, 10am-4pm Sat & Sun), in a large, modern building in the town center. On the ground floor is an interesting collection of sculptures and paintings by the Margarita-born artist Francisco Narváez (1905–82) and some of his contemporaries, while the upper floor is used for temporary exhibitions.

### Sleeping

Despite boasting a huge number of hotels, Porlamar's accommodation options are almost entirely a depressing bunch. Prices are high and standards are very low. Cheapies are mostly located in the older town center, west of Av Santiago Mariño, while standards are generally better at hotels to the east. Three kilometers out of town in Urbanización Costa Azul you'll find the four- to five-star hotels.

Prices given are for the low season. Expect to pay around another 30% or more when visiting around vacation or holiday times (August, December, Semana Santa and Carnaval).

#### BUDGET

**Hotel Jinama** (☎ 261-7186; Calle Mariño; s/d/tr/q BsF50/100/120/140; ❄) Here's a good budget choice that's quiet inside despite being on a busy commercial street. Rooms are basic but decent, each has a private bathroom, and it's friendly enough. Cable TV and fridges sweeten the deal.

**Residencias Virginia Mar** (☎ 261-2373; Calle Fermín; r from BsF80; ❄) A rather large, unappealing hotel with sizable but boring budget rooms, some quite dark. Top-floor doubles, facing a covered balcony over the street, are the best choices. Staff can be rather gruff.

**Hotel Central** (☎ 264-7162; Blvd Gómez; r/tr/q BsF100/140/160; ❄) Located on bustling Blvd Gómez, this good option has a pleasant airy feel to its public areas with their tiled floors and kitschy art. Rooms are very simple with pretty bad bathrooms, but they're absolutely fine for a night or two. The best part is the large balcony overlooking the pedestrian street.

**Hotel Flamingo City** (☎ 264-5564; Av 4 de Mayo; s/d/tr BsF140/160/180; ❄) Strategically placed on the main shopping street, Flamingo City has uniform, carpeted rooms with a fridge and a safe. It's recognizable by the bright-blue paint job and its position in the shadow of an enormous bank building next door.

**Casa Lutecia** (☎ 263-8526; Calle Campos; d/ste BsF140/180; ❄) One of the most pleasant stays in Porlamar, this pretty little Mediterranean-like spot is strewn with flowers, hanging vines and palm trees, which gives it a tropical feel and relaxed atmosphere. The highlight is an excellent rooftop pool boasting a sunny bar-terrace. Rooms are pleasant and comfortable, and come with cable TV, though we found the air-con wasn't good enough to properly cool the rooms.

**Hotel Boulevard** (☎ 261-0522; hotelboulevard@cantv.net; Calle Marcano; s/d/tr/q BsF158/168/188/208; P ❄ 💻) Not a luxurious choice, but it does have 48 clean, dated but decent rooms. Rooms at the back have a view of urban blight plus distant mountains. There's cable TV and air-con in all rooms, and though there's no wi-fi, there is an internet cafe downstairs.

#### MIDRANGE

**Hotel María Luisa** (☎ 261-0564; www.hotelmarialuisa.com.ve; Av Raúl Leoni; s&d/tr BsF210/240 ste BsF280-320; P ❄ 💻 🏊 📶) Waterfront hotel with bright, white-tiled rooms sporting big windows (some with sea views) and cable TV. There's wi-fi in the lobby alongside a quirky display of antique technology. The hotel is good value for money, and within strolling distance of seafront restaurants.

**Hotel Imperial** (☎ 261-6420; www.hotelimperial.com.ve; Av Raúl Leoni; s&d/tr/ste BsF220/250/280; P ❄) A large white hotel with decent but rather tired-looking rooms. Higher-up rooms come with a balcony and a sea view.

**our pick** **Hotel Colibrí** (☎ 261-6346; www.hotelcolibrimargarita.com; Av Santiago Mariño; s&d/tr BsF250/300; P ❄ 💻 📶) For our money the best midrange place in town, the Colibrí is central, squeaky clean and has spacious rooms featuring wooden furniture, cable TV and fridges. Corridors are decorated with mosaics, art and pastel-pink paint, and there's free wi-fi in the lobby.

### TOP END

Most of Porlamar's upmarket hotels and nightclubs are located 3km east of the city in a large area called Urbanización Costa Azul. These destinations, some located at the beach, tend to be spread out from each other and the area still has some large, ugly bare patches, so it's not a great place in which to stroll around. Margarita's most famous hotel, the Hilton Margarita, was nationalized in 2009 and is not currently recommended. Similarly we don't recommend the Hotel Bella Vista, a Porlamar landmark that is overpriced and has been the subject of some reader complaints in the past.

**La Samanna de Margarita** (☎ 262-2222; www.lasamannademargarita.com; Av Francisco Esteban Gómez; r incl breakfast from BsF834; P ⊠ ❄ 💻 🏊) This Mediterranean-style hotel offers airy rooms with balconies (get a sea view) and romantic four-poster beds draped in curtains. Bathrooms have quirky fish themes and give you the choice to bathe in either (filtered) salt or fresh water – very unique. Plus there's an on-site spa that offers facials, massages, reflexology and mud baths, along with a large Jacuzzi pool – a very pampering experience indeed.

## Eating

Porlamar has great eating options catering for every price range. While most of the restaurants in town are pitched at tourists to a degree, be aware that eating along the seafront will mean that this is definitely the case.

### RESTAURANTS

**Restaurant Punto Criollo** (☎ 263-6745; Calle Igualdad 19; mains BsF20-60; 🕐 10:30am-10:30pm; ❄) Deservedly popular with locals for its solid food and great prices, this busy and efficient restaurant has a homey, comfortable atmosphere and a wealth of menu choices. Try the *churrasco a la llanera* (grilled steak), garlic shrimp, veggie pizza or spaghetti Alfredo. Portions are large.

**La Casa de Rubén** (☎ 264-5969; Av Santiago Mariño; mains BsF30-70; 🕐 11am-6pm Mon-Sat) This charming, hidden-away family-run restaurant comes complete with a massive collection of kitschy art and old photos on the walls. But come here for the top-notch seafood, all prepared using traditional island recipes, and featuring treats such as fish roe and fresh mussels.

**Restaurant Rancho Típico Mandinga** (☎ 263-9755; Av Raúl Leoni; mains BsF33-90; 🕐 noon-11pm) A large, barn-like eatery on the beach, Mandinga is fun when it's busy, but can feel like an aircraft hanger when it's not. Seafood is the speciality here.

**Positano** (☎ 264-0951; Calle Fermin; mains BsF35-90; 🕐 noon-11pm Mon-Sat; ❄) Serving up some of the best pizza in the country, Positano is an Italian restaurant that offers a full menu of pasta, meat dishes and multiple delicious pizzas cooked in a wood-fired oven. You can eat inside to escape the heat of the day, or take a table outside under the terracotta-tiled awning in the evenings. Take-away is available.

**our pick** **Mediterraneo Bluu Café** (☎ 264-8848; Calle Campos; mains BsF35-100; 🕐 10am-10pm Mon-Sat; ❄) By far the best place to eat in town, this smart, friendly and excellent Mediterranean-fusion restaurant has a sumptuous and innovative menu and the choice of tables in a shaded courtyard or in its North African–style interior. There's a good selection of South American wines and a stylish ambience to any meal here.

**El Rancho de Pablo** (☎ 263-1121; Av Raúl Leoni; mains BsF36-158; 🕐 noon-10pm Mon-Sat, daily in high season) Right on the beach, this relaxed and friendly bar-restaurant has good service and pleasant wooden fittings. There's a large menu of seafood, grills and pasta, and kicking cocktails.

### CAFÉS & QUICK EATS

**Panadería 4 de Mayo** (Calle Fermín at 4 de Mayo; pastries from BsF3; 🕐 7am-11pm) Of several bustling *panaderías* (bakeries) in the vicinity, this invariably popular spot comes up trumps. It also has beautiful pastries, sandwiches and cakes and its terrace is one of Porlamar's top people-watching spots, though you may have to fight for a table.

**Vivaldi Panadería** (☎ 263-3150; Calle Patiño at Calle Malavé; pastries from BsF4; 🕐 7am-10pm Mon-Sat, to 2pm Sun; ❄) A tranquil spot for frothy cappuccinos, excellent pastries and a morning newspaper. Vivaldi's bakery has a pleasant little terrace or air-con interior from which to choose.

**4D** (☎ 261-5805; Calle Malavé; ice cream from BsF4; 🕑 11:30am-11pm) Opposite Vivaldi is this popular ice-cream parlor with a large, shaded terrace. The enormous and luminous range comprises every imaginable flavor.

**Jumbo Arepa** (☎ 263-2701; Calle Campos; arepas BsF12-20; 🕑 24hr) If all else fails, you can eat anytime at this *arepera* (restaurant selling *arepas;* stuffed corn pancakes) that never closes. Even if you're not hungry at 3am, this is a good choice – delicious fillings and low prices that also make for a great-value lunch.

**Pollos El Cacique** (Calle Igualdad; mains from BsF15; 🕑 10am-10pm) A reasonably good-value chicken affair, this time in a popular and modern fast-food environment with identically uniformed staff. There are just a couple of side dishes and some juices, otherwise it's only *pollo*.

**El Pollo de Carlitos** (Calle Marcano; mains from BsF20; 🕑 noon-1am Mon-Sat) This rustic restaurant does great grilled chicken and meats and has an airy front patio, but it's located in an unattractive area. Try the half chicken with *hallaca* (chopped meat and vegetables in corn dough, steamed in banana leaves) and salad.

## Drinking & Clubbing

Nightlife in and around Porlamar is hardly cutting-edge. Most of the popular nightclubs and bars are beyond Porlamar center, and some are open in high season only. There's always a collection of rustic shacks, well stocked with cold beers, on the beach for something simpler. There are several smaller huts and bars nearby, though nothing here runs very late.

**British Bulldog** (☎ 267-1527; Centro Comercial Costa Azul, Av Bolívar; 🕑 9pm-late Thu-Sat, Tue-Sat in high season; ⚄) Plastered with Union Jacks, Margarita's first and only British-style pub has live rock Wednesday through Saturday, but no pints.

**Cheers** (☎ 261-0957; Av Santiago Mariño; 🕑 noon-11pm Mon-Sat; ⚄) Ripping off the US sitcom's logo and identity is this surprisingly pleasant restaurant-bar with a dark pub atmosphere, good food and a great U-shaped bar. The decor is one of tasteful wood and brick, along with sports on the TV. It's on the 2nd floor.

**El Rancho de Pablo** (☎ 263-1121; Av Raúl Leoni; 🕑 noon-10pm Mon-Sat, daily in high season) It's hard not to slip into a mellow holiday mood at this beachside bar and restaurant, or indeed an alcohol-induced coma with the strong cocktails.

**Kamy Beach** (☎ 267-3787; Av Aldonza Marique, Playa Varadera, Pampatar; 🕑 9pm-4am Thu-Sat, nightly in high season) This slick, beachside nightclub has a distinct tropical feel, with swaying palms, thatched-roofed bars and square beds (with romantic curtains) on the sand. White lounge sofas and airy terraces overlook the beach – great for chilling out and listening to the waves. Live bands and DJs also.

**Señor Frog's** (☎ 262-0451; Centro Comercial Costa Azul, Av Bolívar; 🕑 6pm-4am Tue-Sun, nightly in high season; ⚄) One of Porlamar's most popular party destinations is this brightly colored building accented with cartoon figures inside and out. It's a restaurant until 11:30pm, then a thumping Latin-pop-oriented *discoteca* (disco) by night.

## Shopping

Venezuelans are crazy for shopping on Isla de Margarita, though foreigners may not always feel the same – you'll find few international brands, and the local fashion scene, while decent and good value, won't always be inspiring. Look for sales and pluck up the nerve to ask for *'su mejor precio'* ('your best price'), even in boutiques.

The most elegant and expensive shopping areas are on and around Avs Santiago Mariño and 4 de Mayo. Here you'll find jewelry, imported spirits, clothing, electronics etc. Right in town is the huge six-level **Ciudad Comercial Jumbo** (Av 4 de Mayo at Calle Campos). Or catch a bus out to **Centro Comercial Sambil** (Av Bolívar; 🕑 10am-9pm Mon-Sat, noon-8pm Sun), which is one of the shiniest of the island's shopping malls.

The old center has some of the cheapest shops and is more of a fun local experience. The streets south of Plaza Bolívar bustle all day long, especially the two central pedestrian malls, Blvd Guevara and Blvd Gómez.

For local crafts, in the afternoon, **handicraft stalls** open along the southern part of Av Santiago Mariño, selling their wares until 9pm or 10pm.

## Getting There & Around

The airport is the hub for both international and national routes to Isla de Margarita; see p195 for details.

Frequent buses link Porlamar to the rest of the island, including Pampatar, La Asunción, Playa El Agua and Juangriego. They leave from different points in the city center; see the Porlamar map (p198) for bus stops.

Porlamar is a great place to rent cars, as there are lots of competing agencies, keeping prices low. As well as all the big international firms at the airport, there are several local car-rental

**FINDING YOUR OWN PARADISE**

Isla de Margarita has 167km of world-famous coastline endowed with some 50 beaches big enough to bear names, not to mention countless smaller stretches of sandy coast. Many beaches have become highly developed tourist magnets with swish hotels, beachside restaurants, bars, and deck chairs and sunshades for rent. However, though the island is far from a virgin paradise, with a little legwork you can still find relatively deserted strips of sand, too.

Margarita's beaches have little shade, and some are virtually barren. Those on the northern and eastern coasts are generally better than those skirting the southern shore of the island. You can camp on the beaches, but don't leave your tent unattended, as theft can occur. Swimmers should be aware of the dangerous undertows on some beaches, including at Playas El Agua and Puerto Cruz.

Top destinations include **Playa Manzanillo** and **Playa Puerto Cruz**, the latter of which has arguably the widest, whitest stretch of sand and still isn't too overdeveloped. **Playa Parguito**, next to Playa El Agua, has strong waves good for surfing, and **Playa Caribe** is a 1.5km-long gem with a few open restaurants but no posadas – yet.

If you want to escape from people, head for the largely unpopulated **Península de Macanao**, which is the wildest part of the island – and so are some of its beaches, which are mostly shadeless and deserted. A reasonable road skirts right around the barren peninsula so travelers with their own transportation can easily explore the whole coastline.

companies in front of the Hotel Bella Vista, but you'll find other places in town.

## PAMPATAR

**pop 50,000**

While less built up than its neighbor Porlamar, which lies 10km to the southwest, Pampatar also suffers from the urban blight that has afflicted so many parts of once wild Margarita. The small colonial center shelters some historic buildings that nostalgically hint at bygone days (though they're increasingly swamped by new hotels and housing complexes). A nearby beach features calm waters and fishing boats with roosting pelicans, and also provides views of islets in the distance. Founded in the 1530s, Pampatar was one of the earliest settlements on Margarita, and within 50 years it grew into the largest shipping center in what is now Venezuela.

If you decide to swim at the beach, ask about water quality – pollution has been a problem in the past.

### Sights

Pampatar's fort, the **Castillo de San Carlos Borromeo** (🕑 8am-6pm), is in the center of town, on the waterfront. It was built from 1663 to 1684 on the site of a previous stronghold that was destroyed by European pirates. It's the best-preserved fort on the island, and a classic example of Spanish military architecture. Check out the 800kg front door (a reproduction). Admission is free but donations are appreciated.

Opposite the fort is the **parish church**, a sober, whitewashed construction from 1748. Go inside to see the crucifix, Cristo del Buen Viaje, over the high altar. Legend has it that the ship that carried the crucifix from Spain to Santo Domingo called en route at Pampatar, but despite repeated efforts it couldn't depart until the Christ image had been unloaded. It has remained in Pampatar since. To the right of the church is the **Casa de la Cultura** (admission free), in the old customs house, worth a peek for its occasional art exhibits.

The beach extends for 1km east of the fort, and exudes old-world charm, with rustic boats anchored in the bay and fishermen repairing nets on the beach. The cape at the far eastern end of the bay is topped by another fort, the ruined **Fortín de la Caranta** (built from 1586 to 1626). It provides sweeping views of the area.

The theme park **Diverland** (off Map p198; ☎ 262-0813; Av Jóvito Villalba, Pampatar; under-35s/over-35s/over-65s BsF35/60/5; 🕑 6pm-11:30pm Fri-Sun), 3km west of Pampatar center, has a modest collection of rollercoasters and other attractions. One of the biggest draws within this complex is the separately run **Waterland** (☎ 262-5545), which – by reservation only – lets you swim with dolphins and seals in the attached swimming pool. A basic video, briefing and 30 minutes with the dolphins costs around BsF200.

### Courses

**Centro de Lingüística Aplicada** (CELA; ☎ 262-8198; www.cela-ve.com; Calle Corocoro, Quinta Cela, Urbanización

Playa El Ángel) offers intensive Spanish-language courses at different levels (two weeks about BsF2300). There are also specialized courses in subjects ranging from medical Spanish to legal Spanish. Excursions and cultural activities liven things up, and family stays are available.

### Sleeping & Eating

While there's plenty of sleeping options in Pampatar, little of it is charming and much of it is in large, expensive hotels crowded around the beaches.

**La Posada de Aleja** (☎ 262-7078; Calle Nueva Cadiz; r from BsF160; ❄) This colorful, family-run posada has an odd, mishmash facade. There is nice tiling in the common area and a grassy patio out back, next to the beach, from where you can swim. It's a hard place to find: near the town's entrance, look for the nine-story Bahia Azul building (near the Circulo Militar) and follow the road in front one block, then turn right and go 20m.

**Café Colonial** (☎ 262-2064; Av Joaquin Maneiro; Calle Nueva Cadiz; mains BsF30-60; 🕑 7am-midnight Tue-Sun) This is by far Pampatar's most charming eating option and it's well worth stopping off for a meal here on your way through the town's historic center. The place is bright and airy, with a delicious menu of modern Venezuelan cooking and friendly staff.

### Getting There & Away

There are very frequent buses to Porlamar (BsF1.50, 20 minutes); they run north along Av 4 de Mayo. Taxis cost BsF15 to Porlamar and BsF40 to the airport.

## EL VALLE DEL ESPÍRITU SANTO

**pop 15,000**

Commonly called 'El Valle,' this small town is Margarita's spiritual capital and home to the island's patroness, the miraculous Virgen del Valle. The image of the Virgin was originally kept in the church in Nueva Cádiz on the nearby island of Cubagua in the 16th century. When a hurricane destroyed the church and town in 1541, the image miraculously survived and was taken to Margarita, where a safe home was built to house it. Her image, kept in the mock-Gothic church on the plaza, draws pilgrims from all around eastern Venezuela year-round – but especially on September 8, the Virgin's day. The whole week afterward sees the village packed with revelers camped out on the streets. El Valle is the first Marian religious sanctuary in the Americas.

The fanciful, gingerbread house–like **Basílica de Nuestra Señora del Valle**, standing out in its twin-peaked glory on the central plaza, was built from 1894 to 1906 and is the current home of the Virgin. According to local history, the image of the Virgin was brought to the town around 1510. Her statue is to the right of the high altar, usually surrounded by a huddle of devotees. You can buy rosaries, amulets and crafts – along with a few hundred images of the Virgin – from a crowd of religious stalls next to the church. Shops around the main plaza are also good places to buy crafts.

The **Museo Diocesano** (admission BsF2; 🕑 9am-noon & 2-5pm Tue-Sat, 9am-1pm Sun), behind the church, has objects related to the Virgin, plus various offerings from the faithful asking for favors.

In a different vein, diagonally opposite the church is the **Casa Museo Santiago Mariño** (admission BsF1; 🕑 8am-5pm), the house where its namesake hero of the War of Independence was born in 1788. The sizable country mansion has been painstakingly reconstructed and fitted with vintage furniture and well-displayed period memorabilia. Look for the effeminate painting of Generalissimo Francisco de Miranda, posing suggestively on a bed.

Buses between Porlamar and El Valle shuttle frequently (BsF1, 15 minutes).

## LA ASUNCIÓN

**pop 25,000**

Although Porlamar is by far the largest urban center on the island, the small, sleepy town of La Asunción is actually the state capital of Nueva Esparta. This tranquil spot is set in a fertile, verdant valley.

Built in the second half of the 16th century is the **catedral**, located on the attractive, tree-shaded Plaza Bolívar. It's one of the oldest surviving colonial churches in the country and widely thought to be the second-oldest after Coro's cathedral. Note the unusual bell tower and a portal with a delicate Renaissance facade.

On the northern side of the plaza is the **Museo Nueva Cádiz** (☎ 416-8492; Plaza Bolívar; 🕑 9am-4pm Mon-Fri, to 1pm Sat & Sun), named after the first Spanish town in South America, which was established around 1500 on Isla Cubagua, south of Margarita. An earthquake in 1541 completely destroyed the town. The museum displays a small collection of exhibits related to

---

**ISLAND TOP PICKS**

There's a lot more to Margarita than just its fine beaches. If you've overdone the tan and need a day off, consider some of the following activities.

- Dive or snorkel around the **Archipiélago Los Frailes** (right)

- Try your hand at windsurfing or kitesurfing off **Playa El Yaque** (p207)

- Escape the crowds to remote **Península de Macanao** (p207)

- Drift through the mangrove tunnels of **Parque Nacional Laguna de la Restinga** (p206)

- Catch the sunset with an ice-cold beer at **Juangriego** (opposite)

---

the region's history and culture. Admission is free, but donations are always appreciated.

Just outside town, a 10-minute walk southward up the hill, is the **Castillo de Santa Rosa** (admission free; ☼ 9am-5pm), one of seven forts built on the island to protect it from pirate attacks. It provides great views and has some old armor on display.

Buses from Porlamar will let you off on Plaza Bolívar (BsF1.50, 25 minutes).

## PARQUE NACIONAL CERRO EL COPEY

If you have your own wheels (or are willing to hire a taxi) and want to leave the crowds behind, head up into this fresh, hilly **national park** ( ☎ 242-0306), southwest of La Asunción. The old road climbs up through cool, scented woodland, and near the top a side road branches off to the west and up toward some radio towers. There's potential bird-watching (look for the yellow-shouldered parrot) and hiking in the area, though there were no accommodation or eating options on our last visit, so bring your own food and water.

## PLAYA EL AGUA

This beautiful 3km-long stretch of white sand has in recent years gone from being a well-kept secret to becoming one of Margarita's most popular beaches. Indeed, if you come here during high season, you'll often have to fight for a spot. Out of season it's a wonderfully laid-back place: the shoreline is shaded with coconut groves and densely dotted with thatched-roof restaurants and bars that offer

a good selection of food, cocktails and music. The northern, less developed part of the beach tends to have fewer crowds.

With the crowds have come numerous new hotels, posadas and restaurants. Choose carefully – many can be overpriced. There's also no real center to Playa El Agua: its hotels and restaurants are spread out along the beach road. Beware also that it can be dangerous to walk around after dark here – robbery is common, so travel after dark only with a trusted taxi company (ask at your hotel for a number).

There's no bank, but you can change money at one of the many shops along the beach near the craft market, just ask the owners discretely.

One of the most popular activities in Playa El Agua is taking a boat trip to **Los Frailes**, a small archipelago of coral islands north of Margarita. It's a great place for scuba diving (around BsF400 per dive) and snorkeling (around BsF200) and there are some marvelous beaches to explore. Travel agents along the beach offer the trips, as do many posadas and hotels.

### Sleeping

Across the street from the beach is a swath of midrange to luxury, top-end hotels and holiday homes. Backpackers should head to Juangriego (opposite) instead. The following prices are for low season: expect tariffs to rise 25% or more in high season, unless otherwise stated.

**Posada Nathalie** ( ☎ 249-1973, 0416-291-6717; www.posadanathalie.com; Calle Camino Real; d/q BsF130/220; ⊠ ☑ ) Priding itself on being a refuge from the real world, this charming place has no TV or internet and is a perfect place to relax. The 12-room posada is run by a friendly Dutch family and features clean, tidy rooms with fridges. There's an outdoor common area with a barbecue and a small, nearby swimming pool. Look for the posada up the dirt road that runs from the souvenir stalls' parking lot. There's a minimum two-night stay.

**Hotel Miramar Village** ( ☎ 249-1797; Calle Miragua; s/d/tr BsF190/280/310; ℗ ⊠ ☑ ) This all-inclusive, Mediterranean-like hotel features 35 spacious but unexciting rooms – some with walk-in closets. Wooden bridges connect the two-story buildings, and despite the resort atmosphere there's also an intimate feel of sorts. The restaurant is airy and there's a triangular pool area beyond. It's about a one-minute walk to the beach. Minimum stay is two nights.

**Hotel Cocoparaiso** (☎ 249-0117; Blvd Playa el Agua; s/d/tr/q incl breakfast BsF200/300/400/500; P) A very pleasant stay, this spot is just across the street from the beach. Twenty-six comfortable, spacious rooms enjoy a large front patio complete with a hammock; others might have private back patios off their bathrooms. There is also a good pool, attractive gardens and free wi-fi.

**our pick** **La Posada de Doña Romelia** (☎ 249-0238; yoya37@cantv.net; Av 31 de Julio; d incl buffet breakfast BsF220; P) Just outside Playa El Agua proper, on the main coast road toward Playa Manzanillo, is this charming and intimate blue-painted posada. The rooms are arranged around a pool, and are divided into two floors – upstairs rooms have great balconies, and downstairs rooms have patios. There's friendly service and a good breakfast is served. It's a 1km walk to the beach.

**Chalets de Belén** (☎ 249-1707; Calle Miragua; d BsF250, 6-person casa BsF450; P) This rustic place is run by a Venezuelan woman named Belén and her poodles. Belén has just four clean, comfortable and small rooms with homey touches; they come with shared patios. There's one *casa* (two-bedroom apartment) with kitchenette. They're all in an overgrown garden, and it's a short walk to the beach. Minimum stay is three nights. Prices are negotiable in low season.

## Eating

Sadly much of the eating along the beach is extremely lackluster and overpriced, catering to wealthy tourists in high season and rather indifferent to quality. Those listed below are the best of the bunch.

**Margarita's Café** (☎ 249-0173; Blvd Playa el Agua; mains BsF18-45; 7am-9pm) For no-nonsense, reasonably priced eating try this busy joint on the beach road, which cooks up a good selection of breakfasts (BsF22 to BsF26) and other casual dishes. It's across from the beach near Cambio Cussco and has a shady front-sidewalk area.

**Restaurant Marlin** (☎ 249-5491; Blvd Playa el Agua; mains BsF30-60; 11am-11pm) Definitely aimed at tourists, this place is nevertheless pleasant enough with its big, barn-like structure on the beach open to the elements. The lobster here is good, as are the fresh shrimps cooked in garlic.

**La Isla Restaurant** (☎ 249-0035; Blvd Playa el Agua; mains BsF35-80; 9am-11pm) This is a good, thatched-roof restaurant right on the beach. Seafood is big here – try the jumbo shrimp, crab linguini or lobster with cognac. Those not fond of shellfish can go for the pizza, pasta or paella.

## Getting There & Away

The beach has regular bus transportation from Porlamar (BsF3.50, 45 minutes), so you can easily come for the day if you can't afford to stay overnight. Taxis from the airport cost BsF60; they're BsF40 from Porlamar.

# JUANGRIEGO

**pop 45,000**

Some of Margarita's most fabulous sunsets are seen from this humble town, set along the edge of a fine, sandy bay in the northern part of Margarita. Juangriego's harbor is home to a fleet of rustic fishing boats as well as many resting pelicans, and far away on the horizon the peaks of Macanao are visible and make for a spectacular sight when the sun sets behind them.

Crowning the hill just north of town is the **Fortín de la Galera** (admission free; dawn-dusk). These days little remains of the colonial fort (destroyed by the Spanish royalist army in 1817) other than some stone walls with a terrace and a refreshment stand, but it sees a steady trail of couples arriving in the late afternoon for a sweeping view of the sunset.

All in all Juangriego is a good backpacker destination, as accommodations are more affordable than in places like Playa El Agua and it's less congested than Porlamar. Nearby, **Playa Caribe**, about a 10-minute taxi ride away, is one of the island's best beaches – relatively pristine, but with a few services for comfort. Another fantastic nearby beach is **Playa Zaragoza**, a perfect crescent of sand backed by a charming little village. A couple of houses on the seafront offer bed and breakfast – ask around for a true local experience.

## Sleeping

Juangriego has two highly recommended hotels. Prices for accommodation can rise about 25% in high season.

**El Caney** (☎ 253-5059, 0416-795-6379; http://elcaney.free.fr; Calle Guevara 17; r BsF120;) Behind a gated front on a street perpendicular to the seafront is this colorful little Peruvian-run posada. There's a sweet stone patio in front, complete with thatched roof, plus a small palm garden out back. The 10 rooms are very rustic and dark but comfortable, and a tiny basic kitchen is open to guests. Look for it half a block from Juangriego's main street and a block from the beach.

our pick **Hotel Patrick** (☎ 253-6218; www.hotelpatrick.com; Calle El Fuerte; s/d BsF120/160; ) Not far from the beach is this perennial favorite, run by a friendly and voluble Irishman and his Venezuelan wife. There are 10 colorful and attractive rooms (those upstairs have fantastic views toward the sunset from outside on the balcony), plus a good hangout area with tables, sofas, hammocks and a popular bar. It serves breakfast, does tours and is a great place to meet other travelers.

### Eating & Drinking

The bay in Juangriego is lined by eateries where you can have a drink while watching the sunset or eat a meal with the waves lapping just meters from your feet. The best (but also the most expensive) of these is **El Viejo Muelle** (☎ 253-2962; Calle La Marina; mains BsF38-120; 10:30am-11pm) with its little mock lighthouse and tables on the sand. Nearby you'll find **El Fortin** (☎ 253-4632; Calle La Marina; mains BsF35-85; 11am-10:30pm) and **El Bonguero** (☎ 253-2536; Calle La Marina; mains BsF30-70; 11am-11pm), two other good places for a fresh fish supper with a view of the bay and tables on the sand. At other times of the day, Hotel Patrick serves breakfasts and has a bar open to nonguests.

### Getting There & Away

Frequent buses run between Porlamar and Juangriego (BsF2.50, 45 minutes) via La Asunción, while a por puesto will cost BsF4.50 per seat. Taxis from Porlamar and the airport both cost around BsF50.

## CARAPACHO

Carapacho is a small, sleepy village away from the island's coast that enjoys some lovely views toward the mountains in distance. It's also home to the wonderful **La Casona** (☎ 259-0333; www.hotel-lacasona.homeip.net; Calle Miranda 134; 2-person apt BsF200, additional person BsF30; ), a much-needed charmer among Margarita's surfeit of expensive and mediocre posadas. Run by a German-Venezuelan couple, the extensive property takes in a popular **restaurant** (mains BsF40-60; noon-9pm), a good pool and several buildings containing 24 rustic apartments amid a well-tended garden. Apartments all have their own balconies or patios and are very pleasant, with white walls and wooden furniture. The entire place is a real refuge from the crowds and over-development that plagues the island elsewhere. Taxis from Porlamar should cost around BsF60, though again you're much better off having your own transportation here given the village's remoteness.

## PARQUE NACIONAL LAGUNA DE LA RESTINGA

This **national park** (7:30am-5pm) covers the lagoon and a large mass of mangroves riddled with narrow, labyrinthine channels at its western end. This is a habitat for dolphins, turtles and over 100 species of bird, including pelicans, cormorants and scarlet ibises, not to mention the park's pride and joy, the Margarita blue-crowned parakeet, which is found nowhere else in the world.

Buses from Porlamar go regularly to La Restinga (BsF3.50, 45 minutes) and will deposit you at the entrance to the embarkation pier (taxis from Porlamar cost around BsF50). From there, five-seat motorboats will take you on a **boat trip** (half-hr/hr per boat BsF120/150) drifting along the interconnecting *caños* (channels) that cut through the mangroves. Sadly the tours are less than informative, focusing on the rather cutesy names given to the various channels, rather than the interesting flora and fauna of the park.

The boats end up at the village of La Restinga itself, a rather run-down place set on a gorgeous 3km stretch of shell beach that is only somewhat marred by the telegraph poles running along it, the odd industrial installation and locals picnicking from the back of their SUVs. Your boat captain will take you back to the park entrance at a time you agree on.

There's a chance to eat your body weight in fried fish (BsF90) at the open-air restaurant, as well as to pick up cheaper snacks from the village. If it's just after beach you're after, it's possible to drive here without taking the expensive boats through the national park. Continue past the turn off to the national park on the main road, cross the bridge over the lagoon and take the next turning to the right.

## MUSEO MARINO

This good **Marine Museum** (Map p196; ☎ 291-3231; Blvd El Paseo, Boca del Río; adult/child BsF20/10; 9am-4:30pm, to 5:30pm in high season) is worth the trip across the island, especially for families. It has a shallow pool of safe-to-handle starfish, snails and other underwater fauna that will thrill the kids. (But don't stick your hands in the outdoor turtle pool as there are a couple of small sharks in the water.) The museum also has a small aquarium of other colorful marine life and large exhibitions of coral, shell and photography. Look out for the blue-whale skeleton in front of you when you enter, though you're unlikely to miss it.

## PENÍNSULA DE MACANAO

The largely undeveloped half of Margarita cries out for exploration, though you'll need your own transport to enjoy it. Many good beaches can be found off the circular road that runs from Boca del Río around the entire peninsula.

From the main road follow a signed dirt road down to **Playa Auyana**, where a wonderfully wild stretch of beach awaits you, totally untouched save for a few shacks. Further along off the main road is the friendly village of **San Francisco**, framed by the inaccessible mountains of the peninsula. Here you'll find Macanao's only hotel, **Posada Penicao** (☎ 311-5530, 0412-357-7710; r incl breakfast BsF160; ), a charming place with twelve comfortable and rustically designed rooms surrounding a pleasant courtyard **restaurant** ( noon-9pm daily) that serves up a decent menu of seafood and grilled meats. It's open to the public, too, though it's best to call ahead and check they're open. This posada makes a great base for exploring this side of the island, though you'll need a car if you want to stay here.

Further on, **Playa El Tunal** is another attractive beach, though the dilapidated village nearby and the rather cloudy water rather mar the paradise factor. **Playa La Pared** is a gorgeous crescent of golden sand, again with a rather scruffy village attached. There's a bar and simple restaurant overlooking the beach here, too.

Arguably the best beach on Macanao is **Playa Punta Arenas**, at the island's most westerly point. Here you'll find two long stretches of sand on either side of a spit of land. The southern beach is lined with several beach restaurants and bars, while that on the northern side is far less developed, with just a couple of bars.

## PLAYA EL YAQUE

**pop 1500**

One of the world's best places for windsurfing and kitesurfing, this pleasant and well-developed beach is located just a few kilometers south of Margarita's airport. Tranquil, shallow waters and steady winds have given El Yaque an international reputation, and it's become a hangout for these wind-sport communities. A couple of important national and international competitions take place here every year, attracting big sports stars and spectators.

Several professional outfits on the beachfront have **windsurfing rental** (per hr/day BsF150/400). There is also **kitesurfing** (half-day rental BsF315).

El Yaque is also secure compared to many places on Margarita, with its own private security force keeping tabs on who comes into the village after nightfall. This, along with the great surfing conditions and pleasant hotels, has made El Yaque the current beach of choice for backpackers.

### Sleeping & Eating

As elsewhere on the island, expect prices to jump in the high season.

**our pick** **El Yaque Motion** (☎ 263-9742, 0416-596-5139; www.elyaquemotion.com; Calle Principal; s/d/tr BsF130/150/210, apt BsF250; ) The absolute best deal in town and one of Margarita's most pleasant stays is this German-run posada near the entrance into town (a 10-minute walk to the main beach). It's a well-run place offering clean, neat rooms with good furniture. Three very private apartments are available, and there's a well-equipped rooftop kitchen and terrace for everyone to use. Credit card advances are available if you've run out of money.

**Windsurfer's Oasis** (☎ 263-9216; www.windsurfersoasis.com; Calle Principal; s/d/tr incl buffet breakfast BsF200/220/240; ) This three-story white hotel is one of the most prominent buildings in town. It's right on the beach but you can also hang out in the pool, surrounding patio and Jacuzzi. Rooms are modern and simple and come with cable TV and fridge; most have balconies and sea views. The hotel has its own restaurant/bar over the beach.

**Windsurf Paradise** (☎ 263-9760; www.hotelwindsurf-paradise.com; Calle Principal; s/d/tr incl buffet breakfast BsF200/290/350; ) This pleasant mini-resort boasts a restaurant with a great deck overlooking the beach. The pool area, with its wood and stone walks, also has a relaxing feel. Standard rooms are attractive and feature hammocks outside, but also line the hotel's entrance – go for superior rooms if you want higher ceilings, private balconies, more space and possible poolside location.

**Surfhotel Jump'n Jibe** (☎ 263-8396; www.jumpnjibe.com; Calle Principal; s/d incl buffet breakfast BsF350/525; P ✗ 🖳 ᯤ) Of several midrange hotels fronting onto El Yaque beach, this cool, relaxed choice is one of the best. It has 15 sparkling rooms (including one apartment), a palm-filled garden and terrific sea views (even better if you can afford a private balcony). A small terrace overlooks the beach area.

**Café Beach Local** (☎ 263-2847; Calle Principal; mains BsF35-70) The restaurant of the El Yaque Beach Hotel has a great situation right on the beach, and serves up a great selection of international cuisine and cocktails strong enough to satisfy even the most demanding party animals. This is the favored hangout for the local water-sports crowd.

### Getting There & Away

Several buses per day run between Porlamar and El Yaque (BsF4, 30 minutes). Taxis from Porlamar cost BsF50; from the airport it's BsF30.

# ANZOÁTEGUI STATE

## PUERTO LA CRUZ

☎ 0281 / pop 254,700

This glitzy, busy city is the main gateway to Venezuela's favorite holiday destination, Isla de Margarita (p195), as well as a springboard to the beautiful Parque Nacional Mochima (p211), which stretches just north and east of the city. Up until the 1930s Puerto La Cruz was no more than an obscure village, but it boomed after rich oil deposits were discovered to the south, and port facilities were built just east of town to serve as a main terminal to ship oil overseas. Nowadays, this city is a youthful, dynamic and quickly expanding place.

Taking advantage of its position, it has grown into a big water-sports center, boasting half a dozen marinas and yacht clubs. Most people only visit on their way through – there's nothing much to keep you here. The city itself is not noted for its beauty, though it features a lively 10-block-long waterfront boulevard, Paseo Colón, packed with hotels, restaurants and shops. This seafront area, which borders a decent beach, comes to life in the late afternoon and evening, when kitschy craft stalls open and a gentle breeze sweeps away the heat of the day.

### Information

#### EMERGENCY

**Policia Estado Anzoátegui** (☎ 266-1414; Calle Los Cocos)

#### INTERNET ACCESS

**Centro Commercial Cristoforo Colombo** (upper fl, Paseo Colón; per hour BsF4; ⏰ 9am-9pm Mon-Fri, 11am-9pm Sat) Pick your internet cafe from among the cluster on the 2nd floor.

**Internet Café** (Hotel Neptuno, Paseo Colón; ⏰ 8am-8pm) In the lobby of the Hotel Neptuno; charges BsF3 per hour.

#### LAUNDRY

**Lavandería La Libertad** (☎ 265-5204; Calle Libertad 100; ⏰ 8am-noon & 2-7:30pm Mon-Fri, 8am-8pm Sat)

#### MEDICAL SERVICES

**Farmatodo** (Plaza Colón; ⏰ 24hr) Modern and bright, this is a well-stocked pharmacy.

#### MONEY

Most major banks are within a few blocks south of Plaza Colón.

**Banco de Venezuela** (Calle Miranda)

**Banco Mercantil** (Calle Arismendi)

**Banesco** (Calle Freites)

#### POST

**Ipostel** (☎ 268-5355; Calle Freites; ⏰ 8am-noon & 1-5pm Mon-Fri)

#### TELEPHONE

**CANTV** (Paseo Colón; ⏰ 7:30am-10pm)

### Tours

Travel agencies can be found on Paseo Colón and offer tours around Parque Nacional Mochima as well as further afield. Full-day boat tours include snorkeling, lunch and drinks, and cost around BsF200. Note that tours organized from Santa Fe and Mochima (p213) are cheaper. Some of the most popular destinations are Playa El Saco and Playa Puinare (both on Isla Chimana Grande), as well as Playa El Faro (on Isla Chimana Segunda), which all have nice beaches and food facilities. Playa El Faro also has curious iguanas and the best snorkeling grounds.

These destinations all have boat services that run to and fro (per person BsF20 to BsF35), so you don't need to take a formal tour. Excursions depart from piers on either end of Plaza Colón, leaving around 8am and returning in the afternoon. Inexpensive camp-

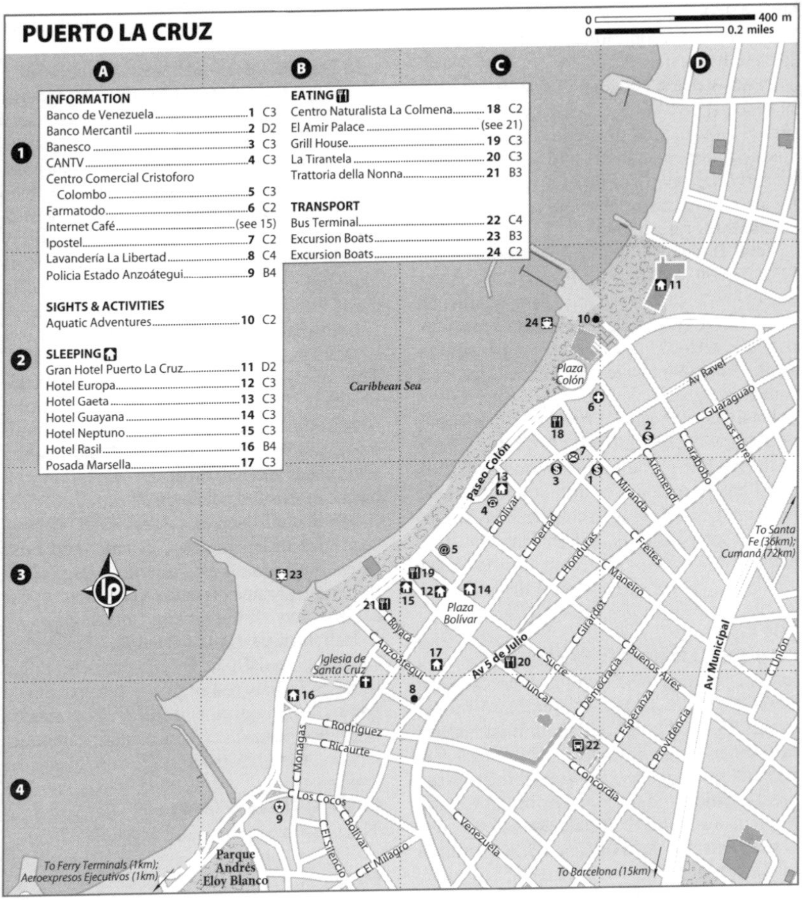


ing is possible on the islands; negotiate with boat operators for a later pickup date.

**Aquatic Adventures** (☎ 0414-806-3744), located at the marina and run by an American woman, organizes diving courses and tours.

Boat-lovers looking for guidance can contact **Allen McLay** (☎ 0416-893-2886; www.yachting-venezuela.com) who does custom boat tours in the area and beyond.

## Sleeping

Puerto La Cruz is an expensive place to stay by Venezuelan standards, and hotels fill up fast in the high season. Even out of season it's not a bad idea to book a room in advance. Many hotels are on Paseo Colón and the adjoining streets, and this is the most lively and safe area to stay. Be careful walking the inland blocks at night because of the risk of robbery – use taxis.

### BUDGET

**Hotel Guayana** (☎ 265-2175; Plaza Bolívar; s/d/tr BsF55/75/95; ❄) A cheap stay with eight rooms, located on Plaza Bolívar. You won't be bowled over by the welcome, but at least the place is safe and central.

**Hotel Neptuno** (☎ 265-3261; fax 265-5790; Paseo Colón at Calle Juncal; s/d/tr/ste BsF95/115/130/155; P ❄ 💻 wi-fi) The popular Neptuno offers good-value rooms. Get one facing the street: they are brighter and more spacious. An open-sided restaurant near the top floor boasts sweeping views out to sea. There's free wi-fi throughout.

### MIDRANGE

The following accommodations all have cable TV and hot water.

**Posada Marsella** (☎ 268-8401; Calle Libertad; s/d/tr BsF105/150/175; ) This excellent value place is tucked away behind the main strip, but offers a large number of smart and secure rooms, even though many of them are windowless. All are clean, comfortable and come with private bathrooms, though.

**Hotel Europa** (☎ 268-8157; Plaza Bolívar; s/d/tr BsF120/135/170; P ) Pass through the parking lot entrance to reach this sparsely adorned hotel, where very basic but clean and spacious rooms overlooking the city's main square await. All rooms have private facilities, and some have great balconies.

**Hotel Gaeta** (☎ 265-0411; Paseo Colón at Calle Maneiro; s/d/tr incl breakfast BsF250/400/500; P ) Smack in the middle of the seafront boulevard, this hotel has four floors of decent and clean, if rather pokey, rooms with colorful bedspreads, ancient air-con units and wicker furniture. Sea-view rooms cost more, but are also bigger and better. There's free wi-fi in the lobby.

### TOP END

**Hotel Rasil** (☎ 920-1600; www.hotelrasil.com.ve, in Spanish; Calle Monagas at Paseo Colón 6; s/d with city/sea view BsF350/450; P ) The standard rooms at this 25-floor hotel remain unimaginative, even after progressive refits in the past few years. The main reason to stay here is for the great location and the views from some of the higher rooms and their balconies.

**Gran Hotel Puerto La Cruz** (☎ 500-3611; www.granhotelplc.com.ve; Paseo Colón; r incl breakfast from BsF700; P ) This ship-shaped, five-star option is located just beyond the marina. Almost all of the 206 rooms have beautiful sea views (with balcony and see-through shower). Other services include a casino, a spa, a business center and good wheelchair accessibility, not to forget the swimming pools and the private beach.

## Eating

There's an unsurprising concentration of restaurants and cafes along Paseo Colón. This area stays alive well into the evening, when fresh breezes alleviate the heat and people gather in the establishments overlooking the boardwalk. It's mostly an upmarket area, but it also shelters some inexpensive Middle Eastern fast-food eateries serving set lunches. Cheap food carts open at night near Plaza Colón.

**La Tirantela** (☎ 265-3812; Av 5 de Julio; pastries BsF5; 7am-9pm Mon-Sat) An old school *panadería* (bakery) set a short distance back from the seafront, La Tirantela offers good coffee, croissants and cake for all occasions, but makes for a great breakfast and people-watching spot.

**El Amir Palace** (Paseo Colón 123; mains BsF15-45; 8am-11:30pm Tue-Sun) Crisply dressed waiters shuttle Middle Eastern specialties to your table like shawarma and falafel, though its long menu also includes pasta, fish and salads.

**Centro Naturalista La Colmena** (Paseo Colón at Calle Miranda; 3-course menu BsF20; 11:45am-2pm Mon-Fri) This lunch-only vegetarian cafe and natural-products shop has flowery tables and a tiny covered terrace looking out across the boulevard to the sea. It serves good and healthy set lunches and will thrill any vegetarian who has been existing solely on *arepas*.

**Grill House** (☎ 265-3314; Paseo Colón at Calle Sucre; mains BsF20-35; 11am-10pm) A large and busy eatery on the main drag offering a large selection of good value pizzas, *cachapas* (corn pancakes), *arepas* and *parrillas* (mixed grills)

**Trattoria della Nonna** (☎ 265-2623; Paseo Colón at Calle Boyacá; mains BsF35-70; 11am-10pm) This rather touristy Italian restaurant is nevertheless a good choice, with lots of different pizzas on offer, rich pasta dishes and a good seafood selection. Venezuelan specialties also available.

## Getting There & Away

The nearest airport is in Barcelona.

### BOAT

Puerto La Cruz is the major departure point for Isla de Margarita, with services offered by **Conferry** (☎ 267-7847; www.conferry.com; Sector Los Cocos; 24hr) and **Gran Cacique Express** (☎ 267-7286; www.grancacique.com.ve; Sector Los Cocos). Smaller excursion boats leave from the small piers in town. See p195 for fare details and travel times. Be aware that buying tickets on Conferry services can be an extremely time-consuming process in Puerto La Cruz, due to high demand and long lines. The ticket office is open around the clock though, so go late at night for an easier experience. You'll need a photocopy of your car documents and passport to get a ticket (there are photocopying services available at the ticket office).

The ferry terminals are accessible by por puesto from the center (taxis BsF10). Try to take a ferry during the daytime – it's a spectacular journey between the islands of Parque Nacional Mochima.

### BUS

The busy bus terminal is four blocks from the beach. Bus destinations include Caracas (BsF30 to BsF55, five hours), Carúpano (BsF20 to BsF35, 4½ hours), Ciudad Bolívar (BsF50, four hours), Cumaná (BsF10 to BsF20, 1½ hours) and Maturín (BsF25 to BsF40, three hours). Sit on the left for views on the trips to Carúpano and Cumaná.

Por-puesto destinations include Caracas (BsF60, four hours), Carúpano (BsF60, four hours), Ciudad Bolívar (BsF90, 3½ hours), Cumaná (BsF30, 1¼ hours), Los Altos de Sucre (BsF7, 40 minutes) and Maturín (BsF50, two hours).

**Aeroexpresos Ejecutivos** (☎ 267-8855) has one of the best services to Caracas (BsF70 to BsF90, five departures daily), leaving from the ferry terminal west of town.

## CLARINES & PÍRITU

The small towns of Clarines and Píritu, both by the Caracas–Barcelona highway, have two of the best restored and most interesting small-town colonial churches in the region.

Founded in 1694, **Clarines** is an old colonial town about 1km south of the highway. Its church, **Iglesia de San Antonio** (⌚ 9:30-11:30am & 3-6pm), is at the upper end of the historic town. Built in the 1750s, the church is a massive, squat construction laid out in a Latin-cross floor plan, and is one of only a few examples of its kind in Venezuela. Twin square towers border the austere facade. The most unusual features of the structure are the two external arcades running between the towers and the transepts on both sides of the church. The single-nave interior is topped with a wooden cupola and is refreshingly well balanced in proportion. Over the high altar is a three-tier main retable dating from around 1760. It is placed against the wall, which still bears its original painting depicting a curtain.

**Píritu**, 16km east of Clarines, lies just north of the highway (but the access road branches off from the highway 2km before the town and rejoins it 2km beyond). The town was founded in 1656, and about half a century later, the fortresslike **Iglesia de Nuestra Señora de la Concepción** (admission free; ⌚ 8am-11am & 5-6:30pm) was built. This three-nave church has quite a number of remarkable colonial altarpieces. The main retable and the two side retables date from about 1745 and are richly gilded.

Scattered around each town center are small local restaurants serving cheap set meals.

### Getting There & Away

Clarines and Píritu are usually visited as a daytrip from Puerto La Cruz. As both towns are just off the Caracas–Barcelona highway, access is easy. Apart from the long-distance buses running between these two cities, there are hourly buses from Barcelona to both Píritu (BsF6) and Clarines (BsF4).

## PARQUE NACIONAL MOCHIMA

☎ 0293

About three dozen arid islands dot the clear, warm waters of Mochima, a 950-sq-km national park covering the offshore belt of the Caribbean coast between Puerto La Cruz and Cumaná. Most of the islands are barren and rocky in parts, and strewn with brush and cacti, but some also have fine beaches for soaking up the tropical sun. Coral reefs, which offer good snorkeling and diving opportunities, surround a few of the islands; Isla Venado is an especially good destination. Pods of dolphins are a common sight in the area's waters.

Roughly bisected by the border of Anzoátegui and Sucre states, the park also includes a strip of mountainous hinterland lined with appealing bays and beaches. The area offers year-round warmth and the waters are usually calm, abounding with marine life. Tranquility seekers will be happy midweek, when only a handful of beachgoers are to be found on the more far-flung islands.

Be warned that deserted beaches can be unsafe, particularly at night. There have been reports from campers of robberies on island and mainland beaches, so ask a local for the current situation. At the time of research, it was wiser not to hang around in Santa Fe or Playa Colorada, both of which are not considered safe and where violent robbery against foreigners has increased in recent years. Also, note that there are no banks in the area: bring money from Puerto La Cruz or Cumaná.

See under individual towns for transportation information.

### ORIENTATION

The mainland park lies along the Puerto La Cruz–Cumaná highway, serviced frequently by cheap buses and por puestos – it's a spectacular drive. A dozen beaches lie off the road, one of the most popular of which is the palm-studded Playa Colorada, 27km east of Puerto La Cruz.

About 8km east of Playa Colorada is the town of Santa Fe, which has a decent stretch of sand but which has also been plagued by robberies in recent years. Another 15km east along the Cumaná highway, a side road branches off 4km downhill to the small and very safe village of Mochima, a jumping-off point for nearby beaches (it doesn't have a beach of its own).

#### TOURS

Trips to the park's islands are organized by boat operators from Puerto La Cruz (p210) and Mochima (opposite).

The following operators conduct tours around the park's waters:

**Allen McLay** (☎ 0416-893-2886) A Scot based in Playa Colorada, McLay can organize customized boat tours to anywhere in Venezuela for sailors and yachties.

**Diving & Safari** (☎ 0414-816-3713; gregtur2000@hotmail.com) An Italian company based in Playa Colorada that offers boat tours, along with local diving, snorkeling, dolphin watching and fishing trips.

**Jakera Lodge** (☎ 808-7057; www.jakera.com) Run by some British and based in Playa Colorada, this outfit does boat tours along with kayaking/snorkeling trips to nearby destinations.

**Tony Martin** (☎ 642-5541, 0414-831-3026; www.hosteltrail.com/extremexpeditions) Based out of Santa Fe, Martin does area boat tours (though he specializes in hands-on Los Llanos adventure trips).

### Isla de Plata

This is one of the most popular islands among Venezuelans, thanks to the beach and coral reefs, as well as its proximity to the mainland. There are food and drink stalls here but no drinking water. It also has a startling, surreal view of the huge cement plant nearby, which mars the tropical beach experience a bit.

Isla de Plata is about 10km east of Puerto La Cruz and is accessible by frequent boats from the pier at Pamatacualito, the eastern suburb of Guanta. This suburb is serviced by regular por puestos from Puerto La Cruz (BsF1.50, 10 minutes). Boats run regularly, especially during weekends, taking 10 minutes to get to the island (roundtrip BsF15). Excursion boats from Puerto La Cruz are more expensive and less regular.

### Playa Colorada

This pleasant beach on the main Cumaná–Puerto La Cruz coastal road has fine orange sand shaded with coconut groves. One of the top coastal destinations for locals, it has been populated with a colony of souvenir kiosks and a line of rustic restaurants. The main village itself lies across the highway and up the hill from the beach, though we'd recommend avoiding it, as it's not the safest place for foreigners. The beach itself should be fine, but keep an eye on your belongings and don't flash your wealth.

On weekends, the beach swarms with a young crowd looking to party and enjoy the spectacular sunset. You may also find boats willing to take you out to La Piscina, a snorkeling destination between the two nearby islands of Arapo and Arapito.

### Los Altos de Sucre

This mountain hamlet sits at an altitude of about 900m and has a fresh climate that's wonderfully cool compared to the coast's. It's a typical one-street village, snaking up and down the rugged terrain for almost 5km without any pronounced center. The surrounding highlands are verdant and sprinkled with coffee and cacao haciendas.

Although Los Altos de Sucre is only 4km back from the coast as the crow flies, it doesn't provide many panoramic views of the coast and the islands beyond. The best vistas are from the winding access road as you approach the village. Once you enter it, about 7km from the turnoff at the coastal highway, the road gradually descends inland. Jeeps continue for about 5km to their terminus on the opposite end of the village.

Los Altos de Sucre is serviced regularly throughout the day by jeeps from Puerto La Cruz (BsF5, 40 minutes).

### Santa Cruz

There's not much in this plain, hilly village for the tourist – exactly how some folks like their vacation. It does have a small beach next to the National Guard, which keeps it clean and safe. The one posada in town is **Villa La Encantada** (☎ 0416-781-0430; christian@insightsvenezuela.com; d BsF200; 💻 🅿), offering 12 good rooms with fans spilling down a hillside. There's even a pool to splash around in, and an outside kitchen BBQ area. It's 500m down the main street from the highway; any bus or por puesto can let you off here.

### Mochima

The peaceful village of Mochima, within the national park itself (entry BsF2) is a small community on a beautiful bay where everyone knows everyone else. It has no beach of its own, but is a jumping-off point to half a dozen isolated mainland beaches inaccessible by road. The beaches are beautiful, though shadeless, and are solitary except during major holiday peaks. Only the more built-up Playas Blanca and Las Maritas have food facilities open daily year-round, so if you're going to more isolated beaches remember to take snacks and water.

#### TOURS

Transportation to the beaches is provided from the wharf in the village's center, where boats anchor and *lancheros* (boatmen) sit on the shore and wait for tourists. They can take you to any beach among Playa Las Maritas (BsF65), Playa Blanca (BsF65), Playa Manare (BsF85) and Playas Cautaro and Cautarito (BsF75). Or you can take a tour of five to six islands (BsF130 to BsF150). These are round-trip fares per boatload, and you can be picked up whenever you want. Don't hesitate to bargain. To camp on the islands, pick up a permit (BsF2 per person nightly) at the Inparques office across from the wharf.

A three-hour tour, which includes snorkeling, costs around BsF50 per person for six to 10 people. Longer tours, which can include cruises to Islas Caracas, La Piscina and Playa Colorada, plus snorkeling, are also available. Most hotels can organize boat tours for their guests.

Mochima is also a good place to dive and has two scuba-diving operators, **Aquatics Diving Center** (☎ 430-1649, 0426-581-0434; info@scubavenezuela.com) and **La Posada de los Buzos** (☎ 416-0856, 0414-180-6244; mochimadivecenter@hotmail.com), located next to each other opposite the wharf. Both charge BsF400 per dive, including all equipment, transport and lunch. Subsequent dives cost BsF380, and diving courses are also available. The latter also runs full-day rafting trips (BsF250 per person) and kayaking trips (BsF200 per person) on the Río Neverí.

#### SLEEPING

**Posada El Mochimero** (☎ 417-3339, 0414-773-8782; r BsF100; ❄) Facing the restaurant of the same name (despite being separately run), this budget posada is right by the water and has 17 basic, colorful rooms with cold-water bathrooms. Those upstairs are much lighter and better tiled.

**Posada Villa Vicenta** (☎ 416-0868; s/d BsF120/140; ❄) Located one block back from the wharf, this place has four levels stepping their way up the hillside, each with a small rustic terrace boasting fine bay views (better on the higher floors). The 11 fairly charmless, stone-walled rooms have open, cold-water showers.

**Posada Girasol** (☎ 416-0535, 0414-795-6371; posadagirasol@hotmail.com; r BsF130-250; ❄ 💻) Run by Brigitte and Roger, a Swiss woman and her Venezuelan husband, this small posada has four comfortable rooms with sunflower themes, cable TV, fridge and private bathroom. The two newer rooms on the top floor are larger and more expensive – both have kitchen facilities and a great terrace with bay views. Good breakfasts are available and you can pay to use the internet at reception.

**Posada El Pozo** (☎ 0414-773-7643; s/d/tr BsF140/160/180; ❄) This friendly family-run place, located near the basketball court you'll pass on the way into the village, has clean rooms with pretty tiles, pastel colors and cable TV.

#### EATING

**Brasero** (Calle Principal; arepas BsF6-12, mains BsF20-40; 🕒 6am-10pm) For coffee and *arepas* throughout the day, check out this little fast food joint. *Parrilla* is the house speciality.

**Los Bohios de Kine** (☎ 416-0810; mains BsF35-80; 🕒 11am-9pm daily in high season, lunch Mon, Wed & Fri in low season) Right near the wharf, this outdoor, colorful restaurant offers a huge range of seafood dishes and a great selection of freshly landed fish.

**El Mochimero** (☎ 0414-774-9133; Calle La Marina; mains BsF40-85; 🕒 11:30am-9pm) Definitely the most atmospheric place in town to eat, this rather pricey Spanish-run restaurant has a fantastic spot on the seafront, with water virtually spilling into the dining room. The food is good – try the fresh fish and seafood dishes.

#### GETTING THERE & AWAY

Buses from Cumaná cost BsF3.50 and take 40 minutes. To Santa Fe or Puerto La Cruz, first take a bus to the *crucero* (highway crossroad), then flag down the proper bus.

## ISLA LA TORTUGA

This desolate paradise lies about 85km from the mainland and has yet to be discovered by mass tourism. It's composed of an arid, flat island

(Venezuela's second largest at 160 sq km) and three smaller islets, and harbors rich reefs teeming with colorful corals and many varieties of fish. There are almost no services on the island and not much to do other than swim, snorkel and enjoy the beautiful sunsets.

La Tortuga was first discovered in 1499 by Alonso de Ojeda, a Spanish explorer and an old sailing buddy of Christopher Columbus. In the 17th century the area became a pirate hideout, even sheltering the infamous raider Henry Morgan. The island was also used by Dutch profiteers for salt harvesting until 1631, when they were ousted by the governor of Cumaná.

Today, La Tortuga is even more virgin that Los Roques and practically uninhabited – a few fishermen hang around in lobster season and one posada has recently claimed ground. There are few buildings, mostly fishermen's huts. One of these huts might have rooms to rent, but you'll need to bring your own sheets. In fact, unless you're staying at the posada, you'll need to be completely self-sufficient. Bring a swimsuit, towel, snorkeling equipment, sun protection (there's little shade on the island), toilet paper, medications, insect repellent and all food and water you'll need – and remember to take it all away with you again.

The one posada on the island is the understandably expensive **Rancho Yemaya** (☎ 0414-339-5574, 0414-793-6379, in Caracas 0212-993-4757; per person incl all meals & drinks BsF800). It's a simple one-story place with seven rooms and outside hammocks. There's a generator for electricity and drinking water is available. Reserve in advance.

You can always camp, but remember there's no water or electricity. Seafood might be available from fishermen who can cook it for you, but otherwise you'll need to bring all your own food and water.

## VENEZUELA'S BEST CARNIVALS

Every year carnival fever grips Venezuela as street parties explode across the country in the run up to Lent, culminating in Mardi Gras ('Fat Tuesday'), the last day of carnival. If you're in Venezuela at this time then you're in for a treat – and a soaking – as water fights are the order of the day.

Carúpano's colorful **Carnaval**, quite possibly the most lively, boisterous and crazy rave you'll ever experience, is the largest of its kind in Venezuela, and encompasses four full days of heavy drinking, steamy dancing and general nonstop, blowout partying. It's had some influences from rowdy neighbor Trinidad, which probably explains much of the riotous atmosphere.

Thousands upon thousands of revelers arrive from all over the country to take part in these fanatical celebrations. They don extravagant papier-mâché masks and dress up in dazzling costumes of animals, monsters, Spanish conquistadores and even well-known celebrities. Parades with dressed-up floats set the stage for skimpily clad performers gyrating to sexy music rhythms and heady drum beats – try to spot the trannies, who'll often have the best (ie skimpiest) outfits and rowdiest attitudes. Marching bands also tramp down the streets, adding to the din by making as much noise as they can.

Elsewhere in the country carnival is no less celebrated. The Brazilian-flavored street party of Santa Elena is famous across the country too, as is the utterly crazy Carnaval of the otherwise desolate Gran Sabana mining town of El Callao.

Carnaval is craziest on its last two days, always Monday and Tuesday (the latter of which is Mardi Gras and the last day of Carnaval). The floats become more elaborate and there are masquerade balls, impromptu bands, people throwing water balloons and food stalls selling their wares to hungry partiers. Of course Carnaval is always attended by pickpockets as well, so keep your wits about you and your money safely hidden.

Carnaval falls on the four days before Ash Wednesday, which is 46 days before Easter Sunday. The following list has Carnaval dates for the coming years, so you'll have plenty of time to prepare – and find that perfect, skimpy feathered dress.

- 2011: March 5-8
- 2012: February 18-21
- 2013: February 9-12
- 2014: March 1-4
- 2015: February 14-17

## Getting There & Away

Getting to La Tortuga is not easy, which is why it's still a paradise. If you don't own a private yacht or small plane you'll have to rely on the little public transportation to the island, and all of it is expensive. It takes about six to seven hours in a small motor boat and 10 to 12 hours in a sailboat or yacht to reach the island. Most transport to and from La Tortuga leaves from Puerto La Cruz, Mochima and Playa Colorada. Ask at hotels or travel agencies for connections, as schedules are erratic.

If you're short on time and would rather fly, contact **Jean-Luc Tersin** (☎ 0281-263-5181, 0426-583-1824; jeanluctersin@hotmail.com), a Frenchman based out of Puerto La Cruz. He does flights from the airport at Barcelona to La Tortuga that leave at 9am and return at 5pm (BsF3000 roundtrip for up to five people, 30 minutes). You can stay and return another day, but remember there are few overnight services on the island, so ensure you've got accommodation or camping equipment and supplies sorted out.

# SUCRE STATE

## CUMANÁ

**☎ 0293 / pop 322,000**

Founded by the Spanish in 1521, Cumaná has the interesting distinction of being the oldest existing town on the South American mainland. Although several devastating earthquakes in the past have destroyed much of the city's historic architecture, there are still a number of streets that retain their colonial charm. There is also a large fort crowning a hillock above the town center. Today the city is both the capital of Sucre state and an important port for sardine fishing and canning.

Cumaná has some beaches nearby, the closest being Playa San Luis, southwest of the city. More beaches, like Santa Fe and Playa Colorada, are in the Parque Nacional Mochima, a little further down the coast, though they've both declined in safety in recent years and are both best visited only with locals. The city is also one of the jumping-off points to Isla de Margarita and a convenient gateway to the nearby Península de Araya. Much further inland but a possible day trip away is the Cueva del Guácharo.

### Information

#### INTERNET ACCESS

**Conydel Internet Café** (Centro Comercial Real Gil, Calle Comerico; 🕑 8am-6:30pm Mon-Sat) Hidden away on the second floor, this is one of several internet cafes in this shopping mall.

#### MONEY

Most major banks are on Calle Mariño and Av Bermúdez, including:

**Banco de Venezuela** (Calle Mariño at Calle Rojas)
**Banesco** (Calle Mariño at Calle Carabobo)

#### POST

**Ipostel** (☎ 432-2616; Calle Paraíso; 🕑 8am-noon & 2-6pm)

#### TOURIST INFORMATION

**Dirección de Turismo** (☎ 808-7769; Calle Sucre; 🕑 8am-noon & 2:30-5:30pm Mon-Fri) An extremely friendly office, with some English spoken, giving advice about trips throughout Sucre state.

### Sights

The grandest and best-restored colonial structure in town is the coral-rock **Castillo de San Antonio de la Eminencia** (admission free; 🕑 7am-7pm), with good views over the city and coastline from a hill just southeast of the center. Constructed in 1659 on a four-pointed-star plan, it has survived repeated pirate attacks and destructive earthquakes.

There were originally four such forts in the area, and the remains of nearby **Castillo de Santa María** (built in 1669) are within the grounds of Santa Inés church – sweet-talk the priest and he may let you through to have a peek at what remains.

Next to Castillo de San Antonio is the small, concrete **Museo de Arte Contemporáneo de Cumaná** (☎ 416-4376; admission free; 🕑 9am-noon & 3-6pm Tue-Fri, 9am-2pm Sat & Sun). It stages changing exhibits of modern art, and is only open on weekends if there are events.

The streets around the **Iglesia de Santa Inés** have retained their colonial appearance. The church itself dates from 1929 and has few objects from earlier times inside, apart from the 16th-century statues of *El Nazareno* (Christ with the Cross) and the patron saint, Santa Inés – both are in the chapels in the right-hand aisle. The **catedral**, on Plaza Blanco, is also relatively young and has a hodgepodge of altarpieces in its largely timbered interior.

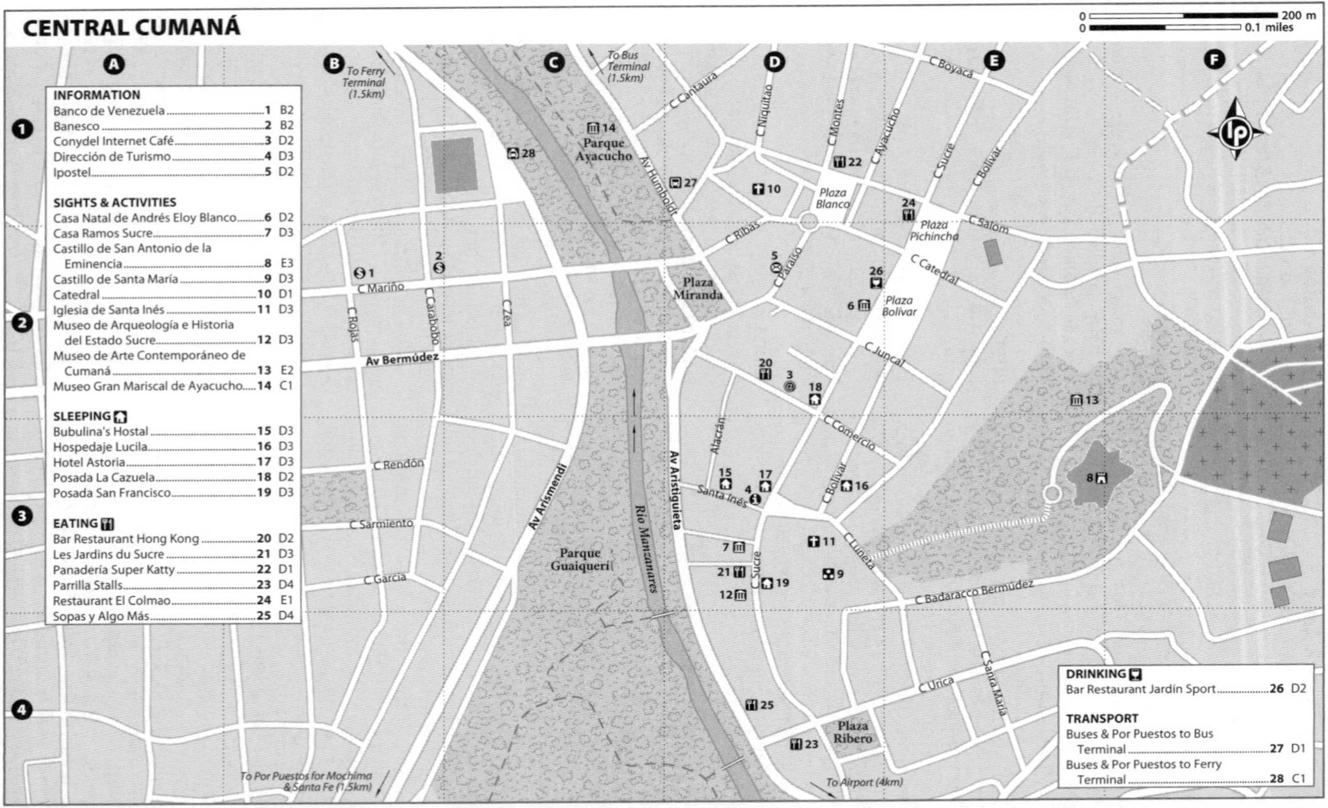
CENTRAL CUMANÁ
0 200 m
0 0.1 miles
INFORMATION
Banco de Venezuela 1 B2
Banesco 2 B2
Conydel Internet Café 3 D2
Dirección de Turismo 4 D3
Ipostel 5 D2
SIGHTS & ACTIVITIES
Casa Natal de Andrés Eloy Blanco 6 D2
Casa Ramos Sucre 7 D3
Castillo de San Antonio de la Eminencia 8 E3
Castillo de Santa María 9 D3
Catedral 10 D1
Iglesia de Santa Inés 11 D3
Museo de Arqueología e Historia del Estado Sucre 12 D3
Museo de Arte Contemporáneo de Cumaná 13 E2
Museo Gran Mariscal de Ayacucho 14 C1
SLEEPING
Bubulina's Hostal 15 D3
Hospedaje Lucila 16 D3
Hotel Astoria 17 D3
Posada La Cazuela 18 D2
Posada San Francisco 19 D3
EATING
Bar Restaurant Hong Kong 20 D2
Les Jardins du Sucre 21 D3
Panadería Super Katty 22 D1
Parrilla Stalls 23 D4
Restaurant El Colmao 24 E1
Sopas y Algo Más 25 D4
DRINKING
Bar Restaurant Jardín Sport 26 D2
TRANSPORT
Buses & Por Puestos to Bus Terminal 27 D1
Buses & Por Puestos to Ferry Terminal 28 C1
To Ferry Terminal (1.5km)
To Bus Terminal (1.5km)
To Por Puestos for Mochima & Santa Fe (1.5km)
To Airport (4km)
Parque Ayacucho
Plaza Miranda
Plaza Blanco
Plaza Pichincha
Plaza Bolívar
Parque Guaiquerí
Plaza Ribero
Río Manzanares
Av Humboldt
Av Bermúdez
Av Arismendi
Av Aristiguieta
C Mariño
C Rojas
C Carabobo
C Zea
C Rendón
C Sarmiento
C Garcia
C Cantaura
C Niquitao
C Montes
C Ayacucho
C Sucre
C Bolívar
C Boyacá
C Salom
C Ribas
C Paraíso
C Catedral
C Juncal
C Comercio
Alacrán
Santa Inés
C Luneta
C Badaracco Bermúdez
C Urica
C Santa María

The city has more museums, though they are pretty modest. The **Casa Natal de Andrés Eloy Blanco** (Plaza Bolívar; admission free; ⌚ 9am-noon & 3-6pm Mon-Fri) is a historic house where one of Venezuela's most extraordinary poets was born in 1896 (see p37).

**Casa Ramos Sucre** (Calle Sucre No 29; admission free; ⌚ 8-11:30am & 2-5:30pm Mon-Fri) is dedicated to another local poet, José Antonio Ramos Sucre, born here in 1890. Sucre's poetry was well ahead of his time, and it was only in the 1960s that his verses attracted the attention of scholars, publishers and finally readers. Long before that, he committed suicide at the age of 40. The well-preserved house is stuffed with beautiful period furniture.

Next door to the Casa Ramos Sucre, the **Museo de Arqueología e Historia del Estado Sucre** (Calle Sucre; admission free; ⌚ 8:30am-noon & 2:30-5:30pm Mon-Fri) has a small archaeological collection, though it was closed for renovations at the time of research.

The **Museo Gran Mariscal de Ayacucho** (☎ 432-1896; Av Humboldt; admission free; ⌚ 9am-noon & 3-6pm Tue-Fri, 3-7pm Sat & Sun) is dedicated to the Cumaná-born hero of the War of Independence, General Antonio José de Sucre (1795–1830), who liberated Peru and Bolivia. His statue is nearby in the park.

## Sleeping

**Hospedaje Lucila** (☎ 431-2044; Calle Bolívar; d without/with air-con BsF70/80; ❄) This very simple little hostel has 21 small rooms around a courtyard strewn with family washing. Rooms are basic and dark, and mattresses saggy, but there's cable TV. It can be noisy at times, too.

**Hotel Astoria** (☎ 433-2708; hotelastoria_7@hotmail.com; Calle Sucre 51; s/d/tr BsF75/120/140; P ❄ wi-fi) This is by far the best of the cheap hotels in Cumaná; its 23 rooms are sufficiently no-frills and windowless but do have cable TV and air-con. There's free wireless throughout and a delicious pizza restaurant downstairs.

**Posada La Cazuela** (☎ 432-1401, 0416-090-1388; Calle Sucre 63; r/tr BsF120/140; P ❄ internet) This small, homey family posada has just four simple rooms with cable TV and bamboo ceilings. The hostess is very welcoming and allows guests to use the internet on reception's computer. It's excellently located and all rooms have private facilities.

**our pick** **Posada San Francisco** (☎ 431-3926; posadasanfrancisco@hotmail.com; Calle Sucre 16; s/d/tr/q BsF160/170/180/200; ❄) This beautiful posada, located in a renovated old *casona* (large house), has nine spacious rooms with tall cane ceilings. They're all arranged around a tranquil, palm-filled patio with traditional-style tiles. There's an attractive bar and a good restaurant, too.

**Bubulina's Hostal** (☎ 431-4025, 0414-883-7174; bubulinas@cantv.net; Callejón Santa Inés; s/d/tr BsF170/180/220; P ❄ wi-fi) A great choice in the center is in this intimate, one-story historical building down a narrow colonial street. There's a bright, indoor-plant-filled hallway with 12 comfortable rooms around it; all have flowery decorations and curvy ironwork furniture. The hostess speaks German and some English and there's free wi-fi. This is also the securest joint in town – nobody comes in or out without the hostess unlocking the door for them.

## Eating & Drinking

The city center has few upper-range restaurants; most are budget eateries. The cheapest (and grungiest) grills are the *parrilla* stalls near Plaza Ribero (open 12:30pm to 11pm), though one restaurant – the superb Les Jardins de Sucre – is arguably the best in the region.

**Panadería Super Katty** (☎ 431-2955; Plaza Blanco; pastries from BsF4; ⌚ 6am-10pm) A small bakery with good pastries and enough frosted cakes to cater for a dozen weddings. Good coffee, but you'll have to sip it standing up – head for a bench in the shady square outside.

**Sopas y Algo Más** (Av Aristiguieta; mains BsF15-35; ⌚ 11am-6pm) Just three soups, three main dishes and four desserts are available at this small but hopping restaurant set in a shady concrete patio. The menu is on the wall, the service is quick and the food is cheap and delicious. Look for the green garage door.

**Bar Restaurant Hong Kong** (☎ 433-1952; Calle Comericio; mains BsF25-35; ⌚ 11am-10pm) A reliable mainstay in the center of town, this new Chinese restaurant has a huge menu and great-value set meals that keeps it busy with locals throughout the day.

**Restaurant El Colmao** (☎ 432-2005; Calle Sucre at Plaza Pichincha; mains BsF35-60; ⌚ noon-2am Mon-Sat) This windowless Spanish restaurant serves up the usual specialties like shellfish stew, grilled prawns and squash Provençal. The second dining room comes with a stage for live music; otherwise there's just soccer on the TV.

**our pick** **Les Jardins de Sucre** (☎ 431-3689; Calle Sucre 27; mains BsF40-80; ⌚ 6:30-10:30pm Mon, noon-2:30pm &

**ARRIVING IN VENEZUELA BY FERRY**

The otherwise forgettable town of Güiria on the Península de Paria is a useful port for connections around the Golfo de Paria. The most popular service here is the weekly boat to Trinidad, though there are other services available including informal fishing boat services to Macuro on the peninsula's eastern tip and irregular services to the Delta del Orinoco port of Pedernales. **Acosta Asociados** (☎ 0294-982-1556; Calle Bolívar 31; 🕑 9am-noon & 2-5:30pm) operates the Sea Prowler, a comfortable and air-conditioned passenger boat that runs between Güiria and Chaguaramas, near Port of Spain, Trinidad. It leaves Trinidad at 9am every Wednesday, arriving around 12.30pm in Güiria and then leaving again for Trinidad at 3.30pm. Fares are BsF720 one way, BsF1185 return. There's also a port tax payable on departure from Trinidad of US$16 per passenger. There is no departure tax payable when leaving Venezuela by boat.

6:30-10pm Tue-Sat) This beautifully designed and exceptionally good French restaurant has its diners discreetly spread out over a shaded patio around a small water garden. Delicious seafood, classic French cooking and a range of crepes make for a great meal, complemented by French and Chilean wines. Daily specials like duck and rabbit are available.

**Bar Restaurant Jardín Sport** (Plaza Bolívar; 🕑 6am-midnight) The locals' favorite for chatting the day away is this informal open-air bar in a courtyard off Plaza Bolívar. It has a few pool tables in back and serves inexpensive snacks, but it's the cheap beer that keeps punters returning for more.

## Getting There & Away

### AIR

The airport is about 4km southeast of the city center. Connections are mainly to Caracas and Porlamar on Avior, Venezolana and Rutaca. A taxi here from the city center should cost you BsF20.

### BOAT

**Naviarca** (☎ 431-5577; www.grancacique.com.ve) runs ferries to Isla de Margarita's dock at Punta de Piedras; see p197 for details. Naviarca also operates a ferry to Araya on the Península de Araya, although it's much easier to go by the small boats called *tapaditos* (see p197).

To get to the ferry docks in Cumaná snag a bus or por puesto (BsF2) from just north of the bridge, or take a taxi (BsF10).

### BUS

The bus terminal is 1.5km northwest of the city center and is linked by frequent buses and por puestos (BsF1) along Av Humboldt; go outside the terminal and take them going right (south).

Bus destinations include Caracas (BsF37 to BsF70, seven hours), Carúpano (BsF15, 2½ hours), Santa Elena (BsF80, twenty hours), Maracay (BsF40, seven hours), Mérida (BsF85, 15 hours) and Puerto La Cruz (BsF10, 1½ hours).

Por puesto destinations include Puerto La Cruz (BsF35, 1½ hours) and Caripe (BsF45, three hours). For the Cueva del Guácharo, take a por puesto bound for Caripe and ask to be let off at the entrance. Busetas to Santa Fe (BsF5, 45 minutes) and Mochima (BsF5, 40 minutes) depart from near the Mercadito, one block off the Redoma El Indio.

## PENÍNSULA DE ARAYA

☎ 0293

Lying just across the deep and intensely blue Gulf of Cariaco from Cumaná, the Península de Araya comprises a 70km-long and 10km-wide finger of strikingly barren land characterized by arid red sands and scrubby dunes. Punta Arenas, on the peninsula's end, is just 5km northwest of Cumaná as the crow flies, but it's some 180km by road. The peninsula's sparse population is scattered through a handful of coastal villages on the northern coast, along which the solitary and rather rough road runs. The town of Araya is the largest settlement here and easy to get to by boat or ferry from Cumaná.

The peninsula's two major attractions – a huge colonial fort, the Castillo de Santiago, and the vast Salinas de Araya – are both near the town of Araya, at the western end of the peninsula. However, if you have time and your own transportation, it's well worth driving the length of the peninsula to see a side of Venezuela most people never do, with its eerie landscapes, tumbledown villages and haunting vistas.

## Araya

The chief town of the peninsula, Araya manages to feel surprisingly lively despite its relative isolation. It sits on the Bahía de Araya, with its pier in the middle the Castillo de Santiago is 750m to the south and the *salinas* (salt pans) spread outward to the north.

There's a decent beach between the town and the fort, but it doesn't come with a lot of shade. Most places to stay are located near this beach and toward the fortress.

### SIGHTS

#### Salinas de Araya

This sprawling salt-extraction site is run by **Sacosal** (☎ 437-1123) and includes three areas: the *salinas naturales* (natural salt lagoon; referred to as Unidad 1), *salinas artificiales* (artificial salt pans; Unidad 2) and the main complex near the pier (not open to the public), where salt is sorted, packed and stored.

The *salinas naturales,* about 1km east of town, consist of a pink-hued salt lagoon, from which the salt is dragged to the shore by specially constructed boats, cleaned and then left to dry in enormous glistening heaps. Walk five minutes behind town to the blue-and-white 'Unidad Laguna Madre' building, which is down the hill and near the green-and-yellow chapel. If you're lucky someone will have time to explain the process to you (in Spanish); they're less busy on weekends.

The *salinas artificiales,* a few kilometers north of the town, are a colorful array of rectangular pools filled with salt water. The intense strength of the sun evaporates this water, leaving behind pure salt, which is then harvested; the pool is then refilled and the process begun again. Numerous pools in different stages of evaporation create a variety of color tones, from rich creamy pinks to deep purple. The water coloration has a lot to do with *artemia,* a microscopic saltwater shrimp found in the water.

A poorly maintained old *mirador* (lookout) is on the hill to the east of the *salinas,* providing a good view over this chessboard of pools. It's on the road to Punta de Araya, 2km north of Araya. Hard-core salt aficionados can hire a taxi for a look around; just be prepared for baking heat and don't forget to take plenty of water, sunscreen, sunglasses and a hat.

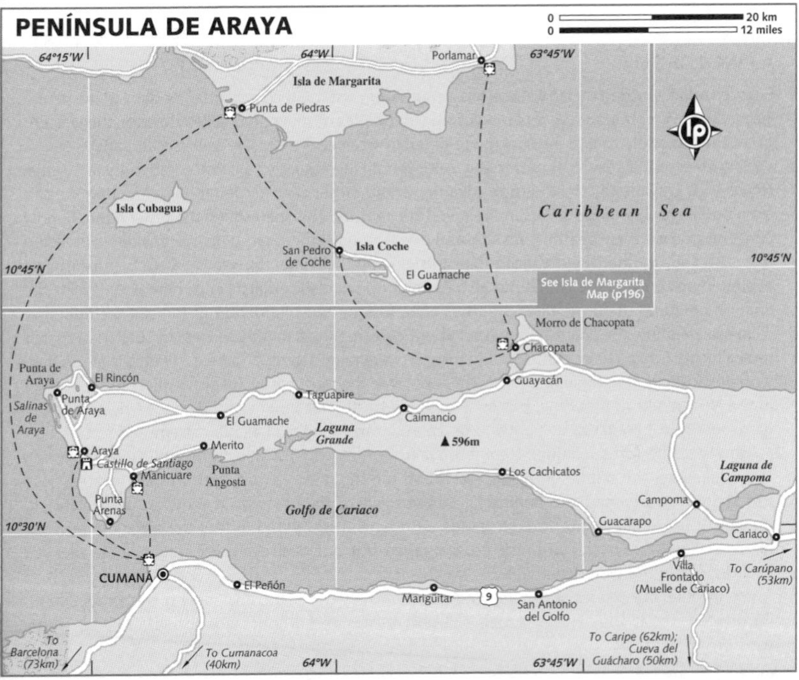

 



### Castillo de Santiago

This, the biggest and oldest colonial fort in the country (see the boxed text, below), is commonly referred to as El Castillo (The Castle). The four-pointed structure stands on the waterfront cliff at the southern end of the bay, a hot 20-minute walk from town. Although damaged, the gargantuan coral-rock walls are an awesome sight and give a good impression of how the fort must have once looked. You can wander freely around the site, as there's no gate.

### SLEEPING & EATING

**Posada Araya Wind** (☎ 437-1132, 0414-189-0717; Calle El Castillo; d/tr incl breakfast BsF120/130; ) The most stylish posada in town, the neatly decorated Araya Wind is located right next to the fortress and offers up 14 good rooms with cane roofing. Some rooms are in the lovely main house, while others are in a block in the garden. Most rooms have private facilities and air-con, while five are fan-cooled and share bathrooms.

**Posada Helen** (☎ 437-1101, 0414-189-3867; Calle El Castillo; r/tr BsF120/140; ) This homey posada has very clean and pleasant rooms complete with private bathrooms and TV, all in a rather kitsch and parrot-heavy environment

our pick **El Refugio del Marinero** (Calle El Castillo; meal BsF20; 9am-4pm) Located near the port right on the beach where the catch of the day is brought in, this fantastic place will serve you up a sublime lunch of freshly caught fish, plantains and rice cooked up by the friendly women who run the place. On Mondays fishermen sing songs and play music on the terrace outside, the perfect accompaniment to a meal.

**Restaurant Araya Mar** (☎ 437-1382; Calle El Castillo; mains BsF30-45, r BsF120; 8am-8pm) This airy, modern restaurant has an open front that catches the breeze. It also offers nine clean, air-con rooms with cable TV.

### GETTING THERE & AWAY

**Naviarca** (☎ in Cumaná 431-5577; www.grancacique.com.ve) runs several ferries daily between Cumaná and Araya (BsF6/28 per person/car, one hour); there are usually three departures daily in each direction, but schedules aren't dependable. A better bet is the small *tapadito* boats, which offer frequent, faster and more reliable service. They go between Cumaná and Manicuare (BsF4, 20 minutes) every 10 to 20

### A PINCH OF SALT

For such a lifeless stretch of land, Araya has a compelling history. The Spaniards first claimed the peninsula in 1499. After the discovery of fabulous pearl fisheries offshore, they sailed down to the western tip of the peninsula to find another, quite different treasure – extensive *salinas* (salt pans).

Salt, an essential means of preserving food, was an increasingly valuable commodity in Europe. However, it was the Dutch who took advantage, and rather cheekily set about extracting the salt from under the Spaniards' noses in the mid-16th century. The Spanish, on the other hand, blindly concentrated on their pearl harvesting and it wasn't until the pearl beds were wiped out in the late 16th century that they realized their mistake. By that time, the *salinas* were being furtively exploited not only by the Dutch but also by the opportunistic English, and there wasn't a lot the Spanish could do about it. Various battles were fought, but plundering of the salt continued.

In exasperation, the Spanish Crown set about constructing a mighty fortress in 1618. However, it took almost 50 years to be completed thanks to pirate raids, storms and heat so fierce that the men worked mostly during the night. The fortress became the most costly Spanish project to be realized in the New World to that time, but once equipped with 45 cannons and defended by a 250-man garrison, La Real Fortaleza de Santiago de León de Araya repelled all who attempted to take it.

However, the fort's fortunes changed again in 1726 when a wild hurricane threw up a tide that broke over the salt lagoon, flooding it and turning it into a gulf. With the salt reserves lost, the Spanish abandoned the peninsula. Before leaving, they set about blowing up the fort to prevent it from falling into foreign hands. Although they ignited all the available gunpowder, however, the sturdy structure resisted. Damaged but not destroyed, the mighty bulwarks still proudly crown the waterfront cliff.

Meanwhile, the *salinas* slowly returned to their previous state, and mining was gradually reintroduced. Today they are Venezuela's largest *salinas* and produce about half a million metric tons of salt per year.

minutes from 6am to 6pm, and the remaining Manicuare–Araya leg is covered by frequent por puestos (BsF2, 10 minutes).

Although there's a (badly) paved road between Araya and Cariaco (95km), there's little traffic traveling along it. There are occasional por puestos from Araya to Cariaco, but you can't rely on them. Traffic dies completely after 3pm.

There's a boat service between Chacopata and Porlamar, on Isla de Margarita (see p197).

## RÍO CARIBE

**☎ 0294 / pop 14,000**

Río Caribe is a colorful colonial seaside town within easy driving distance of some of Venezuela's best beaches. It makes a good base for exploring the area, or serves as a good stop over on the way to the Península de Paria as it has a good range of services and a pleasant and relaxed feel. If you come, visit the 18th-century church on Plaza Bolívar.

The town is an old port that grew fat on cacao exports, and the air of the former splendor is still palpable in the wide, tree-shaded Av Bermúdez, with its grand and brightly painted mansions. Many people find themselves spending longer in this friendly town than they had planned.

### Tours

So far there's little tourist infrastructure in town, which makes for a laid-back feel. Area tours are organized by most mid- to upper-range posadas; shop around, as routes, services and prices may vary. Day tours include a boat trip to a few beaches, the buffalo ranch, hot springs, Playa de Uva and an interesting cocoa plantation (for descriptions of these places see Around Río Caribe, p222).

### Sleeping

The town has a good range of accommodations, including several charming posadas.

**Pensión Papagayos** (☎ 646-1868; cricas@web.de; Calle 14 de Febrero; per person BsF50; ) This tiny family home rents out just four good, well-kept rooms sharing two bathrooms, and you can use the kitchen and fridge. There's a tiny garden and pleasant common dining area.

**Posada San Miguel** (☎ 416-6344; posadasanmigul@hotmail.com; Calle Zea 83; d/tr BsF80/120; ) Eleven clean, simple and tiled rooms with small baths are available at this new and rather antiseptic place. Get an outside window for light. Guests are free to use the family kitchen and there's even a rooftop terrace.

**Posada Don Chilo** (☎ 646-1212; Calle Mariño 27; d/tr BsF90/120; ) A family place with seven cheap, no-frills (but decent) fan rooms and a terrace to hang out on. Home-cooked meals are available.

**Villa Antillana** (☎ 646-1413; Calle Rivero 32; s/d/tr/q incl breakfast BsF100/200/350; ) Set in a restored 19th-century mansion, quiet Villa Antillana has some very attractive mezzanine rooms at the front of the house, while those at the back were being renovated on our last visit. The centerpiece of the posada is its pretty tiled courtyard with hammocks. Services include bike rental and area trips; in season you can take a tour to set baby turtles free.

**our pick** **Posada Shalimar** (☎ 646-1135; www.posada-shalimar.com; Calle Bermúdez 54; s/d/tr/ste BsF150/200/250/350; ) Easily the most charming posada in town, this Moorish paradise has 15 attractive, pastel-colored rooms decorated with tasteful art and gorgeous tilework. There's a pretty restaurant-bar in front that does excellent food, and a pool and numerous tours and activities are available.

**Posada Caribana** (☎ 646-1242; www.parquenivaldito.com; Av Bermúdez 25; per person incl half board BsF355; P ) This upmarket posada is located in a gorgeous *casona* from the 19th century and is run by the posh Parque Nivaldito group. It has 11 good-sized, simply (but stylishly) decorated rooms that line a traditional-style patio. The lounge area is decorated with rattan furniture, and there's a garden and a restaurant out back (where the best rooms are). There's excellent food here (order ahead for dinner).

### Eating

**Restaurant Manos Benditas** (☎ 646-1162; Av Gallegos; mains BsF15-40; noon-10pm) On the seafront a block from Bermúdez, this is the town's most popular restaurant and bustles with local life throughout the day. Its menu is pure *comida criolla*, with dishes including *pastel de chucho* (shredded ray with plantain and cheese) and a delicious *pollo a cacao* (chocolate chicken).

**Da More** (☎ 646-1622; Av Bermúdez; pizzas BsF25-35; 6-10pm) This relaxed and airy place cooks up great pizzas and pastas. You can create your own topping combination or choose from the menu. There's no alcohol served, though.

**Posada Shalimar** (☎ 646-1135; Calle Bermúdez 54; mains BsF25-40; 3-10pm) Unsurprisingly, the best posada in town also has the best eatery. The charming Shalimar's bar-restaurant is open for nonguests in the evenings, when you can choose from a great menu of international dishes, including their signature 'ass-kicking' hamburger.

### Getting There & Away

Río Caribe has no bus terminal and transportation departs from Plaza Bolívar. Crucero Oriente Sur has an office on the square where you can buy tickets for its daily morning service to Puerto La Cruz (BsF40, five hours) and Caracas (BsF80, 10 hours). There are also por puestos to Carúpano (BsF5 per person, 30 minutes) and Cumaná (BsF40 per person, three hours); taxis to Carúpano cost BsF25, while one to Cumaná will set you back BsF200.

For details on transportation to the beaches around Río Caribe, see below.

## AROUND RÍO CARIBE

☎ 0294

East of Río Caribe lies the breathtaking scenery of the Península de Paria, a wonderfully off-the-beaten track landscape of thick vegetation covering dramatic mountainsides that look down onto the best beaches of Venezuela's Caribbean coastline, many of which are nesting sites for green turtles. There are perhaps two dozen separate sandy stretches on the 50km coastal stretch between Río Caribe and San Juan de Unare, the last seaside village accessible by road. The very best are Playa Pui Puy, Playa Medina and the beach at San Juan de las Galdonas, but there are plenty of other lesser-known patches of paradise – all it takes is an adventurous spirit to find them.

There are over a dozen posadas scattered across the region, but roads are few and are in bad shape, and transportation is infrequent. While this makes getting around tricky, it means that the region is, in general, blissfully free of tourists.

#### GETTING THERE & AWAY

Given the bad roads and long drives needed to get to the different beaches, by far the best way to explore the area is by boat; tours are organized by hotels and posadas in Río Caribe (p221).

Getting around using por puestos will just be a frustrating experience as they fill up slowly and won't take you all the way to the beach, leaving you a long, hot walk wherever you're dropped. Much easier is to drive yourself or to hire a taxi for the day – though roads are bad you won't need a 4WD to get to anywhere as far as San Juan de Las Galdonas.

### Playa Loero & Playa de Uva

Side-by-side Playa Loero and Playa de Uva are nevertheless miles apart in atmosphere. They lie 6km from Río Caribe by the road to Bohordal, then another 6km by a paved side road that branches off to the left. The road splits just before you come to both beaches – Playa de Uva is accessible only for guests of the posh **Campamento Playa de Uva** (☎ 416-2888; www.parquenivaldito.com; per person incl half board BsF370, per person incl breakfast in the 'VIP' rooms BsF400; P ✣ ) – look for the name Parque Nivaldito on the main gates. This gorgeous place is something of an anomaly here, but also a treat. The 12 standard rooms surround a pool and restaurant area just moments from the beach, while the new 8 hilltop 'VIP' rooms have their own private plunge pools and feel very sumptuous indeed. The beach itself is small but wonderful.

Just to the west of Playa de Uva, Playa Loero is another pleasant, though less memorable, beach. It has no facilities, but you can string your hammock under the roof of the *churuata* (traditional palm-thatched, large circular hut) and enjoy the breeze.

### Museo del Cacao Pariano

Near the small village of Chacaracual, 14km from Río Caribe, the **Museo del Cacao Pariano** (☎ 988-0404; admission BsF20; 8:30am-5pm) is a cocoa plantation and chocolate factory still in operation. Hour-long tours are given daily and they include a fascinating demonstration of processing cacao and, more importantly, a tasting.

Next door is the **Hacienda Paria Shakti Case Bukare** (☎ 611-8767; www.pariashakti.com; r per person BsF180; P ✣ ), a yoga and meditation retreat in the old cocoa plantation hacienda. The four rooms are simple, with little balconies overlooking the woods outside. It's a peaceful spot and there's a nice pool in the small garden.

### Playa Medina

Proceeding east, a paved road branches off 4km beyond Hacienda Bukare and goes 5km to the village of Medina then northward for 1km to a fork. The left branch goes for 2km to the stunning crescent-shaped Playa Medina. This 400m-long stretch of paradise appears on more postcards in Venezuela than any other beach.

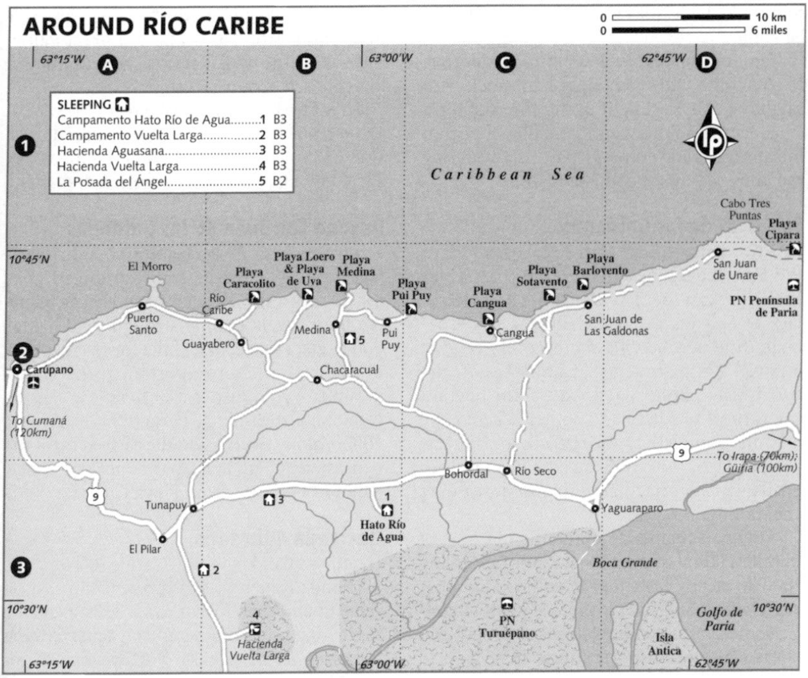


It is indeed picture-perfect, set in a glorious deep bay fronted by a gentle arc of golden sand shaded with a forest of swaying coconut palms. And despite the soft sand, cleanliness and sheltered location, the isolated Playa Medina rarely gets overrun by beachgoers.

Amid the palms at the far end of the beach are some stylish cabañas and a restaurant at **Corpomedina** (☎ 0294-331-5241; playamedina@cantv.net; r per person incl half board BsF207; ). There are eight rustic two-floor cabañas, each housing up to four people and boasting patios, two bedrooms and a basic kitchen; the rooms are a little musty and it's pricy, but this truly is an idyllic spot. It's usually important to reserve in advance.

The beach can be used by anybody, though camping is not allowed. Señoras from the surrounding hamlets come and serve basic meals and snacks (such as delicious fried fish empanadas) for day-trippers.

For those on a more modest budget wanting to be near the beach, 3km from the beach, in the middle of the village of Medina, is the colorful 20-room **La Posada del Ángel** (☎ 417-3179; r per person incl half board BsF150; ). It has a large, pleasant restaurant and bar area with hammocks and thatched roof. Only five of the rooms have air-con.

## Playa Pui Puy

Taking the right branch of the fork 1km beyond the village of Medina, a 6km potholed road leads to the village of Pui Puy and continues for 2km to the beautiful Playa Pui Puy. One of the best beaches around, Pui Puy is a 1.3km-long arc of fine white sand lined with coconut groves. The sea is less sheltered here, and waves can get big enough for bodysurfers – especially from November to January. It also has a colony of 18 very pleasant holiday cabañas and a restaurant operated by **Corpomedina** (☎ 0294-331-5241; playamedina@cantv.net; r per person incl half board BsF207). All cabañas are simple, two-room deals with fan and hammocks; reserve in advance. The restaurant serves average budget meals.

At the very far end of the beach is **Posada Rincón de Pui Puy** (☎ 0414-598-0874, 0414-294-0674; s/d/tr BsF150/250/300, r per person incl half board BsF180; ), a charming place with a panoramic view of the bay from its patio. The 20 colorful rooms range from tiny to large; the cheapest have showers outside, the best have their own huge balconies.

Camping on this beach is permitted for free. If you come with your own hammock, you might be able to sling it under the roof for a small fee. Mosquitoes and sand flies appear in the mornings and evenings, particularly during the rainy season, so come prepared.

## San Juan de las Galdonas

Few travelers venture further east than Playa Pui Puy, though beaches dot the coast as far as the eye can see. The charming seaside village of San Juan de las Galdonas has especially fine beaches. Its main access road is a paved 23km stretch that branches off the Río Caribe–Bohordal road 6.5km beyond the turnoff to Medina. Another access is by a badly potholed 22km road that connects to Río Seco, but you'll need a 4WD. Both roads wind spectacularly up and down over the mountain range.

Tiny San Juan is an authentic old port of about 1700 inhabitants that continues living its own sleepy little life. It's a good spot for travelers to hang out – there is a choice (albeit small) of accommodations and food, and there's more transportation to here than to anywhere else in the area. And you won't miss out on beaches, either – relatively nearby are several gorgeous, isolated stretches of sand.

Local tour operators can also take you further into both Parque Nacional Península de Paria (opposite) and Parque Nacional Turuépano (opposite).

### SLEEPING & EATING

**Posada Las Tres Carabelas** (☎ 511-2729, 211-2622; lastrescarabelas3@gmail.com; s/d BsF80/120, r per person half board BsF130) A few hundred meters beyond the Hotel Playa Galdonas is this friendly posada. It's a basic and rustic spot that sits spectacularly on top of a cliff high above the beach, providing gorgeous views over the sea. There are 15 good budget rooms with fans; room 5 is the best, with its kitchen and great views. Area tours are available, along with three-day trips to Parque Nacional Turuépano (see opposite). There's also a restaurant here that serves up delicious dishes – try their sublime fish soup.

**Hotel Playa Galdonas** (☎ 889-1892; www.littlesecrets.com.ve; s/d/tr BsF103/216/236; ) Looming over the beach is this large, 30-room hotel, a surprisingly classy establishment for such a remote location. Many of the spacious rooms have great balconies with stunning views; all have good bathrooms and are great value. There's a large pool, a terrace restaurant and direct beach access as well.

To eat try **Restaurant Mediterránea** (mains BsF20-40; 11am-3pm & 6-10pm), between Posada Las Tres Carabelas and Hotel Playa Galdonas. It's a friendly place serving up fresh fish dishes.

## Beyond San Juan de las Galdonas

From San Juan de las Galdonas, a dirt road (serviced by sporadic transportation) goes for 20km to the village of **San Juan de Unare**. An hour's walk east by a rough road brings you to **Playa Cipara**, one of the longest beaches in the area and an important turtle-laying grounds. From just east of here, the Parque Nacional Península de Paria (p225) stretches 100km along the coast to the eastern tip of the peninsula. A path to the park's nearest village, Santa Isabel, runs from Playa Cipara.

## Hacienda Aguasana

Heading inland from Río Caribe to Tunapuy, Hacienda Aguasana is a further 5km east on the Tunapuy–Bohordal road. This hacienda has a long trail of mineral-rich **aguas termales** (hot springs; day-use fee BsF30; 8:30am-6pm). There are 17 ponds of various sizes with water of different temperatures scattered around the hacienda's grassy lands and linked by paths. Some ponds are natural, while others have been shaped. There are also bubbling hot mud pools for you to achieve that instant elephantine look. Bring your bathing suit, though nudity is OK, too (towels available).

Other services, such as acupressure and mud massage, are available. The hacienda also has four simple double rooms to rent for BsF200 per person, including breakfast and dinner at the on-site restaurant.

## Hato Río de Agua

A further 8km east beyond Hacienda Aguasana, you'll find the entrance to Hato Río de Agua. This buffalo ranch, which occupies a 1000-hectare chunk of marshland to the south of the Tunapuy–Bohordal road, has 380 water buffalo as well as caimans and abundant bird life. The ranch's usual occupation has been the production of buffalo meat and cheese, but it has also turned to tourism. An attractive **campamento** (☎ 331-3847; d incl breakfast BsF250), consisting of five conical cabañas and a thatched restaurant, sits 2km off the road.

Day visits (without accommodations and meals) are also possible between 7am and 6pm daily; they cost BsF20 per person. The visit includes a brief look around the ranch, a short trip in a dugout canoe, the chance to sit on top of a water buffalo, a soft drink or fruit juice and a piece of the distinctively tangy buffalo cheese.

### Hacienda Vuelta Larga

Heading west from the town of Tunapuy, after about 2.5km a paved side road branches off to the south and goes for 1km to Campamento Hacienda Vuelta Larga. The road runs another 7km to the hacienda proper.

Operated by Klaus Müller, **Hacienda Vuelta Larga** (☎ 666-9052; vueltalarga@cantv.net) is a 10-sq-km ecological ranch with water buffalo and about 230 bird species. The **campamento** (d BsF180, half board per person extra BsF80) provides lodging and hearty traditional food. Birding trips are conducted by Klaus' son, Daniel, who is an experienced bird-watcher (per person BsF120).

### Parque Nacional Turuépano

East of Hacienda Vuelta Larga stretches the wilderness of 726-sq-km Turuépano National Park. It's a rarely visited marshland crisscrossed by a maze of natural water channels and populated by a wealth of wildlife, mainly birds and fish. The habitat is similar to that of the Delta del Orinoco, characterized by high temperature and humidity, along with a significant tide that gives rise to a peculiar type of vegetation. The park lacks any real tourist facilities.

To arrive, get to the village of El Pilar in the early morning, then catch a por puesto to Guariquén, where boats leave to explore the wetlands. For more information you can ask Billy of Hacienda Bukare (p222), who knows the area. Posada Las Tres Carabellas (in San Juan de las Galdonas, opposite) does multiday tours to the park but can also give advice for independent travel.

## PARQUE NACIONAL PENÍNSULA DE PARIA

This 375-sq-km park stretches for 100km along the northern coast of the peninsula, right up to its eastern tip. It encompasses a coastal mountain range, which looms up almost right from the sea and reaches its maximum elevation point at Cerro Humo (1257m). The coast is graced with many coves, in which tiny fishing villages have nestled.

The mountain is largely covered with forest, and the higher you go, the wetter it is. The upper reaches of the outcrop (roughly above 800m) form a typical cloud-forest habitat that's largely unexplored and intact, with rich and diverse wildlife. The southern foothills are being increasingly cleared by local farmers. An additional threat is the discovery of offshore oil, the exploitation of which may alter this remote, bucolic peninsula completely.

### Orientation

The park has no tourist facilities and access is not straightforward. The villages on the northern coast are best (or only) accessed by boat, the closest points of departure being Macuro and San Juan de Unare. However, boat trips are irregular and expensive. Access from the south is via the Carúpano–Güiria highway, but there are few gateways here leading into the park.

A few trails cross the park north to south, and these are the best way to get deeper into the wilderness. Ideally you should hire a guide, as the trails are not always easy to follow.

### Walking Trails

One of the trails goes between the villages of Manacal and Santa Isabel, in the western end of the park. The rough road to Manacal branches off the Carúpano–Güiria highway 20km east of Yaguaraparo and winds uphill to the village at 750m. There are few vehicles along this road, so you may need to walk (three hours). There are no hotels in Manacal, but informal accommodations can usually be arranged. If you have a hammock, you may be allowed to sling it under somebody's roof.

The trail from Manacal winds to the hamlet of Roma and then uphill to the 1000m crest, before descending to **Santa Isabel**, on the coast. Guides can be found in Manacal, and the hike will take about six hours. Stuck to the hillside high above the bay and dotted with rocky islets, Santa Isabel is a tiny fishing village. It shelters the rustic **Posada de Cucha** (d incl breakfast & dinner BsF120), which offers beds and meals and a marvelous view over the rugged coast from its balcony.

There are no roads from the village, but a path goes westward to Boca del Río Cumaná (four hours), then along the shore to Playa Cipara (1½ hours) and onward to San Juan de Unare (one hour). The first part of the trail is faint, so a guide is recommended (available in Santa Isabel). Otherwise, negotiate for a boat to San Juan de Unare, then continue to San Juan de las Galdonas.

On the opposite, eastern end of the park is a path from Macuro to Uquire on the northern coast (four hours). Uquire has a good beach, and you may be able to arrange a room or hammock for the night. You can either walk back or hunt for a boat to return you to Macuro around the peninsula's tip.

If you don't fancy walking, hire a boat in Macuro to take you to Uquire and other nearby places, such as Don Pedro and San Francisco. Tours along the coast are organized from San Juan de las Galdonas (see p224).

# MONAGAS STATE

## MATURÍN

☎ 0291 / pop 410,000

Founded in 1760 as a Capuchin mission, the prosperous commercial city of Maturín is the state capital of Monagas and the regional economic motor. Large deposits of oil exploited in the region have added to the city's coffers, and the center is very well-to-do by Venezuelan standards. Maturín is also a busy regional transportation hub, connecting routes from the northeastern coast to the Delta del Orinoco and the Gran Sabana. It's not an overly interesting place and most travelers pass through quickly.

### Sleeping & Eating

Should you find yourself having to overnight here, there are plenty of hotels to choose from. Budget hotels around central Plaza Ayacucho are easily accessible from the bus terminal by frequent city buses; get off at the intersection of Avs Juncal and Bolívar, two blocks from the plaza. Taxis to the center cost about BsF10.

**Hotel Puerto España** (☎ 642-2476; Calle Cantaura 11; d/tw BsF70/110; ❄) Decent budget rooms with cable TV and private bathrooms, well located just one block from Plaza Ayacucho.

**Hotel Royal Place** (☎ 643-8822; Av Bolívar 133; royalplace@cantv.net; s/d incl breakfast BsF140/180; ❄ wi-fi) This surprisingly excellent hotel is your best bet in town, with a good location in the city center; large, clean and well-maintained rooms; a decent restaurant and bar on the premises and free (though admittedly unreliable) wi-fi.

Most of the city's better eating options are located some way out of the center, so for a simple and cheap dinner head down to the late-night food stalls around the Plaza Ayacucho, or for something more substantial, try the restaurant at the **Hotel Royal Place** (mains BsF40-80; 🕐 7am-11pm).

### Getting There & Away

#### AIR

The airport is in the middle of the city, just 2km east of the city center; eastbound buses 1 and 5 from Av Bolívar will let you off near the terminal, or a taxi will cost BsF20. The airport has several daily flights to Caracas, Porlamar and Ciudad Guayana.

#### BUS

The bus terminal is on Av Libertador, 2km southwest of the city center. There are plenty of buses to the center – cross Av Libertador to pick one up heading the right way.

Several buses run to Caracas daily, mostly in the evening (BsF60, 8½ hours). Other destinations include Ciudad Guayana (BsF30, 3½ hours), Tucupita (BsF45, four hours) and Caripe (BsF35, three hours).

## CARIPE

☎ 0292 / pop 17,500

Nestled in a verdant mountain valley halfway between Maturín and the Caribbean coast, Caripe is a very pleasant, easygoing town renowned for its agreeable temperatures, coffee and orange plantations, and its proximity to Cueva del Guácharo, Venezuela's most visited cave.

Caripe's cool climate makes an inviting weekend escape for Venezuelans from the steamy lowlands, and will often fill up during its elaborate Easter celebrations. The village itself is little more than two parallel streets, on which most activities and services are centered.

If you need cash, **Banesco** (Av Guzmán Blanco) has an ATM. For internet and telephone there's **Sala Web and Intely** on Av Chaumer.

### Sights & Activities

Caripe's number-one attraction is the Cueva del Guácharo (opposite), 12km from the town.

Save for a beautiful colonial high altar in the modern **parish church**, there's not much to see in town, but the rugged surroundings are ripe for **hiking**. If you want to explore and need an escort, try asking the guides at the Cueva del Guácharo, as they're often open to other work. Or drop in at the *ferretería* (hardware store) next to the Hotel Saman; if he's not busy, the effusive Oscar Gregori might have a lead on someone who can help with area tours.

**El Mirador** (1100m), to the north of the town, commands sweeping views over the Valle del Caripe; taxis here cost BsF15 to BsF20. Among the other sights are two beautiful waterfalls: the 30m-high **Salto La Payla**, near the Cueva del Guácharo, and the 80m-high **Salto El Chorrerón**, an hour's walk from the village of Sabana de Piedra. Further away are the **Puertas de Miraflores**, a spectacular river canyon, and the **Mata de Mango**, which features 22 caves, including the impressive Cueva Grande and Cueva Clara.

## Sleeping & Eating

Caripe has a few central hotels and there are plenty of upmarket chalets scattered around the surrounding countryside. Prices may rise on weekends.

### IN CARIPE

**Hotel San Francisco** (☎ 744-9185; Av Chaumer; s/d/tr BsF70/80/100) Don't look for a sign for this place – it's located unmarked across from the church in the town's main square. Behind its doors 18 good, brightly painted rooms with cable TV and fan are available.

**Hotel La Perla** (☎ 0424-414-2204; Av Chaumer; r/q BsF70/140) Functional budget rooms are on offer here – very basic, but clean enough, although don't expect much from the bathrooms. There are also plenty of cockroaches to keep you company at night.

**Hotel Samán** (☎ 545-1183; www.hotelsaman.com, in Spanish; Av Chaumer No 29; r/tr BsF160/175; P wi-fi) This long-running hotel is still the best in town. It has 24 colorful, comfortable rooms (the best ones are upstairs) with firm beds and fans, and a pleasant courtyard packed with plants. There's free wi-fi throughout.

**Restaurant Mogambo** (☎ 545-1021; Av Chaumer; mains BsF25-70; 7am-11pm Wed-Mon, daily in high season; P) Across from Hotel La Perla is this eatery set in a pink chalet-style building, where good quality cooking (something of a godsend here) is served up, including tasty soups, grills and daily specials. There's a good range of breakfasts here, too (BsF17 to BsF35).

**Trattoria Pastas Orence** (☎ 414-6107; Calle Cabello; mains BsF30-80; 11am-6pm Mon-Thu, to 10pm Fri-Sun) This pleasant place serves great pasta, such as ravioli with mushroom sauce and spaghetti with mussels, and has a comfortable dining area. It also features meats and fish on the menu, along with pizzas.

### AROUND CARIPE

There are more places to stay outside town, particularly along the road between Caripe and the village of El Guácharo. Some have cabañas good for large groups. Reserve ahead for weekend stays.

**Cabañas La Floresta** (☎ 414-8878; Sector La Peña; d/tr/q/cabaña BsF130/140/150, cabaña BsF190-430; P) Down a flowery lane and across a stream lies this peaceful place set on a grassy hillside. The simple cabañas (which sleep up to seven) are fitted with cable TV, well-equipped kitchens and outdoor barbecues. It's 2km from town on the road to Maturín.

**Pueblo Pequeño** (☎ 545-1843; pueblopequeno1@cantv.net; Sector Amanita off Via Cocollar; r BsF245, cabaña BsF265-460; P pool) This sweet, village-style collection of rustic cabañas in the hills above Caripe is a haven of rest and relaxation, popular with vacationing Venezuelans. The place is made up of cobblestone streets, comfy rooms and plenty of green space. There's a sauna, restaurant and pool, as well.

**El Rincón de Walter** (☎ 545-1797; 8am-9pm) Just outside town, on the road to Maturín, is this small joint dishing out tasty cups of strawberries and cream. It's worth the 20-minute walk from center, and has a restaurant nearby.

## Getting There & Away

The bus terminal is at the northeastern end of the town, behind the market. Other than Maturín, Caracas and Puerto La Cruz, there aren't many direct bus destinations linking Caripe to the outside world.

Frequent buses run to Maturín (BsF20, three hours), or faster por puestos (BsF30, 2½ hours). There's a daily bus to Puerto La Cruz (BsF70, four hours) and a bus to Caracas every other day (BsF75, eight hours).

# CUEVA DEL GUÁCHARO

Venezuela's longest, largest and most magnificent cave, the **Guácharo Cave** (admission BsF15; 8am-4pm Tue-Sun; P) is 12km from Caripe on the road toward the coast. It was declared Venezuela's first natural monument in 1949, and a 627-sq-km area around the cave was decreed the Parque Nacional El Guácharo in 1975. Alexander von Humboldt, the eminent scientist, penetrated 472m into the grotto in September 1799, and it was he who first classified its namesake inhabitant, the *guácharo,* or oilbird. You're only able to visit the cave as part of a guided tour, given in Spanish only (though some guides do speak English). The tours are frustratingly infantile and are basically an excuse to make smutty jokes about the more phallic stalactites, meaning you get to find out relatively little about the bizarre creatures that dwell here.

The eerie shrieking and flapping that echoes in the high galleries of the first chamber of the Cueva del Guácharo is made by a curious, reddish-brown species of bird that is the only one of its kind in the world. The *guácharo,* or oilbird *(Steatornis caripensis),* is a nocturnal, fruit-eating bird that inhabits caves in various tropical parts of the Americas, living in total darkness and leaving the cave only at night for food. It has a radar-location system (similar to bats) that enables it to navigate. It has a curved beak and enormous whiskers, and grows to about 60cm long, with a wingspan of a meter.

This colony is by far the biggest in Venezuela. From August to December, the population in this single cave is estimated at 10,000 birds, and occasionally up to 15,000. In the dry season the colony diminishes, but at least 8000 birds remain in March and April. The birds inhabit only the first chamber of the cave, 750m-long Humboldt's Hall. And the name of the first chamber following this area, *El Silencio* (Silence), echoes the relief felt by explorers to leave the birds' unsettling screeches behind.

Apart from this unique bird, the cave houses fish, crabs, spiders, ants, centipedes and bats. You'll likely see rodents scampering boldly along the ground. The cave also shelters a maze of stalactites and stalagmites that shine with calcium crystals.

All visits are by guided tours in groups of up to 20 people; tours take one to 1½ hours. A 1200m portion of the total 10.2km length of the cave is normally visited, though occasionally water rises in August and/or September, limiting sightseeing to half a kilometer. Bring nonslippery shoes for tramping over the mud and guano. A flashlight is also a good idea – the cave itself is very badly lit. The reception building also has a small museum and cafeteria. Large bags must be left by the ticket office. Cameras with flash can be used only beyond the *guácharos*' gallery, so as not to blind the birds.

You can camp at the entrance to the cave after closing time; it costs BsF5 per tent and the bathroom is open 24 hours. If you do camp, watch the hundreds of birds pouring out of the cave mouth at around 6:30pm and returning at about 4am. You can also take a short trip to the waterfall of **Salto La Payla**, a 25-minute walk from the cave.

### Getting There & Away

A roundtrip taxi from Caripe to the cave costs BsF20; the driver will return in two hours after setting you down. Buses linking Cumaná and Caripe pass by the cave and can drop you at the entrance, which is 12km north of Caripe.

If coming by car it can be hard to find the turn off from the main road to/from Caripe. The small side road going uphill to the cave is only signposted to drivers coming from Caripe (and even then it's easy to miss). If you're coming from elsewhere in the country, the turn off isn't signed at all, and can be found approximately 3km before reaching Caripe proper.

# Guayana



The vast wildernesses of Guayana are Venezuela's dazzling trump card – a spectacularly beautiful natural wonderland of steamy rainforest, rolling highland savanna and soaring table mountains, or tepuis. It's also home to many of Venezuela's greatest outdoor attractions, including the world's highest waterfall, Angel Falls. No trip to Venezuela is complete without coming here.

Guayana extends throughout the whole of Venezuela's southeast, encompassing the states of Delta Amacuro, Bolívar and Amazonas. While it comprises half of the country's land, it is home to just 6% of Venezuela's population. A majority of the country's indigenous peoples live and thrive here, including the Warao, Pemón, Yekuana and Yanomami.

The sheer natural beauty of this region is hard to overstate. A twenty-minute Cessna flight over the Parque Nacional Canaima will have your jaw dropping, while the trek to the ethereal top of Roraima, the most extraordinary of the tepuis, will stay with you forever. The waterfalls of the Gran Sabana, the exotic animals of the Delta del Orinoco and the pristine wilderness and traditional indigenous settlements of Amazonas are all further reasons to make the effort to come here.

**HIGHLIGHTS**

- Marvel at awe-inspiring **Angel Falls** (Salto Ángel; p247), the world's highest waterfall
- Explore the mysterious cloud-draped table mountain of **Roraima** (p253)
- Trace the lush rainforest waterways of sweltering **Amazonas** (p259)
- Cruise the wildlife-rich channels of the **Delta del Orinoco** (p231)
- Visit the spectacular **Cueva de Kavac** (p249), nestled deep in soaring Auyantepui

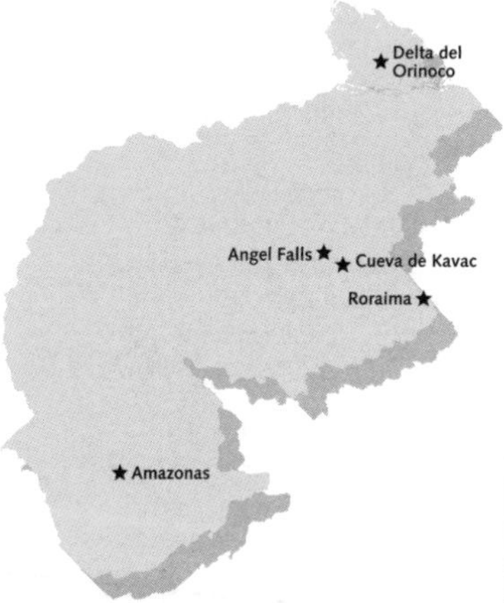

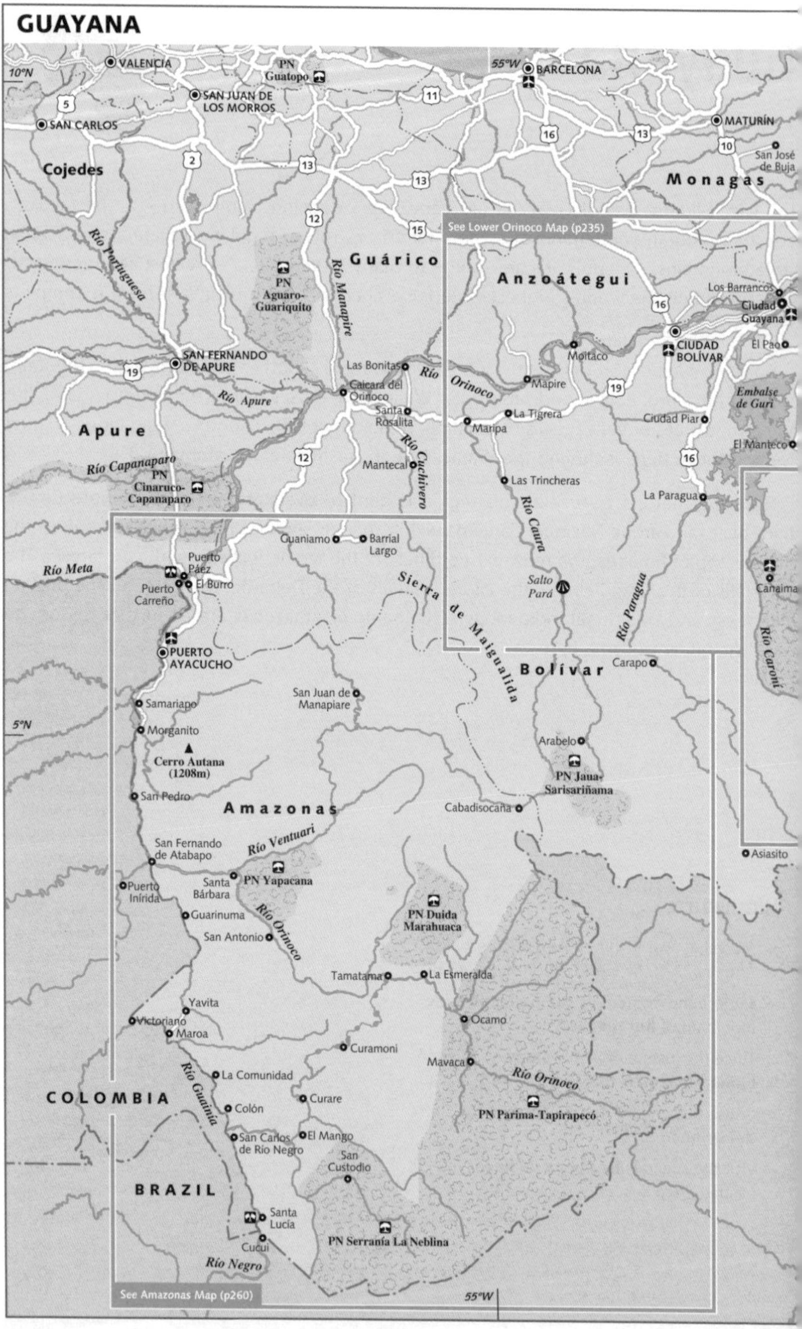
GUAYANA
VALENCIA
PN Guatopo
BARCELONA
SAN JUAN DE LOS MORROS
SAN CARLOS
MATURÍN
San José de Buja
Cojedes
Monagas
Guárico
Anzoátegui
Apure
Bolívar
Amazonas
COLOMBIA
BRAZIL
See Lower Orinoco Map (p235)
See Amazonas Map (p260)
PN Aguaro-Guariquito
Río Portuguesa
Río Manapire
SAN FERNANDO DE APURE
Río Apure
Las Bonitas
Caicara del Orinoco
Santa Rosalita
Río Cuchivero
Mantecal
Río Capanaparo
PN Cinaruco-Capanaparo
Río Orinoco
Mapire
Moitaco
La Tigrera
Maripa
CIUDAD BOLÍVAR
Los Barrancos
Ciudad Guayana
El Pao
Embalse de Guri
Ciudad Piar
El Manteco
Las Trincheras
La Paragua
Río Caura
Salto Pará
Río Paragua
Canaima
Río Caroní
Guaniamo
Barrial Largo
Sierra de Maigualida
Río Meta
Puerto Páez
El Burro
Puerto Carreño
PUERTO AYACUCHO
Carapo
San Juan de Manapiare
Samariapo
Morganito
Cerro Autana (1208m)
Arabelo
PN Jaua-Sarisariñama
San Pedro
Cabadisocaña
San Fernando de Atabapo
Río Ventuari
Santa Bárbara
PN Yapacana
Puerto Inírida
Guarinuma
San Antonio
PN Duida Marahuaca
Asiasito
Tamatama
La Esmeralda
Yavita
Victoriano
Maroa
Ocamo
Curamoni
Mavaca
La Comunidad
Río Guainía
Colón
Curare
PN Parima-Tapirapecó
San Carlos de Río Negro
El Mango
San Custodio
Santa Lucía
Cucui
PN Serranía La Neblina
Río Negro
10°N
5°N
55°W

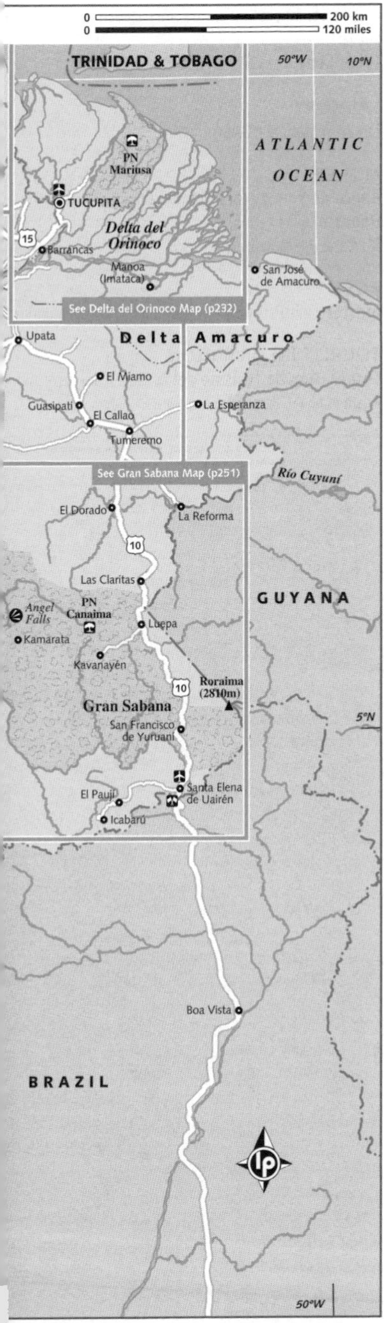


# DELTA DEL ORINOCO

Roaring howler monkeys welcome the dawn. Piranhas clamp onto anything that bleeds. Screaming clouds of parrots gather at dusk, and weaving bats gobble insects under the blush of a million stars. For wildlife viewing on the water's edge, it's hard to outshine the Delta del Orinoco.

A deep green labyrinth of islands, channels and mangrove swamps engulfing nearly 30,000 sq km – the size of Belgium – this is one of the world's great river deltas and a mesmerizing region to explore. Mixed forest blankets most of the land, which includes a variety of palms. Of these, the *moriche* palm is the most typical and important, as it is the traditional staple food for the delta's inhabitants, the Warao people, and provides material for their crafts, tools, wine and houses.

The Río Orinoco reaches a width of 20km in its lower course before splitting into about 40 major channels (and perhaps 250 smaller ones), which flow out along 360km of Atlantic coast. The southernmost channel, Río Grande, is the passage used by ocean-going vessels sailing upriver to Ciudad Guayana.

The best time to see the wildlife in the delta is in the dry season, when wide, orange, sandy beaches emerge along the shores of the channels. In the rainy months, when rivers are full, boat travel is easier, but the wildlife disperses and is more difficult to see.

Curiously enough, the state that encompasses the delta is not named after the Orinoco; rather it's named after the Amacuro, a small river that runs along part of the Guyana border and empties into the Boca Grande, the Orinoco's main mouth. Tucupita is the state capital and a base for Delta del Orinoco adventures.

## TUCUPITA

**☎ 0287 / pop 77,300**

There is only one reason that travelers find themselves in Tucupita – before or just after a Delta del Orinoco trip. The capital of the Delta Amacuro state is a hot, steamy river port and while it may be the only sizable town in the Delta del Orinoco, there is very little to see or do here. Still, the Plaza Bolívar is wide and shady and there are pleasant strolls along the Paseo Mánamo riverbank esplanade.

Tucupita sits beside the westernmost channel of the Delta del Orinoco, Caño Mánamo, which flows northward for 110km and empties into the Golfo de Paria near the town of Pedernales. The town evolved in the 1920s as one of a chain of Catholic Capuchin missions founded in the delta to convert the indigenous peoples. The missions established social programs that focused on providing education and health services; they opened up the region for both governmental activities and *criollo* colonists and, ultimately, for tourism.

## Information

### EMERGENCY

**Emergency Center** (☎ 171)

### INTERNET ACCESS

Rates for access to the internet average around BsF4 per hour.

**Compucenter.com** (Centro Comercial Delta Center, Plaza Bolívar)
**Cyber Copy** (Cnr Calle La Paz & Paseo Mánama)

### LAUNDRY

**Lavandería** (Calle Delta)

### MONEY

**Banco de Venezuela** (Calle Mánamo)
**Banesco** (Calle Petión)
**Mi Casa** (Plaza Bolívar)

### POST

**Ipostel** (Calle Pativilca; 8am-noon & 2-4pm Mon-Fri)

### TOURIST INFORMATION

**Corporación de Turismo del Estado Amacuro** (Av Arismendi; 8am-noon & 2-5pm Mon-Fri)

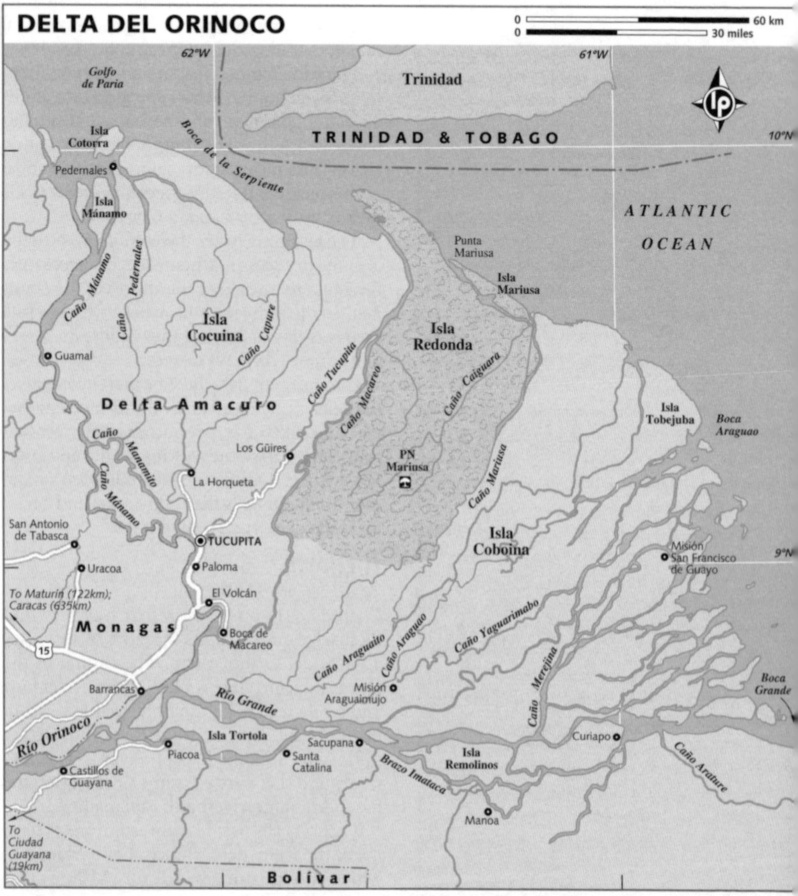

DELTA DEL ORINOCO

## Sights

The oldest building in town is the charmingly rickety-looking **Iglesia de San José de Tucupita** (Calle Mánamo), the Capuchin mission church constructed in 1930. It functioned as a parish church until the huge and rather charmless **Catedral de la Divina Pastora** (Av Arismendi) was completed in 1982, after almost 30 years of construction.

## Tours

Trips to the delta drive the regional tourism economy, and there are plenty of local tour operators ready to set you up with a journey to match your wallet and comfort level, although increasingly agencies aren't bothering to maintain a presence here, preferring to work out of Caracas or Margarita instead, where there's a steadier supply or tourists.

If you're pressed for time, book in advance or pay more to go in a smaller group, as tours can take a while to fill up here. Some travelers buy delta tours in Ciudad Bolívar or Ciudad Guayana, which may not be much more expensive and will save you time and money in the long run. Avoid the independent guides, known locally as *piratas*, who will approach you on the street to ask if you want to buy a delta tour – these trips are best undertaken with an established and trusted agency.

The following agencies have offices in Tucupita. For other tour companies that have *campamentos* (camps) in the delta, see p234.

**Abujene Tours** (☎ 0416-287-6964, 0416-102-3191; www.abujenetours.com; Calle Primera Transveral, Sector Los Cocos) Offers a large variety of activities and tours based at Campamento Abujene, its friendly camp on a narrow channel off the main river complete with a charming bridge across the water & 24 rustic rooms with private bathrooms.

**Aventura Turística Delta** (☎ 0416-897-2285; www.aventuraturisticadelta.com; Calle Centurión) One of the cheaper and more popular agencies, Aventura Turística Delta sends travelers to two simple camps where sleeping is in hammocks only.

**Campamento Mis Palafitos** (☎ 721-5166, 721-1733; www.deltaorinocomispalafitos.com; Centro Comercial Delta Center, Plaza Bolívar) One of the more expensive companies, it has boats leaving almost daily for either its Mis Palafitos Lodge, with 56 thatch-roofed cabins and private bathrooms, or the newer Orinoco Bujana, with 21 cabins, a five-minute boat ride away.

**Cooperativa Osibu XIV** (☎ 721-3840, campamentomaraisa@hotmail.com; cnr Calles Mariño & Pativilca) The oldest local tour company in town, this family-owned business conduct tours to the far eastern part of the delta. It's a five-hour boat ride to their 10-cabaña camp with beds and bathrooms.

## Sleeping

**Pequeño Hotel** (☎ 721-0523; Calle La Paz; s/d/tr BsF30/40/60) These simple rooms are clean but have fairly unpleasant bathrooms. It's the cheapest deal in town though, so it may be worth putting up with the 9:30pm curfew!

**Hotel Amacuro** (☎ 721-0404; Calle Bolívar; s/d/tr BsF80/100/120; ❄) A pleasant option just off Plaza Bolívar, this unremarkable place offers clean, simple rooms, all with private bathrooms. The front door isn't always well guarded, so keep your valuables safe.

**Posada Turistica Oasis** (☎ 721-1871; Av Casacoima; s/d/tr BsF140/140/170; P ❄) A little further out than the other lodging options, the Oasis is a simple, friendly place offering decent rooms with private bathrooms and TV around a small car park. There's a handy restaurant here too. Follow Av Casacoima south about 250m from the town center.

## Eating

In the evening, food stalls open along Paseo Mánamo, turning it into a lively spot where locals gather to meet friends, eat and drink by the river.

**our pick** **Mi Tasca** (☎ 721-1645; Calle Dalla Costa; mains BsF20-40; 🕑 11:30am-10:30pm Mon-Sat, until 8pm Sun) One of Tucupita's best eateries, with a varied menu, good prices, generous portions and friendly service. Try the *lau lau* (catfish) – it's delicious.

**Laredo Grill** (☎ 0414-879-0071; Calle Dalla Costa; mains BsF20-40; 🕑 11:30am-3pm & 6-11:30pm Mon-Thu, until late Fri & Sat, closed Sat lunch & Sun) As you'd expect there are all manner of grills on offer here. Less expected is the TARDIS-like interior and the live music at the weekends – this is one of the few places to party in Tucupita.

**La Mariposa Café** (☎ 721-3810; Centro Comercial Delta Center; mains BsF20-50; 🕑 8:30am-5pm Mon-Fri) A welcoming culinary oasis tucked away in an easy-to-miss shopping arcade, Mariposa's *comidas internacionales* include stroganoff, vegetarian pastas and excellent soups.

To stock up on food for a delta trip:

**Automercado Don Pancho** (☎ 721-1612; Calle Dalla Costa; 🕑 8am-12:30pm & 3-7:30pm Mon-Sat, 8am-noon Sun)

**Supermercado Unión** (☎ 721-1861; Calle Tucupita; 🕑 8am-6:30pm)

### THE CANOE PEOPLE OF DELTA DEL ORINOCO

The Delta del Orinoco is inhabited by the Warao (or Guarao) peoples, who have lived here from time immemorial. Today numbering about 25,000, they are Venezuela's largest indigenous group after the Guajiro of Zulia. Two-thirds of the Waraos live in the eastern part of the delta, between the Caño Mariusa and the Río Grande, where they are distributed across about 250 tiny communities.

The Waraos dwell along the small channels, constructing their open-sided, wooden huts on stilts on riverbanks and living mostly off fishing. Water is pivotal in their lives, as indicated by the tribe's name; in the local language *wa* means 'canoe' and *arao* means 'people.' They are excellent boat builders, making their dugout canoes from logs of large trees, using fire and simple axes.

Only half the Waraos speak Spanish. Most of the indigenous community still use their native language, officially classified as 'independent' because it doesn't belong to any of the major linguistic families. Linguists have not yet determined the origins of the language.

The Waraos are skillful craftspeople, renowned for their basketry and woodcarvings, especially animal figures carved from balsa wood. Their *chinchorros* (hammocks), made from the fiber of the *moriche* palm, are widely known and sought after for their quality and durability, and are sold at markets and craft shops across the country.

### Getting There & Away

The **Terminal de Pasajeros** (cnr Carrera 6 & Calle 10) is 1km southeast of the center; walk or take a taxi (BsF5). About half a dozen buses go to Caracas (BsF55 to BsF75, 11 hours) via Maturín, mostly in the evening. Some continue on to Maracay (BsF80) and Valencia (BsF85).

Por puestos serve Ciudad Guayana's San Felix terminal (BsF45, 3½ hours). For Caripe and Cueva del Guácharo, take a bus to Maturín (BsF20 to BsF30, four hours), or a por puesto (BsF15, three hours), and change there.

## AROUND TUCUPITA

There are plenty of companies offering tours in the vast waterways of the Orinoco Delta, though many are run from elsewhere in the country and don't have offices in Tucupita. You'll have to book a tour here in advance, simply as a boat transfer is necessary from either Tucupita or the small town of San José de Buja (a convenient pick-up point if you're arriving from Isla de Margarita via the airport at Maturín).

Tours usually consist of all-inclusive two- to four-day excursions. Prices fluctuate enormously depending on the company, the routes and conditions, and particularly on the number of people in the group. Activities tend to incorporate a jungle walk/slog (made possible with borrowed Wellington boots), a visit to a local Warao community, a trip in a typical wooden canoe and a stab at piranha fishing. While a trip here is fascinating, bear in mind that there are limited activities and *campamentos* are on small islands, meaning that you're limited to what's laid on by the tour. All those except very keen bird-watchers and wildlife spotters will usually find that two days and one night is the perfect amount of time to spend here.

**Campamento Boca de Tigre** (☎ 0212-524-5032; www.campamentobocadetigre.com) The otherwise remote delta position of this camp is somewhat marred by a large boat building operation next door, but the place itself is very pleasant, with Warao decorative arts brightening up the rooms, soaring ceilings and good bathrooms. The camp is also on a large island, so there's plenty of room to walk about.

**Orinoco Delta Lodge** (☎ 0295-249-1823, 0414-879-0044; www.orinocodelta.com) Tucupita Expeditions may have shut their Tucupita office, but their excellent camp remains, booked through either of their offices in Margarita or Maturín. The camp has spacious rooms with bright interiors, decent bathrooms and great river views. There's a large restaurant and even a small zoo where you can see Toby the Puma and two resident crocs.

**Ubanoco** (☎ 0212-237-2648, 0295-261-4419; www.naturaraid.com) Run by the Caracas- & Margarita-based Natura Raid travel company, Ubanoco has 42 simple chalets along the riverbank, all with private bathrooms. There's a large *churuata*-style restaurant and a beach in dry season.

# LOWER ORINOCO

The industrial engine of the Guayana region, the Lower Orinoco comprises the region's main population and commercial centers. Massive hydroelectric projects such as the Represa de Guri take advantage of powerful rivers, generating a huge part of the country's electricity.

Ciudad Bolívar and Ciudad Guayana are the major cities, and together they account for almost 90% of the population of Bolívar, the country's largest state. Both cities sit on the south bank of the Río Orinoco, and each now has its own bridge spanning the mammoth river. Yet here the similarities end; Ciudad Bolívar is a charming colonial city with well-preserved architecture in its historic center, while Ciudad Guayana is a more modern urban sprawl. Located in the middle of the area's limited road network, they are busy transit hubs for jumping off to the rest of the region.

## CIUDAD BOLÍVAR

☎ 0285 / pop 356,000

The proud capital of Venezuela's largest state, Ciudad Bolívar has an illustrious history as a center of the independence struggle and wears its status proudly. The Casco Historico (historic center) is one of the country's finest, a gorgeous ensemble of brightly painted colonial buildings, shady squares and the fine Paseo Orinoco, overlooking the country's greatest river. Travelers on their way through to Angel Falls and the Parque Nacional Canaima are usually glad to have made a stopover here.

### History

Founded in 1764 on a rocky elevation at the Orinoco's narrowest point, the town was named Santo Tomás de la Guayana de Angostura – *angostura* means 'narrows.' It grew as a lonely beacon on a great river, hundreds of miles away from any major cities, and within 50 years was a thriving port and trade center. Then, suddenly and unexpectedly, Angostura became the spot where much of the country's (and the continent's) history was forged, not to mention the origin of the namesake bitters, a cocktail ingredient that has taken the city's former name around the world.

Libertador Simón Bolívar came here in 1817, soon after the town had been liberated from Spanish control, and set up the base for the military operations that led to the final stage of the War of Independence. The town was made the provisional capital of the yet-to-be-liberated country. It was in Angostura that the British Legionnaires joined Bolívar before they all set off for the battle of Boyacá in the Andes, which secured the independence of Colombia. The Angostura Congress convened



LOWER ORINOCO

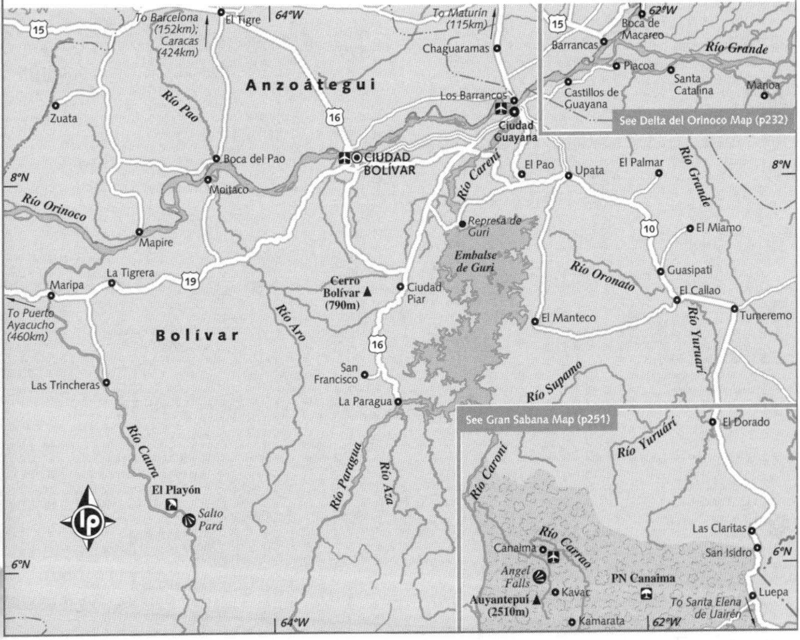

here in 1819 and gave birth to Gran Colombia, a unified republic comprising Venezuela, Colombia and Ecuador. The town was renamed 'Ciudad Bolívar' in 1846, in honor of the hero of the independence struggle. Today it's the capital of Bolívar state, which occupies over a quarter of the country's territory.

## Orientation

Located on the Río Orinoco approximately 420km upstream from the Atlantic, the city's northern boundary is the mighty Orinoco itself. The wide Paseo Orinoco boulevard lines the riverbank, buzzing with shops and street hawkers. To the south the spiffed-up historic quarter spreads over a hillside, with houses coated in a vibrant painter's palette. Modern suburbs surround the historic center, with the bus terminal to the southwest and the airport at the southern end of Av Táchira.

There are a number of excellent accommodations in the historic center, but unfortunately the neighborhood closes up in the early evening. It becomes a very attractive colonial ghost town: few restaurants are open, foot and car traffic peters out and some streets are not well lit – wander cautiously after sunset and avoid the empty Paseo Orinoco.

## Information

### EMERGENCY

**Emergency Center** (☎ 171)

### INTERNET ACCESS

Internet connections are generally fast and cheap (around BsF3 to BsF4 per hour).

**Ciber Play** (Map p236; Paseo Orinoco btwn Calles Igualdad & Libertad)

**Conexiones.net** (Map p236; Calle Venezuela)

**Panadería Pastel King** (Map p236; Paseo Orinoco)

### LAUNDRY

**Lavandería Woo Lee & Co** (Map p236; ☎ 632-3014; Calle Zea btwn Calles Piar & Roscio)

### MEDICAL SERVICES

**Hospital Ruiz y Páez** (☎ 632-4146; Av Germania)

### MONEY

**Banco de Venezuela** (Map p236; cnr Paseo Orinoco & Calle Piar)

**Banco Guayana** (Map p236; Calle Igualdad)

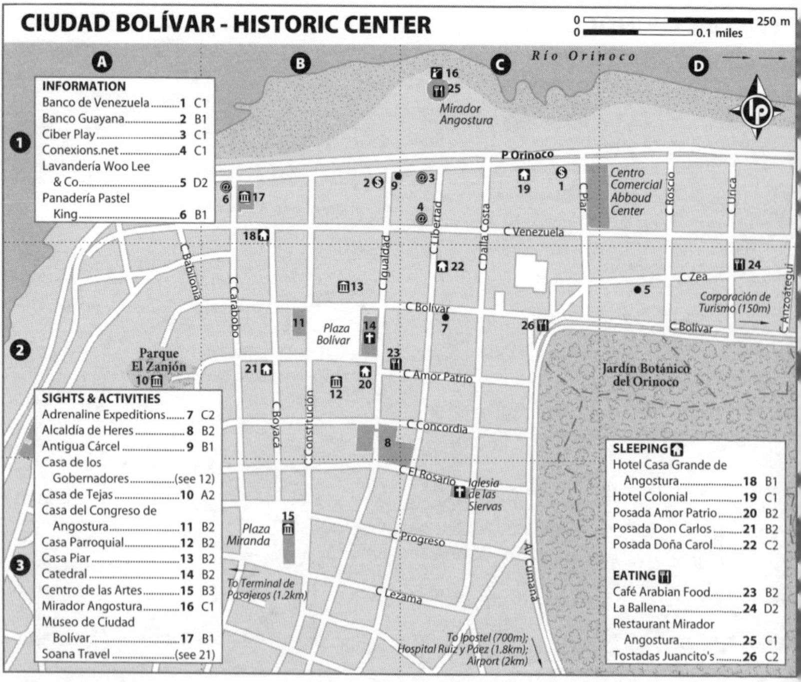

### POST

**Ipostel** (Av Táchira btwn Avs Cruz Verde & Guasipati)

### TOURIST INFORMATION

**Corporación de Turismo** (Map p236; ☎ 800-674-6626; www.turismobolivar.gob.ve; Calle Bolívar; 8am-noon & 2-5:30pm Mon-Fri) In addition to this office just inside the city's botanical garden, the very helpful Bolívar state tourism office runs a toll-free information line (8am to 8pm Monday to Saturday), with operators who speak English, German and Italian. The easy-to-navigate website has loads of useful information as well, though currently only in Spanish.

## Sights

### PASEO ORINOCO

A pulsing waterfront boulevard shaded by arcaded houses, the Paseo Orinoco is the border between the Colonial Quarter and the broad shore of the Río Orinoco. During the day boisterous street vendors pack the sidewalks hawking an A to Z of household goods and tasty nibbles. Before dusk residents take their evening *paseo* (promenade) along the side closest to the river; the sunset views are fantastic. Sadly after dark this area is dangerous simply as it's so deserted, so don't go wandering here after sunset.

In the middle of the Paseo is the **Mirador Angostura viewpoint** (Map p236), a rocky headland that protrudes into the narrowest point of the river. In the month of August the river level peaks and the water laps just below your feet. In March, by contrast, the water level can be as much as 15m lower. Just west is the **Piedra del Medio islet**, and you can easily see the graceful span of the **Puente de Angostura** 5km upstream. As the only bridge across the entire 2140km length of the Orinoco for almost 30 years, it was a source of local pride. However, a second bridge opened at Ciudad Guayana in late 2006, and a third is currently under construction in Puerto Ayacucho.

Across the street from the lookout is the **Antigua Cárcel** (Map p236; cnr Calle Igualdad & Paseo Orinoco; admission free; 9am-5pm Tue-Sun), a restored 18th-century prison building that functioned as a jail until 1952 and now contains the Bolívar state culture offices.

Three blocks west on the Paseo, another example of impressive colonial architecture is the Casa del Correo del Orinoco, which houses the **Museo de Ciudad Bolívar** (Map p236; ☎ 632-4121; Paseo Orinoco; admission BsF10; 9am-noon & 2-5pm Mon-Fri), a hodgepodge of modern art and historic objects. The most interesting artifact is the original printing press of the *Correo del Orinoco*, the new republic's first newspaper, published from 1818 to 1821. Fascinating old city maps decorate the walls around it. Also of interest is a pre-Colombian petroglyph unearthed near the Represa de Guri.

### HISTORIC CENTER

The Casco Historico (Historic Center), or colonial quarter, is where you want to roam around. A compact and hilly section of the city, it has grand old homes splashed in bright, beautiful colors and could pass for Havana were it not for all the modern cars. Most of the tourism infrastructure is situated here but, frustratingly, all commerce halts at dusk and at night the streets become quite deserted.

The district's center is the slightly recessed **Plaza Bolívar** (Map p236), which contains the requisite statue of El Libertador as well as five allegorical statues personifying the five countries Bolívar liberated. On the east side of the plaza rises the large yellow **catedral** (Map p236), begun right after the town's founding and completed 80 years later.

The brash pink **Casa del Congreso de Angostura** (Map p236; admission free; 9am-5pm Tue-Sun) dominates the western side of the plaza. Built in the 1770s, in 1819 it was home to lengthy debates by the Angostura Congress. You can still sense the air of those days while strolling about the formal rooms, wide corridors and elegant courtyards.

On the northern side of the plaza is the **Casa Piar** (Map p236; admission free; 9am-5pm Tue-Sun), where General Manuel Piar was kept prisoner in October 1817 before being positioned against the cathedral wall and executed by firing squad. Piar liberated the city from Spanish control, but rejected Bolívar's authority and was sentenced to death in a controversial and much criticized trial. The plaque on the cathedral's wall marks the spot where he was shot dead, while Bolívar watched the execution from the Casa del Congreso de Angostura.

The 18th-century **Casa de los Gobernadores** and **Casa Parroquial** (both Map p236), next to each other on the upper side of Plaza Bolívar, are other fine historic buildings, but are not open to the public. The presence of all the state politicos contributes to the high number of security personnel and sedan cars in the immediate vicinity.

GUAYANA

One block south is the **Alcaldía de Heres** (Map p236; cnr Calles Igualdad & Concordia), a pair of fine old buildings on both sides of the street, connected by the graceful arch of an aerial walkway.

**Parque El Zanjón** (Map p236) is an unusual city park strewn with massive *lajas* (boulders). The red-tile-roofed **Casa de Tejas** (Map p236), a former 19th-century home constructed on one of the boulders, now holds a small art gallery, complete with pieces of art spread out over the boulders in the open air.

On the southern edge of the colonial sector is the tree-shaded **Plaza Miranda** (Map p236). Positioned at the halfway point between the cathedral and the cemetery, it was once known as the Plaza Descanso (rest), because funeral pallbearers would stop to break here along the way to burials. A sizable building on its eastern side was constructed in 1870 as a hospital, but it never served that purpose. It has had a bizarre list of tenants instead, having been used as a prefecture, theatre, army barracks and police station. Eventually it opened in 1992 as the **Centro de las Artes** (Map p236; ☎ 632-9735; admission free; 🕒 8am-5pm Mon-Fri, 9am-4pm Sat) and stages temporary exhibitions of modern art, though it was being given a renovation on our last visit and should reopen again in 2010.

### OUTSIDE THE HISTORIC CENTER

The **Fortín El Zamuro** (admission free; 🕒 9am-5pm Tue-Sun) is a small fort built in the late 18th century atop the highest hill in the city, just south of the colonial quarter. It provides fine views over the old town. The entrance is from Paseo Heres.

The **Museo de Arte Moderno Jesús Soto** (☎ 632-0518; cnr Avs Germania & Briceño Iragorry; 🕒 9:30am-5:30pm Tue-Fri, 10am-5pm Sat & Sun) has an extensive collection of kinetic works by this internationally renowned artist.

One of the city's most impressive sights is the gigantic **Monumento a Simón Bolívar** (cnr Avs Cumaná & 5 de Julio). Erected in 1999, this 10m-high bronze statue is by far the tallest monument to the hero ever built in Venezuela.

If you're passing through the city's airport, don't miss the **Río Caroní airplane** (Av Jesús Soto), conveniently parked in front of the terminal building. This is the part original, part replica of the plane Jimmie Angel crash-landed on top of Auyantepui in 1937 (see the boxed text, p247) as he sought to prove the existence of an enormous waterfall that nobody believed existed. The plane was removed from the tepui in 1970, restored in Maracay and brought here, though bizarrely its engine remains in Maracay.

## Tours

Ciudad Bolívar is the main gateway to Angel Falls, and tours to the falls are the staple of virtually all the tour operators in the city. The most popular tour is a three-day package that includes a boat trip to the foot of Angel Falls. These trips are normally run in the rainy season only, but depending on weather patterns they can sometimes operate longer. Trips generally wind down between January and April.

Another popular option offered mainly in the dry season is a one-day package that includes a roundtrip flight to Canaima, a flight over Angel Falls, lunch, a short boat excursion in Canaima and a walk to other nearby falls. Tours depart from Ciudad Bolívar between 7am and 8am and return between 4pm and 5pm.

Most agents will offer a variety of other tours that include Angel Falls (eg Angel Falls and Kavac), and may tailor tours to suit your particular requirements. For example, if you don't want to come back to Ciudad Bolívar but would rather continue to Santa Elena de Uairén, the tour operators can replace the Canaima–Ciudad Bolívar return portion with the Canaima–Santa Elena ticket, charging the difference in airfares.

Tour companies use the services of small local airlines, all of which are based at Aeropuerto Ciudad Bolívar. The planes are generally five-seater Cessnas with a luggage allowance limit of 10kg (this is not always very strictly enforced, however). These airlines can fly you to Canaima, and can include a pass over Angel Falls for an additional fee. You can buy tickets directly from the airlines or from tour operators, but prices vary enormously, so shop around and try dealing both directly and through an agency to find the best price.

All the tour companies offer a range of other tours. Trips to the Gran Sabana are possibly the most popular – though they will cost less if bought in Santa Elena de Uairén.

Another tour appearing on the itinerary of various operators is Río Caura, normally scheduled as a five-day trip. Also popular is the trek to the top of Roraima, a six- to seven-day tour that's cheaper to buy in Santa Elena de Uairén. Some agencies also sell Delta del Orinoco tours. Rates for all tours fluctuate widely based on group size and the amenities and lodging type provided.

### TOUR COMPANIES

A tourism hub, Ciudad Bolívar has a large number of operators, and many of them work together. Shop around before booking a tour, as prices and the inclusion of items such as transfers can vary. Most tour offices are in the airport terminal or the historic quarter. Cash, either in *bolívares fuertes* or US dollars, provides the best tour rates, though a few operators have European bank accounts that let you pay by credit card without a surcharge.

Recommended operators:

**Adrenaline Expeditions** (Map p236; ☎ 615-5191, 0414-886-7209; www.adrenalinexpeditions.com; Calle Bolívar) An agency that offers great value tour packages and is particularly good for those into extreme sports. The owner Luis speaks great English and is very helpful.

**Eco Adventures** (☎ 651-9546, 0414-851-3656; www.adventurevenezuela.com; bus terminal, cnr Avs República & Sucre) This friendly agency at the bus terminal offers trips to Angel Falls, Roraima and the Orinoco Delta.

**Energy Tours** (☎ 654-8418, 0424-945-6310; www.energytour.com; airport terminal, Av Jesús Soto) Energy has been operating for 12 years and has a fleet of cars for the Gran Sabana as well as offering Canaima and Orinoco Delta trips.

**Gekko Tours** (☎ 632-3223, 0414-854-5146; www.gekkotours-venezuela.de; airport terminal, Av Jesús Soto) Run by the seemingly untiring Pieter Rothfuss, Gekko offers a wide range of good-quality tours. It also has its own planes.

**Sapito Tours** (☎ 0414-854-8234, 0414-854-8562; www.sapitotours.com; airport terminal, Av Jesús Soto) Representative of Bernal Tours from Canaima.

**Soana Travel** (Map p236; ☎ 632-6017, 0414-854-6616; soanatravel@gmx.de; Posada Don Carlos, cnr Calles Boyacá & Amor Patrio) Based at the posada and run by its German owner, Martin Haars, Soana specializes in Río Caura tours.

**Turi Express Dorado** (☎ 634-1243, 0414-893-9576; www.turiexpressdorado.com; airport terminal, Av Jesús Soto) A reliable company offering both local and regional trips at good prices.

## Festivals & Events

August is prime time for celebrations here, and the city's largest yearly party, the **Feria del Orinoco**, takes place late in the month to coincide with the river's peak *sapoara* (or *zapoara*) season. Brace yourself for *sapoara* fishing competitions, tons of delicious *sapoara* on the local menus, aquatic sports, an agriculture fair, and a range of cultural and other popular events. This is also the time to watch fishermen cast their *atarrayas* (circular fishing nets). On August 5 the city honors its patron saint in the **Fiesta de Nuestra Señora de las Nieves** – though it's doubtful the city has ever experienced snow.

## Sleeping

**Posada Doña Carol** (Map p236; ☎ 634-0989, 0412-696-3916; www.hosteltrail.com/posadadonacarol; Calle Libertad; s&tw with fan BsF70, s with air-con BsF80, d with air-con BsF100; ❄ 💻) Much more like a Cuban *casa particular* (private homestay) than a hotel, this friendly establishment in the heart of town has five simple rooms with use of a kitchen and free internet access. Downstairs rooms have no exterior windows, but one of the large upstairs room has a breezy terrace.

**Hotel Colonial** (Map p236; ☎ 632-4402; Paseo Orinoco; r BsF83; ❄) This large hotel has seen better days, but the faded corridors lead to clean, enormous and weirdly empty rooms with high ceilings and TVs. Ask for an upper-floor room facing the Orinoco.

**Posada Amor Patrio** (Map p236; ☎ 761-1915, 0414-854-4925; www.amorpatriotravel.com; Calle Amor Patrio; s&d/tr BsF90/115; 💻) A popular backpacker's haunt in a wonderful colonial building overlooking Plaza Bolívar, this relaxed posada has five playfully themed rooms with shared bathrooms. Guests can lounge in the airy Salon de Ritmo, a homage to Cuban jazz, cook in the kitchen, quaff cold beer from the honor bar or book a tour. Hammocks (BsF35) are also available on the rooftop terrace.

our pick **Posada Don Carlos** (Map p236; ☎ 632-6017, 0414-854-6616; www.posada-doncarlos.com; Calle Boyacá; s with fan BsF100, d with fan/air-con BsF120/150, tr with fan/air-con BsF150/180; P ❄ 💻 📶) An atmospheric colonial mansion surrounding a lush garden courtyard. Rooms have soaring ceilings, sections of exposed adobe and enormous wooden doors, and the common spaces have gorgeous old-world furniture, including an antique bar. If the visuals weren't enough, it also has free high-speed internet, meals upon request, a kitchen, and drinks to peruse in the honor bar. There's also a large area for hammocks and bunk beds (both BsF40) on the first floor.

**Hotel Casa Grande de Angostura** (Map p236; 632-6706; www.cacaotravel.com; cnr Calles Venezuela & Boyacá; s/d/tr/ste BsF350/390/465/580; ❄ 💻 🏊 📶) The stunning lobby of this colonial-era hacienda was rather let down on our recent visit by an empty rooftop pool and a bad breakfast. That said, the rooms are very comfortable

GUAYANA

and this is definitely the most stylish place to bed down in the Historic Center. There's a second, smaller and slightly less expensive posada run by the same company a little further up Calle Boyacá.

### Eating

**Restaurant Mirador Angostura** (Map p236; ☎ 511-4843; Paseo Orinoco; mains BsF15; 7am-6.30pm Tue-Sat, until 5:30pm Sun) Right next to the Orinoco this open-air restaurant serves up basic but decent meals and ice-cold beers under a *churuata*-shaped roof. There's sometimes live *criollo* and *folklórico* music on the weekends.

**Tostadas Juancito's** (Map p236; ☎ 632-6173; cnr Av Cumaná & Calle Bolívar; arepas BsF15-25; 7am-6pm Mon-Sat) A bright yellow wedge of an *arepera*, with outdoor seating on a busy bend across from the botanical garden. Relax with a newspaper and munch on *arepas* with a choice of over two dozen different fillings.

**La Ballena** (Map p236; ☎ 632-0231; cnr Calles Urica & Zea; mains BsF15-25; 11:30am-10pm Mon-Sat, until 8pm Sun) La Ballena is a rather dark and seedy place to say the least, but within its fiercely air conditioned walls you'll get a decent range of seafood and steaks. It's also one of the few places to eat in the historical center later in the evening.

**Café Arabian Food** (Map p236; ☎ 632-7208; cnr Calles Amor Patrio & Igualdad; mains BsF20-35; 7am-7pm Mon-Fri, 10am-8pm Sat, 11am-8pm Sun) This family run gem of a café is manna from heaven for vegetarians and anyone enjoying Middle Eastern cuisine. The large mixed plates are great value and feature delicious falafel and kebab meat.

When the historic center shuts down for the evening, grab a taxi to the **Calle del Hambre** (Estacionamiento del Estadio Heres, Av Rotaria; dinner), a block-long carnival of bright lights and a few dozen fast-food stalls that buzzes and sizzles until the wee hours of the morning.

### Getting There & Around

#### AIR

The **Aeropuerto Ciudad Bolívar** (☎ 632-4978; Av Jesús Soto) is 2km southeast of the riverfront and is linked to the city center by local buses. A number of tour agencies operate charter flights to Canaima. Flights to and from Caracas are annoyingly few. Rutaca operates flights (BsF300) via Maturín. Rutaca also has a daily Cessna service from here to Santa Elena (BsF600), often stopping at Canaima.

#### BUS

The **Terminal de Pasajeros** (cnr Avs República & Sucre) is 1.5km south of the center. From Paseo Orinoco until 6pm, take the westbound buseta marked 'Terminal.' There is a small departure tax (BsF1) that you'll need to pay at a separate booth before you board your bus.

Plenty of buses go to Caracas (BsF66 to BsF75, nine hours, 591km), the majority in the evening. There are also direct buses to Maracay (BsF75, 9½ hours, 627km) and to Valencia (BsF55 to BsF75, 10½ hours, 676km), which don't go through Caracas, but via the shorter Los Llanos route. These are the buses to take if you want to go to Venezuela's northwest or the Andes and avoid connections in Caracas. Eight daily buses service Puerto Ayacucho (BsF55, 11 to 12 hours, 728km).

Buses depart every 15 to 30 minutes to Ciudad Guayana (BsF10, 1½ hours, 115km); from the parking lot, faster por puestos go to San Félix for BsF20, but will usually drop you off in Puerto Ordaz on the way through.

Buses for Puerto La Cruz (BsF50, four hours, 302km) leave four times a day, but you can also go to the front of the terminal for carritos (BsF60), and if you pay a bit more they will drop you off directly at the Isla Margarita ferry.

Several buses per day head south to Santa Elena de Uairén (BsF70, 12 hours, 716km), mostly in the evening. Note that there are at least five military checkpoints along the way where you need to show ID and sometimes disembark for random baggage rummaging. This isolated road has also known to be unsafe at night with occasional highway robbery – so keep your money well hidden if you travel after dark.

## RÍO CAURA

The picturesque Río Caura offers a variety of natural and cultural experiences few other rivers can match. The thick jungle setting resembles what you might find around Canaima, but unlike Angel Falls it is a year-round boat destination that's not seriously affected by the dry season. The birding is excellent, and tour groups are smaller and more personalized.

A right-bank (south) tributary of the Río Orinoco, the Caura joins the Orinoco about 200km southwest of Ciudad Bolívar. It's graced with islands, beaches and huge granite boulders, and cut by rapids and waterfalls. The most spectacular is Salto Pará. At the end of the lower Caura, two rapids form a huge lagoon and the long sandy beach of El Playón.

For a good part of its course, the Caura flows through wildlife-rich rainforest, with riverbanks inhabited by indigenous communities. The major groups here are the Yekuana, particularly renowned for their fine basketry, and the Sanema, who are descended from the Yanomami. It's also one of Venezuela's least-polluted rivers, as yet unaffected by gold mining, though prospectors have been combing the region for a while. Finally, the Caura is a 'black river', so mosquitoes are scarce.

## Tours

Various travel operators in Caracas, Ciudad Bolívar and other cities offer Río Caura tours. These are most often a five-day all-inclusive package costing BsF300 to BsF400 per day, with simple accommodations in hammocks.

Río Caura tours usually start in Ciudad Bolívar. From there, you venture west for 205km along the Puerto Ayacucho road, then along a small side road branching off to the south and running for about 50km to Las Trincheras. There are several *campamentos* in the area, where tours stay the first and last nights. On the second day, boats go 130km upriver (a five- to six-hour ride) to the vast sandbank of El Playón, where you spend the night. The following day, there's a two-hour walk uphill to the amazing Salto Pará, consisting of five 50m-high falls.

The following are recommended trips and operators (also see p282 for more):

**Jonás Tours** (☎ 0285-651-0237, 0414-099-5904; jonastours54@hotmail.com) The pioneer of Río Caura tours, Jonás Camejo has over 15 years' experience in the Caura region. He leads four- to five-day trips, as well as custom tours; visitors stay in indigenous villages.

**Miguel Estaba** (☎ 0424-901-7710) A native of the Río Caura himself, Miguel Estaba is based in Ciudad Bolívar but runs trips that get good reports from travelers. He enjoys unrivalled access to indigenous villages, though he doesn't speak English.

# CIUDAD GUAYANA

**☎ 0286 / pop 789,500**

Made up of two very different cities fused together for administrative purposes, Ciudad Guayana officially dates from 1961 when the rich iron-ore port of Puerto Ordaz merged with the working class San Félix across the river to form one single conurbation. Half a century later and the divide is still keenly felt, and so while on the map it's Ciudad Guayana, you'll most likely only hear about Puerto Ordaz, where the city's good hotels, restaurants and a smattering of sights are located – San Félix remains poor and unsafe after dark.

While there's little to interest most visitors, anyone traveling to the Canaima National Park, Orinoco Delta or Gran Sabana is likely to pass through, however briefly, simply as it's a large transport hub.

All the listings below are in Puerto Ordaz.

## Information

### EMERGENCY

**Emergency Center** (☎ 171)

### IMMIGRATION

**Brazilian Consulate** (☎ 961-2995, 961-9233; Edificio Eli-Alti, Oficina 04, Carrera Tocoma, Alta Vista Norte; 🕑 9am-noon & 2-6pm Mon-Fri)

### INTERNET ACCESS

Internet connections are generally fast and cheap (BsF4 per hour), and wi-fi is widely available in hotels.

**Big Hat.com** (Map p242; Carrera Padre Palacios) Has phones as well.

**Cyber Café Latin World** (Map p242; Av Principal de Castillito)

### MONEY

**Banco de Venezuela** (Map p242; cnr Avs Las Américas & Monseñor Zabaleta)

**Banco Provincial** (Map p242; cnr Av Ciudad Bolívar & Carrera Upata)

**Banesco** (Map p242; Vía Caracas btwn Calle Guasipati & Av Las Américas)

## Sights

Situated along the Río Caroní, Ciudad Guyana's three stunning parks (all open 5.30am to 5.30pm Tuesday to Sunday) are a calming respite from urbanity, and all have free entry. Escape the heat with a stroll in the 52-hectare **Parque Cachamay** (Av Guayana), a shady canopy of tropical trees dotted with blue morpho butterflies and scampering lizards. Then drink in the spectacular view of the river's 200m-wide waterfalls. Pushy monkeys enliven the adjoining **Parque Loefling** (Av Guayana), which has roaming animals like capybaras and tapirs and a small zoo of native wildlife. Taxis (BsF15 to BsF20) can take you to both parks. The 160-hectare **Parque La Llovizna** (Av Leopoldo Sucre Figarella) is on the other (eastern) side of the

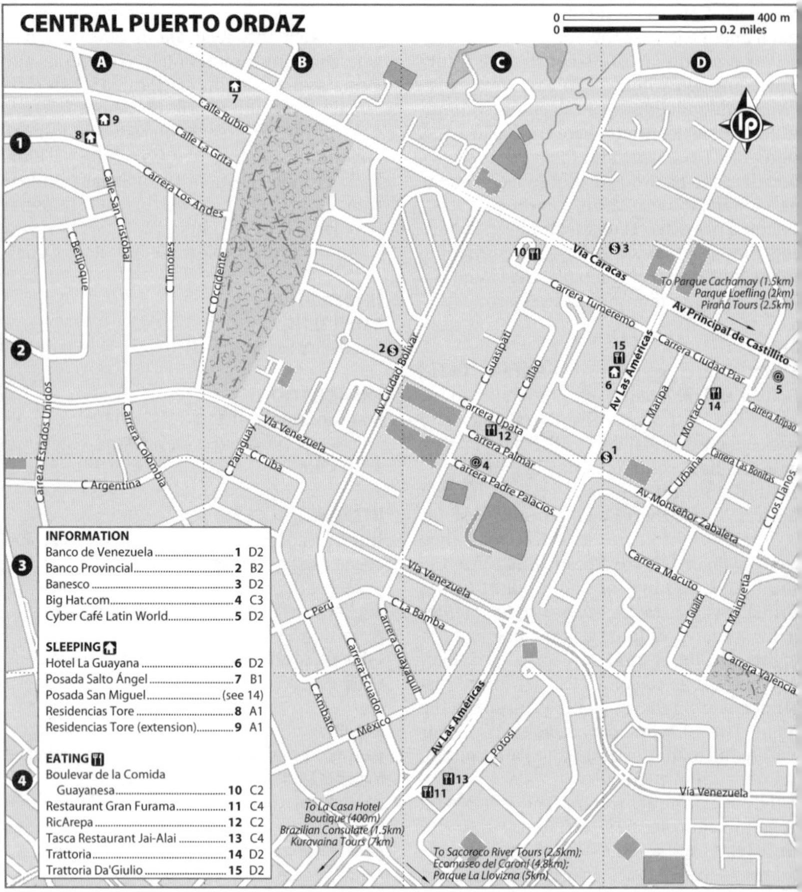


Río Caroní. It has 26 wooded islands carved by thin water channels and linked by 36 footbridges. The 20m-high Salto La Llovizna kicks up the namesake *llovizna* (drizzle) of the park and waterfall. Enter the park from Av Leopoldo Sucre Figarella. Taxis here from the center shouldn't cost more than BsF25.

Nearby Parque La Llovizna and the enormous Macagua dam, the **Ecomuseo del Caroní** (☎ 964-7656; www.edelca.com.ve/ecomuseo; Av Leopoldo Sucre Figarella; admission free; 🕑 9am-6pm) contains an interesting art gallery with a photographic history of the dam and samples of pre-Hispanic ceramics unearthed during construction. A balcony looks out over the huge turbine room.

The most fascinating sight in San Félix is the confluence of the Ríos Orinoco and Caroní. At the bank of the Río Orinoco, just off the Plaza Bolívar, you can see the dark waters of the Caroní swirling into the much lighter Orinoco current. **Paso a Nado Internacional de los Ríos Orinoco-Caroní**, a massive swim competition across the two rivers, takes place in April.

## Tours

Most local tour operators organize expeditions to Guayana's highlights such as Angel Falls, Gran Sabana and Delta del Orinoco. They're often a bit more expensive than tours originating in Ciudad Bolívar, but convenient if you're already in town.

Recommended tour companies:

**Kuravaina Tours** (☎ 717-4463; kuravaina@telcel.net.ve; Centro Industrial Sierra Parima Transversal 'C' Galpón

No 6 Sector 321) Sells all the regional tours, as well as packages to Los Roques and Margarita; will pick you up from anywhere in the city.

**Piraña Tours** (☎ 923-3650; www.piranatours.com; Hotel Intercontinental Guayana, Av Guayana) Offers relaxed local boat tours of the Ríos Caroní and Orinoco as well as regional trips.

**Sacoroco River Tours** (☎ 961-5526; 0416-806-1211; www.deltaorinoko.com.ve; Calle Gahna No 19, Villa Africana, Manzana 32) Runs trips in the Río Grande area of the Delta del Orinoco, staying at its Campamento Oridelta in Piacoa. The owner, Roger Ruffenach, is an authority on the wildlife of the delta, speaks English, German and French, and personally guides all the trips, which never have more than 10 guests.

## Sleeping

**La Casa del Lobo** (☎ 961-6286, 0414 871 9339; www.lobo-tours.de; Calle Zambia No 2, Villa Africana, Manzana 39; r without/with air-con BsF100/120; ) Something of a backpacker institution in these parts – especially for German speakers. The German owner, Wolf, has five fan-cooled rooms with private bathrooms and offers free pickups from the Puerto Ordaz bus terminal when arranged in advance. There's a well-stocked bar on the patio, a kitchen and a great selection of tours available.

**Hotel La Guayana** (Map p242; ☎ 923-4866; Av Las Américas; s/d/tr/q BsF110/130/140/150; ) 33 simple, spartan but clean and safe rooms in the center of town, all with private bathrooms (no hot water) and TV.

**Posada San Miguel** (Map p242; ☎ 924-9385; Calle Moitaco; s/d/tr BsF120/150/180; ) This largely subterranean posada may not win any awards for charm, but it's right in the center of town and is good value, offering seven clean rooms all with private bathrooms and cable TV.

**Residencias Tore** (Map p242; ☎ 923-1389, 923-1780; residenciastore@hotmail.com; cnr Calle San Cristóbal & Carrera Los Andes, Campo A-2; r BsF185-210; ) This posada encompasses two very secure buildings across the street from each other, and while it's a mainstay with tour groups, our last stay wasn't particularly satisfying, with dysfunctional air-con and a strange smell in the room. Despite that it's a popular place, and there's a friendly restaurant.

**our pick Posada Salto Ángel** (Map p242; ☎ 923-6948, 922-6516; posadasaltoangel@canTV.net; Vía Caracas, Campo A-2; s&d BsF224, tr/q BsF275/298; ) This friendly place, housed in a striking building with an art deco feel, is a great place to bed down. The twenty rooms are spacious, clean and have fridges, cable TV and hot water. To top it off, breakfast is delicious too.

**La Casa Hotel Boutique** (☎ 922-1135, 717-9001; www.lacasahotelboutique.com; cnr Av Estados Unidos & Calle Taxco; s/d/tr incl breakfast BsF330/340, ste incl breakfast BsF450-500; ) Opening in 2009, La Casa has bought some much-needed style to the local hotel scene. Its 15 rooms are minimalist and sleek, miles ahead of the competition with flat-screen TVs and clever design touches. It's a short journey from the center by cab.

## Eating

**Boulevar de la Comida Guayanesa** (Map p242; Calle Guasipati; meals BsF15-35; breakfast & lunch) A dozen covered food stalls vie for your business with typical food such as empanadas, *arepas*, soups and fresh juices. Great for breakfast.

**RicArepa** (Map p242; ☎ 923-1483; Carrera Upata; arepas BsF16-26, mains BsF20-40; 24hr) We love this place – a reliable option that never closes and where you can get a good breakfast, choose from almost two dozen types of *arepa* fillings and a good menu of grills, soups and salads.

**Restaurant Gran Furama** (Map p242; ☎ 922-3097; Av Las Américas; mains BsF20-40; 11am-10:30pm) This popular place has a surprisingly large and impressive dining room where the flamboyant *platos calientes* send fireballs leaping to the chandeliers.

**Trattoria** (Map p242; ☎ 922-6193; Calle Moitaco; mains BsF25-45; 11am-4pm) Mix and match with a dozen types of fresh pasta and 15 yummy sauces at this friendly family-run Italian restaurant. Self-caterers can also take delicious fresh sauces away with them.

**Trattoria Da'Giulio** (Map p242; ☎ 923-5698; Av Las Américas; mains BsF30-50; 11:30am-3pm Mon-Sat & 6:30-9pm Wed-Fri) Italian comfort food that hits the spot, with warm and attentive waiters fussing over you like an honored guest. Pizzas are only available on Thursday and Friday nights, for some odd reason.

**Tasca Restaurant Jai-Alai** (Map p242; ☎ 717-3072; Edificio Amazonas, Av Las Américas; mains BsF40-80; 11:30am-3pm & 6-11pm Mon-Sat) Always full of local food-lovers, this bustling outpost of Spanish cuisine is rather pricey, but the food is excellent. Specialties include *pulpo a la gallega* (Galician-style octopus) and a mouth-watering *brocheta de mero* (seafood skewers).

## Getting There & Around

Don't look for 'Ciudad Guayana' in air and bus schedules, because there's no such destination – the airport is called Puerto Ordaz and the bus terminals are either Puerto Ordaz or San Félix.

#### AIR

The **Aeropuerto Puerto Ordaz** (Av Guayana) sits at the western section of Puerto Ordaz on the road to Ciudad Bolívar. From the airport terminal, taxis to the city center are BsF20, but you're likely to be overcharged, so agree the price beforehand. Local buses into town run along the Paseo Caroní, but it's not the closest walk with heavy luggage, and you have to cross two busy highways as well.



Puerto Ordaz is the major air hub of eastern Venezuela, with service by most major domestic airlines. Some popular direct flights include Caracas (BsF250 to BsF350), Porlamar (BsF300), Barcelona (BsF480), Maracaibo (BsF530) and Valencia (BsF390).

#### BUS

Ciudad Guayana has two bus terminals. The **Terminal de Pasajeros San Félix** (Av José Gumilla) is the city's main transit stop. It is unsafe here after dark, with local buses stopping service around 9pm. Taxis are recommended. The **Terminal de Pasajeros Puerto Ordaz** (Av Guayana) is 1km east of the airport and the less busy of the two stations. It's smaller and safer, but has fewer connections than the San Félix station and not all buses pass through here. However, the 2006 opening of the second bridge over the Orinoco, just west of the city, made it faster to take northbound por puestos and buses from this terminal.

From the San Félix terminal, departures to Caracas (BsF55 to BsF80, 10½ hours, 706km) start in the morning, but there are many more at night. The majority of them go through the Puerto Ordaz terminal. Originating in Ciudad Bolívar, nine daily buses stop on their way to Santa Elena de Uairén (BsF40 to BsF70, nine to 11 hours, 601km); all call at San Félix, but not all stop in Puerto Ordaz. Por puestos to Tucupita (BsF45, 2½ hours) run on demand and leave when full. Buses to Maturín depart regularly (BsF25 to BsF50, 3½ hours, 176km); there are also por puestos (BsF55, two to three hours). There's also a daily bus to Guiria (BsF50, seven hours), Valencia (BsF80, 12 hours) and Maracaibo (BsF150, 15 hours).

From Puerto Ordaz there are connections to Puerto La Cruz (BsF57, six hours) and a daily 8pm bus to Puerto Ayacucho (BsF70, 12 hours). Direct buses to Maracay (BsF80, 11 hours, 742km) and Valencia (BsF80, 12 hours, 791km) don't pass through Caracas, taking a shorter route via Los Llanos, and are convenient if you're going to Venezuela's northwest or the Andes. There's also a daily bus at 12.30pm to Mérida (BsF165, 16 hours).

From both terminals, buses leave for Ciudad Bolívar every half-hour or so (BsF10, 1½ hours, 115km); faster por puestos are BsF20.

## PARQUE NACIONAL CANAIMA

The vast Parque Nacional Canaima contains many of Venezuela's highlights and is a natural wonder world of roaring waterfalls, raging rivers, virgin rainforest and spectacular scenery with vast tepuis rising vertically from the jungle, often cloaked in thick mist. The park is on almost every visitor's itinerary as it's home to the incredible Angel Falls, but arguably its less well-known attractions, from mountain gorges that open up to reveal lost worlds of rushing waterfalls and swimming holes to the Pemón villages of the Kamarata Valley are equally worth your time. Whatever you do, don't miss out on coming to Venezuela's most impressive national park.

### CANAIMA

☎ 0286 / pop 1500

The closest population center to Angel Falls, Canaima is a remote indigenous village from where most boat trips to Venezuela's greatest natural attraction begin. Although it's used primarily as a staging post to reach the falls, Canaima is a gorgeous place in itself, with many people being as equally impressed by the series of waterfalls facing the town across its impressive lagoon as they are with Angel Falls itself. The Laguna de Canaima sits at the heart of everything, a broad blue expanse framed by a palm-tree beach and a dramatic series of seven incredibly powerful cascades, with a backdrop of anvil-like tepuis. Make sure to hike behind one of the falls and get the backstage experience of the hammering curtains of water. Their color is a curious pink, caused by the high level of tannins from decomposed plants and trees.

The rambling Campamento Canaima is on the west of the lagoon, with the best beach for swimming and taking photos. When swimming, stay close to the main beach – a number of drownings have occurred close to the hydroelectric plant and the falls. From the airport (the only means of getting here), there is a cluster of posadas about 15 minutes' walk to the north, and a few more on the north end of the water. The southern end is the residential area for about 150 Pemón families, though there are a few posadas here too.

## Information

Canaima has no tourist office and no banks. Tour operators are the primary source of information and the larger posadas can change US dollars. The tour companies calculate their prices in USD but accept payment in both dollars and *bolívares fuertes.* Those that accept credit cards will likely charge a big surcharge for the privilege, so bring cash. The **Tienda Canaima** (☎ 962-0443, 0414-884-0940), a grocery and knickknack outpost at the crossroads near the airport, changes multiple currencies at mediocre rates and traveler's checks at a bad rate. It sells useful double-sided maps depicting both the town and the Parque Nacional Canaima. Some posadas offer internet access, but if yours doesn't try Esedantok (BsF10 per hour; 8pm-noon and 3pm-10pm), which is just by the church in the center of the village.

## Tours

Angel Falls can be reached either by plane or boat, and all Canaima-based tour companies run boat trips and can arrange flights. Trips vary in length and cost, but boat trips tend to last two days, while overflights take just an hour.

Boat tours are definitely the way to go unless you're there in the dry season – they allow you to see the waterfall from up close and, more importantly, enjoy it at a leisurely pace. The boat trip itself is great fun and the scenery is spectacular, particularly in the Cañón del Diablo.

From Canaima you'll be driven the short distance to Ucaima, above the Canaima waterfalls, where you'll board a motorized canoe and go up the Ríos Carrao and Churún to Isla Ratoncito, at the foot of Angel Falls, a journey of around three hours. From there, an hour's walk will take you uphill to Mirador Laime, the outcrop right in front of the falls. You'll normally then spend the night at one of the campsites on the river before making your way back to Canaima the following morning. Always dress for rain, and be sure to have sunscreen, a hat, insect repellent and water with you for the journey.

Boats operate only when the water level is sufficiently high, usually nine to 10 months a year, with some breaks between January and April. The all-inclusive boat package from Canaima costs from BsF800 per person for a one-night tour to BsF1600 per person for a two-night tour. Most packages include a trip to Salto El Sapo as well, the most popular waterfall in the Canaima area. It's a 10-minute boat trip from Canaima plus a short walk. Salto El Sapo is beautiful and unusual in that you can walk under it. Be prepared to get drenched by the waterfall in the rainy season – wear a swimsuit and protect your camera by putting it inside a good quality plastic bag.

Flights are in five-seater Cessna *avionetas,* most of which originate in Ciudad Bolívar. During the 40-minute roundtrip ride from Canaima, the pilot will fly over the falls a few times, circle the top of Auyantepui and then return. These trips can be arranged directly with the pilots at the airport or with local tour operators. For those opting for a flyover of Angel Falls, most operators also run day trips on the lagoon to see the nearby waterfalls.

Reputable local tour operators include the following. Nearly all operators offer far more than just Angel Tours trips – they usually offer other a wide variety of itineraries in the Canaima National Park and the Gran Sabana.

**Bernal Tours** (☎ 0285-632-6890, 0414-899-7162; www.bernaltours.com) Small family-run company based on an island in Laguna de Canaima, where participants stay and eat before and after the tour. Bernal Tours has its well-placed *campamento* on Isla Ratoncito, opposite Angel Falls.

**Canaima Tours** (☎ 962-5560, 0414-868-6943; www.wakulodge.com) Based at its upmarket Wakü Lodge, this is by far the most expensive operator and its tours should be bought in advance in Ciudad Guayana. Its mainstay is a day trip by boat to Angel Falls, with lunch in its comfortable restaurant below the falls before returning to Canaima.

**Excursiones Kavac** (☎ 0289-808-9205, 0416-685-2209; exc.kavac@hotmail.com) Agency managed by the indigenous Pemón community. Marginally cheaper than Bernal Tours, it too has its *campamento* in front of Angel Falls. Trips originate in either Ciudad Bolívar or from its Canaima hotel. It also does longer boat trips within the park and to Kavac and Uruyén.

**Jungle Rudy** (☎ 0289-808-9251, 962-2359; www.junglerudy.com) With their great *campamento* in Ucaima and the only *campamento* at Angel Falls with beds to sleep in rather than hammocks, this is an upmarket and well-run agency offering a large range of tours.

**Tiuna Tours** (☎ 0424-916-9792, 0416-586-1752; tiunatours@hotmail.com) Under new management, this friendly company, with a large *campamento* in Canaima, a camp on Isla Ratoncito and a jungle camp up the Río Carrao at the Aonda (being refurbished at the time of research), is also one of the cheapest.

Representatives from most tour operators can be found at the airport, playing cards with the Cessna pilots on standby and hustling up business from morning until midafternoon. Prices can be negotiated to some extent. Some agencies have outlets at Ciudad Bolívar's airport – although all the agencies there have links to Canaima agencies and can book tours for you. See p238 for tours organized from Ciudad Bolívar, which are likely to work out to be cheaper and more convenient than coming to Canaima and buying a tour.



## Sleeping & Eating

Canaima has lots of accommodation options, ranging from *campamentos* to posadas and smart hotels. As many are geared toward tour groups, some prices start to look painful when not discreetly folded into Angel Falls packages, because rates are per person instead of per room. Most places also serve meals, but all supplies are flown in, so food prices aren't cheap either.

Because all food is imported, the few shops selling groceries mark them up to cover the costs. If you plan to cook your own food, try to bring it, but pack light: there's a 10kg luggage-allowance limit on Cessna flights. Saving money by camping on the lagoon is no longer possible.

**Posada Wey Tupü** (☎ 0289-540-1263, 0426-997-9565; weytupu@hotmail.com; r per person without/with full board BsF150/350) This recently expanded posada now has 17 fan cooled rooms, each sleeping two to four people. Rooms lack charm, but all have private bathrooms and share attractive communal areas.

**Posada Kusary** (☎ 962-0443, 0414-884-0940; r per person without/with meals BsF150/350) Run by the owners of the Tienda Canaima, this well-maintained posada in the northern end of town has 13 decent rooms with fans.

**Campamento Tiuna** (☎ 0424-916-9792, 0416-586-1752; tiunatours@hotmail.com; dm per person BsF200) Now with a young and progressive management team, this no-frills *campamento*, located in the northern part of the village just off the lagoon, is set to give itself a much needed spruce up in the near future. As it is, the six-bed dorms are basic but fine. There's free hammock lodging on the terrace if you take your meals here (BsF180 per day).

**Campamento Churúm** (☎ 0289-8089205, 0416-685-2209; exc.kavac@hotmail.com; hammocks/r per person BsF150/250, hammock/r per person incl full board BsF250/400; ) The Excursiones Kavac *campamento* has 15 well-kept rooms (doubles, triples and quads) with private bathrooms and serves up decent meals in its large dining room. It's also one of the few places you can sleep in a hammock.

**Posada Restaurant Morichal** (☎ 808-9233; morichal25@canTV.net; r per person without/with full board BsF300/680; ) This attractively set out posada moments from Canaima's landing strip is nestled in well-tended gardens and has nine comfortable and clean rooms with traditional-style wooden fittings and pleasant patios. There's a relaxed bar-restaurant and use of the internet at BsF20 per hour.

**Campamento Canaima** (☎ 0426-520-6912, 0416-281-0025; r per person without/with full board BsF340/680; ) The largest lodging in Canaima, with 109 rooms, this '*campamento*' (it's in fact much more of a hotel than a camp) has lovely palm-thatched duplex cabañas that are virtually on the lagoon beach. A large open *churuata* picks up the breeze at the pricey buffet restaurant, but the view from the bar across the lagoon to the waterfalls is truly spectacular – even if you don't stay here, make sure you come for a drink.

**Tapuy Lodge** (☎ 0416-798-6132; kakotours@hotmail.com; s/d per person incl full board BsF810/710; ) A recent addition to Canaima's accommodation scene, the Tapuy lodge is an upmarket 17-room complex with thatched roofs and pretty gardens right on the beach. Rooms are smart and stylish, and all stays include a free lagoon trip.

**Campamento Parakaupa** (☎ 961-4963; www.parakaupa.com.ve; r incl all meals) In the northern part of town, ground-floor rooms have small hammock areas out front, and two gorgeous 2nd-floor suites have spacious floor plans and inspiring views of the surrounding tepuis. All rooms have hot water and fans; transfers from the airport are included. Contact the office for rates.

**Wakü Lodge** (☎ 962-5560, 0414-868-6943; www.wakulodge.com; ) It's hard to fault the Wakü, the best and most expensive hotel in Canaima. A lush and flowering estate, the grounds have prime views of the waterfalls, beach access and a suite of peacocks wandering around just for your pleasure. You need to book in advance to stay here – contact the office for prices as they do not release their rates.

**Mentanai** (mains BsF10-20, 🕑 2pm-11pm) This loud bar and cafe next to Campamento Churúm is Canaima's only place to get food outside a posada, and while the burgers and sandwiches are nothing special, if you're on a budget it can work out well.

## Getting There & Away

Flights between Canaima and Ciudad Bolívar are the most common, with a number of regional carriers flying in daily or as charters (from BsF350). Flights to Kamarata, Kavac and Uruyén can also be chartered in Canaima. Aerotuy flies daily to and from Porlamar (BsF840), while irregular charters come direct from Caracas in the high season. Rutaca has five-seat Cessna flights between Canaima and Santa Elena de Uairén (BsF950), though these do not always fly if demand is low. However, if you're lucky enough to take this flight the journey to Santa Elena is absolutely stunning, taking you over virgin rainforest and past soaring tepuis.

# ANGEL FALLS

Until bush pilot Jimmie Angel crash-landed his plane on top of Auyantepui in 1937, only the Pemón knew about the existence of Angel Falls, which they termed Kerepakupai-Merú ('waterfall of the highest place' in Pemón). With a total height of 979m and a continuous drop of 807m, Angel Falls (Salto Ángel) is the world's highest waterfall. Leaping from the heart-shaped table mountain of Auyantepui and funneling into the moody rock skyscrapers of the Cañón del Diablo (Devil's Canyon), the flume is 16 times the height of Niagara Falls. Buried in a remote and roadless area of river-etched jungle, just getting here is an incredible adventure.

In late 2009 President Hugo Chávez announced that the indigenous name Kerepakupai-Merú would be restored, although popular opinion widely backs the notion that this was more to strip the country's most famous tourist attraction of a Yankee name rather than any real desire to restore its Pemón one. Despite this, the falls formerly known as Angel remain Venezuela's top tourist destination and are an unforgettable site.

## Planning

### WHEN TO GO

In the dry season (typically January through May) the volume of the falls lessens and fizzles out to mist as it drops. This is the time of year with the best chance of actually seeing it in a plane. Boat trips are slowly phased out during this period because the waterways are too shallow to navigate. If you go by boat at the beginning or the end of the dry season, expect a longer travel time because of the need to portage. In the rainy season, especially in August and September, the flow turns to a gushing torrent and portage can also be necessary to avoid certain rapids. However, this is also when Angel Falls is frequently covered by a veil of mist and clouds.



### AN ANGEL FALLS TO EARTH

Angel Falls (Salto Ángel) was not named, as one might expect, after a divine creature, but after an American bush pilot, Jimmie Angel. Returning from a remote expedition, he claimed to have seen a mother lode of gold capping a gargantuan jungle waterfall.

But alas, Angel was a chronic teller of tall tales, and nobody believed his starry-eyed story of gold nuggets and mammoth waterfalls. So in 1937, to prove them wrong, a determined Angel loaded his wife and two friends into his four-seater airplane and went to look for his mythic falls. On this trip he managed to locate Auyantepui, the site of his previous discovery, but when he landed the plane stuck fast in the marshy surface and Angel couldn't take off again. Without food or supplies, the dazed gold-diggers trekked through rough, virgin terrain to the edge of the plateau, then descended a steep cliff, returning to civilization after an 11-day odyssey when they wandered into the village of Uruyén (see p249) to the surprise of locals.

His larger-than-life claim was verified in 1949 and the falls were named in his honor. Angel's plane was later removed from the top of the tepui by the air force, restored and placed in front of the airport terminal in Ciudad Bolívar, where it now resides. Amazingly you can still meet people in the Kamarata Valley today who remember Angel's arrival in their village more than 70 years ago. Even though the name officially reverted to Kerepakupai-Merú in 2009, in practice almost everybody still uses the name Angel Falls today.

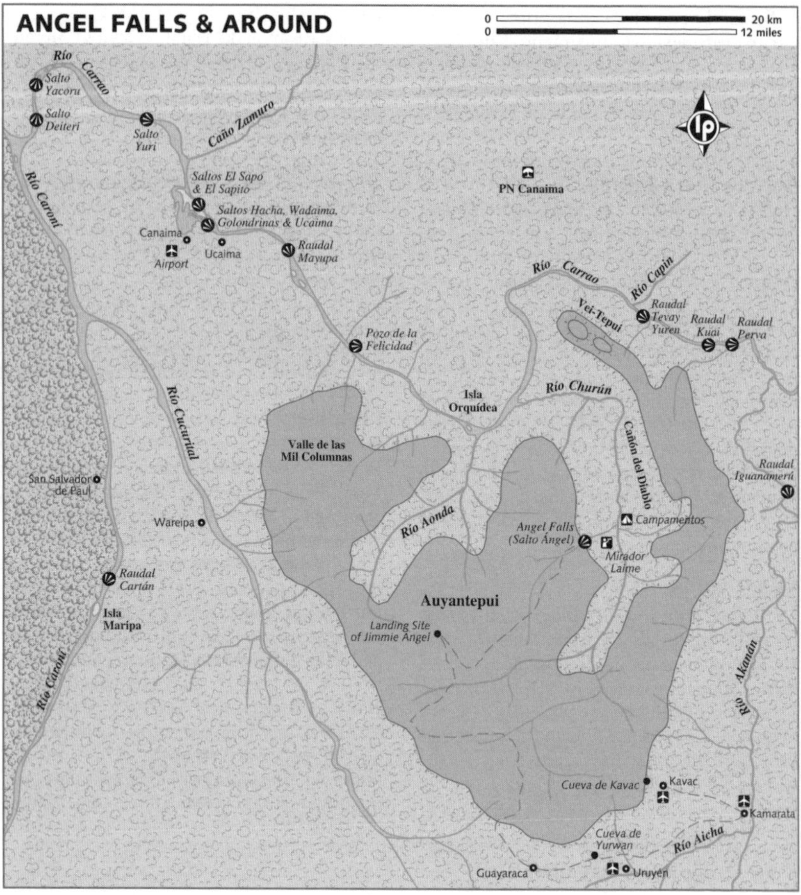


Keen photographers should note that Angel Falls faces east, and is in direct sunlight from sunrise until midday.

#### WHAT TO BRING

At the very least, pack a bathing suit, sun protection and good insect repellent. If you're taking a boat trip, you'll want a rain jacket or poncho, sun hat and plastic bags for your camera and gear. Walking shoes are recommended for the hour-long hike to the viewpoint at the bottom of the falls; it's not tough going, but it can be muddy and slippery. A water bottle and flashlight are also useful. At night in the jungle, the temperature drops after dark; pants and a light jacket ward off chills. Blankets in the hammocks often need a washing, so a lightweight sleep sheet isn't a bad idea.

## KAMARATA VALLEY

The Kamarata Valley, on the other side of massive Auyantepui, is a wonderworld of massive waterfalls, traditional indigenous settlements and virgin rainforest only accessible by air taxi to one of the valley's tiny airstrips. This is where to come to explore the Parque Nacional Canaima without the crowds, and it's even possible to get to Angel Falls from here.

### Kamarata

Kamarata is the chief settlement on the eastern side of Auyantepui, an old Pemón village on

**CLIMBING THE DEVIL'S MOUNTAIN**

All the camps in the Kamarata Valley are starting points for the fascinating and grueling trek to the top of Auyantepui (Devil's Mountain in Pemón), a true once-in-a-lifetime experience. Guides for this adventurous hike can be contracted in either of the villages. The trail leads from Kavac via Uruyén to Guayaraca, from where it approaches the foot of the tepui before snaking uphill, following roughly the same route Jimmie Angel used for his descent in 1937 (see the boxed text, p247). On the third day, you'll reach a place called El Libertador, named after Bolívar, whose bust is placed here. You need another three days to get to the point from where Angel Falls plunges, and will also be able to visit Jimmie Angel's landing site. Count on roughly BsF150 a day per guide for the group, plus another BsF140 per porter. One reliable English-speaking guide is Arturo Berti who is based in Kamarata and can be contacted on auyantepuyexpeditions@gmail.com.



the Río Akanán with a few basic services such as a small clinic and a shop. It is a growing access point for Angel Falls, and attracts travelers wanting to avoid the crowds of Canaima. There are a few simple places to stay and eat in town, including a new posada being built at the time of research by Jimmie Angel's grandson, Santos. The only way to reach Kamarata is by air – the airstrip is serviced daily by air taxis and charter flights on six-seater planes from Canaima and Ciudad Bolívar.

Visiting Kamarata is an interesting chance to see how the modern Pemón live, though it's not the most charming place to stay. Most travelers instead stay at the nearby tourist camp at Kavac. Kavac is a two-hour walk from Kamarata, or a short drive on a dirt road by the town's service jeep.

## Kavac

The camp nearest to Kamarata, Kavac consists of 20-odd *churuatas* built in the traditional style, resembling a manicured Pemón settlement and sitting at the bottom of Auyantepui with some fabulous views toward the summit. There's no village here (most of the staff live in Kamarata and other nearby settlements), but it's a gorgeous spot.

The area's major attraction is the spectacular **Cueva de Kavac**, which, despite its name, is not a cave but a deep gorge with a waterfall plunging into it. There's a natural pool at the foot of the waterfall, which you reach by swimming upstream in the narrow canyon; be sure to bring your swimsuit with you. It's a pretty straightforward half-hour walk from Kavac to the gorge. A second, longer and equally impressive hike follows the Kamarata water pipe up the side of the tepui and along the river to a selection of rock pools and small cascades culminating in a giant waterfall plunging into a rocky gorge, another great swimming spot. The waterfall is an hour's walk from Kavac.

### TOURS

Kavac plays host to three small tour/hotel operators that organize tours in the region – Asociación Civil Kamarata Kavac, Makunaima Tours and Excursiones Pemón. All three offer similar services, though Civil Kamarata Kavac is owned by the local Pemón community while the other two are private.

The tour to Cueva de Kavac is a 2½ hour roundtrip from Kavac (BsF100 per person), while a two-day package at the camp with tours to both waterfalls, accommodations and all food costs BsF380.

Boat trips to Angel Falls can be organized in the rainy season. The boats depart from Kamarata down the Akanán and Carrao Rivers, then up the Churún to Isla Ratoncito. Following a walk to the Mirador Laime, the boats then sail down the Ríos Churún and Carrao to Canaima, where the tours conclude.

### SLEEPING

Any of the three tour operators will put you up for the night at the **Campamento Turístico Kavak** (kavaccampamento@yahoo.es; per person BsF75) with meals costing an extra BsF115 per day.

## Uruyén

This newer development is another community-owned *campamento* at the foot of gorgeous Auyantepui by a small river with a great swimming hole. The **Uruyén Lodge** (reservaciones_uruyen@hotmail.com; per person full board BsF275), has four *churuatas*, each divided into two rooms each sleeping two to four people. There's a newly constructed restaurant and communal area too, and a tiny airstrip for getting there and away.

Uruyén's stellar attraction is the easy hike to the **Cueva de Yurwan**, a breathtaking river gorge that culminates in a spectacular waterfall an hour's walk from the camp.

### Getting There & Away

Both Kavac and Uruyén have airstrips where six-seaters land several times a week from Ciudad Bolívar and Canaima.

# GRAN SABANA

A wide-open grassland that seems suspended from endless sky, the Gran Sabana (Great Savanna) invites poetic description. Scores of waterfalls appear at every turn, and its trademark tepuis sweep across the horizon, their mesas both haunting and majestic. More than 100 of these plateaus dot the vast region from the Colombian border in the west to Guyana and Brazil in the east, but most of them are here in the Gran Sabana. The most famous of the tepuis, Roraima, can be climbed in a thrilling six-day hike – an extraordinary natural adventure.

Throw in a few sheep or cows, and in some places the undulating green landscape could be mistaken for lush Irish fields. But the prickly grasses of the Gran Sabana are not suitable for grazing or farming (amazingly the entire area is actually classed as a desert), and many Pemón families travel a considerable distance to tend small plots called *conucos*.

### Getting Around

The Gran Sabana was virtually inaccessible by land for many years. It wasn't until 1973 that a road between El Dorado and Santa Elena de Urairén was completed, and the last stretch of this road was finally paved in 1992. Today it's one of the best highways in the country, and one of the most spectacular. If you're on a daytime bus, make sure you nab a window seat. The road is signposted with kilometer marks from the El Dorado fork (km 0) southward to Santa Elena de Urairén (km 316) – a great help in orientation.

Although the El Dorado–Santa Elena de Uairén highway provides access to this fascinating land, public transportation on this road is infrequent (and often runs at night), making independent sightseeing inconvenient and time-consuming. Traveling away from the highway (eg to Kavanayén or Salto Aponguao) is still more difficult, as there are no buses at all on these secondary roads and traffic is sporadic. An easy solution is a tour from Ciudad Bolívar or Santa Elena de Uairén.

If you're driving, keep one eye on the road markers. Between km 88 and Santa Elena (km 316), there is only one reliable place to refuel – km 172. Because of the lively gas-smuggling trade along the border, you can't bring extra tanks of gas, and if found, they may be confiscated. Don't let that filling station pass you by!

However you choose to explore the region, bring plenty of good insect repellent. The Gran Sabana is infested by small gnats known as *jejenes* or *puri-puri*, commonly (and justifiably) called *la plaga* (the plague). They are ubiquitous and voracious in the morning and late afternoon, and their bites itch horribly for days.

## SALTO APONGUAO

One of the Gran Sabana's most spectacular sights is Salto Aponguao, a 105m-high wall of water nearly 80m wide during the wet season and spectacular year round.

Getting to the falls takes some work – it's off the highway, 32km along an unpaved (but recently much improved) road toward Kavanayén, plus another 11km south to the indigenous hamlet of Iboribó (for which a 4WD is necessary).

Locals will take you in a *curiara* (dugout canoe) the 5km to the falls, which takes 20 minutes each way and costs BsF150 per boat roundtrip, making it well worth waiting for other tourists at Iboribó if you're in a small group. The boat fee includes the services of a (mandatory) guide who'll take you past the top of the falls and down to the foot of them, where you can bathe in natural pools depending on the strength of the water. For a perfect sun-lit photo, come between midmorning and very early afternoon.

You can pitch your hammock in the *churuata* at Iboribó for BsF50 per person, and you can eat very well at **Restaurant de Mati y Claudio** (try the excellent barbecued oregano chicken, BsF35), a short distance from the harbor.

## KAVANAYÉN

By far the most attractive settlement in the Gran Sabana, Kavanayén is a remote indig-

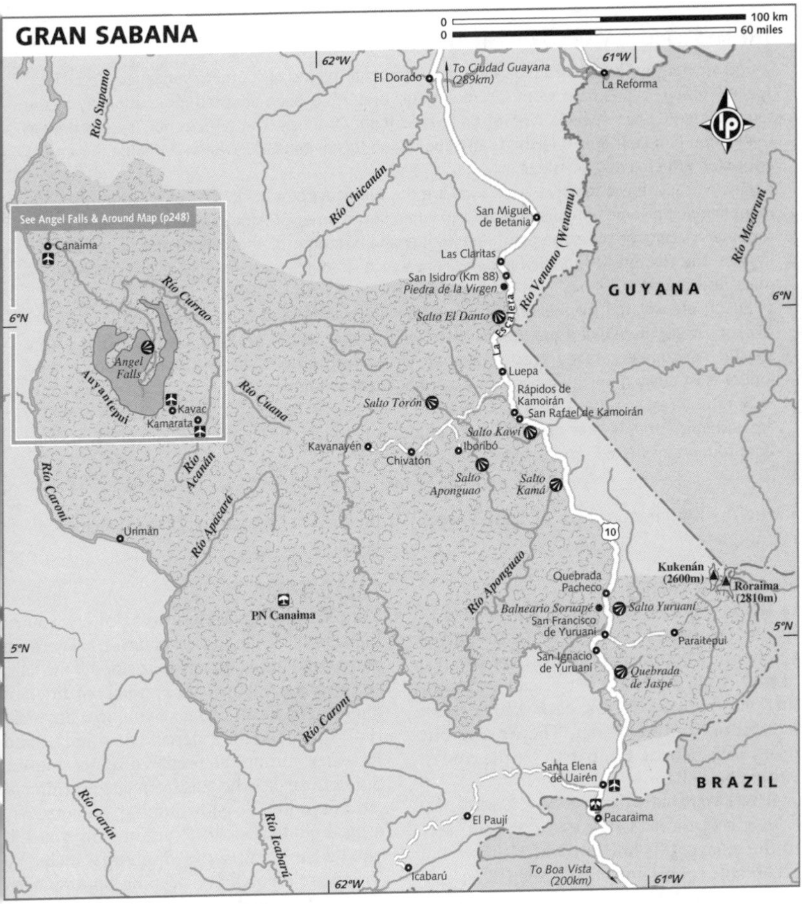


enous village with a spectacular setting on top of a small plateau with great views toward the surrounding tepuis. The village is about 70km west of the highway, and accessible by a recently much-improved dirt road.

Kavanayén developed around the Capuchin mission established here half a century ago. The missionaries erected a massive stone building for themselves that still dominates the village today, and local people constructed stone houses in a similar style for themselves as well, making the place look very different to the thatched adobe *churuatas* you'll see elsewhere in the region.

A rough jeep trail leads from Kavanayén to the **Karuai-Merú**, a fine waterfall at the base of Ptari Tepui, 20km away. The road is bad and the trip may take up to 1½ hours, but the scenery is fabulous.

### Tours

Local Pemón collective **Turismo Pemón** (turismopemon@hotmail.com), based in the Información Turística building opposite Guadalupe's is a group of guides offering unique trekking opportunities to waterfalls they claim are known only to the Pemón, as well as dug-out canoe trips through the spectacular surrounding valleys. You can also book these trips through Mérida-based **Andes Tropicales** (☎ 0274-263-8633; www.andestropicales.org).

Most Santa Elena tour companies can organize trips to and around Kavanayén, including on an adventurous trail going between

### THE MYSTERIOUS WORLD OF THE TEPUIS

Tepuis are flat-topped, cliff-edged sandstone mountains typical of southern Venezuela. Tepui (also spelled 'tepuy') is a Pemón word for 'mountain,' and it has been adopted internationally as the term to identify this specific type of table mountain. Curiously, the term 'tepui' is used only in the Pemón linguistic area – in the Gran Sabana and its environs. Elsewhere, the table mountains are called either *cerros* or *montes*.

Geologically, these massive tablelands are the remnants of a thick layer of Precambrian sediment laid down some two billion years ago when South America, Africa and Australia were joined together as part of the supercontinent Gondwana. Warping of the continental plates created fissures and fractures in the sandstone plain, which gradually eroded, leaving behind only the most resistant rock 'islands' – present-day tepuis.

Effectively isolated for millions of years from each other and from the eroded lower level, the tops of tepuis allowed the independent evolution of fauna and flora. Developing in such a specific environment, many species have preserved features of their remote ancestors, and no longer exist away from the table tops except as fossilized remains.

Botanical research has found roughly 2000 plant species on top of the tepuis, half of which are endemic – that is, they grow nowhere else. This is almost the highest percentage of endemic flora found anywhere in the world.

Karuai to Kamarata, which at least a week to complete.

### Sleeping & Eating

**La Misión** (☎ 0286-963-3763; dm per person BsF30) By far the best place to stay in town, the Capuchin Mission that looms over the rest of the village offers five very clean and comfortable five-bed dorms, each with private bathrooms and hot water. There's also one room with 12 beds. Drop in to see the church while you're here.

**Hotel Kavanaruden** (☎ 0286-963-4585, hotelkavanaruden@hotmail.com; r BsF80) Located at the entrance to the village, this hotel provides simple but acceptable rooms and is only open when reservations have been made. It's a much less attractive prospect than the Misión, with only two hours of electricity in the evenings and no hot water.

our pick **Restaurant de la Señora Guadalupe** (☎ 0286-963-4585; breakfast BsF25, lunch & dinner BsF35) Local celebrity Guadalupe has built up the best loved eatery in the Gran Sabana. Join her for a feast and (if you speak Spanish), some memorable conversation over great home cooking here at Kavanayén's only restaurant.

### Getting There & Away

Kavanayén is a two-hour drive from the highway and hitchhiking isn't the most reliable option due to low traffic. A better bet is a tour, though most of the standard Gran Sabana tours don't come this far. The last stretch of the road to Kavanayén is in poor shape – 4WD is recommended.

## SALTO KAMÁ

Salto Kamá (Kamá-Merú) is a powerful 50m-high waterfall, 200m west of km 202. There are paths descending on opposite sides of the falls, so you can size it up from a number of different angles. The locals can take you on a boat trip (BsF20) around the waterfall's pool and behind its water curtain; be prepared to get doused. Sunlight strikes the falls from late morning to late afternoon. To go swimming, you must pay a local guide (BsF20) to accompany you – if you take the boat then swimming is included. There are a couple of sleeping options here, the **Posada El Kamá** (dm & r per person without bathroom BsF50, r per person with bathroom BsF70), a six-room place with a great *criollo* restaurant (mains BsF30) attached. There are also a couple of cheaper, but very basic *campamentos* here too.

## QUEBRADA PACHECO

Also known as Arapán-Merú, this is a handsome multistep cascade just 100m east of the road at km 237. It looks all right from the road, but it gets better up close. The best light for photos is in the afternoon. Unfortunately this is an extremely popular spot with Venezuelan holidaymakers at Easter and in the summer months, when it can be ruined by littering and loud parties. From here it's a 20-minute walk to the gorgeous Pozo Azul (Blue Well) swimming hole.

## SALTO YURUANÍ

This rushing wall of a river falls is about 6m high and 60m wide, with amazing beer-colored water. It's at km 247, where you cross a bridge over the Río Yuruaní. From the bridge you'll see the waterfall, about 1km to the east, with the Yuruaní tepui in the background. The way to the falls is along both the southern and northern banks of the river. With a guide you can explore behind the water curtain – a thrilling walk, swim and crawl – but only during low-water periods. There's a place for camping next to the falls, but bring a lot of insect repellent as this waterfall is notorious for *jejenes*. The best sunlight strikes the falls in the late afternoon. This is a popular spot for body-surfing and rafting – agencies in Santa Elena can organize trips.

## PARAITEPUI

The last settlement before Roraima shoots majestically up into the heavens, Paraitepui is a rather backward Pemón village 26km east of San Francisco. Treks to Roraima begin from here and so the locals are well used to seeing travelers, though the local tourism scene is decidedly wanting: get all your supplies and equipment in Santa Elena as you'll have little luck here!

The new but already rather sorry-looking **Campo Turistico Paraitepui** (per person without/with food BsF80/120) has 19 duplex cabañas with bathrooms and tepui views. You can in theory come to Paraitepui yourself and organize guides to Roraima in the village, thus cutting out the middleman, but this isn't recommended. Travel agencies usually only work with guides they know and trust, and the extra you pay for peace of mind is well worth it. If you're determined to organize the trip yourself, the Inparques office can round up available guides and porters, or direct you to the *cooperativa* that rents out tents and sleeping bags.

The rutted road requires a high-clearance vehicle, and you can organize one in Santa Elena for a set fee of BsF600 one way per vehicle, carrying up to six people. There is very little traffic here, so hitching is not a solid bet. Jeeps are usually full, and on this rough road they are likely to ask for payment anyway. You could walk to Paraitepui from San Francisco de Yuruaní, but it's seven hours of heat and hills.

## RORAIMA

A stately tepui towering into churning clouds, Roraima lures hikers and nature-lovers looking for Venezuela at its natural and rugged best. Unexplored until 1884, and studied extensively by botanists ever since, the stark landscape contains strange rock formations and graceful arches, ribbon waterfalls, glittering quartz deposits and carnivorous plants. Frequent mist only accentuates the otherworldly feel.

Tropical rainforest clings to the walls of the tepui, but the area was once heavily wooded on a scale unimaginable today. In 1925 one legendary Pemón fire reached such magnitude that it scorched the upper reaches of Roraima, decimating forests that once blanketed its slopes. Local elders can remember this dense landscape, and guides can point out charred roots that remain.

Although it's one of the easier tepuis to climb and no technical skills are required, the trek is long and demanding. However, anyone who's reasonably fit and determined can reach the top. Be prepared for wet weather, nasty *jejenes* and frigid nights at the summit. And give yourself at least five days roundtrip so you have sufficient time to explore the vast plateau of the tepui – you'll want to spend a full day on the top exploring.

### Orientation

Roraima lords over the eastern border of Venezuela and straddles sections of Brazil and Guyana too. The base of the mountain is approximately 47km east of San Francisco de Yuruaní and the El Dorado–Santa Elena highway, and 22km northeast of Paraitepui. The smaller Kukenán tepui sits just to the west. Maps highlighting Roraima's landmarks and hiking distances are widely available throughout the region.

### Planning

#### WHEN TO GO

The dry season lasts from about December through April, but the top of the tepui receives rain throughout the year. The weather is highly temperamental, with intense sun giving way to rainy deluges in a matter of minutes. Peak holiday periods (see p13) are better avoided, when access to the tepui can become harder. There is a limited number of people allowed on the tepui at one time, and so groups can be held by Inparques in Paratepui until a returning group re-enters the village.

#### WHAT KIND OF TRIP

Visitors cannot hike here independently. There are two ways to climb Roraima: join a tour-company group or go solo with a local guide. How you do the trip is a matter of preference, price and ability. On the one hand, tour companies arrange all your gear and food, and carry most of it. They are more expensive, but take care of all the transfers, food shopping and other logistics – no small feat. Groups generally have a minimum number of participants, and if you haven't booked in advance, you may need to wait a few days or pay more if there aren't enough people. Alternatively, you can bring your own equipment and food, hire a guide, and backpack on your own schedule for a lot less money. Camping gear is also available to rent locally, though the cumulative costs can add up. If you want to go with a tour company and still keep costs low, many offer a discounted trip for those willing to carry up to 12kg of equipment, saving money that would be paid to a porter.

The best place to organize tours is in Santa Elena (see p257) where rates are the best in the country. Packages start from BsF500 per person for the most basic package (which only includes transport to Paratepui and a guide for the climb – you'll bring all your own equipment and food, and carry it) and go up to BsF1800 for all-inclusive tours using the very best quality equipment, portable toilets and English-speaking guides.

Though we'd recommend going with a travel agency, guides (BsF250 per day for a group of up to six people) can be arranged in either San Francisco or Paraitepui, as well as porters (BsF150 per day), who are able to carry up to about 15kg.

#### WHAT TO BRING

Think hot, cold and wet. The top of the tepui generates its own microclimate, with rain and fog making multiple or constant daily passes over the eerie landscape. Temperatures hover toward freezing after dark, and soggy clothes may never dry. On the open savanna below, hot and humid conditions rule the day. So in addition to the usual camping gear, make sure you have a waterproof tent with fly, a warm sleeping bag, a ground pad, full rain gear, extra pairs of socks and some flip-flops or lightweight camp shoes to wear while hiking shoes recover from puddle plunges.

Toward the end of the trip, an extra camera battery will come in handy for digital cameras. Stash enough plastic bags for packing out all your garbage and waste, and bring extra food in case you choose to extend your stay – or the weather decides for you. Buy any food in Santa Elena de Uairén, Ciudad Guyana or Ciudad Bolívar. Neither Paraitepui nor San Francisco has any decent shops. And although you won't need insect repellent on Roraima itself, the bugs bite something fierce along the way, so pack some for the journey there and back.

### Climbing Roraima

Once you have a guide or have joined a tour, you must sign in with the Inparques officer in Paraitepui and pay a BsF10 entrance fee before setting out. Departures from Paraitepui are permitted only between 7:30am and 2pm to guarantee enough time to reach the first campsite at Río Tök (four hours from Paraitepui). The top can be reached in two days (total walking time is about 12 hours up and 10 hours down), but most tour companies stretch it out over three days each way. There are several established campsites along the way with water sources for drinking and bathing. The next campsite is at the Río Kukenán (30 minutes past Río Tök). A majority of groups spend the second night at the so-called *campamento base* (base camp) just before the mountain (three hours uphill from the Río Kukenán).

The Río Kukenán can throw a snag in your plans, as the water level rises sharply with rainfall and the resulting runoff from the Kukenán and Roraima tepuis. The river can quickly become furious and impassable, and you may need to cool your heels for several hours, or even a day, until the level drops. Generally, the water level is lower in the evening than in the morning. Sometimes local villagers will haul in a rubber raft (and charge) for the crossing, but don't count on it. When camping next to the river here, do not pitch tents on the shore side of the painted white rocks – they signify the river's high-tide mark.

From the base camp it's about four grueling hours to the top and the most demanding part of the hike. The trail leaves open savanna and enters thick steamy rainforest, and the path becomes a continuous scramble up a steep slope. When the clouds part and you can see the valley below, the views are magnificent.

### THE MOTHER OF ALL WATERS

Sitting on the three-way border between Venezuela, Guyana and Brazil, the 34-sq-km Roraima is the highest of all the tepuis – its plateau is at about 2700m and the tallest peak at 2810m. The indigenous Pemón people call it the 'Mother of all Waters,' presumably because Roraima is the source of rivers that feed all three of the surrounding great river basins – the Orinoco, the Essequibo and the Amazon.

Like most other tepuis in the region, Roraima has a rocky barren surface, swept by rain and wind, and few living organisms have adapted to these inhospitable conditions. Those that have include curious endemic species such as a little black frog *(Oreophrynella)* that crawls instead of jumps, and the *heliamphora (Sarraceniaceae)*, a carnivorous plant that traps unwary insects in beautiful, bucket-shaped, red flowers filled with rainwater.

German explorer Robert Schomburgk was the first European to reach the base of Roraima, in 1838, yet he considered the summit inaccessible. Various expeditions then failed to climb the plateau, until British botanists Everald Im Thum and Harry Perkins made it to the top in 1884 in a two-month-long expedition and discovered its unique plant and animal life.

The news fired the imagination of Sir Arthur Conan Doyle, the creator of Sherlock Holmes. Inspired by the fabulous stories of the explorers, he wrote his famous adventure tale, *The Lost World,* in which dinosaurs were still living on a remote plateau in the Amazon basin – giving Roraima an aura of mystery and romance.



Once you arrive at the top of the tepui, your guide will lead you to one of several 'hotels' to set up camp. The hotels are sandy areas protected by cliffs or ridges of eroded rock, where you'll appreciate the cover when rain lashes the mesa.

It appears desolate, but life thrives here. Roots dart from crevices and thirsty bromeliads inhabit the boughs of sinuous trees. Strips of pink sand meander between soaring boulders and chilly pools of clear water. Vaulting rock to rock over rain deposits, you see tiny black frogs, curious sparrows and tiny blooming flowers.

Getting lost here is easy, so your guide will lead the way to the mountain's natural highlights. On a sunny day, **La Ventana** (Window) has some of the best and most vertiginous views. Three hours to the north, you'll pass through the lush riverbed of the **Valle Arabopo** on the way to the **El Foso** (Pit), a round deep sinkhole with interior arches. Just past this pool are **Valle de los Cristales**, **Laberinto**, **El Abismo** (Abyss) and the meeting point of Venezuela, Guyana and Brazil, **Punto Triple**. In the southwestern sector closer to most of the hotels, you can dunk into freezing quartz-lined ponds called **Jacuzzis**.

## SAN FRANCISCO DE YURUANÍ

An industrious indigenous village on the highway 66km north of Santa Elena de Uairén, San Francisco is a convenient staging area for Roraima trips, and a place to hire local guides. Modern market stalls line the roadside, catering to Venezuelans who visit the Gran Sabana in peak holiday periods, when local accommodations pump up their prices. There are a few basic posadas along the main road near the bus stop.

Many buses a day run in each direction along the Ciudad Guayana–Santa Elena highway, stopping in San Francisco.

## QUEBRADA DE JASPE

One of the most unusual and popular waterfalls in the Gran Sabana, **Quebrada de Jaspe** (7am-5pm, entry BsF2) isn't known for a dramatic plunge but for the brilliant orange and red jasper rock beneath its waters. Kako Paru, its Pemón name, means 'fire creek,' and the design carved by the current creates a slick surface resembling stripes on a tiger. It's located at km 273 between San Francisco and Santa Elena, 300m to the east of the highway, hidden in a stretch of woodland.

## SANTA ELENA DE UAIRÉN

☎ 0289 / pop 30,000

Right on the Brazilian border, Santa Elena is the unofficial capital of the Gran Sabana, a pleasant frontier town with rugged habits and a lilting Portuguese accent. It's the base for travelers exploring the waterfalls and tepuis of the area, particularly Roraima, and is a handy transport hub. The streets are safe and

Brazilian influence runs high, as many residents speak Portuguese as a first language.

Santa Elena was settled as a mining outpost in 1924, and it grew slowly until diamonds were discovered in the 1930s in the Icabarú region, 115km to the west. But the lack of a good road kept the town in a state of suspended development until the highway from El Dorado was completed in 1992. This is the only road link between Venezuela and Brazil, so you'll be passing through Santa Elena if you travel overland between them.

You can cross easily into Brazil here (there's no passport control to visit the town of Pacaraima on the other side) – on your way look for the lot of impounded cars, trucks and passenger buses caught sneaking over with multiple tanks of smuggled gas from Venezuela's cheaper-than-water pumps.

## Information

### EMERGENCY

**Emergency Center** (☎ 171)

### IMMIGRATION

**Brazilian Consulate** (☎ 995-1256; Calle Los Castaños, off Av Perimetral; ⏰ 8am-2pm Mon-Fri) A yellow-fever vaccination certificate and two passport photos are required for a visa (see p289).

### INTERNET ACCESS

Internet connections are slow and cost BsF4 per hour.

**SANTA ELENA DE UAIRÉN**

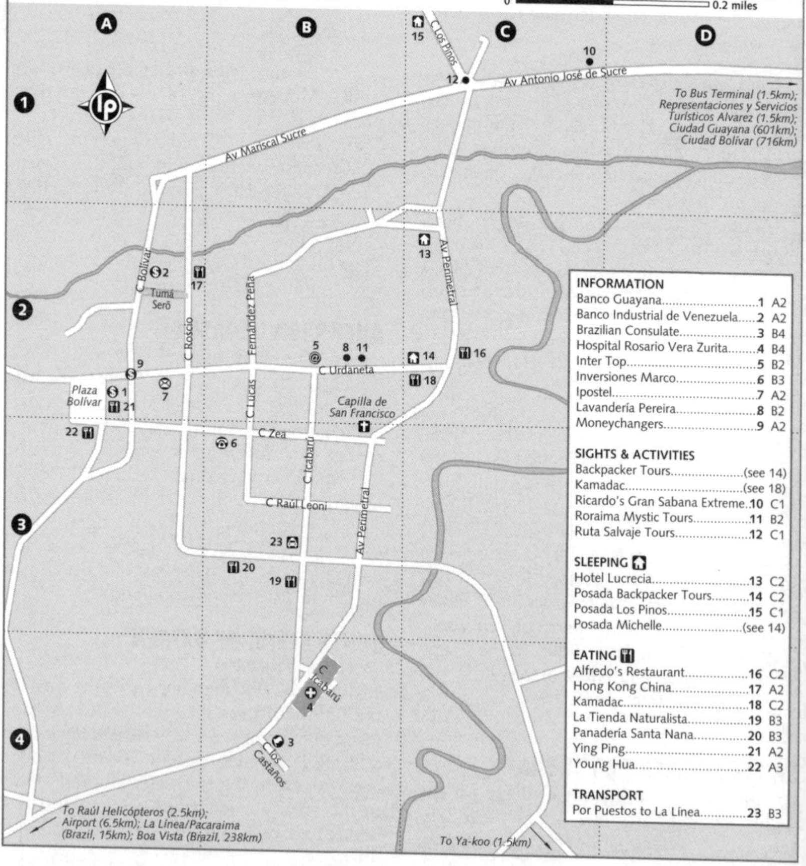

**Inter Top** (Calle Urdaneta)
**Posada Backpacker Tours** (Calle Urdaneta)

### LAUNDRY
**Lavandería Pereira** (Calle Urdaneta)

### MEDICAL SERVICES
**Hospital Rosario Vera Zurita** (Calle Icabarú) No phone; linked to ☎ 171 emergency services via radio.

### MONEY
Moneychangers populate the intersection of Calle Bolívar and Calle Urdaneta, popularly known as Cuatro Esquinas. Expect to be collared by men flashing cash every day except Sunday afternoon. However, it's not a pressured or sketchy scene, and they offer some of the best exchange rates in the country for US dollars. It's also a good place to sell your *bolívares fuertes* and buy Brazilian currency if you're crossing the border.
**Banco Guayana** (Plaza Bolívar)
**Banco Industrial de Venezuela** (Calle Bolívar)

### POST
**Ipostel** (Calle Urdaneta btwn Calles Bolívar & Roscio)

### TELEPHONE
**Inversiones Marco** (Calle Zea btwn Calles Roscio & Lucas Fernández Peña)

## Tours
Santa Elena has about a dozen tour agencies and they all do some type of day or multiday jeep trips around the Gran Sabana, mostly touring the area's spectacular waterfalls and far-flung swimming holes, though there's also a growing number of extreme sports outfits here offering everything from whitewater rafting to paragliding. All companies offer Roraima trips, of course, and this is what the vast majority of travelers are here to do.

Recommended local tour companies:

**Posada Backpacker Tours** (☎ 995-1415, 0414-886-7227; www.backpacker-tours.com; Calle Urdaneta) An excellent German-run company with comfortable Roraima treks and some of the best camping equipment. English is spoken.

**Kamadac** (☎ 995-1408, 0414-886-6526; www.abenteuer-venezuela.de; Calle Urdaneta) A German- and Venezuelan-owned agency, it offers staples (Gran Sabana, Roraima) as well as some more adventurous tours (Auyantepui, Akopán Tepui).

**Representaciones y Servicios Turísticos Alvarez** (☎ 0414-385-2846, 0414-854-2940; www.saltoangelrsta.com; Bus Terminal, Av Perimetral) A personable and helpful presence in the bus terminal, English-speaking Francisco Alvarez organizes regional tours and his costs are some of the cheapest available. He's very happy to deal with small groups and has his own posada too.

**Ricardo's Gran Sabana Extreme** (☎ 0426-894-8143, 0414-886-7209; www.adrenalinexpeditions.com; Av Antonio José de Sucre) Brother to Luís of Ciudad Bolívar's Adrenaline Expeditions, Ricardo handles the Gran Sabana with great passion and knowledge, offering all manner of tours, with an emphasis on extreme sports.

**Roraima Mystic Tours** (☎ 416-0558, 0414-886-1055; Calle Urdaneta) This agency has some of the lowest prices for Roraima treks. Fluent-English speaker Roberto's interest in UFO sightings and the mysteries of the Gran Sabana is infectious.

**Ruta Salvaje Tours** (☎ 995-1134, 0414-889-4164; www.rutasalvaje.com; Av Mariscal Sucre) As well as offering Gran Sabana and Roraima trips, Ruta Salvaje offers very professionally-run rafting, paragliding, canyoning and kayaking excursions. The friendly owner speaks English.

If you have money to burn and no time to spare, **Raúl Helicópteros** (☎ 995-1912, 0414-886-7174; www.raulhelicopteros.com; Hotel Gran Sabana, Vía Brasil) will get you there in its fleet of light planes and helicopters. Trips available include Angel Falls and the top of Roraima.



## Sleeping
**Posada Michelle** (☎ 416-1257, 414-5425; Calle Urdaneta; s/d/tr/q BsF45/70/100/120) The undisputed backpacker headquarters, and the best place to fill out a tour group. A clean and surprisingly quiet posada with 23 rooms with fans, private bathrooms with hot water and a basic kitchen downstairs. Half-day shower-and-rest rates (r per person BsF50) and a shower-only option (per person BsF10) are great for cleaning up after a Roraima trek or grabbing a nap before the night bus to Ciudad Bolívar. Bulletin boards from all the travel agencies in town announce upcoming trips.

**Posada Backpacker Tours** (☎ 995-1415, 0414-886-7227; www.backpacker-tours.com; Calle Urdaneta; s/d/tr/q BsF60/80/120/180; 💻) Another traveler favorite, all rooms here have bathrooms with hot water, fans and are painted in bright colors.

**Hotel San Marco** (☎ 995-1611, 0414-185-2614; Calle Raúl Leoni; s&d/tr BsF100/130; P ❄) This motel-style place offers 22 clean and modern rooms with comfy beds, hot water, fridge, and painted walls.

**Hotel Lucrecia** (☎ 995-1105, 0414-886-6937; hotellucrecia@canTV.net; Av Perimetral; r BsF120; P ❄ 💻 🏊) Far more charming inside than out, with a beautiful courtyard garden and comfortable rooms, the Lucrecia offers a small pool, hot water showers and free internet to guests. The dressing gown-clad matriarch who runs the place suggests an era of bygone fabulousness.

**L'Auberge Posada** (☎ 995-1567; Calle Urdaneta; s/d/tr/q BsF160/250/330/380; ) This new French-run posada is a comfortable option in the center of town. There are eight good-sized rooms, some of which have mezzanines, and all of which come equipped with fridge and TV. There's free use of the internet downstairs and breakfast across the road at the Backpackers for BsF20.

**Posada Los Pinos** (☎ 808-8817, 0289-995-1524; www.backpacker-tours.com; Calle Los Pinos; s/d/tr BsF190/350/450; ) This wonderful new place is a short walk from the center and one of the most comfortable options in town. Ten colorful rooms (a further eight are planned) have fridge and TV and are painted in lively colors. There's a large garden and a small pool here too. Mountain bikes can also be hired for BsF90 a day.

**Ya-koo** (☎ 995-1332, 995-1742, www.ya-koo.com; Vía Sampay, Piedra Canaima; s/d/tr BsF390/600/900; ) The best of several smart posadas outside the town, Ya-koo has 18 very pleasant cabañas in lovely gardens. However, the idyll is somewhat marred by a recently-formed shantytown at the bottom of the hill, which makes the area rather unsafe at night.

## Eating

Santa Elena has plenty of good food available. For a cheap meal in a fun atmosphere head to **Tumá Serö** (off Calle Bolívar; 7am-11pm), a 'boulevard of food' with dozens of different outlets serving everything from *arepas* to noodles.

**Panadería Santa Nana** (Calle Roscio; pastries from BsF5; 8am-9pm) This friendly bakery has great coffee, sublime fresh pastries and also serves as a good supermarket.

**La Tienda Naturalista** (Calle Icabarú; snacks from BsF5; 8am-noon & 3-6pm Mon-Sat) A small health-food store and bakery with great vegetarian empanadas, fresh yogurt and fresh fruit juices.

**Kamadac** (☎ 995-1408; Calle Urdaneta; pizza BsF18-88, noon-10pm Wed-Mon) This tour operator runs a delicious pizza parlor with a huge choice of toppings.

**Ying Ping** (☎ 995-2230; Pl Bolívar; set meals BsF35, 11am-10pm) One of two good Chinese restaurants on the main square (the other, Young Hua, is also recommended), Ying Ping does fantastic homemade rice noodles and has an encyclopedic menu.

**Alfredo's Restaurant** (☎ 995-1042; Av Perimetral mains BsF25-65; noon-3pm, 6-10pm Tue-Sun; ) Another place that looks far better inside than out, Alfredo's is the best restaurant in town There's a lengthy menu and a dish of tortellin with ricotta and spinach that melts in your mouth.

There are a number of supermarket in town for stocking up on supplies for a Roraima trek. The best selection is availabl at **Hong Kong China** (Calle Roscio, 8:15am-12:15pm & 2:15-7pm Mon-Sat, 8:15am-12:15pm Sun).

## Getting There & Away

### TO/FROM BRAZIL

Venezuelan and Brazilian immigration control points are at the border, nicknamed La Línea, 15km south of Santa Elena. Going a far as Pacaraima, the Brazilian border town there is no need for a visa (if required fo nationals of your country) but you must show your passport and proof of yellow fever vaccination, though you won't be stamped ou of Venezuela or into Brazil. Onward traveler will need to get a passport exit stamp fron the Venezuelan immigration point and the a Brazilian entry stamp a few blocks ove There are no through buses between Brazi and Venezuela, instead you have to take a tax or por puesto to Pacaraima bus station fron where there are three daily buses to Boa Vist (three to four hours, 223km); two of thes continue on to Manaus (12 hours, 758km) Brazilian bus companies in Pacaraima chec passport stamps before selling tickets. It' not possible to buy tickets for Boa Vista o Manaus in Venezuela.

In Santa Elena taxis (around BsF50 t BsF70) to Pacaraima congregate in front o the bus terminal and will wait at both immigration checks before dropping you off a the terminal in Brazil. From the Santa Elen city center, cheaper por puestos (BsF10) leav from Calle Icabarú but go only as far as th Venezuelan immigration point.

### AIR

The smart new airport is 7km southwest o town, off the road to the border with Brazi There are no buses; taxis cost BsF15 to BsF2 Tour operators often wait for incoming fligh and offer free lifts to town in the hope of sell ing tours. Rutaca has flights on five-seate Cessnas to Ciudad Bolívar (BsF900), ofte via Canaima (BsF600).

### BUS

Santa Elena's bus terminal is on the Ciudad Guayana highway about 2km east of the town's center. Buses run all the way along the main road through the Gran Sabana, stopping at Ciudad Guayana's San Félix Terminal (BsF40 to BsF70) and continuing to Ciudad Bolívar (BsF45 to BsF70, 10 to 12 hours). Other routes include the mammoth journey to Caracas (BsF130, 20 hours), and daily overnight buses to Puerto La Cruz (BsF75 to BsF115), Maturín (BsF50) and Cumaná (BsF80). Night buses stop up to five times per trip for comically useless identification checks, so keep your passport handy. From here a taxi to the center costs BsF15.

# AMAZONAS

Sparsely populated by humans but teeming with diverse and exotic animal and plant species, the southernmost state of Amazonas is Venezuela's untamed jungle wilderness. Predominantly a thick rainforest, the road-forsaken region is crisscrossed by rivers and inhabited by a mosaic of indigenous communities, whose primary form of transportation is the dugout canoe called a *bongo*.

The current indigenous population, estimated at 40,000 (half of what it was in 1925), comprises three main groups – the Piaroa, Yanomami and Guajibo – and a number of smaller communities, among them the Yekuana (Maquiritare), Curripaco and Piapoco. Following a checkered history of mistreatment by Spanish missionaries and successive Creole governments, the Venezuelan constitution was amended in 1999 to accord special status to the nation's indigenous peoples. There are now guarantees of political, cultural, economic and language rights, as well as the recognition of collective ownership of their lands.

Amazonas covers an area of 180,000 sq km – one-fifth of the national territory – yet it's home to less than 1% of the country's population. Despite its name, most of the region lies in the Orinoco basin, while the Amazon basin occupies only the southwestern portion of the state. The two basins are linked by the unusual 320km-long Brazo Casiquiare, a natural channel that sends a portion of the water from the Orinoco to Río Negro and down to the Amazon. Amazonas boasts four large national parks that cover 30% of the state area.

In contrast to the central Amazon basin in Brazil, Venezuelan Amazonas is quite diverse topographically, with towering tepuis. Though not as numerous as those in the Gran Sabana, they do give the green carpet of rainforest a distinctive and spectacular appearance.

At the southernmost part of the Amazonas, along the border with Brazil, is the Serranía de la Neblina, a scarcely explored and virtually unknown mountain range. The highest peak reaches 2994m, making it the tallest mountain range on the continent east of the Andean chain, and the canyon running through its middle is one of the world's deepest. La Neblina has some of the richest endemic plant life in the world.

The climate is not uniform throughout the region. At the northern edge there's a distinctive dry season from December to April; April is the hottest month. Heading south, the dry season becomes shorter and not so dry, and eventually disappears. Accordingly, the southern part of Amazonas is wet year-round. The best time to explore the region is from October to December, when the river level is high but rains are already easing.

## Getting Around

Amazonas is an enormous region with very few roads, and almost all transportation is by air or riverway. Other than a few short hops from Puerto Ayacucho, there are no regular passenger boats. Independent travel is difficult, if not impossible, but tour operators in Puerto Ayacucho can take you just about everywhere – at a price, of course. Note that you need government permits to visit the majority of Amazonas, as many areas are restricted to indigenous residents (see the boxed text, p264).

## PUERTO AYACUCHO

**☎ 0248 / pop 83,500**

The hot and humid capital of evocative Amazonas, the gateway city of Puerto Ayacucho has an unhurried tempo born of isolation and the contemplation of colossal distances. Founded as a river port in 1924, the town began life as a center for timber shipment from the upper Amazonas down to the country's center. Only in the late 1980s, when a track road linking it to the rest of the country was improved and surfaced, did Puerto Ayacucho start to grow dramatically.

Puerto Ayacucho is the only significant urban center in Amazonas state, and it's set on a colorful section of the Orinoco, just down from the spectacular rapids of Raudales Atures. The town is the regional tourist center, home to a dozen tour companies that can take you up the Orinoco and its tributaries, and deep into the jungle. It is also a transit point on the adventurous back routes to Colombia and Brazil. The town itself has a few interesting sights, including an indigenous craft market and an ethnographic museum.

## Orientation

Puerto Ayacucho is a small city with a lot of small-scale commercial activity. The main thoroughfare is the Av Orinoco, which begins

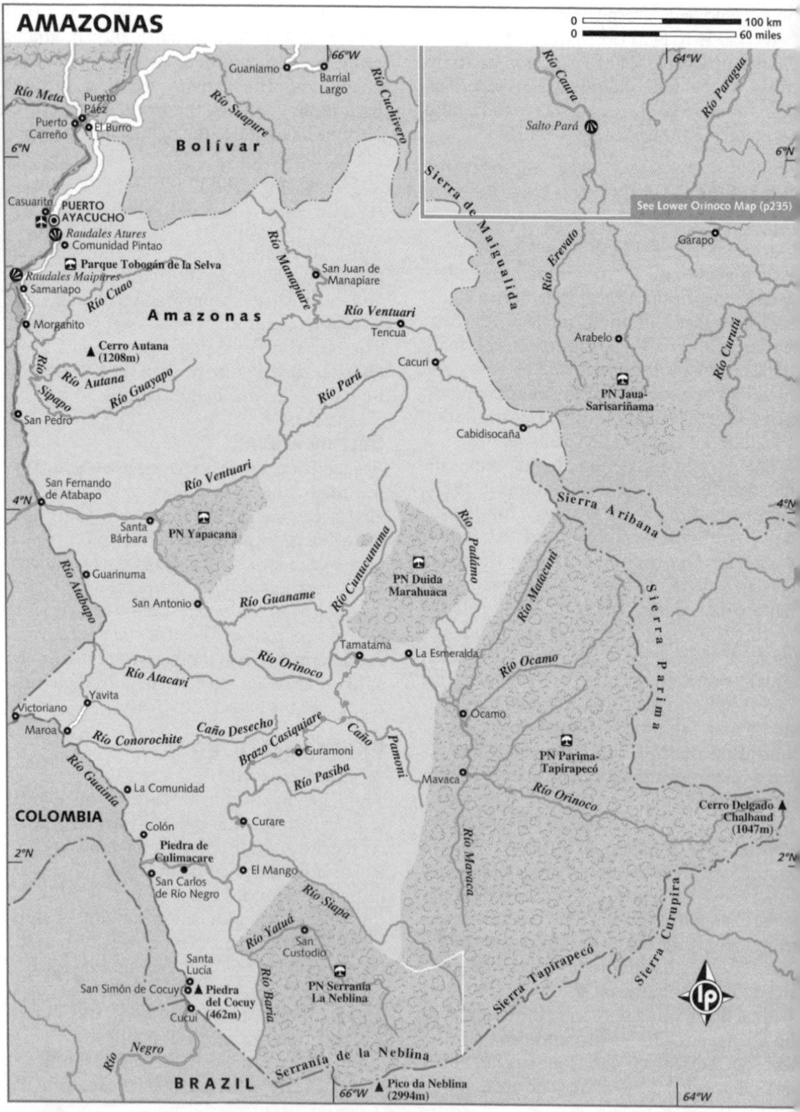

to the north at the *muelle* (dock). The town of Causarito, Colombia is a short distance across the Río Orinoco. Passing a wetlands overrun by dive-bombing birds, the road continues on, becoming busier as it approaches the city's main intersection at Av 23 de Enero. From here, sidewalk vendors camp out under sun-obscuring tarps and sheets, building a continuous arcade a block or so south past the Mercadito stalls. Further south, large bulbous hills seem to pop out of nowhere, and the Raudales Atures churn up the Orinoco.

The bus terminal is 6km east of the center and the airport is almost 6km south. It's rare for a taxi ride anywhere in town to cost more than BsF10.

## Information

### EMERGENCY

**Emergency Center** (☎ 171)

### IMMIGRATION

**Colombian Consulate** (☎ 521-0789; Calle Yapacana, Quinta Beatriz; 🕑 8am-1pm & 3-6pm Mon-Fri)

**ONIDEX** (☎ 521-0198; Av Aguerrevere; 🕑 8am-noon & 2-5pm Mon-Fri) You must have your passport stamped here when leaving or entering Venezuela. No fee.

### INTERNET ACCESS

**Biblionet** (Biblioteca Pública, Av Río Negro) 45 minutes free internet access.

**CANTV** (cnr Av Río Negro & Calle Atabapo) Offers both telephone & internet

**CANTV** (Av Orinoco) Offers both telephone & internet (BsF4 per hour)

### LAUNDRY

**Lavandería Aquario** (Av Aguerrevere)

### MONEY

**Banco de Venezuela** (Av Orinoco)

**Banco Provincial** (Calle La Guardia)

**Banesco** (Av Orinoco)

### TOURIST INFORMATION

**Dirección de Turismo** (☎ 521-0033; Plaza Bolívar; 🕑 8am-noon & 2-5:30pm Mon-Fri) On the ground floor of the Gobernación (government offices). Don't expect much.

## Sights

A fascinating display of regional indigenous culture, the **Museo Etnológico de Amazonas** (Av Río Negro; admission BsF1; 🕑 8-11:30am & 2:30-6pm Tue-Fri, 9am-noon & 3:30-6pm Sat, 9am-1pm Sun) is one place you absolutely shouldn't miss. There are several exhibition rooms, with each one displaying personal items and model housing replicas of the Piaroa, Guajibo, Yekuana and Yanomami groups. Maybe a photo of Yanomami men blowing *yoppo* (a hallucinogenic snuff drug), through a 1m-plus-long wooden pipe will be motivation enough to visit.

Across the street from the museum, the **Mercado Indígena** (Av Río Negro) sells indigenous crafts, but you need to pick through a bit in order to find anything worthwhile, like handmade hammocks and human figures carved in wood. Nearby on the shady Plaza Bolívar, the **Catedral de María Auxiliadora** (Av Río Negro) has a colorful interior worth seeing.

You don't get a true sense of the city and its river history until you get a bird's-eye view. The **Cerro Perico**, just southwest of the town's center, provides good views over Río Orinoco and the town. Another hill, Cerro El Zamuro, commonly known as **El Mirador**, 1.5km south of the center, overlooks the **Raudales Atures**, the feisty rapids that defy river navigation. The rapids are most impressive in the wet season, when the water is high, and they encompass a sprawling chain of wooded islands with gorgeous boulder beaches.

## Tours

Although Puerto Ayacucho is the only major city in Amazons, it doesn't get a reliable stream of tourists, so you need to plan ahead in order to visit off-the-beaten-path destinations. Amazonas covers a huge amount of territory, and tour operators can develop all sorts of itineraries according to your interests and time.

Among the popular shorter tours are a three-day trip up the Río Cuao and a three-day trip up the Sipapo and Autana Rivers to the foot of Cerro Autana. Expect to pay from BsF500 to BsF700 per person per day all-inclusive, and try to negotiate bonus side trips to Piedra Pintada, La Tortuga and/or Parque Tobogán.

The Ruta Humboldt, following the route of the great explorer Alexander von Humboldt is a longer and more adventurous trip. It goes along the Orinoco, Brazo Casiquiare and Guainía Rivers up to Maroa. The boat is then transported overland to Yavita, and returns down the Atabapo and Orinoco rivers to Puerto Ayacucho. This trip can take from 10 to 15 days and tour operators don't usually do the whole loop, but only its most attractive fragments, including Brazo Casiquiare, skipping over the less interesting parts by plane.

Much of Amazonas is not open to independent travelers. The far southeastern part of Amazonas beyond La Esmeralda, including all the Parque Nacional Parima-Tapirapecó, where the Yanomami live, is a restricted area; you need special permits that are virtually impossible to get. Some agents get around the ban by visiting Yanomami villages on the Río Siapa off Brazo Casiquiare. Some exceptions are made for scholarly research groups, but resident indigenous communities have the right to deny visits to their area. For adventurous river journeys, tour companies will acquire any required permits necessary. Make sure you carry your passport and tourist permit on all trips.

Recommended tour operators:

**Axel Expedition** (☎ 414-5036, 0416-785-5033; www.axel-expedition.com; Valle Verde Triángulo) A 25-year veteran of the region, Axel Keleman arranges all kinds of expeditions throughout Amazonas and has wonderful stories to tell. Tour participants can stay in his self-catering guesthouse the night before and after trips. The office is 5km east of the center.

**Coyote Expediciones** (☎ 521-4583, 0414-486-2500; coyotexpedition@canTV.net; Av Aguerrevere) A busy and popular outfit operating here for almost 20 years, it specializes in three-day trips to Autana and has frequent departures. English is spoken.

**Eco Destinos de Venezuela** (☎ 521-3964, 0416-448-6394; henryamazonas@hotmail.com; Calle Principal) Specializes in Cerro Autana trips; a minimum of three people needed. The office is 1km north of town, in the suburb of La Bolivariana.

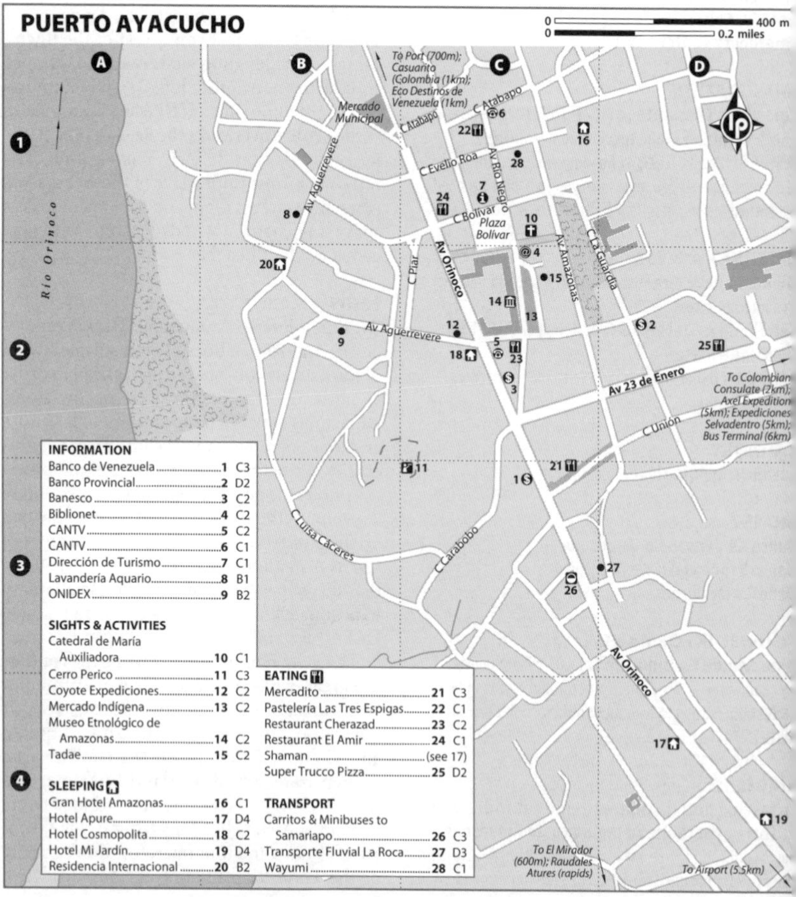

**xpediciones Selvadentro** (☎ 414-7458, 414-487-810; www.selvadentro.com; Vía Alto Carinagua) Long, dventurous trips to distant destinations aboard the *uana*, its 17m-long comfortable catamaran with toilet nd kitchen, personally guided by the experienced manger Lucho Navarro. The office is 5km east of the center. he excellent website gives a great run down.

**adae** (☎ 521-4882, 0414-486-5923; tadaevenezuela@otmail.com; Av Río Negro) Apart from the staple Autana nd Cuao tours, this highly recommended company offers afting on the Raudales Atures.

## leeping

**esidencia Internacional** (☎ 521-0242; Av Aguerrevere; s ith fan/air-con BsF80/100, d/tr/q with air-con BsF100/150/250; P ✱) This friendly, family-operated place on quiet residential street has a rainbow palette f 20 simple rooms arrayed along a long courtard. Borrow a candle and wait out the frequent ity power outages on the rooftop terrace.

**Hotel Mi Jardín** (☎/fax 521-4647; Av Orinoco; s&d/tr sF140/200; P ✱) South of the center, this welllesigned five-story hotel has 66 rooms with vindows that catch the breeze and take in views f nearby hills. Enjoy the night air in the openir courtyard crawling with bougainvillea.

**Hotel Apure** (☎ 521-4443; fax 521-0049; Av Orinoco; s&d/ BsF140/200; P ✱) Slightly sterile but spotlessly lean, the Apure has 17 good-sized rooms with ir-con and cable TV. Comfy lounges and a ramatic wooden entryway add nice touches, nd the tasca restaurant downstairs (see right) s wonderful and convenient.

**Hotel Cosmopolita** (☎ 521-3037; Av Orinoco; d sF180-210, ste BsF210; P ✱) A central if somewhat bland midrange option, it offers three loors of comfortable executive-style rooms vith phones, TVs fridges.

**Gran Hotel Amazonas** (☎ 809-0099, 521-5633; cnr Avs velio Roa & Amazonas; s/d/tr BsF180/250/280; P ✱ ) Puerto Ayacucho's finest, the Gran Amazonas vas partially remodeled in 2008 and now has 5 rooms, all painted in tasteful tropical colors, vith refrigerators, cable and good bathrooms. To top it all, there's a large pool and a good estaurant, though no internet access.

## ating

**asterlería Las Tres Espigas** (Av Río Negro; pastries BsF3; 6am-8pm Mon-Sat, 6am-noon Sun) Four powerful ir-conditioners keep you cool as you recharge n strong coffee and morning pastries.

**Restaurant Cherazad** (cnr Avs Aguerrevere & Río Negro; ains BsF25-40) One of the best restaurants in own, Cherazad provides a sizeable choice of pasta, steaks and fish, plus Middle Eastern dishes and pizza (from BsF10).

**Super Trucco Pizza** (☎ 521-4721; Av 23 de Enero; pizza BsF25-65; 4-10:30pm Wed-Mon) A small fan-cooled patio eatery set back from the road, it makes calzones, burgers and delicious pizza.

**Restaurant El Amir** (Av Orinoco; sandwiches BsF17, mains BsF33-55) Serving decent falafels, this local favorite has plastic tables and chairs a reliably surly waitress.

**Shaman** (☎ 521-3569; Hotel Apure, Av Orinoco; mains BsF65-70; noon-10:30pm Mon- Weds, until 11pm Thu-Sat) The restaurant of the Hotel Apure is also one of the best in town, serving up local specialties including river fish in Amazon curry, and *buñuelos* (fritters) of cassava with a sauce made from *tupiro* (a fruit similar to passion fruit). For the less adventurous there are also more familiar dishes such as a range of pastas and meat grills.

For an inexpensive meal or a quick empanada fix, duck into the **Mercadito** (Av Orinoco), or visit one of the basic *criollo* eateries next door on the Av Amazonas.

## Getting There & Away

### TO COLOMBIA

From Puerto Ayacucho, the nearest large Colombian town, Puerto Carreño, is accessible via El Burro, a Venezuelan village 90km to the north, at the confluence of the Meta and Orinoco Rivers. Take a San Fernando–bound bus and get off at the wharf in El Burro, where traffic loads on ferries to cross the Río Orinoco north to Puerto Páez. Catch a *lancha* across the Río Meta to Puerto Carreño (BsF10); boats runs regularly until about 6pm. Remember to get an exit stamp in your passport at ONIDEX in Puerto Ayacucho before setting off.

In the small town of Puerto Carreño, go to the DAS office (Colombian immigration), for an entry stamp in your passport. The office is located on Av Orinoco in front of the Casa de la Cultura. A number of shops will change bolívars to pesos.

**Satena** (www.satena.com) has two flights per week from Puerto Carreño to Bogotá. Buses go only in the dry season, roughly from mid-December to mid-March, but they are not recommended because of the continued presence of guerrillas in the region.

### TO BRAZIL

Take a flight from Puerto Ayacucho south to San Carlos de Río Negro, from where irregular

**INDIGENOUS AMAZONAS: DO NOT DISTURB**

In order to protect indigenous land and culture, most of Amazonas is off limits to tourism. Europeans first entered Amazonas during the colonial period, and missionaries went to great (and often violent) lengths to convert the local people, pressing many into forced labor. And during the regional gold rush of the 1980s, mining prospectors trespassed onto indigenous lands, bringing disease and environmental damage.

Based on this history, a 1989 law designated eight permissible tourism routes within Amazonas. Outside of these areas, visitors must obtain a government permit, in addition to consent from specific indigenous communities to be visited or affected.

These routes are:

- El Burro – Puerto Ayacucho – Samariapo (northwest)
- Samariapo – San Fernando de Atabapo (northwest)
- San Fernando de Atabapo – Yavita – Maroa (central west)
- San Fernando de Atabapo – San Antonio – La Esmeralda (central/west)
- The mouth of the Río Ventuari (in the Río Orinoco) – Tencua (north/northeast)
- The Río Manapiare valley (north central)
- Río Guainía – Río Negro (Maroa – San Carlos de Río Negro – San Simón del Cocuy; southwest)
- The Brazo Casiquiare from Tamatama to the Río Negro (central/southwest)

However, Amazonas is a vast region, which makes enforcement and monitoring difficult.

boats will take you to San Simón de Cocuy, on the border. From here take a bus to São Gabriel da Cachoeira (Brazil) and continue by boat down the Río Negro to Manaus (three boats per week). Most of Puerto Ayacucho's tour companies can tailor a tour that concludes in San Carlos de Río Negro, or even escort you to São Gabriel.

### Air

The airport is 6km southeast of town; taxis charge BsF15 to get there. Conviasa handles flights to Caracas (BsF250) every day but Saturday. One small local carrier, **Wayumi** (☎ 521-0635; Calle Evelio Roa), operates scheduled and charter flights within Amazonas to a few smaller destinations.

### Boat

**Transporte Fluvial La Roca** (☎ 809-1595; Pasaje Orinoco, Centro Comercial Rapagna, Av Orinoco) runs a daily 6am service to San Fernando de Atabapo (BsF60, 2½ hours) on a 28-person boat. The Sunday service costs an extra BsF5 per ticket.

### Bus

The bus terminal sits 6km east of the center, on the outskirts of town. City buses go there from Av 23 de Enero, or take a taxi (BsF15). Eight buses a day link Puerto Ayacucho to Ciudad Bolívar (BsF55 to BsF70, 10 to 1 hours, 728km). There are a few mornin departures and one night bus daily to Sa Fernando de Apure (BsF60, seven hour 299km), from where you can connect wit buses to Caracas, Maracay, Valencia, Barina and San Cristóbal.

## AROUND PUERTO AYACUCHO

The best known and most commonly visite tepui in Amazonas is **Cerro Autana**, about 80k south of Puerto Ayacucho. It is the sacre mountain of the Piaroa peoples, who conside it the birthplace of the universe. From on side the tepui looks like a gigantic tree trun growing 700m above the surrounding plain (1208m above sea level). About 200m belo the top is the mouth of an enormous cav system, with a labyrinth that passes all th way through the tepui.

Another massive rock called the **Piedra Pintad** boasts pre-Columbian petroglyphs carved hig above the ground in a virtually inaccessib place. They include a 40m-long serpent and 10m-long centipede. From Puerto Ayacuch take the Ruta 17 bus from Av Orinoco to th village of Comunidad Pintao, 17km south the city on the Samariapo road, and then tak a side road left (east) for 3km. The monumen is a 10-minute walk from the village.

# Directory

CONTENTS



## ACCOMMODATIONS

Hotels are not hard to come by in Venezuela and there are budget and midrange options in most towns (though Caracas is conspicuously short on quality budget accommodations). Popular tourist areas like Isla de Margarita and Canaima can become quite full on major holidays, but it is almost always possible to find a vacant room. Campgrounds are rare, but camping on the beach is popular – just be cautious and don't leave your tent unattended. Venezuela has almost no youth hostels.

Places to stay can legally charge a 16% VAT (value-added tax) on top of the room price, though few budget hotels or posadas (small, family-run guesthouses) actually do it. The prices listed in this book have included this tax already. Most top-end hotels will accept payment by credit card, but this is rarely an option in budget places so make sure you have cash.

Hotels in the popular holiday destinations increase their rates during holiday periods (see p271). On the other hand, in the slow season it's possible to bargain, both in the budget and five-star hotels.

### PRACTICALITIES

- Venezuela uses the metric system for weights and measures.
- Electrical current is 110V, 60 cycles AC throughout the country. Plugs are the US type (with two flat prongs).
- The two leading Caracas newspapers, *El Universal* and *El Nacional,* have country-wide distribution; both have reasonable coverage of national and international affairs.
- Many hotels have cable TV and English-language stations.
- Radio Nacional de Venezuela (RNV) is the government-operated national radio station, heard on several dials throughout the country. The news-only Radio Caracas Radio (RCR; 750am) is perhaps the most storied national station, at odds with the government on and off throughout the years.

### Budget

In this book, budget category generally covers places where a double room costs about BsF150 or less (this rises to about BsF200 in areas like Caracas and Gran Roque). Budget places to stay have a variety of names, such as *hotel, residencia, hospedaje,* posada and *pensión*. The last two are meant to be small, family-run guesthouses as well. Budget countryside *campamentos* (literally 'camps') can be anything from a rustic shelter with a few hammocks to private rooms and bathrooms.

Budget hotels tend to be grouped together in certain areas, usually around the market and bus terminal and in the backstreets of the city center. Most of the cheapies have a private bathroom, which includes a toilet and shower. Venezuelans love TV, so most budget hotels provide TVs in the rooms. As most of the country lies in the lowland tropics, rooms have either a fan or air-con, but there's no hot water.

Few budget hotels have single or twin rooms, but many do have *matrimoniales* (rooms with a double bed intended for couples). This type of room usually costs the same for one person as for two, so traveling as a couple significantly reduces the cost of accommodations. Single travelers are at a disadvantage.

Many cheap hotels double as 'love hotels' (that rent rooms by the hour), and it may be impossible to avoid staying in one from time to time.

### Midrange

In this guide, midrange covers the places where double rooms and/or *matrimoniales* generally cost between BsF200 and BsF400.

Many of the midrange hotels nestle conveniently in city centers – you'll often find a few of them in the environs of the local Plaza Bolívar. Some of them can be booked online and paid for by credit card.

Although sometimes lacking in character, midrange hotels usually provide better rooms and more facilities than budget establishments, and virtually every room will have a TV, often with cable. They will almost always have private bathrooms and air-con.

Midrange hotels in tourism destinations with a lower number of accommodations, such as Canaima or Los Roques, or those in Caracas, can have prices on par with top-end hotels in the rest of Venezuela.

### Top End

Any hotel with double rooms costing BsF400 or more is considered top end. By and large, top-end hotels are outside downtown areas, in greener and wealthier residential suburbs sometimes quite a way from the center.

Standards of these hotels vary, but you can expect central air-con, hot water, a reception desk open around the clock; and proper facilities to safeguard guests' valuables. An increasing number of these hotels have wi-fi/internet connections in rooms or in a business center and you can usually book these hotels online.

Prices vary greatly and don't always reflect quality. You can normally grab quite a good double with facilities for somewhere between BsF300 and BsF500, except in Caracas and Isla de Margarita, where prices are generally higher. Los Roques also has higher prices but due to development restrictions (it's in national parkland), there are no five-star accommodations – though the bill might look like it comes from a world-class hotel. Only Caracas and Isla de Margarita, and to a lesser extent Puerto La Cruz and Maracaibo, have a choice of five-star hotels. Sometimes top-end hotels have much lower weekend rates.

## ACTIVITIES

Venezuela has much to offer those who love the great outdoors. Mérida (p153), in particular, is known as Venezuela's adventure-sports capital.

### Fishing

Los Roques (p88) is renowned as one of the world's finest areas for game fishing, particularly for bonefish. You can also go piranha fishing in the *hatos* (large cattle ranches typical of Los Llanos; p182) and trout fishing in the mountain lakes around Mérida.

### Hiking & Trekking

Many of Venezuela's 40-odd national parks provide a choice of walks ranging from easy, well-signposted trails to wild jungle paths. Parque Nacional El Ávila (p82), near Caracas, offers some of the best easy walking trails, while Mérida's surrounds (p155) offer fabulous opportunities for high-mountain trekking. Other hiking possibilities include Parque Nacional Guatopo (p93), Parque Nacional Henri Pittier (p101), Sierra de San Luis (p127), Parque Nacional Península de Paria (p225) and – one of the most adventurous and fascinating treks – to the top of Roraima (p253) and the alternative Auyantepui route (p248) jaunt to the top of Angel Falls (Salto Ángel) via Jimmie Angel's crash site.

### Mountain Biking

The region around Mérida is excellent for mountain biking, and the tour operators in the city organize biking trips and rent bikes (see p157).

### Paragliding

Mérida (p155) is the best place in Venezuela to go paragliding, though you can also now go in Gran Sabana (p257). Double gliders are available, so even greenhorns can try this breathtaking experience.

### Rafting & Canyoning

Rafting trips are run on some Andean rivers (arranged in Mérida; p157) and in the Parque Nacional Mochima (arranged in Mochima; p213). There are new rafting opportunities opening in the Amazonas region, too (ask travel agencies in Puerto Ayacucho; p259). The Mérida region is also the home of canyoning.

### Snorkeling & Scuba Diving

Venezuela has excellent snorkeling and scuba diving all over its coast. The Archipiélago Los Roques (p88) is the most famous areas, but there is also excellent snorkeling and diving around the islands closer to the mainland, including in Parque Nacional Mochima (p211) and Parque Nacional Morrocoy (p129).

### Wildlife- & Bird-Watching

Los Llanos is one of the best regions to see wild animals, including caimans, capybaras (aquatic rodents), anacondas, anteaters and birds. Wildlife safaris are organized from the *hatos* (p182) and from Mérida (p158). If you are particularly interested in bird-watching, consider Parque Nacional Henri Pittier (p101), Parque Nacional Yacambú and the Orinoco Delta (p231 ). There are also some good bird-watching spots around Mérida (p158).

Serious birdwatchers and enthusiasts will want to pop into **Colección Ornitológica Phelps** (Map p63; ☎ 0212-761-5631; www.fundacionwhphelps.org; Blvd de Sabana Grande, Edif Gran Sabana, Piso 3; 🕒 8am-4pm Mon-Fri) in Caracas, an extensive research library that is also home to an astonishing 80,000 different taxidermies of birds, some dating back to 1890.

### Windsurfing & Kitesurfing

Venezuela has some windsurfing and kitesurfing areas of international reputation, including Adícora (p126) and El Yaque (p207). There is also fine windsurfing at Los Roques (p88).

## BUSINESS HOURS

Fixed business hours may exist theoretically in Venezuela, but in practice opening and closing hours are relatively fluid. The working day is supposedly eight hours, from 8am to noon and 2pm to 6pm, Monday to Friday, but many businesses work shorter hours. Almost all offices, including tourist offices, are closed on Saturday and Sunday.

Usual shopping hours are 9am to 6pm or 7pm weekdays, and a half-day on Saturday (9am to 1pm). Many shops close for lunch but some work without a lunchtime break. Restaurants normally open from around noon to 9pm or 11pm, but many are closed on Sunday.

Most museums are open on Sunday but closed on Monday.

For opening hours of banks, post offices, telephone centers and internet cafes, see the respective sections in this chapter (for banks, see Money, p271).

## CHILDREN

Very few foreigners travel with children in Venezuela, but any visiting parents will easily find plenty of local companions for their kids. Venezuelan culture is very family oriented and children will likely be welcomed in most locations.

Children enjoy numerous privileges on local transportation and in accommodations and entertainment. Age limits for discounts or freebies vary from place to place, but are rarely rigidly enforced. Officially children can ride free on buses and the Caracas metro if they don't occupy a separate seat.

For more comprehensive advice on traveling with children, get Lonely Planet's *Travel with Children* by Brigitte Barta et al.

## CLIMATE CHARTS

See p13 for general information about climate. Venezuela is close to the equator, so average temperatures vary little throughout the year. They do, however, change with altitude, dropping about 3°F with every 1000m increase. Since over 90% of Venezuela lies below 1000m, you'll experience temperatures between 70°F (21°C) and 85°F (30°C) in most places. The Andean and coastal mountain ranges have more moderate temperatures.

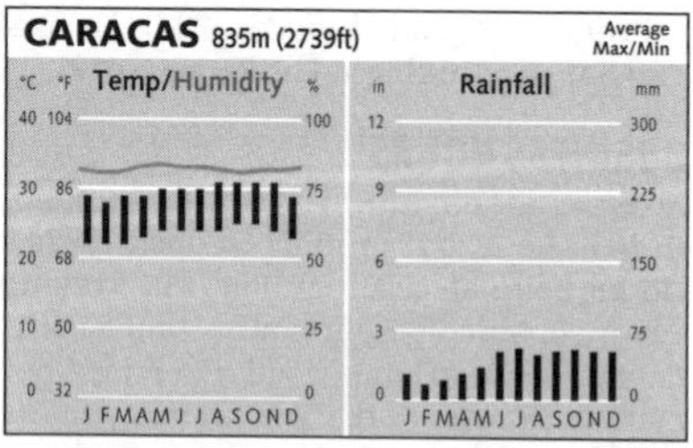


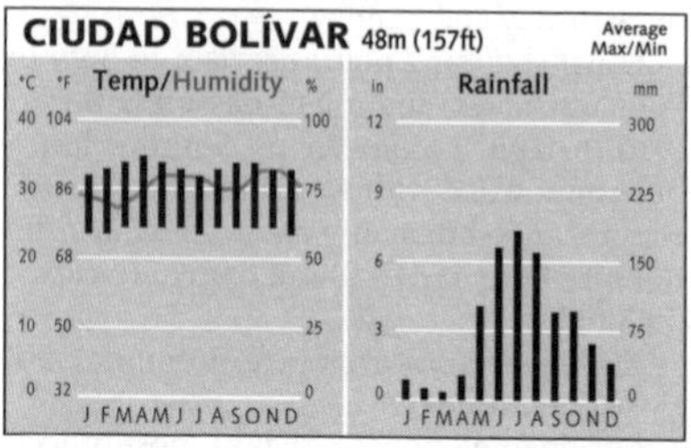


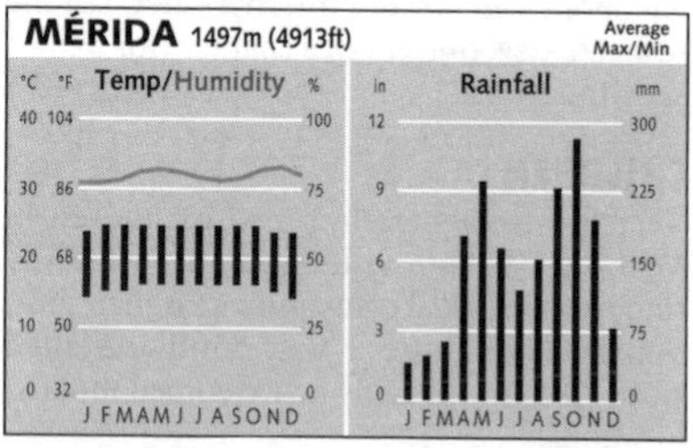


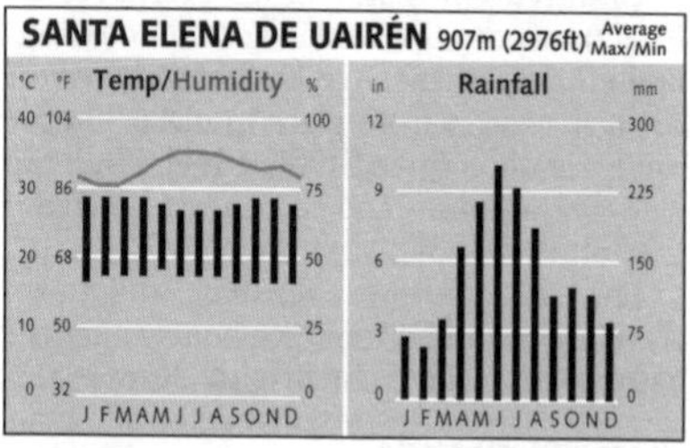


## CUSTOMS

Customs regulations don't differ much from those in other South American countries (namely, 25 cigars and 200 cigarettes, two bottles of alcohol, four bottles of perfume and gifts to the value of US$1000). You are allowed to bring in personal belongings and presents you intend to give to Venezuelan residents, as well as personal and professional camera gear, camping equipment, sports accessories, a personal computer and the like.

According to Venezuelan law, possession, trafficking and consumption of drugs are all serious offenses subject to heavy penalties. The government is trying to stem the flow of drug trafficking from neighboring countries. There are random searches of vehicles and buses inside the borders, too.

## DANGERS & ANNOYANCES

Venezuela on the whole is a somewhat safe place to travel, with notable digressions in Caracas and other large urban areas. However, theft, robbery, kidnapping and common crime are on the increase, particularly in major cities. Caracas is one of the most dangerous capitals in the Americas, and you should take care while strolling around the streets, particularly at night (see p56).

The most common methods of theft are snatching your daypack, camera or watch; taking advantage of a moment's inattention to pick up your gear and run away; or pickpocketing. Thieves often work in pairs or groups; one or more will distract you while an accomplice does the deed. Theft from hotel rooms, cars and unattended tents are also potential dangers.

If you can, leave your money and valuables somewhere safe before walking the streets. In practice, it's good to carry a decoy bundle of small notes, around BsF20 to BsF50, ready to hand over in case of an assault; if you don't have anything, robbers can become frustrated and unpredictable.

Armed hold-ups in the cities can occur even in upmarket suburbs. If you are accosted by robbers, it is best to give them what they are after. Don't try to escape or struggle, and don't count on any help from passers-by. There have been reports of armed robbery on remote hiking trails and deserted beaches or even in a few posadas in tourist towns, but they are considerably less frequent. Also be aware of your surroundings when withdrawing cash from an ATM at any time of the day.

When traveling around the country, there are plenty of *alcabalas* (checkpoints), though not all are actually operating. They check the identity documents of passengers, and occasionally the luggage as well. In the cities, police checks are less common, but they do occur (especially in central Caracas), so always have your passport or a photocopy with you.

### COPIES

All important documents (passport, credit cards, travel insurance policy, air tickets, driver's license etc) should be photocopied before you leave home. Leave one copy at home and keep another with you, separate from the originals.

If you don't, you may end up at the police station. Police are not necessarily trustworthy (though many are), so do not blindly accept the demands of these authority figures.

If your passport, valuables or other belongings are stolen, go to the nearest Policía Técnica Judicial (PTJ) office to make a *denuncia* (report). The officer on duty will write a statement according to what you tell them. It should include the description of the events and the list of stolen articles. Pay attention to the wording you use, make sure you include every stolen item and document, and carefully check the statement before signing it to ensure it contains exactly what you've said. They will give you a copy of the statement, which serves as a temporary identity document, and you will need to present it to your insurer in order to make a claim. Don't expect your things to be found, as the police are unlikely to do anything about it.

All said, your biggest dangers are the standard risks of international travel: sunburn, food-borne illness and traffic-related concerns.

## DISCOUNT CARDS

Students and senior citizens can get small discounts on airfares with some domestic carriers and on ferry tickets to Isla de Margarita, but that's about it. There are no discounts on intercity bus fares, urban transportation or cinema tickets, and most museums have free admission anyway.

## EMBASSIES & CONSULATES IN VENEZUELA

The following embassies are located in Caracas. Consulates are at the same address as the embassies unless otherwise noted. If you can't find your home embassy, check a Caracas phone directory.

**Brazil** (Map p72; ☎ 0212-918-6000; www.embajadabrasil.org.ve; Centro Gerencial Mohedano, Piso 6, cnr Calle Los Chaguaramos & Av Mohedano, La Castellana, Caracas; Ⓜ Chacao); Consulate in Santa Elena de Uairén (Map p256; ☎ 0286-995-1256; Calle Los Castanõs, off Av Perimetral) Consulate in Ciudad Guayana (Map p236; ☎ 0286-961-2995; Edificio Eli-Alti, Oficina 04, Carrera Tocoma, Alta Vista Norte)

**Canada** (Map p72; ☎ 0212-600-3000; www.canadainternational.gc.ca/venezuela; cnr Avs Francisco de Miranda & Sur Altamira, Altamira, Caracas; Ⓜ Altamira) Provides consular assistance to Australians.

**Colombia** (Map p72; ☎ 0212-216-9596; www.consuladocolombiacaracas.com.ve; Torre Credival, cnr 2nd Calle de Campo Alegre & av Francisco de Miranda, Campo Alegre, Caracas; Ⓜ Chacaíto); Consulate in Maracaibo (☎ 0261-792-1483; Av 3Y No 70-16); Consulate in Puerto Ayacucho (☎ 521-0789; Calle Yapacana, Quinta Beatriz)

**France** (Map p72; ☎ 0212-909-6500; www.francia.org.ve; Edificio Embajada de Francia, cnr Calle Madrid & Av La Trinidad, Las Mercedes, Caracas)

**Germany** Consulate (Map p72; ☎ 0212-219-2500; www.caracas.diplo.de; Torre La Castellana, Piso 10, Av Eugenio Mendoza con Calle José Angel Lamas, La Castellana, Caracas; Ⓜ Altamira)

**Guyana** (☎ 0212-977-1158; www.guyana.org/spanish/venezuela_embassy.html; Quinta Roraima, Av El Paseo, Prados del Este, Caracas)

**Ireland** (☎ 0212-951-3645; Torre Clement, Piso 2, Ofc 2A-2B, Av Venezuela, El Rosal, Caracas)

**Italy** Consulate (Map p72; ☎ 0212-212-1104; www.conscaracas.esteri.it; Quinta El Ancla, Av Mohedano btwn 1a & 2a Transversal, La Castellana, Caracas; Ⓜ Chacao)

**Japan** Consulate (Map p72; ☎ 0212-261-8333; www.ve.emb-japan.go.jp/esp; Edificio Bancaracas, Piso 11, Plaza La Castellana, Av San Felipe, La Castellana, Caracas; Ⓜ Altamira)

**Netherlands** Consulate (Map p72; ☎ 0212-276-9300; www.mfa.nl/car; Edificio San Juan, Piso 9, cnr 2a Transversal & Av San Juan Bosco, Altamira, Caracas; Ⓜ Altamira)

**New Zealand** Consulate (☎ 0212-277-7965; Av Francisco de Miranda, C/C Av Libertador, Torre KPMG, Piso 7, Chacao, Caracas)

**Spain** (Map p72; ☎ 0212-263-2855; embespve@correo.mae.es; Quinta Marmolejo, Av Mohedano 64 btwn 1a & 2a Transversal, La Castellana, Caracas)

**Suriname** (Map p72 ; ☎ 0212-261-2724; embsur1@cantv.net; Quinta Los Milagros, 4a Av btwn 7a & 8a Transversal, Altamira, Caracas)

**Trinidad & Tobago** (Map p72 ; ☎ 0212-261-3748; embassytt@cantv.net; No 22-12, Quinta Poshika, 3a Av btwn 6a & 7a Transversal, Altamira, Caracas)

**UK** (Map p72; ☎ 0212-283-8411; http://ukinvenezuela.fco.gov.uk/en; Torre La Castellana, Piso 11, Av Principal de la Castellana, La Castellana, Caracas; Ⓜ Altamira)

**USA** (Map pp52-3; ☎ 0212-975-6411, 975-7811; http://caracas.usembassy.gov; cnr Calle F & Calle Suapure, Colinas del Valle Arriba, Caracas)

**YOUR OWN EMBASSY**

It's important to realize what your own embassy – the embassy of the country of which you are a citizen – can and can't do to help if you get into trouble. Generally speaking, it won't be much help if the trouble you're in is remotely your own fault. Remember that you are bound by the laws of the country you are visiting. Your embassy will not be sympathetic if you end up in jail after committing a crime locally, even if such actions are legal in your own country.

In genuine emergencies you might get some assistance, but only if other channels have been exhausted. For example, if you need to get home urgently, a free ticket home is exceedingly unlikely – the embassy would expect you to have travel insurance. If all your money and documents are stolen, it should assist you with getting a new passport, but a loan for onward travel is out of the question. See also Legal Matters, opposite.

## FESTIVALS & EVENTS

Given the strong Catholic character of Venezuela, many feasts and celebrations follow the Church calendar – Christmas, Carnaval, Easter and Corpus Christi are celebrated all over the country. The religious calendar is dotted with saints' days, and every village and town has its own patron saint and will hold a celebratory feast on that day.

One of Venezuela's most colorful festivals is the Diablos Danzantes (see p93). It's held on Corpus Christi in San Francisco de Yare, located about 70km southeast of Caracas. The ceremony consists of a spectacular parade and the dance of the devils, performed by dancers wearing elaborate masks and costumes.

Cultural events such as festivals of theater, film or classical music are almost exclusively confined to Caracas. Venezuela's main religious and cultural festivals and events are listed on below. See the respective sections for more information.

### JANUARY

**Feria de San Sebastián** Main event of San Cristóbal, taking place in the second half of January (p175).

**Fiesta Patronales de la Divina Pastora** Barquisimeto's major feast, held in mid-January (p135).

**Paradura del Niño** Celebrated for the whole month in Mérida state (p158).

### FEBRUARY/MARCH

**Carnaval** Celebrated throughout the country on the Monday and Tuesday prior to Ash Wednesday; particularly elaborate in Mérida, El Callao and Carúpano.

### MARCH/APRIL

**Festival Internacional de Teatro** Cultural festival held in Caracas on even years.

**Semana Santa** Easter week (the week leading up to Easter Sunday) sees solemn celebrations in the churches all around the country and processions on Maundy Thursday and Good Friday.

### MAY/JUNE

**Festival de los Diablos Danzantes** Colorful dancing devils invade San Francisco de Yare, Chuao and some other villages in the northern-central region on Corpus Christi (60 days after Easter, in May or June; see p93).

### SEPTEMBER

**Fiesta de la Virgen de Coromoto** Major pilgrimage gathering in Guanare on September 8, to honor the anniversary of the Virgin's appearance (p189).

**Fiesta de la Virgen del Valle** Another focus of religious fervor, on September 8 at Valle del Espíritu Santo on Isla de Margarita (p203).

### NOVEMBER

**Feria de la Chinita** Maracaibo's major annual bash, held for a week and culminating with the coronation of Zulia's patron saint on November 18 (p145).

## FOOD

See the Food & Drink chapter (p41) to see what you can eat, where and when. In this guide we have divided eating sections into budget, midrange and top end in major cities such as Caracas. Expect main dishes to cost under BsF40 in a budget eatery, BsF40 to BsF60 in a midranger, and over BsF60 in a top-end place (more so in Caracas and top tourist spots).

## GAY & LESBIAN TRAVELERS

Homosexuality isn't illegal in Venezuela, but the overwhelmingly Catholic society tends to both deny and suppress it. The gay and lesbian movement is at present still very underdeveloped. Caracas has the largest gay and lesbian community and the most open gay life, and is the best place to make contacts and get to know what's going on (see the boxed text, p77). Get as much information there as you can, because elsewhere in Venezuela it can be difficult to contact the gay community.

**Viajando en Ambiente** (www.viajandoenambiente.com.ve) is a recommended GLBT travel agency.

## HOLIDAYS

Keep in mind that Venezuelans usually take holidays over Christmas, Carnaval (several days prior to Ash Wednesday) and Semana Santa (the week before Easter Sunday). In these periods, you'll have to plan ahead, as it can be tricky to find a place to stay in more popular destinations. The upside is that they really come alive with holiday merrymakers.

Official public holidays include:

**Año Nuevo** (New Year's Day) January 1
**Carnaval** Monday and Tuesday prior to Ash Wednesday, February/March.
**Pascua** (Easter) Maundy Thursday and Good Friday, March/April.
**Declaración de Independencia** (Declaration of Independence) April 19
**Labor Day** May 1
**Batalla de Carabobo** (Battle of Carabobo) June 24
**Día de Independencia** (Independence Day) July 5
**Cumpleaños de Bolívar** (Bolívar's Birthday) July 24
**Discovery of America** October 12
**Navidad** (Christmas Day) December 25

## INSURANCE

A travel insurance policy to cover theft, loss and medical problems is a good idea. Some policies specifically exclude 'dangerous activities,' which can include scuba diving, motorcycling, even trekking. Check that the policy covers ambulances or an emergency flight home. See p284 for more details.

## INTERNET ACCESS

Virtually all cities and most towns have cybercafes. An hour of internet access will cost between BsF2 and BsF10, depending on the region, city and particular place. Mérida and Caracas have the most widespread number of cybercafes and some of the best prices. Also note that CANTV and Movistar, the two major local telephone operators (see the Telephone section under each town), often provide internet facilities. The **Infocentro** (www.infocentro.gob.ve) program offers free 30-minute blocks at locations nationwide.

Wireless internet connections are fairly common. Mérida and Caracas offer the best chance of finding a hotel with wi-fi, although it can be found elsewhere.

## LEGAL MATTERS

Venezuelan police are to be treated with respect, but with a healthy dose of caution, too. Cases of police corruption, abuse of power and use of undue force are unfortunately common. Same goes for the military (Guarda Nacional). Do not expect any 'just cause' or 'due process' that may exist in your home country.

Some travelers associate the tropics with open and relaxed drug policy. That is far from the truth in Venezuela. Penalties for trafficking, possessing and using illegal drugs are some of the heaviest in all of Latin America (and probably heavier than in your home country). Soldiers often stop and search travelers or buses on the highways. They are looking for drugs (mainly cocaine) and are known to hand-search every piece of luggage on the bus – even at 3am. It is in your best interest to keep your passport on hand for identification purposes.

Venezuelan prisons are not the most pleasant places you've ever seen. Also be aware that your embassy is of limited help if you get into trouble with the law – foreigners here, as elsewhere, are subject to the laws of the host country.

While your embassy or consulate is the best stop in any emergency, bear in mind that there are some things it cannot do for you. These include getting local laws or regulations waived because you're a foreigner, investigating a crime, providing legal advice or representation in civil or criminal cases, getting you out of jail, and lending you money. An embassy or consulate can, however, issue emergency passports, contact relatives and friends, advise on how to transfer funds, provide lists of reliable local doctors, lawyers and interpreters, and visit you if you've been arrested or jailed.

## MAPS

The best general map of Venezuela (scale 1:1,750,000) is published by International Travel Maps (Canada). Within Venezuela, folded road maps of the country are produced by several local publishers and are available in tourism offices, some hotels and stores that cater to foreign visitors.

## MONEY

In 2008, Venezuela lopped three zeros off its currency and issued new money called *bolívares fuertes* (strong bolívares), abbreviated to

BsF. There are now coins of 1, 5, 10, 12½ and 50 *céntimos* and BsF1, and paper notes of 2, 5, 10, 20, 50 and 100.

However, many people cling to the old ways and will still quote prices in *miles,* or thousands. You may occasionally encounter the old currency (50-, 100- and 500-bolívar coins, and 1000, 2000, 5000 and 10,000 bolívar notes), which is still good. A 100-bolívar coin and 10-*céntimo* coin (and the 500-bolívar and 50-*céntimo*) are worth the same amount; the new coins have the denominations in large type. There's a helpful conversion chart with pictures at www.reconversionbcv.org.ve.

In 2010, the *bolívares fuertes* was significantly devalued, creating a two-tier exchange rate system within Venezuela. See p14 for more information.

Unless you're near the border, it's impossible to get Venezuelan currency before you enter the country.

For information on monetary costs in Venezuela, see p13.

### ATMs & Banks

*Cajeros automáticos* (ATMs) are the easiest way of getting cash, though they use the official exchange rate. ATMs can be found at most major banks and are normally open 24 hours.

Some ATMs will ask you to enter the first or last two digits of your national ID document (referred to as *cédula*) in order to process the transaction.

The usual opening hours for banks are 8:30am to 4pm Monday to Friday, though there are some exceptions to this.

### Black Market

There is a thriving black market for American dollars – and, to a lesser extent, euros – and many people will ask to change currency in airports, bus stations or the center of towns. You can get a much better rate with these money traders, but do so at a higher risk of getting ripped off. Travelers using the black market need to be familiar with current Venezuelan currency before changing money on the black market so as not to come away with bad bills. Almost every tour agency dealing with foreigners will also offer to change your money and this is always the best way to go. On the ground, one of the best places to change money is Santa Elena de Uairén (p257).

Before exchanging money on the black market, talk to in-the-know locals or check websites like www.dollar.nu and www.venezuelafx.blogspot.com for current exchange rates – and thus how much you are being lowballed. See p14 for more info.

### Cash

The usual official place to change your cash is at a *casa de cambio* (an authorized money-exchange office). They exist in most major cities and buy foreign currency (but don't sell it) at the official exchange rate. There are a number of them in Caracas, Puerto La Cruz and Porlamar, but there may be just one or two in other large cities. Italcambio is the biggest and best-known company, with branches all over the country. See p14 before changing money.

US dollars or euros are often accepted by tour operators as payment for tours, and hotels may also accept dollars – though in both situations, discreetly.

### Credit Cards

Visa and MasterCard are the most useful credit cards in Venezuela, though it's important to note that credit card transactions will always be more costly because they are calculated using the official exchange rate. Cards are accepted as a means of payment for goods and services, though many tour operators may refuse payment by credit card or charge 10% more for the service.

### Traveler's Checks

*Casas de cambio* (such as Italcambio) are often the only place that will accept traveler's checks, and will charge a commission of about 3% or more. Some tour operators will accept traveler's checks as payment.

## POST

The postal service is run by **Ipostel** (www.ipostel.gob.ve), which has post offices throughout the country. The usual opening hours are 8am to noon and 1pm to 4:30pm Monday to Friday, with regional variations. Some offices in the main cities may open longer hours and on Saturday. Airmailing a letter up to 20g costs BsF1.60 to anywhere in the Americas, BsF1.90 to Europe or Africa and BsF2.35 to the rest of the world. Sending a package of up to 500g will cost BsF13.44/14 to the Americas and Europe, respectively. The service is unreliable and slow. Airmail to Europe can take up to a month to arrive, if it arrives at all.

Ipostel also handles poste restante (general delivery mail). This service is also slow and not very reliable. Letters sent to Venezuela from abroad take a long time to be delivered and sometimes simply never make it. If you decide to use poste restante, stick to the main offices in major cities.

## SHOPPING

A quick perusal of street stalls in Caracas would lead you to believe that Venezuela sells little more than pirated DVDs and t-shirts with portraits of *reggaetón* stars or Chávez with the tagline: Patria o Muerte (Fatherland or Death). In fact, Venezuela offers varied, good-quality craftwork. It's particularly renowned for its fine basketry, pottery and woodcarving, which differs significantly from region to region. Other attractive crafts include hand-woven hammocks of the Guajiros, papier-mâché devil masks from San Francisco de Yare and woolen ponchos from the Andes.

Try to buy crafts in their region of origin, ideally from the artisans themselves: not only are the crafts more authentic, but they are also cheaper, and the money goes directly to the artisan. If you can't get to the remote communities, shop in the markets in nearby towns. However, don't ignore handicraft shops in the large cities, particularly in Caracas, where you can find the best collections and best-quality crafts from around the country.

If you are interested in local music (*joropo, gaita,* salsa), the Caracas CD shops have the best selection. The price of locally produced CDs ranges from about BsF35 to BsF60.

Venezuela is noted for gold and diamonds, but don't expect to find great bargains everywhere. Possibly the cheapest place to buy gold jewelry is El Callao, but you'll find better quality in Ciudad Bolívar and Caracas.

## SOLO TRAVELERS

While traveling on your own, you need to be more alert to what's going on around you and more cautious about where you go. You also face more potential risks, whether you're walking the city streets or trekking remote mountains. Solo females may face an additional problem of being the target of unwanted attention; see Women Travelers (p275).

Traveling solo is likely to be more expensive, principally due to the higher accommodations costs. Few hotels have single rooms, so you will need to pay for a *matrimonial* or double.

Mérida, Puerto Colombia, Canaima and other major destinations are more accustomed to solo travelers and are generally easier to navigate by yourself.

## TELEPHONE

Venezuela's telephone system is operated by CANTV and is largely automated for both domestic and international connections. All phone numbers in the country are seven digits and area codes are three digits (though, for whatever reason, you will see some domestic airlines with eight digit numbers). A three-minute local call within a city costs about BsF2.25. The cost of long-distance calls is around BsF2.50 per minute, and it doesn't depend on the distance, so calling the neighboring city costs the same as calling anywhere within the country.

### Area Codes

Area codes are listed under the headings of the relevant destinations throughout this guide.

The country code for Venezuela is ☎ 58. To call Venezuela from abroad, dial the international access code of the country you're calling from, Venezuela's code (☎ 58), the area code (drop the initial 0) and the local phone number.

If making an international call from Venezuela, dial the international access code (00), the country code, the area code (without the initial 0), then the local number.

### Cell Phones

Those who plan to stay a longer period of time in Venezuela may opt to purchase a cell phone or buy a local SIM card (around BsF25; passport required) for their own handset. The malls all have numerous competing cell-phone offices. Cell-phone reception is good and services are very cheap. **Movistar** (numbers begin with ☎ 0414/0425) is the major operator of mobile telephone services, followed by the government-subsidized **Movilnet** (☎ 0416/0424) and **Digitel** (☎ 0412). Venezuela has one of the highest cell-phone-per-capita rates in Latin America. Note that calling cellular numbers is expensive and eats quickly into a phonecard. Prepaid cell phone cards are sold by the second, not the minute. A 3000-second top-up on a prepaid cell phone can last for weeks.

### Public Phones

Shiny metallic CANTV public phones are everywhere, though only about half of them work. Phone cards for these phones come in values of BsF2 and BsF5 and can be purchased at most stores and kiosks. The latter nets about 30 minutes of local calls to a fixed line, and a mere six to cell phones.

During the day, entrepreneurs set up small tables on street corners with a few cell phones chained to the tabletop. They charge by the minute for calls. This can be more convenient than using a card in a public phone, but can get expensive unless you are calling a domestic number.

### Phone Centers

Call centers (owned by Movistar, the nationalized CANTV or independents known as *centros de comunicaciones*) are the best for international calls. In large cities, these centers are everywhere and are normally open from about 7am to 9pm daily.

During the day entrepreneurs set up small tables at street corners and bus terminals with a few mobile phones and charge by the minute for calls. For domestic calls, this can be more convenient (but usually noisier) than seeking out a call center, and you can also send text messages.

Sample per-minute phone rates of CANTV are BsF0.26 to the USA, BsF0.72 to the UK and BsF1.26 to Australia.

## TIME

As of late 2007, Venezuela has a unique time zone and is now 4.5 hours behind Greenwich Mean Time. There's no daylight-saving time.

## TOILETS

Since there are no self-contained public toilets in Venezuela, use the toilets of establishments such as restaurants, hotels, museums, shopping malls and bus terminals. The most common word for toilet is *baño*. Men's toilets will usually bear a label reading *señores* or *caballeros*, whereas women's toilets will be marked *señoras* or *damas*.

You can't rely on bathrooms being stocked with toilet paper (particularly in more remote areas), so it is worth carrying a small stash with you. Some toilets charge fees (normally not exceeding BsF1), for which you receive a piece of toilet paper. If it doesn't seem like enough, don't hesitate to ask for more.

Except for toilets in upmarket establishments, the plumbing might not be of a standard you are accustomed to. The tubes are narrow and water pressure is weak, so toilets can't cope with toilet paper. A wastebasket is normally provided.

## TOURIST INFORMATION

**Inatur** (Instituto Autónomo de Turismo de Aragua; www.inatur.gob.ve) is the Caracas-based government agency that promotes tourism and provides tourist information; see p55 for contact details. Outside the capital, tourist information is handled by regional tourist bodies, which have offices in their respective state capitals and in some other cities. Some are better than others, but on the whole they lack city maps and brochures, and the staff members rarely speak English.

## TRAVELERS WITH DISABILITIES

Venezuela offers very little to people with disabilities. Wheelchair ramps are available only at a few upmarket hotels and restaurants, and public transportation will be a challenge for any person with mobility limitations. Hardly any office, museum or bank provides special facilities for disabled persons, and wheelchair-accessible toilets are virtually nonexistent.

## VISAS

Nationals of the US, Canada, Australia, New Zealand, Japan, the UK and most of Western and Scandinavian Europe don't need a visa to enter Venezuela; a free Tarjeta de Ingreso (Tourist Card, officially denominated DEX-2) is all that is required. The card is normally valid for 90 days (unless immigration officers note on the card a shorter period). Extensions beyond this had been discontinued at the time of research. Airlines flying into Venezuela provide these cards to passengers while on the plane. Overland visitors bearing passports of the countries listed above can obtain the card from the immigration official at the border crossing (it's best to check this beforehand at the nearest consulate). Of course, visa requirements are particularly subject to change; see loneyplanet.com for more up-to-date visa info.

On entering Venezuela, your passport and tourist card will be stamped (make sure this happens) by Dirección de Identificación y Extranjería (DIEX or DEX) border officials. Keep the yellow copy of the tourist card while traveling in Venezuela (you may be asked for it during passport controls), and return it to immigration officials when leaving the country (although not all are interested in collecting the cards).

## VOLUNTEERING

It is difficult to find volunteer opportunities from outside the country, partially because many organizations don't respond to queries. The government literacy program, **Mission Robinson** (www.misionrobinson.me.gob.ve), is one option for Spanish-speakers. For those who want to change the world, try the **Prout Research Institute** (www.priven.org), dedicated to researching and discovering the world's next great socioeconomic model. In Santa Elena de Uairén, grassroots NGO **Aldeas de Paz** (☎ 0289-416-0718; www.aldeasdepaz.org; Lomas de Piedra Canaima) runs year-round community development volunteer programs within the local and Pemón indigenous communities.

## WOMEN TRAVELERS

Like most of Latin America, Venezuela is very much a man's country. Women travelers will attract more curiosity, attention and advances from local men than they would from men in North America or Western Europe. Local males will quickly pick you out in a crowd and are not shy to show their admiration through whistles, endearments and flirtatious comments. These advances are usually lighthearted, though they can seem rude (or actually be rude).

The best way to deal with unwanted attention is simply to ignore it. Dressing modestly will make you less conspicuous to the local piranhas. Even though Venezuelan women wear revealing clothes, they are a lot more aware of the culture and the safety of their surroundings. A cheap, fake wedding band is also a good trick to quickly end awkward chat-ups.

## WORK

Travelers looking for a paid job in Venezuela will almost always be disappointed. The economy is not strong enough to take on foreigners for casual jobs. Qualified English teachers have the best chance of getting a job, yet it's still hard to arrange work once in the country. Try English-teaching institutions such as the **British Council** (Map p63; ☎ 0212-952-9965; www.britishcouncil.org; Torre Credicard, 3rd fl, Av Principal de El Bosque, Chacaíto, Caracas), private language schools or linguistic departments at universities. Note that you need a work visa to work legally in Venezuela. Sure, it's possible to get a job without a visa, but you run the risk of exploitation or refusal to pay by your employer – with no legal recourse.

# Transportation

CONTENTS



# GETTING THERE & AWAY

## ENTERING THE COUNTRY

Entering Venezuela by air, sea or land is pretty straightforward. Most visitors from Western countries don't need a visa, just a *tarjeta de ingreso* (tourist card), officially known as DEX-2, which is free and will be provided upon entry to the country. Fill the card in and present it, along with your valid passport, to the immigration officials, who will then stamp the passport and card. At the time of writing, visa extensions had been discontinued. For information on visas, see p274.

Upon departure, make sure they put an exit stamp in your passport; without one you may have problems entering Venezuela next time. Travelers departing Venezuela by air are charged a BsF162.50 *impuesto de salida* (departure tax) as well as international air departure tax of BsF162.50. Land crossings charge a BsF55 *impuesto de salida,* though the Venezuela–Brazilian border in Santa Elena de Uairén wasn't charging this at the time of writing for one of three reasons: it is exempted as a Tax-Free Zone; all foreign tourists who have stayed in the country for more than seven days are exempted from exit taxes according to a new 2008 tourism law; or the Ministry of Tourism just 'doesn't know why.' (Straight answers are not Venezuela's strong suit.)

## AIR

### Airports & Airlines

Most international visitors arrive at Caracas' **Aeropuerto Internacional 'Simón Bolívar'** (www.aeropuerto-maiquetia.com.ve) in Maiquetía, 26km from Caracas. Venezuela has several other airports servicing international flights, but these change frequently and unexpectedly. Isla de Margarita's airport is used by charter flights bringing international package tourists, but few independent travelers fly in here.

Following is a non-inclusive list of national and international airlines flying to/from Venezuela. Of the local airlines, Santa Barbara has the widest international coverage, serving Funchal (Portugal), Madrid, Miami, Panama, Quito and Tenerife.

**Aerolíneas Argentinas** (ARG; Map p72; ☎ 0212-951-3005; www.aerolineas.com.ar)
**Air Canada** (ACA; Map p72; ☎ 0800-100-4918; www.aircanada.ca)
**Air France** (AFR; Map p72; ☎ 0212-208-7200; www.airfrance.com)
**Alitalia** (AZA; Map p72; ☎ 0212-312-5000; www.alitalia.it)
**American Airlines** (AAL; Map p72; ☎ 0212-209-8000; www.aa.com)
**Aserca** (OCA; Map p72; 0212-905-5333; www.asercaairlines.com)
**Avianca** (AVA; Map p72; ☎ 0800-648-8356; www.avianca.com)
**Avior** (ROI; Map p72; ☎ 0501-284-67737, 0212-953-3221; www.avior.com.ve)
**Caribbean** (BWA; Map p63; ☎ 0212-762-4389; www.caribbean-airlines.com)
**Continental Airlines** (COA; Map p72; ☎ 0800-826-7200; www.continental.com)

**THINGS CHANGE**

The information in this chapter is particularly vulnerable to change. Check directly with the airline or a travel agent to make sure you understand how a fare (and ticket you may buy) works and be aware of the security requirements for international travel. Shop carefully. The details given in this chapter should be regarded as pointers and are not a substitute for your own careful, up-to-date research.

**onviasa** (VCV; Map pp58-9; ☎ 0500-2668-4272; www.onviasa.aero)
**opa Airlines** (CMP; Map p72; ☎ 0800-826-7200; www.copaair.com)
**ubana** (CUB; Map p72; ☎ 0212-793-6319; www.ubana.cu)
**elta Airlines** (DAL; Map p72; ☎ 0800-100-3453; www.delta.com)
**iol/Varig** (GLO; Map pp52-3; ☎ 0212-202-2800; www.oegol.com.br)
**beria** (IBE; Map p72; ☎ 0212-284-0020; www.iberia.om)
**LM** (KLM; Map p72; ☎ 0212-208-7200; www.klm.com)
**AN** (LAN; Map p72; ☎ 0212-267-9526; www.lan.com)
**ufthansa** (DLH; Map p72; ☎ 0212-210-2188; www.ufthansa.com)
**lexicana** (MXA; Map p72; ☎ 0212-285-2132; www.nexicana.com)
**anta Bárbara** (BBR; Map p72; ☎ 0800-865-2636; www.sbairlines.com)
**ACA/LACSA** (TAI; Map p72; ☎ 800-000-8222; www.aca.com)
**am** (TAM; Map p72; ☎ 0800-100-8586; www.tam.om.br)
**AP Air Portugal** (TAP; Map pp52-3; ☎ 0212-951-108; www.flytap.com)

## Tickets

Venezuela is not a good place to buy international air tickets – avoid arriving on a one-way icket as you may be disappointed: airfares to Europe and Australia are high, and there are virtually no discounted tickets available. It's always better to have the whole route covered by a ticket bought at home.

Just about every travel agency in Caracas will sell you tickets for flights with most airlines and, consequently, will know which is the cheapest carrier on a particular route. When it comes to more complex intercontinental connections, however, not all agencies are experts, so shop around or use online ources.

It may be cheapest to fly to Miami and take one of the relatively cheap transatlantic flights to Europe (eg with United Airlines). Some Caracas travel agencies will sell combined tickets for the whole route.

## Australia & New Zealand

The shortest route between Australia and South America goes over the South Pole. You can fly with either LAN to Santiago or Aerolíneas Argentinas to Buenos Aires. Both carriers fly from Sydney through Auckland and have connections to Caracas. Expect to pay between A$2200 and A$2800 for the Sydney–Caracas roundtrip flight, depending on the length of stay and the season. The Auckland–Caracas fare will be only marginally lower.

Another possible route goes via Los Angeles and Miami, and will cost much the same as those via Chile or Argentina, though you will probably need to change planes twice, in both LA and Miami. You can also fly to Venezuela through Europe – it's the longest route, but not as absurd as it may sound. You can stop in London, Amsterdam or Paris, and the total fare may be comparable to or even lower than traveling via Los Angeles. Finally, you can buy a RTW (round-the-world) ticket that includes South America, or at least Miami, from where you can make a side trip to Venezuela.

### DEPARTURE TAX

Venezuela's international *tasa aeroportuaria* (airport tax) is BsF162.50. On top of it, an additional *impuesto de salida* (exit tax) of BsF162.50 must be paid by all visitors and is *usually* included in the price of your ticket. The taxes are payable in cash (BsF or USD) or domestic credit card. Children over the age of two must pay fees the same as adults. Check the Caracas airport website (www.aeropuerto-maiquetia.com.ve) for likely increases.

## Canada

Air Canada flies from Toronto to Caracas. Tickets range from C$500 to C$1400 depending on time of year.

## Caribbean

### NETHERLAND ANTILLES

Avior and Venezolana fly from Caracas to Aruba (BsF760 to BsF845 roundtrip). Venozolana flies direct from Maracaibo to Aruba. Avior and Santa Barbara fly from Curaçao.

### TRINIDAD

Caribbean Airlines flies daily between Port of Spain and Caracas (BsF512 one way, BsF918 roundtrip). Conviasa flies between Porlamar and Port of Spain (BsF439 one way, BsF520 roundtrip).

## South America

### BRAZIL

Gol/Varig flies direct from Sáo Paulo to Caracas. TAM (as well as Gol/Varig) also offers the same route via Manaus. Fares are usually around R$900 one way and R$1200 to R$1400 roundtrip.

### COLOMBIA

Avianca flies Bogotá and Caracas (roundtrip from COL$1,230,110). Most flights between the two countries require you to fly through Caracas or Bogotá, regardless of whether this takes you out of your way. If you have sufficient time and are already traveling near the border it's much more affordable to cross the border by land and then take a domestic flight from the first major border city to your desired destination.

### ECUADOR

Santa Barbara flies from Quito to Caracas for around US$350 roundtrip.

### GUYANA

There are no direct flights between Venezuela and Guyana. From Caracas, you must fly via Port of Spain (Trinidad) with Caribbean Airlines (BsF870 one way, BsF1447 roundtrip).

## UK

At the time of writing, there are currently no direct flights between London and Caracas. Discounted connecting flight options include via Madrid on Iberia Airlines, Paris on Air France and Miami on American. Fares hover around UK£450 to UK£800 for a roundtrip.

Recommended ticket agencies:

**Austral Tours** (www.latinamerica.co.uk)

**Journey Latin America** (☎ 020-8747-3108; www.journeylatinamerica.co.uk)

**South American Experience** (www.southamericanexperience.co.uk)

## USA

The major US gateway for Venezuela is Miami, from where several airline carriers, including American Airlines, Avior and Santa Barbara, fly direct to Caracas. Avianca, Caribbean, Copa, LAN, Mexicana and TACA all offer connecting flights. Roundtrip tickets average from around US$700, but Santa Barbara may offer cut-down airfares. Other US cities serving direct flights to Caracas include Atlanta (Delta Airlines) and Houston (Continental Airlines). A dependable agency to try is **eXito** (www.exitotravel.com).

### CLIMATE CHANGE & TRAVEL

Climate change is a serious threat to the ecosystems that humans rely upon, and air travel is the fastest-growing contributor to the problem. Lonely Planet regards travel, overall, as a global benefit, but believes we all have a responsibility to limit our personal impact on global warming.

#### Flying & Climate Change

Pretty much every form of motor travel generates $CO_2$ (the main cause of human-induced climate change) but planes are far and away the worst offenders, not just because of the sheer distances they allow us to travel, but because they release greenhouse gases high into the atmosphere. The statistics are frightening: two people taking a return flight between Europe and the US will contribute as much to climate change as an average household's gas and electricity consumption over a whole year.

#### Carbon Offset Schemes

Climatecare.org and other websites use 'carbon calculators' that allow jetsetters to offset the greenhouse gases they are responsible for with contributions to energy-saving projects and other climate-friendly initiatives in the developing world – including projects in India, Honduras, Kazakhstan and Uganda.

Lonely Planet, together with Rough Guides and other concerned partners in the travel industry, supports the carbon offset scheme run by climatecare.org. Lonely Planet offsets all of its staff and author travel.

For more information check out our website: www.lonelyplanet.com.

## LAND

### Brazil

Only one major road connects Brazil and Venezuela; it leads from Manaus through Boa Vista (Brazil) to Santa Elena de Uairén (Venezuela) and continues to Ciudad Guayana.

You can also enter Venezuela from Manaus via the Río Negro at San Simón de Cocuy. This is an adventurous river/road route seldom used by travelers; see p263.

### Colombia

You can enter Venezuela from Colombia at four border crossings. In the northwest is a fairly popular coastal route between Maicao in Colombia and Maracaibo in Venezuela (see p148). Further south is the most popular border crossing, between Cúcuta and San Antonio del Táchira (see p178). There is a crossing from Arauca to El Amparo de Apure, but it is inconvenient and dangerous (because of Colombian guerrilla activity) and is rarely used.

Finally, there's an uncommon but interesting outback route from Puerto Carreño in Colombia to Puerto Páez in Venezuela (see p263).

Remember to wind your watch forward one half-hour when crossing from Colombia to Venezuela.

### Guyana

The only crossing between Venezuela and Guyana is the remote, difficult and dangerous road between Bochiche and Mabaruma; you're better off going through Brazil.

## SEA

Weekly passenger boats operate between Güiria in Venezuela and Port of Spain on Trinidad (p218), but there are no longer ferries between Venezuela and Netherlands Antilles.

# GETTING AROUND

## AIR

Venezuela has a number of airlines and a reasonable network of air routes. Caracas (or, more precisely, Maiquetía, where Caracas' airport is located) is the country's major aviation hub and handles flights to most airports around the country. Cities most frequently serviced from Caracas include Porlamar, Maracaibo and Puerto Ordaz (Ciudad Guayana). The most popular destinations with travelers are Mérida, Ciudad Bolívar, Canaima and Porlamar.

Fares vary between carriers (sometimes substantially), so if the route you're flying is serviced by several airlines, check all fares before buying your ticket. Approximate fares are given in the relevant sections in the book; see p78 for fares on the main routes out of Caracas.

Some airlines offer discount fares for students and/or senior citizens, but these change frequently and may apply only to Venezuelans; check with the airlines or agencies. Arm yourself with patience, as not all flights depart on time.

### Airlines in Venezuela

Venezuela has half a dozen major commercial airlines servicing main domestic routes, and a dozen minor provincial carriers that cover regional and remote routes on a regular or charter basis. Mostly large, modern jets serve the big cities, while light planes fly to obscure destinations. The airline safety record is appreciably good – you can check www.airsafe.com for statistical data.

The airline situation changes frequently. Always check with a reliable travel agency as the companies come and go and their routes and schedules are malleable.

Venezuelan airlines include the following (the addresses and phone numbers listed are for Caracas):

**Aereotuy** (LTA; Map p63; ☎ 0212-212-3110; www.tuy.com; Blvd de Sabana Grande, Edificio Gran Sabana, Piso 5) Serves the tourism hotspots of Canaima, Los Roques & Porlamar.

**Aeropostal** (Map p72; ☎ 0800-284-6637, 0212-708-6202; www.aeropostal.com; 1st fl, Torre ING Bank, Av Eugenio Mendoza, La Castellana; Ⓜ Altamira) Flies to Maracaibo, Barquisimeto, Porlamar & Puerto Ordaz.

**Aserca** (OCA; Map p72; ☎ 0800-648-8356; www.asercaairlines.com; ground fl, Edificio Taeca, Calle Guaicaipuro, El Rosal; Ⓜ Chacaíto) Airline operating jet flights between several major airports, including Barcelona, Maracaibo, Porlamar, San Antonio del Táchira and Santa Domingo del Táchira, as well as Aruba, Curaçao and the Dominican Republic.

**Avior** (ROI; Map p72; ☎ 0501-2846-7737, 0212-953-3221; www.avior.com.ve; Torre Clement, ground fl, Av Venezuela, El Rosal; Ⓜ Chacaíto) Destinations include Barcelona, Barinas, Barquisimeto, Coro, Cumaná, Maturín, Porlamar, Puerto Ordaz and Valera.

**Conviasa** (VCV; Map pp58-9; ☎ 0500-2668-4272; www.conviasa.aero; Hotel Alba Caracas, Av Sur 25 at Av México, Parque Central; Ⓜ Parque Central) State-owned airline

TRANSPORTATION

with destinations such as Barinas, El Vigía, La Fria, Las Piedras, Maracaibo, Maturín, Puerto Ayacucho & Puerto Ordaz.

**Laser** (LER; Map pp52-3; ☎ 0212-202-0011; www.laser.com.ve; Av Francisco de Miranda, Torre Bazar Bolivar, Piso 8; Ⓜ La California) Carrier with service between Caracas and Porlamar.

**Rainbow Air** ( ☎ 0424-146-6249; makorotours@gmail.com; Maiquetía Airport, domestic terminal) Flights to Gran Roque.

**Rutaca** (RUC; Map pp52-3; www.rutaca.com.ve); Maiquetía Airport ( ☎ 0800-788-2221, 0212-355-1838); Caracas (Map pp52-3; ☎ 0414-624-5800; Centro Seguros La Paz, Av Francisco de Miranda, Nivel Mezzanina; Ⓜ Los Cotijos) Serves Barcelona, Barinas, Canaima, Ciudad Bolívar, Cumaná, Curúpano, Maturín, Porlamar, Puerto Ordaz, San Antonio del Táchira and Santa Domingo del Táchira.

**Santa Bárbara** (BBR; Map p72; ☎ 0212-204-4000; www.sbairlines.com; Miranda level, Centro Lido, Av Francisco de Miranda; Ⓜ Chacaíto) Flies to El Vigía and Las Piedras domestically.

**Venezolana** (Map p72; ☎ 0212-208-8400; www.venezolanaonline.com; Centro Comercial Centro Plaza, Mezzanina, Altamira; Ⓜ Altamira) Flights to Cumaná, El Vigía, Porlamar, Maracaibo & Maturín.

TRANSPORTATION

## BICYCLE

Unfortunately, Venezuela is not the best place for cyclists. There are almost no bike tracks, bike rentals or any other facilities. Drivers don't show much courtesy to cyclists, either. Cycling is not a popular means of transportation among locals, and foreign travelers with their own bikes are a rarity. Mérida is currently one of the few places where mountain biking tours are organized and bikes can be hired (see p157).

## BOAT

Venezuela has many islands off its Caribbean coast, but only Isla de Margarita is serviced by regular boats and ferries; see p195.

The Río Orinoco is the country's major inland waterway. It's navigable from its mouth up to Puerto Ayacucho, but there's no regular passenger service on any part of it.

## BUS & POR PUESTO

As there is no passenger train service in Venezuela, most traveling is done by bus. Buses are generally fast, and they run regularly day and night between major population centers. Bus transportation is reasonably cheap in Venezuela; you probably won't go wrong if you allow BsF8 to BsF16 per hour (or roughly 60km) on a bus.

Venezuela's dozens of bus companies own buses ranging from archaic pieces of junk to the most recent models. All major companies offer *servicio ejecutivo* (executive service) in comfortable air-conditioned buses, which now cover virtually all the major long-distance routes and are the dominant means of intercity transportation. Still better is the so-called *bus-cama*, where seats can be reclined almost into beds. These buses are the most comfy means of transportation – they have air-conditioning, TV and often a toilet. Note that the air-con is often very efficient, so have plenty of warm clothing at hand to avoid freezing.

If various companies operate the same route, fares are much the same though some may offer discounts. Figures given in the regional sections of this book are approximate minimum-to-maximum fares you are likely to pay on a given route.

All intercity buses depart from and arrive at the *terminal de pasajeros* (bus terminal). Every city has such a terminal, usually outside the city center, but always linked to it by local transportation. Caracas is the most important transportation hub, handling buses to just about every corner of the country. In general, there's no need to buy tickets in advance for major routes, except around Christmas, Carnaval and Easter.

Many short-distance regional routes are served by por puesto (literally 'by the seat'), a cross between a bus and a taxi. Por puestos are usually large US-made cars (less often minibuses) of the '60s and '70s vintages that ply fixed routes and depart when all seats are filled. They cost about 40% to 80% more than buses, but they're faster and usually more comfortable. On some routes, they are the dominant or even the exclusive means of transportation. Depending on the region and the kind of vehicle, por puestos may also be called carros or carritos.

## CAR & MOTORCYCLE

Traveling by car is an inexpensive way of getting around Venezuela. Gas stations are numerous and fuel is the world's cheapest – US$0.070 to US$0.097 per liter (fixed since 1998), depending on the octane level. A liter of milk will cost you 25 times more (just for perspective). Call it Venezuela spreading the love.

This rosy picture is slightly obscured by Venezuelan traffic and local driving manners. Traffic in Venezuela, especially in Caracas, is wild, chaotic, noisy, polluting and anarchic.

Bringing a car to Venezuela (or to South America in general) is expensive and time-consuming and involves plenty of paperwork, and few people do it. It's much more convenient and cheaper to rent a car locally.

### Rental

You should think seriously about safety, road conditions and poor signage, and the country's aggressive driving style, before renting a vehicle in Venezuela. If you feel you're up for the challenge, a number of international and local car-rental companies, including Hertz, Avis and Budget, operate in Venezuela. They have offices at major airports and in city centers, often in top-end hotels. (See individual destinations for details.) As a rough guide, a small car will start from BsF381 or so per day, with discount rates applying for a full week or longer. A 4WD vehicle is considerably more expensive and difficult to obtain.

Rental agencies require a credit card and driver's license (your home-country license is valid in Venezuela). You need to be at least 21 years of age to rent a car, although renting some cars (particularly 4WDs and luxury models) may require you to be at least 23 or 25 years. Some companies also have a maximum age of about 65 years.

Read the rental contract carefully before signing (most contracts are in Spanish only). Pay close attention to any theft clause, as it will probably load any loss onto the renter. Look at the car carefully, and insist on listing any defects (including scratches) on the rental form. Check the spare tire, and take note of whether there is a jack.

That said, it's a good idea to contact the international rental companies at home before your trip and check what they can offer in Venezuela. It's likely to be more convenient and cheaper to book at home rather than in Venezuela, and you can be pretty sure that the car will be waiting for you upon arrival.

### Road Rules

Watching Venezuela's crazy traffic, reminiscent of F1 racing, you'd never suspect that there are speed limits, but they do legally exist. Unless traffic signs say otherwise, the maximum speed limit in urban areas is 40km/h, and outside built-up areas it's 80km/h. Officially, traffic coming from the right has priority, unless indicated otherwise by signs. In practice, however, it seems that right-of-way depends on the size of vehicle rather than the regulations.

Cars must be equipped with seat belts for front seats (which always have to be used), and they must have a spare tire, wheel block, jack and a special reflector triangle, which in case of accident or breakdown has to be placed 50m behind the car. Motorcyclists have to wear a crash helmet, and motorcycles cannot be ridden at night. However, once again all of this is theoretical.

As in the rest of the Americas, Venezuela uses right-hand drive.

## HITCHHIKING

Hitchhiking is never entirely safe in any country and is not recommended. Travelers who decide to hitchhike should understand that they are taking a small but potentially serious risk. People who do choose to hitchhike will be safer if they travel in pairs and let someone know where they are planning to go. Women traveling on their own should not hitchhike at all.

Safety apart, Venezuela is not good for hitchhiking. Although many people have cars, they are reluctant to stop to pick up strangers. As bus transportation is fast, efficient and relatively cheap, it's probably not worth wasting time hitchhiking.

## LOCAL TRANSPORTATION

### Bus & Metro

All cities and many major towns have their own urban transportation systems, which in most places are small buses or minibuses. Depending on the region, these are called busetas, *carros*, carritos, *micros* or *camionetas*, and fares are usually no more than BsF1.50. In many larger cities you can also find urban por puestos, swinging faster than buses through the chaotic traffic. Caracas, Maracaibo and Valencia are the only cities in Venezuela with a subway system.

### Taxi

Taxis are inexpensive and worth considering, particularly for transportation between the bus terminal and city center when you are carrying luggage. Taxis don't have meters, so always fix the fare with the driver before boarding the cab. It's a good idea to find out the correct fare from a terminal official or a hotel reception desk beforehand. Prices are often posted at reception kiosks, especially in Caracas.

 



## TOURS

Independent travelers who've never taken an organized tour in their lives will find themselves signing up with a group in Venezuela. As vast areas of the country are virtually inaccessible by public transportation (eg the Delta del Orinoco or Amazon Basin) or because a solitary visit to scattered sights in a large territory (eg the Gran Sabana) may be inconvenient, time-consuming and expensive, tours are a standard option in Venezuelan travel.

Although under some circumstances it makes sense to prebook tours from Caracas (as when stringing together various tours in a short period of time), it is most cost-effective to arrange a tour from the regional center closest to the area you are going to visit.

### Tour Companies

Some Caracas-based agencies (the so-called *mayoristas*, or wholesalers) simply sell tours organized by other companies. Many agencies use some of the services of selected regional operators, adding their own guides and transfers, and sometimes altering routes and upgrading lodging facilities. Some Caracas operators, though, organize the entire trip themselves, using their own camps and means of transportation. Some companies can prepare tailor-made trips, which will cost considerably more than standard tours. Prices vary significantly depending on the number of people in the tour.

The following companies focus on responsible tourism and offer English-speaking guides:

**Akanan Travel & Adventure** (Map p72; ☎ 0212-264-2769; www.akanan.com; Edificio Grano de Oro, grnd fl, Calle Bolivar, Chacao, Caracas; Ⓜ Chacao) These Caracas/Puerto Ayacucho veterans specialize in quality adventure and extreme-sport trips, including treks to the top of Auyantepui (seven days from BsF7900) and Roraima (six days from BsF2800), as well as boat trips to Angel Falls (BsF2200), Río Caura (BsF2300) and Cerro Autana (BsF1200). It's worth stopping in to browse the voluminous library, free maps and internet and last-minute hiking and climbing gear.

**Alpi Viajes** (Map pp52-3; ☎ 0212-283-1433, www.alpi-group.com; 1st fl, Torre Centro, No 11, Centro Parque Boyacá, Av Sucre, Los Dos Caminos) This company specializes in fishing trips, but also offers a range of mainstream packages and some adventurous tours in the Amazonas.

**Angel Eco-Tours** (☎ in Caracas 0212-762-5975, in New York 212-656-1240; www.angel-ecotours.com) This English-led sustainable-tourism specialist, also based in New York City, has over a decade of experience in fostering true ecotourism in Venezuela and runs one- to 14-day trips throughout the country (BsF950-12,000), including a design-your-own-adventure option.

**Autana** (☎ 0212-347-6475; www.autana.org) Run by an international team of paragliders, adventure-sports enthusiasts and nature lovers, this extreme company offers adventure tours, including BASE-jumping Angel Falls and many less nerve-wracking trekking, rafting, canyoning and paragliding excursions. English, Italian and German are spoken.

**Biotrek** (☎ 0212-642-3115; www.biotrek.com.ve) Venezuela's first and only fully specialized kayak outfitter offers solo and group kayak tours throughout the country, including Choroní–Chuao–Cepe (two days from BsF1100), Parque Nacional Mochima (two days from BsF750) and an adventurous Karuai River trip (12 days from BsF8000).

**Cacao Travel Group** (☎ 0285-632-6706; www.cacaotravel.com; Posada Angostura, Calle Boyaca No 8, Casco Historico, Ciudad Bolívar) This agency, 2.5km south of Las Mercedes, has expertise in Río Caura tours (five days in total, BsF2590 per person from Ciudad Bolívar, minimum four persons), where it has its own lodge. It also has a lodge in the Amazonas, serving as a base for boat trips in the region, and in Parque Nacional Canaima.**Natoura** (☎ 0274-252-4216; www.natoura.com) A full-service adventure tourism agency specializing in ecotours, with emphasis on treks and mountain expeditions with specialist guides and naturalists (including mountain biking and canyoning). Popular treks include Pico Bolívar (from BsF1125 per person), Pico Humboldt (from BsF1260 per person) and multi-day, multi-adventure trips to San Jose (from BsF720 per person) and Los Llanos (from BsF945 per person). English, German, French and Italian are spoken.

**Osprey Expeditions** (Map p63; ☎ 0414-310-4491; www.ospreyexpeditions.com; Edificio La Paz, office 51, Av Casanova at 2a Av de Bello Monte, Bello Monte, Caracas; Ⓜ Sabana Grande) Small, personable, Venezuelan-owned agency attuned to a budget traveler's perspective (but with offerings ranging the gamut). It can organize tours throughout Venezuela but it's particularly strong on Los Roques, Canaima and the Orinoco Delta.

**Sociedad Conservacionista Audubón de Venezuela** (SCAV; Map pp52-3; ☎ 0212-272-8708; www.audubonvenezuela.org; Edificio Sociedad Venezolana de Ciencias Naturales, Calle Arichuna, Urb El Marques) Organizes bird-watching tours.

**Tucaya** (☎ 0212-234-9401; www.tucaya.com; Quinta Santa Marta, 1a Av Urbanización Campo Claro, Los Dos Caminos, Caracas) Caters principally to French-speaking clients, but also organizes English-speaking tours. Major destinations include Canaima and Angel Falls (three days from BsF1150), Delta del Orinoco (three days from BsF900), the Andes (three days from BsF500) and Los Llanos (3 days from BsF900).

### ANGEL FALLS TOUR OPERATORS

Angel Falls (Salto Angel) is one of Venezuela's top tourist attractions, so many Caracas tour companies (including most listed earlier) have it in their program. You can also find a couple of agencies in the domestic terminal at Maiquetía airport. See Ciudad Bolívar (p238) for more tour options.

### LOS LLANOS TOUR OPERATORS

If you plan on taking tours to the *hatos* (ranches) in Los Llanos (see p182), note that some may require you to book and pay beforehand through a Caracas agent.

**Hato La Garza** (☎ 0273-414-1176; www.hatogarza.com; r per person incl meals BsF1600) The priciest *hato* is absolutely top-shelf. Go ahead, spoil yourself.

**Hato El Cedral** (☎ 0212-781-8995; www.elcedral.com; r per person incl meals BsF392) The government has taken over, but the wildlife still is outstanding.

**Hato Cristero** (☎ 0273-223-5066; www.hatocristero.com; r per person incl meals BsF550) A midrange option, of all the *hatos* closest to Barinas. A cascading waterfall next to the pool and butterfly-friendly walking paths make for a relaxing, comfortable option.

### LOS ROQUES TOUR OPERATORS

Archipiélago Los Roques is serviced from Maiquetía airport's domestic terminal by a number of small airlines. Besides the flight-only option, the following offer tours as well.

**Aerotuy** (LTA; ☎ 0212-212-3110; www.tuy.com)

**Rainbow Air** (☎ 0424-146-6249; makorotours@gmail.com)

## Excursion Centers

An alternative to tour companies, *centros excursionistas* (excursion centers) are associations of outdoor-minded people who organize independent excursions in their spare time. These are essentially one- or two-day weekend trips around Caracas and the central states, but longer journeys to other regions are often scheduled for long weekends and holiday periods. The focus is usually on nature and walking, though cultural sights are often part of the program. Each trip is prepared by a member of the group, who then serves as a guide. The *excursionistas* use public transportation and take their own food and camping gear if necessary. Foreign travelers are welcome, and you can usually find a companion for conversation in English, German etc.

**Centro Excursionista Caracas** (CEC; www.centroexcursionistacaracas.org.ve, in Spanish) Founded in 1929, this is the oldest and best-known club of its kind. It organizes regular weekend trips to places like Parque Nacional El Ávila, Mérida and Parque Nacional Henri Pittier, and its members include people of all ages. You can contact Aurora Gonzalez (cecaracas@gmail.com) for information on participating.

## Guides

**Asociación Venezolana de Instructores y Guías de Montaña** (www.avigm.com) An association consisting of 50 or so experienced guides for mountaineering, rock climbing and trekking, most of whom are listed on the website with their email addresses.

**Explora Treks** (☎ 0212-285-3718; www.exploratreks.com) A climbing agency consisting of seven highly seasoned Venezuelan climbers who can organize and guide expeditions to several tepuis (flat-topped sandstone mountains with vertical flanks), including a 14-day strenuous trek to the top of Auyantepui in Parque Nacional Canaima, with a descent by rappel alongside Angel Falls (from BsF9300 per person depending on group size).

# Health

Dr David Goldberg

## CONTENTS





Prevention is the key to staying healthy while traveling abroad. Travelers who receive the recommended vaccines and follow commonsense precautions on their journey usually come away with nothing more than a little diarrhea.

# BEFORE YOU GO

Most vaccines will not produce immunity until at least two weeks after they're given, so visit a physician four to eight weeks before departure. Ask your doctor for an International Certificate of Vaccination (otherwise known as 'the yellow booklet'), which will list all the vaccinations you've received. This is mandatory for countries that require proof of yellow-fever vaccination upon entry, but it's a good idea to carry it wherever you travel.

## INSURANCE

If your health insurance does not cover you for medical expenses abroad, consider supplemental insurance. Check the Bookings & Services section of the **Lonely Planet website** (www.lonelyplanet.com/travel_services) for more information. Find out in advance if your insurance plan will make payments directly to providers or reimburse you later for overseas health expenditures.

## MEDICAL CHECKLIST

- acetaminophen/paracetamol (eg Tylenol) or aspirin
- adhesive or paper tape
- antibacterial ointment (eg Bactroban) for cuts and abrasions
- antibiotics
- antidiarrheal drugs (eg loperamide)
- antihistamines (for hay fever and allergic reactions)
- anti-inflammatory drugs (eg ibuprofen)
- bandages, gauze, gauze rolls
- DEET-containing insect repellent for the skin
- iodine tablets (for water purification)
- oral rehydration salts
- permethrin-containing insect repellent for clothing, tents and bed nets
- pocket knife
- scissors, safety pins, tweezers
- steroid cream or cortisone (for poison ivy and other allergic rashes)
- sunblock
- syringes and sterile needles
- thermometer (digital)

## INTERNET RESOURCES

There is a wealth of travel-health advice on the internet. For further information, the **Lonely Planet website** (www.lonelyplanet.com) is a good place to start. A superb book called *International Travel and Health,* which is revised annually and available online at no cost, is published by the **World Health Organization** (www.who.int/ith/).

Another health website of general interest is **MD Travel Health** (www.mdtravelhealth.com), which provides a complete set of travel-health recommendations for every country. The site is updated daily and is also available at no charge.

It can also usually be a good idea to consult your own country's government travel health website before departure, if one is available.

**Australia** (www.dfat.gov.au/travel/)
**Canada** (www.hc-sc.gc.ca/pphb-dgspsp/tmp-pmv/pub_e.html)
**UK** (www.doh.gov.uk/traveladvice/index.htm)
**USA** (www.cdc.gov/travel/)

### RECOMMENDED VACCINATIONS

There are no required vaccines for Venezuela, but a number are recommended. Note that some of these are not approved for use by children or pregnant women – check with your physician.

| Vaccine | Recommended for | Dosage | Side effects |
|---|---|---|---|
| chickenpox | travelers who've never had chickenpox | 2 doses 1 month apart | fever; mild case of chickenpox |
| hepatitis A | all travelers | 1 dose before trip; booster 6-12 months later | soreness at injection site; headaches; body aches |
| hepatitis B | long-term travelers in close contact with the local population | 3 doses over 6 months | soreness at injection site; low-grade fever |
| measles | travelers who have never had measles or completed a vaccination course | 1 dose | fever; rash; joint pain; allergic reactions |
| rabies | travelers who may have contact with animals and may not have access to medical care | 3 doses over 3-4 weeks | soreness at injection site; headaches; body aches |
| tetanus-diphtheria | all travelers who haven't had booster within 10 years | 1 dose lasts 10 years | soreness at injection site |
| typhoid | all travelers | 4 capsules orally, 1 taken every other day | abdominal pain; nausea; rash |
| yellow fever | travelers to all areas, but especially rural areas of the following states: Apure, Amazonas, Barinas, Bolívar, Sucre, Táchira, Delta Amacuro, Angel Falls | 1 dose lasts 10 years | headaches; body aches; severe reactions are rare |

Bring medications in their original containers, clearly labeled. A signed, dated letter from your physician describing all medical conditions and medications, including generic names, is also a good idea. If carrying syringes or needles, be sure to have a physician's letter documenting their medical necessity.

HEALTH

## FURTHER READING

For further information, see *Central & South America: Healthy Travel Guide*, published by Lonely Planet. If you're traveling with children, Lonely Planet's *Travel with Children* may also be useful. The *ABC of Healthy Travel*, by E Walker et al, and *Medicine for the Outdoors*, by Paul S Auerbach, are other valuable resources.

# IN TRANSIT

## DEEP VEIN THROMBOSIS (DVT)

Blood clots may form in the legs during plane flights, chiefly because of prolonged immobility. The longer the flight, the greater the risk. Though most blood clots are reabsorbed uneventfully, some may break off and travel through the blood vessels to the lungs, where they could cause life-threatening complications.

The chief symptom of deep vein thrombosis (DVT) is swelling or pain of the foot, ankle or calf, usually (but not always) on just one side. When a blood clot travels to the lungs, it may cause chest pain and difficulty breathing. Travelers with any of these symptoms should immediately seek medical attention.

To prevent the development of DVT on long flights you should walk about the cabin, perform isometric compressions of the leg muscles (ie contract the leg muscles while sitting), drink plenty of fluids, and avoid alcohol and tobacco.

## JET LAG & MOTION SICKNESS

Jet lag is common when crossing more than five time zones, and can result in insomnia, fatigue, malaise or nausea. To avoid jet lag try drinking plenty of fluids (nonalcoholic) and eating light meals. Upon arrival, get exposure to natural sunlight and readjust your schedule (for meals, sleep etc) as soon as possible.

Antihistamines such as dimenhydrinate (Dramamine) and meclizine (Antivert or Bonine) are usually the first choice for treating motion sickness. Their main side effect is drowsiness. A herbal alternative is ginger, which works like a charm for some people.

# IN VENEZUELA

## AVAILABILITY & COST OF HEALTH CARE

Good medical care is available in Caracas, but may be difficult to find in rural areas. Public hospitals are free, but the quality of medical care is better in private facilities. For an online list of physicians, dentists and other health-care providers, most of whom speak English, go to the **US embassy website** (http://caracas.usembassy.gov). Many doctors and hospitals expect payment in cash, regardless of whether you have travel health insurance.

For an ambulance in Venezuela, call ☎ 171. If you develop a life-threatening medical problem, you'll probably want to be evacuated to a country with state-of-the-art medical care. Since this may cost tens of thousands of dollars, be sure you have insurance to cover this before you depart. You can find a list of medical evacuation and travel insurance companies on the **US state department website** (www.travel.state.gov/medical.html).

Venezuelan *farmacias* (pharmacies) are identifiable by a red light in the store window. The quality and availability of medication is comparable to that in most other countries. The pharmacies keep a rotating schedule of 24-hour availability, so that different pharmacies are open on different nights. To find a late-night pharmacy, you can either look in the local newspaper under 'Turnos,' call ☎ 800-88766 (that is, 800-TURNO), check the list posted on most pharmacy doors or search for a pharmacy with its red light still on.

## INFECTIOUS DISEASES

### Brucellosis

This is an infection of domestic and wild animals that may be transmitted to humans through direct animal contact or by consumption of unpasteurized dairy products from infected animals. In Venezuela, most human cases are related to infected cattle. Symptoms may include fever, malaise, depression, loss of appetite, headache, muscle ache and back pain. Complications may include arthritis, hepatitis, meningitis and endocarditis (heart-valve infection).

### Cholera

Cholera is an intestinal infection acquired through ingestion of contaminated food or water. The main symptom is profuse, watery diarrhea, which may be so severe that it causes life-threatening dehydration. The key treatment is drinking an oral rehydration solution. Antibiotics are also given, usually tetracycline or doxycycline, though quinolone antibiotics such as ciprofloxacin and levofloxacin are also effective.

Cholera sometimes occurs in Venezuela, but it's rare among travelers. Cholera vaccine is no longer required, and is in fact no longer available in some countries, including the US, because the old vaccine was relatively ineffective and caused side effects. There are new vaccines that are safer and more effective, but they're not available in many countries and are only recommended for those at particularly high risk.

### Dengue Fever (Breakbone Fever)

Dengue fever is a viral infection found throughout South America. In Venezuela, large numbers of cases are reported each year, especially from the states of Barinas, Amazonas, Aragua, Mérida, Táchira and Lara, and the Caracas district. Dengue is transmitted by Aedes mosquitoes, which bite preferentially during the daytime and are usually found close to human habitations, often indoors. They breed primarily in artificial water containers, such as jars, barrels, cans, cisterns, metal drums, plastic containers and discarded tires. As a result, dengue is especially common in densely populated, urban environments.

Dengue usually causes flu-like symptoms, including fever, muscle ache, joint pain, headache, nausea and vomiting, often followed by a rash. The body aches may be quite uncomfortable, but most cases resolve uneventfully in a few days. Severe cases usually occur in children under the age of 15 who are experiencing their second dengue infection.

There is no treatment as yet for dengue fever, except to take analgesics such as acetaminophen/paracetamol (Tylenol) and drink plenty of fluids. Severe cases may require hospitalization for intravenous fluids and supportive care. There is no vaccine. The cornerstone of prevention is protecting against insect bites; see p290.

### H1N1

The H1N1 virus (commonly referred to as 'Swine Flu') was given a 'Phase 6' rating by the World Health Organization in June 2009. A 'Phase 6' alert means the virus is considered a global pandemic. As with most countries, accurate figures on H1N1 cases and deaths in Venezuela are hard to come by, but as in most of South America, the number of cases were declining as at the time of time and Venezuela fared far better than many of its neighbors during the initial outbreaks.

At press time, airport staff in some countries were screening arriving passengers for symptoms of the H1N1 flu. Check with the embassy of the country you're visiting to see if they have imposed any travel restrictions. It's best not to travel if you have flu-like symptoms of any sort.

For the latest information, check with the **World Health Organization** (www.who.int).

### Hepatitis A

Hepatitis A is the second most common travel-related infection (after travelers' diarrhea). It's a viral infection of the liver that is usually acquired by ingestion of contaminated water, food or ice, though it may also be acquired by direct contact with infected persons. The illness occurs throughout the world, but the incidence is higher in developing nations. Symptoms may include fever, malaise, jaundice, nausea, vomiting and abdominal pain. Most cases resolve without complications, though hepatitis A occasionally causes severe liver damage. There is no treatment.

The vaccine for hepatitis A is extremely safe and highly effective. If you get a booster six to 12 months later, it lasts for at least 10 years. You really should get it before you go to Venezuela or any other developing nation. Because the safety of hepatitis A vaccine has not been established for pregnant women or children under the age of two, they should instead be given a gammaglobulin injection.

### Hepatitis B

Like hepatitis A, hepatitis B is a liver infection that occurs worldwide, but is more common in developing nations. Unlike hepatitis A, the disease is usually acquired by sexual contact or by exposure to infected blood, generally through blood transfusions or contaminated needles. The vaccine is recommended only for long-term travelers (on the road more than six months) who expect to live in rural areas or have close physical contact with the local population. Additionally, the vaccine is recommended for anyone who anticipates sexual contact with the local inhabitants or a possible need for medical, dental or other treatments while abroad, especially if a need for transfusions or injections is expected.

Hepatitis B vaccine is safe and highly effective. A total of three injections however, are necessary to establish full immunity. Several countries added hepatitis B vaccine to the list of routine childhood immunizations in the 1980s, so many young adults are already protected.

### HIV/AIDS

This has been reported in all South American countries. Be sure to use condoms for all sexual encounters.

### Leishmaniasis

This disease occurs in the mountains and jungles of all South American countries except Chile, Uruguay and the Falkland Islands. In Venezuela it is widespread in rural areas, especially the west-central part of the country. The infection is transmitted by sand flies, which are about one-third the size of mosquitoes. Leishmaniasis may be particularly severe in those with HIV. There is no vaccine. To protect yourself from sand flies, follow the same precautions as for mosquitoes (see p290), except that netting must be finer mesh (at least 18 holes to the linear inch).

### Malaria

Malaria occurs in every South American country except Chile, Uruguay and the Falkland Islands. It's transmitted by mosquito bites, usually between dusk and dawn. The main symptom is high-spiking fevers, which may be accompanied by chills, sweats, headache, body aches, weakness, vomiting or diarrhea. Severe cases may involve the central nervous system and lead to seizures, confusion, coma and death.

Taking malaria pills is strongly recommended for those visiting Angel Falls and for rural areas in the states of Apure, Amazonas, Barinas, Bolívar, Delta Amacuro, Sucre, Táchira and Zulia. In general, the risk of malaria is greatest between February and August, especially after the onset of the rainy season in late May.

There is a choice of three malaria pills, all of which work equally well. Mefloquine (Lariam) is taken once weekly in a dosage of 250mg, starting one to two weeks before arriving in Venezuela and continuing until four weeks after departure. A certain percentage of people (the number is controversial) develop neuropsychiatric side effects, which may range from mild to severe. Atovaquone/proguanil (Malarone) is a newly approved combination pill; it's taken once daily with food, starting two days before arrival and continuing until seven days after departure. Side effects are typically mild. Doxycycline is a third alternative, but may cause an exaggerated sunburn reaction.

In general, Malarone seems to cause fewer side effects than Lariam and is becoming more popular. The chief disadvantage is that it has to be taken daily. For longer trips, it's probably worth trying Lariam; for shorter trips, Malarone will be the drug of choice for most people.

Protecting yourself against mosquito bites (see p290) is just as important as taking malaria pills since none of the pills are 100% effective.

Since you may not have access to medical care while traveling, you should bring along additional pills for emergency self-treatment; take these if you can't reach a doctor and you develop symptoms that suggest malaria, such as high-spiking fevers. One self-treatment option is to take four tablets of Malarone once daily for three days. However, Malarone should not be used for treatment if you're already taking it for prevention. An alternative is to take 650mg quinine three times daily and 100mg doxycycline twice daily for one week. If you start self-medication, see a doctor at the earliest possible opportunity.

If you develop a fever after returning home, see a physician, as malaria symptoms may not occur for months.

## Measles

All travelers should be sure they have had either two measles vaccinations or a blood test proving they're immune. Although measles immunization usually doesn't begin until the age of 12 months, children between six and 11 months should probably receive an initial dose of measles vaccine before traveling to Venezuela.

## Rabies

Rabies is a viral infection of the brain and spinal cord that is almost always fatal. The rabies virus is carried in the saliva of infected animals and is typically transmitted through an animal bite, though contamination of any break in the skin with infected saliva may result in rabies. Rabies occurs in all South American countries. In Venezuela, most cases are related to dog bites.

Rabies vaccine is safe, but a full series requires three injections and is quite expensive. Those at high risk for rabies, such as animal handlers and spelunkers (cave explorers), should certainly get the vaccine. In addition, those at lower risk for animal bites should consider asking for the vaccine if they might be traveling to remote areas and might not have access to appropriate medical care if needed. The treatment for a possibly rabid bite consists of rabies vaccine with rabies immune globulin. It's effective, but must be given promptly. Most travelers don't need rabies vaccine.

All animal bites and scratches must be promptly and thoroughly cleansed with large amounts of soap and water, and local health authorities contacted to determine whether or not further treatment is necessary.

## Schistosomiasis

This parasitic infection is acquired by exposure to contaminated fresh water, and is reported from isolated spots in the north-central part of the country, including the areas around Caracas (but not Caracas itself) and the states of Aragua, Carabobo, Guárico and Miranda. When traveling in these areas, you should avoid swimming, wading, bathing or washing in bodies of fresh water, including lakes, ponds, streams and rivers. Salt water and chlorinated pools carry no risk of schistosomiasis.

## Tick-Borne Relapsing Fever

This fever, which may be transmitted by either ticks or lice, is caused by bacteria that is closely related to those that cause Lyme disease and syphilis. The illness is characterized by periods of fever, chills, headache, body aches, muscle aches and coughs, alternating with periods when the fever subsides and the person feels relatively well. To minimize the risk of relapsing fever, follow tick precautions as outlined on p290 and practice good personal hygiene at all times.

### Typhoid Fever

Typhoid is caused by ingestion of food or water contaminated by a species of salmonella known as *Salmonella typhi.* Fever occurs in virtually all cases. Other symptoms may include headache, malaise, muscle aches, dizziness, loss of appetite, nausea and abdominal pain. Either diarrhea or constipation may occur. Possible complications include intestinal perforation, intestinal bleeding, confusion, delirium or (rarely) coma.

Unless you expect to take all your meals in major hotels and restaurants, typhoid vaccine is a good idea. It's usually given orally, but is also available as an injection. Neither vaccine is approved for use in children under the age of two.

The drug of choice for typhoid fever is usually a quinolone antibiotic such as ciprofloxacin (Cipro) or levofloxacin (Levaquin), which many travelers carry for treatment of traveler's diarrhea. However, if you self-treat for typhoid fever, you may also need to self-treat for malaria, since the symptoms of the two diseases may be indistinguishable.

### Venezuelan Equine Encephalitis

This viral infection, transmitted by mosquitoes, reached epidemic levels in 1995 after unusually heavy rainfalls, especially in the northwestern states of Zulia, Lara, Falcón, Yaracuy, Carabobo and Trujillo. The greatest incidence was reported among the Warao population. Cases still occur, but in smaller numbers, chiefly in the west between the Península de la Guajira and the Río Catatumbo. This illness comes on suddenly and symptoms are malaise, fevers, rigors, severe headache, photophobia and myalgias. Possible complications can include convulsions, coma, and paralysis.

### Yellow Fever

Yellow fever is a life-threatening viral infection transmitted by mosquitoes in forested areas. The illness begins with flu-like symptoms, which may include fever, chills, headache, muscle aches, backache, loss of appetite, nausea and vomiting. These symptoms usually subside in a few days, but one person in six enters a second, toxic phase characterized by recurrent fever, vomiting, listlessness, jaundice, kidney failure and hemorrhage, leading to death in up to half of the cases. There is no treatment except for supportive care.

**TRADITIONAL MEDICINE**

The following are some traditional remedies for common travel-related conditions.

| Problem | Treatment |
|---|---|
| altitude sickness | gingko |
| jet lag | melatonin |
| motion sickness | ginger |
| mosquito-bite prevention | oil of eucalyptus or soybean |

Yellow fever is still present in Venezuela and the yellow-fever vaccine is strongly recommended for all travelers (except pregnant women), especially anyone traveling beyond Caracas and the northern coast.

Yellow-fever vaccine is given only in approved yellow-fever vaccination centers, which provide validated International Certificates of Vaccination (yellow booklets). The vaccine should be given at least 10 days before any potential exposure to yellow fever, and remains effective for approximately 10 years. Reactions to the vaccine are generally mild and may include headache, muscle ache, low-grade fevers or discomfort at the injection site. Severe, life-threatening reactions have been described, but are extremely rare. In general, the risk of becoming ill from the vaccine is far less than the risk of becoming ill from yellow fever, and you're strongly encouraged to get the vaccine.

Taking measures to protect yourself from mosquito bites (p290) is an essential part of preventing yellow fever.

## TRAVELER'S DIARRHEA

To prevent diarrhea, avoid tap water unless it has been boiled, filtered or chemically disinfected (iodine tablets); only eat fresh fruit or vegetables if cooked or peeled; be wary of dairy products that might contain unpasteurized milk; and be highly selective when eating food from street vendors.

If you develop diarrhea, be sure to drink plenty of fluids, preferably an oral rehydration solution containing lots of salt and sugar. A few loose stools don't require treatment but, if you start having more than four or five stools a day, you should start taking an antibiotic (usually a quinolone drug) and an antidiarrheal agent (such as loperamide). If diarrhea is bloody or persists for more than 72 hours or is accompanied by fever, shaking chills or severe abdominal pain, you should seek medical attention.

## ENVIRONMENTAL HAZARDS

### Altitude Sickness

Altitude sickness may develop in those who ascend rapidly to altitudes greater than 2500m. Being physically fit offers no protection. Those who have experienced altitude sickness in the past are prone to future episodes. The risk increases with faster ascents, higher altitudes and greater exertion. Symptoms may include headaches, nausea, vomiting, dizziness, malaise, insomnia and loss of appetite. Severe cases may be complicated by fluid in the lungs (high-altitude pulmonary edema) or swelling of the brain (high-altitude cerebral edema).

The best treatment for altitude sickness is descent. If you are exhibiting symptoms, do not ascend. If symptoms are severe or persistent, descend immediately.

One option for the prevention of altitude sickness is to take acetazolamide (Diamox). The recommended dosage ranges from 125mg (twice daily) to 250mg (three times daily). It should be taken 24 hours before ascent and continued for 48 hours after arrival at altitude. Possible side effects include increased urinary volume, numbness, tingling, nausea, drowsiness, myopia and temporary impotence. Acetazolamide should not be given to pregnant women or anyone with a history of sulfa allergy. For those who cannot tolerate acetazolamide, the next best option is 4mg of dexamethasone taken four times daily. Unlike acetazolamide, dexamethasone must be tapered gradually upon arrival at altitude, since there is a risk that altitude sickness will occur as the dosage is reduced. Dexamethasone is a steroid, so it should not be given to diabetics or anyone for whom steroids are contraindicated. A natural alternative is gingko, which some people find quite helpful.

When traveling to high altitudes, it's also important to avoid overexertion, eat light meals and abstain from alcohol.

If your symptoms are more than mild or don't resolve promptly, see a doctor. Altitude sickness should be taken seriously; it can be life-threatening when severe.

### Insect Bites

#### MOSQUITOES

To prevent mosquito bites, wear long sleeves, long pants, hats and shoes (rather than sandals). Bring along a good insect repellent, preferably one containing DEET, which should be applied to exposed skin and clothing, but not to eyes, mouth, cuts, wounds or irritated skin. Products containing lower concentrations of DEET are as effective, but for shorter periods of time. In general, adults and children over 12 years of age should use preparations containing 25% to 35% DEET, which usually lasts about six hours. Children between two and 12 years of age should use preparations containing no more than 10% DEET, applied sparingly, which will usually last about three hours. Neurological toxicity has been reported from using DEET, especially in children, but appears to be extremely uncommon and generally related to overuse. DEET-containing compounds should not be used on children under the age of two.

Insect repellents containing certain botanical products, including oil of eucalyptus and soybean oil, are effective but last only 1½ to two hours. DEET-containing repellents are preferable for areas where there is a high risk of malaria or yellow fever. Citronella-based products are not effective.

For additional protection, you can apply permethrin to clothing, shoes, tents and bed nets. Permethrin treatments are safe and remain effective for at least two weeks, even when items are laundered. Permethrin should not be applied directly to skin.

Don't sleep with the window open unless there is a screen. If sleeping outdoors or in accommodations that allow entry of mosquitoes, use a bed net, preferably treated with permethrin, with edges tucked in under the mattress. The mesh size should be less than 1.5mm. If the sleeping area is not otherwise protected, use a mosquito coil, which will fill the room with insecticide through the night. Repellent-impregnated wristbands are not effective.

#### TICKS

To protect yourself from tick bites, follow the same precautions as for mosquitoes, except that boots are preferable to shoes, with pants tucked in. Be sure to perform a thorough tick check at the end of each day. You'll generally need the assistance of a friend or mirror for a full examination. Ticks should be removed with tweezers, grasping them firmly by the head. Insect repellents based on botanical products (described under Mosquitoes, left) have not been adequately studied for insects

HEALTH

other than mosquitoes and cannot be recommended to prevent tick bites.

### Snake Bites

Snakes and leeches are a hazard in some areas of South America. In the event of a venomous snake bite, place the victim at rest, keep the bitten area immobilized, and move the victim immediately to the nearest medical facility. Avoid tourniquets, which are no longer recommended.

### Sun

To protect yourself from excessive sun exposure, you should stay out of the midday sun, wear sunglasses and a wide-brimmed sun hat, and apply sunblock with SPF 15 or higher, with both UVA and UVB protection. Sunblock should be generously applied to all exposed parts of the body approximately 30 minutes before sun exposure, and should be reapplied after swimming or vigorous activity. Travelers should also drink plenty of fluids and avoid strenuous exercise when the temperature is high.

### Water

Tap water in Venezuela is not safe to drink – buying bottled water is your best bet. If you have the means, vigorous boiling for one minute is the most effective means of water purification. At altitudes greater than 2000m, boil for three minutes. Another option is to disinfect water with iodine pills: add 2% tincture of iodine to 1L of water (five drops to clear water, 10 drops to cloudy water) and let stand for 30 minutes. If the water is cold, longer times may be required.

## TRAVELING WITH CHILDREN

Children under nine months should not be taken to areas where yellow fever occurs, since the vaccine is not safe for this age group. Although measles immunization doesn't begin until the age of 12 months, children between the ages six and 11 months should probably receive an initial dose of measles vaccine before traveling to Venezuela.

When traveling with young children, be particularly careful about what you allow them to eat and drink, because diarrhea can be especially dangerous in this age group and because the vaccines for hepatitis A and typhoid fever are not approved for use in children under the age of two.

The two main malaria medications, Lariam and Malarone, may be given to children, but insect repellents must be applied in lower concentrations.

## WOMEN'S HEALTH

There are English-speaking obstetricians in Venezuela, listed on the **US embassy website** (http://caracas.usembassy.gov). However, medical facilities will probably not compare favorably to those in your home country. It's safer to avoid travel to Venezuela late in pregnancy, so that you don't have to deliver here. Yellow-fever vaccine should not be given during pregnancy because the vaccine contains a live virus that may infect the fetus.

Also it isn't advisable for pregnant women to spend time at altitudes where the air is thin. If you need to take malaria pills, mefloquine (Lariam) is the safest during pregnancy.

# Language

CONTENTS



Spanish is Venezuela's official language, and with the exception of some of the more remote areas, it's spoken throughout the country. There are also more than 25 indigenous languages spoken in Venezuela. English speakers can be found in large urban centers, but it's certainly not a commonly understood or widely spoken language, even though it's taught as a mandatory second language in the public school system.

Spanish is quite easy to learn and a predeparture language course can considerably enrich your travels. Courses are also available in Venezuela (see p158). Even if you don't get around to doing a course, make the effort to at least learn a few greetings and civilities. Don't hesitate to practice your new skills – in general, Latin Americans meet any attempts to communicate in their language with enthusiasm and appreciation.

Lonely Planet's *Latin American Spanish* phrasebook is a worthwhile addition to your backpack. Another useful resource is the *University of Chicago Spanish–English, English–Spanish Dictionary*. For a food and drink glossary, see p44.

## SPANISH IN VENEZUELA

In Latin America, the Spanish language is generally referred to as *castellano* rather than *español*. Probably the most notable difference between the pronunciation of Latin American Spanish and the language of Spain is that the letters **c** and **z** are never lisped; attempts to do so could well provoke amusement or even scorn.

Venezuelan Spanish is not the easiest to understand. The locals (except those from the Andes) speak more rapidly than most other South Americans and tend to drop some word endings, especially for plurals.

The use of the forms *tú* (informal 'you') and *usted* (polite 'you') is very flexible in Venezuela. Both are used, but with regional variations. Either is OK, though it's best to answer using the same form in which you are addressed. Always use the *usted* form when talking to the police and the Guardia Nacional.

Greetings in Venezuela are more elaborate than in Spain. The short Spanish *hola* has given way to a number of expressions, which are exchanged at the beginning of a conversation. Listen to how the locals greet people, and you'll quickly pick up on some of their local idioms.

Although Venezuelans don't seem to be devoutly religious, the phrases *si Dios quiere* (God willing) and *gracias a Dios* (thanks to God) are frequently heard in conversation.

## PRONUNCIATION

Latin American Spanish is easy, as most of the sounds are also found in English. If you follow our pronunciation guides (included alongside the Spanish phrases), you'll have no problems being understood.

### Vowels

There are four sounds (**ai**, **ay**, **ow**, **oy**) that roughly correspond to diphthongs (vowel sound combinations) in English.

| | |
|---|---|
| **a** | as the 'a' in 'father' |
| **ai** | as in 'aisle' |
| **ay** | as in 'say' |
| **e** | as the 'e' in 'met' |
| **ee** | as the 'ee' in 'meet' |
| **o** | as the 'o' in 'more' |
| **oo** | as the 'oo' in 'zoo' |
| **ow** | as in 'how' |
| **oy** | as in 'boy' |

### Consonants

Pronunciation of Spanish consonants is similar to their English counterparts. The exceptions are given in the following list.

| | |
|---|---|
| **kh** | as the throaty 'ch' in the Scottish *loch* |
| **ny** | as the 'ny' in 'canyon' |
| **r** | as in 'run' but stronger and rolled, especially at the beginning of a word and in all words with *rr* |
| **s** | not lisped |

The letter 'h' is always silent (ie never pronounced) in Spanish.

Note also that the Spanish **b** and **v** sounds are very similar – they are both pronounced as a very soft 'v' in English (somewhere between 'b' and 'v').

There are some variations in spoken Spanish as part of the regional accents across Latin America in general. The most notable of these variations is the pronunciation of the letter *ll*. In some parts of Latin America it's pronounced as the 'll' in 'million,' however in Venezuela it's pronounced as 'y' (eg as in 'yes'), and this is how it's represented in our pronunciation guides.

### Word Stress

In general, Spanish words ending in vowels or the consonants *-n* or *-s* are stressed on the second-last syllable, while those with other endings have stress on the last syllable. Written accents denote stress, and override the rules above, eg *sótano* (basement), *América, porción* (portion).

In our pronunciation guides the stressed syllable is indicated with italics, so you needn't worry about these rules.

## GENDER & PLURALS

In Spanish, nouns are either masculine or feminine, and there are rules to help determine gender. Feminine nouns generally end with *-a*, *-ad*, *-z* or *-ión*. Other endings, particularly *-o*, typically signify a masculine noun. Endings for adjectives change to agree with the gender of the noun they modify (masculine/feminine *-o/-a*). Where both masculine and feminine forms are included in this chapter, they are separated by a slash, with the masculine form given first, eg *perdido/a*.

If a noun or adjective ends in a vowel, the plural is formed by adding *-s*. If it ends in a consonant, the plural is formed by adding *-es* to the end of the word.

## ACCOMMODATIONS

| | | |
|---|---|---|
| **I'm looking for a ...** | *Estoy buscando ...* | e·*stoy* boos·*kan*·do ... |
| **Where's a ...?** | *¿Dónde hay ...?* | *don*·de ai ... |
| **camping ground** | *un terreno de cámping* | oon te·*re*·no de *kam*·peen |
| **guesthouse** | *una pensión/ una casa de huéspedes* | *oo*·na pen·*syon*/ *oo*·na *ka*·sa de *we*·spe·des |
| **hotel** | *un hotel* | oon o·*tel* |
| **youth hostel** | *un albergue juvenil* | oon al·*ber*·ge khoo·ve·*neel* |

| | | |
|---|---|---|
| **I'd like a ... room.** | *Quisiera una habitación ...* | kee·*sye*·ra *oo*·na a·bee·ta·*syon* ... |
| **double** | *doble* | *do*·ble |
| **single** | *individual* | een·dee·vee·*dwal* |
| **twin** | *con dos camas* | kon dos *ka*·mas |

| | | |
|---|---|---|
| **How much is it per ...?** | *¿Cuánto cuesta por ...?* | *kwan*·to *kwes*·ta por ... |
| **night** | *noche* | *no*·che |
| **person** | *persona* | per·*so*·na |
| **week** | *semana* | se·*ma*·na |

**Does it include breakfast?**
*¿Incluye el desayuno?* een·*kloo*·ye el de·sa·*yoo*·no
**Can I see the room?**
*¿Puedo ver la habitación?* *pwe*·do ver la a·bee·ta·*syon*
**I don't like it.**
*No me gusta.* no me *goos*·ta
**It's fine, I'll take it.**
*OK, la alquilo.* o·*kay* la al·*kee*·lo
**I'm leaving now.**
*Me voy ahora.* me voy a·*o*·ra

| | | |
|---|---|---|
| **cheaper** | *más económico* | mas e·ko·*no*·mee·ko |
| **discount** | *descuento* | des·*kwen*·to |
| **full board** | *pensión completa* | pen·*syon* kom·*ple*·ta |
| **private/shared bathroom** | *baño privado/ compartido* | *ba*·nyo pree·*va*·do/ kom·par·*tee*·do |
| **too expensive** | *demasiado caro* | de·ma·*sya*·do *ka*·ro |

## CONVERSATION & ESSENTIALS

In their public behavior, South Americans are very conscious of civilities, sometimes

**MAKING A RESERVATION**

(for phone or written requests)

| | |
|---|---|
| **From …** | *De …* |
| **To …** | *A …* |
| **Date** | *Fecha* |
| **I'd like to book …** | *Quisiera reservar …* |
| **in the name of …** | *en nombre de …* |
| **for the nights of …** | *para las noches del …* |
| **credit card** | *tarjeta de crédito* |
| **expiry date** | *fecha de vencimiento* |
| **number** | *número* |
| **Please confirm …** | *¿Puede confirmar …?* |
| **availability** | *la disponibilidad* |
| **price** | *el precio* |

to the point of ceremoniousness. Never approach a stranger for information without extending a greeting and use only the polite form of address, especially with the police and public officials. Young people may be less likely to expect this, but it's best to stick to the polite form unless you're sure you won't offend by using the informal mode. The polite form is used in this chapter; where options are given, the form is indicated by the abbreviations 'pol' and 'inf.'

| | | |
|---|---|---|
| **Hello.** (inf) | *Hola.* | *o*·la |
| **Good morning.** | *Buenos días.* | *bwe*·nos *dee*·as |
| **Good afternoon.** | *Buenas tardes.* | *bwe*·nas *tar*·des |
| **Good evening/ night.** | *Buenas noches.* | *bwe*·nas *no*·ches |
| **Goodbye.** | *Adiós.* | a·*dyos* |
| **See you later.** | *Hasta luego.* | *as*·ta *lwe*·go |
| **Yes./No.** | *Sí./No.* | see/no |
| **Please.** | *Por favor.* | por fa·*vor* |
| **Thank you.** | *Gracias.* | *gra*·syas |
| **Many thanks.** | *Muchas gracias.* | *moo*·chas *gra*·syas |
| **You're welcome.** | *De nada.* | de *na*·da |
| **Pardon.** | *Perdón.* | per·*don* |
| **Excuse me.** (asking permission) | *Permiso.* | per·*mee*·so |
| **Sorry.** (apologizing) | *Disculpe.* | dees·*kool*·pe |
| **How are things?** | *¿Qué tal?* | ke tal |

**What's your name?**
*¿Cómo se llama?* — *ko*·mo se *ya*·ma (pol)
*¿Cómo te llamas?* — *ko*·mo te *ya*·mas (inf)
**My name is …**
*Me llamo …* — me *ya*·mo …
**It's a pleasure to meet you.**
*Mucho gusto.* — *moo*·cho *goos*·to
**The pleasure is mine.**
*El gusto es mío.* — el *goos*·to es *mee*·o
**Where are you from?**
*¿De dónde es/eres?* — de *don*·de es/*e*·res (pol/inf)
**I'm from …**
*Soy de …* — soy de …
**May I take a photo?**
*¿Puedo sacar una foto?* — *pwe*·do sa·*kar oo*·na *fo*·to

## DIRECTIONS

**How do I get to …?**
*¿Cómo puedo llegar a …?* — *ko*·mo *pwe*·do ye·*gar* a …
**What's the address?**
*¿Cuál es la dirección?* — kwal es la dee·rek·*syon*
**Can you show me (on the map)?**
*¿Me lo podría indicar (en el mapa)?* — me lo po·*dree*·a een·dee·*kar* (en el *ma*·pa)
**Is it far?**
*¿Está lejos?* — es·*ta le*·khos
**Go straight ahead.**
*Vaya todo derecho.* — *va*·ya *to*·do de·*re*·cho
**Turn left/right.**
*Voltée a la izquierda/ derecha.* — vol·*te*·e a la ees·*kyer*·da/ de·*re*·cha

| | | |
|---|---|---|
| **north** | *norte* | *nor*·te |
| **south** | *sur* | soor |
| **east** | *este/oriente* | *es*·te/o·*ryen*·te |
| **west** | *oeste/occidente* | o·*es*·te/ok·see·*den*·te |
| **here** | *aquí* | a·*kee* |
| **there** | *allí* | a·*yee* |

## EATING OUT

**I'm a vegetarian.**
*Soy vegetariano/a.* — soy ve·khe·ta·*rya*·no/a
**Do you have any vegetarian dishes?**
*¿Tienen algún plato vegetariano?* — *tye*·nen al·*goon pla*·to ve·khe·ta·*rya*·no
**I don't eat meat, chicken or fish.**
*No como carne, pollo ni pescado.* — no *ko*·mo *kar*·ne *po*·yo nee pes·*ka*·do
**Is this water purified?**
*¿Ésta agua es purificada?* — *es*·ta *a*·gwa es poo·ree·fee·*ka*·da
**Do you have a menu (in English)?**
*¿Tienen una carta (en inglés)?* — *tye*·nen *oo*·na *kar*·ta (en een·*gles*)
**I'd like the set meal.**
*Quisiera el menú.* — kee·*sye*·ra el me·*noo*
**Does that come with salad/fries?**
*¿Viene con ensalada/ papas fritas?* — *vye*·ne kon en·sa·*la*·da/ *pa*·pas *free*·tas

## EMERGENCIES

| | | |
|---|---|---|
| **Help!** | *¡Socorro!* | so·*ko*·ro |
| **Fire!** | *¡Incendio!* | een·*sen*·dyo |
| **I was robbed.** | *Me robaron.* | me ro·*ba*·ron |
| **Go away!** | *¡Déjeme!* | *de*·khe·me |
| **Get lost!** | *¡Váyase!* | *va*·ya·se |

| | | |
|---|---|---|
| **Call …!** | *¡Llame a …!* | *ya*·me a … |
| **an ambulance** | *una ambulancia* | *oo*·na am·boo·*lan*·sya |
| **a doctor** | *un médico* | oon *me*·dee·ko |
| **the police** | *la policía* | la po·lee·*see*·a |

**It's an emergency.**
*Es una emergencia.* es *oo*·na e·mer·*khen*·sya

**Can you help me, please?**
*¿Me puede ayudar, por favor?* me *pwe*·de a·yoo·*dar* por fa·*vor*

**I'm lost.**
*Estoy perdido/a.* es·*toy* per·*dee*·do/a

**Where are the toilets?**
*¿Dónde están los baños?* *don*·de es·*tan* los *ba*·nyos

**What do you recommend?**
*¿Qué me recomienda?* ke me re·ko·*myen*·da

**Not too spicy, please.**
*Sin tanto picante, por favor.* seen *tan*·to pee·*kan*·te por fa·*vor*

**I didn't order this.**
*No pedí esto.* no pe·*dee* *es*·to

**The bill, please.**
*La cuenta, por favor.* la *kwen*·ta por fa·*vor*

**That was delicious.**
*Estaba sabroso.* es·*ta*·ba sa·*bro*·so

## HEALTH

**I'm sick.**
*Estoy enfermo/a.* es·*toy* en·*fer*·mo/a

**I need a doctor.**
*Necesito un médico.* ne·se·*see*·to oon *me*·dee·ko

**Where's the hospital?**
*¿Dónde está el hospital?* *don*·de es·*ta* el os·pee·*tal*

**I'm pregnant.**
*Estoy embarazada.* es·*toy* em·ba·ra·*sa*·da

**I've been vaccinated.**
*Estoy vacunado/a.* es·*toy* va·koo·*na*·do/a

| | | |
|---|---|---|
| **I'm allergic to …** | *Soy alérgico/a a …* | soy a·*ler*·khee·ko/a a … |
| **antibiotics** | *los antibióticos* | los an·tee·*byo*·tee·kos |
| **nuts** | *las nueces* | las *nwe*·ses |
| **penicillin** | *la penicilina* | la pe·nee·see·*lee*·na |

| | | |
|---|---|---|
| **I'm …** | *Soy …* | soy … |
| **asthmatic** | *asmático/a* | as·*ma*·tee·ko/a |
| **diabetic** | *diabético/a* | dya·*be*·tee·ko/a |
| **epileptic** | *epiléptico/a* | e·pee·*lep*·tee·ko/a |

| | | |
|---|---|---|
| **I have (a) …** | *Tengo …* | *ten*·go … |
| **altitude sickness** | *soroche* | so·*ro*·che |
| **cough** | *tos* | tos |
| **diarrhea** | *diarrea* | dya·*re*·a |
| **headache** | *un dolor de cabeza* | oon do·*lor* de ka·*be*·sa |
| **nausea** | *náusea* | *now*·se·a |

## LANGUAGE DIFFICULTIES

**Do you speak English?**
*¿Habla/Hablas inglés?* *a*·bla/*a*·blas een·*gles* (pol/inf)

**Does anyone here speak English?**
*¿Hay alguien que hable inglés?* ai *al*·gyen ke *a*·ble een·*gles*

**I (don't) understand.**
*Yo (no) entiendo.* yo (no) en·*tyen*·do

**How do you say …?**
*¿Cómo se dice …?* *ko*·mo se *dee*·se …

**What does … mean?**
*¿Qué quiere decir …?* ke *kye*·re de·*seer* …

| | | |
|---|---|---|
| **Could you please …?** | *¿Puede …, por favor?* | *pwe*·de … por fa·*vor* |
| **repeat that** | *repetirlo* | re·pe·*teer*·lo |
| **speak more slowly** | *hablar más despacio* | a·*blar* mas des·*pa*·syo |
| **write it down** | *escribirlo* | es·kree·*beer*·lo |

## NUMBERS

| | | |
|---|---|---|
| **0** | *cero* | *se*·ro |
| **1** | *uno* | *oo*·no |
| **2** | *dos* | dos |
| **3** | *tres* | tres |
| **4** | *cuatro* | *kwa*·tro |
| **5** | *cinco* | *seen*·ko |
| **6** | *seis* | seys |
| **7** | *siete* | *sye*·te |
| **8** | *ocho* | *o*·cho |
| **9** | *nueve* | *nwe*·ve |
| **10** | *diez* | dyes |
| **11** | *once* | *on*·se |
| **12** | *doce* | *do*·se |
| **13** | *trece* | *tre*·se |
| **14** | *catorce* | ka·*tor*·se |
| **15** | *quince* | *keen*·se |
| **16** | *dieciséis* | dye·see·*seys* |
| **17** | *diecisiete* | dye·see·*sye*·te |
| **18** | *dieciocho* | dye·see·*o*·cho |
| **19** | *diecinueve* | dye·see·*nwe*·ve |

| | | |
|---|---|---|
| **20** | *veinte* | *vayn*·te |
| **21** | *veintiuno* | vayn·tee·*oo*·no |
| **30** | *treinta* | *trayn*·ta |
| **31** | *treinta y uno* | trayn·ta ee *oo*·no |
| **40** | *cuarenta* | kwa·*ren*·ta |
| **50** | *cincuenta* | seen·*kwen*·ta |
| **60** | *sesenta* | se·*sen*·ta |
| **70** | *setenta* | se·*ten*·ta |
| **80** | *ochenta* | o·*chen*·ta |
| **90** | *noventa* | no·*ven*·ta |
| **100** | *cien* | syen |
| **101** | *ciento uno* | syen·to *oo*·no |
| **200** | *doscientos* | do·*syen*·tos |
| **1000** | *mil* | meel |
| **5000** | *cinco mil* | *seen*·ko meel |
| **10,000** | *diez mil* | *dyes* meel |
| **50,000** | *cincuenta mil* | seen·*kwen*·ta meel |
| **100,000** | *cien mil* | syen meel |
| **1,000,000** | *un millón* | oon mee·*yon* |

## SHOPPING & SERVICES

**I'd like to buy ...**
*Quisiera comprar ...* kee·*sye*·ra kom·*prar* ...
**I'm just looking.**
*Sólo estoy mirando.* *so*·lo es·*toy* mee·*ran*·do
**May I look at it?**
*¿Puedo mirarlo?* *pwe*·do mee·*rar*·lo
**How much is it?**
*¿Cuánto cuesta?* *kwan*·to *kwes*·ta
**That's too expensive for me.**
*Es demasiado caro para mí.* es de·ma·*sya*·do *ka*·ro *pa*·ra mee
**Could you lower the price?**
*¿Podría bajar un poco el precio?* po·*dree*·a ba·*khar* oon *po*·ko el *pre*·syo
**I don't like it.**
*No me gusta.* no me *goos*·ta
**I'll take it.**
*Lo llevo.* lo *ye*·vo

| | | |
|---|---|---|
| **Do you accept ...?** | *¿Aceptan ...?* | a·*sep*·tan ... |
| **American dollars** | *dólares americanos* | *do*·la·res a·me·ree·*ka*·nos |
| **credit cards** | *tarjetas de crédito* | tar·*khe*·tas de *kre*·dee·to |
| **traveler's checks** | *cheques de viajero* | che·kes de vya·*khe*·ro |

| | | |
|---|---|---|
| **more** | *más* | mas |
| **less** | *menos* | *me*·nos |
| **large** | *grande* | *gran*·de |
| **small** | *pequeño/a* | pe·*ke*·nyo/a |

**SIGNS**

| | |
|---|---|
| **Abierto** | Open |
| **Cerrado** | Closed |
| **Comisaría** | Police Station |
| **Entrada** | Entrance |
| **Información** | Information |
| **Prohibido** | Prohibited |
| **Salida** | Exit |
| **Servicios/Baños** | Toilets |
| **Hombres/Varones** | Men |
| **Mujeres/Damas** | Women |

| | | |
|---|---|---|
| **I'm looking for (the) ...** | *Estoy buscando ...* | es·*toy* boos·*kan*·do ... |
| **ATM** | *el cajero automático* | el ka·*khe*·ro ow·to·*ma*·tee·ko |
| **bank** | *el banco* | el *ban*·ko |
| **bookstore** | *la librería* | la lee·bre·*ree*·a |
| **chemist** | *la farmacia* | la far·*ma*·sya |
| **embassy** | *la embajada* | la em·ba·*kha*·da |
| **exchange office** | *la casa de cambio* | la *ka*·sa de *kam*·byo |
| **general store** | *la tienda* | la *tyen*·da |
| **laundry** | *la lavandería* | la la·van·de·*ree*·a |
| **post office** | *el correo* | el ko·*re*·o |
| **(super)market** | *el (super-) mercado* | el (*soo*·per·) mer·*ka*·do |
| **tourist office** | *la oficina de turismo* | la o·fee·*see*·na de too·*rees*·mo |

**What time does it open/close?**
*¿A qué hora abre/cierra?* a ke *o*·ra *a*·bre/*sye*·ra
**I want to change some money/traveler's checks.**
*Quiero cambiar dinero/cheques de viajero.* *kye*·ro kam·*byar* dee·*ne*·ro/*che*·kes de vya·*khe*·ro
**What is the exchange rate?**
*¿Cuál es el tipo de cambio?* kwal es el *tee*·po de *kam*·byo
**I want to call ...**
*Quiero llamar a ...* *kye*·ro ya·*mar* a ...

| | | |
|---|---|---|
| **airmail** | *correo aéreo* | ko·*re*·o a·e·re·o |
| **black market** | *mercado negro/paralelo* | mer·*ka*·do *ne*·gro/pa·ra·*le*·lo |
| **collect call** | *llamada a cobro revertido* | ya·*ma*·da a *ko*·bro re·ver·*tee*·do |
| **email** | *correo electrónico* | ko·*re*·o e·lek·*tro*·nee·ko |
| **letter** | *carta* | *kar*·ta |
| **local call** | *llamada local* | ya·*ma*·da lo·*kal* |
| **long-distance call** | *llamada de larga distancia* | ya·*ma*·da de *lar*·ga dis·*tan*·sya |
| **parcel** | *paquete* | pa·*ke*·te |
| **postcard** | *postal* | pos·*tal* |
| **registered mail** | *certificado* | ser·tee·fee·*ka*·do |
| **stamps** | *estampillas* | es·tam·*pee*·yas |

## TIME & DATES

Times are modified by morning *(de la mañana)* or afternoon *(de la tarde)* instead of 'am' or 'pm.' Use of the 24-hour clock, or military time, is also common, especially with transportation schedules.

| | | |
|---|---|---|
| **What time is it?** | *¿Qué hora es?* | ke *o*·ra es |
| **It's one o'clock.** | *Es la una.* | es la *oo*·na |
| **It's (two) o'clock.** | *Son las (dos).* | son las (dos) |
| **It's half past (two).** | *Son las (dos) y media.* | son las (dos) ee *me*·dya |
| **It's quarter to (three).** | *Son las (tres) menos quarto.* | son las (tres) *me*·nos *kwar*·to |
| **midnight** | *medianoche* | me·dya·*no*·che |
| **noon** | *mediodía* | me·dyo·*dee*·a |

| | | |
|---|---|---|
| **yesterday** | *ayer* | a·*yer* |
| **today** | *hoy* | oy |
| **now** | *ahora* | a·*o*·ra |
| **tonight** | *esta noche* | *es*·ta *no*·che |
| **tomorrow** | *mañana* | ma·*nya*·na |

| | | |
|---|---|---|
| **Monday** | *lunes* | *loo*·nes |
| **Tuesday** | *martes* | *mar*·tes |
| **Wednesday** | *miércoles* | *myer*·ko·les |
| **Thursday** | *jueves* | *khwe*·ves |
| **Friday** | *viernes* | *vyer*·nes |
| **Saturday** | *sábado* | *sa*·ba·do |
| **Sunday** | *domingo* | do·*meen*·go |

| | | |
|---|---|---|
| **January** | *enero* | e·*ne*·ro |
| **February** | *febrero* | fe·*bre*·ro |
| **March** | *marzo* | *mar*·so |
| **April** | *abril* | a·*breel* |
| **May** | *mayo* | *ma*·yo |
| **June** | *junio* | *khoo*·nyo |
| **July** | *julio* | *khoo*·lyo |
| **August** | *agosto* | a·*gos*·to |
| **September** | *septiembre* | sep·*tyem*·bre |
| **October** | *octubre* | ok·*too*·bre |
| **November** | *noviembre* | no·*vyem*·bre |
| **December** | *diciembre* | dee·*syem*·bre |

## TRANSPORTATION

### Public Transportation

| | | |
|---|---|---|
| **At what time does the ... leave/arrive?** | *¿A qué hora sale/llega el ...?* | a ke *o*·ra *sa*·le/*ye*·ga el ... |
| **boat** | *bongo/bote* | *bon*·go/*bo*·te |
| **bus** | *autobus* | ow·to·*boos* |
| **minibus** | *carrito/por puesto* | ka·*ree*·to/por *pwes*·to |
| **plane** | *avión* | a·*vyon* |
| **ship** | *barco/buque* | *bar*·ko/*boo*·ke |
| **train** | *tren* | tren |

**GEOGRAPHICAL EXPRESSIONS**

The expressions below are among the most common you'll encounter in Spanish-language guides and maps.

| | | |
|---|---|---|
| **avenida** | a·ve·*nee*·da | avenue |
| **bahía** | ba·*ee*·a | bay |
| **calle** | *ka*·ye | street |
| **camino** | ka·*mee*·no | road; highway |
| **campo** | *kam*·po | farm |
| **carretera** | ka·re·*te*·ra | highway |
| **cascada** | kas·*ka*·da | waterfall |
| **cerro** | *se*·ro | hill; mount |
| **cordillera** | kor·dee·*ye*·ra | mountain range |
| **estancia** | es·*tan*·sya | ranch |
| **estero** | es·*te*·ro | marsh; estuary |
| **finca** | *feen*·ka | farm |
| **fundo** | *foon*·do | farm |
| **granja** | *gran*·kha | ranch |
| **hacienda** | a·*syen*·da | farm |
| **lago** | *la*·go | lake |
| **montaña** | mon·*ta*·nya | mountain |
| **parque nacional** | *par*·ke na·syo·*nal* | national park |
| **paso** | *pa*·so | pass |
| **playa** | *pla*·ya | beach |
| **puente** | *pwen*·te | bridge |
| **rancho** | *ran*·cho | ranch |
| **río** | *ree*·o | river |
| **ruta** | *roo*·ta | highway |
| **salto** | *sal*·to | waterfall |
| **seno** | *se*·no | sound |
| **valle** | *va*·ye | valley |

| | | |
|---|---|---|
| **airport** | *aeropuerto* | a·e·ro·*pwer*·to |
| **bus stop** | *parada de autobuses* | pa·*ra*·da de ow·to·*boo*·ses |
| **bus terminal** | *terminal de pasajeros* | ter·mee·*nal* de pa·sa·*khe*·ros |
| **luggage check room** | *guardería de equipaje* | gwar·de·*ree*·a de e·kee·*pa*·khe |
| **ticket office** | *boletería* | bo·le·te·*ree*·a |
| **train station** | *estación de ferrocarril* | es·ta·*syon* de fe·ro·ka·*reel* |

**I'd like a ticket to ...**
*Quisiera un boleto a ...* kee·*sye*·ra oon bo·*le*·to a ...

**What's the fare to ...?**
*¿Cuánto cuesta hasta ...?* *kwan*·to *kwes*·ta *a*·sta ...

| | | |
|---|---|---|
| **1st class** | *primera clase* | pree·*me*·ra *kla*·se |
| **2nd class** | *segunda clase* | se·*goon*·da *kla*·se |
| **one-way** | *ida* | *ee*·da |
| **roundtrip** | *ida y vuelta* | *ee*·da ee *vwel*·ta |
| **taxi** | *taxi* | *tak*·see |

## ROAD SIGNS

Traffic signs are invariably in Spanish and may not be accompanied by international symbols. Pay attention in particular to *Peligro* (Danger), *Ceda el Paso* (Give Way; prevalent on one-lane bridges) and *Hundimiento* (Dip; often a euphemism for 'axle-breaking sinkhole').

| | |
|---|---|
| **Acceso** | Entrance |
| **Alto** | Stop |
| **Aparcamiento** | Parking |
| **Ceda el Paso** | Give Way |
| **Curva Peligrosa** | Dangerous Curve |
| **Derrumbes en la Vía** | Landslides/Rockfalls |
| **Despacio** | Slow |
| **Desvío** | Detour |
| **Dirección Única** | One Way |
| **Hundimiento** | Dip |
| **Mantenga Su Derecha** | Keep to the Right |
| **No Adelantar** | No Passing |
| **No Estacionar** | No Parking |
| **No Hay Paso** | No Entrance |
| **No Rebase** | No Passing |
| **Peaje** | Toll |
| **Peligro** | Danger |
| **Prohibido Aparcar** | No Parking |
| **Prohibido el Paso** | No Entry |
| **Pare** | Stop |
| **Salida de Autopista** | Freeway Exit |
| **Trabajos en la Vía** | Roadwork |
| **Tránsito Entrando** | Entering Traffic |

## Private Transportation

| | | |
|---|---|---|
| **I'd like to** | *Quisiera* | kee·*sye*·ra |
| **hire a …** | *alquilar …* | al·kee·*lar* … |
| **4WD** | *un todo terreno* | oon *to*·do te·*re*·no |
| **bicycle** | *una bicicleta* | *oo*·na bee·see·*kle*·ta |
| **car** | *un auto/carro* | oon *ow*·to/*ka*·ro |
| **motorbike** | *una moto* | *oo*·na *mo*·to |
| | | |
| **gas** | *gasolina* | ga·so·*lee*·na |
| **hitchhike** | *hacer dedo* | a·*ser de*·do |
| **pickup (truck)** | *camioneta* | ka·myo·*ne*·ta |
| **truck** | *camión* | ka·*myon* |
| **unleaded/** | *sin/con plomo* | seen/kon *plo*·mo |
| **leaded** | | |

**Is this the road to …?**
*¿Se va a … por*    se va a … por
*esta carretera?*    es·ta ka·re·*te*·ra
**Where's a gas station?**
*¿Dónde hay una*    *don*·de ai *oo*·na
*gasolinera?*    ga·so·lee·*ne*·ra

**Please fill it up.**
*Lleno, por favor.*    *ye*·no por fa·*vor*
**I'd like (20) liters.**
*Quiero (veinte) litros.*    *kye*·ro (*vayn*·te) *lee*·tros
**(How long) Can I park here?**
*¿(Por cuánto tiempo)*    (por *kwan*·to *tyem*·po)
*Puedo aparcar aquí?*    *pwe*·do a·par·*kar* a·*kee*
**I need a mechanic.**
*Necesito un mecánico.*    ne·se·*see*·to oon me·*ka*·nee·ko
**The car has broken down (in …).**
*El carro se ha averiado*    el *ka*·ro se a a·ve·*rya*·do
*(en …).*    (en …)
**The motorbike won't start.**
*No arranca la moto.*    no a·*ran*·ka la *mo*·to
**I have a flat tyre.**
*Tengo un pinchazo.*    *ten*·go oon peen·*cha*·so
**I've run out of gas.**
*Me quedé sin gasolina.*    me ke·*de* seen ga·so·*lee*·na
**I've had an accident.**
*Tuve un accidente.*    *too*·ve oon ak·see·*den*·te

## TRAVEL WITH CHILDREN

**Are children allowed?**
*¿Se admiten niños?*    se ad·*mee*·ten *nee*·nyos

| | | |
|---|---|---|
| **Is there (a) …?** | *¿Hay …?* | ai … |
| **babysitter** | *una niñera* | *oo*·na nee·*nye*·ra |
| **(who speaks** | *(que habla* | (ke *a*·bla |
| **English)** | *inglés)* | een·*gles*) |
| **car seat for** | *un asiento* | oon a·*syen*·to |
| **babies** | *de seguridad* | de se·goo·ree·*dad* |
| | *para bebés* | *pa*·ra be·*bes* |
| **child-minding** | *un servicio* | oon ser·*vee*·syo |
| **service** | *de cuidado* | de kwee·*da*·do |
| | *de niños* | de *nee*·nyos |
| **(disposable)** | *pañales (de* | pa·*nya*·les (de |
| **diapers/** | *usar y tirar)* | oo·*sar* ee tee·*rar*) |
| **nappies** | | |
| **highchair** | *una trona* | *oo*·na *tro*·na |
| **milk formula** | *leche en polvo* | *le*·che en *pol*·vo |
| **potty** | *una pelela* | *oo*·na pe·*le*·la |
| **stroller** | *un cochecito* | oon ko·che·*see*·to |

phrasebooks

Latin American
**Spanish**

with 3500-word two-way dictionary

Also available from
Lonely Planet:
*Latin American Spanish*
phrasebook

# Glossary

See the Food & Drink chapter (p41) for useful words and phrases dealing with food and dining. See the Language chapter (p292) for general-use words and phrases.

**andino/a** – inhabitant of the Andes
**araguaney** – trumpet tree *(Tabebuia chrysantha)*, a large tree with yellow flowers; Venezuela's national tree
**arepa** – hamburger-sized corn pancake stuffed with juicy fillings
**arepera** – restaurant selling *arepas*

**baloncesto** – basketball
**barrio** – shantytown
**béisbol** – baseball
**bodega** – warehouse; also used to mean 'grocery store,' especially in small localities and rural areas
**buseta** – small bus, frequently used in city transportation

**cajero automático** – automated teller machine (ATM)
**calle** – street
**callejón** – alley or narrow, short street
**camioneta** – minibus
**campamento** – countryside lodging facility, usually in cabins, with its own food services and often a tour program
**CANTV** – the national telecommunications company
**capybara** – a tailless, largely aquatic South American rodent
**carabobeño/a** – inhabitant of Carabobo state, particularly Valencia
**caraqueño/a** – person born and/or residing in Caracas
**casa** – house; used for anything from a rustic hut to a rambling colonial mansion
**castillo** – fort
**caudillo** – South American dictator; normally a military man who assumes power by force and is noted for autocratic rule; caudillos governed Venezuela from 1830 to 1958
**CC** – common abbreviation for Centro Comercial, or shopping mall
**cédula** – identity document of Venezuelan citizens and permanent residents
**chavistas** – supporters of President Hugo Chávez
**cheque viajero** – traveler's check
**chinchorro** – hammock woven of cotton threads or palm fiber like a fishing net; typical of many indigenous groups, including the Warao and Guajiro
**churuata** – a traditional circular palm-thatched hut common to many of Venezuela's indigenous cultures
**coleo** – form of rodeo practiced in Los Llanos, also known as *toros coleados*; the aim is to overthrow a bull by grabbing its tail from a galloping horse
**comida criolla** – typical Venezuelan cuisine
**cónchale** – informal tag word used on its own or added to the beginning of a sentence to emphasize emotional involvement
**corrida** – bullfight
**costeño/a** – inhabitant of the coastal regions
**criollo/a** – Creole, a person of European (especially Spanish) ancestry but born in the Americas
**cuadra** – city block
**Curripaco** – indigenous community living in Amazonas state

**denuncia** – official report/statement to the police
**DIEX** or **DEX** – Dirección Nacional de Identificación y Extranjería, the Venezuelan immigration authority

**embarcadero** – landing dock
**esquina** – street corner

**farmacia** – pharmacy
**flor de mayo** – species of orchid that is Venezuela's national flower
**fortín** – small fort
**fuerte** – fort
**fútbol** – soccer

**gaita** – popular music played in Zulia state
**garza** – heron
**gavilán** – sparrow hawk
**gringo/a** – any foreigner, especially white ones; sometimes, not always, derogatory
**guacamaya** – macaw
**Guajibo** – indigenous group living in parts of Los Llanos and Amazonas along the frontier with Colombia
**Guajiro** – Venezuela's most numerous indigenous group, living in Zulia state (Venezuela) and Península de la Guajira (Colombia)
**guarda equipaje** – left-luggage office; checkroom
**Guardia Nacional** – military police responsible for security

**hacienda** – country estate
**hato** – large cattle ranch, typical of Los Llanos
**hospedaje** – cheap hotel

**iglesia** – church
**impuesto** – tax
**impuesto de salida** – departure tax
**Ipostel** – company operating a network of post offices
**IVA** – *impuesto de valor agregado*, a value-added sales tax (VAT)

**jején** – species of small biting gnat that infests the Gran Sabana and, to a lesser extent, some other regions
**joropo** – typical music of Los Llanos, today widespread throughout the country; considered the Venezuelan national rhythm

**lanchero** – boatman
**lavandería** – launderette
**liqui liqui** – men's traditional costume, typical of most of the Caribbean; a white or beige suit comprising trousers and a shirt with a collar, usually accompanied by white hat and shoes
**llanero/a** – inhabitant of Los Llanos
**loro** – parrot

**mal de páramo** – altitude sickness
**malecón** – waterfront boulevard
**manta** – long, loose, usually colorful dress worn by Guajiro women
**mapanare** – venomous snake common in Venezuela
**maracucho/a** – person from Maracaibo; often extended to mean anyone from the Zulia state
**margariteño/a** – person from the Isla de Margarita
**matrimonial** – hotel room with a double bed intended for couples
**médanos** – sand dunes near Coro
**menú del día** – set lunch or dinner
**merengue** – musical rhythm originating from the Dominican Republic, today widespread throughout the Caribbean
**mestizo/a** – person of mixed European-Amerindian blood
**micro** – in some regions, a term for a minibus or van used as local transportation
**mirador** – lookout, viewpoint
**mochilero** – backpacker
**módulo** – dormitory-style accommodations, popular with school groups
**monedero** – originally a term referring to a public telephone operated by coins, now means any public phone
**moriche** – oily palm common in Los Llanos and the Delta del Orinoco, used by indigenous people for construction, food, household items, handicrafts etc
**morrocoy** – tortoise typical of some regions, including Los Llanos and Guayana
**mucuposadas** – traditional rural lodges

**Onidex** – Oficina Nacional de Identificación y Extranjería (see also DIEX)

**palafito** – house built on stilts over the water; a typical Warao dwelling in the Delta del Orinoco. Also found in Zulia state, especially in Laguna de Sinamaica.
**panadería** – bakery
**parada** – bus stop
**parrilla** – mixed grill
**paseo** – promenade
**pastelería** – pastry shop
**Pemón** – indigenous group inhabiting the Gran Sabana and neighboring areas
**peñero** – open fishing boat made from wood
**Piapoco** – indigenous community living in Amazonas state
**Piaroa** – indigenous community living in Amazonas state
**playa** – beach
**plaza de toros** – bullfight ring
**por puesto** – cross between a bus and taxi that travels fixed routes and departs when full
**por rato** – love motel
**posada** – small, family-run guesthouse
**propina** – tip
**puri-puri** – small biting sand flies, similar to *jejenes*

**quinta** – house with a garden; *quintas* originally took up a fifth of a city block, hence the name

**ranchería** – indigenous hamlet
**refugio** – rustic shelter in a remote area, mostly in the mountains
**residencia** – cheap hotel or, more often, apartment building
**río** – river
**roqueño/a** – inhabitants of the Archipiélago Los Roques
**rumba** – party

**Semana Santa** – Holy Week, the week before Easter Sunday

**tarjeta de crédito** – credit card
**tarjeta de ingreso** – tourist card
**tasa aeroportuaria** – airport tax
**tasca** – Spanish-style bar-restaurant
**teleférico** – cable car
**tepui** – flat-topped sandstone mountain with vertical flanks; the term is derived from the Pemón word for 'mountain'
**terminal de pasajeros** – bus terminal
**tienda** – small store that sells food, toiletries, batteries etc
**trapiche** – traditional sugarcane mill
**turpial** – small black, red and yellow bird; Venezuela's national bird

**vallenato** – typical Colombian music, now widespread throughout Venezuela
**vaquero** – cowboy of Los Llanos
**viajero** – traveler

**Warao** – indigenous group living in the Delta del Orinoco

**Yanomami** – indigenous group living in the Venezuelan and Brazilian Amazon
**Ye'Kwana** or **Yekuana** – also referred to as Maquiritare; an indigenous group inhabiting parts of Amazonas and Bolívar states

# The Authors

## KEVIN RAUB **Coordinating Author, Caracas, The Central North**

Kevin Raub grew up in Atlanta and started his career as a music journalist in New York, working for *Men's Journal* and *Rolling Stone* magazines. The rock 'n' roll lifestyle took its toll, so he needed an extended vacation and took up travel writing. He'd thought he'd seen it all in South America, until he watched the pilot of his flight to Canaima walk up to the plane holding a seat above his head or his pilot from Los Roques work his Blackberry shortly after takeoff! This is his 7th Lonely Planet title.

## BRIAN KLUEPFEL **The Northwest, The Andes, Los Llanos**

Brian Kluepfel has worked across the Americas as a travel writer and has lived in the Bronx, Berkeley and Bolivia (as the managing editor of the late, great *Bolivian Times*). He's written for various international periodicals, including *Guitar Player, Acoustic Guitar* and Frontier Airlines' in-flight magazine, *Wild Blue Yonder*. He is currently the music editor for the *Examiner News* in Westchester County, NY, and is working on a biography of the Irish guitar legend Rory Gallagher. During his travels in Venezuela, Brian was bitten by one dog and five mosquitoes, lost 5kg, and visited 19 Plaza Bolívars. He added several birds to his life list, including the amazing hoatzin.

## TOM MASTERS **The Northeast, Guayana**

Having traveled to Venezuela as both a backpacker in the pre-Chávez days and as a documentary producer in more recent times, Tom was delighted to return to a diet of *arepas* (hamburger-sized corn pancake stuffed with juicy fillings) and Polar Solera while researching the Guayana and Northeast chapters of this book. Traveling through the Canaima National Park, the Orinoco Delta and exploring the Península de Paria and de Araya were all unforgettable experiences. Tom currently lives in Berlin and more of his work can be seen at www.mastersmafia.com.

**LONELY PLANET AUTHORS**

Why is our travel information the best in the world? It's simple: our authors are passionate, dedicated travelers. They don't take freebies in exchange for positive coverage so you can be sure the advice you're given is impartial. They travel widely to all the popular spots, and off the beaten track. They don't research using just the internet or phone. They discover new places not included in any other guidebook. They personally visit thousands of hotels, restaurants, palaces, trails, galleries, temples and more. They speak with dozens of locals every day to make sure you get the kind of insider knowledge only a local could tell you. They take pride in getting all the details right, and in telling it how it is. Think you can do it? Find out how at **lonelyplanet.com**.

## CONTRIBUTING AUTHORS

**David Goldberg MD** wrote the Health chapter. Dr Goldberg completed his training in internal medicine and infectious diseases at Columbia-Presbyterian Medical Center in New York City, where he also served as voluntary faculty. At present he is an infectious diseases specialist in Scarsdale, NY, and the editor-in-chief of the website MDTravelHealth.com.

**Tobias Mendelovici** wrote the Environment chapter. He was born in Caracas and became an avid traveler while still a teenager. He has traveled extensively in Latin America and Australia and has put his passion for nature into practice over the last decade through a number of environment-related projects in Israel, Australia and Venezuela. For the last four years Tobias has been at the forefront of ecotourism development in Venezuela.

# Behind the Scenes



## THIS BOOK

This 6th edition of *Venezuela* was researched and written by Kevin Raub (coordinating author), Brian Kluepfel and Tom Masters. Kevin wrote all the front and back chapters as well as Caracas and the Central North. Brian covered the Northwest, the Andes and Los Llanos. Tom researched and wrote the Northeast and Guayana. Dr David Goldberg MD contributed the Health chapter. Tobias Mendelovici wrote the Environment chapter for the 5th edition. This guidebook was commissioned in Lonely Planet's Oakland office, and produced by the following:

**Commissioning Editors** Catherine Craddock-Carrillo, Kathleen Munnelly, Emily Wolman
**Coordinating Editor** Jeanette Wall
**Coordinating Cartographer** Andrew Smith
**Coordinating Layout Designer** Jacqui Saunders
**Managing Editor** Brigitte Ellemor
**Managing Cartographer** Alison Lyall
**Managing Layout Designers** Sally Darmody, Indra Kilfoyle
**Assisting Editors** Ali Lemer, Helen Yeates
**Cover Research** Naomi Parker, lonelyplanetimages.com
**Internal Image Research** Sabrina Dalbesio, lonelyplanetimages.com
**Project Manager** Rachel Imeson
**Language Content** Branislava Vladisavljevic
**Thanks to** David Carroll, Daniel Corbett, Lisa Knights, Annelies Mertens, Raphael Richards, John Taufa

## THANKS

### KEVIN RAUB

Special thanks to my wife, Adriana Schmidt. At Lonely Planet, Kathleen Munnelly, Tom Masters and Brian Kluepfel. Along the way: massive thanks to Maria Renjifo, an impossibly invaluable savior; Enmar Perez, Rafael Abella, Steven Bodzin, Juan Restrepo, Ben Rodriguez, Leo Lameda, Eustoquio Ferrer, Juan Carlos Ramirez, Oscar Maza, Arleth Espinoza, Claudia Beckmann and Emilio Espinoza, Daniel Mendes, Alejandra Basciani, Karina Zavarce, Veronica Crepinsek and Thomas Schwarzer.

### BRIAN KLUEPFEL

Brian Kluepfel wishes to thank the folks at Lonely Planet who hired him, the generous people of Venezuela who were kind enough to open their hearts, homes and restaurants to him during his stay, and every person who works to keep the travel industry moving – in hotel lobbies, airport ticket counters, bus station windows and many

### THE LONELY PLANET STORY

Fresh from an epic journey across Europe, Asia and Australia in 1972, Tony and Maureen Wheeler sat at their kitchen table stapling together notes. The first Lonely Planet guidebook, *Across Asia on the Cheap,* was born.

Travelers snapped up the guides. Inspired by their success, the Wheelers began publishing books to Southeast Asia, India and beyond. Demand was prodigious, and the Wheelers expanded the business rapidly to keep up. Over the years, Lonely Planet extended its coverage to every country and into the virtual world via lonelyplanet.com and the Thorn Tree message board.

As Lonely Planet became a globally loved brand, Tony and Maureen received several offers for the company. But it wasn't until 2007 that they found a partner whom they trusted to remain true to the company's principles of traveling widely, treading lightly and giving sustainably. In October of that year, BBC Worldwide acquired a 75% share in the company, pledging to uphold Lonely Planet's commitment to independent travel, trustworthy advice and editorial independence.

Today, Lonely Planet has offices in Melbourne, London and Oakland, with over 500 staff members and 300 authors. Tony and Maureen are still actively involved with Lonely Planet. They're traveling more often than ever, and they're devoting their spare time to charitable projects. And the company is still driven by the philosophy of *Across Asia on the Cheap*: 'All you've got to do is decide to go and the hardest part is over. So go!'

### SEND US YOUR FEEDBACK

We love to hear from travelers – your comments keep us on our toes and help make our books better. Our well-traveled team reads every word on what you loved or loathed about this book. Although we cannot reply individually to postal submissions, we always guarantee that your feedback goes straight to the appropriate authors, in time for the next edition. Each person who sends us information is thanked in the next edition and the most useful submissions are rewarded with a free book.

To send us your updates – and find out about Lonely Planet events, newsletters and travel news – visit our award-winning website: **lonelyplanet.com/contact**.

Note: we may edit, reproduce and incorporate your comments in Lonely Planet products such as guidebooks, websites and digital products, so let us know if you don't want your comments reproduced or your name acknowledged. For a copy of our privacy policy visit lonelyplanet.com/privacy.

others – who do many things and often get little thanks for it.

### TOM MASTERS

First of all a huge thank you to Ben Rodríguez of Osprey Expeditions and his team in Caracas for all the help, advice, logistical support and general assistance given over my entire time in Venezuela – I couldn't have done it without you. Thanks also to Paul Stanley and Anthony Ippolito of Angel Conservation for being such fantastic guides and great company in the Kamarata Valley, along with Clemente, Arturo, Wilson and all the Pemón I was honored to meet in the PN Canaima. In Canaima and Angel Falls thanks to Expediciones Kavac and Nathanial Masterson. Huge gratitude also to Ricardo, Eric, Jonás and Ivan in Gran Sabana, Luis and Cosimo in Ciudad Bolívar; Antonio, Robin & Tomás in Delta del Orinoco, Juan in Maturín and Ricardo Rudas Alvarado in Margarita. Finally thanks to Kevin Raub for coordinating with such good humor, and to Kathleen Munnelly for sending me to Venezuela.

## OUR READERS

**Many thanks to the travelers who used the last edition and wrote to us with helpful hints, useful advice and interesting anecdotes:**

Kate Adlam, Clare Anderson, Julie Berranger, Lea Bonnington, Walt Bosmans, Hope Boylston, Peter De Ruiter, Laurent Depond, Paul Dobson, Enrico Fardella, Jayne Fisher, Henning Füllers, Steven Fulmer, Julius Garde, David Gavin, Jean-Yves Girard, Daniel Griesser, Thomas Hägg, Bernard Herman, Patrick Hess, Maeve Hoelscher, Lee Inserto, Vicky Joseph, Marco Klarenbeek, Sophie Lemberger, Stephanie Mitter, Solveig Niemann, Roger Noonan, Imogen Nulty, Francisco Ortiz, Julien Pain, Hanna Parson, Jamie Peters, Sand Pomeroy, Lutz Poppelbaum, Cesar Rodriguez, Malcolm Rood, Pinc Russo, Eivind Rutle, Shawn Sanders, Dina Sinigallia, Katrin Sippel, Mario Sobacchi, Loredana Spadola, Matt Steiman, Helen Stone, Michael Stout, Maria Thomas, Angelo Rodolfo Tomaselli, Bert Ungerer, Andy Wand, Doris Wisher, Alan Wood

## ACKNOWLEDGMENTS

**Many thanks to the following for the use of their content:**

Globe on title page ©Mountain High Maps 1993 Digital Wisdom, Inc.

# Index

**000** Map pages
000 Photograph pages

**000** Map pages
000 Photograph pages



INDEX

INDEX

## GREENDEX

Venezuela's incredible variety of natural attractions and biodiversity makes it an understandably attractive destination for nature lovers, and a growing number of tour operators include ecotourism tours and accommodations in their packages. But do be aware that not all tours marketed as 'eco' are committed to high standards of ecological conservation or to local community participation.

Lonely Planet is committed to expanding our sustainable-tourism content and the following list represents Venezuela's best-chance opportunities for ecotours, sustainable lodges and hotels, and environmentally friendly and responsible points of interest. If you think we've omitted someone who should be listed here, or if you disagree with our choices, email us at www.lonelyplanet.com/contact. For more information about sustainable tourism and lonely Planet, see www.lonelyplanet.com/about/responsible-travel.

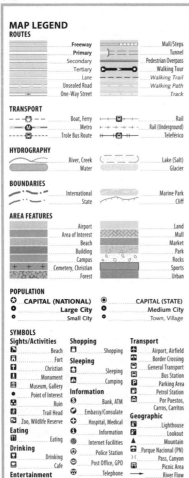

## MAP LEGEND

### ROUTES

Freeway
Primary
Secondary
Tertiary
Lane
Unsealed Road
One-Way Street
Mall/Steps
Tunnel
Pedestrian Overpass
Walking Tour
*Walking Trail*
*Walking Path*
*Track*

### TRANSPORT

Boat, Ferry
Metro
Trole Bus Route
Rail
Rail (Underground)
Teleférico

### HYDROGRAPHY

River, Creek
Water
Lake (Salt)
Glacier

### BOUNDARIES

International
State
Marine Park
Cliff

### AREA FEATURES

Airport
Area of Interest
Beach
Building
Campus
Cemetery, Christian
Forest
Land
Mall
Market
Park
Rocks
Sports
Urban

### POPULATION

CAPITAL (NATIONAL)
**Large City**
Small City
CAPITAL (STATE)
**Medium City**
Town, Village

### SYMBOLS

**Sights/Activities**
Beach
Fort
Christian
Monument
Museum, Gallery
Point of Interest
Ruin
Trail Head
Zoo, Wildlife Reserve

**Eating**
Eating

**Drinking**
Drinking
Cafe

**Entertainment**
Entertainment

**Shopping**
Shopping

**Sleeping**
Sleeping
Camping

**Information**
Bank, ATM
Embassy/Consulate
Hospital, Medical
Information
Internet Facilities
Police Station
Post Office, GPO
Telephone
Toilets

**Transport**
Airport, Airfield
Border Crossing
General Transport
Bus Station
Parking Area
Petrol Station
Por Puestos, Carros, Carritos

**Geographic**
Lighthouse
Lookout
Mountain
Parque Nacional (PN)
Pass, Canyon
Picnic Area
River Flow
Waterfall

## LONELY PLANET OFFICES


**Australia** (Head Office)
Locked Bag 1, Footscray, Victoria 3011
☎ 03 8379 8000, fax 03 8379 8111
talk2us@lonelyplanet.com.au

**USA**
150 Linden St, Oakland, CA 94607
☎ 510 250 6400, toll free 800 275 8555
fax 510 893 8572
info@lonelyplanet.com

**UK**
2nd fl, 186 City Rd,
London EC1V 2NT
☎ 020 7106 2100, fax 020 7106 2101
go@lonelyplanet.co.uk



**Published by Lonely Planet**
ABN 36 005 607 983





Cover photograph: Parrot sitting at window, Caracas, Venezuela, David Mendelsohn/Masterfile. Many of the images in this guide are available for licensing from Lonely Planet Images: lonelyplanetimages.com.





Printed by Toppan Security Printing Pte. Ltd.
Printed in Singapore